COMPARATIVE HUMAN RIGHTS

Also by Richard P. Claude
The Supreme Court and the Electoral Process

COMPARATIVE
HUMAN RIGHTS

Edited by
RICHARD P. CLAUDE ,1934-

The Johns Hopkins University Press
Baltimore and London

Copyright © 1976 by The Johns Hopkins University Press

All rights reserved. No part of this book may be
reproduced or transmitted in any form or by any means,
electronic or mechanical, including photocopying,
recording, xerography, or any information storage and
retrieval system, without permission in writing
from the publisher.

Manufactured in the United States of America

The Johns Hopkins University Press, Baltimore, Maryland 21218
The Johns Hopkins University Press Ltd., London

Library of Congress Catalog Card Number 76–7043
ISBN 0–8018–1784–6

Library of Congress Cataloging in Publication data
will be found on the last printed page of this book.

To Our Parents

There are certain words,
Our own and others', we're used to—words we've used,
Heard, had to recite, forgotten,
Rubbed shiny in the pocket, left home for keepsakes,
Inherited, stuck away in the back-drawer,
In the locked trunk, at the back of the quiet mind.

Liberty, equality, fraternity.
To none will we sell, refuse or deny, right or justice.
We hold these truths to be self-evident.

I am merely saying—what if these words pass?
What if they pass and are gone and are no more . . .?

It took long to buy these words.
It took a long time to buy them and much pain.

Stephen Vincent Benét

From "Nightmare at Noon" in *The Selected Works of Stephen Vincent Benét,* Vol. 1, Holt, Rinehart and Winston. Copyright 1933 by Stephen Vincent Benét; copyright renewed © 1961 by Rosemary Carr Benét. Reprinted by permission of Brandt & Brandt.

CONTENTS

PREFACE

The diverse beliefs of nations and classes, the world divisions, and the racial rivalry reflected in various systems of law and politics all give changing meaning to such phrases as "human rights" and "fundamental freedoms." Writing in 1789, Edmund Burke commented, "Of all the loose terms in the world, liberty is the most indefinite." From the point of view of scholarship it is distressing that the situation has changed little since the time of Burke's famous observation. To some scholars, the historically unique and various circumstances surrounding the development of legal guarantees of rights from country to country all but foreclose meaningful comparison. Even with twentieth century hindsight, it would be a most challenging task, for example, to compare the Virginia Bill of Rights of 1776, steeped in a pioneering spirit which was fired by religious fervor, with the French principles of 1789, reflecting the revolt of the Third Estate. To those who see only diversity or coincidence in the worldwide field of rights and liberties, a "science of rights"—to use J. G. Fichte's ambitious term—is either impossible or premature. Two responses are available to the objections which are leveled at the assumptions of comparative human rights research. First, an admission is in order that such study is indeed academically underdeveloped. Second, a plea must be made for a beginning, however modest, of the systematic study of human rights and basic freedoms. The reason for urgency is that *homo sapiens* is also *homo faber,* making ever more ingenious devices for both the benefit and oppression of man's liberties and welfare.

Cooperation among scholars in many disciplines is needed to initiate as broad a field as comparative human rights. Even cooperation, however, brings its own difficulties. Scholars in such varied areas as law and the social sciences have tended to use quite different sets of professional vocabulary, and even to employ incompatible methods of analysis. Nevertheless, a willingness to try cooperation is the first requisite for multidisciplinary work. Agreement on some bases for cooperation is another primary requisite, and the work by eight political scientists, six legal scholars, one psychologist, and one sociologist reflected in this volume grows out of accord on a few starting points.

First, we recognize that the term "human rights" is confusing. As the successor concept to "natural rights," the newer title has acquired an emotional appeal surpassing any fixed meaning which analytical philosophers and scholars of international and domestic law have tried to assign to it. Like earlier entitlements to various natural or moral rights, some claims are asserted under the label "human rights" so as to assist politically the cause of justification and incorporation into a legal system. Although efforts are made at various points throughout this volume to refine further the title phrase of the book, we begin from a tolerant, if somewhat tentative, assumption that "human rights" is not the exclusive terminological domain of international law or political philosophy. It is as convenient a generic term as is available to embrace the universe of civil rights, civil liberties, and newly emerging social and economic rights which enjoy or are moving toward legal sanction from country to country.

Second, we acknowledge that comparative human rights research has not been systematic. From this premise, we impose upon ourselves a methodological restriction: it is necessary to begin systematic comparative work within a narrowly defined radius for research. To initiate the comparative study of human rights, something less than the globalism of international law and something more than the parochialism of traditional public policy studies is needed. The basic strategy relied upon in this volume reflects an admittedly controversial decision to launch comparative inquiry from the relatively restricted foundation of a small class of countries. We are generally involved in studying human rights and freedoms among the liberal democracies which profess in constitutional or other legal terms to advance them. Since comparative research in this field can only be called an academic fledgling, the initial need is to generate analysis out of detailed case work—a standard prescientific task. In this instance, we generally focus on politico-legal systems which are functionally comparable, though structurally as diverse as those found in Mexico, Uganda, Japan, and India, and among civil code, Scandinavian and Germanic, and common law countries.

Third, the worldwide humanitarian concern for human rights transcends the differences among political and economic systems. We start from this assumption, carrying as it does unblushing normative implications about common human dignity. Although we may defend in pragmatic terms the choice of political systems for inquiry here, it is hoped that a research strategy which partially excludes developing countries from its purview will not be seen as reflecting cultural paternalism. We recognize with Latif Adigbite of Lagos University that, however recent may be the written record of legal rights in third world politics, the love of freedom is universal. Precolonial African history is rich in examples of remedies against tyrannical rules. The ancient Hindu teaching that freedom is necessary because authority is not creative attests to the same universality of freedom values. Clearly, to arrogate the origins of the notion of human rights to a particular peoples, that is, to Europeans, would be both erroneous and dysfunctional to the general effort to secure acceptance of human rights worldwide.

The kinds of questions that engage scholarly concern in a research area can be decisive in its development. The reason, of course, is that once the focus of inquiry is clear, research may more economically proceed to the fruitful level of problem-oriented description and analysis, if not explanation. In each study that follows, a carefully defined problem area has been examined from comparative perspectives. Equipped with the tools of his or her profession, each author has given intense attention to a single topical area within the field of human rights, and where possible, comparisons have been drawn between two or more politico-legal systems. Selectivity in the bases for comparison and division of labor reflecting various authors' tastes are discernible from essay to essay. This is natural enough, since the questions we pose are quite varied in kind.

At one level, we are concerned with genetic questions. Here the preoccupation is with matters of origin and development. As a point of introduction, the first essay describes the liberal pattern of human rights development classically typified by France, Great Britain, and the United States. This familiar foundation supplies a useful base for comparison as the range of countries reviewed is expanded in subsequent chapters. Richard P. Claude's essay, in chapter 1, on comparative history involves the presentation and analysis of what he calls a "four-stage model of transition" to the mature human rights systems associated with advanced postindustrial democracies. By linking each stage of human rights development to critical social changes, the author illustrates the interaction of social and legal variables over time.

The four phases of human rights development which Claude isolates are (a) constitutionalism, (b) negative liberties, (c) civil rights, and (d) positive rights. Where these stages of legal progress are concerned, the sequence and pace of development will vary from country to country. But even among countries of the widest diversity, priority attaches to the problem of political freedom or constitutionalism. Chapter 2 by James C. Strouse and Claude further examines the theme of comparative human rights development. However, the method of approach is entirely different and more nearly scientific. Regression analysis is used to clarify some of the socioeconomic conditions associated with advances in civil liberties and political rights among 122 countries today. The emergence of a "communications infrastructure" is found to be a requisite for the advance of human rights. The data show that developing countries are often faced with painful trade-off dilemmas between rapid economic modernization and libertarian political goals.

The chapters in part II are policy-oriented. That is, they are written by scholars (lawyers as well as social scientists) who have become professionally involved in a substantive policy area. Their work shows a commitment to look beyond the narrow reach of legal prescriptions and to examine specific problems in terms of the policy-making process and in terms of policy effectiveness. The tendency in most of the essays in part II is to turn from the genetic question of how standards and systems of rights originate to the functional question of how particular rights can be preserved and enhanced. These comparative policy studies help to spotlight many of the social as well as the legal conditions for sustaining various rights under different systems of protection.

Chapter 3 by Fletcher Baldwin, Jr., develops the thesis that political freedom conditions other forms and variations of human rights guarantees and institutions. His essay connects the idea of constitutionalism with three highly disparate political systems: Mexico, Uganda, and the United States. Although each nation evolved from radically different historical origins, each today has a constitution which promises to confine governmental power. Baldwin links fulfillment and default on this promise to the press of socioeconomic and political exigencies and to varying national goals. In chapter 4, Lawrence W. Beer's study concentrates on free expression in Japan with comparative reference to the United States. His analysis of speech and assembly rights and the public-welfare standard found in the Japanese Constitution illustrates the critical importance of cultural as well as institutional forces for viable, free expression policy. In chapter 5, social and political factors are likewise comparatively interwoven in the meticulous review by E. Jeremy Hutton, Krishan S. Nehra, and Durvasula S. Sastri of the right to privacy. Concentrating on the United States, Great Britain, and India, the authors assess the effect of social, economic, and technological changes upon standards of protection of privacy. In chapter 6, Otis H. Stephens, Jr. analyzes diverse institutional developments and remedial patterns that characterize policies aimed at implementing the right to legal representation in Canada and the United States. The similar federal structure in these countries makes comparison convenient and interesting. Manfred W. Wenner's study, in chapter 7, of discrimination directed against national minorities emphasizes the link between changing public policy in Great Britain, France, and Switzerland and the policy-making process in these countries. His analysis, relying on social science techniques, shows the impact of politics upon policy affecting the linguistic rights of European minorities. In chapter 8, the focus is on the construction of effective remedies to combat racial discrimination. Ved P. Nanda details recent Anglo-Canadian and American affirmative action programs to ensure equal treatment irrespective of race or color. He offers a careful comparative analysis of enforcement procedures and legislation. In chapters 9 and 10, the concern turns to policy affecting women and children. Patterns of family organization, interpersonal relations, role stereotypes, and governmental institutions are analyzed in the essay on the status of women by Anna P. Schreiber in chapter 9 and in the complementary study on the rights of children by Linda Breeden in chapter 10. In both of these essays, interesting Scandinavian-American comparisons are offered. Chapter 11, by Jay Adrian Sigler, is addressed to the most difficult problem affecting comparative policy research generally. That is the problem of locating and effectively utilizing research resources. Sigler's essay provides the research scholar interested in pursuing policy comparison in the area of human rights with answers to the threshold question of where to begin.

The final section of this volume is composed of four exploratory essays pointing to new directions in behavioral research. In part III, the focus turns to the most difficult questions that can be posed in any new field of study, those associated with explanation. Chapter 11 is written by Judith Gallatin, a psychologist. She asks how the concept of rights develops in terms of the requisite mental constructs and processes. Her essay offers valuable insight into political socialization related to human rights. She sheds new light on the psychological origins and development of the concept of rights, especially among the young in Great Britain, West Germany, and the United States. Chapter 13, by William B. Devall, also eschews institutional and legal considerations and presents a critical and uniquely broad-ranging review of the comparative social science literature associating human rights values with socioeconomic and cultural variables. He assesses the extent to which social scientists have been able to come to grips with questions about the sources of supporting public opinion favorable to human rights. Chapter 14, by Carl Baar, reviews the progress and difficulties associated with recent efforts by political scientists to devise categories of analysis that will so order data as to further the scientific task of foreseeing how the decisional bodies concerned with rights will act. His Canadian-American analysis is carefully marshaled to support the view that comparative research on judicial behavior can benefit greatly by placing it in a developmental context. The final chapter, by the editor, offers some concluding observations based on the preceding essays and the state of the art in interdisciplinary research. While it is premature at this time to speak of comparative human rights research as an academic discipline, the bases for promise and future exploration are discussed. Problems of focus and methodological difficulties are assessed in terms of the intersection points between law and social science implied by comparative work in the field of human rights research.

Taken as a whole, the volume undoubtedly raises more questions than it answers. It is offered as a call to scholars for additional effort. The pressing reasons for such a call confront us daily in the news. Radio dispatches beamed to neighboring countries decry the end of civil liberties as the forces of a dictatorial coup d'état close in on the doomed broadcaster. Artists and writers publicly appeal for people worldwide to keep abreast of human rights developments in countries other than their own. Racial, ethnic, linguistic, and religious minorities face the traumatic experience of exile in the hope that citizens in their new host countries will receive them with good will and understanding. With events such as these becoming commonplace, one would expect to find a well developed scholarly literature on the topic of human rights. The essays in this volume reflect an effort by their respective authors to cooperate in such an interdisciplinary effort. But the task has been made difficult by the fact that there are no precedents for systematic comparative research.

Bethesda, Maryland   R. P. C.

The notes in this book appear at the end of each chapter.

ACKNOWLEDGMENTS

The fifteen essays that compose this volume have not been published previously. Indeed, where several of the chapter topics are concerned, there is little preexisting literature available. A bibliographic note generally precedes each essay pointing the reader selectively to existing material which the respective authors found helpful in comparative study. But more than bibliographic dependency must be avowed in a work as far-flung and experimental as that involved in this collection of essays. Many acknowledgments are in order, and we would like to be explicit about our gratitude.

Problems of locating comparative materials, sources of information, and "people resources" were, to say the least, multiple. Helpful in these regards were Professor Kirsti Bull, Nordisk Institutt for Sjørett, Oslo; Professor Morris L. Cohen, Librarian of The Harvard Law School; Professor Frede Castberg, University of Oslo; Assistant Attorney General Robert Dixon, United States Department of Justice; Dr. Héctor Gross-Espiell, Secretary of the Organization for Proscription of Nuclear Arms in Latin America; Professor Pirkko Koskinen, Law School, University of Helsinki; Eli Lauterpacht, Q. C., of Trinity College, Cambridge; Professor Gerhard O. W. Mueller, Director of the Criminal Law Education and Research Center, New York University; Justice K. R. Rao, High Court of Andhra Pradesh, India; Professor Aharon M. K. Rabinowicz, Hebrew University Faculty of Law; Professor Didier Leuba de Roussillon, Geneva; Mme. Helvi Sipila, Assistant Secretary General for Social Development and Humanitarian Affairs, United Nations; The Right Honorable Lord Shawcross, Chairman of the International Council of the Morgan Guaranty Trust Co.; Dr. Karel Vasak, Secretary General of the International Institute of Human Rights, Strasbourg; Professor H. Frank Way, University of California, Riverside; and Theodore Zoupanos, Associate Human Rights Officer, United Nations.

Professor Thomas Buergenthal of the State University of New York, Buffalo College of Law, deserves our special thanks for his incisive critique of the first draft of this book. Portions of the volume have benefited from the scrutiny of interested scholars. We are indebted to Professors Jerrold Becker, College of Law, and Robert B. Cunningham and T. Alexander Smith, Department of Political Science, University of Tennessee; Lewis Flyr, Yale University; Professors M. Margaret Conway, Theodore McNelly, Mancur Olson, and Stephen Woolpert, University of Maryland; Professor Richard Rosswurm, Marshall University; Professor Walter Tarnopolsky, Osgoode Hall Law School, York University; Professor Tom Truman, McMaster University; Professor Stephen L. Wasby, Southern Illinois University at Carbondale; and Professor James Wolfe, University of Southern Mississippi.

Ellen Baar, Colette Claude, Constance Pitchell, and Mickee Wenner gave valuable editorial assistance as well. Joseph Adelson of The University of Michigan collected the interviews used in Judith Gallatin's essay and aided her in cross-national research. Research for the essay on Japan was supported in part by a Faculty Fellowship from the University of Colorado and a Japan Foundation Fellowship awarded to Lawrence W. Beer. He also wishes to acknowledge the aid of Professor Masami Ito of the Faculty of Law, University of Tokyo. Portions of Carl Baar's comparative material on judicial activism were first presented at the 1970 annual meetings of the Canadian Political Science Association. He received helpful criticism from Eugene Dais, Sidney Peck, and Harold Waller.

The research assistance of numerous young scholars has contributed materially to work reflected in this volume. Among them are Janet Kelly, Chris Mason, and Vico Porco of Cornell University, who assisted Baar. Sewhan Kim of the University of Maryland was instrumental in the data analysis by James C. Strouse. Howard Labow and Jack Isaacs of the University of Maryland, and Glenna White of St. Hugh's College, Oxford all were helpful to Richard P. Claude's work. K. V. P. Sastri, Advocate in Hyderabad, India, assisted in the research on the topic of privacy for Durvasula S. Sastri. William Ris of the University of Denver gave useful support to the research of Ved P. Nanda.

In view of the present affiliation of E. Jeremy Hutton and Krishan S. Nehra and the past affiliation of Linda Breeden with the American Law Division of the U. S. Library of Congress, it is appropriate on their behalf to note that the views represented in their respective essays are solely those of the authors. Further, it should be noted that portions of the essay by Fletcher N. Baldwin, Jr., have been published by the *California Western Law Review,* and they appear here, with the editors' permission, in a different context and in substantially revised form.

Deserving of the editor's special appreciation is the General Research Board of the University of Maryland. It generously supplied a research grant at a critical stage in the development of this book.

The encouragement and aid of many persons, including but not limited to those named, have invariably been welcomed over the five years during which the book has evolved. But the sage words of advice of these well-wishers have perhaps been employed all too selectively. Having maneuvered from the safe harbors of established disciplines into the uncharted waters of a relatively new area of study, the editor and authors of the volume accept responsibility for their respective contributions. Where the comparative study of human rights is concerned, we cheerfully acknowledge that much remains to be done.

PART I POLITICAL-LEGAL
DEVELOPMENT

EDITOR'S INTRODUCTION

It is commonplace among political philosophy and legal scholars to suggest that the antecedents of contemporary rights and liberties are of ancient origin. Some point to the Greece of Plato and Aristotle as the cradle of freedom. Equal respect for citizens (*isotimia*), equal liberty to speak and meet in public (*isogoria*), and equality before the law (*isonomia*) all enjoyed recognition, however short-lived, as communal norms for the privileged class of citizens in classical Athens. Others find embryonic human rights springing from the Roman adoption of stoic notions of equality for all persons (not merely citizens, as in Athens). The Roman jurist Ulpian echoed Cicero in declaring that, according to the law of nature, all men are equal, and by the same law all are born free. Identification of our present concept of rights with early Christian philosophy or the advent of medieval constitutionalism also commands the attention of those who seek the pedigree of human rights. In the thirteenth century, Thomas Aquinas revived and expounded the classical doctrine that human dignity sets moral limits to political rule. Rationality, continuity, and coherence, if not linear sequence, appear to be inspiring features of such intellectual and ethical history.

Unfortunately, these qualities of philosophical history do not coincide with those of political history. As edifying as may be the intellectual lineage of the concept of liberty, such analysis should not be confused with description of the development of liberty and rights as empirical phenomena. There are understandable reasons for such confusion. On the one hand, the enterprise of legitimizing special pleadings on the basis of an idealized version of history is a familiar feature of political rhetoric. On the other hand, there is nothing disingenuous about taking the intellectual position that some ethical values are perennial. For example, philosophical poignancy has endured for 2500 years regarding the plight of Antigone, daughter of Oedipus. When Creon, ruler of Thebes, forbade the burial of her brother, Polynices, Antigone risked her life on his behalf to defy the law. The reason, she declared, was that the laws of man must not interfere with the immortal, unrecorded laws of God. Her story was told in "Antigone" by Sophocles in the sixth century B.C., and with equal appeal by Jean Anouilh in the twentieth century existentialist drama of the same name. Ancient justifications for confronting autocratic and tyrannous rule may enjoy permanent recognition, but obviously the practical problems of how to frame an effective political response change over time.

If we forebear projecting onto actual historical developments the unilinear appearance characteristic of history of ideas scholarship, we are bound to follow a more difficult course of comparative research. It must be grounded on the premise that ideas do not always shape events, influence institutions, or explain behavior. Segmented development and nonrational processes come into focus, for these qualities characterize the construction of the actual institutions of liberty as we know them today. The task for research is to locate human rights policy in the larger context of law and social development, as suggested by such diverse scholars as Wallace Mendelson, David Trubek, and Marc Galanter.[1] The challenge is substantial. As soon as we commit ourselves to the position that human rights development must be examined empirically, we face a difficult problem of scholarly inquiry. Should our research look for discernible serial stages of historical development, or should we seek patterns in cross-sectional analysis which offer clues to the processes of development? In part 1, the first chapter tries to answer the former question, while chapter 2 takes the latter approach.

The "classical model" set out in chapter 1 adds up to a phased typology built upon the experience of modern liberal democracies. The serial approach used there relies on historical analysis to posit one background condition and four common problems of human rights development which appear to have wide import. Each problem is discussed in terms of related sociopolitical processes and problem responses. The sociopolitical problems emphasized in each case rely upon the theoretical analysis of processes identified by Leonard Binder et al. in *Crises and Sequences in Political Development.*[2]

The emphasis in chapter 2 is less upon legal and institutional development and more upon a cross-sectional analysis of rights policies and social indicators worldwide. In this essay, Strouse and Claude move in the direction of building cross-national theory in the field of human rights study. In an exploratory statistical analysis, they rigorously review some of the relationships that appear in cross-national data between levels of economic and social development in a given country and the development there of legal rights and liberties. Among other things, they correlate civil liberties and political rights variables with communications indicators among the 122 countries for which data were available. The research suggests that where a plateau of economic development has already been achieved, social communications may take a three-way set of paths:

government to people; people to government; and people to people. Where deprivation or rapid economic modernization emphasizes only the path from government down to people, conditions militate against the development of a balanced system of formalized human rights.

NOTES*

*In references to legal periodical literature, the number of the *initial* page of the work cited immediately follows the volume title. Page references to material specifically referred to in the text, if any, follow the initial page citation. Legal case citations correspond to *A Uniform System of Citation,* 11th ed. (Cambridge: The Harvard Law Review Association, 1974).

1. Wallace Mendelson, "Law and the Development of Nations," *Journal of Politics* 32 (1970):223–38; David M. Trubek, "Toward a Social Theory of Law: An Essay on the Study of Law and Development," 82 *Yale Law Journal* 1 (1972); David M. Trubek and Marc Galanter, "Scholars in Self-Estrangement: Some Reflections on the Crisis in Law and Development Studies in the United States," 1974 *Wisconsin Law Review* 1062.

2. Leonard Binder, James S. Coleman, Joseph La Palombaro, Lucien Pye, Sidney Verba, and Myron Weiner, eds., *Crises and Sequences in Political Development,* Committee on Comparative Politics of the Social Science Research Council, (Princeton: Princeton University Press, 1971). For similar perspectives, see also Gabriel A. Almond, Scott C. Flanagan, and Robert T. Mundt, *Crisis, Choice, and Change* (Boston: Little Brown and Company, 1973).

Chapter 1 THE CLASSICAL MODEL OF HUMAN RIGHTS DEVELOPMENT

Richard P. Claude

Comparative literature on the politico-legal history of rights and liberties is neither extensive nor systematic. French, German, British, and Scandinavian scholars have shown a greater willingness than have Americans to generalize about staged development of rights and liberties and to scan lengthy historical periods.[1] Any effort to identify such stages is necessarily hazardous as an exercise in historical interpretation. Nevertheless, efforts to abstract identifiable processes and development sequences from historical experience is increasingly recognized as a useful preliminary step toward generating explanatory theory.[2]

The analysis set out in this essay assumes that a set of problems can be identified in terms of differentiated steps towards human rights achievements, and that, in the pattern of industrialized liberal democracies, there has been a tendency to face these distinguishable problems more or less serially. For the progress of human rights development, the only determined point or necessary prerequisite is the existence of a secure legal system. There must be a juridical solution to the problem of social organization for the ambitious march toward human rights to commence. Beyond this, the phased problems which compose the items in the model of transition are four in number. As a matter of convenience and brevity they may be labelled: (1) the problem of political freedom, (2) the problem of legal guarantism, (3) the problem of equality rights and political participation, and (4) the problem of positive (socioeconomic) rights policy.

The reader should be aware that the analysis of segmented development which follows is comprehensive neither with regard to the human rights topics covered nor in relation to the countries reviewed. Since the emphasis is on what Carl Friedrich has called "founding processes,"[3] I selectively focus on critical problems associated with innovating human rights standards. I do not offer a full review of the problems of established ongoing systems. Moreover, discussion draws largely, but not exclusively, upon historical developments in France, Great Britain, and the United States. These three systems supply the framework for what we may term a "classical model" of development. Though they are hardly typical in the respective ways in which they have fostered various rights, still their achievements are among those most widely emulated in liberal democracies. One reason for such emulation lies in the fact that each of these countries, in law if not in fact, has more or less achieved the establishment of a mature legal rights system.

While France, Great Britain, and the United States thus illustrate three variations on the classic path toward human rights development, it must be conceded that there may be and have been many alternatives to these classic patterns. American scholars of law and development have recently begun to issue healthy warnings against "ethnocentric" interpretations of comparative law and politics. David Trubek and Marc Galanter, for example, have counselled against generalizing about the impact of "liberal legalism" upon the social and economic development of third world countries.[4] The twin tenets of "liberal legalism" are the tendency to equate the concept of development with the gradual industrializing advances of the West, and the tendency to equate "modern law" with the legal structures and cultures of the West. The point of this cautionary analysis is that, while liberal democratic regimes supply an apt basis for a model of gradual change, the quest of developing countries for rapid change calls for prescriptions derived from different theoretical assumptions. While the full implications of this observation go beyond the scope of the description set out below, it will nevertheless be appropriate in the concluding section of this essay to acknowledge the limits as well as the utility of the classical model built upon the limited foundation of liberal democratic regimes and systems.

MODEL OF TRANSITION TO HUMAN RIGHTS SYSTEMS

The beginning point for the model is a single background condition, that of a secure and procedurally regularized legal system. That recognized human rights arise, if at all, as an integral part of an established legal order may easily be taken for granted by continental legal scholars. For them, the words *droit, diritto, derecho,* and *Recht* are broad generic terms for the entire field of law. In each case, they also happen to stand for the specific equivalent of the English word, right, so closely tied linguistically is the concept of rights with the system of law.

The background condition. Listing the security of the legal system as a background condition implies nothing fanciful about "government of laws, not of men," nor should the proposition be taken to insinuate a scholarly gloss upon cliches about "law and order." It simply means that, preliminary to any movement towards human rights development, the framework of an operative legal system must be securely established. Where the security of the legal system does not exist, incipient or actual conditions of violence prevail in which *force majeure* capriciously and unpredictably sets up an equation between might and right. There is this grain of truth in Thomas Hobbes's analysis of the state of nature: where human beings strive to satisfy their respective wants under conditions of interdependence, questions of mutual concern will have to be decided in one way or another.[5] To leave their resolution to the play of raw force is always a possibility inherent in every social grouping. Neither the resultant anarchy nor alternative regimes of slaves and master supply a field for freedom. Where law and the authority of its defenders end, neither security nor freedom is possible, Jean-Jacques Rousseau argued, noting that ". . . the strength of the state can alone secure the liberty of its members."[6]

However agreeable Rousseau's point may be in normative terms, it is at least historically correct to say that, as a value promoted by law, security antedates freedom. In Max Weber's analysis, a legal system may be secure even though it is quite primitive, as is the case where "charismatic justice" results in the unpredictable but legitimate settlement of disputes depending on personal relations, or circumstances of "khadi justice" where blind reliance on precedent prevails or an oracle's revelations are relied upon to dictate doom or ordeal.[7] By contrast, a procedurally regularized legal system is closer to Weber's ideal of "rational justice." Where it exists, a constitutive understanding prevails about how members of an interdependent society are to conduct themselves relative to each other. Weber also associates "rational justice" with regularized arrangements to govern the operation of procedures for the settlement of questions of group concern.

Where procedurally regularized legal institutions have taken hold, a necessary, but by no means sufficient, condition exists for human rights development. This point has been effectively made in historical terms by Professor Paolo Colliva of Bologna who has done detailed research on the late medieval constitutions of upper Italy.[8] In his search for medieval antecedents of modern human rights systems, he emphasizes the importance of the development of regularized and rationalized legal procedures under Italian free-community constitutions. In this context, Colliva distinguishes between the setting of human rights standards and the establishment of constitutionalism. Where standards are concerned, primitive forms of rights guarantees found in early sources lack universal applicability. Thus, medieval examples that appear to indicate an ancient tradition of guaranteeing liberties by contract include Magna Carta in the twelfth century, the Golden Bull of Hungary issued in the thirteenth century, and the King's Chapters of the Swedish County Laws dating from the fourteenth century.[9] But as originally formulated, all of these examples involve royal promises on behalf of securing privileges for the peerage. Human rights standards for the common man have no early precedent. On the other hand, Colliva reports that one can speak of incipient constitutionalism and secure legal systems flourishing intermittently throughout the *media tempestas* of the fifth to the fifteenth centuries. Against this background, he scores the assumption that the French and American eighteenth century revolutions mark the first stage of the path towards publicly defined legal rights. His point is that, while such rights are not precisely traceable to medieval continental experience, nevertheless, their requisite legal setting had earlier prevailed in the form of constitutionalism and procedurally regularized institutions of law.

For example, the medieval European revival of Roman law made it possible to create binding contractual agreements and to speak on a purely private basis of mutual rights and duties fixed by law between private parties. Itself the product of a developed commercial system, Roman law contained many principles adaptable to the needs of breaking down the particularism of the feudal order. In Max Weber's terms, the late medieval popularity of Roman law "was due to its rational form and . . . the increasingly complicated nature of the cases arising out of the more and more rationalized economy [which] was no longer satisfied with the old crude techniques of trial by ordeal or oath but required a rational technique of fact-finding such as the one in which . . . university men were trained."[10]

Roman law, while received in Scotland, did not penetrate England. With its distinctive system of judge-made laws, England enjoyed greater continuity in the security of its legal system (since 1066) than elsewhere in Europe. Continuity, the peculiarly public character of English assizes, and the flexible ingenuity of the common law all lent to English judges a greater popular esteem than that attached to continental counterparts. These elite of independent judges were, of course, the key figures in establishing "the rights of Englishmen," especially in the seventeenth century. Such innovation was made possible by the gradual introduction into the legal system of the differentiated systems of legislation and judge-made law as active new instruments in shaping of behavior and institutions.

Flexibility and bureaucratization of the administration of justice were important elements of legal development in France and England. Nevertheless, in Max Weber's view, such development was uneven and retained some nonrational features, for example, the French *lit de justice* and the English and American jury system all demand the rendering of verdicts where the reasons are not pronounced. In comparing Roman and common law development, Weber concluded that the existence of a secure and advanced legal system is a necessary condition for progress towards human rights development. Weber made this point in the following terms: "The demands for 'legal equality' and of guarantees against arbitrariness require formal rational objectivity in [the] administration [of justice] in contrast to personal free choice on the basis of grace, as characterized the older type of patrimonial authority."[11] In these terms, a secure legal system appears to be necessary for the dispensing of justice with regularized procedures for settling disputes. Once that condition obtains, other circumstances intrude to control the outcome of human rights prospects. For example, the more economically simple and socially homogeneous the social structure, the greater the reliance on rule making and rule adjudication based on systems of personal relationships, customary law, and religion, according to

Weber. Alternatively, assuming a secure legal system, the more economically developed the social system, the greater the tendency to develop institutionally differentiated legal structures and flexible and rational settling procedures. Where these conditions prevail, construction of a human rights system becomes possible through the development of legislation, regularized settling procedures, and/or judge-made law—the institutional tools for adapting a legal system to incremental social and political change.

1. The Problem of Political Freedom

Against the single background condition of secure and procedurally regularized legality, the first step toward human rights is worked out in terms of the problem of political freedom. The dynamics of human rights history present the problem of political freedom as a practical one rather than as a philosophic one, yet it is the pragmatic vocabulary of the philosopher John Locke which we can use for a definition. Political freedom is the condition of "not being subject to the inconsistent, uncertain, unknown, arbitrary will of another man."[12] What does this problem have to do with the background requisite of a secure legal system stipulated above? Unfortunately, Locke's fictional "social contract" ideas obscure the prior necessity for legal security if the problem of political freedom is to be managed. The tie between legal security and political freedom lies in the fact that in the liberal tradition the chief institutional solution to limiting the use of power has historically relied on balanced power wrapped up in the stipulations of legal limits. It is a problem of setting legitimate limits to domination.

Problems and processes. Max Weber defines "domination" as the probability that certain specific commands (or all commands) will be obeyed by a given group of persons.[13] He hastens to add that in order to achieve a measure of uncoerced compliance, such domination must be legitimate. It must be believed to be rightful. The establishment of political freedom demands that countervailing power be used to check government absolutism. The problem is tied in with a critical shift in patterns of legitimacy. When old equilibrium points in a traditional society change and a new balance of social forces is institutionalized by legal checks on power, prevailing beliefs about rightful authority are strained. A profound transformation in the legitimacy of restrained power is set in motion, even though such a transformation rubs against the grain of prevailing opinion in older traditional societies.[14] Where social structure is popularly attributed to divine plan, moral sanctions are gratuitously seen as sufficient to punish a tyrannical ruler. In such a traditional social order, no opposition short of treason could seriously arise between the objectives of the common individual and those of the rules of the community. In a traditional society, even where natural law doctrines are invoked against abusive power, it may not be the individual and government that are opposed, but the ruler and eternal moral order.

Normatively diffuse and particularistic in application, traditional late medieval legal systems were so encumbered by religiosity and privilege as to forestall any but the most modest human rights developments. Most importantly, in the middle ages, where the social organization of feudalism was concerned, no clear distinction was discernible between the "private person" and the "public individual." When this differentiation was made in the age of the Reformation, the process of responding to the problem of political freedom was launched on an ideological plane. The private person sought not a new legal definition of his status as a public individual, and still less, political power. He sought assurance of his private existence: to be secure in the family unit by being unencumbered with excessive taxation and by being left alone in religious (and therefore ideological) matters.

Achieving this kind of accommodation between the "private person" and those in power entailed a crisis of political legitimacy growing out of two outmoded features of traditional society. First, the essential norms and guiding principles of the older established legal order were anchored in transcendental standards—difficult to define and even harder to apply. Second, these systems generally lacked universal norms applicable to the whole society rather than to a few of its segments, estates, or classes. The process of overcoming these structural features of earlier politico-legal systems—the process of responding to the problem of political freedom, can be illustrated by historical reference to seventeenth century France and England. Although different results issued in each of the two countries, the dynamic process of achieving political freedom was initiated in both cases by intolerable acts of royal absolutism. Some descriptive detail is in order.

The precipitous issue in France was the St. Bartholomew's Day Massacre of 1572 involving the slaughter of thousands of Huguenots. The event hardly disposed of French Protestantism, but it did result in sharp political divisions among Catholics. Opposed to those who applauded the bloodletting, there developed a politically active group of French intelligentsia, administrators, lawyers, and publicists who made common cause for reform. Called *"les politiques,"* they criticized the royally sponsored program, while at the same time proclaiming their patriotism and Catholicism. Above all, they feared that national division would result from the centrifugal forces of religious fighting and royal family rivalries among *les grands*—the highest ranking nobles and royal princes (notably including some Calvinists). The pamphlets of *les politiques* were among the first widely distributed tracts to promote religious toleration.

Far from seeking constitutional limits on royal power, some writers among *les politiques* such as Jean Bodin ended up reconceptualizing the crown as the key to peace and order, a center of national unity above all religious sects and factions.[15] Reflecting the aspirations of the *bon bourgeois* and nobles, Bodin did speak of the rights of subjects to private property—a right associated with the institution of the family. But in his theoretical formulation, all authority which was not paternal was said to belong to the sovereign and was to be exercised directly by him or through agents. True to this view, royal authority during the reign of Louis XIII was thus conceived in absolute terms, and the king and subsequent regent, Anne of Austria (mother of Louis XIV), claimed to be "absolved" from any formal controls by subjects or their moribund Estates General.

Vestiges of feudalism were supplanted by breaking down the virtually independent status of *les grands*. But as national unity coalesced around newly centralized administration, resistance to the crown continued. The cost to Louis XIII of military forays against Huguenot strongholds included the development of antagonism within the royal administration itself. The collision between the imperious policies of Richelieu and Mazarin on the one hand and overtaxed subjects on the other, stimulated numerous tax rebellions, and finally the major revolt of the 1640s, "*la Fronde.*"[16]

La Fronde was the last attempt prior to the French Revolution to challenge royal absolutism. Beginning in 1643 and approaching success in the critical years 1648 to 1652, *la Fronde* involved a rebellion led by an elite corps of French judges. Most important among them were those associated with the *Parlement* (law court) of Paris. This eminent judicial body was traditionally charged with registering royal decrees. Encouraged by apparent popular sympathy and by contemporaneous political revolution in England, the *Parlement* attempted to establish a primitive form of judicial review for itself by defying Cardinal Mazarin, minister to the Boy-King, Louis XIV. In claiming immunity from royal control, Advocate General Omer Talon noted that the judges were insisting merely upon "freedom to debate" though that claim "will result in the option of modifying [laws] and appending conditions which will render void their execution."[17] Thus the exaction of various public taxes which had not been freely and expressly authorized was said to be illegal. The office of *intendant* (regional tax collectors appointed by the crown to take over a traditional function of *les grands*) was abolished, and various regency ministers were overthrown. Moreover, the movement led to the curbing of arbitrary detentions and baseless arrests. To these demands, Parisians gave support by erecting barricades in anticipation of a policy of retrenchment. Mazarin temporarily sanctioned the new order while his troops were fighting in Germany. Though fleeting and mere paper guarantees, these reforms helped to popularize the liberal cause of restraining tyranny and limiting the powers of government. The idea survived, although temporary political freedom was crushed within six months by Regency troops. With the concessions annulled, the path was cleared for the royal absolutism of Louis XIV's later years.

In England, the question of whether the law reflected merely the king's pleasure and command reached a critical point during the first half of the seventeenth century. The solution of parliamentary supremacy was painfully affected by revolution but eventually worked out in a framework of legality.

Indeed, the central issue of the Civil War of 1642–1649 was the question of whether the king was bound by the law. The practical issue of this crisis involved challenges from the peerage (and eventually from the common man) to the traditional royal prerogative of suspending the law and applying it selectively by arbitrary grants of dispensation.[18]

In 1627, King Charles I called for the arrest of five knights who had resisted the royal demand for a "loan." The argument that the exactions were made without the authorization of Parliament was of no avail in preventing the knights' imprisonment. The jailor justified the detention by reference to the crown mandate, and the judge accepted this explanation as a sufficient return to a writ of habeas corpus.[19] The following year in the Petition of Right, Parliament objected to this style of law by command. But Charles, viewing such efforts to restrict his authority as "impertinent to observe," tried to govern without Parliament from 1629 to 1640. With this institutional irritation effectively dissolved, the king had to face the more difficult task of raising sufficient funds to continue the public business. For example, paying the army in the war with Scotland in the late 1630s proved impossible without supplementary monies. Control of such commercial revenues as customs duties was traditionally a royal prerogative. Charles extended its scope by calling for the collection of "ship money." The new tax applied not only to the ports where such exactions had traditionally helped to outfit the fleet, but also to the landowners in outlying areas as well.

Sir John Hampden was prosecuted in 1637 for his refusal to pay the tax. Was the power to arrest and detain him exercisable at the king's pleasure, or was it subject to rules laid down by the law? A majority of judges in the Court of Exchequer Chamber sided with the crown.[20] In a candid defense of autocracy, Mr. Justice Berkeley said, "The law itself is an old and trusty servant of the king; it is the instrument or means that he useth to govern his people by." Berkeley concluded that it would be very strange and a new proposition to say "that *lex* was *rex*; but it is common and most true that *rex* is *lex*." Justice Vernon added his view that "A statute derogatory from the prerogative doth not bind the king, and the king may dispense with any law in case of necessity." In 1640, when Charles was finally compelled to convene Parliament for financial reasons, it boldly annulled the decision in the Ships Money Case. It also abolished the Court of Star Chamber which was considered a tool of arbitrary rule.

After a series of such critical disputes between Crown and Parliament, civil war resulted within a short time, bringing the issue of the supremacy of law into every English cottage and leading eventually to Charles's execution in 1649.

Dissatisfied with Cromwell's early reluctance to turn military victory to the benefit of the unpropertied, the untitled, and the religiously dissident, the Levellers debated their views in the famous Army Council meeting at Putney Field in 1647. A remarkable verbatim record was preserved that reveals the Levellers as the first "liberals." That is, their scale of values put political freedom first; and freedom was extended to include government by consent of the ruled, who were described as enjoying a natural right to life and property. The program of the Levellers insisted on the need for more nearly uniform application of the law. The "Agreement of the People" used these terms: "That in all laws made, or to be made, every person must be bound alike, and no tenure, estate, charter, degree, birth, or place, do confer any exemption from the ordinary course of legal proceedings whereunto others are subjected." Further building a statement of asserted rights on the basis of specific past complaints, the Levellers called not only for parliamentary supremacy, but also for frequent popular elections of representatives, for religious toleration, and for an end to "impressing any of us to serve in the wars."[21]

This early effort at solving the problem of political freedom by reliance upon a written constitution for England was thwarted by Cromwell's short-lived military dictatorship. The English Bill of Rights, however, eventually established the principle that the king could not tax without the consent of Parliament, nor could he suspend and dispense from the law; in consequence, the king was subject to the law. This understanding of the entitlements won by Parliament and the people during the Civil War was formally accepted by William and Mary when they acceded to the throne in 1689 and accepted the Bill of Rights. The thrust of this effort to solve the problem of political freedom by legislative means was that the Crown thereafter was subject to the law and could not make exceptions to its uniform application. In this form, the problem of supremacy of the law was settled, and according to the English Bill of Rights, political freedom was to be ensured by free and regular elections of Parliament.[22]

In seventeenth century France and England, opposition to unchecked government was led by entrenched forces whose position lent continuity to the struggle. These groups typically represented upper social classes with their histories of superior resources, royal promises, and grants of privilege. From the history of their respective drives for political freedom, it is apparent that two conditions were the requisites of success: the pluralization of power, and the expansion of political communication. French experience suggests that the effort to establish political freedom may fail where centralized bureaucracy is effectively used by status quo forces as a counterweight against centrifugal forces of pluralized opposition. Certainly judicial review as attempted by *la Fronde* was not a necessary condition for political freedom, but some such form of postfeudal pluralized power reflecting otherwise unrepresented social divisions and economically successful groups may be hypothesized as an apt institutional requisite.[23]

Second, both France and England were simultaneously affected by the new social divisions of religious pluralism and broadened patterns of political communication. Where the Huguenot tracts in France failed, the Leveller tracts in England succeeded in extending the circle of dispute beyond noble and privileged elites to the common man. Such French pamphlets as *Vindiciae contra tyranos* and such English writings as "The Agreement of the People" and related Leveller tracts tended to frame their justification for limited political rule, not in the language of external, unaccessible forces, but in man himself and in nature surrounding him. In these broad terms, a critical social process was sparked in Europe to transform the bases of political legitimacy from transcendental to secular norms, and demands were voiced to replace royal command with rule of law. Thus the broadening of political communication was no doubt a critical feature of the move toward political freedom, though initial success prevailed only in England in the pamphleteering effort to reduce the sacred character of political obligation.

Elsewhere in Europe, the same process was being set in motion, but without early success. In his *Age of Democratic Revolution,* Robert Palmer summarized the eighteenth century erosion of royal legitimacy as a breakdown of "confidence in the justice of reasonableness of existing authority; where old loyalties fade, obligations are felt as impositions, law seems arbitrary, and respect for superiors is felt as a form of humiliation; where existing sources of prestige seem undeserved, hitherto accepted forms of wealth and income seem ill-gained, and government is sensed as distant, apart from the governed and not really representing them."[24] Of the many political upheavals of the seventeenth century in Europe, for example in France, Spain, Brandenburg, Sweden, and Russia, rebellion was abortive without an ideology so widely propagandized as in England. In these countries, efforts to popularize ideas about alternatives to royal absolutism were effectively fought with the heavy hand of censorship. On the continent, moreover, the effort to check royal power was diminished for lack of any institution comparable to the English Parliament that could mobilize rebellion by supplying a forum capable of cutting across deep traditional social divisions. By the end of the seventeenth century, only the English rebels proved successful. Their victory encouraged John Locke to give philosophical dress to the conventional and secular basis of government, and thereby simultaneously to expound and justify a solution to the problem of political freedom in terms of limited government, and miscellaneous subject rights emphasizing property, personal security, and religious toleration. From the base of this new secular ideology, Englishmen succeeded in unhinging the entire system of feudal society in favor of a new standard of political freedom, and the lesson was not lost on continental and New World observers.

2. The Problem of Legal Guarantism

What is the relationship of the individual to the government, the place of the citizen in the system of political rule? This is the problem at the core of the second phase of human rights development. Changing socioeconomic conditions impel the individual to see his legal status in a new light. Economic advances motivate the individual to seek adjustments that will bring legal facts into line with socioeconomic and political circumstances—to bring his citizenship role into line with emerging middle class social roles. The German term for civil liberties linguistically reveals these interconnected roles in the word "Bürgher-recht," or "middle-class citizen rights."

Problems and Processes. Significantly, the quest for juridically fixed claims which the individual can make against government arose side by side with the growth of the middle class—inured to an ideology of intolerance to arbitrary power. Acquiring economic resources, members of the middle class sought a marginal share of power and protection by some measure of legal recognition in the form of declarations of rights and privileges. The need, in some such form, to redefine the status of the individual as the institutions of agrarian feudalism declined was made unavoidable principally on account of critical changes affecting the individual in the distribution of material goods. These changes necessitated revised standards for the role of (1) the individual, and (2) the role of government.

(1) The assertion of property rights was the lynchpin which joined the individual's new economic role with his citizenship role as a public individual. Critical to the development of a postfeudal economy was the uneasy competition between monarch and merchants for the control of capital. Under feudalism, the network of distribution was tied to the landed sovereignty of the king; thus the system permitted compensatory privileges and stipends to the king's outlying landed agents for their efficiency in extracting goods and services from reluctant subjects. But to the commercially successful "third estate"—on the rise during the seventeenth and eighteenth centuries—material rewards followed accomplishments in the control and management of capital. With the beginning of mercantile banking and trading success for the propertied (but sometimes unlanded and usually untitled) middle class, the system of material goods distribution began to place a new premium upon ability and achievement. Legal entitlements protecting these values would have to replace the privileges attending the feudal structure of personalized property then giving way to exchange, commerce, and trade. The press of tax obligations sensitized the middle class to the need to use law as an instrument to protect the rights of private property. Thus eighteenth century jurists and publicists portrayed property as a natural right, representing the individual's field of action consonant with marketplace behavior. Only in his economic role as owner of property could the individual approach self-sufficiency and thereby resist the overstepping of others and the encroachments of the state. On this understanding, property rights were given the highest priority among the revolutionary French declarations of the rights of man, not only those of 1791 and 1795, but also the more radical declaration of 1793.

(2) In addition to the problem of harmonizing the economic and political roles of the individual, the relation of these roles where government was concerned also underwent scrutiny and change. In the eighteenth century, from Spain to the German principalities, rulers advanced extravagant claims of divine

right in ideological defense of the new efforts at centralized absolutism. In opposition, Enlightenment philosophic literature contributed to the case, not only for political freedom, but also for religious toleration and even broader civic liberties. A revolutionary novelty in the resulting ideology of natural law was the emphasis placed on the legal nature of the sphere of liberty, and the consequent insistence on government respect and protection of rights. Property, for example, was conceptualized by John Locke not only as a right *in re,* but also as a right against other persons. The role of government was accordingly to supply the necessary enforcement power to give everyone his own. In the lofty terms of the French Declaration of the Rights of Man and of the Citizen: "The aim of all political association is the protection of the natural and imprescriptible rights of man: liberty, property, security, and resistance to oppression." With the business of government thus radically redefined, the individual could get on with his private business. In terms less philosophic than those of the Declaration the need, as perceived economically, was for a system of rule strong enough to guarantee the legal underpinnings for private investment, and yet not so strong as to interfere greatly with the free decisions of men willing to risk their money and careers in the enterprise of commercial ventures.

In England, the fight for political freedom was led by Parliament. It had accumulated independent power as the king's reliance on it for financial support was inflated by the growth of the middle class. Although the role of Parliament was overriding in setting limits to royal power, jurists were pivotal in aiding Parliament to resolve the second problem of human rights development: that of the legal status of the individual. In this area, key judges aided doctrinal development sympathetic to civil liberties and sided with Parliament in its opposition to royal prerogatives. The courts were ultimately rewarded with a statutory guarantee of judicial independence with the Act of Settlement of 1701. The peculiarly English notion of "ascriptive rights"—rights grounded not in philosophical abstractions but in a process of slowly broadening out from precedent to precedent, was reinforced by an elite of reforming judges. As enforcement agents, they were positioned by various procedural characteristics of the legal system, for example, the writ of habeas corpus, to make good on their judicial independence by hampering an executive action. Moreover, English judges enjoyed a new level of popularity among developing English and colonial middle classes because the old common law doctrines of property, contract, and torts favored stable economic development by permitting the accumulation of surplus resources for investment. The common law concepts of trespass, negligence, and liability offered men opportunities under the label of rights to exercise their talents and enjoy the fruits of their efforts.

The strain between the English Crown and the courts dates from the beginning of the Stuart period, when James I came to London trained in the Roman law which then prevailed in Scotland. English judges perceived a threat to both their training and prestige in this foreign king's preference for the abstractions and logic of civil law. In response, segments of the bench combined with parliamentary members of the bar in support of a significant revival of old English law. The movement was led by Sir Edward Coke who effectively laid the legal base for parliamentary opposition to Stuart tax policies. Moreover, in his opinion in *Doctor Bonham's Case* in 1610, Coke set a dramatic example of the power of judicial review—later ignored in England, attempted temporarily by *la Fronde* in France, but adopted with permanence in America.[25] A skillful legal craftsman, Coke gave substance in his writings and decisions to claims on behalf of the "rights of Englishmen" by salvaging the feudal privileges of nobles and turning them into standardized public liberties. In 1628, Coke published his famous restatement of English law, *The Second Institutes,* which gave a libertarian reinterpretation to common law precedents, rationalized diverse elements of English law, and included an influential commentary on Magna Carta. Coke concluded: "Every oppression against law, by colour of any usurped authority is a kindle of destruction . . . and it is the worst oppression that is done by the colour of justice."[26] This was not merely legal obiter dicta, but strong political rhetoric as well.

An historic attempt to make good on Coke's words was asserted by John Lilburne before the Star Chamber Court. Defending himself against their effort to force self-incrimination, Lilburne replied, "I am not willing to answer anymore of these questions. Seeing that the things for which I am imprisoned cannot be proved against me, you try to get other incriminating matters out of my examination." The Star Chamber then condemned the political pamphleteer to be whipped and pilloried. In 1641, the House of Commons affirmed Lilburne's right of silence, voted him a large indemnity, and found that the Star Chamber sentence was "illegal and against the liberty of the subject."[27] In abolishing the special tribunal only months earlier, Parliament relied on Coke's understanding of Magna Carta to find that the actions of the Star Chamber had not been in accordance with "due process of law" and were contrary to the "law of the land." In addition to the silence privilege legislatively affirmed in 1641, Parliament also reformulated the right of personal liberty from unlawful detention in the Habeas Corpus Acts of 1640 and 1679, held the Crown to the Bill of Rights in 1689, established the beginnings of religious liberty in the Toleration Act of the same year, and ensured the freedom of the press by permitting the old Licensing Act to lapse in 1695. The English Bill of Rights sets out a list of complaints against earlier royal abuses. It especially singles out the principle of trial by jury for reaffirmation along with prohibitions on excessive fines and bail and the imposition of cruel and unusual punishments.

These rights and liberties, though inspiring achievements in the eyes of non-English observers, were justified less by resort to "natural rights" concepts than by fictitious legal reference to "the ancient customs of the realm." The right to debate policy freely within Parliament, for example, was but one of many guarantees of the Bill of Rights which, of course, was not sanctioned historically by ancient custom. But the moral basis in tradition for the assertion took second place to the fact that people had come to want to propagandize their own beliefs, maintain or extend the position of their groups in society, and promote a free exchange of men and ideas congruent with market realities and human hopes. Even John Locke's theoretical "natural rights" formulations were of secondary importance compared to the crafting of standards of liberty by English jurists. Nevertheless, Locke fairly reflected the prevailing priority of values by emphasizing the protection of property and slighting personal liberties.

In the secular imagination kindled by Enlightenment reformers, natural rights ideology (as voiced by Rousseau, Siéyès, Paine, and Jefferson) increasingly assumed a programmatic character leading outside of England to formal bills of complaints and declarations of rights. In the hands of an elite American corps of the legal profession, natural rights even took on a revolutionary character. In the American lawyers' eighteenth century text, *Commentaries on the Common Law,* Sir William Blackstone had tied in natural law views with a summary of English law. With rights as the basis of his jurisprudence, Blackstone assumed that there are, strictly speaking, no rights of society, but only individual rights.[28] When American colonists resorted to arms to protest royal tax policies and excessive use of force, they could do so by evoking the immemorial rights of Englishmen which were considered identical with natural rights. Blackstone's view of government as a means to the end of protecting individual rights was particularly appealing to American revolutionaries, among whom were found many members of the Colonial bar.

The demand for professionally trained lawyers came with economic development in the New World and with the growth of trade and commerce.[29] Additionally, the fact that American Colonial legislation was subject to disallowance by the English Privy Council (voiding Colonial law for inconsistency with English law) made the skill of the lawyer a necessity for drafting Colonial legislation. For them, knowledge of English law was equaled by sensitivity to the grants of rights and duties laid down by Colonial charters. In keeping with the common law tradition prevailing in America, rights are invoked by writs and, as the saying goes, lawyers are in the writ business.

The First Continental Congress held in 1774 invoked English law, natural law, and traditional chartered guarantees in support of the rights of settlers to life, liberty, and property. The Declaration of Rights insisted that the rights of Englishmen had not been forfeited by emigration. Their claims included the right of assembly and petition, the right to "the common law," the privilege of the defendants to be "tried by their peers," and the "right in the people to participate in their legislative council." Standing armies in time of peace were declared "against the law" when unsupported by local legislative consent. Finally, it was resolved "indispensably necessary to good government, and rendered essential by the English Constitution, that the constituent branches of the legislative be independent of each other."

After the Declaration of Independence in 1776, Virginia, largest of the American Colonies, was the leader in constitutional innovation. Most of the Virginia Declaration of Rights was written by the planter-lawyer, George Mason. It served as a model for other state bills of rights, the later federal Bill of Rights of 1791, and the famous Declaration adopted in revolutionary France. Several of its articles specified basic principles of government: human equality, the right of revolution, majority rule, the "separation of powers," and the superiority of civil over military power. The remaining provisions set out the most systematic list of the rights of individuals published up to that time (1776). Every man with an interest and attachment to his community was entitled to vote. The rights of an accused were to include the privilege against compelled self-incrimination, the right to notice of the nature and cause of his arrest, and the rights to a speedy jury trial free from excessive bails and fines as well as cruel and unusual punishments. General warrants of search and seizure were condemned as "grievous and oppressive." Civil disputes should be settled by juries. Freedom of the press was promised as "one of the great bulwarks of liberty." The sixteenth and final article—inspired by James Madison, stipulated that "all men are equally entitled to the free exercise of religion according to the dictates of conscience."

The American Constitution drawn up in Philadelphia in 1787 made few references to individual freedoms. While it contained no bill of rights, some safeguards for personal liberty were scattered throughout its brief seven articles: a guarantee of personal liberty supported by the writ of habeas corpus and an assurance of jury trial. Bills of attainder and ex post facto laws are forbidden, as are religious test oaths. The ratification process among the states made explicit a demand for a more systematic bill of rights despite the claim of *The Federalist* that, where the new national government was concerned "things shall not be done which there is no power to do."[30] As the price for state ratification, nonetheless, a federal bill of rights was demanded and largely formulated by James Madison. Adopted in 1791, the American Bill of Rights provides that "Congress shall make no law respecting an establishment of religion, or prohibiting the free exercise thereof; or abridging the freedom of speech or of the press; or the right of the people peaceably to assemble, and to petition the Government for redress of grievances." The second and third amendments respectively affirm a right to keep and bear arms and prohibit the peacetime quartering of soldiers with any unwilling householder. The fourth through the eighth amendments guarantee civil jury trials and repeat the great criminal process rights assured by the Virginia Declaration of Rights—adding a right to defense counsel, the use of grand jury indictments, and banning double jeopardy. More generally, the fifth amendment asserts that no person shall be deprived of "life, liberty or property without due process of law: nor shall private property be taken for public use without just compensation."

Except for the corps of philosophically liberal publicists and lawyers in colonial America and eighteenth century France, no institutional ally of the emerging middle class proved as durable as the British courts and Commons in the task of stipulating the rights of the individual. Elsewhere the task of identifying various rights and liberties was left to the visionary field of natural law. Its terms were explicitly moral, and its earliest adherents were often persons with international perspectives. In 1787, Thomas Jefferson had written from Paris to James Madison about the necessity to safeguard individual liberty: "...a bill of rights is what the people are entitled to against every government on earth."[31] The view reflected not only Jefferson's conviction, but also mirrored opinion favorable to guarantism then gaining ground in France as well.

In the absence of any guarantees of citizens' rights in France, the king could imprison enemies without restriction by the notorious sealed *lettres de cachet*. By this device, critical expression of opinion was silenced by the threat of prison without trial. The law courts (*parlements*) could venture a protest against royal edicts, and sometimes strengthened opposition by printing and selling such pamphlets of protest. In response the king could either accede to the protest or summon the *parlement* into solemn session (*lit de justice*) and command it to register the law. In the autumn of 1787, the revolutionary Parlement of Paris followed the technique of *la Fronde* in refusing to register a loan for the nearly bankrupt Crown. But the condition was attached that the measure would be approved if Louis XVI would promise to assemble the States General within five years. In the face of royal delay, the Parlement boldly drew up a bill of complaints in May 1788. Among other things, it stipulated that taxes could only be imposed voluntarily by consent of the States General. It affirmed the right of judges to stay in office in spite of the king's wishes to the contrary; further, it insisted on the right of every arrested citizen to be brought promptly before a competent court and to be tried only by regular judges. This demand, emphasizing constitutionalism and political freedom, was followed by a meeting of the States General at Versailles. The tremendous upheaval following in the wake of its first meeting in 1789 culminated in the publication of the great Declaration of the Rights of Man and of the Citizen.

Issued by the new National Assembly, the Declaration began with the announcement that "men are born and remain free and equal in rights," and that the "aim of all political association is the conservation of the natural and imprescriptible rights of man" including "liberty, property, security, and resistance to oppression." Liberty is defined as "freedom to do all that does not injure others." Correspondingly, the law is empowered "to prohibit only those actions harmful to society." Law, being the expression of the general will, "all the citizens have the right to assist personally or by their representatives, in its formation and every public agent must be accountable to society." The Declaration specifies that no man should be accused, arrested, or held in confinement except in cases determined by law and according to the forms which it has prescribed; that no one ought to be punished except under a law promulgated before the offense; and that a man is to be presumed innocent until he has been declared guilty. Other articles of the Declaration say that no one shall be disturbed because of his opinions, including religious opinions, as long as their manifestation does not disturb public order as established by law; and that every citizen may speak, write, and publish with freedom, provided he is responsible for abuse of this liberty, in cases determined by law. Tax policy should be fixed by the public or through the citizens' representatives, and taxes "ought to be equally distributed among all citizens according to their means." The final article specifies that "since property is a sacred and inviolable right, no one shall be deprived thereof except where public necessity, legally determined, clearly demands it, and then only on condition of a just and prior indemnification."

Because judicial review had not been part of the French tradition since the failure of *la Fronde,* no effort was made by French revolutionaries to rely upon it. Nevertheless, to ensure consistent interpretation of the law, a Tribunal of Cassation was set up in 1790. However, not until the Napoleonic period did the Court of Cassation take over this function in association with adoption of the Civil Code. The responsibility of ensuring against errors of law in contested judgments and of safeguarding against failures to apply a rule of law are historic functions of the Court. It has exercised them largely on the strength of the power to issue cassation orders (setting aside an earlier judgment) and the order of *renvoi* (sending a case back to be retried on fact and law). With jurisdiction over private law, the Court has decided questions bearing upon the freedom of movement, the right to privacy, personal liberty, and safeguards against abuse of a person's honor or reputation. In mercantile law, the Court has upheld respect for the Commercial Charter of 1791 which established the right of "every person to engage in business, trade or profession of his choice," subject to paying a tax. In criminal law, the Court of Cassation is charged with protecting the citizen in his right to be considered innocent until proved guilty, his right to legal representation, and his right to humane treatment if proved guilty. Moreover, the Court was envisioned as the guardian of the two principles that serious offenses shall not be created ex post facto and that an offense cannot be based upon any but a specific criminal charge (the principles of *nullum crimen* and *nulla poena sine lege*).

Since the eighteenth century inception of guarantism, the techniques of enforcing individual rights, on the one hand, and the standards to be applied, on the other, have been the subject of comparison from one country to another. In 1789, La Fayette, who was then recently returned from America, read to the National Assembly the text of Jefferson's Declaration of Independence and the Virginia Bill of Rights. Mirabeau, who was rapporteur of the drafting committee, was known even earlier to have called upon the Dutch people to resist the domination of Austria, and to frame a "list of rights which belong to you as men."[32] Thus there was a cross-fertilization of interest in guarantism among France, Holland, America, and elsewhere. Georg Jellinek has attempted to show that the French Declaration copied American documents which, in turn, ideologically grew out of Puritan conceptions largely inspired by Luther.[33] French scholars, on the other hand, have dismissed both American and Germanic paternity for their classic Declaration, insisting that it was derived primarily from the European literature of the French Enlightenment.[34]

As sterile as the debate over the origin of French guarantism may seem, it does point to an empirical social phenomenon often associated with institutional innovation: the demonstration effect. Foreign observers, noting successful innovation, seek to emulate its success in their own countries. For example, the French Declaration became a model of constitutional legislation widely adopted elsewhere. That reliance helps to explain why, despite national diversities, the list of basic rights and chartered freedoms in Europe have many commonalities. The development of human rights in the Netherlands (since 1798), in the German states (1818–1850), in Belgium (1831), Switzerland (1848), Italy (1848), and Austria (1867) were based on the French tradition.

The problem of defining the legal status of the individual extended to other countries besides France and America partly because of the "demonstration effect" associated with the apparent success of France and America. The prominence of France in world affairs made notice of its example unavoidable, and the suppressed hopes of colonial areas for national sovereignty made of the American example a carefully studied lesson in achieving independence. In both countries, the demonstration of success in legally defining the status of the individual supplied widely noted solutions to the complex problems of transforming demands previously voiced as moral aspirations into declarations and legislation that promised to shape legal reality. On the grounds that legal formulations reflect social content and not just rhetorical imitation, it should be noted that French and American models also have been followed elsewhere because the socioeconomic conditions associated with efforts to create new political structures extended to other areas as well. For example, as sovereigns became financially dependent upon the support of a growing middle class, the need for legal change became more pressing. The political context of change in France—casting off an over-bearing absolute monarchy—was different from that in America—achieving independence from a colonial master. But the underlying socioeconomic processes associated with these goals had a common basis. Involved was the critical economic problem of altering the distribution of goods and services from a basis of feudal status and privilege in France, and of imperial prerogatives and colonial exactions in America, to the freer market conditions sought by the developing middle class and independent landowners in both countries. From the economic plateau of a strong bargaining position vis-á-vis government, these groups could define and demand from government a set of liberating legal guarantees matched to their interest. For many French revolutionaries, the goal of the Declaration was not only to clarify the status of the citizen and lend dignity to the claims associated with being a man, but additionally to elevate ability and achievement as values that helped to structure the newly rationalized system of material and service distribution.

Article 1 of the French Declaration announces that "social distinctions may be founded only upon common utility." American catalogues of freedoms primarily tended to safeguard the rights threatened by the English (prominently including property, security, and expression rights) so as to be free from restrictions imposed by a distant ruler; but to many, the superior object was so to define the status of the citizen so as to ensure his freedom of action and thereby to create an extensive zone of governmental noninterference in the private management and control of capital on a social scale. Accordingly, in both France and America, liberty was no longer the collective claim of a fixed upper level of society. Property was no longer the object of chartered lease from the sovereign; instead, life, liberty, and property became the inalienable rights of the individual. Under these circumstances, the potentialities for the growth of industrial production attuned to private individual initiative opened wide. Eighteenth and nineteenth century middle class development all over the world was associated with a tendency to equate opportunity with legal guarantees of individual rights.

3. The Problem of Equality Rights and Participation

The promotion of new standards of political and civil rights was worked out in nineteenth century Europe and America in terms of a drive toward democratization. Liberal democracy involves a system that is supposed to ensure that public officials are fairly chosen by the masses of voters casting equally weighted secret ballots in more or less competitive elections which involve public consideration of issues and candidates. Behind this composite of specifications lies a lengthy historical process which has resulted in electoral systems gradually and haltingly exposing government to widespread political participation.

Problems and processes. As new segments of the population are given entrée to the political process, their influx into the system creates strains on existing legal institutions. New interests and new issues arise in association with broadened participation. In particular, the issue of citizenship equality and civil rights becomes an important part of the adaptation required of the legal system to ensure the peaceful expansion of participation. The developmental link between political and civil rights lies in the fact that debate over democratization results not only in exploring alternative electoral arrangements, but also in politicizing issues relating to the legitimacy of social inequalities. The underlying theme of civil rights problems, legal equality, is an issue frequently introduced into political debate as competing elites vie for electoral arrangements favorable to their respective constituent groups.

The suggestion that civil rights issues are genetically connected to the working out of democratic electoral standards may be illustrated by reviewing five such standards as analyzed by Stein Rokkan.[35] First is the protection of the citizen's act: voting is made accessible to those who qualify consistent with a system of voting secrecy and protection against vote buying, tampering, and fraud. Second is the universality of access to the ballot: all accountable adults not in confinement for crimes or mental incapacity are given the vote, however peripheral their concern for public affairs. In the process of moving toward this objective, the inequality of excluded groups increasingly becomes the topic of debate as irrational exclusions are challenged on a group-by-group basis: the poor; aliens; racial, ethnic, linguistic, and religious minorities; the educationally deprived; women; and youth. Third is the weight of ballot influence (the "one person–one vote" problem): each vote cast counts as an equal unit of electoral influence. This standard is achieved only through the process of attacking geographical discrimination and politically sensitizing the electorate to the unfairness inherent in unequal schemes of representation such as rotten boroughs, and systems of legislative malapportionment. Fourth is the problem of organizational capacity: groups are assured the legal competence to nominate political candidates consistent with the legal standards for terms and qualifications of elected public officials. As this electoral standard is recognized, contention focuses on the lack of equal access to the political process—the economic barriers which are inherent in the costs of electioneering, and the invidious discrimination against candidates and would-be voters. Fifth is the modern problem of the public's control over public policy: interelection safeguards (such as lobbying and campaign finance restrictions) are set out to ensure some degree of continued public influence over policymaking and its execution. Inherent in this problem is the politically advantaged status of monied elites whose influence on policy is disproportionately inflated compared to that of the common man.

The histories of political systems moving toward these standards of liberal democracy present an amazing array of responses to the task of giving the people a voice in government. In liberal theory, the desirable sociopolitical order is that which relies on the least possible coercion, which allows the free play of spontaneous social forces, and which ensures controls on government. To the extent that these ideas reflected ideological commitments on the part of prevailing elites in early nineteenth century England, France, and America, they created a political environment conducive to expanding civic participation. More fundamentally, however, whether these benevolent standards of the liberal democratic order could be implemented depended upon a larger process of stabilizing the revolutionary ferment from which ideas of individual liberty had been born. With the expansion of society in terms of the formation of new postfeudal classes and commercial interests which had demonstrated their capacity to use violence against royal crowns and colonial masters, a new political problem crucial for the development of human rights emerged. The problem, in terms of competing social groups and classes, was to isolate conflict, manage it, and noncoercively to routinize it. The problem generated a lengthy process involving critical changes in political participation and equal citizenship rights. The problem of routininzing conflict depended for its resolution on expanding political participation because the related institutions of representation supplied the needed forums into which new social groups could be drawn as they began to express their demands. The routinization of conflict also followed a path of legal development whereby civil rights were defined in terms of minimum standards of equality for members of various groups (such as aliens, religious and racial minorities, and women) and a beginning was thereby made toward regularizing procedures for the settlement of intergroup discord on a premise of equality.

At the opening of the nineteenth century, democratic elections and equal citizenship rights existed nowhere. American merchants and landowners shifted their position from acceptance of de facto autonomy to the insistence on consent in taxing policy. In the absence of vestigial feudal social barriers, broadened political participation developed first in America. English aristocrats moved from a defense of their feudal privileges to their own active inclusion in the decision making associated with limited monarchy. Extended participation was slow to follow. The dominant elite of landed and *haute bourgeoisie* French (with Bonapartist and restoration interludes) eschewed the claims of absolute monarchy in favor of their own participation in the workings of republican constitutionalism. The new assertion of American ex-colonials for self-government on the one hand, and the claims of English and French privilege to control government on the other, gradually gave way to democratic demands for political participation broadened from an exclusive to a mass middle class base. As Guido de Ruggerio writes of the expanding nineteenth century pursuit of liberalism: ". . . liberty would now consist not in being independent of the state, but in taking active part in it."[36] In England, France, and America, the earliest implements of democracy—parliamentary privilege, electoral accountability, and political representation—were at first constructed by the upper classes for their own use in governmental participation. They were gradually and grudgingly redistributed to groups clamoring for inclusion and equality. These aspirations broke out in the bourgeois revolution of 1830 in France and in revolutions in 1848 in western and central Europe where efforts to stamp out Jacobinism were often successful. Acceptance of reform so as to avoid the more threatening danger of violent conflict was variously from country to country subject to multiple pressures. But in France, England, and America, two forces in particular helped to shape civil and political rights development: stress in the dynamics of social stratification and elite competition.

Social stratification. Taking wealth, prestige, and power as the indicators of social status, it is clear that the forces affecting change from country to country vary considerably. Nevertheless, stratification systems in countries with high levels of industrialization have more in common with one another than do systems in countries with low levels of economic development. Simon Kuznets has shown that, in the early stages of industrial development, disparities in income between social extremes tend to grow, while progress in economic development has the effect of bringing the mean, median, and mode of income distribution closer together.[37] In his analysis in *Social Origins of Dictatorship and Democracy,* Barrington Moore sheds additional light on the relationship between early industrial development and nascent democracy.[38] He argues that at the beginning stages of democratic development, the social divisions associated with the commercialization and modernization of the countryside are critical. Where the commercial impulse among the landed aristocracy is quite weak, the continuation of a peasant economy (as in provincial France) or a plantation system (as in the American South) serves as an impediment to the expansion of political and civil rights. Moore stresses that where agriculture has not undergone commercial modernization, the need of the elite to hold the political levers which keep laboring forces on the land is incompatible with concessions to broadened participation and equality rights.

The predominance of rural over town areas precludes the development of urbanization, industrialization, and the spread of literacy which are all precursors of the expansion of political participation and egalitarianism. In France and the American South, where status reversal was inflicted upon the landed upper classes, resistance to liberal reform was particularly strong. But long-term trends worked in the direction of more equality. Once economic development was underway, expanding technology resulted in improved labor productivity and wages. The related demand for higher levels of skills within the work force had an equalitarian effect upon social stratification because of increasing emphasis placed upon education and literacy. Modest rearrangements in income distribution prompted increased pressures toward broadened participation as well. Thus political rights and issues associated with equality developed side by side with industrial development. The fact that the system of social stratification in France centered on class and religion tended to link the struggle for participation with issues of taxation, group associational rights, economic and labor policy, and church-state problems. The French artisans who joined forces with republican groups in the streets of Paris in 1830 sought not only some remedy to unemployment, but also demanded voting rights as a way of gaining respect from other elements of society. In the United States, the Civil War abolished the institution of slavery and introduced a deeply divisive element of racial stratification into the struggle for civic involvement. Because of the basic color divisions characteristic of American social stratification, the quest for democratization gained association with issues of sectionalism, ethnicity, civil rights, and educational policy. The fourteenth and fifteenth amendments to the U. S. Constitution were adopted not only to assure the elimination of voting discrimination based on race, but also to guarantee black political participation as a symbol of newly achieved equal citizenship status and civil rights.

In contrast to rural France and the American South where the landed upper classes resisted the liberalization of political participation and equality rights, the English gentry and landed Whigs of the nineteenth century became a part of democracy's entering wedge. There the move toward extending political power was especially associated with the issue of achieving social status. Leadership for the Reform Bill of 1832 came from Whig aristocrats with commercialized farms, manufacturing interests in the industrializing provinces, and family ties to the banking center of London. Their views reflected a tradition (predating the Puritan Revolution) of opposition to royal bureaucracy and alliance with the upper ranks of town dwellers. Fearful of the example of the Paris barricades of 1830, which reformed the franchise monopoly of the great landlords, the Whigs passed the Bill over the protest of the House of Lords. The Reform Act improved voter equality by abolishing the worst of the rotten boroughs. While it enhanced the representational position of industrial, commercial, and financial groups, property qualifications remained restrictive, notwithstanding some relief in 1867. Urban and rural voters were treated unequally until the Reform Acts of 1884–85, and universal suffrage was not fully adopted until 1919.

In his essay on "Citizenship and Social Class," T. H. Marshall argues persuasively that the inequalities characteristic of the English social class system were made tolerable by the compensatory mechanism of extending political participation and equalizing citizenship rights.[39] An important lesson was drawn from the Reform Act of 1832, which extended suffrage to leaseholders and occupying tenants of substance. The cost to entrenched forces was relatively low compared to the benefit: thirty peaceful and prosperous years followed this experiment in democratization. By enfranchising shopkeepers under its terms, Britain avoided radicalization of the lower-middle class. What is more, economic and political stability contributed to the rising living standards necessary to expand markets toward which incipient industrialism was geared. In France, by contrast, only the upper-middle class could vote during the July Monarchy, and the press of economic and political disadvantage suffered by French shopkeepers fixed them by the 1840s in the mold of republicanism and more radical egalitarianism. Under the adversities which they suffered during the Siege of Paris in 1870, they joined Parisian artisans to form the revolutionary Commune.

In Britain, the Chartist movement sponsored demands for working class participation under a program of universal suffrage, secret ballots, and equalized electoral districts. In T. H. Marshall's interpretation, the impetus sustaining such reform efforts was bound up in the peace-keeping effort to open a path of mobility into the middle class to every law-abiding citizen to earn, save, buy, lease, or sell property and to achieve the political rights attached to economic achievement. The prospect of such apparent social gains was directly tied to the system of social stratification because the perception of class inequalities was softened with the promise of equal citizenship rights. Their extension in Britain is thus seen by Marshall as a politico-legal adaptation to the twin processes of middle class expansion and the assimilation of new groups into the middle class.[40]

Elite competition. The phased development of liberal democracy is the topic of an analysis by Dankwart Rustow which emphasized the importance of elite competition.[41] Constructing a model of transition to democracy, he identifies three successive development stages following upon a "background condition" of political unity. The first is a "preparatory phase" during which opposed entrenched elites engage in protracted and inconclusive struggle. The second, a "decision phase," involves settlement of the latter conflict by a small circle of leaders whose compromise incorporates a number of democratic rules of procedure. The final "habituation phase" is the most important for democratic development. It extends these rules of the game for competition to include an ever broader circle of citizen participants and to affect an ever wider range of issues including civil rights. From the vantage point of Rustow's perspective, it is clear that the decision to extend the vote and to construct legal standards of civil rights is not simply a response to pressures from below growing out of strains in social stratification. It is also the result of contests for influence at the top during the habituation phase of democratic development. During this phase, elites compete on a regularized basis, and they tend to adopt and promote the norms associated with sustaining open channels for leadership change.

Elite competition leading toward toleration for organized opposition was a part of the nineteenth century English pattern of party rivalry, franchise expansion, and democratization. For the Reform Bill of 1832, the Whigs took credit. The Conservative "leap in the dark" resulted in an even broader statute in 1867. The Act of 1867 brought the artisan class in the boroughs into the electorate and thereby created enough voters for political parties to develop organizationally. Disraeli's leadership in this effort was inspired less by Chartist reform ideals than by a conservative reckoning that the admission of the working class to political participation would strengthen national unity and generate new sources of support, however inarticulate, for the Conservative Party. The Liberals were responsible for the reforms of 1884 and 1885. Liberal efforts in the mid-1880s were likewise prompted by the quest for party advantage which resulted from a tripling of the electorate and a demolition of aristocratic influence in Commons because of more nearly equalized electoral districts. Thus, competition among English parliamentary factions helped to mobilize political participation and to make electoral engineering a continuous governmental function.

In the United States, the problem of political and civil rights has historically been affected by tension between federal authority and local control over the electoral process.[42] Conducting elections, defining the scope of the electorate, and protecting civil rights have generally been decentralized functions of state activity. Even before the Civil War, the process of democratization was afoot among state politicians who found it expedient to promote changes in the rules of the political game by increasing the number of participants. Jacksonian Democrats frequently were the originators of liberalized state franchise laws which enacted manhood suffrage or substituted taxpaying qualifications for property tests. But the realignment of voters by party following liberalization of the suffrage remained sufficiently unclear to motivate both Democrats and Whigs to sponsor electoral reform at the state level. Consequently, by midnineteenth century, adult manhood suffrage for all but blacks and females virtually existed under the laws of the states.

The growth of the American electorate has enjoyed bipartisan support, since doubt generally envelops the question of which party will be the lasting beneficiary of any given increment to the electorate, and neither party wishes to let the other take full credit. The classic pattern in the United States of democratizing political parties (acting as brokers in the process of enfranchising more and more groups) has carried Jacksonian democracy into the twentieth century. The consequences for the parties of this process is that, in addition to enlarged numbers of members, their structure, goals, and leadership recruitment may be changed. An internal redistribution of power within the parties tends to promote accommodation to newly entering groups. Thus parties are under pressure to become more responsive to the enlarged electorate. The peculiarly large size and weak organization of American parties, however, means that they are not equipped to handle the adjustment of rights and demands which accompany the process of group inclusion. Courts become involved as well. Their role has been to oversee the definition and realization of the rights of political participation and related civil rights.

The role of elite competition associated with political parties does not go far in explaining the development of civil and political rights in France. With the monarchs of Europe allying in 1791 against French liberal tendencies, deputies followed Danton's call to suspend the king and elect a National Convention (by universal manhood suffrage) to prepare a new constitution. With this revolutionary enactment of 1792, France was plunged into forty days of near anarchy and forty years during which the last vestiges of hope for parliamentary government were lost. France was swept in ten years from regularized elite competition through a constitutional monarchy (1792–95), to the constitutional republic of the Directorate (1795–99), and, finally, to the quest for authority and order which culminated in the establishment of the Napoleonic consulate and empire.

In France, full-fledged continuous competitive parties did not develop until late in the nineteenth century. Although the popular assembly under the Second Empire was said by the emperor to be elected by virtue of the most liberal law in the world, the significance of manhood suffrage to which he referred was blunted by restrictions on organized political opposition and by blatant reliance upon le découpage électoral (gerrymandering). Without competitive parties until the fin de siècle years of the Third Republic, the French enjoyed no continuous organizational framework for establishing roles and procedures useful in integrating diverse interests and in bargaining for goals and resources for which those involved might otherwise compete in a mutually destructive manner. Except for cultural traditionalists, the decline of feudalism in nineteenth century France meant popular rejection for fixed social status. The inevitable conflicts over inequalities of status had thus to be resolved without benefit of English-style party leaders viewed as brokers of social status. In the absence of such agents of accommodation in France, the revolutionary tradition had to carry the burden of popularizing assertions of civil and political rights. That tradition included the idea that revolutionary activity may be seen as a legitimate form of citizen participation. Indeed the revered Declaration of The Rights of Man and of the Citizen had asserted that "resistance to oppression" is a "natural and impre-scriptible right." From the many and varied periodic experiments in government during the nineteenth century, the French people gained a political education. From experience they could compare alternating authoritarian regimes and brief episodes of liberal democracy. The consequent evanescence of legally defined and enforced political and civil rights helped to sustain sentimental acceptance in Paris of the one form of participation which remained constant: fighting on the barricades.

On the more conventional side, the French nation was introduced from 1815 to 1848 to practices of a limited form of parliamentary government. However, the prospect of organized and sustained political party competition was imprac-ticable in view of the uncompromising rivalry of Bourbon, Bonapartist, and republican factions. Nevertheless, a taste of the right to political participation was gained by the institution of popular elections for members of municipal councils in 1831 under King Louis Phillipe. Universal suffrage was momentarily enjoyed under revolutionary circumstances during the Republic of 1848. The subsequent constitutional experiment of electing the prince-president, Louis Napoleon, demonstrated the centralizing possibilities inherent in establishing a plebiscitary relationship between the head of government and the mass of voters. The reorganized empire later exhibited some degree of liberalism between 1867 and 1870 when French voters were finally given a real opportunity to vote against official candidates.

In 1870, with the German capture of Napoleon III, government fell by default to the founders of the Third Republic. Although its early years were marked by political deadlock and unproductive factionalism, it eventually suc-ceeded in supplying a constitutional framework for regularly competing political parties. Equally significant, as political elites became habituated to competition, they articulated new ideas affecting French political culture. For example, Leon Gambetta, the founder of French Radicalism, argued that such democratic practices as party competition for office "best ensure social equality in law, in fact, and in custom, because the gradual achievement of social reforms is completely dependent on the kind of regime and on political reforms.[43] Gambetta's late-nineteenth century views, like those characteristic of the earlier English Whigs and Jeffersonian Democrats, had the effect of imbuing key segments of the population with the standards of legal-rational culture. That culture stresses the duty of citizens to exercise their legal rights and to partici-pate in politics. It reinforces a high sense of political efficacy: the belief that individuals can influence the political system. It promotes equalitarian values on the expectation that people should be recruited into politics on account of achievement and competence rather than social position and status. Its equalitarian impulse was unmistakably innovative in Third Republic France since legal-rational political culture was incompatible with the ascriptive views associated with earlier traditions. The day was finished, it was hoped, when people should regularly have access to political power on account of religion, ethnicity, race, and family connections.

4. The Problem of Positive Rights Policy

In times past, ecclesiastical almsgiving and the security reinforced by the extended family supplied the mantle of protection to individuals for basic bodily needs. But under the pressures of industrialization and the consequent adversities of unemployment, sickness, and old age, modern man tends to rely for support upon larger secular associations. The need for safeguards against the unexpected may be met by distributing financial risks among members of private associations: insurance funds distribute benefits to subscribers by the criterion of need; government-supplied security entitlements proliferate in the welfare state. By himself, the individual cannot always obtain employment, adequate education, sufficient medical care, and continuing wages upon retirement from the work force. Positive rights promise such aid and shelter from jeopardy. They are designed to protect the individual from the economic stress that would otherwise by caused by a suspension of income and to ensure to him needed medical care. Private insurance and employer-employee financed pension plans may be widespread, but increasingly the most important of security entitlements flow from government. Of course, the methods of extending such protection vary greatly from country to country, and everywhere are subject to the contingencies of changing social, economic, political, and legal conditions.

Problems and processes. Some theorists, influenced by the needs of the industrial age, have attempted in the speculative context of philosophic justification, to identify specific positive rights in advance of their legal enactment. Thus Jacques Maritain lists as the rights of the working man: rights to form trade unions, to a just wage, to work itself, to relief, to unemployment insurance, to sick benefits, to social security, and even to the ownership and joint management of an enterprise wherever an associative system can be substituted for the wage system.[44] To set a uniform standard of achievement, a number of positive rights are proclaimed in the United Nations Universal Declaration of Human Rights of 1948. A partial listing of these proposals is sufficient to make clear that positive rights generally presuppose an affirmative commitment from the state: the right to social security, the right to work (including free choice of employment), the right to leisure (including holidays with pay), and the right to a reasonable standard of living (including special care for mothers and children in need). Related cultural rights identified by the United Nations also demand government support, such as the right to education, and the protection of scientific, literary, and artistic works.

The development in any one country of schemes of positive rights depends heavily upon three factors: (1) economic potential; (2) political will; and (3) administrative capacity.

(1) Economic Potential. The development pattern of positive rights and welfare policies in various democracies differs from country to country. Genetically, nevertheless, there is a clear link between economic development and the organization of social dependence on a system of continued salaried income and cash wages. Because of the sufferings of many under the stresses and strains of industrial modernization, the idea has grown that protection can justifiably be claimed on behalf of those in the poorest circumstances. The result, in essence, involves governmentally set minimum standards of survival needs under conditions of industrial development.

Under the individual rights guarantees associated with the eighteenth century, security was derived from the right to property. Thus the right served an important social function in service of welfare needs. Since individual security depended greatly upon agricultural self-sufficiency or savings and accumulated reserves, it was hardly enjoyed by the propertyless. For them, the alternative welfare safety nets against disaster ranged from charity to frontier-adventurism. As the movement of workers to urban centers loosened the traditional links of family ties, the problem of poverty, old age, and unexpected destitution generated new social and political pressures. Consonant with minority rights and the process of political assimilation beginning in the nineteenth century, group associations played a significant role in meeting security needs. Efforts were made to minimize work-injury and health and old-age risks by transferring their financial consequences from the family to funds sponsored by the industrial community, the trade union, the farmers' cooperative, or the ethnic and religious association. But for better or for worse, the path toward national affluence has been away from the self-contained unitary economy grounded on property rights (whereby most of the necessities of life, including education, are provided in the home or extended private association). Of critical importance, the path of economically sophisticated systems has been toward nearly universal dependence by all citizens upon a continuing flow of money income for the necessities of life. In the context of the wage system, the circumstances of educational needs, labor injuries, ill-health, and old age increasingly generate economic problems placed at government's doorstep.

Since positive rights put a burden on the resources of government and the social commonwealth, the standard of achievement in responding to welfare needs is differentially related to economic development. Phillips Cutright has readily demonstrated this in a comparative study of broad scope.[45] He shows a positive statistical correlation between development in those countries which have undergone industrial transformation (using energy consumption as the principal indicator) and the length of time during which various social insurance programs have been in force. Cutright's comparative policy indicators were drawn from an American government report entitled *Social Security Programs Throughout the World.*[46] It distinguishes five general categories of government programs for meeting basic needs. An updated version of the report shows that in 1971 work injury compensation laws were in effect in 122 countries; old age, disability, and survivors' benefit programs had been established in 101 countries; sickness and maternity programs prevailed in 68 countries; systems of family allowances were the rule in 63 countries; and 34 unemployment insurance programs were in operation worldwide.[47] The ordering of these five policies does not necessarily reflect the sequence of development, although in most political systems, legislation in the employment injury field has been the pacesetter for other branches of social security.

A controversial point of debate concerning welfare policy in Great Britain has turned on the comparative statistics of benefits.[48] In the field of pension rights, the British have fallen well behind the standards of provision widely available on the continent. Joachim Wedel has shown statistically that the scope and generosity of social security benefits does not invariably relate to economic indicators such as the rate of increase in gross national product.[49] To appraise comparative policy performance, Wedel calls for a look at political considerations. The effective role of political variables in explaining differential social security benefits was originally documented in the comparative research of Henry Aaron, an economist. He has shown that program longevity is the single most important factor which accounts for higher benefits relative to wage levels.[50] The underlying reason is that benefits under existing programs are seldom cut back once they have been increased. Retrenchment is politically too risky. Thus the state of current research and the dynamics of political economy are such that one can say little more than that economic development is a necessary, though hardly a sufficient, condition for a comprehensive system of positive rights.

(2) Political Will. Aside from the field of education (in which the United States led the way in supporting public schools), earliest government reform along systematic welfare lines was initiated in Germany by Bismarck. In 1883 a bill was passed insuring workingmen against sickness and in 1884 employers were compelled to insure their employees against accidents. In 1887 laws were enacted which limited the maximum number of working hours of women and children. Two years later, Germany began to insure workingmen against old age and disability. These policies were represented as increasing industrial efficiency, and the democratic regimes in Austria, the Scandinavian countries, the Low Countries, and finally France and Italy followed suit.

For welfare benefits to be satisfactorily conceptualized as rights, more was needed than the recognition that related policies functionally served industrial development or that moral considerations were involved. The changing jurisprudence of workmen's compensation is illustrative. The original basis for a legal claim for injury compensation in Germany and other continental countries under the influence of Roman law was the principle of "responsibility." Compensation for on-the-job injury of an industrial laborer was due only if the employer were at fault. If the victim failed to satisfy the heavy burden of showing default on responsibility, he could secure no compensation whatever to cover his losses. Under the common law system prevailing in Great Britain, the Commonwealth, and the United States, the victim of an accident generally had to absorb its consequences unless it was demonstrably due to the fault of a second party—the employer in the case of work-related injury. Financial disaster was, thus, often visited on families of injured workers. On the other hand, unpredictably large damages might be assessed against employers. The winner-take-all appearance of such disputes not only provided dramatic newspaper copy, but also exacerbated industrial strife. Consequently, policymakers were sensitive to the need for change. The result, though under quite disparate legal systems, was to regularize (and also to lower) compensation on a principle of no-fault liability. This kind of "occupational risk" policy was written into French law in the Industrial Accidents Act of 1898, thereby modifying the earlier jurisprudence of contractual liability—*responsabilité contractuelle*. In Great Britain, the Workmen's Compensation Act of 1897 had embodied the same idea of no-fault liability, thereby terminating judicial reliance upon the doctrine of contributory negligence.

Widespread unemployment in Great Britain in 1905 prompted a systematic review of the administration of the British Poor Laws. Many of them could be traced back to Elizabethan responsibilities for almsgiving taken over from the Church. Among other things, the *Report of the Royal Commission on Poor Laws and Relief of Distress* proposed the replacement of archaic statutes with a broad program of nationally created insurance.[51] David Lloyd George's sponsorship of the proposal led to a scheme of unemployment and health insurance. The resulting National Insurance Act of 1911 was prepared substantially by Sir William Beveridge, chief architect of the welfare state in the English-speaking world. Many of the recommendations of the famous Beveridge Report of 1942 were enshrined in the health services and social insurance legislation passed by the Atlee Government between 1945 and 1951. Among liberal democracies no other country has embarked on a plan of medical services as ambitious as is the British National Health Service.[52] Moreover, Britain has achieved a scheme of pension rights for retired persons based on a universal compulsory insurance plan whereby recipients receive flat-rate benefits, regardless of means, in return for flat-rate worker contributions without respect to earnings. This basic program of social security is now taken for granted in Britain, and retirement care has come to be seen as a matter of right for the individual, designed to satisfy at least minimum needs. Continuing debate focuses on whether and how the program might be improved to bring retirement income closer to pre-retirement levels.

By the 1930s, only the United States among the economically developed liberal democracies failed to develop a comprehensive program of social security

rights. Wealth, cultural puritanism, a polyglot population, the expanding frontier, and a fragmented system of government combined to postpone basic policy
changes. Furthermore, until recently pressures for welfare programs in America
were deflated by the profile of the voting public. The proportion of lower
income groups casting ballots in national elections, according to Seymour Martin
Lipset, has been significantly below the political participation levels in most
other economically developed liberal democracies.[53] Nevertheless, in the 1930s,
dire economic depression prodded the federal government into action. Over the
years, resulting federal programs have focused on the major components of
social and economic insecurity. For example, inadequate income has been
marginally remedied by a more progressive tax system, and the right to join
labor unions as assured by the National Labor Relations Act of 1935. Jobless-
ness is the focus of the Employment Act of 1946. It declares that it is the
"... responsibility of the Federal Government to use all practicable means
to ... promote maximum employment, production, and purchasing power."
The logic of this general declaration supports an acceptance of fiscal and
monetary policies as a prerequisite for economic growth and as basic for any
welfare program. The expansion of welfare services, such as under the Economic
Opportunities Act of 1964, has developed side by side with judicial scrutiny of
classifications of recipients to ensure that "equal protection" rights are not
violated by arbitrary distinctions.[54] Partial compensation for disabilities resulting from accident, sickness, and old age is supplied by the Social Security Act of
1935 with its many updatings and various systems of insurance with costs
distributed among employers and employees. Federal Medicare and Medicaid
programs of the mid-1960s have encountered numerous difficulties in implementation. Nevertheless, two problems for future resolution already have begun to
press for public attention. First, should publicly aided access to health services
be assured on the basis of right (as a free public service as in Great Britain or
through social insurance), or should it be contingent on financial need? Second,
how much of the financial barrier should be removed? The widespread distaste
for a means or income-tested system suggests that the trend will be toward a
system conferring the right to health services.[55]

(3) Administrative Capacity. In contrast to earlier liberal assumptions about
the necessity for government to leave the individual alone and to refrain from
discrimination, the social and economic claims associated with newer positive
rights often require that the weight of state laws and administration interfere
with many things the individual would like to do. Examples include the collection of taxes, regulation of economic activities, administration of public welfare
services, and enforcement of mandatory education laws. Clearly, positive rights
depend on legislative definition and administrative enforcement. Their realization thus depends upon the depth and extent of government administrative
control and capacity. Will government merely license and standardize private
health insurance programs, or will it take over the administration of health

services? The answer concerns program legitimacy as gauged by shifting electoral majorities and patterns of legislative responsiveness. But the answer in administrative terms depends practically upon program effectiveness gauged by the capacity that government brings to administrative penetration into previously insulated social structures. Since positive rights are only as good as administrative enforcement services, their legal and organizational setting is important.

The penetration of government administration into every phase of society has had an important effect on legal structure. The evolution of positive rights standards has brought about a blurring of older sharp distinctions between private and public law.[56] An analogous blending of private and public organizational principles and procedures also has affected administrative enforcement services, especially during the initial stage of welfare policy development. An illustration may be drawn from French experience. In France since 1946, the existence of independent pension funds of private organizations has been illegal. The social security program of the *régime général,* nevertheless, bears the organizational marks of an earlier period when erstwhile private pension groups made and administered their own rules. Thus, at present the sickness insurance scheme for farmers, and the social security plan for the self-employed (especially shopkeepers) and others allow a certain diversity of standards and administration. Furthermore, the French supplementary retirement systems are based on freedom of choice of institutions, and the plurality of institutions is said not to impede effective government administration.[57] The authority of the funds over the payment of benefits recalls the idea of the freedom of intermediate groups which is characteristic of the pluralism of social institutions and associational groupings authorized by earlier minority rights standards.

An important philosophical question pervades the debate about extension of rights which are dependent upon administrative services. Negative individual rights and the rights of civic equality can largely be enforced by judicial action, such as declaring offensive laws null and void (where judicial review prevails) or (where *droit administratif* is typical) interpreting administrative decrees by reference to *ultra vires* action or other standards of legality and the rule of law. By contrast, positive rights require legislative, administrative, and executive planning to make and enforce new rules. Maurice Cranston has seized upon this institutional difference in the implementation of the older and newer rights as the basis for attacking the latter. He argues that social and economic rights are not "authentic human rights" because "it would be totally impossible to translate them in the same way into positive rights by analogous political and legal action."[58] One answer, offered by the British scholar D. D. Raphael, is that Cranston has unsuccessfully aggravated the philosophical question of the limits of liberalism by offering an Anglocentric institutional answer. How rights are defined and enforced is an important practical question. But Raphael accuses Cranston of erroneously supposing that the process to follow at the legal level, to ensure the exercise of human rights, must be the same everywhere.[59]

These divergent views reflect an old debate. Ever since Article 11 of the abortive French Constitution of 1793 proposed that society is obliged to provide for the livelihood of all its members, European jurists have heatedly discussed the imminent "crisis of legality."[60] Friedrich A. Hayek's *The Road to Serfdom,* supplied a controversial addition to the discussion. First published in Great Britain in 1944 and widely read since in the United States and Western Europe, the book raises serious doubts about prospects for the nonarbitrary administration of welfare rights. Hayek asserts the monumental charge that "any policy aiming directly at a substantive ideal of distributive justice must lead to the destruction of the rule of law."[61] His views have struck a responsive chord, especially among those Americans who prize the cultural tradition of self-reliance. Nevertheless, the American system of social security has substantially withstood the criticism of Hayek's supporters. In the United States, the citizen's personal contributions and salary deductions (in the form of social security taxes) levied during working years support the idea that benefits will be paid as an earned right, without eligibility tests, and in a manner safeguarding his freedom of action and his privacy. Because the conditions under which benefits are paid are clearly defined by law, the detailed definition of legal rights helps to minimize the area of administrative discretion. Moreover, the implementation of the law need not terminate with the rulings of administrative officials; their decisions may generally be tested before the courts, as illustrated by the Supreme Court's ruling on the social security question in *Flemming v. Nestor.*[62]

In response to Hayek's fears about administrative failings, Harry Jones suggests that Hayek offers scant evidence for assuming "that administrative officers are themselves alien to the tradition of honest judgment and fair decision embodied in the rule of law."[63] To redress arbitrary action, most countries lodge the ultimate review of administrative rulings within the jurisdiction of the courts. In France, the *Conseil d'Etat* offers an unusual example of jurisdictional control over administration by an institution which is in the administration but not of it.[64]

There is no denying that problems of administrative inefficiency and overstepping bedevil the claim that socioeconomic entitlements enjoy the status of effective legal rights. For example, in the United States, programs for economic security sometimes emphasize the question of eligibility in such a way as to create rather than to resolve conflict. Where arbitrarily administered means and need tests are used, the burden of obtaining the benefit may fall so heavily upon the would-be beneficiary that one cannot meaningfully speak of "welfare rights."[65] For example, in order to establish the need to receive public assistance benefits, social workers may investigate the property of the applicant and his family. Since many of the visible poor are black, programs for the poor are burdened by connotations of dependency and racial prejudice. The consequent mutual suspicion between the poor and the investigator may so cripple the legitimacy of welfare policy as to affect administration and to propel the program seriously into conflict with privacy rights. In Great Britain, investigation of fraudulent welfare claims has also raised the charge of excessive administrative snooping or Nosey Parkering. Discussion often confusingly blends questions of whether the programs are worthwhile with equally difficult questions about how the efficiency of the program is to be assessed. In these terms, issue resolution is difficult. For example, the *Report of the British Committee on the Abuse of Social Security* points out that by 1973 the number of certified sickness claims had risen sharply over the preceding decade (even allowing for population growth.)[66] But the Committee was unsure of how to evaluate the effectiveness of the National Health Program because it could not discern whether the increase grew out of fraudulent claims or changing attitudes toward health.

Care should be taken not to confuse standards of legitimacy and effectiveness in any analysis of the administration of positive rights. On the effectiveness side, it is true that the new socioeconomic rights cannot be asserted where the presence of government administration is not felt. To remove doubt regarding the equality of such rights, services must extend beyond the modern-sector enclaves of the urbanized middle class and into outlying areas to ensure the registration of claims and complaints by all qualified recipients. But where specialized field administrators are essential, such as in health care or old age assistance, the legitimacy of such rights over time is no more destroyed by temporary inefficiencies than is the legitimacy of the rights of the criminally accused when overcrowded court dockets raise questions about the efficiency of judicial administration. (Even assuming that justice delayed is justice denied, it does not follow that delays in justice are sufficient reason to rewrite the standards of fairness for criminal procedures.)

In the industrially developed liberal democracies today the most frequent, and perhaps the most important, contact between the average citizen and his government is not with the criminal magistrate. Increasingly the significant encounter is with the state establishment in the form of the health insurance administrator, the public assistance social worker, or the social insurance official. The social needs of industrial democracies have generated diverse new positive rights which, to an unprecedented degree, have multiplied citizen interaction with agents of government.

SUMMARY AND CONCLUSIONS

Because the discussion in this essay has been wide-ranging, Table 1 is set out to supply the reader with a panoramic view of the elements of development that have been analyzed. The scheme offers a genetic overview of the classical stages of human rights development which, in the three countries discussed, do not antedate the seventeenth century origins of the legally defined territorial state. In antiquity, what few restrictions were placed upon the use of power, over and

Table 1. THE CLASSICAL HUMAN RIGHTS MODEL:
LEGAL STANDARDS AND REQUISITE SOCIAL ORGANIZATION

	Problem	Background Condition	Political Freedom	Legal Guarantism	Equality and Participation	Positive Rights
Law	Legal Standard	Security of the Legal System	Rule of Law, Constitutionalized Limits on Government	Bills of Rights, Civil Liberties	Civil and Political Rights	Socioeconomic Rights
Society	Ideological Requisites	Support for nonarbitrary, rationalized system of justice	Universalistic and secularized ideology of the rightful bases of political authority	Acceptance of public-private person distinction in politico-economic intercourse	Legitimacy of ameliorating stratified social inequalities by reliance on inclusion of new groups into civic life	Recognition of the need for universal sharing of the risks of industrial development
	Organizational Requisites	Procedurally regularized system of legal administration	Political communication—technologically adequate to educate the populace to rule of law standards	Modernized system of economic distribution of goods and services and capital accumulation by regime-favored elites	Intergroup conflict regularized by setting minimum equality standards with related minority rights enforcement	Economic infrastructure sufficient for and supportive of health, education, and welfare policy planning
		Institutionally differentiated policy-making organizations	Institutional checks and balances consistent with social balance of power	Institutional arbiter of claims on negative government duties and professionalized scheme of remedies	Institutionalized political parties to routinize elite competition	Administrative penetration into every phase of society.
		Social choice processes affected by administration of the law	Social choice processes affected by pluralized power	Social choice processes affected by marketplace behavior	Social choice processes affected by group bargaining	Social choice processes affected by centralized planning

above the practical limits set by technological backwardness, were at most moral postulates. In the Middle Ages, where chartered guarantees of rights were set out in documentary form, the protection was seldom general, but involved privileges for particular towns, estates, or classes. By contrast, the modern solution to the problem of curbing power in the name of political freedom involves an effort to make power impersonal by placing government under law. The classical notion of rule of law thus encompasses protection against arbitrary power, the principle that law should prevail, and that arbitrary power may not be exercised against the individual.[67]

One of the principal difficulties involved in translating moral response to social need into modern legal change lies in society's understanding of the role of the individual. He must be seen, not only in terms of his private needs, but also in terms of his public citizenship role. The process of distinguishing between the private person and public individual (which penetrates social consciousness ideologically during the process of achieving political freedom) enters a new stage of development with the effort to define the role of the public individual in terms of legally fixed rights. To this problem the liberal response was classically framed in seventeenth and eighteenth century declarations and bills of rights. An optimistic faith in such "guarantism" was placed in documentary shields promising to the individual security from overreaching governments. Newly asserted civil liberties were supposed to protect the individual from arbitrary governmental demands (such as unreasonable taxes and military service), from unfair criminal process, and from political interference (such as with the individual's personal security, property, family circle, and freedom of religion and thought).

The liberal idea, born of the eighteenth century, required of government chiefly those limited actions which protect freedom by forbidding interference with the individual. The resulting civil liberties which define the status of the individual are generally correlative to negative duties of the state. They are largely consistent with an optimistic view of man as a self-directing agent living in a materially sufficient environment, coupled with a pessimistic view of government seen as overreaching and potentially tyrannous. By contrast, political and civil rights largely reflect a series of more typically nineteenth century legal accomodations to the demands of various groups for guarantees of equal rights of civic participation. In the main, they are consistent with an egalitarian view of man as a politically competent participant in shaping public policy, coupled with a positive view of government as capable of using the mechanisms of law-making to mitigate the legal consequences of social inequality. The resulting civil and political rights are, by and large, correlative with positive policies of government protection and enforcement. They involve, in a phrase attributed to John Stuart Mill, "arrangements for freedom" although little more may be required of the state than that it place its power behind a set of prohibitions against interference with the exercise of equal rights on behalf of those new groups to which participation rights are extended.[68]

During the twentieth century, new economic and social claims have come to broaden the spectrum of human rights. Because they depend for their fulfillment on affirmative government policy, they may be referred to collectively as positive rights. They are designed in legal terms to meet basic human needs not otherwise satisfied by the socioeconomic system. In the twentieth century, the combined influence of political parties and trade unions has been decisive in promoting positive-rights policies of social welfare. In the earliest phases of such policy development their spokesmen have often been effective in noting that welfare policies promote industrial efficiency, and they have been skillful in applying the symbolism and rhetoric of human rights to the field of welfare security policy. Positive rights place upon government the task of protecting the people from the misfortunes of industrial life. The aim is to remedy by welfare the needs which were privately satisfied in the earlier stages of human-rights development when negative rights were functionally linked to an ideal of individual self-sufficiency.

The classical model as a source of empirical questions. The classical model of developing rights and liberties which has been synthesized in this essay has both uses and limits. It is useful as a teaching device because it helps scholars to overcome the tendency to accept without question the sundry aspects (norms, concepts, and institutions) of their own legal systems. Since the study of comparative human rights seeks to explain differences and similarities, those who pursue it see their own systems in a fresh light. Explanation derived from study is also useful in generating questions for research. Inasmuch as the reasons or causes of divergencies and resemblances are often nonlegal, we must look to the socioeconomic milieu. Reliance on a model helps to supply a beginning step toward framing questions that can usefully be studied empirically.

A few such research questions are set out below. While discussion in this essay has dealt with them, it would be misleading to convert analytical presuppositions into verified propositions. Additional empirical inquiry is needed on hypotheses which can be derived from the classical model. More important for purposes of further extending comparative work, efforts should be made to define or distinguish the applicability of these statements to developing countries. With care and skill, indicators could be developed to verify the following assertions. (1) The larger the proportion of the population involved in the private distribution of goods and services, the greater the tendency to define citizen roles in terms of legal guarantees for the free exchange of men and ideas congruent with existing economic market conditions. (2) The larger the demand for citizenship equality, the greater the claims of centralized government to satisfy civil and political rights demands by undercutting intermediary powers (public and private groups and associations). (3) The more habituated political party elites are to competition, the greater their tendency to promote the legal-rational values associated with popular participation and civic equality rights. (4) The larger the proportion of politically active low-income groups in the electorate, the greater the likelihood of comprehensive positive-rights planning. (5) The less representative a government, the greater the tendency to manipulate positive social and welfare rights to suit the objectives of the ruling group. These scattered hypotheses are set out here to illustrate the point that generalizations that merit research can be derived from a model such as that presented in this essay.

If we set our sights on a world perspective, the narrow bases of the model and derivative hypotheses should be apparent. The model is rooted in the experiences of liberal democratic systems. Projecting it onto third world and socialist people's republics can be done only with caution, if at all. Let us conclude this important point about the limits of the classical model with an example drawn from economics. As suggested by the descriptive analysis in this essay, it appears that classical human rights development has been conditioned materially, perhaps uniquely, by certain reinforcing relationships between legal and economic variables. On the one hand, gradual economic development helps to promote human rights, on the other, human rights development in the classical model helps to promote economic development.

In terms of the promotion of human rights by economic development, our model is instructive. The classical path of human rights development in France, Great Britain, and the United States was favored by gradual economic and industrial development. What brings the experience of these countries together in a coherent model is that three varieties of human rights policies can be clearly linked with three categories to which political economists refer as "public choice processes": market choice, bargaining choice and centralized choice.[69] Thus property rights, liberty of contract, free expression, the right to travel, and related civil liberties developed side by side with processes of choice involving a largely decentralized exchange of goods, services and ideas concomitant with relatively free market economic conditions. The political and civil rights stage of policy development which followed was associated with changing processes that emphasized collective choice: competing labor, political, associational, and social groups engaged in a variety of bargaining processes including competition, compromise, persuasion and electoral participation. The positive rights policies emphasizing health and welfare considerations have become associated in a subsequent stage of human rights development with centralized choice processes where authority is concentrated and where the hierarchical choice processes emphasize planning.

With respect to promotion of economic development by human rights development, the model also is informative. Legal guarantism offered the promise of minimizing individual insecurity wrought by government interference. Without the security of expectations assured by the law in the form of the institutions of property and civil liberties, people are seen from the liberal perspective to be less motivated to work, save and invest. But just as insecurity among the mass of citizens promotes economic stagnation, so does privilege among the few. Electoral rights which encourage participation and civil rights which extend equality and freedom from discrimination help to break down privilege and vested interests which dampen the incentive to attempt change, entrepreneurial risk, and economic development.[70] Modern economic development associated with industrialization requires the aggregation of capital. Where, for purposes of concentrating capital, multiple sources of private financial reserves contribute to the aggregation needed for investment, processes of public choice may usefully rely upon market and bargaining interactions. But what of developing countries which lack pluralized private investment sources? Where the accelerated concentration of capital must rely upon hierarchical choice processes, traditional civil liberties and civil rights may not be seen by government elites as congenial to economic development. David M. Trubek draws the general conclusion: "Today, when laissez-faire has been abandoned in the West, and developed command economies exist in the socialist bloc, contemporary developing nations almost inevitably lean toward a degree of government economic involvement."[71] Whether government economic planning in developing countries necessarily advances at the expense of liberal-style civil liberties and equality rights is a subject which urgently demands future research.

It remains to be seen whether positive rights will acquire an overriding new importance where the expectations created by comprehensive systems of social welfare are more widely dispersed among the citizens than the old rights ever were. This may be less so in political systems where human rights development has been gradual. So long as the citizen-skepticism of government which generated civil liberties and the citizen-participation in politics which bred equal rights reforms are sustained, political pressure for fair and nonarbitrary enforcement of the new rights may usefully be exerted. For example, demands may increase to improve grievance procedures and to ensure responsiveness. But where the stages of human rights development have been rapidly traversed, mass-produced positive rights may be cheapened by capricious or discriminatory action. On the scale of legal values, as popularly conceived, the question of whether the multiple new positive rights will remain outranked by essential civil liberties and civil rights is one of enormous continuing significance.

The classical model as a source of normative questions. There are few problems as difficult to manage satisfactorily in philosophical discourse and legal analysis as that of rights in conflict with other rights. Examples include the right to privacy, which is sometimes at odds with welfare rights that depend upon surveillance for administration; the right to a fair trial versus the possibly contaminating right to free publication of information affecting unbiased judicial hearings; and the right to private property and its use against the right to a healthful environment free from industrial pollution. The problem of attributing a priority of importance to some rights over others is not so easily solved as is the problem of noting the historical priorities of development, although the two priority criteria may be related.

Normative questions about rights in conflict involve very difficult problems of judgment. Nevertheless, the classical model set out in this essay does offer some modest basis for analytical assistance. Most human rights are important in more ways than one. Indeed, their significance may be of three kinds. First, they may serve, in the setting of their historical origins, as basic principles for a scheme of rights by enjoying a logical priority in establishing others: property rights in the Lockean analysis of natural rights when the English middle class carried off the bloodless revolution of 1688; rights of political participation which proliferated into demands for legal equality as industrialization and population change strained the patterns of social stratification; and social welfare policy in the United Nations Declaration of Human Rights against a twentieth century background of administrative expansion to meet the challenges of economic depression and unemployment. Second, human rights may be important in being unsurpassed by other considerations, e.g., few, if any other, moral claims or principles outweigh the right to existence. Issues associated with abortion, euthanasia, and capital punishment touch upon the deepest moral sensitivities. Third, human rights may be related to other rights in a means-ends chain linking rights to one another and to other moral concerns. For example, the assertion of substantive rights depends procedurally upon citizen access to legal process for complaining about the abuse of rights. A French mayor has power in his own commune to enforce the maintenance of the peace. Yet the citizen's access to the *Conseil d'Etat* with its "in excess of power" actions, helps to ensure that a mayor's enforcement decree does not unjustifiably interfere with public freedom. Thus, some rights, such as property, are important because they supply a foundation for many others; some, such as the right to existence, because they cannot be outweighed by other considerations; and others, such as the French principle of legality and the Anglo-American standard of due process of law, because of their instrumental value.

Early rights are neither more nor less important than later rights, simply by virtue of the sequence of development. Thus Maurice Duverger writes that the essential idea of newer economic and social rights, as far as he is concerned, is their instrumental value in assuring to all citizens the material conditions which permit them to exercise their other earlier and more important liberties.[72] The Constitution of the Italian Republic (1947) is explicit in recognizing this kind of link between socioeconomic circumstances and effective participation in political and community life. In Article 3, section 2, it declares that inasmuch as the living conditions of the laboring class inhibit their exercise of traditional rights and liberties, it becomes the task of the state to mitigate those socioeconomic obstacles which circumscribe the liberty and equality of some groups. According to this analysis, there is a reciprocal relationship between civil and social rights which is both functionally and ethically important for the higher goal of improving the quality of political and social life.

The prospect of stepping over the threshold of the postindustrial welfare state demands innovation, not simply reliance upon past lessons and experience. Inasmuch as rights and liberties conflict, and because some in any group of rights cannot be defended as a final good, the future of normative debate in the liberal tradition must focus upon the question of whether and how liberties derived from earlier stages of human rights development can be defended as conditions of the more recent welfare standards.[73]

NOTES*

* In references to legal periodical literature, the number of the *initial* page of the work cited immediately follows the volume title. Page references to material specifically referred to in the text, if any, follow the initial page citation. Legal case citations correspond to *A Uniform System of Citation,* 11th ed. (Cambridge: The Harvard Law Review Association, 1974).

1. The effort to construct theory from historical development in the field of human rights is characteristic of the following titles: Georges Burdeau, *Les Libertés Publiques,* 3d ed. (Paris: R. Pichon et R. Durand-Auzias, 1966); A. J. Carlyle, *Political Liberty, A History of the Conception in the Middle Ages and Modern Times* (London: Frank Cass, 1963); Frede Castberg, "Natural Law and Human Rights: An Idea-Historical Survey," in *Nobel Symposium 7: International Protection of Human Rights,* ed. Asbjörn Eide and August Schou (New York: John Wiley, 1968), pp. 13–34; Rudolph von Ihering, *Geist des römischen Rechts* (Leipsig, 1888); Georg Jellinek, *Allgemeine Staatslehre* (Berlin: O. Haring, 1900); idem., *The Declaration of the Rights of Man and of the Citizen,* trans. Max Farrand (New York: H. Holt, 1901); idem., *The Rights of Minorities,* trans. A. M. Baty and T. Baty (London: P. S. King, 1912); idem., *System der subjektiven öffentlichen Rechte* (Freiburg: B. Mohr, 1892); Leonard Krieger, "Stages in the History of Political Freedom," in *Liberty, Nomos IV,* ed. Carl Friedrich (New York: Atherton Press, 1962), pp. 1–28; Gerhard Oestreich, "Die Entwicklung der Menschenrechte und Grundfreiheiten," in *Die Grundrechte, Handbuch der Theorie und Praxis der Grundrechte* ed., Karl Bettermann, Franz L. Neumann, and Hans C. Nipperdey (Berlin: Dunker und Humbolt, 1966) 1:7–122; A. F. K. Organski, *The Stages of Political Development* (New York: Knopf, 1965); Roscoe Pound, *The Development of Constitutional Guarantees of Liberty* (New Haven: Yale University Press, 1957); Heinrich Rommen, "The Geneaology of Natural Rights," *Thought* 29 (Autumn 1954):114–32; James T. Shotwell, *The Long Way to Freedom* (Indianapolis: Bobbs-Merrill, 1960); Leo Strauss, *Natural Right and History* (Chicago: University of Chicago Press, 1955); Imre Szabó, *The Socialist Concept of Human Rights* (Budapest: Akadémiai Kiadó, 1966).

2. Leonard Binder, James S. Coleman, Joseph La Palombaro, Lucien Pye, Sidney Verba, and Myron Weiner, eds., *Crises and Sequences in Political Development,* Committee on Comparative Politics of the Social Science Research Council (Princeton: Princeton University Press, 1971).

3. Carl Joachim Friedrich, *Man and His Government, An Empirical Theory of Politics* (New York: McGraw–Hill, 1963), pp. 389–405.

4. David M. Trubek and Marc Galanter, "Scholars in Self-Estrangement: Some Reflections on the Crisis in Law and Development Studies in the United States," 1974 *Wisconsin Law Review* 1062. See also, David M. Trubek, "Toward a Social Theory of Law: An Essay on the Study of Law and Development," 82 *Yale Law Journal* 1 (1974).

5. Thomas Hobbes, *Leviathan* (New York: E. P. Dutton and Company, 1950), pp. 101–6.

6. Jean-Jacques Rousseau, *The Social Contract and Discourses,* trans. G. D. H. Cole (New York: E. P. Dutton, 1950), p. 52.

7. Max Rheinstein, ed., *Max Weber on Law in Economy and Society* (Cambridge: Harvard University Press, 1954), pp. 349–56.

8. Paolo Colliva, "Die Rechtsstaatlichheit im Mittelalter," *Internationales Colloquium über Menschenrecht* Association for the United Nations, (Berlin: W. Buxenstein Gmb., 1968), pp. 1–20.

9. J. C. Holt, *Magna Carta* (Cambridge at the University Press, 1969), pp. 43–62. See also Zoltán Péteri, "The Golden Bull of Hungary and the Problem of Human Rights," in *Essays in Legal History in Honor of Felix Frankfurter,* ed., Morris D. Forkosch (Indianapolis: Bobbs-Merrill, 1966), pp. 211–25.

10. Rheinstein, *Max Weber,* p. 353. See also David M. Trubek, "Max Weber and the Rise of Capitalism" 1972 *Wisconsin Law Review* 720.

11. Rheinstein, *Max Weber,* p. 355.

12. John Locke, *Of Civil Government, Second Treatise* (Chicago: Henry Regnery Company, 1955), p. 16.

13. Rheinstein, *Max Weber,* pp. 322–37.

14. This concept of legitimacy is given analytical sharpness by Lucien Pye, "The Legitimacy Crisis," in Binder et al., *Crises and Sequences,* pp. 135–58. Historical illustration is supplied by W. J. Slankiewicz, *Politics and Religion in Seventeenth Century France* (Berkeley: University of California Press, 1960).

15. See the editor's "Historical Introduction" in Harold L. Laski, ed., *A Defense of Liberty Against Tyrants* by Junius Brutus [pseud.] (London: G. Bell and Sons, 1924), pp. 1–60. More generally, see also W. F. Church, *Constitutional Thought in Sixteenth Century France* (New York: Octagon Books, 1969), and idem., *Richelieu and Reason of State* (Princeton: Princeton University Press, 1973).

16. The most useful review of this complex topic is to be found in A. L. Moote, *The Revolt of the Judges* (Princeton: Princeton University Press, 1971).

17. Moote, *Revolt,* p. 111.

18. An apt documentary source book is Samuel R. Gardner, ed., *The Constitutional Documents of the Puritan Revolution* (Oxford: Clarendon Press, 1889). More convenient is William Haller, ed., *The Leveller Tracts* (New York: Columbia University Press, 1944).

19. *King* v. *Thomas Darnell* (Five Knights' Case), 3 State Trials 1 (1627). See generally Joseph Tanner, *English Constitutional Conflicts of the Seventeenth Century* (Cambridge at the University Press, 1962).

20. *King* v. *John Hampton* (The Case of Ships Money) 3 State Trials 825 (1637). See generally, Brian P. Levack, *The Civil Lawyers in England 1603–1641* (Oxford at the Clarendon Press, 1973).

21. A. S. P. Woodhouse, ed., *Puritanism and Liberty: Being the Army Debate (1647–1649) from the Clarke Manuscripts,* (London: J. M. Dent and Sons, 1938), p. 444.

22. For the complete text of the English Bill of Rights see Pound, *Constitutional Guarantees,* pp. 179–83.

23. For an analysis of this proposition in the context of a detailed review of French constitutional thought and developments see Carlyle, *Political Liberty,* pp. 58–80. See also André Tunc, "The Royal Will and the Rule of Law, A Survey of French Constitutionalism under the Ancien Regime," in *Government Under Law,* ed., Arthur Sutherland (Cambridge: Harvard University Press, 1956), pp. 401–21.

24. Robert Palmer, *The Age of Democratic Revolutions,* 2 vols. (Princeton: Princeton University Press, 1959) 1:21.

25. *Dr. Bonham's Case,* 8 Coke 114 (1610); see J. S. Cockburn, *A History of English Assizes, 1558–1774* (Cambridge at the University Press, 1972).

26. Erwin Griswold, *The Fifth Amendment Today* (Cambridge: Harvard University Press, 1955), p. 34. In article 39 of the Great Charter, King John had promised:

> No man shall be taken or imprisoned or desseised or outlawed or exiled or in any way ruined, nor will we go or send against him, except by lawful judgment of his peers or by the law of the land." In Sir Edward Coke's timely new construction, the phrase "law of the land" was equated with the requirements of "due process of law" and the two were combined to represent the legal protection of the subjects' liberties.

27. Ibid., p. 3.

28. William Blackstone, *Commentaries on the Laws of England,* 4 vols., 9th ed. (London: W. Strahan, 1783). The volumes proceed from individual rights through public wrongs: rights of persons, rights of things, private wrongs, public wrongs.

29. Pound, *Constitutional Guarantees,* pp. 55–81. See also Robert Rutland, *The Birth of the Bill of Rights* (New York: Collier Books, 1962).

30. James Madison, Alexander Hamilton, and John Jay, *The Federalist* No. 84 (New York: Modern Library, 1941), p. 559.

31. P. L. Ford, ed., *Writings of Thomas Jefferson,* 10 vols. (New York: G.P. Putnam, 1892–1899), 4:477.

32. Prosper Alfaric, *Les Déclarations françaises des droits de l'homme* (Paris: Union Rationaliste, 1954), p. 7. Mirabeau's "Adresse aux Bataves," which he wrote while in prison at Vincennes, is quoted here.

33. Jellinek, *Die Erklärung,* p. 346.

34. Emile Boutmy, "La Déclaration des droits de l'homme et du citoyen et M. Jellinek," *Annales des Sciences Politiques* 18 (1902): 415–43.

35. Stein Rokkan, *Citizens, Elections, Parties* (New York: David McKay, 1970), pp. 147–68. See also Philip Coulter, *Social Mobilization and Liberal Democracy* (Lexington, Massachusetts: D. C. Heath, 1975).

36. Guido de Ruggiero, *The History of European Liberalism,* trans., R.G. Collingwood (Boston: Beacon Press, 1959), p. 60.

37. Simon Kuznets, "Quantitative Aspects of the Economic Growth of Nations," *Economic Development and Cultural Change,* 11 (January 1963) Part 2, pp. 1–80; see also, idem., "Economic Growth and Income Inequality," *American Economic Review* 45 (March 1955):1–28. See also Mancur Olson, Jr., "Rapid Growth as a Destabilizing Force," *Journal of Economic History* 23 (December 1963):527–47.

38. Barrington Moore, *Social Origins of Dictatorships and Democracy* (Boston: Beacon Press, 1966), pp. 420–21. See also, J. Rogers Hollingsworth, "Perspectives on Industrializing Societies," *American Behavioral Scientist,* 16 (May-June 1973):715–39.

39. T. H. Marshall, *Class, Citizenship and Social Development,* (Garden City, New York: Doubleday Anchor Book, 1965), pp. 71–134.

40. Seymour Martin Lipset, *The First New Nation,* (New York: Doubleday, 1967) pp. 284–312. Allowing for different national and class values, Lipset offers a similar analysis of suffrage and civil rights extension (viewed as a function of social stratification under circumstances of industrialization) in the United States.

41. Dankwart A. Rustow, "Transitions to Democracy," *Comparative Politics,* 2 (April 1970):337–64. Another developmental model of note is presented by Richard Pride in *Origins of Democracy: A Cross-National Study of Mobilization, Party Systems and Democratic Stability* (Beverly Hills: Sage Publications, 1970).

42. See generally, Lee Benson, *The Concept of Jacksonian Democracy* (New York: Atheneum Press, 1964); William N. Chambers, *Political Parties in a New Nation* (New York: Oxford University Press, 1963); Alfred de Grazia, *Public and Republic* (New York: Alfred A. Knopf, 1951); Chilton Williamson, *American Suffrage from Property to Democracy, 1760-1860* (Princeton: Princeton University Press, 1960).

43. Leon Gambetta, "Address to the Electors of Belleville," *Les grandes batailles du Radicalisme, 1820–1901,* ed., Jacques Kayser (Paris: M. Riviere, 1962), pp. 318–20. See generally Maurice Duverger, *Political Parties,* trans., Barbara and Robert North (New York: John Wiley, 1954).

44. Jacques Maritain, *Rights of Man and Natural Law,* trans. Doris Anson, (New York: Charles Scribner, 1943), pp. 113–14. See generally, the proceedings of the International Conference on Social Welfare, *Social Welfare and Human Rights* (New York: Columbia University Press, 1969); C. W. Jenks, "Work, Leisure and Social Security as Human Rights," *Journal of the International Commission of Jurists,* 9 (1968):49–62.

45. Phillips Cutright, "Political Structure, Economic Development and National Social Security Programs," *American Journal of Sociology,* 70 (March 1965):537–51. Cutright found that nations which score high using indicators of political representation generally also score high on measures of social insurance policy, but that when economic development is taken into account, it becomes more precise to say that the impact of

effective representation on social insurance policy is greatest among the more economically developed nations. More generally, see Guy Perrin, "Reflections on Fifty Years of Social Security," *International Labor Review* 99 (1969):249–92. See also Yuichi Nakamura, "Human Rights, Social Welfare and the Level of Socio-economic Development," in *Social Welfare*, pp. 305–8.

46. U. S. Department of Health, Education and Welfare, *Social Security Programs Throughout the World, 1961*, Social Security Administration Report No. 40. (Washington, D.C.: Government Printing Office, 1961).

47. Ibid., 1971, p. *xi*.

48. Shirley William, "The Welfare State in Europe and the United Kingdom," *Contemporary Review* 219 (August 1971):57–63. See also D. L. Capps, "The Citizen, Administration and Politics in Post-Welfare Britain," *Politics in the Post-Welfare State: Responses to the New Individualism* in ed. M. D. Hancock and G. Sjoberg (New York: Columbia University Press, 1972), pp. 117–87.

49. Joachim Wedel, "Social Security and Economic Integration: Their Interaction with Special Regard to Social Cost," *International Labor Review*, 102 (1970):591–614.

50. Henry Aaron, "Social Security in an Expanding Economy," (doctoral dissertation, Harvard University, 1963). See also Charles P. Kindleberger, *Economic Growth in France and Britain, 1851–1950* (Cambridge: Harvard University Press, 1970), pp. 230–33; and generally, Roy Lubove, *The Struggle for Social Security* (Cambridge: Harvard University Press, 1966).

51. Great Britain, *Report of the Royal Commission on Poor Laws and Relief of Distress,* Royal Commission on Poor Laws and Relief of Distress (London: H.M.S.O., Cd. 4499, 1909). Beatrice Webb, one of the founders of the Fabian Society, was a member of the Commission who strongly favored repeal of the poor laws and the abolition of their related means tests in favor of public assistance as a right. On the other hand, the Charities Organization Society and the allied conservatives on the Commission sought merely to make the system of private charity and the poor laws more efficient. Thus the *Report* presages the extensive debate that has developed over welfare and social insurance: whether the individual or the socio-political system should be seen as at fault for poverty. See generally Michael Rose, *The English Poor Law, 1780–1930* (Newport Abbott, England: David and Charles, 1971).

52. Sir William Beveridge, *Social Insurance and Allied Services* (New York: Macmillan, 1942), pp. 287–93.

53. Seymour Martin Lipset, *Political Man* (New York: Doubleday, 1960), p. 189.

54. For local political reasons, many American municipalities and some states enacted residence requirements for eligibility to receive public assistance. However, in 1969, residence requirements for welfare benefits were found to be unconstitutional, not on the basis that welfare involved a constitutionally protected right, but on the ground that such qualifications interfered with the constitutionally protected right to travel from state to state; *Shapiro* v. *Thompson,* 394 U.S. 618 (1969). By contrast, in *Lindsey* v. *Norment,* 405 U.S. 56 (1972)–involving housing; *Dandrige* v. *Williams,* 397 U.S. 471 (1970)–involving welfare assistance; and *Ortwein* v. *Schwab,* 410 U.S. 656 (1973)–involving review of reduced welfare payments, the Supreme Court refused to apply the same strict standards of constitutional scrutiny under the equal protection clause of the fourteenth amendment because, unlike the right to travel, housing and welfare policy were not deemed to involve constitutionally guaranteed interests. Likewise, in *Rodriguez* v. *San Antonio Independent School District,* 411 U.S. 1 (1972), the Court refused to recognize education as a fundamental right under the Constitution.

55. This analysis is based on Eveline M. Burns, "The Nation's Health Insurance and Health Services Policies," *American Behavioral Scientist,* 15 (1972):713–31. Stephen P. Strickland writes: "More and more people seem to accept the principle that unimpeded access to good medical care is tantamount to a civil right," "Health Care and Social Policy," *Science* 180 (1973):629. The best comparative study on this subject of the United States, Sweden and England is by Odin W. Anderson, *Health Care: Can There Be Equity?* (New York: John Wiley, 1972).

56. Walter Leisner, *Grundrechte und Privatrecht* (Munich: Beck, Münchener öffentlich-

rechtliche Abhandlungen, 1960). The author traces lines of development from contract rights in ancient private law to contemporary civil liberties.

57. Jacques Doublet, "Human Rights and Social Security," in *Social Welfare*, pp. 194–210.

58. Maurice Cranston, "Human Rights, Real and Supposed," in *Political Theory and the Rights of Man* ed., D. D. Raphael (Bloomington, Indiana: University of Indiana Press, 1967), pp. 43–53.

59. Ibid., pp. 111–13.

60. The wide-ranging character of literature in this field is illustrated by the following titles: Mario Diaz Cruz, "Rule of Law–Quo Vadis?," *Comparative Juridical Review* 5 (1968):249–81. B. Horvath, "Twilight of Government of Laws," *AFRS Archives for Philosophy of Law and Social Philosophy* 54 (1968):1–30. Cf. Walter Gellhorn, "Poverty and Legality: The Law's Slow Awakening," *Proceedings of the American Philosophical Society* 112 (1968):107–16. Fritz Gygi, "The Rule of Law in the Contemporary Welfare State," *Journal of the International Commission of Jurists*, 4 (Summer 1962):3–32. Bernard Schwartz and H. W. R. Wade, *Legal Control of Government* (Oxford: Clarendon Press, 1972). Robert Paul Wolff, ed., *The Rule of Law* (New York: Simon and Schuster, 1971).

61. Friedrich A. Hayek, *The Road to Serfdom* (Chicago: University of Chicago Press, 1956), p. 79. Further systematic development of Hayek's critique is offered in idem., *Constitution of Liberty* (Chicago: Henry Regnery, 1972), pp. 253–394.

62. *Flemming* v. *Nestor*, 363 U.S. 603 (1960). A statute which ended payment of social security benefits to an alien following deportation was declared not *ex post facto* on the ground that it was not a criminal penalty. American courts have generally held that statutory pension rights may be adversely affected by subsequent legislation, and that they do not enjoy the status of constitutionally protected property, vested, or contract rights.

63. Harry W. Jones, "The Rule of Law and the Welfare State," 58 *Columbia Law Review* 143, 152 (1958).

64. Maxime Letourneur, "The French Conseil d'Etat," *Journal of the International Commission of Jurists* 8, (Special issue 1968):85–112. American and British administrative law and the *droit administratif* are compared in Schwartz and Wade, *Legal Control*, pp. 323–27.

65. Jay Sigler, *The Courts and Public Policy* (Homewood, Illinois: The Dorsey Press, 1970), p. 466.

66. Great Britain, *Report of the Committee on the Abuse of Social Security*, Chrmn., Hon. Sir Henry Fisher, (London: H.M.S.O., Cd. 5528, 1973).

67. Norman S. Marsh, "Working Paper on the Rule of Law," in *The Rule of Law in a Free Society* (New Delhi, International Congress of Jurists, 1959), pp. 187–322. The leading British view is put forth in A. V. Dicey, *Introduction to the Study of the Law of the Constitution*, 9th ed. (London: Macmillan, 1939), pp. 187–96. See also Maxime Letourneur and R. Drago, "Principles of the Rule of Law as Seen by the French Conseil d'Etat," *American Journal of Comparative Law*, 7 (1958):147–77.

68. John Stuart Mill, *On Social Freedom*, ed. Dorothy Fosdick (New York: Columbia University Press, 1941), p. 43. Cf. J. C. Rees, *Mill and His Early Critics* (Leicester: University College of Leicester, 1956), pp. 38–54. Rees attributes authorship of the essay to E. R. Edger.

69. For related analysis, see Stephen L. Elkin, "Political Science and the Analysis of Public Policy," *Public Policy* 4 (1974):399–422.

70. See Kenneth L. Karst, "Law in Developing Countries," *Law Library Journal* 60 (1967):13–20.

71. Trubek, "Social Theory of Law," p. 36.

72. Maurice Duverger, *Droit Public* (Paris: Presses Universitaires de France, 1966), p. 167.

73. These issues have been recently joined in John Rawls, *A Theory of Justice* (Cambridge: Harvard University Press, 1971); and in Brian Barry, *The Liberal Theory of Justice* (Oxford at the Clarendon Press, 1973).

Chapter 2 EMPIRICAL COMPARATIVE RIGHTS RESEARCH: SOME PRELIMINARY TESTS OF DEVELOPMENT HYPOTHESES

James C. Strouse and
Richard P. Claude

In his introduction to the UNESCO publication *Freedom and Culture,* Julian Huxley wrote, "It is no longer possible for us, as it was for our ancestors in the Age of Reason, to conceive of human rights as existing in the abstract, merely waiting to be deduced from first principles by the human intellect."[1] We would add that it is no longer possible for us, as it has been until recently for legalists and institutionally oriented political scientists to conceive of human rights as little more than the documentary results of enlightened legal processes. Although the human aspirations underlying various rights may reflect perennial high goals, and although human rights depend upon formal legal and institutional endorsement, modern social scientists must inquire into the underlying social forces generating human rights development. The means for exploring this kind of analysis in this essay is offered tentatively in the hope that it will encourage future research. We seek to set out a macro-level hypothesis and a related analysis that appear to have theoretical explanatory power in associating human rights policies with political and economic development.

An appreciation of the place of statistical analysis in comparative social science can be gained by an understanding of two different research strategies, dyachronic (longitudinal) and synchronic (cross-sectional). This dichotomy in approach to comparative research has developed in recent years among social scientists concerned with questions about the influences at work in the process of sociopolitical development.[2]

The dyachronic approach is historical. It seeks to identify for a small number of cases the causal factors and the sequence of development of linked changes. Chapter 1 of this volume compares the staged evolution of human rights in France, Great Britain, and the United States. The essay forms the basis for describing the classical model of human rights development. One of the theses of that chapter is that three distinguishable varieties of public choice processes—market choice, bargaining choice, and centralized planning—can be associated with three categories of human rights. This exposition suggests that free expression and related civil liberties constituted human rights policies evolving from an early stage of gradual politicoeconomic development where the processes of choice involved a largely decentralized exchange of goods, services, and ideas associated with relatively free-market economic conditions. The political and civil rights stage of policy development which succeeded was related to changing processes which emphasized collective choice, and in which competing labor, political, associational, and social groups engaged in a variety of bargaining relationships encompassing competition, compromise, persuasion, minority group demands for legal equality, and electoral participation. The positive-rights policies emphasizing health and welfare considerations and social security rights were associated in a more recent stage of human rights evolution with a centralized choice process where authority is concentrated and where the hierarchical choice process emphasizes planning. While this essay on the "classical model of human rights development" links policies and processes of choice in a way that supplies an explanatory review of human rights evolution in gradually industralizing countries, these relationships are difficult to test statistically because the processes of choice—markets, bargaining, and concentrated planning—may have developed serially, whereas contemporary institutions are usually composed of combinations.

The model of slowly modernizing liberal democracies supplies a well-known paradigm against which to contrast and compare other countries. Only with great caution can we say that it provides any basis for broad universal generalization. For example, although it may offer a baseline for comparison, it hardly supplies a general theoretical basis for explaining development in the third world countries, as suggested by the analysis of Uganda and Mexico described by Baldwin in chapter 3. Dyachronic comparative studies, such as those in the first and third chapters of this volume, generally rely upon qualitative rather than quantitative analysis.

Synchronic studies avoid these longitudinal characteristics. They tend to employ a cross-sectional statistical, multicase approach. Whereas historically oriented research tends to rely on multiple explanatory variables, synchronic research relies upon a specified number of variables. Quantitative indicators are used, opening up inquiry to sophisticated statistical treatment which uses multiple correlation, regression analysis, factor analysis, and causal modeling.

The capacity of synchronic quantitative analysis to test theory depends upon the accuracy, validity, and comparability of the statistics that are employed. At the present time, both social data and rights data present noteworthy difficulties from the standpoint of accuracy, validity, and comparability. Consequently, analysis must be seen as tentative, suggestive, and preliminary, rather than error-free and conclusive. But to foreswear the use of available, although imperfect, data does not advance scholarship. Moreover, as long as the field of human rights analysis is left to speculation and intuitive discussion, questionable analysis can find no basis for refutation. For example, if solid data were available, one might confidently support (or more likely refine) the following generalization advanced in 1968 by the United Nations Commission on Human Rights, Social Welfare, and the Level of Socioeconomic Development: "Some human rights (the right of peaceful assembly and association), of course, are independent of socioeconomic considerations, but certain social human rights (the right to protection against unemployment and the right to social security) must depend on the level of socioeconomic development."[3] As suggested by the analysis which follows, the right of peaceful assembly and association and other civil liberties are not wholly independent of socioeconomic considerations.

The data from the field of politico-economic development used in the analysis are drawn from a 1972 publication of the Yale University World Data Analysis Program edited by Charles Taylor and Michael Hudson, *World Handbook of Political and Social Indicators*. (The data are hereafter referred to as Taylor-Hudson data.)[4] Sociopolitical and economic variables are available for 122 countries from the decade of the 1960s. Extensive information is supplied by Taylor and Hudson regarding their reliability and validity. The data on civil liberties and political rights pertain to the early 1970s and, as a result, a problem of comparability exists between the two sets of data. Thus the analysis is subject to the margin of error which results from the use of dependent variables (human rights) which are from three to seven years more recent than the independent variables (socioeconomic indicators).

For human rights variables, we rely upon the Freedom House Survey of Human Rights.[5] (Although the Survey includes no data on positive rights such as health, welfare, education, and social security policies, indicators of a worldwide scope of that nature are available.[6]) Produced semiannually by Raymond D. Gastil, the Freedom House survey focuses on civil liberties, political rights, the status of freedom, and associated trends.[7] The civil liberties data taken from Gastil's periodic review are based upon information that is available about the rights of the individual against the state. In the January 1975 survey, civil liberties, rated on a seven-point scale, are defined as: ". . . the rights of individuals or groups vis-á-vis the government. On the one hand, the survey is interested in the extent to which a variety of opinions are expressed and made available to the people, or in other words in the de facto right of the people to communicate and express opinions in areas that are relevant to the political decision process. . . . On the other hand, civil . . . [liberties] also include a broad spectrum of rights to live under a rule of law rather than of whim. . . . Therefore, civil . . . [liberties] include rights to privacy, and rights to form organizations that are not beholden to government."[8] Political rights, also evaluated for each country on a seven-point scale from highest to lowest level, are defined as: " . . . the rights of people to express directly or through the election of representatives how they want government to be legislated and administered. . . . Therefore, in our review of events in the countries of the world, we consider a variety of indicators of the emergence of opposition, such as the existence of opposition parties, and the election of a significant opposition to the legislature. We also look for the general freedom of individuals to stand for election, or of evidence of democratic polling and counting procedures."[9] The "status of freedom" measure (free, partly free, not free) not only aggregates civil liberties and political rights indicators, but rests more broadly on a qualitative and relative judgment. "The key questions are always: How do the freedoms in this particular country compare with those in other countries? Which countries are freer, and which less free? [Here] there is no quantitative process occurring. We are always interested in overall judgment, focusing on which states seem more or less equivalent along the continuums."[10]

While relying upon cross-sectional data, statistical analysis nevertheless permits us to draw some inferences regarding development links and sequence. In the discussion that follows, some problems relating to human rights development are statistically examined using cross-sectional data—the Taylor-Hudson socioeconomic data and the Gastil indicators. First, simple correlations shed interesting light on the relationships between systems of legal rights and socioeconomic development indicators. Second, the more powerful technique of regression analysis is utilized to examine further these data in explanatory terms. The pace of economic development is studied in 122 countries, and the results suggest that the dislocations tied to rapid growth rates may be detrimental to political rights as well as civil liberties. Since the data are dominated by the large number of developing countries, it is not surprising that a picture of human rights development emerges which is at variance with the classical model associated in chapter 1 with gradually modernizing industrialized liberal democracies. Third, there is a detailed inquiry into the social, economic, and political correlates of countries scoring high in political rights and civil liberties. The analysis supports the findings of cognate studies that communication and urbanization variables are importantly associated with the development of institutions connected with liberal democracy.

Correlation analysis. In this section we rely upon simple correlation analysis to examine the components of the following hypothesis. *The greater the level of political stability, social development, and economic development per capita, the more civil and political rights are expressed and made available; but the more rapid the rate of economic development, the less civil liberties and political rights are expressed and made available.* The statistics for political stability are the Taylor-Hudson indicators of regular executive transfer and irregular power transfer. In both cases, the focus is on the national executive; the difference turns upon the frequency of change by conventional legal procedures or irregular change conditioned by actual or threatened violence and by abnormal procedures. Social development indicators isolate urbanization and certain measures of communications such as literacy, foreign mail per capita, domestic mail per capita, and telephones per capita. Economic development includes six indicators. Aggregate energy consumption refers to industrial output and economic size. An alternative measure of development is energy consumption per capita. Fixed domestic capital formation refers to expenditures for capital goods by enterprises, private institutions, and government (excluding defense expenditures.). Taylor and Hudson provide another economic development indicator, the percentage of males in professional and technical jobs. National accounts data are reported as gross national product and GNP per capita. The food supply indicator reports calories and grams of protein per capita per diem. Economic development rates bring together three indicators of rapid-paced development. Rate of growth figures for gross national product and per capita GNP report the average annual rate of change. Data on energy consumption are also expressed in terms of continuous growth.[11]

Table 1 presents the simple correlations between economic and sociopolitical variables and the output variables (civil liberties and political rights). Given the large number of countries for which data were available, and given the plethora of factors affecting human behavior of any sort, it is not surprising that no one of the independent variables shows a strikingly high correlation with human rights development scores. The table shows the index of association for each variable and how closely they are related, either positively or negatively. A correlation coefficient below ±.1800 cannot be considered statistically significant given the number of countries examined and the requirements, at the .05 significance level, of the F test for correlational significance. Coefficients in italics are those which prove statistically significant by these standards.

It appears from table 1 that the political variables chosen do not offer unequivocal insight into human rights development. While civil liberties appear to depend upon the absence of irregular power transfers, and, in a long term sense, upon a secure legal system, nevertheless, irregular power transfers in the national executive office may have a direct and immediate influence upon positive trends toward improved freedom. The Gastil trend indicator is a short term evaluative score based on progress in the "status of freedom." The anomalous correlation between the trend data and abnormal transfer procedures may be illustrated by abrupt regime changes such as those in Greece and Portugal in 1973 and 1974, so that where previously repressive regimes prevail, only revolution or some unexpected political change can precipitate a radical improvement in civil liberties and political rights. Thus the first portion of the preceding hypothesis regarding political stability is not confirmed in terms that are statistically significant for the correlation analysis. One might guess that if worldwide data were available on such indicators of political stability as an independent judiciary, this institutional variable would score a significant correlation with civil liberties development.[12] Moreover, as Baar suggests in chapter 14, little serious research has been done using multiple cases to examine the correlation between institutional longevity and human rights activism. Democratic development and constitutional longevity have also been consigned to the penumbra of systematic research.[13]

Table 1. SIMPLE CORRELATION COEFFICIENTS FOR 122 COUNTRIES COMPARING RIGHTS VARIABLES AND SOCIOPOLITICAL AND ECONOMIC VARIABLES

	Civil Liberties	Political Rights	Status of Freedom	Trends
Political Development				
Legal executive transfer	−0.0744	0.0475	0.0586	0.0984
Irregular power change	−0.2453[a]	0.0107	*0.2936*	*0.4005*
Social Development-Communications				
Urbanization	*0.2907*	*0.4721*	*0.3585*	*0.2293*
Literacy	*0.3278*	*0.5454*	*0.4959*	*0.2311*
Domestic mail per capita	*0.3521*	*0.6186*	*0.4937*	*0.2017*
Telephones per capita	*0.4516*	*0.6393*	*0.4920*	0.1310
Foreign mail per capita	*0.5259*	*0.4930*	*0.3722*	0.1346
Economic Development				
Aggregate energy consumption	−0.0558	−0.0659	−0.0502	−0.0014
Gross national product	0.0968	0.1838	0.1584	0.0324
Fixed domestic capital formation	0.1311	*0.3848*	0.1138	0.1785
Percent males in professional-technical	*0.2667*	*0.5354*	*0.4295*	0.1233
Energy consumption per capita	*0.2724*	*0.3893*	*0.3508*	0.1588
GNP per capita	*0.3756*	*0.5802*	*0.4699*	0.1667
Economic Development Rates				
Growth rate GNP per capita	−0.1213	−0.1558	−0.1497	−0.0157
Growth rate total GNP	−0.0871	−0.1726	−0.1710	−0.0116
Growth rate energy per capita	−0.1133	−0.2373	−0.2545	−0.0893

[a]Figures in italics are statistically significant.

The correlation coefficients for the socioeconomic indicators are sufficient to confirm the relevant part of the hypothesis. All of these variables (excluding the aggregate energy indicator) correlate positively with political rights. Two economic distribution indicators—energy per capita and GNP per capita—reflect an intriguing positive association with civil liberties. The strength of the correlations between political rights development and the social indicators (especially the communications indicators) as well as such economic variables as fixed domestic capital formation, gross national product, food supply, energy per capita and GNP per capita is not surprising given the findings of related preexisting literature.[14] The relationships between the communications variable and political and civil liberties are especially interesting. Telephones per capita, mail per capita, and literacy are all significantly related to civil liberties and political rights, and they are among the highest correlations reported. Communications scholars, such as Daniel Lerner, Lucian Pye, and Karl Deutsch,[15] have emphasized the importance of communications systems in analyzing nation-states. Indeed, Deutsch argues that the communications system forms a central nerve system from which one can predict system stability, social cohesion, and many other aspects of the political system. Strong communications systems keep the citizen informed of both national and international events, and they condition the political system to be responsive to demands for political rights and civil liberties.

In the case of the economic development rate indicators, the correlation coefficients by and large fall short of statistical significance. Strikingly, however, they all reflect a pattern of negative correlation. The growth rate of energy consumption per capita is significantly correlated in an inverse relationship with political rights and the status of freedom variables. To the extent that this relationship holds, it confirms that portion of the hypothesis which attributes an inhibiting effect on human rights development to rapid economic development.

In the preceding discussion, the relative absence of analysis suggesting causal interrelationships may be surprising. What the reported correlations explain is ambiguous. This is because correlation techniques make no assumptions about causality. The hypothesis is stated in terms of elements which coincide; one element does not explain another. Neither the hypothesis nor the significant correlation scores indicate, for instance, whether increases in per capita GNP induce civil liberties development or whether the presence of civil liberties stimulates an increase in per capita GNP. Correlation leaves open the question of whether factor X causes factor Y or whether Y causes X; whether there is mutual causation; whether both are caused by a third variable; or whether there may be another explanatory variable.

Multiple correlation and regression analysis. In his magisterial study, *Philosophy in the Development of Law,* Pierre de Tourtoulon of the University of Lausanne has written, "If it had been necessary to wait until a complete and incontestable doctrine of causality was elaborated before making use of cause as an instrument of research, the greater part of the sciences would still be in a very rudimentary state."[16] It is difficult, if not impossible, to prove causation in the physical sciences no less than in the study of law and the social sciences.[17] However, regression analysis furnishes a framework for explanation. Using it, it is possible to examine the independent variables that explain the variation in the dependent variables and to specify which of the former, and in what order, explain most of the variation in the latter. With regression analysis, we attempt an explanation of development in each of the three dependent variables: civil liberties, political rights, and freedom status.

The step-wise regression program indicates the explanatory power of the independent variables. It shows which variable explains most of the variation in the dependent variable, lists the second most powerful variable, and so on. In the process, occasionally indicators which show high correlation scores in multiple correlations are eliminated, the weaker element being subsumed by the duplication of the stronger explanatory element. It is possible, by this method, to observe the power (in terms of variation explained) of each of the independent variables. Tables 2, 3, and 4 show the dependent variables (civil liberties, political rights, and "status of freedom") related to the most influential independent variables (socioeconomic and political indicators). For purposes of interpreting the tables, the significance of Multiple R, R Square, and R Square change should be noted. Multiple R can be interpreted as a simple Pearson's R correlation; it explains the degree to which the dependent and independent variables vary in the same pattern among all of the cases examined. The Multiple R is the cumulative correlation of the independent variables combined. The R Square is the variance explained. It shows how much of the variation in the dependent variable all of the independent variables account for. R Square change tells us exactly how much additional variation explained is due to that particular independent variable. The tables also show the regression equation which, if reliable, may have predictive value, although each equation should be set up to include an "error term."

A word more of methodological explanation is in order. Regression has often been called the "law of social science" since it takes multitudinous factors into account and produces a resulting explicit statement on what influences the dependent variable. It thus represents a formal theory because it represents a precise set of relationships. It permits us to see exactly how much, and to what extent, the independent variables are affecting the dependent variable. This is spelled out in the regression equation which relies on "beta weights" to describe the pattern of the regression slope. The use of "beta weights" aids in a problem of data comparability which has long vexed social science. The variety of the units of measurement which characterize social data is great. For instance, some variables may be measured in caloric energy units, some in percentages, and some in dollars. To adjust for this problem, each variable is standardized by dividing each measure by its standard deviation to make all the measures comparable. The "beta weights" are the slopes, which tell the observer exactly how much change in the dependent variable is caused by (explainable in terms of) a change in the independent variable. Thus a beta weight of 2.6 means that for each one unit of change in the independent variable, there is a 2.6 unit change in the dependent variable.

In table 2, the cumulative *R Square* shows that the independent variables taken together explain over 50 percent of the civil liberties variance. The regression equation shown at the bottom of the table describes the influences shaping the configuration of the regression slope. All the slopes are steep, indicating considerable change in the dependent variable for each one unit change in the independent variable. All of the positive slopes involve communications indicators: domestic mail per capita with a beta weight of 7.4, telephones per capita (2.3), and foreign mail per capita (2.1). The economic development variables appear to have a depressing effect upon civil liberties, at least where rapid growth is concerned. This set of relationships may seem perplexing. On the one hand, R. B. Nixon has published statistics which show that among economically developed countries, there is a generally greater level of civil liberties (using free speech and press as his reference) than among less well developed states.[18] In fact this relationship also appears in table 1 in the Civil liberties-GNP per capita correlation. On the other hand, the regression analysis notes a negative relationship between civil liberties and economic growth rates. The apparent paradox may be resolved by emphasizing that, while economic development provides the conditions under which greater civil liberties become feasible, nevertheless, rapid development encourages the strengthening of government controls which may preempt more democratic systems of com-

Table 2. STEP-WISE REGRESSION BETWEEN CIVIL LIBERTIES AND INDEPENDENT VARIABLES (N = 122)

Independent Variables	Multiple R	R Square	Increase in R Square Due to Addition of Independent Variable[a]
Foreign mail per capita	0.5259	0.2766	0.2766
Telephones per capita	0.5796	0.3359	0.0593
Professional-technical percent	0.6053	0.3663	0.0303
GNP growth per capita	0.6185	0.3826	0.0162
Irregular power change	0.6436	0.4143	0.0316
Domestic mail per capita	0.7109	0.5054	0.0911

$$
\begin{aligned}
\text{Civil Liberties } (Y) = {} & 2.12 \text{ Foreign mail per capita } (x_1) \\
& +2.3 \text{ Telephones per capita } (x_2) \\
& -3.0 \text{ Professional-technical percent } (x_3) \\
& -3.8 \text{ GNP per capita } (x_4) \\
& -4.6 \text{ Irregular power change } (x_5) \\
& +7.4 \text{ Domestic mail per capita } (x_6)
\end{aligned}
$$

[a]Change in *R square* refers to the additional variance explained due to the addition of an independent variable.

munications. Wilbur Schramm has put the point thus: "Whereas it is easier for a developed country to have a completely free press and free communication, it is much harder for a country in the early stages of development to do so."[19] The political instability that is sometimes associated with third world countries is also reflected in table 2. The strongest negative slope involves irregular executive transition (−4.6). The violence, coups, and irregular procedures which constitute this indicator are often ad hoc and episodic; by definition they are the exception rather than the rule. They may not necessarily reflect long-term trends. For all of these reasons, it is not surprising that, even though it is important, this factor explains only 3 percent of the variance in civil liberties changes (see "R Square Change"). Nevertheless, the occurence of such events as the establishment of rule by decree in Brazil or the displacement of regular democratic constitutional forms in Uruguay, has a dramatic and profound effect on civil liberties in the countries involved.

The regression equation in table 3 shows that the communications variables associated with political participation rights are very strong, and all have a positive impact upon rights related to the electoral process. Economic development variables are not carried forward by the regression program to show substantial explanatory power. This result is in harmony with recent cross-national studies in this area. In 1959, Seymour Martin Lipset, in a study of social and economic requisites of democracy, concluded that the more well-to-do a nation, the greater the chances that it will sustain democracy.[20] The suggestion that the more economically developed a country is the more democratic it also is appears in a cross-national comparative study by Phillips Cutright.[21] Dean Neubauer, however, has more recently refined this view by making clear that, while economic development is important, it constitutes a threshold phenomenon with respect to such liberal democratic institutions as free elections. Once a country crosses the economic development threshold, other factors such as communications are more important than economic development in determining the prevalence of political rights.[22] A newer analysis of these data using causal modeling has been done by Donald J. McCrone and Charles F. Cnudde which clarifies the importance of communications variables in the presence of democratic political development.[23] Given these findings, the absence in the regression equation of strong positive economic development influences is understandable. However, figures in the table affirm the negative influence of rapid economic development on political rights as suggested by the −2.2 slope for growth rate of per capita GNP; a unit increase in growth rate causes a 2.2 unit decrease in political rights. In terms that merit extended quotation, Mancur Olson has commented aptly on this phenomenon:

Rapid economic growth, whatever the nature of the economic system, must involve fast and deep changes in the ways that things are done, in the places that things are done, and in the distribution of power and prestige. Most people spend such a large proportion of their time working for a living and draw such a large part of their social status and political influence from their economic position that changes in the economic order must have great effects on other facets of life. This is especially true in underdeveloped societies, where the institutions that exist were developed in relatively static conditions and are not suited to making rapid adjustments. Therefore, until further research is done, the presumption must be that rapid economic growth, far from being the source of domestic tranquility it is sometimes supposed to be, is rather a disruptive and destabilizing force that leads to political instability.[24]

That the economic dislocation associated with intensive growth often results in repression for the sake of economic development is discussed in chapter 3 in the description by Baldwin of the unfortunate treatment of the Uganda Asians in the early 1970s.

Table 4 reports on the results of a step-wise regression between "status of freedom" and certain other characteristics of society. It should be emphasized that the freedom indicator is particularly subjective as a measure and does not have the useful range of interval data that characterize the civil liberties and political rights indices. Freedom status scores range from "free" to "partly free" to "not free." At the "free" end of the continuum, "persons in the government are to use force only to prevent the destruction of the constitutional system, but not to keep themselves in power." By contrast, at the "not free" end of the continuum, "government is established over a people by a group of persons to achieve their personal goals. The goals may be those of individual or party power, or they may be those of moral uplift or national pride. But in any case, the ruling group is not dependent upon what the majority wants. To an extent they can afford to ignore the majority, for they also assume the right to use violent force both to prevent anarchy and to keep themselves in power through the suppression of political and civil rights."[25] Although this explanation is diffuse and contains elements of ambiguity, it still is useful in order to see which

Table 3. STEP-WISE REGRESSION BETWEEN POLITICAL RIGHTS AND INDEPENDENT VARIABLES (N = 122)

Independent Variables	Multiple R	R Square	Increase in R Square Due to Addition of Independent Variable[a]
Telephones per capita	0.6193	0.3836	0.3836
Literacy	0.6698	0.4487	0.0651
Foreign mail per capita	0.7053	0.4975	0.0476
Growth rate per capita	0.7214	0.5204	0.0229
Domestic mail per capita	0.7517	0.5651	0.0447

Political Rights (Y) = +.52 Telephones per capita (x_1)
+.44 Literacy (x_2)
+1.29 Foreign mail per capita (x_3)
−2.2 Growth rate per capita (x_4)
+1.69 Domestic mail per capita (x_5)

[a]Change in R square refers to the additional variance explained due to the addition of an independent variable.

Table 4. STEP-WISE REGRESSION BETWEEN FREEDOM STATUS AND
INDEPENDENT VARIABLES (N = 122)

Independent Variables	Multiple R	R Square	Increase in R Square Due to Addition of Independent Variable[a]
Literacy	0.4952	0.2452	0.2452
Domestic mail per capita	0.5783	0.3345	0.0892
Aggregate energy consumption	0.6617	0.4378	0.1033
Irregular power change	0.7273	0.5289	0.0910
Gross national product	0.7590	0.5760	0.0471

Freedom status (Y) = .17 Literacy (x_1)
    +2.28 Domestic mail per capita (x_2)
    −1.13 Aggregate energy (x_3)
    −1.3 Irregular power change (x_4)
    −.54 Gross national product (x_5)

[a]Change in R square refers to the additional variance explained due to the addition of an independent variable.

variables explain the variance and to examine the regression equation. Obviously, future empirical analysis will combine this measure with others to construct a more meaningful indicator. However, it is interesting to note that communications data again explain most of the variance and have positive slopes in the regression equation. Indicators of economic development and irregular executive transition have negative slopes.

The development of systems of communications has been described by Daniel Lerner as a source of political and economic change. In industrializing countries, urbanization exposes the uneducated to the media with consequent development of literacy—equipping them to perform the varied tasks required in a modernizing society. "Out of this interaction," he observes, "develop those institutions of participation (such as voting) which we find in all advanced modern societies." Although efforts to quantify Lerner's thesis have relied especially upon mass media indicators, communications development also may be taken to be the technical means for transmitting personal or business messages, such as by domestic and foreign mail and by telephone. In table 5 the latter, along with urbanization, literacy, and professionalization data correlate positively with economic development, especially among the twenty-two countries which score highest on the Gastil rights scale.

Table 5 should be approached cautiously. Because the research is exploratory, it was decided to examine more closely the countries with high scores on political rights and civil liberties compared to the large undifferentiated group of 100 which do not score highly (100 countries). On the high scoring group of 22 and the low scoring group of 100 we ran a correlation program. The figures in table 5 lack perfect statistical comparability because the tests of significance differ slightly for the two groups. Since we examine only the intercorrelations of

Table 5. SIMPLE CORRELATIONS BETWEEN SELECTED INDEPENDENT VARIABLES WITH HIGH RIGHTS SCORES (N = 22) AND LOW RIGHTS SCORES (N = 100)[a]

	Social Development-Communications											
	Professional-Technical Percent		Literacy		Foreign Mail per Capita		Urbanization		Domestic Mail per Capita		Telephones per Capita	
	High Rights	Low Rights	High Rights	Low Rights	High Rights	Low Rights	High Rights	Low Rights	High Rights	Low Rights	High Rights	Low Rights
Political Development												
Legal executive transfer	-0.32	-0.05	-0.16	0.38	0.10	-0.09	-0.11	0.07	-0.05	-0.01	-0.37	0.04
Irregular power change	0.02	-0.03	0.10	-0.05	0.04	-0.09	0.08	0.02	0.15	0.01	-0.04	-0.13
Economic Development												
Aggregate energy per capita	0.60	-0.09	0.15	0.21	-0.21	-0.12	0.38	-0.03	0.56	0.02	0.42	-0.07
Fixed domestic capital	-0.12	0.09	0.41	0.08	0.25	0.13	-0.13	0.05	0.02	0.20	0.13	0.12
Gross national product	0.59	-0.06	0.16	0.63	-0.23	-0.11	0.38	-0.01	0.57	0.01	0.41	-0.02
Food supply (calories)	0.36	0.43	0.59	0.27	-0.09	0.21	0.51	0.54	0.50	0.57	0.25	0.60
Energy per capita	0.51	0.36	0.63	0.39	0.07	0.64	0.40	0.40	0.72	0.31	0.61	0.54
GNP per capita	0.57	0.48	0.74	0.50	-0.09	0.68	0.28	0.46	0.62	0.43	0.90	0.65
Economic Development Rates												
Growth rate per capita	-0.20	0.39	0.01	0.05	-0.17	0.26	0.25	0.01	-0.11	0.53	-0.39	-0.04
Growth rate energy per capita	-0.06	0.22	-0.08	0.16	-0.42	0.18	0.34	0.24	-0.12	0.30	-0.27	0.18
Growth rate	-0.46	0.20	-0.53	-0.05	0.06	0.41	-0.16	-0.10	-0.39	-0.06	-0.52	0.03

[a]Levels of significance are different for the low rights (.43) and high rights (.20) countries.

the independent variables, we avoid to a large extent sampling on the dependent variable, against which Hubert M. Blalock cautions.[26] Because a tabular presentation of 289 correlations is too large, only those variables which explain most of the variance in political rights and civil liberties are reviewed here. The variables in the social development-communications area seem to be most powerful, and we shall, therefore, concentrate on them.

As is shown in table 5, communications indicators, along with urbanization, literacy, and profesionalization data are important. Excluding foreign mail per capita, the correlations between the social development-communications indicators and food supply, energy per capita, and GNP per capita are especially impressive. The economic development rates are negatively associated with social development and communications, particularly among those countries which sustain high standards of civil liberties and political rights. Low scoring countries appear to have abandoned liberal political goals—at least temporarily—in order to place social development at the service of rapid economic modernization. In these countries, the growth rate variables are predominantly positively associated with social development and communications variables. The economic development variables seem to have a higher correlation pattern in the high scoring countries than in the low scoring countries. The reciprocal relationship between social development-communications, and economic modernization is not as strong among developing nations as it is in the economically mature liberal democracies. Precisely why this should be so raises a question which goes beyond the scope of this preliminary analysis.

CONCLUSIONS

According to Robert Seidman, "To promote economic development, governments must rely upon the law, for the legal order is the filter through which policy becomes practice."[27] Since economic modernization is a type of social change, it is peculiarly dependent upon communication. Where a plateau of economic development has already been achieved, communications may indulgently take three pathways: government to people, people to government, and people to people. Effective government communicates its expectations about how citizens and officials are to behave. Correspondingly, literate and politically active citizens communicate to government their interests and needs, and individual rights guarantees ordinarily mark out a zone of spontaneous individual initiative which citizens expect government to reserve for private action and enterprise. Moreover, communications are used to transmit generalizable information from citizens among themselves, using government as an intermediary. In countries with developed systems of human rights, according to the Swedish scholar Karl Olivekrona, ". . . it seems impossible to comprehend how we could go on without information about people's rights." Rights assertions are themselves a special form of communication. Olivekrona observes that in countries with long traditions of respect for civil rights and civil liberties "The sequence of ideas about the acquisition of a right, the existence of a right, and the consequences thereof for behavior, is firmly established with regard to the old, well-known rights. When new rights are introduced through legislation the same scheme of thought is automatically applied to them. Therefore, to legislate in the form of issuing prescriptions for the acquisition, transference, etc., of rights is a suitable means of directing behavior among the general public."[28]

In developing countries and countries undergoing rapid economic modernization under the tutelage of authoritarian regimes, the three-way communication scheme may seem an excessive luxury or a technological impossibility. The downward flow of one-way communication from government to the governed may seem the cheapest, most direct, and, necessarily, the only feasible route to economic development. Yet, it entails a structure of government controls which, at least temporarily, excludes the spontaneity, freedom, and reciprocal communication inherent in systems of civil liberties and political rights in which three-way systems of public communications prevail.

Different societies take separate routes to economic modernization and industrialization. The trade-offs between civil and political rights, on the one hand, and rapid economic growth, on the other, should be examined in subsequent research. Any such inquiry should relate this problem to the various ways in which the elites organize the industrialization and modernization process from country to country. Research should focus on the role of culture in adaptations of society to changing patterns of rights consciousness. It should examine social stratification and cleavages associated with strategies of growth which are, in turn, related to questions about social beneficiaries. Finally, the variation in approaches to economic development should be explored with reference to patterns which prevail among such elites as the middle class, dynastic rulers, revolutionary intellectuals, socialist bureaucrats, colonial administrators, and nationalist leaders.

Political systems of every description must respond to a wide spectrum of changing stimuli. But only among those countries which adhere to human rights only under extreme circumstances, such as external threat or economic adversity, is the response one of suppression or withdrawal of rights. To the extent that freedom, equality, and recognition of human dignity are perceived by legal actors to contribute to public order and general welfare, these human rights will be not only encouraged by the system, but also will be vigorously guarded. In the presence of relatively high economic development and a communications infrastructure which permits multidirectional exchange, it becomes possible for the political system to reach a position of comparative equilibrium. However, if the system is to maintain this homeostatic position, the contending concepts of freedom, equality, and welfare must be channeled so that destructive oscillations from the steady state can be controlled. That mechanism is to be found in the balancing effect of rights and duties and in the integrative functions of politics.

Reciprocating rights and duties provide the quid pro quo, the medium of exchange, the social lubricant which allows systems to function smoothly by human rights standards.

NOTES*

* In references to legal periodical literature, the number of the initial page of the work cited immediately follows the volume title. Page references to material specifically referred to in the text, if any, follow the initial page citation. Legal case citations correspond to *A Uniform System of Citation,* 11th ed. (Cambridge: The Harvard Law Review Association, 1974).

1. Julian Huxley, *Freedom and Culture,* United Nations Educational, Scientific and Cultural Organization (Freeport, New York: Books for Libraries, 1971), p. 7.

2. Sylvia L. Thrupp, "Diachronic Methods in Comparative Politics," *The Methodology of Comparative Research,* ed. Robert L. Holt and John E. Turner (New York: The Free Press, 1970), pp. 343–58.

3. Proceedings of the 14th International Conference on Social Welfare, *Social Welfare and Human Rights* (New York: Columbia University Press, 1969), p. 306.

4. Charles Lewis Taylor and Michael C. Hudson, eds., *World Handbook of Political and Social Indicators,* 2d ed. (New Haven: Yale University Press, 1972).

5. Raymond D. Gastil, "Comparative Survey of Freedom," *Freedom at Issue,* no. 17 (1973), p. 4; no. 20 (1973); p. 14; no. 23 (1974), p. 8; no. 26 (1974), p. 15.

6. See generally, U.S., Department of Health, Education and Welfare, *Social Security Programs throughout the World, 1973,* Social Security Administration Report No. 44 (Washington, D.C.: Government Printing Office, 1973). See also, Phillips Cutright, "Political Structure, Economic Development and National Social Security Programs," *American Journal of Sociology* 70 (March 1965):537–51.

7. For another example of independent reliance upon the Freedom House Survey, see Theodore A. Sumberg, *Freedom in the Third World* (Washington, D.C.: Georgetown University Center for Strategic and International Studies, 1975).

8. Gastil, "Survey of Freedom," no. 29 (1975):3. To maintain consistent usage throughout this book, we have substituted the term "civil liberties" where Gastil uses "civil rights."

9. Ibid. For an analysis of related problems of measurement, see Hayward R. Alker, Jr., and Bruce M. Russett, "Indices for Comparing Inequality," in *Comparing Nations,* ed. Richard L. Merritt and Stein Rokkan (New Haven: Yale University Press, 1966).

10. Gastil, "Survey of Freedom," no. 26 (1974):14.

11. Taylor and Hudson, *World Handbook,* pp. 128–35; 150–53; 219–21; 232–35; 236–38; 239–41; 326–31; 341–43; 332–37; 306–21; 256–58;

12. Mauro Cappelletti, *Judicial Review in the Contemporary World* (Indianapolis: Bobbs-Merrill, 1971). See also "The Judiciary and the Legal Profession under the Rule of Law," in *Executive Action and the Rule of Law,* The Report of Committee 4 (Geneva, Switzerland: International Commission of Jurists, 1962), pp. 12–15.

13. Leslie Wolf-Phillips, *Constitutions of Modern States* (New York: Praeger, 1968), pp. ix–xxvi.

14. See Karl Deutsch, "Communication Theory and Political Integration," in *The Integration of Political Communities,* ed. Phillip E. Jacob and James V. Toscano (Philadelphia: J. B. Lippincott Co., 1964), pp. 46–74; Daniel Lerner, "Communications Systems and Social Systems: A Statistical Exploration in History and Policy," *Behavioral Science* 2 (1957):266–75; Lyle W. Shannon, "Is Level of Development Related to Capacity for Self-Government?" *American Journal of Economics and Sociology* 17 (1958):367–82.

15. Daniel Lerner, *The Passing of Traditional Society: Modernizing the Middle East* (New York: The Free Press, 1958); Lucian W. Pye, ed., *Communications and Political Development* (Princeton, New Jersey: Princeton University Press, 1963); Karl W. Deutsch, *The Nerves of Government* (New York: The Free Press, 1966); see also, idem, *Nationalism and Social Communication* (Cambridge: The M.I.T. Press, 1966).

16. Pierre de Tourtoulon, *Philosophy in the Development of Law* (New York: Augustus M. Kelley, 1969), p. 46.

17. Seymour Martin Lipset, "History and Sociology: Some Methodological Considerations," in *Sociology and History: Methods,* ed. Seymour Martin Lipset and Richard Hofstadter (New York: Basic Books, 1968), pp. 20–58.

18. R. B. Nixon, "Factors Related to Freedom in National Press Systems," *Journalism Quarterly* 37 (1950):13–28.

19. Wilbur Schramm, "Communication Development and the Development Process," in Pye, *Communications,* p. 55.

20. Seymour Martin Lipset, "Some Social Requisites of Democracy: Economic Development and Political Legitimacy," *American Political Science Review* 53 (1959), 69–105.

21. Phillips Cutright, "National Political Development: Measurement and Analysis," *American Sociological Review* 28 (1963), 253–64. The index of political development (which is really an index of liberal democratic development) is found to be highly related ($r=.81$) to an index composed of newspaper circulation, newsprint consumption, telephones, and domestic mail.

22. Deane E. Neubauer, "Some Conditions of Democracy," *American Political Science Review* 61 (1969), 1002–9.

23. Donald J. McCrone and Charles F. Cnudde, "Toward a Communication Theory of Democratic Political Development: A Causal Model," *American Political Science Review* 61 (1967), 72–79.

24. Mancur Olson, Jr., "Rapid Economic Growth As a Destabilizing Force," *The Journal of Economic History* 23 (1963), 529–52.

25. Gastil, "Survey of Freedom," no. 29 (1975):4. The twenty-two countries which had the highest scores in the civil liberties and political rights fields from 1972–1975 were: Australia, Austria, Barbados, Canada, Costa Rica, Denmark, France, West Germany, Iceland, Ireland, Italy, Jamaica, Japan, Luxembourg, Netherlands, New Zealand, Norway, Sweden, Switzerland, United Kingdom, and the United States.

26. Hubert M. Blalock, Jr., *An Introduction to Social Research* (Englewood Cliffs, New Jersey, 1970), pp. 62–85.

27. Robert B. Seidman, "The Communication of Law and the Process of Development," 1972 *Wisconsin Law Review* 686, 686.

28. Karl Olivecrona, *Law as Fact,* 2d ed. (London: Stevens and Sons, 1971), p. 198.

PART II POLICY PROBLEMS IN COMPARATIVE PERSPECTIVE

EDITOR'S INTRODUCTION

In recent years, scholars in the fields of law and the social sciences have expressed interest in moving research on public policy and decisional behavior beyond the parochialism of national study and onto a comparative basis. But the obstacles facing any such expedition are great. Comparative public policy in the field of human rights largely remains terra incognita, and where guiding theory is concerned, we have neither chart nor compass. From the point of view of the social sciences, we stand in the prescientific stage of requiring case studies, although some very useful case studies exist, such as those of Ronald Bunn and William Andrews, focusing on Europe, and of Kenneth Karst and Keith Rosenn, focusing on Latin America.[1] From the point of view of comparative law, the field has remained impoverished by a tendency to focus on a single legal system in a way which avoids explicit intersystem comparisons. Distinguished exceptions are the work of such scholars as Frede Castberg, Walter Gellhorn, and A. H. Robertson.[2] Generally speaking, however, legal scholars in the field of comparative law are strangers to social scientists. Their categories of analysis are different from those used even by political scientists, and, as the *Index of Foreign Legal Periodicals* shows, they often write in French, the language of international law.

To a large extent, the complaint of Moses Moskowitz that human rights, except as a parochial national concern, is "an untrodden area of systematic research" remains unanswered.[3] It is true that scholarly work on human rights at the level of international law has been fruitful, as illustrated by the research of John Carey, Ernst B. Haas, Louis Sohn and Thomas Buergenthal, and Vernon Van Dyke.[4] But comparative work has largely been ignored, although one recent global review by Ivo Duchacek exists,[5] two scholarly journals have been founded to review human rights progress,[6] and a useful comparative casebook edited by Thomas M. Franck is available.[7]

Why has the study of so important a subject as comparative rights and liberties remained academically underdeveloped? There are two separate explanations which have a bearing on the essays that follow in part II. First, there is a

71

dearth of reliable information about human rights development from country to country. A lesson can be taken from United Nations experience with the information gathering it has done to implement the Universal Declaration of Human Rights. Adopted by the General Assembly in 1948, the Declaration was to be strengthened according to a plan set up in 1966 calling for government reports on domestic human rights developments. Unfortunately the fragmentary triennial reports to the U.N. Commission on Human Rights do not form a realistic, reliable, or complete picture. Faulting the reporting sources rather than the Commission, Moses Moskovitz complains sharply, "The irrelevancies contained in the reports are only exceeded by their omissions."[8] Harsh criticism should be tempered in this case by recognition that, in a field with inadequate categories of analysis, the more inclusive the coverage, the shallower it will necessarily be. As a corrective, the essays that follow attempt to explore what is possible in this field by assessing systems actually in force about which reliable information is available.

Second, the scope of the field of human rights remains in dispute. Must the expression of a human need be translated into a legally enforceable claim before we can properly call it a right? Is a legal demand entitled to the designation of human right only if we can somehow philosophically justify it in terms of human dignity? We do not believe such difficult questions need to be finally answered before enlisting the term, human rights, as a worthy generic title for cross-national comparative study of various moral and politico-legal claims. In using the term, human rights, to cover the full range of basic rights and freedoms open to comparative investigation, we follow an increasingly accepted practice. Given the wide area of public policy covered by the term, the essays that follow by no means exhaust the component topics of an ever-expanding field. About the changeable and various character of rights and liberties, the French scholar Georges Burdeau writes that "in any given society at any given time, the dominant sociopolitical thought results in reinforced weighting of certain rights as these rights become reflected in the legal value structure by which they are enforced. Consequently the listing of rights appears to be contingent and subject to constant revision."[9]

In the essay by Claude, the contingency, flux, and diversity about which Burdeau has written is seen to affect rights and liberties in France, Great Britain, and the United States. Such relativism notwithstanding, the classical model of human rights development in part I portrays a pattern of sequential development. The essays in part II are organized to reflect that pattern. The studies begin with the basic problem of setting limits on government. They proceed from the libertarian guarantees of free expression, privacy, and due process associated with individual rights and civil liberties, to the equalitarian guarantees of civil rights associated with such groups as linguistic and racial minorities and women. Finally, the welfare considerations related to the rights of children are reviewed.

No effort has been made to enhance the unity of the studies by uniformity of country selection. On the contrary, some breadth of coverage was encouraged. Each of the authors in part II begins from the assumption that the discrete problem under examination is, in some sense, topical and fundamental to what Justice Cardozo called a "scheme of ordered liberty." Moreover, each attempts to shed new light upon a specific human rights problem by comparing specifically how two or more politico-legal systems treat the same policy problem. Free to develop in any way the topic, each writer has succeeded in presenting information about a subject very seldom included in textbooks on civil rights and civil liberties. The comparative framework has elicited some fresh analysis and insights.

Claude's essay in part I distinguishes four stages of human rights development in a historical survey of four centuries of experience in France, Great Britain, and the United States. In contrast to Claude's historical perspective, that of Fletcher Baldwin, Jr. is essentially cross-sectional. He offers a detailed analysis of the present state of constitutional affairs in three differing political systems— Mexico, the United States, and Uganda—each now at a different plateau of sociopolitical and legal development. Baldwin's approach enables him to indicate how and why (in contrast to the classical model of the preceding essay) legal development may be subordinated to varying national goals dictated by pressing socioeconomic and political exigencies.

The importance of the social and political setting for human rights development is taken into account by each author. Lawrence W. Beer examines in detail legal protection for political demonstrations in Japan, and he contrasts sharply conditions in the United States with the Japanese emphasis "on harmony, self-discipline, teamwork, avoidance of frontal conflict, group conformity and the achievement or at least the appearance of consensus." He stresses that the social system, rather than the official mechanisms of the law, define the parameters of freedom, expression, and assembly in Japan. The essay by E. Jeremy Hutton, Krishan S. Nehra and Durvasula S. Sastri notes that "technology, social needs, cultural and political circumstances all have a bearing on the legal status of privacy." In their comparison of the United States, Great Britain, and India, they examine how the laws of these countries are being shaped to recognize privacy as a right and how their systems of law protect it. Otis H. Stephens, Jr., asserts that "fundamental social forces which cut across national boundaries" have been at work in the field of the due process rights of criminal defendants. In this connection, he traces case law development in Canada and the United States and describes the underlying political bases of support for the development of legal aid programs in the two countries. Manfred Wenner's study of linguistic minorities explores the question of the extent to which political characteristics of specific countries and particular minorities explain the kinds of action taken to meet minority demands for human rights. Ved Nanda's comparative study of affirmative action programs and legislative remedies for racial discrimination contrasts American, British, and Canadian legalities, which represent varying traditions of economic and social laissez-faire attitudes toward the regulation of human relations in society. In her comparison of the status of women in the United States and the Scandinavian countries, Anna P. Schreiber describes legal developments as well as the historical and social setting responsible for "some common roots of sex inequality." Against the background of reviewing the women's movement, she seeks to "assess the effectiveness of various strategies for change." In a complementary essay on the same countries, Linda Breeden distinguishes the egalitarian thrust of the women's movement from the needs reflected in the drive for children's rights where equal treatment is not always indicated. It is the thesis of her essay on the United States and Scandinavian countries that "the rights of children must include the right of each child to fair treatment in his relations with the state, his family, and also with other individuals."

What is needed at the present stage in the comparative study of human rights is to generate analysis from detailed case work. To the criticism from social scientists that the essays do not rely sufficiently on elaborate techniques of inquiry, it must be said that the essays in part II were deliberately based largely on legal methodology to help students of comparative development, behavior, and policy arrive at speaking terms with students of comparative law. We take heart from the comment by Arend Lijphart of the University of Leiden, who writes that, at the earliest stages of systematic comparative research, "the intense comparative analysis of a few cases may be more promising than a more superficial statistical analysis of cases."[10] Contrasting data on countries with minimal or merely incipient human rights protection should be a part of future inquiry at a later stage of comparative research.[11] But for the present, it is generally best to begin studying a phenomenon where it actually exists, and in that context, to try to straighten out the staples of legal analysis. To that end, the final essay in this part by Jay Adrian Sigler offers concrete guidance to the bemused scholar who does not know what research resources are available.

NOTES

1. Ronald Bunn and William G. Andrews, eds., *Political and Civil Liberties in Europe* (Princeton: Van Nostrand, 1967). Kenneth L. Karst and Keith S. Rosenn, eds., *Law and Development in Latin America* (Berkeley: University of California, 1976).

2. Frede Castberg, *Freedom of Speech in the West: A Comparative Study of Law in France, the United States and Germany* (Oslo: Oslo University Press, 1960); Walter Gellhorn, *Ombudsman and Others, Citizen Protectors in Nine Countries* (Cambridge: Harvard University Press, 1966); A. H. Robertson, *Human Rights in Europe* (Manchester: University of Manchester Press, 1963).

3. Moses Moskowitz, *The Politics and Dynamics of Human Rights* (Dobbs Ferry, New York: Oceana Publications, 1958), pp. 98–99.

4. John Carey, *U.N. Protection of Civil and Political Rights* (New York: Syracuse University Press, 1970); Ernst B. Haas, *Human Rights and International Action* (Stanford: Stanford University Press, 1970); Louis B. Sohn and Thomas Buergenthal, *International Protection of Human Rights* (Indianapolis: The Bobbs-Merrill Company, 1973); Vernon Van Dyke, *Human Rights, the United States and World Community* (New York: Oxford University Press, 1970).

5. Ivo. D. Duchacek, *Rights and Liberties in the World Today* (Santa Barbara: The American Bibliographic Center-Cleo Press, 1973).

6. *Human Rights,* American Bar Association, New York; *Revue des droits de l'homme,* International Institute of Human Rights, Strasbourg.

7. Thomas M. Franck, *Comparative Constitutional Process* (London: Sweet and Maxwell, 1968).

8. Moskowitz, *Politics and Dynamics,* p. 94.

9. Georges Burdeau, *Les Libertés Publiques,* 3rd ed. (Paris: R. Pichon and R. Durand-Auzias, 1966), pp. 20–21.

10. Arend Lijphard, "Politics and the Comparative Method," *American Political Science Review* 65 (1971):682–93.

11. John Henry Merryman, "Comparative Law and Scientific Explanation," in *Law in the United States of America in Social and Technological Revolution,* ed. John N. Hazard and Wenceslas J. Wagner (Brussels: Establissement Emile Bruylant, 1974), pp. 81–101. See also, Karl Fox, *Social Indicators and Social Theory, Elements of an Operational System* (New York: John Wiley and Sons, 1975), pp. 8–28.

Chapter 3 CONSTITUTIONAL LIMITATIONS ON GOVERNMENT IN MEXICO, THE UNITED STATES, AND UGANDA

Fletcher N. Baldwin, Jr.

In a multicultural, transitional society in which few values are held in common and in which the advancement of science and technology have fundamentally altered the foundations of social and economic organization, it becomes essential to study the role of constitutionalism in comparative terms.[1] The dependence of human rights upon constitutionalism becomes apparent thereby. Understanding of one's own constitutional environment is facilitated, and it becomes possible to determine what part, if any, legal limitations on government play in the overall scheme of the social process.

The objective of this chapter is to develop a broad-based understanding of ongoing legal systems ostensibly operating under concepts of constitutionalism. Constitutional systems at various stages of development are examined, those of Mexico, Uganda, and the United States. Mexico is a part of the civil-law, Latin American complex. Uganda, a potential force in the third world, has a legal system in which law stems from customary and common-law traditions. The laws of the United States flow directly from a common-law tradition.

An ingredient common to each nation studied is a concept of constitutionalism that reflects a fear of despotism. Although each nation evolved from a different historical reference point, the three constitutions are sophisticated attempts to confine governmental power. The powers of government have been channelled through confined policy paths; the difficulty has come about through the application of the confinements. In the United States Constitution, the essential distrust of government is apparent from the beginning of the preamble "*We* [italics added] the people. . ." to the twenty-sixth amendment. The fear of a dictator is manifest in the Uganda Constitution. Chapter 1, article 1, section 1 makes the Constitution the supreme law of the land.[2] The 1917 Mexican Constitution attempts to fix decentralized power as the result of a bitter revolution.[3] All three constitutions, however, leave the path open for strong executive control.

In each case, chief executives have taken advantage of the broad contours of authority outlined in the respective documents.[4] As this imbalance has grown, constitutional defenses have become, at best, holding actions. At worst, the concept of ordered constitutional government may be a mere philosophical discussion.

In developing nations, numerous military coups have hampered orderly constitutional process. Instability and despotism have become the extreme obstacles encountered by supporters of constitutional government. Ultimately, scholar-leaders have argued in good faith that Western concepts of constitutionalism are an impediment to orderly growth.[5] President J. Nyerere of Tanzania considers the concept of constitutionalism, as developed in Anglo-American political thought, to be alien to the needs of his people.[6] With his party platform he has set about to produce one of the most stable African countries. Nyerere is most unusual, but he does force one to reevaluate the ingredients and implementation provisions of the various constitutions under consideration.

This essay focuses first upon the initial constitutional frameworks of Mexico, Uganda, and the United States. The metamorphosis of constitutional principles into the practical realities of governmental power are traced and a comparison is drawn between the idea and the application of the constitutions of these three nations. Finally, through an examination of the immediate challenges to be met by each nation, it is shown how Mexico, Uganda, and the United States each have balanced the myriad of conflicting demands upon their governments.

HISTORICAL EXPLORATION: MEXICO AND UGANDA

The nations under consideration are in various stages of constitutional development. Although they share similar goals and objectives, they have used strikingly different methods to attain them. The methods chosen perhaps reflect the divergent paths to nationhood.

Mexico, a former Spanish colony,[7] retained the civil-law tradition of Spain after gaining independence in 1821. While the first code of the young nation was primarily adopted from a civil code of European nature, Mexico turned northward to the United States for a guide to constitutional ideals.[8] The drafters of the Constitution of the United Mexican States adopted many of the basic principles of democratic government which are manifested in American constitutional tenets. Henceforth in Mexico there would be a separation of powers, election of the Executive for a fixed term and guarantees of fundamental individual rights. Similarly to the United States, the legislative branch of Mexican government was to be bicameral, with a Chamber of Deputies apportioned on the basis of population and a Senate consisting of two members from each state.[9]

The Constitution provides for a judicial branch of Government headed by a Supreme Court consisting of twenty-one judges appointed for life.[10] Unlike its United States counterpart, the Court is divided into four main divisions: Penal, Civil, Administrative, and Labor, with five judges assigned to each. A trial and appellate court system consisting of forty-two district and eleven circuit courts supplements the Supreme Court.[11] Finally, as the judicial procedure protecting constitutional rights, Mexico chose the concept of *amparo* consisting of a combination of mandamus, habeas corpus, and certiorari.[12]

Whereas Mexico was part of the great European colonization of the North American continent, the nation of Uganda was in part a product of the extension of European power into Africa. The British, upon their arrival in the midnineteenth century in the territory that would become Uganda, found African kingdoms operating under complex political and legal institutions.[13] The English common-law tradition was naturally at odds with the legal and political systems which had developed in the old kingdoms over several centuries.[14] Years of conflict, acceptance, rejection, and compromise between the customary law and the imported common law were the natural results.[15]

Despite the confusion the received law had caused in Uganda's legal, civil, social, and economic life, legal preparation for independence was begun in 1955 with the establishment of a ministerial system that led to an increase of African leadership in the decision-making process. The London Constitutional Conference of 1961 established the dates for independence,[16] and on October 9, 1962, Uganda became an independent nation.[17] Uganda is currently governed by military leaders.[18] Parliament consists of the Chief Executive, who took power by force in 1971, and the unicameral National Assembly.[19]

The High Court of Uganda consists of a Chief Justice and a variable number of Puisne Judges. The High Court usually sits in panels of three, but Puisne Judges sitting alone may also hear cases of first impression.[20] Below the High Court are various magistrate courts.

Although Mexico, Uganda, and the United States vary in political composition, through each nation's constitution runs the common thread of an attempt to insure stability for both the nation and individuals. This purpose is manifested by a basic commitment to the guarantee of those rights which each nation considers implicitly necessary for nationhood.

INITIAL CONSTITUTIONAL SETTING

Each constitution stresses the importance of achieving a specified goal or ideal state.[21] However, the maximization of liberal values associated with individual liberties in the United States may not facilitate the goal of nation building in either Uganda or Mexico.

Difficult questions of nationhood are not dealt with except by historical reference to an implementing ideology: What is the purpose of a nation state? Correspondingly, under what circumstances should the state exercise control over the individual? The unchecked exercise of freedom of expression, so precious a right in United States constitutional theory, could result in tribal war in Uganda and in Mexico might result in riot or death. Social factors become important to the implementation of constitutionalism.[22] One of the foremost aims of the power structure in an emerging nation is that of the nation's self-preservation. Consequently, to meet this goal a redefinition of individual liberty often takes place.[23] This is so in Uganda as well as Mexico.

The United States has a long history of defining and refining its concepts of constitutionalism. The ideal emerged historically from a philosophical theory of a contract-compact. The attempt to breathe life into a democratic system encompassing freedom, dignity, and equality met with strong resistance as the new nation grew, but with less as the nation matured and stabilized. The consumer became the democratic man. This ideal of a consumer combined with a constitutional concept of representative self-government was able ultimately to succeed. But, it began to succeed only when it appeared that the theories in practice were concepts that reflected the will of the people of the new nation and that citizens' demands, in turn, were based upon contemporary needs.

While the concept of nation building emerged from Philadelphia, the criteria for the governing principles which originated there have been shifted and turned ever since. Concepts of freedom, justice, dignity, and responsibility were slow to take root. The same struggle is manifested in the newly emerging countries of Africa as leaders argue against ill-defined values.[24] They point out that the basic document should establish the rules to be followed in nation building and should not concern itself with philosophically confused discussions of the rights of man which reflect western attitudes toward constitutionalism.

The constitutions of Africa are, for the most part, imported from the western colonial powers and reflect western ideals of government. For example, the Uganda Constitution of 1962, the first constitution of independence, reflects the influence of the former colonial power.[25] After the first coup in 1966,[26] the new constitution that was drafted and approved September 8, 1967, continued to reflect the imported "Westminster" system of government. However, the constitution appears to take no cognizance of the machinery by which values are changed into reality. Consequently, the present government tends to ignore constitutional concepts of nation building.[27]

The difficulty in analyzing the constitutions of Mexico, Uganda, and the United States lies in the ever-present issue of whether or not there are attractive alternatives for social growth and nation building. What does the Constitution offer and what does it ignore? What are and what should be specific national priorities? Are they reflected in the constitutions? Has there been a restructuring of constitutional theory in the political context while the basic document has remained unchanged? A review of the constitutions themselves can help to understand these questions.

CONSTITUTIONAL ANATOMY

The most obvious difference between the constitutional documents of Uganda, Mexico, and the United States is in length. Both the 1917 Constitution of the United Mexican States, with more than 136 articles, and the 1967

Constitution of the Republic of Uganda, with more than 130, contain minute, detailed descriptions. This makes them much longer than the United States Constitution which has 7 articles and 25 amendments. In the United States, the accepted concept of judicial review has enhanced the vitality of such phrases as due process and fair trial.[28] The rationale of the drafters was that future conflicts could not be anticipated and specifically provided for. Therefore, the judicial branch of government was charged with constitutional interpretation for contemporary effect and meaning.[29] The drafters of the Mexican constitution in 1917 and their counterparts in Uganda in 1967 were inclined to place less trust in their ability to sustain review of unclear language. Unlike the Americans, the Mexican and Ugandan drafters had a history of both successful and unsuccessful constitutions on which to draw.

The basic human rights provisions found in each constitution serve as starting points from which to assess the degree of national commitment to constitutional government in an era of nation building; the level of implementation helps to assess governmental stability. Two initial impressions result from a reading of Uganda's constitutional protection of individual rights. First, the third chapter of the Uganda Constitution, which guarantees fundamental human rights, is more complex than the U. S. Bill of Rights and the language is much more qualified. Whereas the Bill of Rights aims to shield individuals from unreasonable governmental interference, the Guarantees of Fundamental Human Rights focuses upon governmental self-preservation.

The first amendment to the U. S. Constitution articulates political and religious freedom. "Congress shall make no law. . . ." is absolute in its wording. Freedoms of expression and association in Uganda are found in articles 17 and 18, respectively. After article 17, a series of exceptions are inserted which are treated as consistent with the main, protected concept. Article 18, respecting freedom of association, follows. Under article 18, an individual is able to assemble and associate freely so long as his actions do not conflict with the interests of others in their private capacities or with government in its public capacity. Freedom of association is prohibited if it conflicts with public safety, good order, morality, or health. Even the primary freedoms are subject to article 21, which provides for suspension of the Constitution in times of public emergency, and to article 10, which permits preventive detention for "political enemies" of the republic.[30]

The first amendment of the U. S. Constitution, which establishes free speech, is worded in the absolute, but is subject to judicial interpretation. Over the years, the exercise of judicial interpretation has established qualifications to the primary freedom.[31] In Uganda the scope of judicial review is potentially broad because the language of the Constitution, even without the qualifications, is subject to interpretation. The delineated interests of the national economy, public safety, and public morality are nebulous terms which require a judicial definition for each actual situation.

In Mexico, the potential for broad judicial power is defined as *amparo,* which is outlined in articles 103–10. *Amparo* is to some extent similar to a combination of declaratory judgment and certiorari.[32] The Mexican Constitution restricts judicial review to suits in *amparo,* thus limiting the court as a primary platform for nation building.

Other noteworthy protections include the right to petition and the right of assembly. In Mexico the right to petition is restricted to citizens who are petitioning in political matters. The right of assembly, which is also subject to the citizen participation limitation, contains, in addition, a restriction disallowing all armed, deliberative meetings and provides for the dissolution of assemblies on such tenuous a ground as insult or threat. These two limitations obviously lend themselves to broad interpretation.

Religious expression in Mexico has been limited by many constitutional provisions. Freedom of religion is provided, but it is limited to the practice of religion in the home: within places of public worship religion is subject to government supervision.[33] The Uganda Constitution expressly provides for the freedoms of religion, speech, and assembly, and may include freedom of the press under the freedom of expression provision.[34] Freedom of religion is included under the freedom of conscience provision. This is similar to that of the United States and differs from that of Mexico only in the allowable public manifestation of religion. There is, however, one major obstacle to the freedom of conscience concept that invades almost all the other provisions. Legislation limiting basic freedoms is permissible if it can be shown that the freedoms in any way interfere with the interests of the national economy, the administration of essential services, defense, public safety, public order, public morality, or public health. Otherwise, the freedoms of expression and assembly are equal to those of the United States.[35]

The constitutions of both Mexico and the United States, utilizing similar language, proscribe the confiscation of personal residence by the military.[36] However, no mention is made of this subject in the Ugandan document. Freedom from unreasonable search and seizure and the security of the person have been well tested in American courts.[37] Mexico and Uganda also provide for this guaranty.[38] The Mexican provision appears more meticulous in its expressed guaranty than that of either the United States or Uganda, including as it does separate requirements for arrest and search warrants.[39] However, these requirements have been incorporated into the U. S. Constitution through judicial interpretation. Uganda's provision against unreasonable search and seizure is followed by a long list of exceptions which include those implied by the United States provision and expressed by the Mexican article.[40] The exceptions extend far beyond those provided for in Mexico, and allow searches where reasonably required to protect the public safety, order, morality, health, planning, and taxation. The freedoms granted by the Uganda Constitution may be restricted by the utilization of terms capable of such broad interpretation as to make the guarantee completely disappear if decision makers are so inclined.

The requirements in the U. S. Constitution prohibiting double jeopardy, self-incrimination, deprivation of life, liberty, or property without due process of law; and requiring compensation for private property taken for public use, are found in both the Ugandan and the Mexican Constitutions.[41] They are nearly identical in both form and substance. In both Uganda and Mexico, the double jeopardy provision is looser than the American view permits and precludes a second trial for the same offense except upon the order of a superior court after appeal of conviction or acquittal. The second deviation occurs in the self-incrimination provision. While the United States accords the privilege against such incrimination in all cases, a strict interpretation of Uganda's provision would seem to provide this protection only when the person is himself being tried for the offense. Thus, he would not be entitled to utilize this privilege if he were compelled to testify in any other action. The guarantees provided for in the U. S. Constitution of speedy and public trial, trial by jury, information as to the nature of the accusation, confrontation of adverse witnesses and assistance of counsel have their equivalent in the constitutions of both Uganda and Mexico.[42]

The sections which provide for information for criminal defendants as to the charged crime and for the confrontation of adverse witnesses do not deviate substantially among the three constitutions. The speedy trial provisions of Mexico and Uganda are specific as to the time period required to satisfy the guarantee, whereas the United States provision is clarified by case law.[43] Again, the main difference between these constitutions is that the provisions of the Mexican and Ugandan Constitutions are expressly stated, whereas the United States provision is subject to judicial interpretation.

In the area of jury trials a more divergent view is found. The Mexican provision allows for jury trials in criminal cases.[44] The Uganda Constitution contains no provision for jury trial. This is the rule in both magistrate and higher court trials.[45]

Assistance of counsel is implied by the provision in the Mexican Constitution which guarantees that the defense of the accused be conducted personally or by counsel.[46] Uganda guarantees the aid of counsel, but only at the financial expense of the defendant.[47] The United States position on state assumption of the cost of counsel is not specified in the Constitution, but has been articulated by judicial decisions and federal legislation.[48] Mexico has no constitutional provision indicating whether the state should furnish counsel.[49]

The U. S. Constitution, on its face, expressly forbids excessive bail. Mexico's provision allows for bail based on the accused's financial status, but limits the allowance of bail to offenses punishable by not more than five years in jail.[50] Uganda has no provision for bail.

Cruel and unusual punishment is feared in all three nations. But while Uganda prohibits torture and inhuman or degrading treatment, political prisoners are not protected because they fall outside the constitutional prohibitions.[51] Prohibitions against slavery, *ex post facto* laws, and titles of nobility are found in all three constitutions. Finally, the concept of equality of the law is shared by each country.

These are a few of the similarities of the three constitutions. Implementation is another matter, for it must take into account the complex factors not found among the words of the Constitutions.

THE SHARED IDEAL

A common thread running through each of the constitutions is the acknowledgment of the document as a predetermined rule of limitation upon governmental power. The rule is said to be supreme, and supposedly not subject to the whims of government officials. Normally the vehicles for testing the ebb and flow of governmental limitations are provided for in the constitution with a judiciary headed by a supreme court, the most familiar of constitutional referees.

The concept of a supreme court, balancing and testing governmental action against a constitution, is primarily Anglo-American. Although historically England did not have judicial review in the strict sense of *Marbury* v. *Madison*,[52] English tradition fostered the principle of judicial interpretation of government under law.[53] In the United States, this principle was formalized in article III and in article VI of the Constitution;[54] the impact of the judiciary in the United States has been well-documented and discussed elsewhere. The doctrine of judicial review can be found in most anglophonic African constitutions.[55] Furthermore, these provisions have enabled the judiciary to serve as one of the chief institutions of acculturation for the third world nations by preserving chieftancies and conforming them with customary law. As such, the court structures have provided the methodology by which multiple legal systems have often achieved coexistance within a single sovereign state.[56]

The independence of the judiciary generally receives great emphasis as one of the significant checks on the strong executives created by the constitutions of the new African nations. In the words of the International Commission of Jurists: "An independent judiciary is an indispensable requisite of a free society under the rule of law. Such independence implies freedom from interference by the executive or legislative with the judicial function, but does not mean that the judge is entitled to act in an arbitrary manner."[57] In response to the spirit of this statement, which was made in 1959, most of the first constitutions of the new African nations quite explicitly guaranteed the independence of the judicial system.[58] Those who did not, assured it by implication.[59] Thus the emerging nations adopted the machinery to enable direct adjudication of the constitutional conflicts which would inevitably result from the explosion of nation building. As will be seen, additional factors have influenced the ways in which both Uganda and Mexico have utilized their distinct systems of constitutional review.

CULTURAL AND SOCIAL FACTORS AFFECTING CONSTITUTIONALISM

Within the political boundaries of the African nations are distinct ethnic and cultural groups based upon tribal affiliations as well as those of language, origin, and religion. Tribal language grouping is likely to be one of the major identifying factors. Subgroups based upon race and religion exist within the major language groupings, in addition to which there is the heterogeneous population. African countries shelter a multiple legal system under one political roof.

The legal structures utilized by the colonial powers for administration invariably are those which survived the demands for independence and reconciliation at least through the first stages of nationhood. Constitutional development in Africa has been brought about with difficulty. It is said that the introduction of Westminster parliamentary institutions into anglophonic Africa was an introduction of an alien legal system upon conquered nations.[60] The difficulty of introducing foreign ideas, both political and competitive, into a developing nation did not become clear until after independence. A consequence of this friction was a constitutional evolution that produced strong executive leadership.

The importance of a major national movement to cope with the complexities of the received law was perceived by President Jules Nyerere of Tanzania. Nyerere emerged in the 1950s as *mwalimu,* the teacher. He argues that in the western world the objective is to ensure representative parties. In government the debate occurs within the party, after which the vote is taken in the legislature. Nyerere points out that the vote is usually along party lines. He also attempts to point out what he perceives to be the fundamental differences between the characteristics of democratic, constitutional government and the realities of an emerging nation. The U.S. Constitution and the American political system, he argues, came into being as a result of existing social and economic divisions. African parties had a vastly different origin; they were formed to challenge the foreigners who ruled Africa.

With respect to civil liberties and social change, Nyerere asserts that power in the presidency ensures the rights of the individual. His rationale is that African nations have neither long traditions of nationhood, nor the means of national security which stronger nations take for granted. A handful of people can still jeopardize a nation and reduce it to ashes. Regarding a constitutional bill of rights, he argues that a bill of rights limits national advancement. Constitutional guarantees for the individual in a developing nation tend to defeat the very purpose for which they are set up, for they serve to protect those whose object it is to subvert and destroy democracy itself.

Nyerere believes, furthermore, that a bill of rights results in grave conflict between the judicial and executive branches of government which an emerging nation can ill afford. He deems a luxury the conflict in a developed nation such as the United States. In general terms, the institutions of government which are

emerging in Africa, at least theoretically, follow Nyerere's rationale.[61] Consequently, the trend in Africa is presidentialism with a distinct African flavor.
Nyerere has emerged as an excellent example of a strong executive taking
aggressive action toward stabilization.[62]

Although they sooth the growing pains of emerging nations, the constitutions
can be said at best to symbolize independence. The documents, Nyerere has
argued, provide a measure of legitimacy for the new rulers. However, Nyerere's
country Tanzania, unlike Uganda, is stable and has been able to treat the
concept of constitutionalism much as a treaty between the colonial power and
the independent nation. The real platform for the Tanzanian government comes
from the pronouncements of the Arusha Declaration of 1967. On the other
hand, whenever leadership in Uganda changes, the Constitution is suspended;
thus, the document is not given the force and effect of its writing.[63] Consequently, it can be said that the Constitution reflects at most the aspirations of
the new rulers; or that the colonial powers wanted certain values and principles
to become part of the newly independent nation in order to continue a western
concept of colonialism. In any event, Uganda courts, with their long tradition of
independence, have occasionally rebelled against governmental disregard of constitutional concepts.[64] Implementation of the constitution through judicial
review ended temporarily in Uganda in 1971 with the military take over of the
nation.[65] The take over produced clear constitutional and transnational violations so basic as to make many human rights concerns of the United Nations
pale in comparison. When General Ide Amin came to power in Uganda he
ordered all Asians (decendants of the Punjab, Gujurat and Goa nationalities who
settled in Uganda as railway workers, and subsequently worked their way into
the professions and commerce) to report for classification on October 12, 1971.
As a result, many Asians had their documents and passports taken from them.[66]

On August 9, 1972 President Amin issued a decree revoking entry permits
and resident permits for most noncitizen Asians. Within a period of 90 days
most (approximately 55,000) of the Asian population in Uganda had departed
leaving behind property of every kind.[67] Property was abandoned because of
two decrees which were issued in October, 1972. The first stated that in effect
Asians would not transfer immovable property to anyone.[68] The second decree
allowed the appointment of agents to sell the property; however, agents could
not in their dealings in any way frustrate governmental policy, which was the
Africanisation of all properties.[69] Abandoned property was taken over by
Ugandans, mainly soldiers or their relatives, and no reimbursement ever was paid
for the lost property.[70] Although the government established an Abandoned
Property Custodian Board[71] their work was frustrated by the President and the
army.[72]

It would seem that if a viable nation in a community of nations swiftly expels
thousands of people without permitting them to take money or personal
belongings, the matter could be expected to be aired in the community of

nations, the United Nations, or in the domestic courts of that nation with reference to internal constitutional principles.[73] Despite its concern for the plight of humans everywhere in the world, the General Assembly of the United Nations failed to act on the expulsion of the Asians; furthermore, the Human Rights Sub-Commission on the Prevention of Discrimination and the Protection of Minorities did not care to put the matter on its agenda. The United Nations agreed substantially with the Uganda delegate, Mr. Ibingira, that the matter should be confined to the domestic laws of Uganda.

Chapter 2, article 13 of the 1967 Constitution, which is still in operation, although at present under suspension, deals with expropriation of property. Article 13 section 1 does not permit a taking of any property except for very limited purposes, none of which would fit the Asian taking. Section 3 however permits a taking "in the public interest" of any property. What is in the public interest would presumably be determined by the High Court under article 13, section 1, cl.(c)(ii), which grants right of access to the High Court where the legality of a taking is in question. No case has been considered by the High Court under chapter 2. Indeed, no case of any important constitutional issue has been considered by the High Court since "Phase I" of President Amin's economic war on the Asians began in 1971.[74] Within the present political climate it is doubtful whether any redress can be considered by the domestic courts of Uganda. The fact, however, that the 1967 Constitution remains and that article 13 is intact, coupled with a long history of judicial review, could mean that a change in political climate or leadership would also liberalize access to the courts for the Asians who have lost everything as a result of the effort to turn over businesses and professions in Uganda to Ugandans.[75] Notwithstanding President Amin, who in 1975 expressed admiration for Adolph Hitler, the long and rich tradition in Uganda of fairness and use of the courts to settle disputes cannot be suppressed indefinitely.

The history of the Constitution of Mexico and of the political ramifications surrounding it is similar to that of the emerging nations of Africa.[76] Like Uganda, Mexico is virtually a single party state; like premilitary Uganda, there are minor parties representing specialized political viewpoints. However, the major party and the force and effect of its programs overshadow the representation of other parties in local and national governments. The revolutionary party in Mexico, *Partido Revolucionaro Institutional* (PRI), has taken on a broad political function demanded by the westernization of the country. The PRI acts as an auxiliary constitutional mechanism that makes possible limited and responsible national government. It provides a structured, disciplined, political agency that balances the demands of the three basic sectors in the country: farm, labor, and popular.

The PRI supplies support, at the same time, to the formal governmental agencies which regulate those interests outside the party machinery. It would seem that the vast preponderance of power resides in this party inasmuch as almost all seats in both chambers of the Congress of the Union belong to PRI members. However, the strength of the government lies with the party executive. The party executive is the chief executive of the nation, the President of Mexico. In Mexico, if a dispute arises which involves a constitutional question, the concept of judicial review is of little help if the President wishes to act independently. At best, the doctrine of *amparo* serves the parties to the litigation.

DOCTRINE OF JUDICIAL REVIEW

The philosophic principles embodied in the United States, Mexican, and Ugandan Constitutions are vitally important to the societal direction of each Government. However, aside from party machinery which is transient at best, how are these principles to be translated into realistic programs? The essential characteristics of any constitution are such that they require an interpretative authority.[77] In the United States, in the absence of specific constitutional commands, a doctrine of translation was derived from the principle of constitutional supremacy. It was adjudicated in *Marbury v. Madison* and further justified on the ground that federal courts are required to hear cases or controversies arising under the Constitution. The task of translation settled into article 3 courts.

Judicial review in Uganda and Mexico presents both similar and dissimilar practices. Although the *Marbury* deductive thesis has received some practical acceptance in Uganda, the Mexican federal courts base their practice of constitutional review almost exclusively upon the explicit authorization of articles 103 and 107 of the Constitution of 1917.

Mexican constitutional historians point out that the difficult task of judicial review in a civil-law country is compounded by a long history of instability and, at times, despotism.[78] Both factors act to deter the development of an independent judiciary. While the Constitution of 1917 does not reflect support for an independent judiciary on a general scope, the Constitution does establish an autonomous form of suit where constitutional questions are placed in issue: *juicio de amparo*.[79] Although this review is independent, the limitations placed upon constitutional review by *amparo* centers interpretations, both historically and factually, elsewhere.

Anglophonic African nations present a common-law, traditional approach to judicial review. The 1962 Uganda Constitution of Independence stressed the importance of the judiciary in the political structure of the new nation. The independence of the judiciary was emphasized again in the 1967 Uganda Constitution. The application of judicial review in Uganda closely parallels article 3 of the United States Constitution. Judges of the High Court determine constitutional issues in much the same manner as justices of the United States Supreme Court. The Constitution contains a supremacy clause which, coupled with other provisions, authorizes judicial review by the High Court. Furthermore, the High Court determines the validity of both the presidential election and election of the National Assembly. Unlike the United States Constitution, that of Uganda provides for executive suspension of judicial review.[80] This suspension of basic constitutional provisions occurs upon executive determination of a state of national emergency. But short of national emergencies, the High Court is empowered to adjudicate actively both constitutional matters and political disputes.

The role of the Court in Uganda with regard to political questions is interesting in view of the social and political conditions there. The Judicative Act of 1967, section 3 (1), gives the court power to determine any type of dispute that is brought to it. This includes the raising of matters that are political in nature. Thus, traditional political issues which often are fraught with special dangers, find their way to the High Court. However, to date, the chief executives of Uganda have respected the independence of the judicial branch and the courts have retained the power to shape the country's development.

The case of *Uganda v. Commissioner of Prisons Ex Parte Matovu*,[81] demonstrates that the High Court of Uganda was, as long as a Constitution was operating, willing to interpret it even in a politically complex and sensitive area. Interestingly enough, the Chief Justice of the High Court of Uganda who wrote the opinion was Sir Udo Udoma, a Nigerian contract judge who wanted to Africanize the law of Uganda. The case arose out of a resolution of the National Assembly in 1966 which abolished the 1962 Uganda Constitution and adopted the 1966 Constitution. Before the resolution the President and Vice-President of Uganda had been overthrown, which was in contradiction to the 1962 Constitution. Their offices were abolished and the authority of government was transferred to the Prime Minister with the consent of the Cabinet. After the 1966 Constitution was adopted by the National Assembly, a state of public emergency was declared, and the Emergency Powers Regulations of 1966, which were detention laws, were enacted. Michael Matovu was one of those government officials detained under the Emergency Detention Act. He argued in his petition that the detention powers of the new government were outside of the constitutional powers; that is, the detention powers were unconstitutional under the 1962 Constitution. He did not argue the validity or the invalidity of the 1966 Constitution. The Attorney General argued, however, that in a successful revolution a court has no jurisdiction. The Attorney General further argued that the validity of the 1966 Constitution was a political question, which would mean the detention laws were valid. The court could only interpret, he noted, that which is brought before it. Attorney-General Labowa argued that after the initial detention by Dr. Obote (the then President) of five cabinet ministers under a law invalid by standards of the earlier constitution, the National Assembly immediately passed the new Constitution, which permitted detention. Sir Udo's written opinion is a mixture of praise and condemnation of the actions of Dr. Obote. It is also interesting to note that the opinion by Sir Udo supplies a curious counterpart to the position of Chief Justice Marshall in *Marbury* v. *Madison*. Certainly the conditions under which *Ex Parte Matovu* was written presented some rather interesting parallels.

Initially Sir Udo accepted the concept of the revolution as a fact. He therefore declared the 1966 Constitution to be valid. He would at this juncture seem to have completely undermined the Court's authority. However, it must be noted, that the Chief Justice in making his ruling did not leave the interpretation of the Constitution to the political branch or to the Attorney General himself. Indeed, the Chief Justice went to great pains to ensure that the judiciary would make the interpretation, even though the interpretation itself was a politically expedient one. The Court ultimately upheld the detention order under the 1966 Constitution. The Court then proceeded to scold the Attorney General for arguing that this was a political question after having held in his favor. The Court pointed out that the Attorney General was in error in "relying on certain American cases in supporting the proposition that the issue as to the validity of the 1966 Constitution was purely a political matter outside the scope of the jurisdiction of this court."[82] He distinguished the cases cited by the Attorney General, especially, *Luther* v. *Borden*,[83] noting that there was a contest in the American case between two competing political powers as to which should control the government of Rhode Island. The Court then noted that in Uganda there is no contest because the government of Uganda has no rival. Thus, on that factual basis *Luther* v. *Borden* was said to be inapplicable.

Secondly, the Court argued that in *Luther* v. *Borden* political questions were raised, including the right to vote and the qualifications of voters. There were rival governors appointed and the rivalry between the two governments produced a situation which was tantamount to a state of civil war. In fact, the Court pointed out, insurrection had occurred and war was levied upon the state. Such was not the case in Uganda, Sir Udo concluded. He also distinguished *Baker* v. *Carr* but in distinguishing it, he invoked Justice Clark's language that the apportionment ruling "is in the greatest tradition of this court."[84] After a lengthy analysis of the coup of 1966 and an analysis of the direction of the then present political party in Uganda, Sir Udo held that the 1966 Constitution was the supreme law of the land. It became the new legal order, and its effective date was April 14, 1966. Sir Udo also held that the questions of interpretation found in the new Constitution are subject to judicial review and not political whim. It would have been very easy for the High Court to have held the issue presented to be a political question. However, the Uganda High Court, much in the tradition of *Marbury*, took the matter and refused to skirt the difficult issues.

An active judicial role in nation building is not an option in Mexico.[85] The courts of Mexico do not take part frequently in the major constitutional issues confronting the nation, and when the courts do face the adjudication of a constitutional question, the vehicle of procedure lies in *amparo*. In an *amparo* proceeding the arguments ordinarily are in writing, oral presentations are the exception. The hearing involves a plaintiff, a defendant, and a third party who usually represents the Federal Public Minister.[86] *Amparo* can be divided into two categories: direct and indirect.[87] Direct *amparo* can go to the Supreme Court and collegial circuits, and proceeds from a final civil judgment or final criminal sentence. Indirect *amparo* originates as a particular litigant's challenge in district court to the constitutionality of an act affecting him, and may be pursued on appeal to The Supreme Court.

In Mexico the doctrine of *amparo* has existed in some form since its incorporation into article 102 of the Constitution of 1957, but it stems from the Yucatan Constitution of 1841. In theory, any citizen in Mexico may bring a writ of *amparo* for the redress of infringement upon his constitutional rights. Also in theory, the writ is fair and effective.[88] However, in the Mexican judicial system there are several pragmatic factors which prevent the writ of *amparo* from being an adequate method of enforcing constitutional guarantees within the governmental structure of Mexico.

The concept of judicial review as it is known in the United States or as practiced in some African countries does not exist in Mexico. As noted earlier, the executive branch dominates the government with the President initiating almost all legislation. He appoints all important administrative officials and controls the political party in power. The Supreme Court Ministers, as well as those of the superior courts for the federal district and federal territories, are appointed by the President. The appointed ministers in turn select the lower court judges.

The constitutional separation of powers in Mexico is not nearly as complete as it is in the United States and in many of the African countries, inasmuch as the drafters of the 1917 Constitution refused to grant full judicial review to the judicial branch of Government.[89] That decision seems to have been based upon two factors. First, the concept of judicial review was foreign to the roots of Mexican law. Second, the cultural and social characteristics of the Mexican people led the drafters of the Constitution to believe that the system would not work. They argued that judicial review would create friction between the Mexican Supreme Court and the executive, and that this conflict would weaken the stability of the nation. Consequently the writ of *amparo* was all that remained. Under *amparo,* if in a single case before the court a law is found to be unconstitutional, the holding of the court is limited in application to the particular case. The specific law is still considered valid and enforceable to all who are not parties to the suit. Initially then, each citizen wishing to challenge the constitutionality of the law must bring a separate *amparo* action. The cumulative effect of several similar *amparo* actions, however, may be to establish the constitutional rule which they announce as a judicial precedent.

The functioning of *amparo* is illustrated by *Compania Minera De San Jose.*[90] *Amparo* was brought under section 5(b)(c) of chapters 2 and 3 of the judiciary law. Under Mexican law there is a general tax on exports. The Minister of Finance, after consulting other authorities, assesses what the export tax should be in each case. It had been the custom of the Minister to set the taxes on a monthly basis with the tax established about midmonth for the particular period. In the case at bar, the official rate for December, 1959, was established by a circular published on December 14. The rate for January, 1960, was established by a circular published on January 12. Inasmuch as jurisdiction is usually determined by the nature of the act complained of rather than the arguments employed to demonstrate unconstitutionality, this was a case of indirect *amparo*. The plaintiff companies brought a writ of *amparo* in the federal district court contending that the publication of these circulars in the fashion described had the effect of making them, at least in part, retroactive, which is a violation of article 14 of the Constitution, which forbids retroactive laws. Their position was sustained and the government appealed to the Supreme Court. The government argued that article 14 of the Constitution must be read to include the principle that first an injury must occur to a person; since prices were not fixed until the middle of the month, an injury did not occur. In other words, where no law exists, no rights will follow. The Constitution, said the government, cannot be followed unless there is some law involved, and since the prices were not fixed until the middle of the month, no law was involved. The Court rejected the government's argument. They adopted the civil law interpretation and found that since the government did not set the prices until the middle of the month, at the beginning of each month there were no rules to regulate the general tax on exports for that month. Therefore, the complainants could disregard the government's tax for the first half of the month when set in the middle of the month. The Court noted that the civil law was clear: where there is no rule, there can be no punishment, and until the government sets an established rule, the parties are not required to rely on the export tax rate published after the fact.[91]

It should be mentioned that there were five complaints consolidated in this one case. In comparison, had this been a case decided by the United States Supreme Court or the High Court of Uganda, the precedent would have been well settled for all future cases. However, after this case, the Court decided two similar cases on the same facts. Professor Butte notes that this would suggest the Minister of Finance continued his former practice respecting all other corporations not affected by the initial *amparo* action.[92] The precedent did not apply to any other case. Thus complaints had to be brought on an individual basis. However, had two more such decisions been rendered by the Supreme Court, making a total of five, under articles 192 and 193 of the law on *amparo,* the rule laid down would have been binding *jurisprudencia.*[93] In theory, the five-decision rule would have made the law binding in all courts, but even then not necessarily binding upon administrative activities. Furthermore, laws which have been declared unconstitutional by the Supreme Court are almost never repealed by the federal government. The legislative branch will not alter legislation simply because the judiciary has found the legislation to be unconstitutional.

Amparo has several positive features, even though there are numerous reasons for precluding such action. First, the *amparo* in criminal, labor, and agrarian cases is very simple. There is no time limit within which the *amparo* must be brought. The judge has the power to correct any deficiencies in the petition in favor of the weaker party, and thus, many technical errors are found and removed in criminal, labor, and agrarian proceedings. Second, once *amparo* has been granted, the federal courts have powerful procedures enforcing the decision. The Supreme Court has the power to remove from office any official, including the President, who refuses to obey a Supreme Court decision. In practice, the power of removal is used only in cases involving municipal officers or unimportant state officials. The Supreme Court has never attempted to remove from office any important federal official.

CONCLUSION

At this point the crucial question may be raised: *What do constitutions, in our time, mean to the people?* Are they "living" in the sense that they are essential for the life, not of the professionals manipulating them, but, of the common people? Or, as expressed more emotionally: Is the constitution instrumental for the pursuit of happiness of the people? Karl Loewenstein writes:

> The new constitutions will find it difficult to integrate themselves in the minds of the people. They mean next to nothing, or very little, to the little man ground between the nether and the upper millstones. . . . (T)he constitutions are indifferent toward the realities of the life of the people, incapable of satisfying the minimum of social justice and economic security that the common people believe themselves entitled to, the pretentious bills of rights notwithstanding. . . . The constitution cannot, and does not bridge the gap between poverty and wealth. . . . (T)he people distrust their governments, their officials, their parties and parliaments, and their constitutions.[94]

Does this pessimistic observation reflect the general concept of constitutionalism in the developing nations? If implemented, can the constitutions serve the needs of those who now distrust their importance? To apprehend the importance of constitutionalism in a nation, one must first consider what factors motivate a people to nationhood. Constitutional maturity depends upon economic growth and national stability, and the term that continually emerges in the writings of intellectuals and political activists is "nation building."

"Nation building" is the primary consideration of most African countries inasmuch as transnational demands are for economic and social development. This indeed is a special form of social change. Although individual African nations reached independence at differing stages of national development, almost all shared the same burden of the social and legal legacies of colonialism.

The aftermath of colonialism was a pluralistic legal system because the new nation states adopted systems of colonial-imposed law. An exception had been made: the right to have customary law applied to disputes between Africans. As a result, in anglophonic African countries, customary law affected only Africans, whereas common law was utilized by the colonial ruling power. For this reason, two Ugandas arose. The pluralistic social, political, economic, and legal legacy of colonialism eventually generated the current demands for change. Therefore, instead of examining the concept of constitutionalism in Uganda via its antecedents, the question really should be, what are the goals of nationhood? By far the overriding goal is to improve the country's standard of living. Second in importance is a transformation from the plural economic, social, and legal system. In a comment on customary law, Nyerere argues that the law, as applied today, inevitably supports a subsistence economy. The real need is for African policy makers who are sensitive to the basic rights of the people. The real power in African nation building, and in Mexico, as well, is not found in constitutions. Nor will it be found in the concept of judicial review such as in *amparo* in Mexico or in appeals in Africa. The real power lies with the political manifesto of the ruling party. In Africa there has been a proliferation of party manifestoes to advance the cause of African nationhood, to articulate the concept of national revolution, and to identify what is thought to be an African revolution.

From a political standpoint, Mexico is quite similar to Uganda in both executive power and goals, as well as in party control of national direction. In Mexico, with its single party system, the success of the major party completely overshadows the minor parties that represent specialized political viewpoints and seldom capture more than token representation in local or national elections. However, size of membership and electoral success is but an end product of a revolutionary process that has produced a broadly based, nationally oriented party attracting large numbers of supporters and wielding greater political influence than its more narrowly conceived counterparts. Under such circumstances, the major party platform serves as an auxilliary constitutional mechanism that makes possible limited and responsible national government. By providing a structured and internally disciplined political agency, the party forces a certain amount of adjustment and balance among the demands of the three basic sectors: agricultural, labor, and popular.

The importance of the PRI in Mexico's political system is not simply that it has been able to form interest associations into sector organizations. It also has been able to convince the varied interest groups that they share enough political characteristics to adopt common political goals. Those goals contemplate economic and social progress in the world community. However, throughout the developing stage the Mexican Constitution has gently nurtured preparation for implementing the final ingredients of democratic nationhood: the protection of human rights from governmental interference. Uganda and Mexico seem to plan primarily for economic and political stability and only secondarily for the constitutional promotion of individual dignity. But Uganda, throughout its early national history, had never lost sight of the latter. The High Court continually established precedents of judicial review, a situation which suggests the attainability of successful constitutional protections.

At present, both Mexico and Uganda challenge constitutional involvement in economic development. The sacrifices growing out of the challenge will perhaps result in the achievement of present expectations much more quickly. Along the path to constitutional stability, a government must impose sanctions that compel unity. Resistance will occur where the government commitment is unpopular. But if a government is focusing upon the ultimate quality of life for each individual, then the constitution and the court can serve as interpreters, just as they should serve as defenders of individual rights once the government has the potential of achievement in the field of promoting acceptable standards of the quality of life.

The three constitutions which have been examined retain the important doctrine of judicial review, the ingredients of which serve as a necessary concommitant to nationhood. Lacking this service as a Republican Schoolmaster, a nation's people could quite understandably reject the Constitution and all it stands for.

Finally, the courts and the constitutions, if operating as intended, reflect the aspirations of nations seeking the achievement of a total quality of life for their citizens.[95] Mexico, Uganda and the United States, although at quite different stages in their development, certainly are to be included in the list of such nations.

NOTES*

* In references to legal periodical literature, the number of the *initial* page of the work cited immediately follows the volume title. Page references to material specifically referred to in the text, if any, follow the initial page citation. Legal case citations correspond to *A Uniform System of Citation*, 11th ed. (Cambridge: The Harvard Law Review Association, 1974).

1. The field of comparative constitutionalism is rich in scattered materials but poor in major works of synthesis. Nevertheless, see Mauro Cappelletti and Denis Tallon, *Fundamental Guarantees of the Parties in Civil Litigation* (Dobbs Ferry, New York: 1973); also Mauro Cappelletti, *Judicial Review in the Contemporary World* (Indianapolis: Bobbs-Merrill, 1971); and Edward McWhinney, *Judicial Review*, 4th ed. (Toronto: University of Toronto Press, 1969). For source materials, see: Asian African Legal Consultative Committee, Constitutions of African States, 2 vols. (Dobbs Ferry, New York: Oceana, 1972); Benjamin Obi Nwabnese, *Constitutionalism in the Emergent States* (London: C. Hurst, 1973); Felipe Tena Ramírez, *Leyes fundamentales de Mexico, 1808–1967,* 3rd ed. (Mexico City: Editorial Porrúa, 1967). For regional materials, see A. N. Allott, *New Essays in African Law* (London: Butterworths, 1970); L. J. Brinkhorst and J. G. Schermers, *Judicial Remedies in the European Community* (Hackensack, New Jersey: Rothman Co., 1969); Kenneth Karst,

Latin American Legal Institutions (Los Angeles: University of California Latin American Center, 1966); B. S. Strayer, *Judicial Review of Legislation in Canada* (Toronto: University of Toronto Press, 1968). For developing countries, see David H. Bayley, *Public Liberties in the New States* (Princeton, New Jersey: Norton Co., 1964); and the symposium edition of "Law and Society in Developing Nations," in 1972 *Wisconsin Law Review* 2. On the broad theoretical problems of research strategies, see David M. Trubek and Marc Galanter, "Scholars in Self-Estrangement: Some Reflections on the Crisis in Law and Development Studies in the United States," 1974 *Wisconsin Law Review* 4.

2. The Republic of Uganda, *Constitution* (1967).

3. The United Mexican States, *Constitution* (1917). See generally Senriago Roel, "History of Mexican Constitutional Experience: From Zitacuaro, 1811, to Queretero, 1917," 4 *California Western Law Review,* 251 (1968).

4. See generally Herbert Spiro, "Political Stability in the New African States," 354 *The Annals* 97, 109 (1964); and W. R. Duncan, "The Mexican Constitution of 1917: Its Political and Social Background," 5 *Revista Juridica Interamerican* 277 (1963).

5. Julius Nyerere, *Freedom and Unity: Uhuru na umoia* (New York: Oxford University Press, 1966).

6. Ibid., 162–70.

7. The Latin American and Mexican social, religious, and political heritage has been well documented elsewhere. Much of the analysis of the Mexican Constitution is taken from two major works: W. L. Butte, "Selected Mexican Cases" (unpublished, University of Texas School of Law, 1970) and Richard D. Baker, *Judicial Review in Mexico* (Austin: University of Texas Press, 1971).

8. Butte, *Mexican Cases* at 1.

9. United Mexican States, *Constitution* (1917), Title 3. ibid., Title 3, chapter 3, article 83; ibid., Title 1, chapter 1; ibid., Title 3, chapter 2.

10. Ibid., Title 3, chapter 4.

11. W. Butte, *Mexican Cases,* p. 26.

12. Baker, *supra* note 8, at 267–73.

13. A. Moorehead, *The White Nile* (London: Sweet and Maxwell, 1960) 316–25.

14. See J. B. Byamugisha, "Introduction to the Law of Uganda" (Unpublished for Makerere University Kampala, Uganda, 1970). Compare Gordon Woodman, "Some Realism About Customary Law–The West African Experience," 1969 *Wisconsin Law Review* 128. See also Ian R. Macneil, "Research in East African Law," 3 *East African Law Journal* 47 (1967).

15. Robert B. Seidman, "Law and Economic Development in Independent, English-Speaking Sub-Saharan Africa," 1966 *Wisconsin Law Review* 1006–1007; *supra* note 14; Byamugisha, "Law of Uganda." See *Mayambala* v. *The Buganda Government,* 1962 *East Africa Law Report* (EAL) 283; and J. F. Scotton, "Judicial Independence and Political Expression in East Africa," 6 *East African Law Journal* (1970).

16. H. F. Morris and James S. Read, *Uganda: The Development of Its Law and Constitution* (London: Stevens, 1966) pp. 74–75.

17. Ibid., pp. 80–81. See also T. N. Karleson, "Sources for African Constitutional Studies," 6 *African Legal Studies* 165 (1972).

18. "Legal Notice No. 1 of 1971," 7 *African Law Digest* 101 (1971). Proclamation concerning the change in the Uganda government. While some scholars have compared the ending of "rule of law" in Uganda to the demise of constitutional parliamentary government in Italy, Germany and, during the Vichy regime–in France after World War I, a more useful explanatory model can be found in Lucian W. Pye, "Armies in the Process of Political Modernization," in *The Role of the Military in Underdeveloped Countries* ed. J. J. Johnson (Princeton: Princeton University Press, 1962), pp. 69–89.

19. Republic of Uganda, *Constitution* (1967) ch.5, art.39.

20. Ibid., ch.8, art.83, 87.

21. See especially the Preamble to the Uganda Constitution: "Our aspirations for national unity, peace, prosperity and progress. . . .," to that of Mexico (Art. 1): "Every person . . . shall enjoy the guarantees granted by this Constitution. . . ." The United States Constitution: "We the People of the United States, in Order to form a more perfect Union,

establish Justice, insure domestic Tranquility, provide for the common defense, promote the general Welfare, and secure the Blessings of Liberty to ourselves and our Posterity, do ordain and establish this Constitution."

22. See, for example, Y. Ghai and T. P. McAuslan, *Public Law and Political Change in Kenya* (Oxford at Clarendon, 1969).

23. Nyerere, *Freedom and Unity*, pp. 162–70.

24. See, for example, Julius Nyerere, "How Much Power for a Leader," 7 *Africa Report* 5 (1962).

25. Morris and Read, *Uganda*, pp. 80–83.

26. *Uganda v. Commissioner of Prisons, Ex Parte Matovu* 1966 *EAL Report* 514.

27. At least since the proclamation concerning the 1971 coup, the 1967 Constitution has been suspended. 7 *African Law Digest* 101 (1971). See also, International Commission of Jurists, *Violations of Human Rights and Rule of Law in Uganda* (Geneva: The International Commission of Jurists, 1974).

28. See for example *Palko v. Connecticut,* 302 U.S. 319 (1937) overruled in *Benton v. Maryland,* 395 U.S. 784 (1969), and see *Gideon v. Wainwright,* 372 U.S. 335 (1963).

29. Fletcher Baldwin, "The United States Supreme Court: A Creative Check of Institutional Misdirection?" 45 *Indiana Law Journal* 550 (1970).

30. *Shah v. Attorney General* (No. 2), 1970 *EAL Report* 523.

31. See, for example, *Brandenburg v. Ohio,* 395 U.S. 444(1969). See also, *United States v. O'Brien,* 391 U.S. 367(1968).

32. Pedro P. Camargo, "The Claim of 'Amparo' in Mexico: Constitutional Protection of Human Rights," 6 *California Western Law Review* 201(1970).

33. Mexico, *Constitution,* art. 24.

34. Uganda, *Constitution,* art. 16(1).

35. Ibid., art. 8(2)(b) and art. 17.

36. U.S., *Constitution,* amend. 2 and 3; cf. Mexico, *Constitution,* art. 10 and 26.

37. See, for instance, *Mapp v. Ohio,* 367 U.S. 643(1961); and *Katz v. United States,* 389 U.S. 347(1967).

38. Mexico, *Constitution,* art. 16; see also, Uganda, *Constitution,* art. 8(2)(a) and art. 14.

39. For example the Mexican Constitution in art., 16 ch. 2 states that: "Administrative officials may enter private homes for the sole purpose of ascertaining whether the sanitary and police regulations have been complied with." Health codes are quite common in the United States and accomplish the same end as art. 16. The debate as to whether an administrative entry is constitutionally permissible continues, however. See *Frank v. Maryland,* 359 U.S. 360 (1959) overruled in *Camara v. Municipal Court,* 387 U.S. 523(1967) and *See v. Seattle,* 387 U.S. 541(1967). Compare *Wyman v. James,* 400 U.S. 309 (1971).

40. Uganda, *Constitution,* art. 14.

41. Uganda, *Constitution,* art. 8(2)(c); 10; 13 and 15(5)(7); see also, Mexico, Constitution title I, ch. I, art. 20(2); 23 and 27.

42. Ibid., ch. 20(6)(8)(9); and Uganda *Constitution,* art. 10(3)(b) and 15.

43. Uganda, *Constitution,* art. 10(5)(a): "he shall, not more than twenty-eight days after the Commencement of his detention or restrictions, be furnished with a statement in writing in a language that he understands specifying the grounds upon which he is detained or restricted and shall be afforded an opportunity of making representations in writing to the authority by which his detention or restriction was ordered; (b) his case shall be reviewed by an independent and impartial tribunal established by law and presided over by a person appointed by the Chief Justice and such review shall be held, (i) as soon as reasonably practicable where the person detained or restricted has made representations to the authority by which his detention or restriction was ordered; or (ii) in any other case not more than two months after the commencement of his detention or restriction, and thereafter during his detention or restriction, at intervals of not more than six months. . . ." and Mexico, *Constitution,* art. 20(8) ". . . he shall be tried within four months if charged with an offense whose maximum penalty does not exceed two years imprisonment, and within one year if the maximum penalty is greater." The speedy trial portion of the sixth

amendment to the U.S. Constitution as incorporated into the fourteenth amendment was analyzed in *Klopfer* v. *North Carolina,* 386 U.S. 213(1967).

44. Mexico, *Constitution,* art. 20(6). Jury trial, "provided the penalty for such offense exceeds one year's imprisonment."

45. See generally, Richard L. Abel, "Case Method Research in the Customary Laws of Wrongs in Kenya," 5 *East African Law Journal* 247(1969).

46. Mexico, *Constitution,* art. 70(9).

47. Uganda, *Constitution,* art. 10(5)(c).

48. See, for example, *Argersinger* v. *Hamlin,* 407 U.S. 25(1972); and *Tate* v. *Short,* 401 U.S. 395(1971); and *Coleman* v. *Alabama,* 399 U.S. 1 (1970). See, also, 18 U.S.C.A. 3006 A(1969).

49. Camargo, "Claim of 'Amparo.' "

50. Mexico, *Constitution,* art. 20(1).

51. *Ex Parte Matovu, supra* note 26.

52. See, for example, *Marbury* v. *Madison* 5 U.S. (1 Cranch) 137(1803); *Martin* v. *Hunter's Lessee,* 14 U.S. (1 Wheat). 304(1816) and *Cohens* v. *Virginia,* 19 U.S. (6 Wheat.) 264(1821). For an example of the doctrine strikingly reasserted, see *United States* v. *Nixon,* 418 U.S.683(1974).

53. Karl Llewellyn, *The Common Law Tradition Deciding Appeals* (Boston: Little, Brown, 1960). "Magna Carta" in *Sources of our Liberties,* ed. Richard L. Perry, ed. (Chicago: American Bar Association, 1960), pp. 1–5.

54. See, for example, Charles Warren, *The Supreme Court in United States History* (Boston: Little, Brown, 1972), and James B. Thayer, "The Origin and Scope of the American Doctrine of Constitutional Law," 7 *Harvard Law Review* 129 (1893).

55. For example, Uganda, *Constitution,* art. 85.

56. Antony N. Allott, *New Essays in African Law* (London: Butterworths, 1970), pp. 70–103. Robert B. Seidman, "The Communication of Law and the Process of Development," 1972 *Wisconsin Law Review* 686, 693–706; *Baumann & Co.* v. *Nadiope* 1968 EAL Report 306; *Shah* v. *Attorney General of Uganda (No. 3)* 1970, EAL Report 544.

57. International Commission of Jurists, *African Conference on the Rule of Law* (Geneva: International Commission of Jurists, 1961) p. 21.

58. Cameroun, *Constitution,* art. 32; Dahomey, *Constitution,* art. 77; Guinea, *Constitution,* art. 35; Togo, *Constitution,* art. 77; Senegal, *Constitution,* art. 80; Somalia, *Constitution,* art. 93.

59. Burundi, *Constitution,* art. 90; Ghana, *Constitution,* art. 45; Nigeria, *Constitution,* sec. 113; Uganda, *Constitution,* art. 92.

60. See generally, Julius Nyerere, *Freedom and Development* (New York: Oxford University Press, 1973); idem, *Man and Development* (New York: Oxford University Press, 1974).

61. P. T. Georges, "The Court in the Tanzania One-Party State" in *East African Law and Social Change,* ed. G.F.A. Sawyer (London: Butterworths, 1967), p. 26.

62. *The Arusha Declaration of the Tanganyikan African National Unity* (TANU) (1967) outlined the strong role the executive was to play in Tanzania.

63. See *Namwandu* v. *Attorney General* 1972, EAL Report 108, 111.

64. *Uganda* v. *Commissioner of Prisons, Ex Parte Matovu* 1966, EAL Report 514.

65. See generally, Y. P. Ghai, "Constitutions and the Political Order in East Africa," 21 *International and Comparative Law Quarterly* 403(1972).

66. For a complete analysis of the expulsion of Ugandan Asians and its implications for international human rights, see Vishnu D. Sharma and F. Wooldridge, "Some Legal Questions Arising from the Expulsion of the Ugandan Asians," 23 *International and Comparative Law Quarterly* 397(1974).

67. "Uganda, Economic War" in *Africa* 24 (1973):33–40.

68. Uganda, *Decree,* 27, art. 1(a).

69. Uganda, *Decree,* 29, s.1.

70. Sharma & Wooldridge, "Some Legal Questions," 402–3. See also, "Uganda, Economic War," 33–40.

71. Uganda, *Decree,* 29, s.16(5)(c).

72. "Uganda, Economic War," 35.

73. The control of businesses now seems to be in the hands of new soldier committees made up of soldiers from Amin's ethnic group—the Nubians. The common man so lionized in the common-man's charter of Obote now appears worse off than before.

74. Sharma & Wooldridge, "Some Legal Questions," p. 423.

75. Ghai, "Political Order in East Africa," pp. 428–31.

76. See generally, Francisco Porrúa Perez, *Doctrina politica de las garantias individuales* (Mexico City: Editorial Porrúa, 1961); and Conference of African Jurists, *Legal Process and the Individual* (Addis Ababa: Haile Selassie University, 1972).

77. See Baldwin, "U.S. Supreme Court".

78. Duncan, "The Mexican Constitution."

79. Luis Cabrera and W. C. Headrick, "Notes on Judicial Review in Mexico and the United States," 5 *Revista Jurisdicia Interamericana* 253 (1963). See also, Carl Schwartz, "Judges under the Shadow: Judicial Independence in the United States and Mexico," 3 *California Western International Law Journal* 160 (1973).

80. Uganda, *Constitution,* art. 1, 87, and 21.

81. *Ex Parte Matovu, supra* note 26, 514.

82. Ibid., 533.

83. *Luther v. Borden,* 7 Howard 1 (1849).

84. *Baker* v. *Carr,* 368 U.S. 186 (1962). *Ex Parte Matovu, supra* note 26, 534.

85. Concepts here of the role of the judiciary in Mexico are formed from Baker, *Judicial Review* (1971).

86. "Section IV of article 5 of the Amparo Law states that the Federal Public Ministry shall be a party in *amparo* suits that, in the judgement of that agency, involve the public interest."

87. Baker, *Judicial Review,* 49–50.

88. *Ibid.,* 12–13 and 267–73. See also, Camargo, "Claim of Amparo," p. 201.

89. Baker, *Judicial Review,* pp. 46–54.

90. Butte, "Mexican Cases," p. 41.

91. Ibid., p. 43.

92. Ibid., p. 45.

93. Baker, *Judicial Review,* p. 270.

94. Karl Loewenstein, "Reflections on the Value of Constitutions in Our Revolutionary Age" in *Comparative Politics,* ed. Harry Eckstein and David E. Apter. (New York: The Free Press of Glencoe, 1963).

95. See, for example, Gilbert P. Verbit, "Tanu Builds the Nation," 81 *Yale Law Journal* 334 (1971).

Chapter 4 FREEDOM OF EXPRESSION IN JAPAN WITH COMPARATIVE REFERENCE TO THE UNITED STATES

Lawrence W. Beer

Political demonstrations in Japan take many forms. They range from small student marches on Tokyo sidewalks to large clusters of fishing boats drawing attention to polluting effluents. Television has broadcast examples of vast and vociferous throngs milling about government buildings. Bright banners and headbands, the singing and chanting of slogans, inspirational speeches by bullhorn-wielding leaders, and chains of orderly groups stretching along thoroughfares or swinging into formation in a park area make worker demonstrations a noteworthy tourist attraction. There is both flamboyance and ritual even in unruly illegal gatherings. Yet serious violence has been rare in post-1945 Japan. The political confrontations between students and police in this modern island country have become commonplace in the international news media. With freedom of expression so frequently tested, Japan presents an interesting case study of the legal and social limits of tolerance.[1] This study examines the constitutional rights of free expression in contemporary Japan with some comparative reference to the United States.[2] The study will focus particularly on the law of political demonstrations and the patterns of group behavior and rights consciousness. The basic contention of the study is that freedom of expression is viable and protected in Japan.

LAW AND JAPANESE CULTURE

The Japanese constitutional setting. The Constitution of Japan is the most authoritative theoretical reference point in Japan, and it therefore appears in the rhetoric of most political debates. Supreme Court decisions setting forth the limits of freedom of speech and assembly under the public welfare clauses of the 1947 Constitution of Japan have been major points of controversy over the years. Chapter 3 (articles 10 through 40) of the Constitution establishes an impressive array of rights, freedoms, and ideals.[3] Although the Constitution has some indigenous roots in prewar Japan and was overwhelmingly approved by the

Diet in 1946, it reflects American constitutionalism as understood by the "Occupationnaires" who helped write the charter after World War II. In article 21, freedom of assembly and association, as well as speech, press, and all other forms of expression are guaranteed. Moreover, it is said there that "No censorship shall be maintained, nor shall the secrecy of any means of communication be violated." Article 16 establishes the right of peaceful petition; article 28 grants workers the right to bargain and act collectively.[4] But the principle that human rights shall be the supreme consideration in legislation and in other governmental affairs (article 13) is qualified by the public welfare (*kōkyō no fukushi*) doctrine.

In articles 12, 13, 22, and 29, the rights of the individual are counterbalanced by the requirement that they be exercised for and within the limits of the public welfare.[5] Articles 22 and 29 are specific, protecting property rights and the rights to choose one's occupation and place of residence. But articles 12 and 13 are comprehensive, and both are invoked by the Supreme Court in applying the public welfare doctrine in freedom of expression cases. No right is put in a preferred position in relation to the public welfare.

Inasmuch as article 13 makes the individual's right "to life, liberty and the pursuit of happiness" the supreme consideration to the extent that it does not interfere with the public welfare, it appears to fix national priorities. Indeed, the public welfare would seem to be the supreme consideration. However, the spirit of the Constitution rules out any notion of the public welfare antithetic to the primacy of human rights. Article 11 specifies that the people shall not be prevented from enjoying fundamental human rights. "These fundamental human rights guaranteed to the people by this Constitution shall be conferred upon the people of this and future generations as eternal and inviolable rights."[6]

Unlike the "general welfare" in the U.S. Constitution, the public welfare provisions in the Japanese Constitution are commonly more than didactic, and have provided a judicial standard for judging the constitutionality of laws and ordinances regulating freedom since the late 1940s. In a 1950 decision, the Supreme Court explicitly defined the public welfare as: "the maintenance of order and respect for the fundamental human rights of the individual—it is precisely these things which constitute the content of the public welfare."[7] In a 1949 decision later used as precedent, the Supreme Court invoked the public welfare as a legally relevant positive clause regulating freedoms and rights, although the option was not foreclosed to interpret it as merely declaratory of a moral obligation on the part of the people. The Court held that incitement not to sell to the government a staple foodstuff at a time of food shortage exceeded permissible criticism of government policies. Accordingly, it constituted inciting the nonobservance of an important legal duty borne by citizens. Since it is thus "harmful to the public welfare . . . (it) exceeds the bounds of freedom of expression." The Court concluded that "freedom of speech under the new

Constitution, therefore, does not allow the people to act entirely as they wish, but rather must always be subject to coordination with the public welfare. . . ."[8] The theoretical meaning, the governmental use, and the judicial interpretation of the public welfare as the determinative phrase in a wide range of subject areas and problems, have continued to spark controversy in Japan.[9]

Many intellectuals have feared that officials and bureaucratic judges with a *kanson minpi* ("look-up-to-officials-and-down-on-the-people") mentality would use the public welfare standard to revert to prewar patterns of state supremacy and suppression of free speech, when similar phrases were used to unite the people behind policy. Others consider such worries exaggerated.[10] Small pockets of extremists to left and right either consider the public welfare an exploitive tool of the capitalist state or decry the excesses of freedom under the "imposed" Constitution. The latter would return to unity and pride under an emperor-centered constitution. However, opinion polls over the years suggest that there is both popular opposition to constitutional revision restrictive of rights and support for more emphasis by fellow citizens on the public welfare than on rights.[11]

The Constitution of Japan is based on respect for the individual. But this emphasis need not imply nor does it manifest itself in terms of individualism as understood in the United States. Traditionally, the Japanese have stressed the "social nexus" and identification with the group rather than individualism.[12] This remains true today. Opposition to the public good or to group consensus through over assertion of individuality is viewed as unprincipled and reprehensible egotism. Presumptions in doubt may be less on the side of the individual's rights than in the United States. On the other hand, vocal but nonviolent dissent and advocacy through group activities are more fully accepted as legitimate than in America. It is unlikely that an individualistic rights consciousness closely paralleling that in America will develop in Japan.

Since 1945 the Japanese have modified, not jettisoned, the values and social structure necessary to their sense of belonging, identity, well-being, and self-respect. The only fundamental change in Japanese ideals under the Constitution of Japan is the elevation of the individual as a person to the position of highest constitutional value, in place of such dominant prewar values as service to the Emperor, loyalty to the nation, and strict adherence to hierarchy in family and society. Loyalty, hierarchy, and Emperor remain on the scene in diminished or changed capacities.[13] Critical to freedom of expression under the rule of law is the perception of a necessary relationship between the individual and law (viewed as protective of rights) in such a way that this perception will mesh with and influence Japanese community standards.

Traditional Japanese rights consciousness. The implications of freedom vary according to cultural context and depending on the ways people integrate freedom and their consciousness of rights with law and public welfare consciousness.[14] These cultural factors, in turn, affect enforcement policy and judicial thought and behavior. Moreover, cultural factors inevitably bear traces of the historical past. Japan changed in many ways after its isolated Tokugawa era (ca. 1600–1868).[15] Still, the Tokugawa experience has affected the contemporary Japanese appreciation of rights, although to a lesser degree than the formative mixture of indigenous and foreign legal, political, and intellectual forces that influenced Japan in the twentieth century. The pervasive imperative in Tokugawa Japan was to fulfill one's duties according to one's place in the elaborate status hierarchy. It was not to recognize the rights of the individual. Indeed, no word for a "right" existed in the Japanese language until the midnineteenth century. In many villages, local customary law probably admitted little gap between the equivalents of perceived and protected rights. The traditional view of the functional group of landlords and tenants, masters and servants, was that inasmuch as all were in the same boat, everyone enjoyed communal rights. As Chie Nakane observes of the traditional peasant outlook, "There is strong opposition to the formation of status groups within a single community, although the order of higher and lower in relationship between individuals is readily accepted."[16]

Every Japanese had some recognized duties under *dōri* ("natural justice," "reason"), and Confucian duties were understood to be in some degree reciprocal. Duties differed with one's status, but persons in a higher status had duties to peers and to royalty above and common men below. Although rights were not enforceable through suits against authorities, irresponsibility was not accepted in Tokugawa law and government. The loyalty so essential to the operation of the system, then as now, was given in return for adequately benevolent treatment. Thus, a real rights consciousness existed, despite the extent to which rights and duties failed to include the concept of equal rights. To some extent, these traditional perceptions, which can be termed reciprocal duty consciousness, modify present perceptions and practices.

In such a context, self-realization is achieved by freely fulfilling duties to others with a correlative expectation that others will do likewise. This mutual awareness is one of diffuse, interpersonal responsibilities, rather than of clearly and narrowly defined duties, as in American law. The *desideratum* for the Japanese is the right not to a high degree of autonomy, but the right to belong to a world of loyalties and duties which, while demanding much at times, surrounds, stimulates, provides for, and protects the individual.

Japan's social structure is a meticulously and minutely differentiated hierarchy, not of clearly discernible classes, but of quasi-parent-child (*oyabun-kobun,* "patron-client") relationships. Cohesive groups are formed usually by the multiplication of vertical relations between two individuals like the structure of the figure below. Over time, horizontal relations often develop which intensify group ties.

A motive force that permeates this vertical society (*tate shakai*) is *amae* ("dependency;" verb form, *amaeru*). *Amae* refers to the individual's need and desire to be passively loved, to be sheltered and cared for, to be indulged, to be able to assume and presume on the good will of others, to remain warmly wrapped in an optimistically conceived environment. To some extent, this type of orientation, characteristic of mother-child relationships from early infancy in most cultures, is in Japan " . . . prolonged into and diffused throughout adult life . . . ," and shapes basic perspectives on people and reality much more than in the West.[17]

Freedom (*jiyu*) traditionally meant the freedom to *amaeru*, "to behave as one pleases, without considering others."[18] A duty consciousness is not intrinsic to the *amae* mentality, but derives from a benevolent, mature sense of duty to indulge the *amae* of others. It generates the feeling that one must fulfill duties to others if one is to be indulged by them.

The individual does not transcend the group; rather, group life typically raises the self from a sense of nothingness to greater felt significance. The individual prefers a context which enables uninhibited presumption on others, but is disciplined in carrying out duties to the in-group and the family. Both are referred to by the term "*uchi*" ("my family" or "our house"). In this context, the insider opts for anonymity and shows restraint in most relationships with outsiders as an individual in the larger community.

The status of freedom of expression depends primarily on the relationship of the individual with his in-group, but not with government, the law, or the community at large, and on the relationship of the in-group with the community at large, but not with government or the law. The individual is oriented toward expressing himself in and with the group, not as an individual in the larger community. Thus the right to free expression may face pervasive restraints from within the group. For example, the pressure on the individual to comply after consensus is reached is considerable. Only a rare nonconformist speaks out of turn during the decision-making process. Emphasis upon conformity with the group, to the point of psychological coercion, is perhaps the principal problem for the individual's self-determination with respect to expression. Such socio-psychological force is legitimized by unwritten rules which support *amae*, loyalty, and reciprocal duty consciousness, and oppose egotism in hierarchically organized in-groups. Still, it is usually not attended by physical coercion, or by governmental, legal, or theoretical sanctions.

In contrast, American rights consciousness, which is also an influence in present-day Japan, emphasizes the autonomy of the individual and the propriety of maximum self-assertion consonant with law and the autonomy of others.[19] The stress is upon individual rights, such as the imperative, to stand up for one's rights, the right casually to join or to leave an association or a job; and the right not to belong or to conform. Freedom from the encroachments of other persons or government is considered essential for self-realization. Anonymity within the group and self-discipline are less valued than in Japan. The notion of duty is often seen in a somewhat negative way. To do something because it is a duty is often thought to imply that the action is not done freely, but because one has to. Not to act freely is not to act authentically as a person. Duties are carefully limited lest they interfere with the right to fulfillment through individual freedom and independence. Carried to an extreme, excessive individualism, with its lack of emphasis on man's interdependence would seem as destructive of freedom as extreme group dependency.

The role of conciliation also contrasts with that in the United States. Disputes in Japan from the Tokugawa period to the present have been more often settled by voluntary or compulsory conciliation (mediation) than by adjudication or arbitration.[20] The aim of the conciliator—not a judge or outside arbitrator, but a local status bearer—has been to involve himself with disputants in a quasi-group relationship of harmony, as a means of restoring, at least external and ideally emotive, interpersonal harmony between the parties. Most Japanese still prefer conciliation to litigation or arbitration. This preference for conciliable rights over justiciable rights often meshes with a modern legal consciousness in the parties' expectation that official mediation will result in a resolution which is in conformity with objective facts or the law (or which at least reflects the legal rights of the parties involved).[21] Although compulsory conciliation in dispute settlement and in-group relations today is not legally binding, powerful pressures usually assure the individual's compliance. Relatively few demonstration cases go to trial. This is true, in part, because of distaste for court confrontations, but also because black-white judgments backed by force are not always as morally authoritative as are the results of informal discussion.[22]

Some tensions in Japanese rights consciousness. The elements of duty and right, freedom and restraint, independence and *amae,* conciliation and litigation, the individual and the group, group welfare and the public welfare all collide with one another in daily Japanese life. The resulting conflicts cannot be understood without some appreciation of Japanese political concepts. For example, freedom in Japanese traditionally carried a pejorative implication of wilfulness. In more recent years, it has acquired favorable implications of liberty from arbitrary paternalism. Today, the word *jiyu* partakes of both its positive western sense and its negative traditional Japanese meaning. The resulting ambiguity ever since the Meiji Restoration is a sense of conflict concerning freedom. Indeed, according to Takeo Doi, the theme of the bittersweet qualities of freedom is clearly illustrated in modern Japanese literature.[23] The word, right, carries equal crosscurrents of meaning. Thus the term *kenri*, "a right," was created and first employed in Japanese constitutional thought in the midnineteenth century.[24] In previous uses of *ken* (the first ideograph in the compound *kenri*), it implied might or power without any connotation of moral or legal claim. Although *ken* is also now in common use in such terms as *jinken* ("human rights") and *jiyuken* ("civil liberties"), its use to mean a right is not historically deep and is unrelated to the traditional usage of *jiyū*.

At present, individual rights consciousness, especially in the sense of reciprocal duty consciousness and awareness of one's right to expect something (such as the right to speak) from superiors and peers, is operative in Japanese democracy. Nevertheless, the group's sense of its rights vis-à-vis the individual and society is very often incomparably stronger. Appreciation for social structure explains this group emphasis. For example, modern Japanese scholars never overcome sensitivity to the distinction between *sempai* and *kohai* (based on who graduated first from university). Seniority in other social relations is equally important. Indeed, in group meetings, the frequency with which a person offers an opinion and the order in which those present speak, often are indicators of how rank is perceived within the group. Thus, ranking may stifle the free expression of individual thought. Moreover, Chie Nakane, in describing the "social grammar" of Japan, tells that it "often happens that, once a man had been labelled as one whose opinions run contrary to those of the group, he will find himself opposed on any issue and ruled out by majority opinion."[25]

Although deference is paid to the leader's opinions and feelings in group decision making (for example, in companies, unions, and ministries), by no means does a Japanese leader have the right to act in an authoritarian, one-sided way. He is obliged to consider the views of other group members. The leader's influence is essential to group cohesion, but the leader is not equally important in the determination of the group's views.[26] Democracy in Japanese decision-making processes seems to mean consensus building within the group, at whatever the structural level of society, in an atmosphere in which deference does not substantively interfere with openness, and in which each member's sense of self is taken seriously.

However, to dissent on grounds of honest disagreement from a consensus of, say, 70 percent is to fail to understand the higher moral values of group harmony and loyalty. One may, of course, retain private views, but they must not interfere with group action and should not be "obnoxiously" emphasized. Nakane writes; "An individual, however able, however strong his personality and high his status, has to compromise with his group's decision, which then develops a life of its own."[27] In practice, a majority in the United States also likes a cooperative minority when a job is to be done, but stresses the right to independent opinion more than would a Japanese group. The consequences of serious deviation from loyalty to consensus in Japan can be painful ostracism.

Being cut off from the group is onerous to the individual. In a society where *amae,* belonging, and loyalty are so central, isolation can be a shameful and frightening prospect.

The forms and contexts of ostracism in Japan are many, and it is just as common among the urban, the young, and the modern and democratic as among other Japanese. For example, a newsman may be transferred because peers in other companies object to a report.[28] *Mura hachibu,* village ostracism, is still fairly common. It may extend to a man's wife and children.[29] Equally, a housewife in a modern apartment complex may be ostracized by neighboring women. Examples of the intensity of group feelings among some youth include several killings: of a youth group member who wanted to leave a college athletic club, of radical students by members of a rival faction, of a student by members of his own faction because of ideological impurity. Obviously, such tragic interference with the "freedom of dissociation" is decried in Japan, but the pattern in less violent form is widespread.

In a 1973 comparative study made in eleven nations of attitudes of youths between eighteen and twenty years old, the Japanese respondents indicated a distinct preference for closer relationships with fewer friends (70 percent, as compared to an average of 30 percent among the youth of other nations), rather than "not so close" friendly relations with "a large number of people."[30] The primary goal for Japanese youth was "worthwhile work"—the occupational group is the most common center of a man's group life—whereas all other nationalities opted for showing "love and sincerity to fellow citizens." The Japanese manifests his "love and sincerity" within the group context. As the survey confirmed, the Japanese tends toward distrust and uneasiness with the unfamiliar outsiders.[31] Consequently, it may be said that the individual's freedom of expression in Japan revolves around his in-group relations. As we shall see, that freedom also revolves around the relationships between his own and other groups.

In-Group relations with the outside. The stress on conformity encourages the individual to identify his personal rights with the rights of his group. As western ideas of individualism and litigious behaviour have become influential in Japan they have reinforced group chauvinism and encouraged what some perceive as exaggerated ideas of group rights. Since 1945, imported individualism has heightened the consciousness of individual rights, but it has also had the effect of enhancing the sense of political efficacy of groups. In a society where the primary social unit is the group, it is not unusual to hear of group rights vis-à-vis the government, other groups, and society at large.

There is less conciliation, conformity, and duty consciousness between groups than within groups. Important exceptions exist to the extent that leaders of clusters of groups occasionally are able to constitute themselves as a secondary group (for instance, faction leaders of political parties, unions, or student groups).[32] The group tends to be cliquish, exclusive, and closed rather than open, and to emphasize collective maintenance of the honor, rights, and interests of the group. Those outside the group are not clearly recognized as having rights. The group's rights tend to be limited only by its power, untempered by the strong social awareness displayed within groups and by the restrained politeness of the individual relations. The individualistic element in rights consciousness may thus intensify intergroup conflict and ideological antagonisms in labor, government, and politics.

One example is *seisan kanri* ("production control"), illegal worker seizure and operation of a place of business, and ejection of management and owners.[33] A former director of the Civil Liberties Bureau notes: "Among the intelligentsia and the classes which provide leaders there is a tendency for violation of human rights ... to be used as a stick with which to beat one's adversary or the organization to which he belongs. One example of this is, as everyone knows, where in labor disputes, etc., one union fights another ... whereas one's adversary's violations of human rights are listed with neurotic precision, one is almost indifferent to the violation of human rights by one's own union. ... We have a mixture of undue sensitivity to human rights on the one hand and complete indifference on the other."[34] Indifference, or even hostility, to the rights of others has been most striking since the late 1960s in gang warfare confrontations between student factions.

When two or more groups oppose one another, or when a union or student demonstration or strike takes place, the groups manifest intergroup hostility. But they also display an *amae* expectation of indulgence and support from the people (*kokumin*) that is different from an appeal for support in an individualist democracy. A "confrontation is like a domestic discord, so that it tends to be very emotional and radical."[35] Japan is no longer the patriarchal family state that it was under the Emperor from the late 1800s until 1945.[36] But Japan is still a family state, albeit without a father. Political groups present petitions and protests to their superiors or to society as a whole asking for the good will and indulgence of the "Japanese family" (the largest so-conceived group) and appealing for a benevolent response. For example, adult indulgence of student activist *amae* precludes the angry resentment sometimes manifested for even peaceful protests against student activists in the United States. Japanese employees wear armbands to dramatize their dissatisfaction and to appeal to management while staying on the job. National Railway Worker Union strikes are usually slowdowns of a few hours duration and are accompanied by repeated public apologies and appeals for public understanding and support.[37]

Another feature of Japan's social organization that affects freedom of expression is the openness of usually conflicting groups to the possibility of cooperating for the welfare of a larger, more inclusive "we." This is so particularly when a threat from outsiders is perceived. Factions within a political party or union and subdivisions within a business firm, a ministry, a university, or a mass media company compete with one another with strong in-group consciousness under ordinary circumstances, but in dealings with outsiders, unanimous loyal support of the larger unit normally is expected. For example, although factions within a political party compete for power and differ among themselves on issues, in Diet voting there is often unanimous party support for the party's position. Another illustration is a 1969 court order affecting the mass media industry. The order to four television companies to present newsfilm as evidence triggered instant unanimity in opposition thereby ending fair debate of the issue.[38] The face-to-face in-group serves as the model in the dynamics of the inclusive group which counterbalances the individualistic group under circumstances of special challenge. Sometimes various group clusters are fenced off from each other in ways that seem strange to western observers. For example, members of a trade union may at times be too loyal to their own company to join forces with other unions.[39]

Freedom to dissent *during* the consensus-building process, free competition for public support among primary groups and among more inclusive clusters of groups, and freedom to petition private or public authorities for benevolent response seem to be core elements in Japan's system of freedom of expression.

The expansion of the duty of tolerance. The Japanese structural system tends to protect the freedom of expression of groups. There the problem for individual freedom presented by the group is different in degree, not in kind, from the problem of infringement on freedom in the United States. A problem of balance is involved. In the United States, a greater emphasis on sociality may be as needed as is stress on individuality in Japan.

Analytically, there are two central problems for individual freedom of expression in Japan. The first is whether the individual's right to self-determination in preconsensus discussion is honored by the group. The second problem is whether postconsensus dissent is punished unpersuasively, that is, arbitrarily without reasons being given.

In a dialogue situation, sensitivity to the need for respectful treatment of the individual *within* the group framework of reciprocal duties is important. Deepened responsiveness to the value of the person as such does not imply abrogation of interdependence in a social world characterized by the presence of groups. It does imply expansion of consciousness of duty to others beyond the particularistic confines of any group. Such expanded consciousness implies recognition of a duty to be tolerant of the right of an individual or of another group to its self-determination regarding expression, and it implies a system of reciprocal duties that is tolerably demanding. Responsiveness to substantial demands on time, energy, and resources is expected by the Japanese, in what they term their "wet" (close and emotional) human relations. These contrast with the "dry" (casual and less emotional) relations of Americans. The demands upon the individual implicit in the Japanese model of responsive relationships are so great that they must be engaged in with only a very limited number of people, lest the demands on total resources become impractical and intolerable. Expansion of duty consciousness may strain binding loyalties and thereby diminish demands in a model relationship, which, in turn, may loosen particularistic group bonds. The loosening of such bonds might facilitate more widely diffused trust and tolerance in interpersonal and intergroup relations. This is so only if such a nexus is seen as natural within the evolving system. The rights of others in the community might come into peripheral vision more easily, if the individual, as such, is not conceived of as a basically incomplete entity, a submerged part of a group, but as a social whole and, as such, the ultimate reference point in public life. The closed nature of political groups militates against their recognizing and accepting the legitimacy of laws and community standards unless they sense their own participation in consensus-building through representative "consultation" within the most inclusive group, Japan. Demonstrations and other group activities provide that sense of participation in postwar Japan.

Whatever the forms of future rights consciousness, it is likely that freedom of expression in Japan will be maintained by its frequent exercise. Free expression has the support of pluralized group interests and it is reinforced by a powerful mass media system which relishes its freedom. Moreover, it is supported by a highly professionalized police, prosecutorial, and judicial system; by respected intellectual elites who rationalize freedom in the Japanese milieu through the education system and the mass media; and by leaders and citizens who, at least vaguely, support legally protected freedom and, at most, consider it essential for Japan.

FREEDOM OF ASSEMBLY AND THE PUBLIC WELFARE

Political demonstrations have supplied the most dramatic examples of group activity in post-1945 Japanese politics. Some leaders of illegal demonstrations have viewed any type of regulation, even of group violence, as an unconstitutional infringement of article 21 which deals with freedom of expression. Political support for limitless free speech may spring from multiple motives: frustration with political impotence; a sense of *amae* which generates a claim and expectation of special leniency; and, in particular, early in the postwar period, ideological rejection of or unfamiliarity with the constitutional system. An absolutist view of free expression often accompanies a calculated civil disobedience strategy, as does a posture of self-defense under perceived threat of attack by police. An inability to see a relationship between democracy and the regulation of freedom under law may underlie an uncompromising view of free speech. Single-minded preoccupation with group emotion and the issue at hand may explain unawareness of the legal factor.

So unaccustomed were many citizens in the early postwar period to freedom of assembly under ordinance permit systems that unnecessary formal applications were often made for meeting permits. Examples of such applications from Tokyo in the early 1950s include a social held by the film club of an insurance company, a film review in a temple compound sponsored by a Tokyo education society, a high school reunion held in a city office building, a lecture on nutrition at a private home, and a film evening of a social club which was held in the garden of the person who sponsored it.[40]

Although the Constitution of Japan speaks of the Diet as "the highest organ of state power" (article 41), it also empowers the Supreme Court "to determine the constitutionality of any law, order, regulation, or official act" (article 81). All laws are national laws, and all courts come under the administrative authority of the Supreme Court. Even though Japan's legal system and methods of legal interpretation and application resemble those of continental code-law countries, precedent binds the courts in certain situations and the Anglo-American common-law approach has steadily increased in importance since 1945.[41] For example, a sizable number of judges at all levels are familiar with American case law, and some judges make use of American doctrine, but usually without explicit reference. The voluminous body of scholarly commentary ranges from very abstract exegesis to meticulous case analyses, and reflects very sophisticated understanding of European (particularly German) and American legal experience. Controversial decisions concerning "collective activities" (*shūdan kōdō*) handed down by "progressive" lower court judges are sometimes accorded an importance in political discourse that they do not enjoy in law, and they are often overturned by subsequent appellate court decisions.

Most of the cases discussed below involved violations of local public safety ordinances (*kōan jōrei*) which regulate parades and other gatherings by means of either a notification or a permit system.[42] Postwar occupation officials initially required the repeal of legislation and ordinances that restricted freedom of expression, but after the middle of 1948, encouraged passage of such municipal and prefectural ordinances because of their concern about leftist violence.

At the time, neither courts nor lawyers were accustomed to the ideas of judicial review and freedom of expression. Reactions to events and court actions were sometimes infected with ideological bias. District court decisions between 1951 and 1954 more often found ordinances unconstitutional, whereas high court decisions usually upheld their validity and emphasized a flexible public welfare doctrine, the propriety of permit systems, the need for public order, and the dangers of mob psychology.[43] In two pivotal decisions of 1954 and 1960, upholding the public safety ordinances of Niigata Prefecture and Tokyo respectively, the Supreme Court clarified for the courts broad principles of interpretation regarding freedom of assembly cases. Since 1960, judges and scholars gradually have been filling in the interstices of public welfare abstractions with legal distinctions and specific standards developed in considering new cases. Almost all of these many cases, affecting law and politics throughout Japan, have arisen in Tokyo, which can be termed Japan's central nervous system.

The freedom of assembly guaranteed by the Japanese Constitution has raised legal problems not unlike those familiar to western legal systems. For example, the problem of prior restraint is a subject of lively debate, as is the distinction between a notification system and a licensing system. Debatable, also, may be the proper legal instrumentality for regulating collective activities: whether local ordinances, national law, or traffic regulations apply. The problem of establishing acceptable judicial and regulatory standards has focused on the time, place, and manner of regulated demonstrations. Regulation may go so far as to include the imposition of conditions on the conduct of demonstrations by public safety commissions (sometimes applying unpromulgated standards and internal rules). The problems associated with administrative discretion are multiple: the propriety of delegation of authority by public safety commissions to police for the administration of an ordinance; the appropriate limits of on-the-spot police discretion in dealing with demonstrations; the absence of redress when a permit is refused arbitrarily; and the refusal of a permit on the formalistic grounds that the application is not properly drawn. Issues that have received considerable publicity and have gone to litigation include the lack of a speedy trial causing needless suffering; entry by the police of university grounds to regulate collective activities; and the constitutionality of special restrictions and administrative penalties where the free expression rights of public employees are concerned.[44]

Particularly noteworthy for purposes of our discussion is judicial use of abstract theory in delineating the public welfare respecting freedom of assembly where no application or notification has been made and, therefore, no denial of permission or attachment of conditions upon notification is at the base of the controversy. In responding to appellant challenges of the prima facie constitutionality of such ordinances, the Supreme Court has employed its theories of the public welfare, not to make judgments concerning specific ordinance provisions, administrative or police enforcement of ordinances, or criminal acts of the accused, but to determine the reasonableness of the general intent of the ordinance taken as a whole.[45] The core of the judges' public welfare notion respecting freedom of assembly is the protection of individual rights both to assemble and to be free from coercive or violent group activities. To charges of disproportionate fear of crowd tendencies toward disorder and "reverse course" (that is, toward prewar patterns), the Supreme Court has countered through decisions which stress the *duty* of local public safety commissions to grant permits with a minimum of regulation. Exceptions arise where there is clear danger to the public welfare, balanced against the greater weight attaching to the general intent of a permit ordinance to grant permission for gatherings.

The spring crisis of 1952, the security treaty crisis of 1960, and the university crisis of 1968 to 1970, will be remembered as historic periods involving demonstrations and group violence. Best known is the May Day incident of 1952, during which there were violent demonstrations, car burnings, and clashes with the police in which two were killed. Additionally, 2,300 persons were injured, another 1,232 arrested, and 261 indicted for crimes of violence and demonstrating without a permit. Many of the substantive court decisions on this and similar incidents of the time were not handed down until the 1969–1973 period. Litigation has been slow because of the number of the accused, the political sensitivity of related issues even years later, and such knotty legal problems as those relating to establishing a conspiracy "crime of riot" (*sōranzai*). The Tokyo May Day Trials extended over 1,792 court sessions before the first decisions (including many acquittals) were handed down in January, 1970.[46]

The earliest Supreme Court decision bearing directly on the freedom of assembly dealt with an aspect of the Tokyo May Day events. The May Day decision of 1953 is most notable for its clear refusal to recognize unreviewable administrative discretion to regulate collective activities.[47] The General Council of Japan Trade Unions (*Sōhyō*) was denied permission to hold a mass demonstration for "500,000 people." (Less than 10 percent of that number actually assembled). The proposed location was the Imperial Palace Plaza, a national public park in Tokyo, and the demonstration was to extend from 9:00 A.M. to 5:00 P.M. on May 1, 1952, under regulations of the Ministry of Welfare. *Sōhyō* contended in court that refusal to allow the demonstration was an unconstitutional abridgement of freedom of assembly, while the Minister of Welfare questioned the power of the Court to review the denial.

The Supreme Court upheld the Tokyo High Court decision of November 15, 1952, which said the suit presented "no legal interest requiring adjudication" since the day of the proposed demonstration had passed. But in lengthy obiter dicta the Court noted that, although the Minister had acted legally in keeping the park open for the public, he did not have the unreviewable power he claimed. Neither here nor in the later ordinance decisions does the Court suggest an avenue of relief when an abuse of discretion results in denial of a permit and the day of the proposed public gathering arrives.[48]

The Niigata ordinance decision of 1954 concerned the arrest in 1949 of approximately 30 Koreans in Takada, Niigata prefecture, on a charge of "illicit brewing."[49] Release of the accused was demanded the following day by a crowd of several hundred people who gathered in front of the police station. Two of the accused actually led the demonstration, which included speeches against the government as well as the singing of communist and Korean patriotic songs.[50] The Niigata ordinance provided that no demonstration or parade be held without a permit in places to which the public has free access. In upholding a lower court conviction, the Supreme Court denied the appellant's contention that the ordinance establishes an unconstitutional prior restraint on freedom of assembly. Debate concerning this decision turns on the interpretation put on the Court's statement of principles: "It is against the intent of the Constitution and impermissible to place prior restraints upon parades, processions, and mass public demonstrations . . . under an ordinance that provides for a general system of licensing rather than a system of simple notification, because the people have the basic freedom to demonstrate unless the purpose and manner of the demonstration are improper and against the public welfare."[51]

The Court qualified this statement by maintaining that regulations established by ordinance that might prohibit such activities or require a license or notification are constitutional as long as they deal with "the place and procedure under reasonable and clear criteria in order to maintain public order and to protect the public welfare." An unconstitutional "general system of licensing" is one which *intends* "to control all such activities" or which has "the effect of restricting such activities in general" and which gives the public safety commission a "very broad" area of discretion. The Court emphasized the intent of the ordinance as an "organic whole," and not the words "license" or "notification," as the crux of the problem. This and other ordinances are constitutional apparently because public gatherings "must be licensed, unless there is a specific reason for not doing so," that is, unless "it is foreseen that they may involve a clear and present danger to public safety."

Justice Hachiro Fujita notes approvingly the use of notification systems in West Germany, France, Italy, and the United States, and maintains the Niigata ordinance is unconstitutional as a licensing system and is thus "a general prohibition of such activity (*ippanteki kinshi*)." The supplementary opinion of Justices Inouye and Iwamatsu played down the distinction between a permit and notification system, noting that the Niigata ordinance allowed a demonstration if, after application for a permit, no response was forthcoming from the public safety commission within twenty-four hours of the proposed activity (article 4, paragraph 4). In his dissent from the later *Tokyo* decision, Justice Fujita harkened back to this provision as the Court's basis for judging the "organic whole" of the Niigata ordinance as equivalent to a notification system and therefore constitutional, despite its reservations about the generality of other provisions.[52] Because the Tokyo ordinance contains no such provision, Justice Fujita concluded that, for the sake of consistency, the Supreme Court should have held the Tokyo ordinance unconstitutional.

The *Niigata* Court did note that article 1, paragraph 1 "has quite general aspects" and that article 4, paragraph 1 "especially, sets forth an extremely abstract standard": that a permit must be granted when "the parade or demonstration concerned involves no threat to public order." The ordinance would not be "in accord with the spirit of the Constitution" if that were the only standard provided by the ordinance, and consequently, it may be desirable to revise the ordinance into clearer and more concrete terms. However, *Niigata* nowhere links the constitutionality of the "organic whole" with the provision stressed by Justices Inouye, Iwamatsu, and Fujita, or with any other provision stating "reasonable and clear criteria." In both the *Niigata* and *Tokyo* decisions, the ambiguous flexibility of a general public welfare standard was apparently preferred, and used to support the conclusion that a primary intent of the ordinance was to grant permits. Further specificity was considered desirable, but not necessary.

The Supreme Court's ordinance decisions between *Niigata* and *Tokyo* tend to corroborate its doctrinal consistency. Nevertheless, between 1954 and 1960, disagreements arose between lower courts concerning which elements of the *Niigata* decision to stress—the statement of principles or the Court's flexible application of criteria. During the late 1950s, the ordinance rulings of the lower courts ran both favorably and unfavorably to free expression claims—like the zig-zag path of a Japanese garden.

The Supreme Court's 1955 decision on the Saga prefectural ordinance—a petty bench decision and therefore, necessarily consonant with *Niigata* grand bench doctrine[53] —upheld the constitutionality of a notification system granting officials broad discretionary power to "attach appropriate conditions it deems necessary for the maintenance of order" (article 4).[54] On April 19, 1950, a communist-led demonstration of approximately 300 persons took place in front of the Saga Tax Office following local rumors of official corruption. After about an hour, police attempted to disperse the crowd, and a violent confrontation ensued. As in the *Niigata* and *Tokyo* cases, appellants had made no attempt to comply with the ordinance.

Another petty bench decision in 1955, quoting *Niigata* almost verbatim, upheld the Tokuyama municipal permit ordinance and the conviction of local communists who had been granted a permit for a March 6, 1950, demonstration.[55] In violation of the condition that the gathering stay at least 200 yards from any government building, demonstration leaders entered the Tokuyama Tax Office to persuade officials to negotiate about tax problems. As in *Niigata*, the Court deemphasized the distinction between permit and notification systems and stressed provisions "concerning the place and procedure under reasonable and clear criteria in order to maintain public order and to protect the public welfare against serious harm," while not identifying any "reasonable and clear criteria." In light of Justice Fujita's contention about *Niigata* doctrine in *Tokyo,* it is notable that the *Tokuyama* case involved the absence of any provision allowing public gatherings when officials fail to act on a permit application.

The Saitama prefectural ordinance at issue in a 1955 Grand Bench decision establishes a notification system with relatively specific provisions.[56] It requires more information on the notification form than other ordinances, but exempts more assemblies from the prior notification requirement, sets out procedures and conditions to be observed in carrying on collective activities, and allows the police chief discretion "to take necessary steps to maintain public order" should a demonstration violate other ordinance provisions.

On March 27, 1950, about 150 day laborers had gathered before Kawaguchi City Hall to petition for labor reforms. Since the local officials were not responsive, the crowd forced its way into a meeting of city officials, and its leader delivered a speech from atop the secretary's desk. The demonstration continued into the night and involved considerable scuffling with police. Next day a related demonstration was held without prior notification. The appellants were convicted for failing to comply with limitations set forth on the notification form. Against the contention that the ordinance establishes an unconstitutional "general licensing system," the Supreme Court, with Justice Fujita participating, unanimously held all provisions constitutional, establishing clear standards for protecting the public welfare.

In 1960, a landmark free assembly ruling was delivered. The *Tokyo Ordinance Case* came about against a politicized background of almost daily demonstrations focusing on policy debate in several areas: revision of the United States-Japan Security Treaty, judicial and scholarly debate on *Niigata* doctrine, failure of the ruling party to revise the controversial Police Duties Law thereby increasing police discretion with respect to demonstrations, the U-2 incident, the downfall of the Syngman Rhee government in Korea and of the Menderes government in Turkey, and the cancellation of President Eisenhower's visit to Japan.[57] The 1960 demonstrations against the "undemocratic" anticonsensual handling of issues by Prime Minister Nobusuke Kishi involved the largest mass movement in Japanese history. Certainly it reflected a powerful affirmation of Japanese expectations for consensual democracy, and it resulted in the resignation of the prime minister.

Tokyo district court judgments in 1958 and 1959 had held the Tokyo public safety ordinance unconstitutional, and in November 1959, in the early stages of the Security Treaty drama, a Tokyo district court refused to allow police detention of students who had demonstrated without a permit. Out of concern for the urgency of the matter, the Supreme Court of Japan reviewed three assembly cases simultaneously. The Tokyo student detention case came up on appeal along with a Shizuoka trial ruling which also found local regulations unconstitutional. Appeal was heard in a third case against a Hiroshima decision upholding assembly restrictions.[58]

Focusing on the Tokyo regulation, the Supreme Court held all three ordinances constitutional, with Justices Fujita and Tarumi dissenting.[59] More fully than other decisions, the *Tokyo* judgment presents the Court's theoretical analysis of the freedom of assembly, the intent of the ordinance involved, and the public welfare within Japan's sociopolitical context. Because *Tokyo* offers the classic example of Supreme Court jurisprudence at a time and in a problem area peculiarly critical for freedom of expression in Japan, and because of its continuing impact on Japanese legal and political life, the essentials of the Court's opinion deserve extended presentation. The opinion sets out nine important propositions.

One, the guarantee of freedoms such as the freedom of assembly "is the most important feature that distinguishes democracy from totalitarianism . . ."

Two, the people may not abuse such rights as freedom of assembly, " . . . but have a responsibility at all times to exercise them for the public welfare; in this respect they do not differ from other fundamental rights. . . ." (see article 12 of the Constitution).

Three, the task of the courts is "to draw a proper boundary between freedom and the public welfare," to guarantee the freedom to hold gatherings character-ized by "pure freedom of expression" with groups comporting themselves "peacefully, respecting order," and to determine whether and to what extent legal restrictions should be placed on public gatherings.

Four, the degree and kind of restriction the law places on given activities depends on their nature; "expression" refers to activities quite varied in nature. Collective activities are not the same as mere speech or writing, because they involve "the might of a large number of people actually assembled together in a body, a type of latent physical force . . . [which] can be set in motion very easily" and can result in excitement, anger, and even a violent "mob whose own momentum impels it toward the violation of law and order, a situation in which both the crowd's own leaders and the police are powerless. So much is clear from the laws of crowd psychology and from actual experience." Therefore, it is "unavoidable that local authorities, in due consideration of both local and general circumstances," adopt by means of public safety ordinances "prior to the fact the minimum measures necessary to maintain law and order."

Five, in determining whether measures are within the bounds of what is minimum and necessary, those engaged in judicial review of such disputes must not be distracted from the real problem by emphasis upon words such as "license" and "notification," but rather must "consider the spirit of the ordi-nance as a whole, not superficially, but as a functional entity."

Six, the provisions of the Tokyo ordinance are within constitutional bounds. Article 3 makes it an obvious duty for the public safety commission to grant a license unless "it is clearly recognized" that the collective activity in question "will directly endanger the maintenance of the public peace." By contrast, the Niigata ordinance standard applied "in cases wherein the . . . demonstration concerned involves no threat of disturbance to public order." To the *Tokyo* Court, the circumstances under which the commission can refuse are "strictly limited," so this licensing system is essentially the same as a notification system. But "the prerequisites for collective activities . . . are immaterial so long as freedom of expression is not thereby improperly restricted."

Seven, the public safety commission must use its discretion after "concrete study and consideration of the various factors operating in the particular situation," with "maximum respect to freedom of expression" and a sense of its "responsibility to the inhabitants to maintain law and order." The ordinance was described by the Court as not "entirely free from the danger" of abuse, but that was thought insufficient reason for holding it unconstitutional.

Eight, there is no provision permitting a group activity when the commission has not indicated refusal of permission by a certain time. Prosecution can result from any unlicensed collective activity, and the court of first instance "inferred from this that the ordinance is a general prohibition on collective activities" and therefore unconstitutional. The lower court also held it invalid because "the applicant is provided with no means of redress when the appointed day arrives and the decision is still deferred." This thinking, said the Supreme Court, "mistakenly evaluates the problem and is quite wrong."

Finally, the Court said that article 1 of the Tokyo ordinance is not, as contended, unconstitutionally general in regulating collective activities "in streets and other places" and mass demonstrations "in any place whatsoever." Constitutionality does not hinge on the specificity of references to place. Some degree of generality in place designation is unavoidable; it is "completely profitless" to debate such a matter.

The *Tokyo Ordinance Case* has continued to have substantial impact on Japan's law of demonstrations since 1960. Some ordinances, such as those of Hiroshima, Gumma, and Aichi, were revised or written anew to conform with the Tokyo ordinance. Although their perceptions were modified by the extremes of the 1968–1970 period, critics of the decision contended its doctrine unduly strengthens the hand of the police vis-à-vis activist elements. Some have suggested that the *Tokyo* decision established by judicial holding and local ordinance the controversial 1958 Police Duties Bill which failed to come to a vote in the Diet. On balance, it should be noted that demonstrations continue in freedom, that police casualties are usually much higher than activist injuries, and that police have not caused a single political death since 1952, while ultraradical killings (usually of one another) continue to be a problem.

Before 1960, most judicial decisions on public safety ordinances responded to prima facie constitutional challenges in light of article 21 guarantees of freedom of assembly.[60] With the *Tokyo* decision, however, such challenges have markedly decreased. Liberal and reform-minded defense lawyers, judges, and scholars who must now test their hopes by the rough-hewn but firm touchstone of public welfare doctrine, have sought more sharply honed cutting tools. On the rare occasions since 1960 when the constitutionality of a public safety ordinance has been attacked on its face, article 31 of the Constitution has been used: "No person shall be deprived of life or liberty, nor shall any other criminal penalty be imposed, except according to procedure established by law."

Supreme Court and lower court decisions have turned most often on such issues as constitutionality under article 1 or article 31, or both, or correctness from the standpoint of legal interpretation, or applications of the ordinance in specific cases.[61] In a 1966 case, the Supreme Court upheld convictions for a 1952 demonstration by young leftist workers who had no permit and who fought with the police.[62] The convictions were sustained despite appellants' arguments. They said that article 2 of the Tokyo ordinance required a permit only of the sponsor (*shusaisha*) and not of the leaders or inciters of a demonstration. Appellants also argued that the ordinance was not operative law when the case arose inasmuch as no one could receive a permit under an Occupation ban. Further, they contended that the case should be dismissed for lack of speedy trial. Not until December, 1972, did the Supreme Court finally recognize lack of a speedy trial as a basis for dismissing charges. The incident involved in the

Takada Case occurred during the violent political activities of the faraway summer of 1952.

The recent trend has been toward clarification of narrower points of law. An apt illustration is provided by the petty bench decision of July 16, 1970, concerning the meaning of "public place" (*kōkyō no basho*) in the Hiroshima prefectural ordinance.[63] A demonstration was staged by approximately 700 public employees without a permit in front of the Hiroshima prefectural building in July, 1961. The accused contended that the site of the demonstration is for the use of local public employees and people there on business with the local governments. By this view it is, therefore, not "a public place" within the meaning of the ordinance; the Hiroshima High Court agreed. The Supreme Court held the ordinance applicable to the environs of such local government buildings which are under local government supervision. The Court defined a "public place" in the ordinance as "a place which in reality is generally open and can be used and entered freely by unspecified people."

A unanimous Grand Bench decision of December 24, 1969, reflects the reliance of Japan's law of demonstrations on *Tokyo* doctrine. In the case at hand, a student demonstration group had disregarded a condition that they march down one side of a street by marching in the middle of a thoroughfare. It upheld the prima facie constitutionality of a Kyoto ordinance under articles 21 and 31 of the Constitution.[64] The Court said that although the ordinance established "prior regulation" (*jizen no kisei*), the public safety commission "must permit'. . . (collective activities) as a matter of duty except in cases (of) . . . direct danger (*chokusetsu no kiken*) to property or freedom, life or limb, of the public. . . ." (article 6). The ordinance does not violate article 31 due process requirements by allowing imposition of conditions on a permit. Nor does it offend the law by authorizing the police chief to issue warnings or exercise controls in case of violation or intent to violate conditions, and by legitimizing penalties based on police interpretation of violations of permit conditions.

In a related field of legal development, it must be noted that numerous lower court and Supreme Court decisions have upheld significant limitations on the freedom of assembly and political activities of public employees. Restrictions have been sustained in a wide range of categories under various civil service laws.[65] For example, in the famous *Sarufutsu Decision* of November 6, 1974, the Supreme Court, divided eleven to four, reversed lower court acquittals and held a postal employee in violation of the National Public Employees' Law. His offense was that he distributed a few fliers during his off-duty hours on behalf of a socialist candidate for the House of Representatives in 1967. Such restraints have not been a chilling deterrent. "Spring offensives" (nationwide union struggles for wages and the like) occur annually. Political demonstrations by civil servants, such as teachers, court employees, and mailmen continue, even when forbidden collective activities are followed by government disciplinary measures. In this line of cases, as in all others affecting freedom of expression doctrine in

Japan, the courts turn to what critical scholars call the "abstract-formalistic" public welfare standard. Enduringly, lower courts and some justices in the Supreme Court have continued to emphasize that freedom of expression is essential to the public welfare.

CONCLUSION

Elimination of the public welfare standard from judicial chambers or from the Constitution, as some have suggested, would not soften politically charged disputes about legal criteria for resolving conflict.[66] It would not end political trials.[67] It would have little, if any, appreciable effect on the vigorous freedom of group expression in Japan. Supportive laws, bureaucrats, police, courts, pluralistic elites, and citizens are essential to the future of freedom of expression in Japan. About that there is no question, but collective activities in opposition to the present sociopolitical system or government of Japan manifest the persistence of perennial social patterns. Although some judicial decisions have been widely criticized as too restrictive and others as too liberal, there is no evidence that the Japanese social system, characterized by such features as hierarchy, prevalence of groups, and *amae,* is ready to give way to revolutionary discontent. The Constitution of Japan seems acceptable in Japan because it is not divorced from sociopolitical reality. Japanese patterns of thought and behavior—the unwritten Constitution of Japan—create the problem of myopic groupism, yet ensure the vigor of intergroup competition and recurrent waves of vibrant dissent. They limit the individual's freedom within the group and within society at large, but define the outer parameters of legitimate power assertion by leaders and followers in both official and private in-groups. Those like Professor Miyazawa who "every day enjoys breathing freedom again" as he remembers the repressive pre-1945 situation, realize from experience that restriction of self-determination with respect to freedom cuts deeply into the energy, trust, and hope that support free dissent. Whether the problem be authoritarian government, in-group oppression of the individual, or callousness of society, it is society more than law that determines the status of free expression, although both are essential. Japan's experience and problems seem instructive in all the above contexts.

It appears that accurate and ultimately useful comparative legal knowledge cannot be developed or communicated across cultural barriers unless the approach to the study of law integrates nonlegal factors in some manner, and transcends a unicultural perspective. A transcultural approach should incorporate four elements for comparison: (1) the status of law and judicial doctrine; (2) general social conditions which tend to affect freedom of expression; (3) patterns of behaviour and rights consciousness in the country under study; and (4) theoretical presuppositions of constitutional democracy in whatever time or place.

By theoretical presuppositions are meant principles which underlie and, indeed, are almost taken for granted in a particular political system. For example, free expression is presupposed for the operation of constitutional democracy, and hence is an essential standard for good government in such a system; but freedom is not thereby a self evident truth nor is it essential in all types of political systems. Even in constitutional democracies, however, cultural context is important, because it can cause different values or weightings to be given to these presuppositions. One example is the idea of tolerance, which is subjected to great strains if the clash of the doctrines being tolerated seems to be dangerous. In *Freedom and Culture,* Dorothy Lee writes, "As a concept or as a recognized value, freedom is seldom if ever present in non-Western cultures, but the thing itself is present and carefully implemented . . . as autonomy, or otherwise as a dimension of self."[68] While the presuppositions of Japan and America with respect to the person's intrinsic value are the same, enhancement of freedom of expression in the rights consciousness of their respective legal cultures may rest on opposite perspectives: independence in America, interdependence in Japan. This radical polarity in nations which subscribe to self-determination respecting expression recommends such freedom, politically and perhaps in theory, as a transcultural human political value.

NOTES*

* In references to legal periodical literature, the number of the *initial* page of the work cited immediately follows the volume title. Page references to material specifically referred to in the text, if any, follow the initial page citation. Legal case citations correspond to *A Uniform System of Citation,* 11th ed. (Cambridge: The Harvard Law Review Association, 1974).

1. The western-language literature on freedom of expression in Japan, and on Japanese law in general, is not extensive. See Lawrence W. Beer, "Freedom of Information and the Evidentiary Use of Film in Japan: Law and Sociopolitics in an East Asian Democracy," *The American Political Science Review* 65, (1971):1119–1134; idem., "Defamation, Privacy, and Freedom of Expression in Japan," *5 Law in Japan: An Annual* 192 (1972); and idem., "The Public Welfare Standard and Freedom of Expression in Japan," in *The Constitution of Japan: Its First Twenty Years, 1947–1967,* ed. Dan F. Henderson (Seattle: University of Washington Press, 1969), pp. 205–38, which served as a basis for parts of this essay. See also Lawrence W. Beer and Hidenori Tomatsu, "A Guide to the Study of Japanese Law," *The American Journal of Comparative Law* (April 1975); Hiroshi Itoh and Lawrence W. Beer, *The Constitution of Japan: Major Judicial Decisions, 1961–1970* (n.p., 1976); Lawrence W. Beer, "Education, Politics and Freedom in Japan: The Ienaga Textbook Review Cases," 8 *Law in Japan: An Annual* (1975). Also particularly useful for the study of freedom and civil liberties in Japanese constitutional law today are: John M. Maki, *Court and Constitution in Japan: Selected Supreme Court Decisions* (Seattle: University of Washington Press, 1964); Y. Okudaira, "The Japanese Supreme Court: Its Organization and Function," *3 Lawasia* 67 (April 1972); Frank O. Miller, *Minobe Tatsukichi: Interpreter of Japanese Constitutionalism* (Berkeley: University of California Press, 1965); Shigemitsu Dando, *The Japanese Law of Criminal Procedure,* trans. B. J. George (South Hackensack, N.J.: Fred B. Rothman and Co., 1965); and M. Ito, "The Rule of Law in Japan" in *Law in Japan,* ed. Arthur T. Von Mehren

(Cambridge: Harvard University Press, 1963), pp. 205–38; and David Danelski, "The Supreme Court of Japan: An Exploratory Study," in *Comparative Judicial Behavior,* ed. Glendon Schubert and David J. Danelski (New York: Oxford University Press, 1970), pp. 121–56. American social science specialists on Japan have not generally manifested sustained interest in freedom or constitutional law under the American-influenced Constitution of Japan, a notable irony. For a unique and excellent study of courts and politics, see Chalmers Johnson, *Conspiracy at Matsukawa,* (Berkeley and Los Angeles: University of California Press, 1972).

2. Concerning freedom of speech and assembly in other nations, there are few works which compare two or more systems. But see, Ivo D. Duchacek, *Rights and Liberties in the World Today: Constitutional Promise and Reality* (Santa Barbara: ABC-CLIO, Inc., 1973); David H. Bayley, *Public Liberties in the New States* (Chicago: Rand McNally & Co., 1964); R. F. Bunn and W. G. Andrews, eds., *Politics and Civil Liberties in Europe* (Princeton: Van Norstrand, 1967); Harry Street, *Freedom, The Individual and the Law* (New York: Penguin Books, 1963); Frede Castberg, *Freedom of Speech in the West* (New York: Oceana Publications, 1960); Haig A. Bosmajian, *The Principles and Practice of Freedom of Speech* (Boston: Houghton-Mifflin, 1971); L. A. Stein, "Municipal Controls over Freedom of Assembly in Canada and the United States," 1971 *Public Law* 115; J. Carson, "Freedom of Assembly and the Hostile Audience," 15 *New York Law Forum* 798(1969). D. G. T. Williams, "Protest and Public Order," 78 *Cambridge Law Journal* 96 (April 1970); J. Velasco, Jr., "The Right of Free Speech and Assembly," 45 *Philippines Law Journal* 501 (1970). An enormous body of literature on freedom of expression, including substantial comparative work, exists in Japanese, but it is inaccessible to all but a handful of the world's legalists because of the difficulty of the written Japanese language.

3. All references to articles of the Constitution of Japan are taken from *The Constitution of Japan,* Supreme Court, Tokyo, 1968. Article 97 is of special interest: "The fundamental human rights by this Constitution guaranteed to the people of Japan are fruits of the age-old struggle of man to be free; they are conferred upon this and future generations in trust, to be held for all time inviolate."

4. Japan, *Constitution,* article 16: "Every person shall have the right of peaceful petition for the redress of damage, for the removal of public officials, for the enactment, repeal, or amendment of laws, ordinances or regulations and for other matters; nor shall any person be in any way discriminated against for sponsoring such a petition." article 28: "The right of workers to organize and bargain and act collectively is guaranteed."

5. Whether or not the term "public welfare" in articles 22 and 29 means the same thing as it means under articles 12 and 13 has not been authoritatively determined, and opinion differs. See Lawrence W. Beer, "The Doctrine of the Public Welfare and the Freedom of Assembly Under the Constitution of Japan" (dissertation, University of Washington, 1966). Article 1 of the Civil Code provides that "All private rights shall conform to the public welfare," concerning which see S. Wagatsuma, "Kōkyō no fukushi shingisoku kenri-ranyō no sōgo no kankei" ("The relationships among public welfare, good faith, and abuse of rights"), 1 *Kenri No Ranyō* ("*Abuse of Rights*") 46 (1960).

6. For representative views of Japanese scholars regarding the public welfare, see Isao Sato, *Kempō Kenkyū Nyūmon* ("*Introduction to Constitutional Studies*") 3 vols. (Tokyo: Nippon Hyoron Sha. 1964–68)2:25–117; and Beer, "Doctrine of Public Welfare," pp. 191–227.

7. *Japan* v. *Sugino,* 4 *Keishū* 2012, 2014 (1950). "The public welfare" is the official translation of *kōkyō no fukushi,* which can also be translated as "communal well-being" or "prosperity." According to one Japanese scholar, "Before the establishment of the Constitution of Japan words like '*kōkyō no kōfuku*' [the public happiness] or '*kōkyō no fukuri*' [the public benefit, welfare or prosperity] were used, but instances of *kōkyō no fukushi,* at least in legal enactments, are not to be found." Kelichi Yamamoto, "Kokyo no fukushi," *Nihonkoku Kempō Taikei,* ed. Jirō Tanaka (Tokyo: Yūhikaku, 1961)8:16.

8. Okudaira, "Japanese Supreme Court," p. 86.

9. Professor Toshiyoshi Miyazawa clarifies the controversial background of the public welfare as a standard: "There can be no objection to translating such words as *salus publica, bonum commune,* and *Gemeinnutz* as '*kōkyō no fukushi*'; but these words have often been

used in a more or less anti-individualist sense. Similarly, words used in Japan during the war, such as 'kōeki' in 'kōeki yūsen' [forget yourself and revere the community], are not significantly different from 'kōkyō no fukushi', considered simply as words. Perhaps some of that wartime coloring has stuck to the phrase 'kōkyō no fukushi'. . . . But the 'kōkyō no fukushi' of the Constitution of Japan differs significantly from those wartime expressions in that its meaning is firmly grounded in individualism." Toshiyoshi Miyazawa, Nihonkoku Kempō ("The Constitution of Japan") (Tokyo: Nihon Hyoron Shinsha, 1963), p. 205. Miyazawa's views on individualism conceive of political man as highly socialized, rather than individualistic. His teachings have been among the most influential in postwar Japan. One reason for controversy in Japan is difference of opinion on interpretive methodology. As Takayanagi pointed out, Japanese civilian methods differ from Philippine common law approaches, "even in cases in which the constitutional text is the same." See Kenzo Takayanagi, "A Century of Innovation: the Development of Japanese Law, 1868–1961" in Von Mehren, Law in Japan, pp. 5–40. For similar results in constitutional theory, compare Miyazawa with Edward S. Corwin. Miyazawa develops a systematic state theory, while Corwin's constitutional theory flows out of legal history and case law and is not highly systematized. See Edward S. Corwin, The 'Higher Law' Background of American Constitutional Law (Ithaca: Cornell University Press, 1959), and idem., The Constitution and What it Means Today, ed. Harold W. Chase and Craig R. Ducat (Princeton: Princeton University Press, 1973). Among recent American discussions of the public interest as theory, Carl Friedrich, ed., The Public Interest (New York: Atherton, 1962), and Richard Flathman, The Public Interest (Chicago: University of Chicago Press, 1966).

10. See Jurisuto ("The Jurist") (Tokyo: Yūhikaku, 1970), special issue concerning kōkyō no fukushi.

11. For Japanese public opinion on rights questions, see, for example: Japan, Office of the Prime Minister, Information Section, "Some Materials of Public Opinion Census," January, 1963, which was prepared for the Commission on the Constitution, concerning which see the following periodicals: 419 Horitsu Jiho 363 (1964), 303 Jurisuto 10 (1964), and Journal of Asian Studies, 24:3 (1965). See also, Nobuyoshi Ashibe, "Consciousness of Human Rights and Problems of Equality," in Hiroshi Ito, ed., Japanese Politics: An Inside View (Ithaca: Cornell University Press, 1973).

12. Hajime Nakamura, Ways of Thinking of Eastern Peoples (Honolulu: East-West Center Press, 1964), p. 407. Chie Nakane, Japanese Society (Berkeley: University of California Press, 1970). Y. Scott Matsumoto, Contemporary Japan: The Individual and the Group (Philadelphia: American Philosophical Society, 1960); Kazuko Tsurumi Social Change and the Individual: Japan before and after Defeat in World War II (Princeton: Princeton University Press, 1970).

13. The imperial family is now a model nuclear family to many Japanese. For poll data, see Lawrence W. Beer, "Japan Turning the Corner," Asian Survey (January 1971), pp. 74–75. The persistence and depth of Japanese loyalty, as Ryuichi Nagao notes in a discussion of Hozumi, has been a block to understanding Japan: 5 Law in Japan: An Annual 209 (1973);

14. Dan Fenno Henderson, Conciliation and Japanese Law: Tokugawa and Modern, 2 vols. (Seattle: University of Washington Press, 1965), Dan Fenno Henderson, "Law and Political Modernization in Japan," in Ward, Political Development, pp. 387–456; and more generally, Burton M. Leiser, Custom, Law and Morality: Conflict and Continuity in Social Behavior (Garden City, N.Y.: Doubleday-Anchor, 1969).

15. Particularly useful sources on Japan and social change are Nakane, Japanese Society; Takeo Doi, The Anatomy of Dependence, trans. John Bester (Tokyo: Kodansha International, 1973); Chikio Hayashi et al., Nipponjin No Kokuminsei (A Study of Japanese National Character), vol. 2 (Tokyo: Institute of Statistical Mathematics and Shiseido, 1970) which contains surveys conducted every five years; Japan Regional Development Center, ed., Nihonjin No Kachikan ("The Sense of Values of the Japanese People"), (Tokyo: Shiseido, 1970); and Gekkan Seron Chosa ("Opinion Research Monthly") (Tokyo: Finance Ministry Printing Office, from 1969). Good descriptive studies are Ronald Dore, City Life in Japan (Berkeley: University of California Press, 1965); James Abegglen, The Japanese

Factory (Glencoe, Ill.: Free Press, 1958). See also Robert E. Ward, ed., *Political Development in Modern Japan* (Princeton: Princeton University Press, 1968); Nobutaka Ike, *The Beginnings of Political Democracy in Japan* (Baltimore: The Johns Hopkins University Press, 1950); Masao Maruyama, *Thought and Behavior in Modern Japanese Politics,* ed. Iram Morris (New York: Oxford University Press, 1969); George Totten, *Socialist Movements in Prewar Japan* (New Haven: Yale University Press, 1967); Robert Scalapino, *The Japanese Communist Movement, 1920–1966* (Berkeley: University of California Press, 1967).

16. Nakane, *Japanese Society,* p. 147 and pp. 42–44: "The *kobun* receives benefits or help from his *oyabun,* such as assistance in securing employment or promotion, and advice on the occasion of important decision-making. The *kobun,* in turn, is ready to offer his services whenever the *oyabun* requires them."

17. Takeo Doi, *Anatomy of Dependence,* pp. 8–9.

18. Ibid., pp. 84–87.

19. This emphasis in America is sometimes read into Japanese ideals, as when an author judges Japan should develop "the aggressive individualism required for effective citizenship in a democracy." H. Quigley and J. Turner, *The New Japan* (Minneapolis: University of Minnesota Press, 1956), p. 175. See also, T. Kawashima and R. Wargo, "Symposium on Law and Morality: East and West," *Philosophy East and West,* October 1971, pp. 493–511.

20. Henderson, *Conciliation;* Takeyoshi Kawashima, "Dispute Resolution in Japan," in Von Mehren, *Law in Japan,* pp. 41–72; and idem., *Nihonjin No Hōishiki ("The Legal Consciousness of the Japanese")* (Tokyo: Iwanani Shoren, 1967).

21. Kahei Rokumoto, "Problems and Methodology of Study of Civil Disputes (1)," trans. Tōru Mori 5 *Law in Japan: An Annual* 109 (1973).

22. While there is very little police brutality in Japan, extended detention before indictment, and pressure to confess is a problem at times. Before indictment, one has no right to bail or to a public defender.

23. Doi, *Anatomy of Dependence,* pp. 84–87.

24. Carmen Blacker, *The Japanese Enlightenment* (Cambridge: Harvard University Press, 1964), p. 105; and Kawashima, *supra,* n. 45.

25. Nakane, *Japanese Society,* pp. 33–35.

26. One example of limited influence of authorities is the *ringisei* system whereby lower bureaucrats in government and business "pile up" seals of approval before a superior sees a proposal. See Kiyoaki Tsuji, "Decision-Making in the Japanese Government," in Ward, *Political Development,* pp. 457–76.

27. Nakane, *Japanese Society,* p. 150.

28. Beer, "Freedom of Information," pp. 1119–20 and n. 2; Richard Halloran, *Japan: Images and Realities* (New York: Alfred Knopf, 1969), pp. 159–84.

29. See Beer, *"Defamation, Privacy, and Freedom,"* pp. 194–96; K. Igarashi & H. Tamiya, *Meiyo To Puraibashi ("Reputation and Privacy")* (Tokyo: Yūhikaku, 1968), pp. 204–16, 269–77, 290–96; for a more recent case, see *Asahi Shimbun* (evening edition), March 24, 1970.

30. Ibid., July 29, 1973; *Japan Times,* July 31, 1973. The survey was conducted in October and November, 1972, by the Prime Minister's Office, in the United States, Britain, West Germany, France, Switzerland, Sweden, Yugoslavia, India, Brazil and the Philippines.

31. Concerning *taijin kyōfu* ("anxiety in dealing with other people"), see Doi, *Anatomy of Dependence,* pp. 104–9.

32. H. Fukui, *Party in Power: The Japanese Liberal-Democrats* (Berkeley: University of California Press, 1970); R. Scalapino and J. Masumi, *Parties and Politics in Contemporary Japan* (Berkeley: University of California Press, 1962).

33. Concerning *seisan kanri,* see K. Ishikawa, "The Regulation of The Employee-Employer Relationship," in Von Mehren, *Law in Japan,* pp. 439–479.

34. David Sissons, trans., "Human Rights Under the Japanese Constitution," *Papers on Modern Japan* (Canberra: Australian National University, 1965), pp. 68–69.

35. Nakane, *Japanese Society,* p. 149.

36. For the flavor of prewar times, see David Titus, *Palace and Politics in Prewar Japan* (New York: Columbia University Press, 1974); Nobushige Hozumi, *Ancestor Worship and*

Japanese Law (Tokyo: Hokuseido Press, 1940); and Richard Minear, *Japanese Tradition and Western Law: Emperor, State and Law in the Thought of Yatsuka Hozumi* (Cambridge: Harvard University Press, 1970).

37. L. Beer, "Japan, 1969: 'My Homeism' and Political Struggle," 10 *Asian Survey* 43 (1970) and idem., "Japan Turning the Corner," 11 *Asian Survey* 74 (1971).

38. Beer, "Freedom of Information," pp. 1131–34.

39. Nakane, *Japanese Society,* p. 149.

40. Maki, *Court and Constitution,* p. 98.

41. See, in general, Okudaira, "The Japanese Supreme Court;" David J. Danelski, "The People and the Court in Japan" in *Frontiers of Judicial Research,* ed. J. Grossman and J. Tanenhaus (New York: John Wiley & Sons, 1969), pp. 45–72; Maki, *Court and Constitution,* n. 1. For a discussion of Supreme Court interpretive methodology, see Kenzo Takayanagi, "The Conceptual Background of the Constitutional Revision Debate in the Constitution Investigation Commission," 1 *Law in Japan: An Annual,* 1(1967). See also, Beer and Tomatsu, "Guide to Japanese Law."

42. Freedom of assembly is regulated under the *Dōro Kōtsūhō* ("Road Traffic Law"), art. 7 (law no. 105, 1960); *Densembyō Yobōhō* ("Communicable Disease Prevention Law"), art. 19 (law no. 36, 1897); *Hakai Katsudō Bōshihō* ("Subversive Activities Prevention Law"), art. 5, 7 (law no. 240, 1952); *Keihō* ("Penal Code"), art. 106, 107; *Kokumin Kōen Kanri Kisoku* ("National Public Park Regulations"), art. 4 (Ministry of Welfare Order no. 19, 1949, *Official Gazette* (no. 938); and public safety ordinances. Concerning rights protection agencies, see T. Horiuchi, "The Civil Liberties Bureau of the Ministry of Justice and the System of Civil Liberties Commissioners," *Effective Realization of Civil and Political Rights at the National Level—Selected Studies* (New York: United Nations, 1968), pp. 51–92; *Jinken Hakusho* ("Human Rights White Paper"), Japan Bar Association (Tokyo: Nihon Hyoronsha, 1973); *Hanzai Hakusho* ("Crime White Paper") Ministry of Japan, Justice, Legal Affairs Research Office (Tokyo: Finance Ministry Printing Office, 1972). These latter sources provide detailed data on collective activities involving legal problems.

43. See Takashi Ebashi, "Kōan Jōrei Hanketsu no Dōkō" ("Trends in Judgments concerning Public Peace Ordinances"), 377 *Jurisuto* 66 (1967); ("*A Collection of the Main Points of Judicial Precedents concerning Public Safety Ordinances*") Secretariat of the Supreme Court, Japan, "*Kōan Kōrei Kankei Saibanrei Yōshishū*" (Tokyo: August, 1968, by courtesy of Justice Toshio Iriye.)

44. Concerning the applicability of public safety ordinances to university campus activities, see *Tokyo Public Prosecutor v. Senda* (the so-called *Popolo Case*), 17 *Keishu* 370 (1963). See "Daigaku no Jichi" ("University Autonomy"), *Horitsu Jiho,* special issue (1970), for background and for commentary on the 1968-70 university crisis; see also, Beer, "Japan, 1969," pp. 44–47; Y. Okudaira, "Daigaku to Keisatsu" ("The University and the Police"), 426 *Jurisuto* 63 (1969). In the early 1950s the Education Ministry, after consultation with the Tokyo police, notified universities of the policy with respect to collective activities on campus and the Tokyo ordinance, to the effect that in some cases permits would not be needed, and that police would enter campus only at the president's request. With the university crisis of the late 1960s came erosion of this guideline so as to allow campus intervention without the university president's request. H. Tomatsu, "University Autonomy in Japan" (Seminar paper, University of Colorado, May 1973).

45. Okudaira, "The Japanese Supreme Court," pp. 83–94; Sato, *Constitutional Studies.*

46. Concerning the May Day case, see Sakae Wagatsuma, ed., "Mē Dē Jiken" ("The May Day Case"), 446 *Jurisuto,* (1970); Jiho, "Chian to Jinken;" Beer, "Japan Turning the Corner," p. 78. *Asahi Shiumbun* (evening ed.), Nov. 21, 1972, and *Japan Times,* Nov. 22, 1972, tell of acquittal by a Tokyo High Court judgment of 84 out of the 100 persons who appealed district court conviction, and reversal of convictions for the "crime of riot" (*sōranzai*).

47. *Sohyo v. Minister of Welfare* 7 *Minshu* 1561 (1953). See K. Hashimoto, "The Rule of Law: Some Aspects of Judicial Review of Administrative Action," in Von Mehren, *Law in Japan,* pp. 239–273.

48. In 1967, a Tokyo district court indicated a remedy when it issued an injunction against the Tokyo Public Safety Commission for conditions it had imposed on a demonstra-

tion intended for the environs of the Diet. However, Prime Minister Eisaku Sato overrode the court, and a subsequent court decision quashed an appeal on grounds that the law legitimizing Sato's act was a political matter determined by the Diet. *Asahi Shimbun* (evening ed.), Sept. 27, 1969.

49. *Japan* v. *Yamaoka* 8 *Keishu* 1886 (1954), hereinafter cited as *Niigata*; see Maki, *Court and Constitution*, p. 70, for a translation.

50. Ibid.

51. Ibid., pp. 70–78. See Ebashi, "Public Peace Ordinances," concerning debate.

52. Maki, *Court and Constitution*, pp. 79–82, 92–97.

53. Ibid., pp. *xxii–xxix;* Okudaira, "The Japanese Supreme Court," pp. 74–80. There are fifteen justices on the grand bench, who divide into three petty benches. See especially Japan, Supreme Court, *Saibanshohō ("Court Organization Law")* no. 59, 1947. Under article 10, a petty bench cannot rule contrary to grand bench constitutional doctrine. See also Japan, Supreme Court, "Rules Concerning the Conduct of Business."

54. *Japan* v. *Miyake*, 9 *Keishu* 119 (1955).

55. *Japan* v. *Sasaki*, 9 *Keishu* 967 (1955).

56. *Japan* v. *Kuroshiro*, 9 *Keishu* 562 (1955).

57. Concerning the Security Treaty crisis, see John M. Maki, *Government and Politics in Japan* (New York: Praeger, 1962); Scalapino and Masumi, *Parties and Politics;* and George Packard, *Protest in Tokyo* (Princeton: Princeton University Press, 1966).

58. Maki, *Court and Constitution*, p. 84.

59. *Japan* v. *Ito*, 14 *Keishu* 1243 (1960). See Maki, *Court and Constitution*, pp. 85–87, for text of the ordinance.

60. See Ebashi, "Public Peace Ordinances."

61. For example, the Supreme Court decisions on the Mie prefectural ordinance (Nov. 15, 1963), the Aichi prefectural and Nagoya city ordinances (Dec. 6, 1963), and the Tokyo ordinance (Mar. 3, 1966) upheld constitutionality under the article 31 due process clause. On Sept. 29, 1960, the 1950 Kyoto ordinance was held valid on its face in relation to article 21; 14 *Keishu* (no. 11) 1515 (1960).

62. *Japan* v. *Kayano* 20 Keishu 57 (1966).

63. See *Asahi Shimbun,* July 17, 1970, concerning a case involving a gathering to which the Tokyo ordinance is held not to apply because it was not a demonstration but "preparatory to" a demonstration; but the court also indirectly held the ordinance applicable to a commercial building, *viz.,* Haneda airport, for the first time, *Asahi Shimbun,* December 19, 1969. Some 300 dissenters had gathered to "see off" the prime minister on a controversial trip abroad.

64. 577 *Hanrei Jiho* 18 (1970).

65. Concerning recent decisions affecting workers' rights, see 536 *Jurisuto ("The Jurist"),* (Tokyo: Yūhikaku, 1973). Also Yoshiharu Tsujimoto, *Rōdō Hanrei Jiten ("Dictionary of Labor Decisions in the Courts")* (Tokyo: Romugyosei Kenkyujo, 1973); 33 *Koho Kenkyu ("Studies in Public Law"),* (Tokyo: Yūhikaku, for the Public Law Assn. of Japan, 1971). In restricting expression rights, the government and Supreme Court tend to place all types of public employees in the same category without reference to function, while unions do the same but think all instead of none should have full rights to political expression. See, for example, *Japan Times,* Apr. 26, 1973 and Sept. 29, 1973. In the spring of 1973, a railway workers' slowdown strike led to the first spontaneous explosion into violence of the unorganized public and, although no one was injured, train stations suffered substantial damage. Concerning the *Sarufutsu Decision,* see *Asahi Shimbun* (evening ed.) Nov. 4 and 6, 1974; and *The Japan Times,* Nov. 7, 1974.

66. See, for example, *Kempō Chōsakai Hōkokusho Fuzoku Bunsho (Report on Rights and Duties of the People and the Judiciary)* (Tokyo: Ōkurashō Insatsukyoku, 1964); *Kempō Mondai Kenkūkai, Constitutional Problems Study Society* (Tokyo: Iwanami Shoten, 1961); *Kempō o Ikasu Mono,* "Giving Life to the Constitution" (Tokyo: Iwanami Shoten, 1961).

67. See Wagatsuma, "Public Welfare," n. 10.

68. Dorothy Lee, *Freedom and Culture* (Englewood Cliffs, N.J.: Prentice–Hall, 1959), p. 53. The presuppositions described above are in harmony with, but also supplement, the

analysis of William Spinrad. He offers several sociological conclusions regarding conditions for maintaining individual rights in the United States. Three of his conclusions provide a useful basis for assessing also, or at least examining, the status and problems of freedom in Japan. His first conclusion is that, although a general adherence in society to the principle of freedom and to supportive convictions is essential, the maintenance of the desire for dissent is even more important. In Japan, this first need is met by the general support for constitutional values and the persistence of political conflict. Second, Spinrad analyzes the political factor. "Serious conflict," he writes, "especially if it poses any question of legitimacies and intense value conflict, . . . may spur suppressions." But conflict is necessary to encourage freedom of expression by arousing people's interest, and it is more likely to have adequate outlets in a large and complex society such as Japan. Spinrad continues: "The tyranny of a 'small government' can be more complete than that of a large body, for it may provide less of an option for either pluralistic insulation or pluralistic conflict. . . . Civil liberties . . . rest on competitive politics and the rules for their operation." Although the government is assumed to be the most frequent threat to freedom in the Japanese political rhetoric, the "small government" of the in-group in the social system seems to present greater problems. Third, Spinrad comments on the law. Formalized and just legal structures are essential because they are clear and predictable, and "never a carbon-copy reflection of the libertarian or anti-libertarian attitudes of politicians or any general public consensus." This condition also is met in Japan, which has an independent judiciary generally favorably inclined towards liberalism. See William Spinrad, *Civil Liberties* (Chicago: Quadrangle Books, 1970), pp. 5–26, 292–306.

Chapter 5   THE RIGHT OF PRIVACY IN THE UNITED STATES, GREAT BRITAIN, AND INDIA

E. Jeremy Hutton,
Krishan S. Nehra, and
Durvasula S. Sastri*

As newspapers the world over almost daily attest, privacy is fragile. It has only recently begun to come into its own as a legal right. This changing status reflects a response to social need. As Watergate revelations of "enemy lists", "national security" wiretaps, and burglaries have dramatized in the United States, the threats to privacy are of a serious nature. The technology of surveillance has increased in sophistication to include the microphone secreted in a cocktail olive; the "emotional stress evaluator" to probe our innermost emotions; the message-carrying laser beam capable of piercing the thickest wall and transmitting information over the expanse of the continents. Technology, social needs, and cultural and political circumstances all have a bearing on the legal status of privacy. This essay examines how the laws of three countries have been and are being shaped to recognize privacy as a right and how these systems protect it.[1]

Privacy rights in the United States, Great Britain, and India supply an interesting range for comparison because of differences among them in terms of industrial and technological as well as constitutional development. If the existence of privacy safeguards depends upon the stimulus provided by some degree of threat, then the legal responses should be greatest in the United States, nearly as great in Britain, and nearly nonexistent in India, because the level of technological and economic development of India, compared to the other two countries, does not establish the conditions necessary for the legal safeguard of privacy rights. A casual student of Indian law might conclude that the right of privacy is unknown except for a few isolated instances in that system. Nevertheless, an alternative conclusion is in order. Privacy as a basic human right touches upon fundamental needs and values associated with man's gregarious nature. Certainly the level of technological and economic development creates pressures

---

* The views expressed are those of the authors and do not necessarily reflect those of the Congressional Research Service or the Library of Congress.

to protect these privacy values through legal enforcement techniques. But even in the absence of such development, the value of and the basic human right to privacy may prevail irrespective of legal recognition. On the other hand, active claims for legal enforcement of the right seem to have a very direct relationship to the degree of threat posed to its survival. Certainly this relationship holds at the level of legal development, and it supports the thesis that human rights such as privacy, although recognized by laws, are enforced only when the danger to underlying values is perceived. The values, themselves, may also be shared and implied in cultural norms, but often they are not articulated as legal norms until threatened.

The three countries reviewed here provide contrasts in the manner in which their basic charters of government have been formulated and, more importantly, in the ways in which power flows to government. The United States government was created as one of limited powers, with certain functions enumerated in a basic charter reserved to the federal government, and with the remainder delegated to the states unless specifically prohibited to them. Individual rights are not given by the Constitution; they result indirectly from restrictions on the federal government which have been applied to the states through incorporation in the fourteenth amendment to the Constitution. Thus, the first amendment does not give anyone freedom of speech, it merely prohibits Congress from passing any law "abridging the freedom of speech," and the fourteenth amendment applies the same limitation to the states. With the focus on limiting government, an American's legal rights are uninvolved if hecklers interfere with his delivery of a speech unless they are recruited by the government.

The British Constitution, by contrast, is unwritten. Governmental structure, limitations on political powers, and enumeration of the rights of Her Majesty's subjects depend upon centuries of custom and tradition developed from court decisions and statutory law which form the ever-evolving common law. With the overriding principle of parliamentary supremacy prevailing, British constitutional law is easy to change legally, but difficult to document. The chief barrier to the erosion of rights lies in custom. Thus, in Britain, human rights, including privacy, are more a matter of tradition, education, and everyday behavior than of constitutional guarantees.

India's Constitution is a lengthy and comprehensive document which, unlike the U. S. Constitution, was designed to prescribe all individual rights and powers. Coming nearly two centuries after the American innovation of a written constitution, and after more than one and one-half centuries of experience with British rule, the Indian Constitution has a hybrid quality. Its language resembles that of the U.S. Constitution, but the process of constitutional interpretation in India has not yet involved use of the document as an outline from which additional powers can be implied and from which individual rights evolve. The Supreme Court of India has not yet adopted the philosophy of Bishop Hoadly who preached that "whoever hath an *absolute authority* to *interpret* any written or spoken laws, it is *he* who is truely the Law-Giver to all interests and purposes, and not the person who first wrote or spoke them."[2]

Since the primary thrust of any study on human rights should track the relationship of the individual to the state, the analysis is less concerned with tort remedies that private citizens have against one another than with governmental intrusions upon individual privacy. Where little public law has been developed in the area of privacy rights, we survey remedies to find hints of what developments may occur in the future in the public sector.

PRIVACY RIGHTS IN THE UNITED STATES

Origins of the right of privacy. Recent U. S. Supreme Court decisions establish the existence of a constitutional right of privacy. Nevertheless, the origins, dimensions, and effects of legal privacy claims are mired in controversy. Credit for fathering the concept has been attributed to such a diverse set of historical figures as John Locke, Thomas Cooley, Louis Brandeis, Samuel Warren, and William O. Douglas. Professor Alan F. Westin is one of the leading advocates of the position that the value of privacy was fully appreciated by the eighteenth century framers who intended to constitutionalize it in the Bill of Rights, for example, in the first amendment on free expression, the third amendment limiting the quartering of soldiers, and the fourth amendment banning unreasonable searches and seizures. Westin ably shows the influence of John Locke's writings by defining the context for privacy in a republican political system.[3]

Since colonial times, doctrines of immunity for certain forms of privileged communications have received recognition, including those between husband and wife and attorney and client. Other forms of communications that have received privileged status by statute or case law later in American legal development include those between priest and penitent and between physician and patient. The privacy of the mails received official sanction by an act of Congress in 1872, which prohibited any postal employee from opening another person's letters while they were being transmitted in the mail. In 1925 the prohibition was extended to all persons.[4] No provision was made in these early statutes for a court order to permit government officials to open the mail. Even when the possibility of surreptitious intelligence gathering increased with the invention of the telegraph immediately prior to the Civil War, American law showed adequate flexibility to deal with the new privacy threats. Many states enacted laws to prohibit the cutting or tapping of telegraph lines or the interception of telegraph messages.

Privacy in the nineteenth century was a prized value which was relatively easy to protect in the wide open spaces of steadily expanding American frontiers. Given the relatively weak influence of government upon the daily life of the frontier citizen, the threat to privacy originated largely from private sources: a prying sensationalist press, puritanical religious authorities, corporations worried about labor activities, and the like. Nevertheless, in Westin's judgment, "American law controlled surveillance in this pre-technological era in a way that continental regimes in the Roman Law-authoritarian tradition did not."[5]

Judge Thomas Cooley probably did more than any other single person in the period after the Civil War to advance the idea that there was a constitutional right of privacy. Cooley saw the two foundations of personal liberty as the "immunity in [one's] home against the prying eyes of government" and prohibitions against "arbitrary control of the person." In his work on torts (1888), he developed the phrase "the right to be let alone"[6] which formed the basis for Louis Brandeis's influential argument in support of a common law right of privacy two years later.

Samuel D. Warren and Louis D. Brandeis are most often credited with "discovering" the right to privacy. In 1890, the two wrote an article in the *Harvard Law Review,* "The Right to Privacy."[7] It was partly inspired by Brandeis's annoyance at the intrusion of the Boston press into his social life. The article examined a number of defamation, implied contract, breach of confidence, and other cases in which relief had been afforded. The conclusion was that, rather than being based on some property right, these cases were based on the broader concept of a right to privacy which Brandeis felt should receive separate legal recognition. The article had a significant impact on the area of tort law in which no American or English court had, up to that time, granted relief solely on the basis of any claim to privacy rights. By 1970, according to Dean William Prosser, "all but a very few jurisdictions" had come to recognize the right to privacy as a broad tort concept. Using Brandeis-style analysis, Prosser identifies four distinct kinds of personal invasion for which the only attributable commonality is the plaintiff's right to be let alone. These torts include: "intrusion upon the plaintiff's physical solitude or seclusion," the unwarranted "public disclosure of private facts," publicity which "places the plaintiff in a false light in the public eye," and "appropriation for the defendant's benefit or advantage, of plaintiff's name or likeness."[8]

The tort "right to privacy" is formally grounded on traditional concepts of contract, trespass, or defamation of character. It is likely that courts would have difficulty in applying these concepts to nonphysical trespasses on a person's privacy such as occur when statistics and facts about individuals are stored in computer data banks. Under traditional concepts, the mere compilation of such knowledge would not form the basis for asserting that probable harm has been done. Indeed, the subject of such files might not even be aware of their existence. But faced with the realities of modern urbanized living and the technological and communications revolutions which more closely than ever link the maintenance of individual freedom and privacy, the courts have been groping toward new legal concepts of privacy that go beyond those traditionally associated with the private law of torts.

Early cases involving privacy rights. Prior to 1965, references were frequently made to "privacy" or the "right to privacy," but these phrases were used as little more than flourishes of rhetoric. They added nothing to already existing rights. Legal researchers could look in vain for a case the outcome of which rested strictly upon privacy concepts. Not surprisingly, most references to privacy have occurred in fourth amendment litigation. In declaring the right of all "to be secure in their persons, houses, papers and effects, against unreasonable searches and seizures," the Constitution provides the primary support for a privacy right. *Boyd* v. *United States* particularly shows that the Supreme Court, as early as 1885, recognized privacy as the underlying principle of the fourth amendment prohibition against unlawful searches and seizures.[9] Writing for the Court, Justice Bradley recognized a concern for privacy as being part of our heritage of British common law. He wrote that the applicable principles (where Boyd's complaint about the government seizure of personal papers was concerned) "affect the very essence of constitutional liberty and security." Bradley said that: "It is not the breaking of his doors and the rummaging of his drawers that constitutes the essence of the offence; but it is the invasion of his indefeasible right of personal security, personal liberty and private property, when that right has never been forfeited by his conviction of some public offense—it is the invasion of this sacred right which underlies and constitutes the essence of . . . the Fourth and Fifth Amendments to the Constitution."[10]

Despite the use of such broad language in the nineteenth century, further constitutional development was slow. Use of the fourth amendment as a vehicle for the right of privacy was inhibited in the 1920s because of the heavy reliance placed on it by bootleggers during Prohibition. Law is never created in a vacuum, and the interpretation of law, like the making of it, is shaped by the pressures and prejudices of the times. During the 1920s much "bad" law was written by judges anxious to support the "noble experiment." In particular, Chief Justice Taft narrowed the fourth amendment to assist federal agents in keeping America dry.[11] The high point of his fight for prohibition came in the Court opinion in *Olmstead* v. *United States.*[12] There Taft condoned obtaining incriminating evidence through the tapping of telephones even though no provision of law or court order authorized it. It took over forty years for the Supreme Court to overrule completely this unfortunate precedent. In the meantime, the sophisticated bugging, eavesdropping, and wiretapping devices that so plague us today were perfected without the deterring effect that a different result in *Olmstead* might have achieved. Justice Brandeis's famous dissent warned that wiretapping represented a serious threat against privacy under the fourth amendment. Had he been heeded by a majority of the Court, the most serious invasion against privacy might have been uprooted in its infancy. But in 1928, the Supreme Court gave the fourth amendment a narrow, technical reading which precluded development of a comprehensive right of privacy for decades. The fourth amendment was seen as protecting individuals from only one type of intrusion on their privacy—the trespass or physical intrusion into a house with seizure of material objects.

Justice Brandeis's dissent is more renowned than the opinion written by Chief Justice Taft because it is more enduring and creative. Brandeis gave privacy rights their first recognition as a separate constitutional principle and their first comprehensive description. He credited the framers of the Constitution as having conferred, as against the government, "the right to be left alone—the most comprehensive of rights and the right most valued by civilized men." Brandeis concluded: "To protect that right, every unjustifiable intrusion by the government upon the privacy of the individual, whatever the means employed, must be deemed a violation of the Fourth Amendment."[13]

In the area of traditional searches and seizures, the Supreme Court has had little trouble in recognizing a right of privacy as the underlying interest protected by the fourth amendment. With *Wolf* v. *Colorado*,[14] the Court extended the federal right against unreasonable search and seizure to the states through the fourteenth amendment. Justice Frankfurter's opinion of the Court then recognized "the security of one's privacy against arbitrary intrusion by the police" as being "at the core of the Fourth Amendment" and "therefore implicit in 'the concept of ordered liberty.' "[15] Over the vigorous dissent of Justices Douglas, Murphy, and Rutledge, the Court left the states free to accept the federal exclusionary rule, first articulated in *Weeks* v. *United States*,[16] or reject it. That rule barred from federal trials all evidence obtained through illegal search and seizure.

Wolf was overruled seven years later by *Mapp* v. *Ohio*,[17] a decision that clearly equated the fourth amendment with the right of privacy. The appellant's conviction for possession of pornographic materials resulted from evidence seized by police who forcefully entered her apartment, apparently without a search warrant. The police had claimed to be looking for a bombing suspect and, in the course of an intensive search through the premises, which included a search of personal papers, had handcuffed the appellant and barred her attorney from entering. In his opinion for the Court, Justice Clark found that *Wolf's* narrow construction of the exclusionary rule was based on the Court's realization that two-thirds of the states were opposed to that rule. In reversing the *Wolf* rule, the Court recognized that over one-half of the states had then adopted the exclusionary rule and gave the right of privacy its strongest fourth amendment victory. He specifically found that the fourth amendment declared a "right of privacy" that would have to be enforced against the states through the due process clause of the fourteenth amendment or else "state invasions of privacy would be so ephemeral . . . as not to merit this Court's high regard as a freedom 'implicit in the concept of ordered liberty.' "[18]

If the "right of privacy" is to be nothing more than a shorthand expression for restrictions against unreasonable searches and seizures, other sources must be found beyond the fourth amendment. Without broader applications of privacy concepts extending beyond traditional unlawful entry, this new constitutional right would have no reason for existence because its protections would not be any greater than those provided by the fourth amendment. Justice Brandeis was the first Supreme Court Justice to suggest that the first amendment had privacy as an underlying concern. When the plaintiff in *Gilbert* v. *Minnesota*[19] was convicted of violating a state law that made advocacy of nonenlistment in the armed forces a crime, Brandeis's dissenting opinion noted that the statute was not limited to public teaching but could extend into the home with effects upon the relationship of parent and child and upon their religious beliefs, thus creating an invasion of the privacy of the home. In a series of cases involving the National Association for the Advancement of Colored People, the Court has found privacy to form a basis for first amendment freedom of association and assembly protections. Where state laws required the NAACP to provide officials with membership lists, the Court held that "inviolability of privacy in group association may, in many circumstances be indispensable to preservation of freedom of association particularly where a group espouses dissident beliefs."[20]

While the first amendment does appear to provide a secondary source for a right to privacy, it should be noted that, prior to 1965, the amendment's status as a privacy safeguard had been recognized only when the particular privacy-related right was also protected by legislation. Thus the individual right of privacy is protected from the "loud and raucous" noise of loudspeakers when the person is at home where the legislature has barred such disturbances, but not from music or speech broadcast in a public bus where no ordinance prohibited the private corporation from providing music.[21]

New scope for the right of privacy. As the early record of the search for a right of privacy indicates, the Constitution alone, as interpreted by the Supreme Court prior to 1965, offered little protection to the privacy of the individual. But social need outpaced the law as modern science and technology increased the powers of government to manipulate or interfere in the lives of individuals to an extent not thought possible at the inception of our republic.

Griswold v. *Connecticut* gave privacy its first and greatest recognition as a constitutional limitation on the power of both state and federal government to interfere in the lives of individuals.[22] In writing the opinion for the Court, Justice Douglas found a right mentioned nowhere in the Constitution to be a peripheral right, just as freedom of association was earlier found to be a right peripherally protected by the first amendment.[23] For the first time, the Court found the right of privacy to be of sufficient importance to overturn a state law, that is, a Connecticut law prohibiting sale or distribution of contraceptives to any person. The unique nature of the *Griswold* decision is more apparent when we realize that the Court did not have to create a new right to overturn the oft-attacked 1879 statute and could have reached the same result on more traditional grounds. In fact, the appellant's brief devoted only ten out of one hundred pages to the right of privacy, the least documented section of the brief.

Griswold's attorneys centered their argument on the contention that the law violated the due process clause of the fourteenth amendment, because it was not reasonably related to a legitimate legislative purpose, and was otherwise unreasonable, arbitrary, and capricious. The brief also contended that by prohibiting instruction in birth control methods, the statute violated the first and fourteenth amendments by abridging freedom of speech.[24] Privacy contentions had been dismissed by the appellee's brief in a sentence[25] that relied on the Connecticut appellate division's decision that there was "no invasion of anyone's privacy in this case."[26] The Connecticut supreme court of errors had not even considered the issue of privacy but had unanimously found the contested statute to be a legitimate exercise of the legislature's police power to "conserve" the public health and morals.[27]

In his opinion for the Court in *Griswold,* Justice Douglas went a step beyond the incorporation theory of Justice Black. The latter had looked to the written guarantees of the first eight amendments for explicit definition of the liberty and due process provision of the fourteenth amendment. Although Douglas examined the wording of the Bill of Rights to define the liberties of state and federal citizens, in *Griswold* he found that these amendments mean more than they specifically say. For the first time, the Court found the right of privacy to be a substantial constitutional right formulated not by any one amendment but by the specific guarantees of at least five amendments (the first, third, fourth, fifth, and ninth) that "have penumbras, formed by emanations from those guarantees that help give them life and substance.... Various guarantees create zones for privacy."[28]

Perhaps the most surprising aspect of *Griswold* was its use of the ninth amendment as an important source of the right of privacy. Justice Goldberg, joined by Chief Justice Warren and Justice Brennan, wrote a concurring opinion, "to emphasize the relevance of that [the ninth] Amendment to the Court's holding."[29] It is arguable, and apparently three members of the Court were willing to take the view in *Griswold,* that the framers intended the court to use the ninth amendment, if necessary, "as a declaration, should the need for it arise, that the people had other rights than those enumerated in the first eight amendments."[30]

Justice Black was most critical of the newly created right of privacy and of the process by which it was created, warning that its creation actually detracted from the protections provided by the Bill of Rights. He wrote: "The Court talks about a constitutional right of privacy as though there is some constitutional provision or provisions forbidding any law ever to be passed which might abridge the privacy of individuals. But there is not."[31] Justice Black's complaint emphasized that "one of the most effective ways of diluting or expanding a constitutionally protected right is to substitute for the crucial word or words of a constitutional guarantee another word or words, more or less flexible and more or less restricted in meaning."[32] Justice Stewart also wrote a dissenting opinion in the case expressing the view that while the Connecticut statute seemed "silly" to him, he could not find any way that it violated the Constitution.

In Griswold's shadow. Has the Court been able through subsequent decisions to define the new right discovered in the *Birth Control Case?* The answer is still evolving. The greatest weakness of the *Griswold* opinion remains that, despite its broad language describing the sources and listing types of privacy protected by the Bill of Rights, the right itself is never defined. Although the Court appeared to be seeking a new constitutional right of possible broad application, its failure to define the right has tended to limit its application to cases involving similar circumstances.

The Supreme Court cases since *Griswold* have done little to define what privacy is but merely suggest factual situations in which related rights arise. When balanced against written constitutional guarantees, the penumbral right usually fares poorly, as, for example, in *Time, Inc.* v. *Hill,*[33] where the Court overturned a New York court's award of $30,000 in damages for invasion of privacy. Involved was a New York family, erroneously identified as the "real life" subjects of a play about a household invaded by escaped convicts. Justice Brennan for the Court held that the protections of the first amendment for speech and press barred application of the relevant New York privacy statute. Redress for false reports of matters of public interest should not be available in the absence of proof that the publication had been made with knowledge of its falsity or in reckless disregard of the truth. The opinion made only passing references to privacy through its recognition that "exposure of the self to others in varying degrees is a concomitant of life in a civilized community. The risk of this exposure is an essential incident of life in a society which places a primary value on freedom of speech and press."[34]

It was left to the dissenting opinion, written by Justice Fortas, with Chief Justice Warren and Justice Clark concurring, to defend the right of privacy as a constitutional right that could limit freedom of the press. The dissenters would have permitted Hill to recover under the New York statute because, "privacy . . . is a basic right. The States may, by appropriate legislation and within proper bounds, enact laws to vindicate that right."[35] Even Justice Douglas, turning against the right he had found so critical the year before, joined in a concurring opinion by Justice Black that warned against creating "by judicial fiat . . . a right of privacy equal to or superior to the right of a free press that the Constitution created."[36]

The area of conflict between pornography laws and the first amendment has provided the basis for some rhetoric concerning privacy. Nevertheless, cases fulfilling President Nixon's campaign promises to appoint a Court that would do something about pornography have so proscribed earlier decisions as to make them meaningless. In *Stanley* v. *Georgia,*[37] a state conviction for possession of pornographic materials (found during a search of Stanley's bedroom for book-making apparatus) was overturned on the basis that the first amendment prohibited making the mere private possession of pornographic materials a crime. Justice Marshall's opinion for the Court cited *Griswold* and Brandeis's dissent in *Olmstead* as the basis for the findings that such statutes would permit illegal intrusions into one's privacy: "Whatever may be the justification for other statutes regulating obscenity, we do not think they reach into the privacy of one's home." Justice Marshall concluded: "Whatever the power of the state to control public dissemination of ideas inimical to the public morality it cannot constitutionally premise legislation on the desirability of controlling a person's private thoughts."[38] In *United States* v. *Reidel,* the Court declared that, while a man may enjoy pornography in the privacy of his home, his right of privacy does not extend to the distributor or seller of these pornographic materials who may be prosecuted under state law for his activities.[39] When the Court was faced in the companion case to *Reidel, United States* v. *Thirty-Seven Photographs,*[40] with consideration of the conviction of a man who was prosecuted for bringing pornographic pictures into the country for private use with the possible intention of using some of them in an illustrated edition of the *Kama Sutra,* a majority of the Court affirmed his conviction. Only three justices, Burger, Brennan, and Blackmun, joined in Justice White's plurality opinion which would have had the effect of overruling *Stanley.* The right of privacy was found by these justices to be limited to a man's home and not to extend to a port of entry.

The "permissive" period of pornography was abruptly brought to an end on June 21, 1973, with five Supreme Court decisions upholding various state antipornography statutes and leaving determination of what is obscene to local authorities.[41] These decisions fulfilled the dissenters' fears in the *Case of the Thirty-Seven Photographs* and left the privacy right of *Stanley* hollow and meaningless. The convoluted legal result is that a person may read novels which might be considered obscene by his community or watch films in his home, but he may well have no legal way to acquire them.

Electronic eavesdropping. Berger v. New York was decided in 1967.[42] It struck down New York's eavesdropping statute which permitted law enforcement officers to obtain an *ex parte* order permitting eavesdropping devices to be used for up to two months. A showing was required of reasonable cause that evidence of a crime can be obtained in this manner, and specification was required of the person or persons whose conversations were to be overheard or recorded. The Court's opinion, written by Justice Clark, which appeared to be a reaffirmation of the existence of a right to privacy, found New York's statute to lack requirements for the officer seeking the order to specify with sufficient particularity the places to be searched or the evidence sought. The statute was also said to be too broad in its authorization of a two-month period for eavesdropping. The Court found this situation to be the equivalent of a series of intrusions, searches, and seizures pursuant to a single showing of probable cause. It could too easily lead to indiscriminate seizure of the conversations of all the persons who come into the area during the period, regardless of their connection with the crime under investigation. As a result of its failure to limit the surveillance powers of the police, the Supreme Court found New York's statute to be "too broad in its sweep resulting in a trespassory intrusion into a constitutionally protected area and . . . therefore, violative of the Fourth and Fourteenth Amendments."[43] Justice Douglas in his concurring opinion called "bugging" of conversations "the greatest of all invasions of privacy" because, unlike the traditional search, "the homeowner is completely unaware of the invasion of privacy,"[44] a factor which could violate the fifth amendment inasmuch as the subject could not be said to be voluntarily testifying against himself. Douglas clearly indicated his belief that no statute authorizing electronic surveillance could ever be constitutional.

Katz v. *United States* overruled the already eroded trespass doctrine of earlier years.[45] Further, it dispelled much of the gloom with which legislators and law enforcement officers had greeted language in *Berger* that many thought made any laws authorizing wiretapping or eavesdropping constitutionally impossible. And it appeared to refute assertions building since *Griswold* that there was a broad constitutional right of privacy.

The Court reversed a conviction for a gambling offense which had relied on evidence obtained from listening and recording devices attached to the outside of a public telephone booth. In overruling *Olmstead,* the Court rejected the concept that there are "constitutionally protected areas." As a result, the fact that the eavesdropping device did not penetrate the telephone booth surface or that the booth was a public telephone was of no constitutional significance. According to Justice Stewart, the fourth amendment "protects people, not places." He reasoned: "What a person knowingly exposes to the public, even in his home or office, is not a subject of Fourth Amendment protection. . . . But what he seeks to preserve as private, even in an area accessible to the public, may be constitutionally protected."[46]

In language narrowly construing the constitutional right of privacy, Justice Stewart's opinion for the Court rejected the concept that the fourth amendment could be translated into a general constitutional "right to privacy." That amendment protects individual privacy against certain kinds of governmental intrusion, Stewart said, and "its protections go further, and often have nothing to do with privacy at all." He concluded that "a person's general right to privacy—his right to be let alone by other people—is, like the protection of his property and of his very life, left largely to the law of the individual States."[47]

The Court, in language which encouraged Congress to authorize court-supervised wiretapping and electronic surveillance, indicated that the telephone booth "bugs" in the case were so limited as to be permissible if a duly authorized magistrate, informed of the need for the investigation, of the basis on which it was to proceed, and of the amount and degree of surveillance required, could have authorized it with safeguards to provide continuing judicial control.

But since no search warrant had been obtained, the resulting search had been illegal even if there was probable cause for making it. Prior judicial approval was found required for all searches, whether electronic or conventional, unless the situation fit within certain well-defined exceptions such as a search incident to an arrest or, possibly, in national security cases.

Justice Black's dissent criticized the Court for its attempts to "bring the Fourth Amendment up to date" by defining eavesdropping by electronic means as a "search" or "seizure." Black penned: "With this decision the Court has completed, I hope, its rewriting of the Fourth Amendment, which started only recently when the Court began referring incessantly to the Fourth Amendment not so much as a law against *unreasonable* searches and seizures as one to protect an individual's privacy."[48] Justice Black concluded his dissent with a warning that, by creating new rights that go beyond those specifically guaranteed by the Constitution, the Court was establishing itself as an "omnipotent lawmaking authority" and that "the history of governments proves that it is dangerous to freedom to repose such powers in courts."[49]

More recently, in *United States* v. *United States District Court,* the Court unanimously reversed the convictions of three defendants charged with bombing a CIA office in Michigan.[50] Fatally defective was the fact that wiretap evidence had been obtained through "national security" taps approved by the Attorney General but by no court, a practice apparently widespread during the first Nixon administration. Justice Powell's decision for the Court weighed the "Government's right to protect itself from unlawful subversion and attack" along with another interest. That is, "the citizen's right to be secure in his privacy against unreasonable Government intrusion." Powell found that, at least as far as domestic security investigations are concerned, privacy rights outweigh security interests, and the detached judgment of a neutral magistrate is still required by the fourth amendment.

Debate over the scope of privacy rights. In one of its most controversial cases, the Supreme Court found unconstitutional a Texas abortion statute which, like laws in force in most states, forbade procuring or attempting an abortion except "by medical advice for the purpose of saving the life of the mother." In *Roe* v. *Wade,* Justice Blackmun said that the state regulation violated the due process clause of the fourteenth amendment which was found to protect the right of privacy against state action.[51] The right of privacy was said to be the basis of a woman's qualified right to procure an abortion free from state interference during most of her pregnancy. As in the *Griswold* case, the Court appeared to go out of its way to reach the constitutional issue despite traditional theories of judicial restraint that usually preclude reaching of constitutional questions particularly when state law is involved. While finding privacy to be a "fundamental right," Justice Blackmun's decision for the Court did not clarify the definitional basis of that right. In some ways, the decision seemed to narrow the scope of the right by cataloguing "certain areas or zones of privacy."

The list of areas in which the right of privacy was found to have some application included marriage,[52] procreation,[53] contraception,[54] family relationships,[55] and child rearing and education.[56] Justice Blackmun concluded that the "right of privacy, whether it be founded in the Fourteenth Amendment's concept of personal liberty and restriction upon state action, as we feel it is, or, as the District Court determined in the Ninth Amendment's reservation of rights to the people, is broad enough to encompass a woman's decision whether or not to terminate her pregnancy."[57] Like written guarantees, privacy rights were found to be subject to limitation when they conflicted with a "compelling state interest." For the first trimester of pregnancy, the Court held the state can only regulate abortion procedures in a manner reasonably related to maternal health but must leave decisions relating to effectuation of an abortion to the woman and her physician. After that point, the state interest increases as the potentiality of human life increases until, in the last trimester, it can limit abortions to those cases in which it is medically necessary in order to preserve the life or health of the mother.

The cases in which the right to privacy has been controlling center predominantly in the area of contraception and abortion. If this trend continues, we may witness the limitation of constitutional privacy rights to mere marital privacy (thus providing little protection against governmental intrusion upon privacy interests not related to sex and family and not completely covered by other constitutional guarantees). The explanation for this development is to be found partly in judicial politics. *Roe* v. *Wade* and its companion case, *Doe* v. *Bolton*, demonstrate that the Supreme Court is divided over the question as to whether there is a constitutional right of privacy and, if it exists, what it means and from where it arises. Justice Stewart, in his concurring opinion in *Roe*, suggested that the right of privacy developed in *Griswold* was merely a device to avoid admitting reliance on the due process clause of the fourteenth amendment and the "substantive due process doctrine" which Justice Douglas had said in 1963 "could not be used to substitute the Court's social and economic beliefs for that of elected legislative bodies."[58] If Justice Stewart is correct that there is no right of privacy apart from traditional constitutional guarantees, then protection from many forms of invasion of privacy will have to come from legislative action rather than from the courts relying on existing constitutional prohibitions. Four examples at the federal level reflect this prospect.

First, the Privacy Act of 1974,[59] marked enactment of the first comprehensive law to regulate use of records of personal information collected and maintained by the federal government. This landmark legislation, which gives citizens the right to see and copy most records about them stored by federal agencies and the right to challenge and correct any inaccurate information, also prohibits nonroutine dissemination and disclosure of personally identifiable information, unless requested by or consented to by the file subject. Each federal agency is required to publish annual notices in the *Federal Register* as to the existence and nature of personal records maintained by it including a description of categories of individuals on whom records are maintained, the routine uses and users of the system, and procedures concerning access to and for correction of such records.

The Privacy Act also established a Privacy Protection Study Commission, prohibited sale of mailing lists by federal agencies, and prohibited denial of privileges or benefits by any governmental agency because of an individual's refusal to disclose his social security number, unless disclosure is specifically required by law or the system in question had been established prior to January 1, 1975. Violations of the Act are punishable by criminal penalties or by civil suits brought against the agency involved by persons adversely affected by Act violations.

Second, title 3 of the Omnibus Crime Control and Safe Streets Act of 1968[60] broke new ground by specifying criminal and civil sanctions against persons who engage in unauthorized wiretapping or electronic surveillance. More important, the Act significantly advances privacy interests by prohibiting virtually all electronic surveillance activities conducted without court authorization and under some degree of judicial control.

Third, the Fair Credit Reporting Act of 1970[61] marked the first attempt by the federal government to control the accuracy of investigative reports made on millions of Americans each year by credit reporting agencies. While the Act does not permit the report-subjects to see the contents of the actual dossier compiled on them, it does require notice to be given to the subjects of such reports. This step is mandated when the report forms part of the basis for denial of insurance, credit, or employment. Criminal and civil damages are available to report-subjects when the credit agency fails to make a reasonable effort to purge inaccurate information from the file. Bills, such as S.2360, 93rd Congress, have been introduced to require written authorization from the subject before an investigative report is begun, and upon completion, to supply him with a copy of the report at the expense of the agency.

Fourth, concern for the detrimental effects that unwarranted dissemination of criminal records can have on an individual's reputation and rights led to enactment of a floor amendment to the Crime Control Act of 1973. Affected are all state law enforcement agencies collecting, storing, or disseminating criminal history information through support received from the Law Enforcement Assistance Administration (LEAA). They must "assure that the security and privacy of all information is adequately provided for and that information shall only be used for law enforcement and criminal justice and other lawful purposes."[62] All LEAA research or statistical information identifiable to a specific private person is barred from use for any purpose other than that for which it was collected. Further, it is immune from legal process, and cannot be used in any judicial or administrative proceeding without the consent of the person furnishing the information. In view of the increasing reliance of all state law enforcement agencies on LEAA funds, this new requirement is likely to mark the first significant protection for computerized criminal records.

The rapid advances made by the Ninety-third Congress in the privacy area toward the end of its session indicate that Watergate, revelations of political surveillance by the F.B.I., and of possible misuse of tax returns by the Internal Revenue Service may have caused a consensus to form. With the resignation of President Nixon, the last barriers to bipartisan cooperation in this area appeared to have been removed and the demand for new laws to protect privacy reached a crescendo comparable to that achieved by environmental concerns a few years earlier.

In 1974 alone, more actions were taken to provide formal protection to privacy than had been achieved in all of the prior history of the United States. President Ford, who as vice-president had chaired a presidentially created Domestic Council Committee on the Right of Privacy, began his new administration with a pledge that, "There will be no illegal tappings, eavesdropping, bugging or break-ins by my Administration. There will be hot pursuit of tough laws to prevent illegal invasions of privacy in both government and private activities."[63] Shortly thereafter, he issued an executive order limiting White House access to income tax returns[64] and indicated interest in bills introduced in the Senate and House to provide more extensive restrictions on access to tax returns.[65] In addition to passage of the Privacy Act, Congress enacted the "Family Educational Rights and Privacy Act of 1974,"[66] which would deny federal funds to any educational institution that prevented parental access to a child's school records or permitted the release of a student's records without parental consent to anyone but another school official or in compliance with a court order. Among over 300 other privacy bills introduced in the Ninety-third Congress relating to privacy, serious consideration was given to a bill to establish rules on the use and dissemination of criminal records[67] and a bill to prohibit military surveillance of civilian activities.[68] At the end of the Ninety-third Congress, it appeared likely that the impetus which led to the first serious legislative and executive consideration of the consequences of technological, societal, and governmental developments on personal privacy would continue through future Congresses with the likely eventual enactment of law to deal with these difficult problems. In the long run, this is the only way that civil liberties can adequately be protected where sufficient informal protections do not exist.

It is a peculiarity of the American policy-making process that the Supreme Court is able to open new avenues of reform by posting directional markers reading "legal rights and liberties." But the more substantial work of smoothing the way for citizens to make use of their rights is often left for legislative follow-up. Of course, executive action and administrative policy also play a role which citizens expect to be constructive. Unfortunately, that has not always been the case; witness the assorted crimes assembled under the title of "Watergate." These politically motivated invasions of privacy and related scandals have damaged public trust and confidence in government. The "bill of complaints" against Watergate-style abuses has generated significant demands for a more secure right to privacy. Popularly esteemed rights and liberties often grow out of deeply felt complaints against very specific executive abuses. This was true of the English Bill of Rights of 1689 no less than the American Bill of Rights of 1791.

THE RIGHT OF PRIVACY IN GREAT BRITAIN

Recent review of government policy. British law recognizes no general right to privacy. Nevertheless, conditions now favor rapid legal development to restrict both public and private intrusions into areas where the individual's interest in protecting information about himself, or in being left alone, outweighs the public's need to know. Recent consideration of privacy legislation in Britain was initiated by a report on privacy and the law published in early 1970 by a Committee of Justice. This British section of the International Commission of Justice includes in its report a draft privacy bill. The bill would create a general legal right of privacy with a right of civil action by a person whose privacy has been infringed. A nearly identical bill was introduced earlier in Parliament by Brian Walden, and it received its second reading debate a week after publication of the Committee of Justice proposal. Also subject to civil suit under the bill would be a person who had knowingly been made a party to the infringement or who had knowingly made use of the infringement for his own benefit to the detriment of the object of the privacy infringement. The proposal, by specifically binding the crown, would authorize suits by private individuals against governmental officials responsible for unlawfully invading their privacy.

During debate on his bill, Walden credited studies in the United States as proving the need for privacy legislation and, after urging the government to forego further investigation on privacy matters, noted, "In America there is far more vogue for, and far more criticism of, the use of advanced technology for what the Justice Committee term 'spying prying, watching or besetting.' "[69] He said that, while industrial espionage was in its infancy in Britain as compared with the United States, the alleged bugging of many boardrooms should lead to prohibition of surreptitious use of bugging devices except for "reasonable" purposes and exclusion of conversations seized in civil actions.

Possibly because of its authorization of suits against the government, the bill was rejected by the Labor Government on its second reading. Public interest in the legislation was so great that Home Secretary James Callaghan appointed a Committee on Privacy, headed by Sir Kenneth Younger, to consider whether legislation of privacy was needed.[70] In establishing the Committee, however, he excluded the public sector from its consideration. Although the succeeding Conservative Government also barred the Younger Commission from considering governmental activities which might endanger privacy, the new home secretary,

Reginald Maulding, recognized that the government should carefully note "recommendations for the private sector in deciding what should be done about the public sector."[71] The 350-page report of the Younger Commission released in July, 1972, is controversial and vague in some of its recommendations. Still, it is enormously important. It is, no doubt, the most comprehensive study ever undertaken by a government on the problems of maintaining individual privacy in a modern, industrial society. The Commission considered written and oral evidence from interested organizations. It reviewed the growing literature on the subject and commissioned a public opinion survey to determine public attitudes toward and definitions of privacy. The laws restricting private intrusions on individual privacy in England and a number of other industrially advanced countries were also considered. The report gave comprehensive coverage to each of the following areas of privacy invasion: unwanted publicity, misuse of personal information including credit rating agencies, intrusions on home and business life, and modern technical developments.

Rather than create a general right of privacy to be balanced against competing public interests, (the course that the U. S. Supreme Court seems to be following) the report favored specific statutory or administrative remedies for specific problems. While leaving the citizen without legal remedy for some invasions of privacy not covered by law, the British approach supplies a more stable and certain body of law and precedent than found in the United States. Legislation was recommended to create new offenses where there were new threats to privacy, such as from new electronic surveillance devices, or to grant an individual access to information gathered and disseminated about him similar to the American credit reporting act. Additional administrative controls were supported, in other cases, over particular types of activities, such as credit rating agencies and private detectives. Reported abuses by the mass media, universities, industrial employers, and the medical profession were felt best handled by self-regulation.

The common-law tradition. At present, British law gives scattered protection to privacy through civil and criminal statutes and common law. As is true with statutory law in the United States, most of the provisions are primarily directed toward ensuring security or toward other goals but incidentally protect privacy too. Consider these three examples: First, trespass laws are primarily designed to protect personal property rights, but in keeping the uninvited off private land they insulate against unwanted physical intrusions on personal solitude and privacy. Trespass laws provide a civil remedy which is only partly reliable as a support to the value of privacy. A right of action for trespass exists only if the victim is the legal occupier of the violated property, and recovery is usually in the amount of damage actually caused by the trespass. The exact scope of damage is always difficult to assess, but if the aggressor's conduct is particularly heinous, "exemplary damages" are available, though they are seldom awarded. Second, privacy of words, drawings, or other matter reduced to writing can be protected by copyright law or, if publication has been restricted by agreement, by contract law. Once again, these laws are primarily designed to sustain property rights although privacy is also protected. Third, libel and slander laws, injurious falsehood and "passing off" (appropriation of a person's professional reputation at his expense) protect against falsehoods which do damage a person's reputation. British defamation laws are not as broad as those in the United States: they are more concerned with reputation than privacy.

Unlike the examples noted above, several British civil law remedies are more closely directed to privacy interests. The most effective is that involving breach of confidence. All specific and reasonably applied confidences are protected by laws providing damages for breach of confidence, except where disclosure of the information confidentially given is shown by the discloser to be in the public interest.[72] The Younger Commission felt that action for breach of confidence offered the greatest potential protection for privacy rights and urged that, instead of waiting for uncertain progress in this area through case law, confidence law be referred to the Law Commissions for clarification by drafting of a new statute. (The Law Commissions have authority similar to the Revision and Codification Subcommittees of the U. S. Senate and House of Representatives. However, the latter do not draft laws, they merely codify those laws enacted by Congress.)

In Britain, as in the United States, the limitations on public authority that most directly protect privacy interests are restrictions on searches and seizures of evidence by policemen. They are restrained by warrant requirements similar to those prevailing in the United States. That is, a search warrant may not be issued except by authorization of a magistrate after consideration of a law enforcement officer's sworn statement as to the reason a search is necessary. The warrant must specify the evidence expected to be seized and the necessary extent of the search. This required intervention of a neutral magistrate between the policeman and the object of his search places a brake on capricious police snooping. Use of the magistrate to determine whether the cause for the invasion of the suspect's privacy justifies the intrusion is part of the common law heritage which has been widely adopted among countries with a Commonwealth tradition and in the United States. Insistence on the warrant procedure traces back to the eighteenth century case of *Entick* v. *Carrington.*[73] The continuing significance of the case is lucidly attested by R. F. V. Heuston, a leading English constitutional law scholar. He writes: "If one case had to be chosen to illustrate more than any other the fundamental principles of English constitutional law, it would be this one. It is . . . the case to take to a desert island."[74] *Entick* v. *Carrington* laid down the proposition that an invasion of a person's liberty, as with any action by the government, can be justified only if authorized by statute or common law. Entick was suspected of editing a seditious publication. But since the sheriff could find no authority other than "long-standing practice of the Secretary of

State" for breaking and entering the plaintiff's house and seizing his books and papers, Entick was awarded £300. damages in his trespass action.

While English common-law tradition would appear to offer as much protection against physical invasion of privacy by governmental officials as in the United States, the absence of written constitutional restrictions to limit governmental arrest and search powers permits the government to seek suspension of usual search restrictions whenever a domestic or international crisis is deemed to make such a course necessary. Such broadening of search and seizure powers has been accomplished through regulations issued under authority of the Special Powers Act of 1922. It was designed to meet dangers posed by the Irish Rebellion. In Northern Ireland, British officers, operating under regulations issued by the Minister of Home Affairs, can order indefinite house arrest or internment of persons believed to have acted, or who are believed about to act, in a manner prejudicial to preservation of the peace. Arrest and searches without a warrant are also authorized in these circumstances. Under regulation 4 (introduced in June, 1954), members of the armed forces or police are authorized to enter houses or other buildings, if necessary, by force, day or night, to search for or seize anything thought to be kept or used in a manner "prejudicial to the preservation of peace or maintenance of order."

The power of the British Government to enact laws such as the Special Powers Act, which suspend normal privacy rights in periods of crisis, would appear to indicate that basic English privacy rights are somewhat more tenuous than those enjoyed under the American constitutional system. However, under the English system, the decision to suspend such liberties is associated with democratic processes of open discussion and parliamentary free debate. Since the Ellsberg break-in, Americans are less assured that the fourth amendment will not be violated whenever a President thinks that the national interest or national security requires it. While Americans believe that the Constitution precludes representatives from taking such actions without ratification of a constitutional amendment, they can no longer be certain of what actions are being taken in secret.

Government eavesdropping. The British executive authority has long claimed an absolute right to intercept letters carried in the royal mail. In fact, during the eighteenth century, the Bishop of Bath and Wells was designated as the chief government decoder. With the advent of modern technology, these claims were extended to cover telephone communications. The theories supporting governmental wiretapping and electronic eavesdropping are unclear and have been disputed in recent years. A special Committee of Privy Councilors in 1956 advanced two theories to support it.[75] The first theory is that the crown has a prerogative or discretionary power to intercept communications as part of its general power to protect the public welfare, limited only by its general power to protect the public interest. In support of this theory, it is said that a long series of statutes have by implication recognized this prerogative since 1710. Section 58(1) of the Postal Act, 1953, permits postal employees to open communications, but only upon express warrant of a Secretary of State. However, under section 9(1) of the Crown Proceedings Act, 1947, state authorities are exempted from liability for interruption of either postal or telephone communications.

Despite the long practice of governmental interceptions, the Special Committee observed that mere usage does not of itself create a discretionary power to make legal an act that would otherwise be illegal. Rather than rely on inherent governmental powers to justify wiretap or mail covers, they suggested that the finding of such a power may be unnecessary, insofar as the interception of messages involves no illegal acts. On this theory, a legal power is needed only if some legally protected rights of the subject are invaded. Since there is no general right of privacy, it is arguable that the subject of a governmental wiretap or seizure of mail has no right that is thereby violated. A 1957 decision of the Court of Appeal, *Triefur and Co.* v. *Post Office,*[76] held that services provided by the Postmaster General are not of a contractual nature. Nor apparently is a trespass committed on chattels because neither the person to whom a letter is sent nor the sender has possession of it. This is reinforced by postal regulations that prevent a person who has mailed a letter from retrieving it. The Younger Commission also adopts the attitude that there are no privacy rights invaded by wiretapping because in England, unlike the United States, telephone users do not regard their conversations as private:

People who use the telephone expect to be heard by the person they are talking to and they are also aware that there are several well understood possibilities of being overheard. A realistic person would not therefore rely on the telephone system to protect the confidence of what he says because, by using the telephone, he would have discarded a large measure of security for his private speech. He might accept these risks or consider them of no consequence.[77]

Until 1937, the General Post Office, which runs England's telephone system, assumed that it had the authority to intercept telephone communications without receiving approval from any other executive or judicial agency. In that year, the government decided, as a matter of policy, that no further interception of telephone calls should occur unless a warrant was first obtained from the Secretary of State for Home Affairs. It was not until 1951 that the Home Office issued a memorandum setting forth criteria for issuance of wiretap warrants: the offense involved would have to be serious, that is, involve a crime that would result in at least three years imprisonment or, if a customs offense, be a substantial and continuing fraud likely to damage the economy if unchecked; normal methods of investigation should have failed or reasonably seem unlikely to succeed; or be a case involving subversive or espionage activity likely to endanger the national interest. These standards were not enforced by legislation and were interpreted by executive rather than judicial officers. Since they were based on policy rather than constitutional compulsion, these advisory regulations are subject to suspension or repeal at any time.

The long-continuing practice of governmental wiretapping exempt from judicial safeguards did not remove the practice from controversy. Official wiretapping practice came in for parliamentary and public examination after an incident in 1956 demonstrated the danger that insufficiently regulated wiretapping can create for privacy interests. A barrister was under investigation for unprofessional conduct by the Bar Council. Among the charges under investigation by the Council was an allegation that the barrister had been improperly in direct telephone communication with a criminal suspect. The suspect was also under investigation by the police, who were intercepting all his telephone conversations, including those with the barrister. The Bar Council requested the transcripts of any telephone conversations held between the barrister and the criminal suspect. Even though the barrister was not suspected of any crime, the Home Secretary authorized release of the transcripts to the Bar Council which, on the basis of evidence contained in the conversations, disbarred the lawyer. As a result of public uproar over the incident, a distinguished Committee of Privy Councillors was established to investigate the extent to which governmental wiretapping could be justified. It was this Committee which formulated the two theories justifying wiretapping which have been discussed and it concluded that transcripts should not be released to persons outside the government and found the Home Secretary's action in the barrister's case "mistaken."[78] No objection was made to the continuing practice of issuance of wiretap warrants by the Home Secretary without judicial supervision. As a result, the government is left with almost unlimited power to intercept telephone conversations.

The lack of statutory controls on wiretapping or electronic eavesdropping in the public sector is matched by a similar lack of direct controls over wiretapping or bugging by private citizens or industry. If the use of such devices involves an unauthorized entry on the property of another, there may be an action in trespass. Of course, some sophisticated listening devices require no entry. Thus, the possibility of seeking a remedy through such an action becomes more remote. Also, since the property would have to belong to the person who would bring the trespass action, hotel rooms, apartments, or offices would usually be excluded from coverage.

The Wireless Telegraphy Act of 1949 approaches the problem by regulating the "emitting or receiving over paths which are not provided by any material substance constructed or arranged for that purpose of electro-magnetic energy." It provides criminal penalties for installing or using any device to transmit such wireless telegraphy signals without a license from the Minister of Posts and Telecommunications (formerly the Postmaster General). Section 5(b)(i) specifically prohibits use of wireless telegraphy to obtain the contents, sender, or addressee of a message, even if the message itself was not originally sent by radio, unless authorized by the Minister of Posts and Telecommunications.

Section 5(b)(ii), like section 605 of the United States Federal Communications Act of 1934, prohibits disclosure of information obtained through unauthorized means covered by section 5(b)(i). This Act does not limit possession or sale of such devices and does not cover wiretapping unless the message is transmitted beyond the telephone wire.

The Wireless Telegraphy Act of 1967, while primarily directed to protecting existing radio broadcast frequencies, could incidentally touch upon privacy interests. It gives the Minister of Posts and Telecommunications the power to make regulations to prohibit the unauthorized manufacture or importation of equipment transmitting over certain designated frequencies. The purpose is to prevent interference with the most heavily used broadcast frequencies.

Section 2 of the Post Office Act (Data Processing Service) is the first law to reach a new type of message interception—from data banks. This law, dated 1967, prohibits disclosure of information obtained by post office personnel from their data processing services. Since it covers only postal workers, it is a small, first step to protect the integrity of computerized data bases.

The only other act indirectly to restrict private wiretapping is section 13 of the Theft Act of 1968. It provides penalties for dishonestly using or causing electricity to be wasted or diverted without authority. One case has tied this statute to the telephone by holding it could be used as the basis of criminal penalties for making telephone calls without paying tolls.[79]

After viewing the British laws relating to wiretapping and electronic surveillance, we can see why the Younger Commission, upon completing a comparative survey of the privacy laws of the United States, France, Germany, Sweden, and Canada, concluded: "One general observation can be made with confidence: that Great Britain has less in its law aimed specifically at invasion of privacy than any other country whose law we have examined."[80]

The principal explanation for the lack of comprehensive legal regulation on behalf of privacy rights can readily be observed by any visitor to Great Britain: the British love and defense of privacy is internalized. Until recently, the Englishman has not felt the need to have his privacy protected by laws. The English citizen has been socialized from infancy to develop inner defenses with which to protect his thoughts. A cultivated personal reserve keeps him from prying into others' privacy or permitting intrusions into his own. He attains by self-restraint and reserve a standard of privacy which elsewhere can be secured only by doors, walls, and trespass rules. Drawing on the comparative cultural research of Edward Hall, Westin notes that, because English children in the middle and upper classes do not usually have separate rooms, but share the nursery with brothers and sisters until they go away to boarding school and live in dormitories, "the Englishman grows up with a concept of preserving his individual privacy within shared space rather than by solitary quarters. He learns to rely on reserve, on cues to others to leave him alone." Westin notes that English political and business figures do not have private offices: "members of

Parliament, for example, do not occupy individual offices, and they often meet their constituents on the terrace or in the lobbies of the House of Commons."[81] Where an American seeking privacy goes to a private room and shuts the door (using a "physical privacy screen"), an Englishman stops talking, and this signal for privacy is respected (by reliance on an "internalized privacy mechanism.")

It is not just the English character that has permitted the growth of a society in which laws are not necessary to protect privacy and other civil liberties. The internalized privacy mechanism is reinforced by the nature of the British society itself, that is, the relative homogeneity of the people and the high level of toleration which exists among classes. Westin describes this phenomenon well in terms of the "deferential democratic balance of British society." It is based on "England's situation as a small country with a relatively homogeneous population, strong family structure, surviving class system, positive public attitude toward government, and elite systems of education and government service." In Westin's view, this combination has produced a democracy balanced by high value attaching to personal privacy in the home and association, and a faith in governmental respect for privacy as well. Moreover, all of these relationships are affected by toleration for nonconformity.

Although ingrained norms tend to be enduring, they may undergo modification. The patterns and traditions of the past appear to be dissolving in the 1970s in Great Britain. Previously unwritten British civil liberties, always understood in the past, are currently under pressure from political, economic, and social changes. Since World War II, Britain has lost her empire; the arrival of waves of immigrants from her economically-deprived former colonies has led to the loss of cultural and ethnic homogeneity. Entry into the Common Market, thought by some to be the path to economic salvation, has been blamed by others for extraordinary inflation, higher taxes, coal workers' strikes and related power shortages. Theatrical productions such as *Room at the Top, Saturday Night and Sunday Morning* and *Look Back in Anger* suggest that many have begun to question the equity of the existing class system. And there are other accumulating developments which indicate an erosion of prized privacy values. Examples include, the trans-Channel tunnel plan which promises an invasion of continental trucks in rural Kent that represents a threat to national as well as individual privacy; disclosures that a newspaper used bugging techniques to obtain information about a sex scandal that led to the resignation of two ministers; and physicians at four Buckinghamshire hospitals who announced their refusal to cooperate in the building of a centralized data bank of confidential information about their patients. The list of such developments grows daily.[82]

Where social systems break down by erosion of understanding and mutual respect between classes and between the government and the governed, unwritten codes are threatened and must be reduced to writing to attempt to preserve something of the larger entity that is gone. For example, on July 17, 1973, when the House of Commons debated the Younger Commission Report, Home Affairs

Minister Robert Carr said that the security of privacy could no longer be taken for granted. He announced that the Government would propose legislation to enact many of the Commission recommendations. These included provisions for criminal and civil penalties for certain forms of surveillance, granting individuals access to credit information about themselves, and protection from harassment by collection agencies. It appears that increased perception of privacy threats may be leading to an accelerated pace of legislative development, as a result of the present dearth of laws specifically protecting privacy, toward a position of greater legal protection than now exists in the United States. But the correlation between the crises that are leading to that position makes one wonder if this change really marks progress in protection of civil liberties.

THE RIGHT OF PRIVACY IN INDIA

Historical perspective. Indian law, while resembling the forms of both American and British law insofar as protection of civil liberties is concerned, is somewhat alien to both of these systems. It reflects ancient Hindu and Mohammedan influences that predate British colonial rule. A lengthy Constitution, which provides detailed descriptions of the powers of the government and rights of the people shows concern for the difficult task of both governing a huge and diverse population and maintaining a democratic rule.[83] Pressures for survival in the face of famine, possible military invasion, and seemingly uncontrollable population growth present problems of an order and magnitude never experienced before or elsewhere. As Indian spokesmen observe, these pressures threaten the very forces of democracy. Since independence from British rule was achieved in 1947, western observers have perhaps too readily predicted that India would have to adopt more authoritarian forms of leadership to overcome these problems. It is a tribute to indigenous stamina, nurtured by long cultural traditions,[84] that India for so long found democratic forms and a tolerant attitude towards the rights of her citizens desirable goals, when economic or political crises might tempt nations without the same moral resources and cultural traditions to turn openly toward dictatorship. Basic to this attitude is the fact that democracy was not introduced to India only in the last fifty years as a western institution. Rather, it existed for several centuries in the form of village *panchayats.* Ancient Hindu kings were ordained to govern the people in accordance with *Dharmashastras* rather than *fiat.*[85]

We have identified the coincidence of development of the right of privacy in the western cultures with the emergence of a technology able to intercept, store, or retrieve confidential communications or information to a degree beyond individual control and perception of dangers created. Yet laws specifically concerned with privacy, while not so elaborate in form, do exist in India despite the relative lag in technological and economic development.

The ancient law givers of the Hindus declared *"Sarvas Sve Sve Grehe Raja"* which means "every man is a king in his own house." The *Dharmashastras* of ancient India and their commentaries expounded the laws of privacy with this concept as the central theme and the king, being bound to uphold *Dharma,* had to respect the privacy of the citizens. Even Kautilya in his *Arthasastra*[86] written around 321–296 B.C. advocated privacy for the king in consultations with his ministers. He prescribed procedures to ensure privacy in consultations. On the subject of citizens' privacy and the king's obligation to know about "national security risks", while advocating the employment of spies, he did not recommend to them the role of eavesdroppers. On the other hand, he urged the loyal spies of the king to infiltrate congregations of people in pairs and stir a debate on the affairs of the state. The people were thereby encouraged to join the debate, and their views could be publicly elicited. Although aspects of privacy in ancient Indian law cannot absorb our attention further, suffice it to say that a high degree of awareness of the need for privacy, as a basic human value, existed in ancient India. The Muslims always maintained the distinction between "public and private" and a high level of consciousness about privacy is reflected in their language, culture, architecture, and other aspects of every day life. This is not to say that formalized suits for redress of "invasion of privacy" were any part of ancient Indian history.

Modern Indian law. While Britain has few laws specifically concerned with privacy, there have been continuing legislative debate and discussion in scholarly journals and public discussion promoting active formulation of laws to counteract recently perceived challenges. In the most technologically and economically advanced society considered, the United States, the courts have declared the existence of privacy rights implied in the Constitution, and the national legislature has approved several laws dealing with specific privacy problems. India is far behind both Britain and the United States in active judicial enforcement, or even public discussion, of privacy laws. The lack of demands for judicial enforcement of the laws safeguarding privacy, and the further lack of public debate on the threat to the right of privacy, may mislead a casual observer to believe that there are no laws safeguarding this human right in India. Nevertheless, research in Indian law on the subject reveals propositions which are somewhat startling.

Consider the following examples which in each instance are more demanding than American and British law. One, section 509 of the Indian Penal Code of 1860 specifically makes it a crime to intrude upon the privacy of a woman intending to insult her modesty.[87] Two, in the case of *In re Ratnamala,* the court ruled legally inexcusable the behavior of a police officer (accompanied by witnesses to observe a raid on a brothel). They proceeded to the bedroom of a girl and pushed open the door, as the Court observed, ". . . without even the civility of a knock or warning to her to prepare for the intrusion."[88] Thus, even a prostitute is entitled to elementary decencies. Three, the fact that a man can command the view of the interior of his neighbor's house does not entitle him to gaze at his neighbor's home at all times.[89] Elaborate easement legislation covers this situation. Four, case law shows that a police officer searching a dwelling without a warrant must take precautions. Prior to the search, he should record reasons why the search cannot be made after obtaining a warrant and state what he expects to find as a result of the search. Strict compliance with this law is necessary to insure against humiliation and reckless searches in disregard of citizens' rights.[90]

A listing of several such propositions taken from Indian law (surpassing in some respects western parallels) supports the conclusion that in the body of Indian law there exist a number of safeguards which enforce the right of privacy of the individual.[91] For almost a century Indian criminal law has embodied some of the modern constitutional safeguards which the United States Supreme Court did not apply as national standards until the 1960s. For example, *Miranda* v. *Arizona,* decided by the American Supreme Court in 1966, is less stringent in some regards than the Indian Evidence Act of 1872.[92] The latter prohibits the admissibility of any confession of guilt made to a police officer, "unless it be made in the immediate presence of a magistrate." Moreover, under Indian law, even an accused person has the privilege of protection of privacy against an arbitrary search. According to section 165 of the *Code of Criminal Procedure,* the power of an officer to conduct a search is limited to quests pursuant to the investigation of an offense.[93] While conducting a search, the officer must enlist two respectable residents of the locality to join him as witnesses. To protect a citizen's privacy, magistrates must comply with the conditions for warranting a search according to section 94 of the *Code.* These conditions are mandatory and not merely directory.[94] Prior to issuing a warrant, the magistrate should examine the informant under oath, and take upon himself the responsibility of considering the weight of the information preparatory to issuing an order of search.[95] The law of searches and seizures, restrictions on the admissibility of evidence procured by improper means, and related rules, act as strong bastions in defence of individual privacy.

From the Indian point of view, the problems for further present-day development of the law of privacy grow out of factors associated with the nature of the courts and the nature of debate over public policy. One reason why Indian law, especially the law of torts, is slow to develop can be traced to the exorbitant expenses associated with litigation. This discourages speculative actions, and offended parties often simply refrain from making demands on the judicial system to meet the needs of changing times. A plaintiff tends to go to court only if there is established law to grant him redress. Since the scope for development of law through adjudication is narrow, the judicial function becomes mechanical on the view that cases that do arise are covered by precedent. Developments in Indian law tend to arise out of petitions for constitutionally provided writs, criminal cases, and through legislation.

A second inhibition on contemporary development of privacy protection lies in the fact that it has not been isolated by influential spokesmen and policy makers as an urgent subject for debate and policy reform. No Indian scholar, in the style of Brandeis and Prosser, has yet synthesized existing privacy law so as to identify those principles which are now recessed in the vaults of the law libraries. Nevertheless, pressing problems associated with privacy and the law are clearly discernible in India today. For instance, there exists in some parts of India a principle, based upon Hindu customary law, that a property owner, to insure his privacy, may acquire an easement over the property of a neighbor preventing him from erecting a window overlooking the window of his own house. This principle in a codified form has existed since 1773 and, in some states of India, it is judicially enforced under the Indian Easements Act, 1882. But this customary right, ancient in origin and appropriate to that society, has not been extended to the present congested urban living. Of value to women, the question has nevertheless not arisen of the applicability of the custom to rooms occupied by males. Similarly, the desirability of extending this customary right to other parts of India where it does not prevail has hardly been debated. The only attempt at provoking a discussion appears to have been made by a decision of the Allahabad High Court, where it was observed that the reason for judicial recognition of the custom appears to be disappearing in that modern unveiled women do not observe *purdha* any more and therefore the customary right may require abrogation.[96] Another example may be cited involving changing law regarding wiretapping. Under the Indian Telegraph Act of 1885, no disturbance or interference of communications was allowed.[97] However, with little public debate or scholarly scrutiny of policy, the right of privacy suffered a setback in 1972 when the Parliament amended the Act and authorized certain officers to intercept such messages or stop their transmission if it was considered to be in the interest of the country, or the public, or for the maintenance of friendly relations with foreign states, etc.[98] Thus, in Indian law there are many aspects of privacy which require a thorough examination from diverse perspectives. However, few public spokesmen argue for such a review. It should not be postponed until abuses, technology, and urbanization force the issue at a later date.

The constitutional basis for privacy rights. The rights to freedom of speech, expression, and movement are guaranteed by article 19 of the Constitution of India. The right to personal freedom is ensured by article 21. All these rights are grouped in part 3 of the Constitution under the title "Fundamental Rights." Article 13 forbids the state from making any law taking away or abridging these rights, and any law or regulation in contravention of these rights may be declared void. As a further safeguard, the Supreme Court of India and other High Courts exercise wide powers for enforcing these rights by issuing writs of habeas corpus, certiorari, mandamus, quo warranto, and the like, under articles 32, 226, and 228 of the Constitution. The preamble of the Constitution assures the "dignity of the individual." The state is directed to recognize and enforce international law as a matter of state policy. In these commands of the constitution lies the necessary basis for affording constitutional protection to the right of privacy. Just as India gained admission to the nuclear club by exploding a single atom bomb, it also gained admission to the privacy defenders club of modern times when its Supreme Court declared that it "does not lend its approval to the police practice of tapping phone wires and setting up hidden microphones."[99]

Although the Indian Supreme Court initially adopted a rather conservative construction on the term, personal liberty, and restricted its meaning to liberty of movement, at least a minority view is on record according to privacy the status of a constitutional right. In *Kharak Singh* v. *State of U.P.*[100] the court considered the constitutional validity of a police regulation which permitted secret surveillence of the house or approaches to the house of criminal suspects. Authorized were domiciliary visits at night, periodical inquiries into repute, habits, associations, income, expenses and occupation, of the suspect. All such information and notations about movements and absences from home could be collected and recorded systematically in the form of a "history sheet." The petitioner was suspected of complicity in crime, but the police were unable to supply the prosecutor with hard evidence. Accordingly, they opened a history sheet and maintained close surveillance on him. Reviewing this practice, the Supreme Court majority merely declared the domicilary visits as unconstitutional, but the minority went further to declare that the right of personal liberty guaranteed by the Indian Constitution encompasses not only the right to move about the country, but also to be free from encroachments on personal liberty, i.e., one's private life. They maintained that nothing is more deleterious to a man's happiness than a calculated interference with his privacy. Accordingly, the proper construction to be placed on the right to move freely is to recognize the right to move in a free country. The word freely, an adverb, enlarged the content of the right. While this thread of reasoning was neither followed in subsequent cases nor elaborated by Indian scholars, a potential exists for its development. The Supreme Court could even construe the words "personal liberty" as meaning "liberty and the security of the person," reading into article 21 of the Constitution of India, article 3 of the Universal Declaration of Human Rights. Although such attractive avenues for enlarging the content of the fundamental rights protected by the Constitution of India exist, the Indian Supreme Court has treated the Constitution as a self-contained document. The tradition has been to avoid speculative constitutional constructions. Nevertheless, the advocates of the right of privacy did not give up their struggle to establish this right as an independent fundamental right. They raised the issue again in a decision of the Supreme Court on March 18, 1975, under circumstances parallel to those in *Kharak Singh's Case.* Asserted was the right of free movement and personal liberty said to be restricted by surveillance and constant police observation of a citizen. As evident from the following holding, the Court went a step further in crystallizing the right of privacy:

The right to privacy in any event will necessarily have to go through a process of case-by-case development. Therefore, even assuming that the personal liberty, the right to move freely throughout the territory of India and the freedom of speech create an independent right of privacy as an emanation from them from which one can characterise a fundamental right, we do not think that the right is absolute.[101]

The appeal was dismissed on the ground that the right of privacy in the circumstances of the case was reasonably restricted.

The Indian Constitution and the manner in which it has been interpreted, do not give much support for development of a constitutional right of privacy as has occurred in the United States. Judicial review powers of the Indian courts are much more restricted by self-imposed limitations than those of the United States. In the United States, the Constitution has been interpreted as providing general limits to governmental power and outlines of authority subject to expansion by judicial interpretation. Indian courts regard their Constitution more literally. The courts have regarded nullification of law to be beyond their power unless the legislature is specifically prohibited from exercising a power by that document.

Chief Justice Kania stated this principle in *Gopalan v. State of Madras* in terms that would indicate rejection of "penumbral rights" of privacy:

Where the fundamental law has not limited, either in terms or by necessary implications the general powers conferred on the legislature, we cannot declare a limitation under the notion of having discovered something in the spirit of the Constitution which is not even mentioned in the instrument. It is difficult upon any general principles, to limit the competence of the sovereign legislative power by judicial interposition, except so far as the express words of a written constitution give that authority.[102]

While the Indian courts will narrowly interpret restrictions on the government and will not invalidate government actions unless they are beyond the express powers granted by the Constitution, they will broadly interpret the powers of the legislature to act. As in the United States, the presumption of constitutionality will attach to any legislative act. The difference is that the U. S. Supreme Court will also broadly interpret individual rights and often curb governmental powers on the basis of some restriction implied in the Constitution. The U. S. Constitution is regarded as an outline, not an exhaustive document. But the Indian Constitution is extremely long and is regarded by its courts as comprehensive, thereby eliminating the necessity to look beyond its language for interpretation.[103]

On June 26, 1975, fundamental rights, including the right of privacy, received a blow when the President of India, exercising his constitutional power, proclaimed an emergency.[104] The basis for the proclamation was said to be a threat of internal disturbance to the unity of the country. The proclamation, its issuance being a political question, was approved by the Parliament in July, 1975. The effect of a proclamation of emergency is that, while in operation, Parliament may make laws for the whole or any part of India on any matter or subject which is otherwise reserved for the states. Moreover, as soon as a proclamation of emergency is issued by the President, under article 358, the provisions of article 19 relating to privacy are suspended.[105] Hence, an order or rule which contravenes fundamental rights cannot be challenged. A further consequence of the emergency is that executive action is insulated from challenge.[106]

Of course, these observations about political interference with basic rights are not made to deprecate the valuable contributions made by the Supreme Court of India toward the development and enforcement of human rights. As correctly pointed out by Dr. Hunnings, representing the United Kingdom at the 1966 Helsinki Conference on Human Rights, the pivotal position in human rights development has not been occupied by the United Nations but by national courts. He said, "If any organ can be said to fill that position it is the Supreme Court of the United States, closely followed by the Supreme Court of India. These two courts between them have examined and analyzed the concept of human rights to such an extent that it is impossible to understand these problems without having mastered their jurisprudence."[107]

CONCLUSION

The study of privacy laws in three countries leads us to a paradox of political power. The United States, the country with the greatest number of laws to preserve privacy, actually protects it least. Indian citizens who are protected by centuries-old privacy customs and laws probably have the greatest degree of privacy with virtually no demands made on courts for protection, at least as far as governmental intrusion is concerned. Englishmen, whose country has few statutes specifically directed toward privacy, are facing increased threats to their privacy as their government moves toward passage of laws to secure what is being rapidly lost. A paradox of political weakness is discernible in the fact that if a government has little ability minimally to grapple with societal problems, it is scarcely in a position to intrude substantially on personal privacy or to interfere with the lives of its citizens, whether for their good or to their detriment. Hence, in India the need for revising privacy laws is not even perceived, because the danger is so remote. By the mid 1970s, the topic of privacy protection is not even on the policy-making agenda. Whether widespread extraordinary detention policies under Premier Indira Ghandi will precipitate later reforms affecting privacy remains to be seen. With the revocation of the emergency proclamation, public consciousness may turn to enacting specific safeguards for privacy. By contrast, Great Britain is in a unique position because a very effective government, in a well-organized society, has not previously perceived the need for laws to limit governmental and individual privacy intrusions, inasmuch as societal controls were internalized. But as controls break down due to factors related to the development of technology, the dissolution of a stratified class system, and the increasing heterogeneity of society, laws have become necessary to replace the internal controls now disappearing as a result of social change. Moreover, given the sensitivity of public issues associated with privacy, the process by which these laws come into being may place considerable strain upon the legal system. For example, the method by which the challenge has been initially met in the United States carries with it some dangers. By overturning laws on the grounds of "privacy rights" in areas about which people have deeply felt convictions, such as birth control and abortion, the Supreme Court has opened itself to the charge of improperly assuming a legislative role—doing what the legislatures themselves have been unable to do. It remains to be seen whether such actions weaken the role of the Supreme Court as institutional guardian of liberties and lessen the protections of the Constitution. The obvious alternative would be to follow the lead of Great Britain in this area: when dangers form a consensus by which laws can be formulated, to let the elected legislatures fashion specific remedies.

NOTES*

* In references to legal periodical literature, the number of the *initial* page of the work cited immediately follows the volume title. Page references to material specifically referred to in the text, if any, follow the initial page citation. Legal case citations correspond to *A Uniform System of Citation,* 11th ed. (Cambridge: The Harvard Law Review Association, 1974).

1. For further comparative study of the right of privacy and related civil liberties, see Thomas M. Franck, *Comparative Constitutional Process, Fundamental Rights in the Common Law Countries* (London: Sweet and Maxwell, 1968); Great Britain, Home Office, *Report of the Committee on Privacy,* Rt. Hon. Kenneth Younger, Chairman (London: H.M. Stationery Office, 1972); C. F. O. Clarke, *Private Rights and Freedom of the Individual* (Oxfordshire: The Ditchley Foundation, 1972); F. R. U. Heuston, *Essays in Constitutional Law,* 2d ed. (London: Stevens, 1964); A. H. Robertson, *Privacy and Human Rights* (Manchester University Press, 1973). Velandai Gopalayyar Ramachandran, *Fundamental Rights and Constitutional Remedies,* 2d ed. (Lucknow, India: Eastern Book Co., 1970); James B. Rule, *Private Lives and Public Surveillance* (London: Allen Lane, 1973). "The Protection of Privacy, a Comparative Survey of Ten Countries," *International Social Science Journal* 24 (1972): 417–583; Krishna Sharma, "Penumbras and Emanations" thesis, Harvard Law School, 1970; Malcolm Warner and Michael Stone, *The Data Bank Society: Organizations, Computers and Social Freedom* (London: George Allen and Unwin, Ltd., 1970); Allan F. Westin, *Privacy and Freedom* (New York: Atheneum, 1967).

2. John C. Gray, *Nature and Sources of the Law,* 2d ed. (New York: Macmillan Co., 1927), p. 102.

3. Westin, *Privacy and Freedom,* p. 330.

4. Act of June 8, 1872, ch. 335, 17 Stat. 302; Act of March 3, 1925, ch. 318, sec. 194, 43 Stat. 977.

5. Westin, *Privacy and Freedom*, pp. 337–38.

6. Thomas Cooley, *Torts*, 2d ed. (Chicago: Callaghan and Co., 1888), p. 29.

7. Samuel D. Warren and Louis D. Brandeis, "The Right to Privacy," 4 *Harvard Law Review* 193 (1890).

8. William Prosser, *Law of Torts*, 4th ed. (New York: Foundation Press, 1971), pp. 804–14.

9. *Boyd* v. *United States*, 116 U.S. 616 (1885).

10. *Id.* at 630 in reference to *Entick* v. *Carrington*, 19 How. St. Tr. 1029 (1765).

11. William Beaney, "The Constitutional Right to Privacy," 1962 *Supreme Court Review* 212, 218 n. 24. This article may have inspired Justice Douglas to use *Griswold* v. *Connecticut* as the forum for development of a constitutional right to privacy. The author suggests cases which challenge the Connecticut anti-birth control statute as a possible vehicle for developing such arguments.

12. *Olmstead* v. *United States*, 277 U.S. 438 (1927).

13. *Id.* at 478.

14. *Wolf* v. *Colorado*, 338 U.S. 25 (1949).

15. *Id.* at 27–28.

16. *Weeks* v. *United States*, 238 U.S. 383 (1914).

17. *Mapp* v. *Ohio*, 367 U.S. 643 (1961).

18. *Id.* at 665.

19. *Gilbert* v. *Minnesota*, 254 U.S. 325, 334 (1920).

20. See *Louisiana* v. *N.A.A.C.P.*, 366 U.S. 293 (1961); *Bates* v. *City of Little Rock*, 361 U.S. 516 (1960); *N.A.A.C.P.* v. *Alabama*, 357 U.S. 449 (1958).

21. *Public Utilities Commission* v. *Polk*, 343 U.S. 451 (1952).

22. *Griswold* v. *Connecticut*, 381 U.S. 479, 484 (1965).

23. *N.A.A.C.P.* v. *Alabama*, 357 U.S. 449, 462 (1958).

24. Brief for Appellants at 79–90, *Griswold* v. *Connecticut*, 381 U.S. (1965).

25. Brief for Appellees at 20, *Griswold* v. *Connecticut*, supra.

26. *State* v. *Griswold*, 3 Conn. Cir. 6, 47 (1964).

27. *State* v. *Griswold*, 151 Conn. 544 (1964).

28. *Griswold* v. *Connecticut*, 381 U.S. 479, 484 (1965).

29. *Id.* at 487.

30. James Wilson, speech of July 8, 1788, before the Pennsylvania Ratifying Convention in Jonathan Elliot, ed., *Debates on the Federal Constitution*, 2d ed. (New Haven: Yale University Press, 1881) 2:436–37.

31. *Griswold* v. *Connecticut*, 381 U.S. at 508 (1965).

32. *Id.* at 509.

33. *Time, Inc.* v. *Hill*, 385 U.S. 374 (1966).

34. *Id.* at 388–89. Extension of this analysis may be seen in *Cantrell* v. *Forest City Publishing Company*, 419 U.S. 245 (1975).

35. *Time, Inc.* v. *Hill*, 385 U.S. at 415 (1966).

36. *Id.* at 400.

37. *Stanley* v. *Georgia*, 394 U.S. 557 (1969).

38. *Id.* at 565–66.

39. *United States* v. *Reidel*, 402 U.S. 351 (1971).

40. *United States* v. *Thirty-Seven Photographs*, 402 U.S. 351 (1971).

41. *Miller* v. *California*, 413 U.S. 15 (1973); *Paris Adult Theatre I* v. *Slaton*, 413 U.S. 49 (1973); *Kaplan* v. *California*, 413 U.S. 115 (1973); *United States* v. *12,200 Foot Reels of Film*, 413 U.S. 125 (1973); *United States* v. *Orito*, 413 U.S. 139 (1973).

42. *Berger* v. *New York*, 388 U.S. 41 (1967).

43. *Id.* at 49.

44. *Id.* at 65.

45. *Katz* v. *United States*, 389 U.S. 347 (1968).

46. *Id.* at 351–52.

47. *Id.* at 350–51.

48. *Id.* at 373.

49. *Id.* at 374.

50. *United States* v. *United States District Court,* 407 U.S. 297 (1972).

51. *Roe* v. *Wade,* 410 U.S. 112 (1973).

52. *Loving* v. *Virginia,* 388 U.S. 1, 12 (1967).

53. *Skinner* v. *Oklahoma,* 316 U.S. 535, 541–42 (1942).

54. *Eisenstadt* v. *Baird,* 405 U.S. 438, 453–54 (White concurring), 460, 463–65 (1972).

55. *Prince* v. *Massachusetts,* 321 U.S. 158, 166 (1944). Cf. *United States* v. *Kahn,* 415 U.S. 143 (1974).

56. *Pierce* v. *Society of Sisters,* 268 U.S. 510, 535 (1925); *Meyer* v. *Nebraska* 262 U.S. 390, 399 (1923).

57. *Roe* v. *Wade* 410 U.S. at 153 (1973).

58. *Id.* at 167 n. 2, quoting *Katz* v. *United States,* 389 U.S. 347, 350, 351.

59. *Privacy Act of 1974;* Public Law No. 93–579, Dec. 31, 1974, 88 Stat. 1896.

60. *Omnibus Crime Control and Safe Streets Act;* Public Law No. 90–351, June 19, 1968; 82 Stat. 197; see particularly 18 U.S.C. secs. 2511–2513, 2520.

61. *Fair Credit Reporting Act;* Public Law No. 91–508, Title VI, sec. 601, October 26, 1970, 84 Stat. 1128.

62. *Crime Control Act of 1973;* Public Law No. 93–83, sec. 524, August 6, 1973; 87 Stat. 197, 215.

63. U.S., Congress, *Presidential Message,* President Gerald R. Ford, August 12, 1974. 120 *Cong. Rec.* H8161 (1974).

64. *Ex.Ord. No. 11805,* Sept. 24, 1974, 39 Fed. Reg. 34261 (1974).

65. U.S., Congress, House of Representatives, H.R. 16602, 93rd Cong. (1974).

66. *Elementary and Secondary Education Act,* Public Law No. 93–389, 512, 88 Stat. 464, 571 Aug. 21, 1974, as amended by Public Law No. 93–568, sec. 2, 88 Stat. 1855, 1858 Dec. 31, 1974.

67. U.S., Congress, Senate, S. 2963, 93rd Cong. (1974).

68. U.S., Congress, Senate, S. 2318, 93rd Cong. (1974).

69. "Privacy: Getting the Bug out of the Rug," *The Economist* 234 (Jan. 17, 1970):18–21.

70. Home Office, *Report on Privacy;* (hereafter cited as Younger Commission).

71. Ibid., p. 2, quoting letter of July 23, 1970, from Reginald Maulding.

72. *Hubbard* v. *Hosper* 2 W.L.R. 389 (1972).

73. *Entick* v. *Carrington,* 19 St. Tr. 1030 (1765).

74. R. F. V. Heuston, *Essays in Constitutional Law,* 2d ed. (London: Stephens, 1964), p. 35.

75. Ibid., pp. 50–52.

76. *Triefur and Company* v. *Post Office,* 2 Q.B. 352 (1957).

77. Younger Commission, p. 168.

78. Great Britain, Home Office. *Report of The Committee of Privy Councillors,* (London: H.M. Stationery Office, Cmnd. 283 1957).

79. *R.* v. *Scolting,* Crim. L.R. 241 (1957).

80. Younger Commission, p. 221.

81. Westin, *Privacy and Freedom,* pp. 29–30.

82. "Britons Worry About Losing Privacy—to Europe, Computers, Detectives and Press," *New York Times,* July 18, 1973, p. 17. See also, Joseph Hanlon, "Doctors Diagnose Data Distress," *New Scientist,* July 5, 1973, pp. 28–29.

83. M. Basu, *Introduction to the Indian Constitution* (New Delhi: Rejhi Publishing, 1960).

84. Sir Sivaswamy Aiyer, *Evolution of Hindu Moral Ideals,* (Calcutta University Press, 1935); Sri Aurobindo, *The Foundations of Indian Culture,* (New York: Sri Aurobindo Library, 1953).

85. J. N. Sarkar, *India Through the Ages,* (London: Sweet and Maxwell, 1959), p. 48.

86. R. Shama Sastri, *Kautilya's Arthasastra* (Mysore: Raghuveer Press, 1951), pp. 19, 26, 68.

87. R. Ratanlal and D. K. Thakore, *Law of Crimes* 22d ed. (Bombay: N. M. Tripathi & Co. and Bombay Law Reporter, 1971), p. 1376. Generally, see Samirendra Ray, *Judicial Review and Fundamental Rights* (Calcutta: Eastern Law House, 1974).

88. *In re Ratnamala,* A.I.R. 1962 (Mad. 31, 35).
89. Trikamial R. Desai, *The Indian Easements Act,* 11th ed. (Ahmedabad: C. C. Vora, 1956), pp. 53–54. Generally, see Vasudha Dhagamwar, *Law, Power and Justice: Protection of Personal Rights under the Indian Penal Code* (Bombay: N. M. Tripathi, 1974).
90. *State of Rajastan* v. *Rehman,* A.I.R. 1960 (S.C. 210).
91. See: *Mhd. Hussain Saheb* v. *Chartered Bank,* A.I.R. 1964 (1 Mad. 1012) for discussion of Secrecy in Banking; Indian Evidence Act, 1872, secs. 121 to 129, 132, on Privileged Communications, secs. 24, 25, 26, 29 on Confessions, secs. 33 of Special Marriage Act, 1959; secs. 53 of Indian Divorce Act, 1869 (in camera proceedings); secs. 96, 95, 127-A, 128, Representation of Peoples Act (Secrecy of Ballot).
92. Compare *Miranda* v. *Arizona* 384 U.S. 436 (1966) with the following: (1) Indian Evidence Act 1872. *Sec. 25.* No confession made to a police officer shall be proved as against a person accused of any offence. *Sec. 26.* No confession made by any person whilst he is in the custody of a police officer, unless it be made in the immediate presence of a magistrate, shall be proved as against such person. (2) *Sec. 164.*(3) of the Code of Criminal Procedure, 1898, dealing with the procedure for recording confessions by magistrate provides: 164(3) A magistrate shall before recording any such confession, explain to the person making it that he is not bound to make a confession and that if he does so it may be used as evidence against him and no magistrate shall record any such confession unless, upon questioning the person making it, he has reason to believe that it was made voluntarily; and when he records any confession, he shall make a memorandum at the foot of such record to the following effect: "I have explained to [name] that he is not bound to make a confession and that if he does so, any confession he may make may be used as evidence against him and I believe that his confession was voluntarily made. It was taken in my presence and hearing, and was read over to the person making it and admitted by him to be correct, and it contains a full and true account of the statement made by him."
93. *Sheonath Prasad* v. *State of Bihar,* A.I.R. 1966 (S.C. 1577).
94. India, *Code of Criminal Procedure* (1973), sec. 94; see *The New Swadeshi Mills of Ahmedabad* v. *S.K.Rattan,* A.I.R. 1968 (Gujarat 117).
95. *Lourenco Rocha* v. *Euclidas Joao Rodrigues,* A.I.R. 1968 (Goa 48).
96. *Basai* v. *Hasan Raza Khan* A.I.R. 1963 (All. 340).
97. 1972 Acts of Parliament 310 (1973).
98. Indian Telegraph Act (Amendment), 1972, sec. 2.
99. *The Hindu,* (Madras) April 20, 1967, p. 7.
100. *Kharak Singh* v. *State of U.P.,* A.I.R. 1964 (S.C. 332) at 360. Dissenting, Justice Subra Rao noted: "If a man is shadowed, his movements are obviously constricted. He can move physically but it can only be a movement of an automaton. A movement under the scrutinizing gaze of a policeman cannot be described as a free movement. The whole country is his jail. The freedom of movement [in article 19] therefore must be a movement in a free country, i.e., in a country where he can do whatever he likes, speak to whomsoever he wants, meet people of his own choice without apprehension, subject of course to the law of social control."
101. *Gopi Nath Paramanik* v. *The District Magistrate, Nodia,* 17 *Supreme Court Notes* 140 (1975).
102. *Gopalan* v. *State of Madras,* A.I.R.1950 (S.C. 27).
103. E.g., *Delhi Laws Case,* A.I.R. 1951 (S.C. 747). See, M. Hidayatullah, *Democracy in India and the Judicial Process* (New York: Asia Publishing House, 1966). See also, Nirmal C. Chatterjee, *Judicial Review and Fundamental Rights under the Constitution of India* (Bangalore: Bharadwaja Publications, 1965).
104. *New York Times,* June 27, 1975, p. 12.
105. *K.Anandan Nambiar* v. *Chief Secretary, Government of Madras,* 1966 (S.C. 406).
106. H. Seervai, *Constitutional Law of India* (Bombay: N.M. Tripathi & Co., 1967).
107. In Nagendar Sing, *Human Rights and International Cooperation* (New Delhi: S. Chand & Co., 1969), p. 44.

Chapter 6 EQUAL JUSTICE AND COUNSEL RIGHTS IN THE UNITED STATES AND CANADA

Otis H. Stephens, Jr.

The ideal of equal justice is elusive. Continually redefined to reflect changing societal values, it has figured prominently in the political and legal traditions of Canada and the United States. Within both systems, major judicial rulings have condemned various forms of discrimination against racial minorities and against groups of political and religious nonconformists. Constitutional and statutory advances have been made toward equality. Moreover, outside of the formal legal process, basic economic, social, and political inequalities have been loudly deplored by political leaders. However, in both Canada and the United States, it remains doubtful whether the formal expansion of rights in accordance with the ideal of equal justice has greatly diminished actual legal inequalities.

These inequalities persist. Nowhere are they more apparent than in the divergent levels of individual and group access to legal representation.[1] Despite the North American professions of concern for equality before the law, it was not until the 1960s that the constitutional right to assistance of counsel in criminal cases received comprehensive recognition. It was not until then that broad programs of legal aid, in civil as well as criminal cases, were undertaken. And it must be acknowledged that in neither Canada nor the United States has the recent emphasis on legal representation been translated into anything approaching a comprehensive, nationwide program of legal services.

Lack of access to legal services is intrinsic to the complex problem of discrimination. It works to the disadvantage of both the very poor who must rely entirely on free legal assistance, to the extent it is available, and persons of moderate means who can neither qualify for legal aid nor afford the quality and quantity of assistance available to affluent clients. What real difference does this gross form of inequality make? From the fragmentary evidence bearing on this important question we must settle for something less than a definitive answer. We do know that in some courts the rights of uncounselled tenants are more vulnerable to abuse than those of landlords. Consumers who are unable to retain attorneys frequently have no recourse for defective products against corporations. And the fact that our prison population is drawn heavily from the ranks of the poor, among whom the most nominal legal representation is the rule and not the exception, carries its own message.[2]

Comparative perspectives. Strongly influenced by the English common law tradition, judges in the United States and Canada have uniformly recognized precepts of fundamental fairness in relations between government and individual, summed up in the principle of due process of law. Only to a narrow extent, however, have they agreed that when these relations take the form of a criminal prosecution, the accused should be provided with an opportunity to be represented by an attorney. Broadly speaking, Canadian courts have confined the right to counsel to those who can afford to pay a lawyer. On the other hand, the U. S. Supreme Court, since its landmark decision in *Gideon* v. *Wainwright,* has enlarged the right of counsel available to indigent persons at all stages of the criminal process and in all trials at which conviction would result in the defendant's imprisonment.[3] Notwithstanding such broad judicial pronouncements, positive efforts to provide legal services, particularly in criminal cases, have been at least as great in Canada. There no rigid separation between criminal and civil matters has been made in providing legal services for the poor. In the United States, however, the Sixth Amendment provision regarding counsel is applicable only to criminal cases, and with its expansion, an artificial cleavage between the right to counsel in criminal and civil cases has emerged.

Beyond identifying broad differences and similarities in approach to legal representation in the two countries, comparative analysis of this subject becomes a difficult task. While the potential advantages of such a comparative study clearly outweigh its disadvantages, it is appropriate at the outset to identify a few historical and institutional differences that suggest the dangers of direct comparison. In spite of the similarity of a sizable body of shared legal traditions drawn from the common law and other English influences, there are great differences in the colonial experiences of the United States and Canada. Among the more obvious are: (1) the early assumption of quasi-independent political status by most of the Thirteen Colonies and the resultant growth of largely autonomous political institutions; (2) the absence of significant French legal influence in the Thirteen Colonies prior to the American revolution, in contrast to the Quebec-centered French influence on early Canadian development; (3) violent revolution resulting in total separation of the American colonies from England and establishment of a legally independent governmental system, in contrast to English control of Canada for almost a century longer and continuation, under the Commonwealth, of at least the rudiments of a formal connection even after independence; and (4) early movement within the United States away from a confederation of largely independent states to a federal republic under a constitution in which powers were delegated to a central government of theoretically limited powers, as compared with the establishment of dominion and provincial governments in Canada under the British North America Act of 1867, a comprehensive measure adopted by the Parliament of the United Kingdom to serve as the basis for constitutional government in Canada.

These and other differences in historical and institutional development have contributed to the continuation of sharp structural distinctions between the governments of the two countries. The ever-changing concept of federalism in the United States—highlighted by economic struggle, social confrontation, civil war, and chronic sectionalism—together with the interplay of forces between president and Congress, have accounted in large part for the prominence of the Supreme Court as a participant in the formulation of broad public policy. In Canada, the theory of parliamentary supremacy, in combination with growing pressures toward decentralization, has heretofore inhibited the development of comparable influence by that country's highest tribunal.

Bearing in mind the hazards of direct legal and institutional comparisons across national boundaries, this study attempts to survey and to analyze counsel-related rights and legal services in these two American democratic systems. Attention will be focused both on the dimensions of formal constitutional development, as reflected chiefly in decisions of the United States Supreme Court and Canadian appellate tribunals, and on the largely extraconstitutional growth of a wide variety of legal aid programs in the two countries.

CONSTITUTIONAL PROTECTIONS

United States developments. Amendment six of the United States Constitution provides in part that: "In all criminal prosecutions the accused shall enjoy the right . . . to have the assistance of counsel for his defense." This brief provision (often in combination with the due process clause of the fourteenth Amendment, and sometimes with the self-incrimination clause of Amendment five) has served as the basis for providing formal right of representation to every criminal defendant regardless of economic status. In theory, the defendant's access to legal counsel is to prevail at every "critical stage" of prosecution from arrest through appeal. No comparable guarantee of a right to counsel appears in the British North America Act, but the Canadian Bill of Rights, a comprehensive statute enacted by the Canadian Parliament in 1960, is relevant. It stipulates that "no law of Canada shall be construed or applied so as to . . . deprive a person who has been arrested or detained . . . of the right to retain and instruct counsel without delay or . . . authorize a court, tribunal, commission, board or other authority to compel a person to give evidence if he is denied counsel. . ."[4]

Although in the United States the right to counsel has undergone vast expansion, this process of constitutional growth did not begin until the 1930s, over one hundred and forty years after enactment of the original sixth amendment provision. Limited judicial application of the relatively recent Canadian provisions regarding counsel may not therefore indicate as sharp a contrast with developments in the United States as the scope of court decisions alone suggests. The institutional independence of the U.S. Supreme Court dates from its opening session in 1790, and its status as the nation's highest appellate tribunal was fully established by 1821.[5] By contrast, the present position of the Canadian Supreme Court as Canada's court of last resort dates only from 1949, when the judicial committee of the British Privy Council was divested of its final appellate authority over the Canadian judicial system.[6]

State governments have traditionally held chief responsibility for the enactment of criminal law within the United States. Despite the steady growth of federal power and activity in this field, the routine application and enforcement of criminal law continues to be performed by local agencies under state authority. Prior to the 1930s, constitutional and statutory recognition of legal representation was confined to the right to retain counsel in criminal cases and thus did not extend to indigent defendants. The first occasion for U.S. Supreme Court involvement and major constitutional development in this area arose in 1932 out of the infamous Scottsborough Case in which seven young, uneducated, indigent black defendants were convicted in a rural Alabama community of the rape of two white women and were sentenced to death. Trials were conducted in great haste, in an atmosphere of mob hysteria, and vividly reflected some of the baser forms of racial prejudice.[7] Relying on the due process clause of the fourteenth amendment, Justice George Sutherland concluded for the Court majority that "in a capital case, where the defendant is unable to employ counsel, and is incapable adequately of making his own defense . . . it is the duty of the court, whether requested or not, to assign counsel for him. . ."[8] For a time, it was widely assumed that this interpretation of the due process clause amounted to the incorporation of the sixth amendment counsel guarantee into the fourteenth amendment, thus making it applicable to the states. But a decade later in *Betts* v. *Brady,* the Court in a noncapital case refused to recognize the claim to appointed counsel as a fundamental right.[9] The majority of the Supreme Court opted instead for a "totality of facts" approach geared to individual cases. This ruling stood in sharp contrast to a 1938 decision in which the Court, speaking through Justice Black, ruled emphatically that "The Sixth Amendment withholds from federal courts, in all criminal proceedings, the power and authority to deprive an accused of his life or liberty unless he has or waives the assistance of counsel."[10] Under this decision, indigent federal defendants in capital and noncapital cases were fully entitled to legal representation free of charge.

Thus by the early 1940s two distinct constitutional standards, one for state cases and the other for federal prosecutions, had emerged. The Supreme Court struggled for more than twenty years with the highly flexible and uncertain due process approach established in the *Betts* decision, attempting to determine whether under the particular circumstances of each state case a denial of counsel rendered the proceedings fundamentally unfair. Under this case-by-case method of analysis, the Court gradually enlarged the scope of constitutional protection theoretically available to indigent defendants, but it did not develop a rule comparable in breadth or clarity to the sixth amendment requirement applied in federal trials.[11] Constitutional uniformity was finally achieved in *Gideon* v. *Wainwright.* In overruling *Betts* v. *Brady,* Justice Black wrote that ". . . in our adversary system of criminal justice, any person hailed into court, who is too poor to hire a lawyer, cannot be assured a fair trial unless counsel is provided for him."[12] This decision fully applied the sixth amendment right to counsel to the states through the fourteenth amendment. Of equal importance, it signaled the rapid extension of this protection to other stages of the criminal process.

Post-*Gideon* expansion of the right to counsel followed two fairly distinct lines. On the one hand, broadened counsel rights were applied to judicial proceedings, including the preliminary hearing and appeal.[13] On the other hand, the right to counsel became useful as a device for protecting suspects from certain abuses of police investigation.[14] Of particular importance under the first of these headings was the 1972 decision in *Argersinger* v. *Hamlin,* requiring the assistance of counsel, unless waived knowingly and intelligently, in all cases "whether classified as petty, misdemeanor, or felony," where conviction would result in imprisonment of the defendant.[15] In view of the large number of minor crimes that fall within the scope of Justice Douglas's "jailable offense" rule, the impact of the decision may be formidable where the legal profession and the administration of justice are concerned. While the ruling aroused some controversy, it hardly compared in this respect with earlier rulings of the 1960s which made either retained or appointed counsel available during police interrogation and postindictment lineup identification sessions.[16] From *Escobedo* v. *Illinois* in 1964 to *United States* v. *Wade* in 1967, a narrow majority of the justices took the position that the presence of a lawyer during these traditionally private stages of investigation would shield suspects from the dangers of coercion and deception. Similar concern regarding widespread abuses within the so-called juvenile justice system led the Warren Court in 1967 to apply several procedural safeguards, including the right to counsel, to juvenile delinquency proceedings.[17]

The 1960s was a decade in which the Supreme Court also enlarged other constitutional safeguards available to criminal defendants and gave formal expression to the ideal of equal justice in such fields as race relations and freedom of expression.[18] Several of the Court's decisions, particularly those in the field of criminal justice, produced criticism and controversy. Some reaction has ultimately been felt within the partially reconstituted Supreme Court of the 1970s.[19] Nevertheless, most constitutional guarantees to the poor remain intact and continue in some instances to grow. The *Argersinger* case provides one example, and another is seen in the Court's condemnation of certain sentencing practices which impose longer jail terms on indigent defendants as a direct result of their inability to pay fines for a variety of minor offenses.[20]

Despite further development of the right to counsel at the preliminary hearing and at trial, the Court under Chief Justice Burger has shown increasing reluctance to grant this protection at such administrative proceedings as hearings on parole and on probation revocation.[21] Most of the justices also appear far less certain than did the Warren majority respecting the importance of defense counsel during police questioning and related procedures.[22] Nevertheless, an impressive number of safeguards remain legally available to the poor, no less than to the affluent, in criminal prosecutions at all jurisdictional levels in the United States. These include, in addition to immunity against self-incrimination during police interrogation, the provision of trial transcripts free of charge for purposes of appeal and the right to confront and cross-examine prosecution witnesses.[23] Obviously these protections are of little value by themselves. From the standpoint of an overwhelming majority of defendants they are highly technical and abstract; and their actual implementation is accordingly dependent on the skill of competent defense counsel. Sensitive to this reality, the Supreme Court has tended to regard the assistance of counsel as a mechanism through which to give life and meaning to otherwise empty procedural forms.

While constitutional development of counsel rights in the United States has been farreaching, limitations on its scope and utility remain formidable. First, the Supreme Court is in no position to assure the availability of legal representation in those situations where it is clearly required. Although, Congress, through the Criminal Justice Act of 1964 and subsequent amendments, has made limited provision for appointed counsel in federal cases,[24] the fifty states have by no means developed uniformly adequate programs in this area. In addition, although the Supreme Court has recognized that a basic standard of quality must characterize the work of appointed counsel, it has been unable or unwilling to define that standard. That is, it has not gone beyond saying that an indigent is entitled to reasonably competent representation and that counsel must perform "in the role of an active advocate on behalf of his client, as opposed to that of amicus curiae."[25] The Court seems to have been easily satisfied on this score, especially in cases based on guilty pleas. While indicating that such a plea should not be accepted in the absence of legal advice to the defendant, the Court has been unwilling to take a critical look at the plea-bargaining device through which the great majority of criminal cases in the United States are routinely decided.[26]

Two points regarding the limited efficacy of counsel as a protection against undue police pressure should be underscored. First, failure to advise suspects of their right to the presence of an attorney during interrogation (or even outright refusal to grant a request for a lawyer) merely bars the admission of any subsequent statement into evidence. In other words the right of counsel, like the immunity against self-incrimination and restrictions against unreasonable searches and seizures by the police, is protected only by the application of an exclusionary rule of evidence. This limited negative approach to the protection of human rights has been of uncertain value as a deterrent to illegal police methods.[27] Second, after being advised of their rights, usually by the very officers who intend to question them, suspects may, in the Court's euphemistic phrase, "knowingly and intelligently" waive the exercise of these rights. The Court has not clearly defined the meaning of a voluntary waiver. It has failed to provide a method by which to check conflicting accounts of officers and suspects as to what takes place between arrest and interrogation. Unfortunately, as Justice Harlan aptly pointed out in his *Miranda* dissent, "Those who use third degree tactics and deny them in court are equally able and destined to lie as skillfully about warnings and waivers."[28] The logical conclusion is borne out by experience under the *Miranda* guidelines. It is that uncounseled persons who are very likely to be unaware of the interests at stake during police interrogation, may easily miss the opportunity to obtain badly needed legal advice. Perhaps these deficiencies could be overcome simply by broadening counsel requirements and making the right nonwaivable. Thus the Court might forbid, as a violation of the sixth amendment, the prosecution of any defendant who is not actually represented by a lawyer during police interrogation. However unacceptable this approach might be to the police (and they would object vehemently), it would at least produce a fair test of the value and importance of legal counsel at the interrogation stage.

Whether the enlargement of a constitutional right to counsel in the United States has had a significant impact on the operation of criminal justice machinery is by no means certain, as some critics have been quick to point out.[29] The question is particularly intriguing for purposes of comparison of United States and Canadian approaches. The Canadian courts have not given extensive application to counsel rights even for persons able to retain their own attorneys. They have found no basis for a constitutional right of appointed counsel for indigents, even in the most serious criminal cases. Yet it does not follow that criminal defendants in Canada are subjected to more arbitrary and abusive treatment by police and prosecution officials than are their counterparts in the United States. Nor does it appear that the absence of judicial leadership in the formulation of policy guidelines regarding counsel rights has prevented the development of substantial legal services programs, including those available to criminal defendants in financial need.

Canadian developments. In the largely undeveloped area of counsel rights adjudication, the Canadian Supreme Court has not assumed a position of leadership vis-à-vis the provincial courts. This, of course, contrasts sharply with the dominant position taken by the U.S. Supreme Court. In addition to institutional differences between these tribunals, this contrast seems to result in large part from two factors—one structural, the other essentially philosophical.

First, the Dominion Parliament, under provisions of the British North America Act, has established a unitary system of criminal law, which is applied in all ten provinces through provisions of the Canadian Criminal Code.[30] Although the administration of criminal justice is left to the provinces, their legislatures do not exercise the comprehensive and largely independent criminal law-making powers of the fifty states. Each provincial court is thus interpreting the same code of criminal law and related parliamentary measures such as the Canadian Bill of Rights. Accordingly, judicial decisions at this level would be expected to attract greater national attention from the bench and bar in other parts of the country. The second point has to do with different conceptions of the proper scope of judicial activity on the part of Supreme Court justices in Canada and the United States. The Canadian justices wield broad authority, including the power of judicial review.[31] Yet they have exercised judicial restraint to a degree that would seem excessive to most students of jurisprudence in the United States. In the tradition of legal positivism, they tend to be mechanistic in approach, according great weight to stare decisis and playing down the potential relevance of social science findings in favor of the formal tasks of adjudication.[32]

It is true, nevertheless, that the Canadian Supreme Court has upheld human rights claims, notably in the area of freedom of expression.[33] Moreover, the Canadian Bill of Rights, while not a constitutional equivalent of the British North America Act, could serve as the basis for further judicial protection of procedural safeguards, including the right to counsel. Through this device the Canadian Parliament attempted to place a variety of protections beyond the reach of routine legislative and administrative action. The Supreme Court gave potentially significant support to this broad intent when it ruled in 1969 that a racially discriminatory provision of the Indian Act was rendered inoperative by the Canadian Bill of Rights.[34] As noted, two provisions of the Bill of Rights deal with the assistance of counsel, one prohibiting the deprivation of an arrested person's "right to retain and instruct counsel," the other making it illegal for a "court, tribunal, commission, board or other authority to compel a person to give evidence if he is denied counsel. . ." This language is admittedly less general than the sixth amendment guarantee of one's right to have the assistance of counsel for his defense, but it is capable of far broader interpretation than the Canadian courts have accorded it. Reference to a few of the Canadian cases may best illustrate divergent judicial approaches in the two countries.

Denial of the right to instruct counsel, even if acknowledged by an appellate court, does not alone assure reversal of a conviction or the dropping of charges. The Nova Scotia Supreme Court made this point emphatically in a 1963 decision.[35] Robert Howard Steeves was apprehended following his involvement in a traffic accident. At the time that he was taken into custody, he was in consultation with his attorney, who accompanied him to headquarters and advised him not to answer certain questions. The attorney was later barred from the interrogation, despite his insistence to the police that under the Canadian Bill of Rights he was entitled to see his client at any time. These circumstances closely parallel the situation in *Escobedo* v. *Illinois* which served as the basis not only for recognition of the right to counsel during interrogation in the United

States but also resulted in an automatic reversal of conviction. On the other hand, while acknowledging that the police had violated Steeves' right to "instruct counsel" and conceding the possibility of civil or criminal remedies against them, Chief Justice Ilsley concluded that "the right to acquittal or dismissal of the charge" did not "accrue" to the defendant. Agreeing in a separate opinion, Justice Coffin elaborated on this line of reasoning. For him, the controlling question was whether Steeves had been accorded a fair hearing—whether, as he put it, "proceedings before the magistrate [were] in order." Since the defendant had counsel at trial and was thus able to present evidence and cross-examine witnesses, Coffin concluded that this requirement was met. In doing so he invoked the widely quoted rationale of English Chief Justice Lord Goddard, ". . . the test to be applied in considering whether evidence is to be admissible is whether it is relevant to the matters in issue. If it is, it is admissible and the court is not concerned with how the evidence was obtained. . ."[36]

The Canadian Supreme Court adhered to this restricted definition of procedural rights in a 1966 decision. It upheld a conviction for driving while under the influence of alcohol.[37] At issue was the admissibility of evidence that police had obtained through a breath test administered before the defendant was told that he was under arrest. After a night in jail following the test, the defendant asked permission to contact an attorney. He was given an opportunity to make one phone call but, when he failed to make contact on his initial effort, he was refused permission to try a second time. The Court found nothing in these circumstances to indicate a violation of the defendant's right to a fair hearing in accordance with principles of natural justice. Even if the absence of an attorney during the breath test had amounted to the denial of certain procedural safeguards, the evidence from the test was still clearly admissible. The right to retain and instruct counsel without delay was thus seen as unrelated to the admissibility of otherwise reliable evidence.[38] Six years later, in *Brownridge* v. *The Queen* the Court was willing to acknowledge a slightly broader application of the right to counsel in another case of "impaired driving."[39] Here, however, the question was not whether the breath analysis itself was admissible, but whether the accused could be convicted of failing, "without reasonable excuse," to provide a breath test on demand of the police. Brownridge had indicated that he would take the test only if given a chance to consult his lawyer, but the police ignored his request. In the opinion of Justice Ritchie, this denial "of his right to retain and instruct counsel without delay . . . constituted a reasonable excuse for his refusal to provide a breath sample." Indeed, it proved sufficient to bring about reversal of the conviction.[40] Still, this limited recognition of a right to counsel did not disturb earlier rulings giving wide scope to the admissibility of evidence obtained by the police.

The Canadian emphasis on a broad standard of natural justice as applied to the factual circumstances of individual cases is reminiscent of the due process approach followed by the U.S. Supreme Court prior to the *Gideon* ruling. Like that approach, it has produced considerable uncertainty. For example, the Manitoba Court of Appeals ruled in 1968 that the action of police in barring repeated efforts by a suspect and his attorney to communicate by telephone prior to interrogation invalidated a subsequent guilty plea.[41] On the other hand, a county court in Ontario held in 1972 that the Bill of Rights was not violated by failure of the police to contact the attorney of an eighteen-year-old suspect before taking a statement, even though they knew that he had previously retained counsel and were aware of where to contact him.[42] As noted, Canadian judges acknowledge a limited right to retain counsel at trial and on appeal. Moreover, it has been recognized that Parliament and provincial legislatures may provide for the appointment of counsel to represent indigent defendants.[43] Yet most judges have been reluctant to view legal representation, per se, as an indispensable prerequisite to fundamental fairness.

One recent Canadian development, technically outside the field of counsel rights, deserves special notice because of its implications for restricted judicial policymaking in this field. As we have seen, evidence of guilt has been admitted, following the English model, primarily on the basis of its reliability, and irrespective of the methods used in obtaining it. Nevertheless, judges have traditionally exercised broad discretion in excluding such evidence if standards of fundamental fairness were believed to have been threatened by its use. With its 1970 decision in *Regina* v. *Wray*[44] the Canadian Supreme Court substantially narrowed this judicial discretion, thereby moving even further away from the possibility of judicial regulation of the law enforcement process. Prior to this decision, the English Judges' Rules, a set of broad guidelines for police interrogation, had been accorded some importance in Canada and had occasionally been used as criteria for the discretionary exclusion of illegally obtained evidence. However, as long as the principle underlying the *Wray* decision is followed, it seems doubtful whether even the modest investigative restrictions contained in the Judges' Rules will be viable in Canada.[45] The current Canadian approach is similar to the position which has been followed for some time in Australia where the Judges' Rules are accorded little more than lip service.[46] Recent criticism of the Judges' Rules, in England as well as Canada, reflects a growing scepticism about the value and legitimacy of judicial efforts to upgrade police methods.[47] This mood also is evident in the United States, as seen in renewed criticism of the exclusionary rules.

As the preceding discussion suggests, in Canada the right to counsel has achieved no broad judicial protection at any stage of the criminal process. In the United States the right has been fully recognized at virtually every stage from arrest to appeal. Its violation, if properly challenged, almost automatically brings a reversal of conviction. But it has not been established empirically that this sharp divergence of judicial activity has produced great differences in the actual availability of legal representation, either retained or appointed. It is perhaps too much to say that formal constitutional protections in the United States have had no relation to the development of legal aid programs. It seems undeniable, however, that more fundamental social forces which cut across national boundaries have been at work in this field, as in the emergence of other forms of human rights protections. A brief examination of the growth of legal aid programs in the two countries may assist in identifying some of these broad influences.

LEGAL ASSISTANCE PROGRAMS

Principles of legal equality in Canada and the United States are deeply rooted in traditions of political and economic individualism. These traditions have heavily influenced the objectives, values, and ethics of the legal profession and are at the core of the judicial process. In large part, lawyers have served the needs or demands of individual or corporate clients as opposed to the broad interests of society. Traditionally, judges have decided cases, even constitutional cases, with reference to the duties and rights of individuals. Struggles for basic racial and economic justice have centered around individual instances of discrimination or oppression and have frequently been resolved through an adversary process that pits the individual against the state. Vast changes produced in this century by accelerated industrial growth, urbanization, and the revolution in communications media have made it clear, however, that the goal of legal equality cannot be pursued realistically without recognizing and dealing with fundamental social problems. Despite this recognition, the approaches to legal assistance in both countries continue to be heavily influenced by what might be called the individual response model.[48]

Emerging Canadian patterns. Emphasis on individual self-help and initiative at the expense of the recognition of overriding social impediments to equality before the law has been a problem throughout North America. In Canada until after World War II, legal aid was seen largely as a form of private charity. But with establishment of the Ontario Plan in 1967, fairly comprehensive legal services programs have recently emerged at the provincial level.[49] Enacted to supplant a more modest effort dating from the early 1950s, the Ontario Plan blends elements of the individualized approach to legal assistance for the poor with elements of a modern social welfare program. The emphasis remains, however, on a traditional relationship between the private attorney and his client. Incorporating some features of the English Legal Aid and Advice Act of 1949,[50] the Ontario Plan provides for government reimbursement of the fees of private attorneys who participate on a voluntary basis. The plan is administered by the Law Society of Upper Canada, the official organization of the Ontario bar. Persons seeking assistance must file applications with local area directors who, on the basis of recommendations by welfare officers, make final decisions regarding the allocation of legal aid. A flexible needs test is applied so that an applicant may receive full or partial support from the government. Lawyers participating in the program are paid 75 percent of the fee that they would charge a paying client of modest means for identical services, as compared with 90 percent under the English system. The successful applicant for assistance is issued a legal aid certificate and is free to employ the lawyer of his own choice. The attorney is likewise free to determine which clients he will represent. The Ontario Plan covers criminal cases as well as civil matters and quasi-judicial proceedings, and a certificate may be issued simply for legal advice or for assistance during formal litigation. On the criminal law side, the plan provides for "duty counsel," a rotating group of attorneys who visit the jails each morning and offer preliminary legal assistance to persons in custody without the requirement of formal application for assistance.[51] In general, the plan is regarded as a significant development in the legal aid field. It has been particularly effective in criminal law where, according to one estimate, it is utilized in about 70 percent of the cases.[52]

This "judicare" approach was initially popular and seemed to provide a model for other Canadian provinces. The alternative "neighborhood law office" approach gained in popularity, however, and in 1972 such a program was established in Quebec.[53] Under this plan more than two hundred lawyers, together with paralegal personnel, were employed on a full-time basis in an effort to meet the legal needs of the poor. Moreover, the plan was placed under the administrative control of regional boards, with heavy representation from the communities being served by the program.

Both the Ontario and Quebec legal assistance plans represent substantial efforts to meet existing needs. They reflect the alternatives of a "juridical" and a "welfare" approach to legal aid. The Ontario Plan has been praised for its flexibility and for its apparent success in accommodating the interests of an autonomous legal profession with the needs of a sizable portion of the community not otherwise able to pay for legal services. It has been criticized primarily because of its domination by the bar, its potential as a form of government subsidy for private legal practice, and its exclusive focus on individual legal needs as opposed to broad social problems. The Quebec Plan on the other hand has been praised for its high level of community participation. Two observers recently concluded that Quebec is "the first province to operationalize with some vigour the view that more than legal expertise is needed to administer and develop a program which, while law-oriented, is also a program of social service and social change."[54] Critics of this approach, primarily representatives of the private bar, deplore the "welfare" dimensions of the program and the threat that it allegedly poses for the traditional independence of the legal profession.

No comprehensive program of legal assistance has been developed at the national level in Canada. The programs in Ontario and Quebec have, however, been given broad province-wide application; and similar efforts, sometimes combining features of the two approaches, have been undertaken in other provinces.[55] Moreover, with grant support from the Federal Department of Health and Welfare, three Canadian law schools launched clinical legal assistance programs in 1971. Following a pattern well established in many law schools in the United States, these universities have begun to rely on law students for the delivery of legal services.[56] Canadian programs for providing legal assistance for the poor have managed to avoid the problems posed in the United States by the largely artificial separation between the categories of civil and criminal law. It seems clear, however, that the chronic problem of limited financing is equally serious in both countries.

Emerging patterns in the United States. Organized legal assistance to the poor began in 1876 with the establishment of a private legal aid office in New York for newly arrived German immigrants.[57] In 1888 a more broadly based legal aid society, the Bureau of Justice, was established by the Ethical Culture Society in Chicago. In 1910 the first publicly financed legal aid program was established, the Municipal Bureau in Kansas City, Missouri; and in 1914 in Los Angeles, the first public defender office was set up. From these modest origins the movement grew to a nation-wide total of 72 legal aid organizations in 1925 and more than 300 legal aid and public defender offices by the middle 1960s. Efforts at national coordination of this highly fragmented movement began in 1911 with the formulation of plans for a National Alliance of Legal Aid societies. This organization ultimately became the National Legal Aid and Defender Association, an affiliate of the American Bar Association and, over the years, a leading force in the movement. In 1940, the House of Delegates of the American Bar Association adopted resolutions supporting legal aid; and since that time the ABA has worked actively through its legal aid committee to strengthen and expand programs at the local level.[58]

Until establishment of a broad legal services program in the United States by the Office of Economic Opportunity in 1965, legal assistance was chiefly supported by private sources and was limited for the most part to service on a traditional individual-client basis. Governmental involvement was largely confined to state and local levels and was limited almost entirely to criminal proceedings. With the Criminal Justice Act of 1964, Congress provided limited compensation for lawyers assigned to represent indigents in federal prosecutions. Subsequent amendments have expanded the scope of this legislation, notably by providing for the establishment of federal public defender offices and for the support of defender organizations at the community level.[59] The OEO Legal Services Program, although limited to civil law, was a far more ambitious effort to provide assistance to the poor. By 1973, it employed more than 2500 full-time attorneys, working out of some 900 neighborhood offices, and provided supplementary funds to numerous other legal aid programs in cities, towns, and rural areas throughout the country. By means of an elaborate grant application and review procedure, the OEO could appropriate up to 80 percent of the cost of local legal services to the poor. Criteria for financing eligibility were flexible and varied widely among localities. Generally speaking, they restricted legal aid to persons unable to defray even a portion of the costs from their own resources. In addition to maintaining neighborhood law offices employing full-time legal staffs, the OEO program supported the experimental alternative judicare approach, in which private attorneys provided legal services to the poor on a basis of partial government reimbursement of fees. Case loads of the OEO attorneys in the neighborhood law offices were extremely heavy, averaging more than 500 a year. In 1965, just before the program went into full operation, private legal aid societies spent only $4.3 million for assistance in civil cases. By contrast Congress appropriated over $27.5 million for the legal services program for fiscal 1966, and by fiscal 1973 the appropriation had climbed to more than $70 million.[60]

Beyond quantitative growth, however, the OEO Legal Services Program introduced a new philosophical dimension to the legal aid movement in the United States. The chief objective of this program, consistent with the "war on poverty" of which it was originally a part, was fundamental sociolegal reform. As Stumpf and Janowitz describe it, the program was originally intended "to reach beyond the individualized services of traditional legal aid by using the instrumentalities of the law, broadly defined, to attack the root causes of poverty."[61] The precise relationship between this reform objective and the provision of legal services, which would remain an integral part of the program, was not clearly defined. Sharp disagreement persisted among supporters of the program regarding the degree of emphasis that should be placed on the poverty lawyer's role in representing the broad interests of the poor. It soon became clear that with the enormous volume of routine legal work expected of them, the neighborhood legal services attorneys would have little time to devote to the broader objective. The reform dimension was given impetus by the establishment of Reginald Heber Smith Community Lawyer fellowships administered by the office of the national director of the legal services program and not subject to control by local program boards. These fellowships enabled a limited number of high-ranking graduates of leading law schools to devote periods of one year or more to full-time test case litigation on behalf of the poor. Since it challenged prevailing legal patterns in many communities, this innovative dimension of the program became one of its most controversial features.

The OEO program was well on its way to formal implementation before American Bar Association and National Legal Aid Association support was actively sought and reluctantly given.[62] These long-time proponents of traditional legal aid proved, however, to be important allies, especially during the early development of the program. On the other hand, opposition from local bar associations in many communities was strong from the start and intensified as time passed. It appears that many trial judges shared this negative view.[63] Moreover, sociolegal reform aimed at changing the conditions that produce poverty aroused strong political opposition within and outside conservative legal circles. Partly as a result of this opposition, the reform dimension of the program, although a significant feature, did not achieve a dominant position and by the early 1970s was distinctly eclipsed.

Apart from the overt opposition of local bar groups and politicians, the legal reform objective was frustrated by the failure of many lawyers and judges to understand it or to accept its basic assumptions. Some observers attributed this factor to the technical emphasis and relatively narrow focus which characterizes the educational programs of many law schools.[64] It must also be remembered that major segments of the legal profession are closely identified with the protection of economic and political interests that would be severely threatened if social reform on behalf of the poor were fully implemented. Achievement of this broad objective requires nothing less than a fundamental reordering of values and priorities within the legal profession itself.

As all OEO programs came under increasing attack during the early 1970s, the future of federally financed legal services became more uncertain. Despite the criticism leveled against it, the legal services program was recognized as one of the more successful OEO enterprises, and even its opponents seemed unwilling to scrap it entirely. The efforts of critics and supporters produced conflicting proposals aimed at retaining a national program through the creation of some type of independent legal services corporation. The ABA backed a proposal that essentially embodied the legal reform objective while the Nixon Administration, in sharp disagreement with this approach, endorsed a restrictive plan containing strong antireform elements.[65] A slightly softened substitute for the Administration bill was passed by the House of Representatives on June 21, 1973. A still less restrictive Senate bill was passed on January 31, 1974, but it was the House version, with minor modifications that, after months of haggling, received final approval by both chambers. Research aimed at furthering the more farreaching and controversial aspects of the legal services program had been provided in large part by "back-up centers" located at major law schools. Support for these centers was excluded from the House version of the bill but was restored by Senate sponsors. In a last-minute compromise with the White House, this controversial feature was dropped and a threatened presidential veto was averted. In one of the last of his major official actions, President Nixon signed the measure on July 25, 1974.

The Legal Services Corporation Act of 1974 provides for the establishment of an independent, private, nonprofit corporation, with an eleven member board of directors, appointed by the President, subject to Senate confirmation. Members of the bar shall comprise a majority of the board, and the same principle would apply to the makeup of advisory councils to be appointed by the fifty state governors. The corporation is authorized to make provision for legal assistance in civil cases by making grants or entering into contracts with "individuals, partnerships, firms, organizations, corporations, state and local governments," and other "appropriate entities. . . ."[66] Among the more controversial provisions of the legislation are restrictions against political protest activities by employees of the corporation and employees of recipient legal service organizations. These persons are prohibited from participating in "any picketing, boycott, or strike . . . rioting or civil disturbance."[67] Other provisions call for the maintenance of sound lawyer-client relations and the establishment of flexible guidelines of financial eligibility. The Legal Services Corporation Act provides for an initial increase over previous legal services appropriations, authorizing the expenditure of $90 million in fiscal year 1975. Nevertheless, the new program represents a repudiation of the broad social reform objective to which the original OEO program of legal assistance was committed.

This overview of major legal services programs in Canada and the United States suggests something of the diversity of approaches that can be followed in providing legal representation for the poor. Perhaps of greater importance, it also underscores the problem of agreeing on a working definition of the very concept of legal representation. The Ontario Plan, while relying on public funds, is based on essentially the same concept of legal service as that which gave rise to the private legal aid movement in the United States: that legal assistance should be confined to the immediate needs of clients and should be handled within the traditional limits of individual legal representation. In far more restricted form, this is the prevailing approach to legal services in Australia. There even greater emphasis is accorded to the independence and prerogatives of the legal profession in administering programs in various states.[68] Governmental involvement is severely limited by comparison with the Ontario Plan. In contrast to traditional approaches the abortive OEO Legal Services Program and the Quebec Plan have applied the principle of legal representation to the broad objective of social reform. Such alternatives are based on the belief that conditions giving rise to legal inequities must be removed, and that this objective cannot be accomplished without fundamental changes in the nature and goals of the law.

CONCLUSION

Recent developments in the United States and Canada strongly support the proposition that the adequate protection of counsel rights requires far more than judicial rulings, however sweeping, and more than formal compliance with conventional legal safeguards. Major expansion of legal services has taken place in both countries since the middle 1960s. During roughly the same period, the U.S. Supreme Court has greatly enlarged the constitutional right to counsel at virtually all stages of a criminal prosecution and has made it clear that government is obligated to provide attorneys for indigent defendants. The Court's decision in *Gideon* v. *Wainwright*, recognizing this broad right in criminal trials, received extensive publicity in Canada as well as in the United States.[69] Unquestionably this decision highlighted some of the more serious inequities and abuses of the adversary system as applied to the uncounseled poor. It does not necessarily follow, however, that even this landmark ruling had decisive influence on the general expansion of legal assistance programs. In the United States this expansion has been more substantial in civil law than in criminal law. Yet *Gideon* and other important constitutional rulings expanding the right to counsel are confined to the latter field. Passage of the Federal Criminal Justice Act and the proliferation of public defender offices have been directly attributable to the Court's enlargement of the right to counsel, but even here a number of broad social forces were at work, quite apart from the judicial recognition of constitutional safeguards.

The U.S. Supreme Court did not begin to give significant constitutional protection to the rights of indigents in civil cases until after establishment of the OEO Legal Services Program. In fact, it was OEO-financed litigation that afforded the Court some of its most important opportunities to apply fundamental principles in this broad area. An illustration is provided by *Boddie* v. *Connecticut,* a class action initiated in 1968 by OEO attorneys on behalf of welfare recipients who sought divorces but who were unable to pay required court fees. After protracted litigation, the Supreme Court held in 1971 that a state violates due process of law when it denies persons access to divorce proceedings solely because of their inability to pay court costs.[70] Although it has only an indirect bearing on the constitutional right to counsel, this ruling has great potential significance for the expansion of broad constitutional safeguards for the poor. It also suggests that causal relationships between judicial decisions and the process of social reform, if they exist at all, may move in either direction.

In Canada, the judiciary has provided little in the way of formal protection of a broad right to counsel. Nevertheless, fairly comprehensive legal services have been made available. Although Canada has not developed a national program of legal assistance, its efforts at the provincial level have been more extensive than those in most states and localities in the United States. Through a judicare approach in Ontario and a neighborhood law office approach in Quebec, legal assistance has been furnished not only in civil cases but also in large numbers of criminal cases. Avoidance of the rigid and often arbitrary distinction between the categories of civil and criminal law (a distinction that has inhibited the development of legal assistance in the United States) is an important feature of Canadian development in provinces which have adopted variations of the Ontario Plan. Beyond provisions for the indigent, legal assistance programs in Canada have given some attention to the problems of those who can afford to pay for a portion of their legal expenses, but are unable to carry the full financial burden. Admittedly, this problem has not received sufficient attention, but Canadian programs seem to have accorded it more recognition than have their counterparts in the United States. Generally speaking, Canadian programs, despite the absence of a coordinated national plan, are designed to meet a broad range of needs. They differ from programs in the United States chiefly in their greater flexibility.

The growing availability of legal services for the poor in Canada might conceivably influence the enlargement of formal constitutional and statutory protections through judicial interpretation. But the limited policy dimensions of Canadian appellate court rulings in this area and, in particular, the reluctance of the Canadian Supreme Court to assume a position of leadership indicate that the enlargement of legal guarantees is likely to be slow in coming. Not only have Canadian judges refused to recognize the right to counsel as a means of protecting suspects against mistreatment by the police, they have even been unwilling to recognize that a person who cannot afford to hire a lawyer has a right to representation of any kind at trial. Counsel might be provided at the discretion of the judge and might, as a practical matter, be furnished through legal assistance programs, but it is not regarded as an explicit right, except for those who can pay for it.

Despite the substantial growth of legal services in both countries and the formal expansion of constitutional rights in the United States, it must be recognized that the amount of emphasis given to human needs in this area is still relatively small. In the United States, according to one estimate, it would be necessary to provide 137,000 attorneys for the poor, rather than the present just over 2,000, if legal representation were to be furnished at the level available to the general population.[71] This quantitative gap obviously results in the imposition of unduly heavy workloads on the limited number of attorneys who are provided for the poor. Not only is the quality of legal assistance thus threatened, but lawyers who have lucrative and less demanding professional opportunities open to them tend to avoid long-term commitments to legal services programs.

The legal profession in North America has a strong and productive tradition of public service. Nevertheless, it remains oriented toward private client representation, whether individual or corporate interests are involved. Full-scale legal assistance to the poor, going beyond a mere "band-aid" approach and undertaking major surgery aimed at removing the causes of legal inequities requires a fundamental change in this restricted professional focus. The individual lawyer-client relationship is, of course, preferred by most segments of the legal profession as the mechanism for furnishing legal aid to the poor. And yet the very condition of poverty usually precludes or seriously discourages the development of such a relationship. An indigent person is unlikely to know any attorney well enough to make even a rough estimate of his competence, and the almost certain differences in education, economic status, and social class often pose insurmountable barriers against full communication and understanding between lawyer and client.

Moreover, a largely unattended problem is that posed by underrepresentation of persons with moderate means in respect to legal services. Despite the flexibility of the Ontario Plan which permits a person to receive either total or partial support in defraying legal costs, this problem has not been effectively confronted in either Canada or the United States. The cost of adequate legal representation, even of routine transactions, is often beyond the reach of persons who do not come close to qualifying for publicly financed legal aid. As the consumer movement grows in influence, this issue might be given more serious consideration in the future. A small step in that direction occurred in the fall of 1973 in hearings before a U.S. Senate Subcommittee chaired by Senator John V. Tunney of California. The hearings, which were subsequently published, focused on abuses to which typical consumers are routinely subjected as a direct result of inadequate legal representation.[72] But whether significant corrective legislation will result from the disclosure of inequities remains to be seen.

The effective protection of counsel rights in accordance with ideals of equal justice in Canada and the United States requires far greater commitment than has yet been shown by agencies and individuals, public or private. It is dependent, first of all, on a reordering of values and priorities identified with the legal profession. Such a fundamental change goes beyond the revision of traditional methods of formal, case-oriented legal education—important though this dimension may be. It involves basic reorientation of attitudes, within and outside the profession, regarding the ends that should be served by lawyers and by the law itself. Recent reaction against the reform objective of the OEO Legal Services Program and the reassertion of older and narrower legal aid objectives, make it clear that little in the way of fundamental change has yet occurred, at least in the United States. Adequate protection of counsel rights also requires the sustained support of governmental institutions including, but by no means confined to, the courts. Legislative and administrative efforts to provide legal services are no less important than the recognition of formal constitutional guarantees through judicial decisions. Finally, if counsel rights are to be protected, their exercise must not be made totally dependent on the assertion of those rights by individuals who are denied them. Of course, every effort should be made to inform individuals of these rights and to increase general awareness of their importance. But individual responsibility and initiative is not sufficient to ensure the legal protections to which all persons within constitutional systems such as Canada and the United States are entitled. Counsel rights, like other procedural safeguards, depend heavily on the shared assumptions and values implicit in the acceptance of social responsibility.

NOTES*

* In references to legal periodical literature, the number of the *initial* page of the work cited immediately follows the volume title. Page references to material specifically referred to in the text, if any, follow the initial page citation. Legal case citations correspond to *A Uniform System of Citation*, 11th ed. (Cambridge: The Harvard Law Review Association, 1974).

1. Few comparative studies deal extensively with legal assistance and counsel rights, and even fewer focus exclusively on the United States and Canada. An excellent recent analysis

of historical trends and current approaches to legal assistance, with emphasis on programs in Western Europe and the United States, is provided by Mauro Cappelletti and James Gordley, "Legal Aid: Modern Themes and Variations," 24 *Stanford Law Review* 347 (1972). For critical analysis of the right to counsel in Canada against the background of recent constitutional developments in the United States, see Brian Donnelly, "Right to Counsel," 11 *Criminal Law Quarterly* 18 (1968), and Brian A. Grossman, "The Right to Counsel in Canada," 10 *Canadian Bar Journal* 189 (1967). A useful summary of Canadian legal provisions and judicial decisions on the right to counsel appears in Walter S. Tarnopolsky, *The Canadian Bill of Rights* (Toronto: The Carswell Company, 1966), pp. 168–82. For discussion of procedural developments in Canada that have potential bearing on the right to counsel, see S. F. Sheppard, "Restricting the Discretion to Exclude Admissible Evidence: An Examination of *Regina v. Wray*," 14 *Criminal Law Quarterly* 334 (1972), and J. Grant Sinclair, "The Queen v. *Drybones:* The Supreme Court of Canada and the Canadian Bill of Rights," 8 *Osgoode–Hall Law Journal* 599 (1970). For discussion of recent trends in Canadian legal aid, see L. Taman and F. H. Zemans, "The Future of Legal Services in Canada," 51 *Canadian Bar Review* 23 (1973); John F. Honsberger, "The Ontario Legal Aid Plan," 15 *McGill Law Journal* 436 (1969); Graham Parker, "Legal Aid–Canadian Style," 14 *Wayne Law Review* 471 (1967); Lee Silverstein, "The New Ontario Legal Aid System and Its Significance for the United States," 25 *The Legal Aid Briefcase* 83 (1967); Frederick H. Zemans and Lester Brickman, "Clinical Legal Education and Legal Aid–the Canadian Experience," 6 *Council on Legal Education for Professional Responsibility* 1 (1974). For early development of the right to counsel in the United States, see William M. Beaney, *The Right to Counsel in American Courts* (Ann Arbor: University of Michigan Press, 1955). An excellent analysis of all aspects of the *Gideon* case is presented by Anthony Lewis in *Gideon's Trumpet* (New York: Random House, 1964). For recent developments see Tom C. Clark, "*Gideon* Revisited," 15 *Arizona Law Review* 343 (1973); Otis H. Stephens, "The Assistance of Counsel and the Warren Court: Post-*Gideon* Developments in Perspective," 74 *Dickinson Law Review* 193 (1970); "*Gideon* and Beyond: Achieving an Adequate Defense for the Indigent," 59 *Journal of Criminal Law, Criminology and Police Science* 73 (1968). For description and analysis of legal services in the United States, see Lee Silverstein, *Defense of the Poor in Criminal Cases in American State Courts* (Chicago: American Bar Foundation, 1965); Emory A. Brownell, *Legal Aid in the United States* (Rochester: Lawyers Cooperative Publishing Company, 1951); A. Kenneth Pye, "The Role of Legal Services in the Antipoverty Program," 31 *Law and Contemporary Problems* 211 (1966). Philip J. Hannon, "The Leadership Problem in the Legal Services Program," 4 *Law and Society Review* 235 (1969); Richard Pious, "Congress, the Organized Bar, and the Legal Services Program," 1972 *Wisconsin Law Review* 418.

2. For documentation of the gross economic and racial discrimination that traditionally characterized judicial imposition of the death penalty in the United States see *Furman v. Georgia*, 408 U.S. 238 (1972).

3. See, for example, *Douglas v. California*, 372 U.S. 353 (1963); *Escobedo v. Illinois*, 378 U.S. 478 (1964); *Miranda v. Arizona*, 384 U.S. 436 (1966); *United States v. Wade*, 388 U.S. 218 (1967); *Gilbert v. California*, 388 U.S. 263 (1967); *Coleman v. Alabama*, 399 U.S. 1 (1970); *Argersinger v. Hamlin*, 407 U.S. 25 (1972).

4. Canada, *Bill of Rights*, S.C. 1960, ch. 44, sect. 2(c)(iii)(d).

5. See *Cohens v. Virginia*, 19 U.S. (6 Wheat.) 264 (1821); cf. *Martin v. Hunter's Lessee*, 14 U.S. (1 Wheat.) 304 (1816).

6. For further comparative analysis of these and related distinctions see Donald E. Fouts, "Policy-making in the Supreme Court of Canada 1950–60," in *Comparative Judicial Behavior*, ed. Glendon Schubert and David J. Danelski (New York: Oxford University Press, 1969), pp. 257–92. For broad analyses of legal and judicial institutions in Canada see Edward McWhinney, ed., *Canadian Jurisprudence: The Civil Law and Common Law in Canada* (Toronto: The Carswell Company, 1958).

7. For background on the Scottsborough episode see Dan T. Carter, *Scottsborough, a Tragedy of the American South* (Baton Rouge: Louisiana State University Press, 1969).

8. *Powell v. Alabama*, 287 U.S. 45, 71 (1932).

9. *Betts* v. *Brady,* 316 U.S. 455 (1942).

10. *Johnson* v. *Zerbst,* 304 U.S. 458, 463 (1938).

11. See, for example, *Chandler* v. *Frether,* 348 U.S. 3 (1954); *Cash* v. *Culver,* 358 U.S. 633 (1959); *Morgan* v. *Chewning,* 368 U.S. 443 (1962); *Carnley* v. *Cochran,* 369 U.S. 506 (1962).

12. *Gideon* v. *Wainwright,* 372 U.S. 335, 344 (1963).

13. For expansion of the right to counsel at the preliminary hearing, see *Coleman* v. *Alabama,* 399 U.S. 1 (1970). For the right to counsel on appeal, see *Douglas* v. *California,* 372 U.S. 353 (1963), and *Anders* v. *California,* 386 U.S. 738 (1967).

14. *Massiah* v. *United States,* 378 U.S. 201 (1964); *Escobedo* v. *Illinois,* 378 U.S. 478 (1964); *Miranda* v. *Arizona,* 384 U.S. 436 (1966); *United States* v. *Wade,* 388 U.S. 218 (1967); *Orozco* v. *Texas,* 394 U.S. 324 (1969).

15. *Argersinger* v. *Hamlin,* 407 U.S. 25, 37 (1972); opinion of the Court by Justice Douglas.

16. Evidence of the sharp reaction that these decisions produced among many congressional leaders and at the grassroots may be gleaned from U.S., Congress, Senate, Subcommittee on Criminal Laws and Procedures of the Committee on the Judiciary, *Controlling Crime through more Effective Law Enforcement,* 90th Cong., 1st sess., 1967. U.S., Congress, Senate, Committee on the Judiciary, *Nominations of Abe Fortas and Homer Thornberry,* 90th Cong., 2d sess., 1968.

17. *In re Gault,* 387 U.S. 1 (1967).

18. See for example, *Edwards* v. *South Carolina,* 372 U.S. 229 (1963); *Katzenbach* v. *McClung,* 379 U.S. 294 (1964); *Loving* v. *Virginia,* 388 U.S. 1 (1967); *Keyishian* v. *Board of Regents,* 385 U.S. 589 (1967).

19. By 1972, an indication of this reaction was already apparent in *Milton* v. *Wainwright,* 407 U.S. 371 in which a narrowly divided Court rejected a defendant's claim that police had denied his right to counsel *after* indictment. In 1974, three rulings produced restrictive sixth amendment results: *United States* v. *Kahan,* 415 U.S. 239; *Fuller* v. *Oregon,* 417 U.S. 40 (1974); *Ross* v. *Moffitt,* 417 U.S. 600 (1974).

20. See for example, *Williams* v. *Illinois,* 399 U.S. 235 (1970).

21. *Morrissey* v. *Brewer,* 408 U.S. 471 (1972) and *Gagnon* v. *Scarpelli,* 411 U.S. 778 (1973).

22. See *Harris* v. *New York,* 401 U.S. 22 (1971), *Kirby* v. *Illinois,* 406 U.S. 682 (1972), and *United States* v. *Kahan,* 415 U.S. 239 (1974).

23. See *Griffin* v. *Illinois,* 351 U.S. 12 (1956) and *Pointer* v. *Texas,* 380 U.S. 400 (1965).

24. *Criminal Justice Act,* 1964, 18 U.S.C. sect. 3006(a).

25. *Anders* v. *California,* 386 U.S. 738, 744 (1967); opinion of the Court by Justice Clark.

26. See *Brady* v. *United States,* 397 U.S. 742 (1970); *Parker* v. *North Carolina,* 397 U.S. 790 (1970); *North Carolina* v. *Alford,* 400 U.S. 25 (1970); *Dukes* v. *Warden,* 407 U.S. 934 (1972). But cf. *Santobello* v. *New York,* 404 U.S. 257 (1971).

27. For a summary of empirical studies generally supporting this conclusion see Otis H. Stephens, *The Supreme Court and Confessions of Guilt* (Knoxville: University of Tennessee Press, 1973), pp. 165–200.

28. *Miranda* v. *Arizona,* 384 U.S. 436, 505 (1966).

29. See generally, Abraham S. Blumberg, *Criminal Justice* (Chicago: Quadrangle Books, 1967); and *Struggle for Justice, a Report on Crime and Punishment in America,* The American Friends Service Committee (New York: Hill and Wang, 1971).

30. See *Canadian Criminal Code,* Secs. 557(3), 709(1) (2), and 590.

31. For discussion of judicial review in Canada, see Edward McWhinney's comparative study, *Judicial Review,* 4th ed. (Toronto: University of Toronto Press, 1969), pp. 61–75.

32. For an excellent assessment of the limited constitutional role of the Canadian Supreme Court, see Edward McWhinney, "Legal Theory and Philosophy of Law in Canada," in McWhinney, *Canadian Jurisprudence,* pp. 1–23.

33. See Donald E. Fouts, "Policy-making in the Supreme Court of Canada, 1950–60,"

in Schubert and Danelski, *Comparative Judicial Behavior,* pp. 257–92. See also Sidney R. Peck, "A Scalogram Analysis of the Supreme Court of Canada, 1958–67," in ibid., pp. 293–334.

34. *Queen* v. *Drybones,* 9 D.L.R. 3d 473 (1969).

35. *Queen* v. *Steeves,* 42 D.L.R. 2d 335 (1963).

36. *Kuruma, Son of Kaniu* v. *The Queen,* 1 A.E.R. 236 (1955).

37. *O'Connor* v. *The Queen,* 57 D.L.R. 2d 123 (1966).

38. For analysis of the *O'Connor* ruling and other right to counsel decisions reflecting divergent approaches in Canada and the United States, see Walter S. Tarnopolsky, "The Canadian Bill of Rights from Diefenbaker to *Drybones,*" 17 *McGill Law Journal* 437,464–68 (1971). See also, Donnelly, "Right to Counsel," p. 20, and Grossman, "The Right to Counsel in Canada," pp. 196, 202–5.

39. *Brownridge* v. *The Queen,* 28 D.L.R. 3d 1 (1972).

40. Ibid., 5,5.

41. *Queen* v. *Ballegeer,* 1 D.L.R. 3d 74 (1968).

42. *Queen* v. *Deleo and Commisso,* 8 Can. Crim. Cas. (n.s.) 264 (1972).

43. See *Queen* v. *Happeney,* 5 Can. Crim. Cas. (n.s.) 353 (1970).

44. *Queen* v. *Wray,* 11 D.L.R. 3d 673 (1970).

45. See Sheppard, "Admissible Evidence," pp. 338–39.

46. See G. L. Teh, "An Examination of the Judges' Rules in Australia," 46 *Australian Law Journal* 489 (1972).

47. For the prevailing British view, see The Criminal Law Revision Committee, *Evidence General,* eleventh report (London: H.M.S.O., 1972).

48. See generally, James Gordley, "Variations on a Modern Theme," in Cappelletti and Gordley, *Legal Aid,* pp. 387–421.

49. For background on the development of the Ontario plan, see Parker, "Legal Aid, Canadian Style," pp. 472–77.

50. Act 1949 (12–13–14 Geo. VI, c.51). For discussion, see Mauro Cappelletti, "The Emergence of a Modern Theme," in Cappelletti and Gordley, *Legal Aid,* pp. 474–76.

51. For discussion of the important function performed by "duty counsel," see Parker, "Legal Aid, Canadian Style," pp. 479–80.

52. See Honsberger, "The Ontario Legal Aid Plan," p. 443.

53. For a more complete description of this program, see Taman and Zemans, "The Future of Legal Services," pp. 33–34.

54. Ibid.

55. Ibid. pp. 32–33.

56. For discussion of this development see Zemans and Brickman, "Clinical Legal Education and Legal Aid—The Canadian Experience," p. 2.

57. For information on the early development of legal aid programs in the United States, see U.S., Department of Labor, Reginald Heber Smith and John S. Bradway, "Growth of Legal Aid Work in the United States" Bureau of Labor Statistics Bulletin No. 398 (1926).

58. See "First Annual Report of the Program of the Office of Economic Opportunity to the American Bar Association" (Annual Convention, Montreal, August, 1966).

59. See 84 Stat. 916–20 (1970).

60. For information on program expenditures, see ABA, *Program of the OEO,* p. 3. Note "Neighborhood Law Offices: The New Wave in Legal Services for the Poor," 80 *Harvard Law Review* 805, 806 (1967), and *Congressional Quarterly Weekly Report,* (March 17, 1973, pp. 564–65.

61. Harry P. Stumpf and Robert J. Janowitz, "Judges and the Poor: Bench Responses to Federally Financed Legal Services," 21 *Stanford Law Review* 1058, 1058–59 (1969).

62. See Pious, "Bar and Legal Services," pp. 418–22.

63. Stumpf and Janowitz, "Judges and the Poor," p. 1075.

64. See Harry P. Stumpf, Henry P. Schroerluke, and Forrest Dill, "The Legal Profession and Legal Services: Explorations in Local Bar Politics," 6 *Law and Society Review* 47, 60 (1971).

65. *Congressional Quarterly Weekly Report,* March 17, 1973, pp. 564–65, and June 8, 1973, p. 1448.

66. See *United States Code Congressional and Administrative News,* September 15, 1974, p. 2695.

67. See *Legal Services Corporation Act of 1974,* sec. 1006 (5)(a)(b); 42 U.S.C.A. 2701.

68. For discussion, see Ross Cranston and David Adams, "Legal Aid in Australia" 46 *Australian Law Journal* 508 (1972).

69. See Parker, "Legal Aid, Canadian Style," p. 473.

70. *Boddie* v. *Connecticut,* 401 U.S. 371 (1971).

71. Leonard Downie, Jr., *Justice Denied: The Case for Reform of the Courts* (Baltimore: Penguin Books, 1971), p. 105.

72. U.S., Congress, Senate Subcommittee on Representation of Citizen Interest of the Committee on the Judiciary, *Effect of Legal Fees on the Adequacy of Representation,* 93d Cong., 1st sess., Parts 1 and 2, September 19–20, October 1–2, 4–5, 1973.

Chapter 7 THE POLITICS OF
EQUALITY AMONG
EUROPEAN LINGUISTIC
MINORITIES

Manfred W. Wenner

The emphasis in this essay is on linguistic minorities and on how some modern European political systems and their political processes have treated the subject of human rights.[1] Accordingly, it becomes important to define and categorize those minorities. The definition of minority in this context will be a common-sense one: a collection of individuals which may be distinguished from the majority or dominant group in a political unit (country) on the basis of their collective possession of differential characteristics. Among such differential characteristics are: (1) language, (2) religion, (3) race, (4) culture, and (5) a collective conviction that they possess some jointly-held characteristic which constitutes grounds for recognition on the part of the majority or dominant group of their distinctiveness. For purposes of easy identification and location of the European minorities which are referred to, table 1 provides some essential background information.

THE POLITICAL CONTEXT

European views on minority rights. Until World War II, and especially during the interwar period of 1919–1939, an important assumption was shared by European leadership elites who dominated the international political arena. They assumed that *international* guarantees of the rights of ethnic minorities (of all types) within their current political domiciles would provide some measure of protection against the likelihood of new wars. This view was based upon the conclusion (only in part substantiated by evidence) that the grievances of ethnic minorities against their current governments were a major precipitant of such international conflicts. With politically destabilizing results, ethnic minorities could relocate or ally themselves with others of their group elsewhere and publicize prejudicial governmental behavior or policies.

The post-World War II era brought about a shift in the assumptions about the role of minorities in provoking international wars. In part, the experience of

European Jewry during the ascendancy of the Nazi Party (NSDAP) in Germany contributed to this change in attitude. The widely shared view now is that the elimination of minorities by absorption and assimilation, not by genocide, is an important strategy in the elimination of potential interstate conflicts. Under the old suppositions and related treaties designed to protect minority *collectives,* it was possible for a government to direct specific public policies at collectives within its borders. As the experience of Europe's Jews at the hands of the NSDAP showed, one such potential public policy could be genocide. This experience generated scepticism regarding international guarantees for the protection of minorities. In the postwar era, attitudes toward international guarantees have changed. It is now often argued that public policy carried out on an *individual* basis (with no special arrangements for collectives) would be more likely to eliminate invidious or prejudicial distinctions than did the former guarantees.

This change of attitude has affected current discussion of human rights. A number of "universal" statements which specified the rights of all *individuals* irrespective of their creed, color, national origin, and other such criteria have been promulgated, and all countries expected to adhere to and enforce such personal guarantees. Although some minorities sought specific guarantees for their collective protection, as well as special privileges which would promote and protect their continued distinctive character (such as separate educational systems), these were opposed by the governments of countries with such minorities. In some cases, this opposition rested on the argument that the introduction of special provisions for any group would negate the validity of the universal guarantees for all citizens. As such it ran counter to liberal democratic theory; in other cases, governments were reluctant to admit the existence of any minority within their frontiers for fear of potential intergroup competition in the political arena. General recognition of group distinctiveness could lead to increased self-consciousness among other potential minorities among which no such sentiment previously had existed.

The postwar era has seen the formulation and ratification of only three international treaties which seek to protect human rights. These are the Universal Declaration of Human Rights, the Genocide Convention, and the European Convention on Human Rights. They are not comparable in purpose or content with the plethora of treaties and international agreements for such purposes which followed World War I. Although a number of draft treaties have been proposed in recent years which more specifically seek to protect collectives, none of these have been ratified.

The Universal Declaration of Human Rights was adopted in 1948 by the General Assembly of the United Nations. It has been supplemented by two additional covenants: the Covenant on Civil and Political Rights, and the Covenant on Economic, Social, and Cultural Rights (both adopted in 1966). None of these are binding on the member states nor on those nations which

Table 1. CHARACTERISTICS OF SELECTED EUROPEAN MINORITIES

Country (Population)	Minority Population	Minority Percentage	Type of Minority	Minority Background
GREAT BRITAIN (55.1 million)				
Scots (Scotland)	5,200,000	9.4	Linguistic/cultural	Gaelic
Welsh (Wales)	2,600,000	4.7	Linguistic	Celtic
Cornish (Cornwall)	350,000	0.6	Cultural/linguistic	Celtic
Manx (Isle of Man)	50,000	0.001	Cultural	Celtic
Normans (Channel Islands)	125,000	0.02	Cultural/Linguistic	French
Catholics (Northern Ireland)	500,000	4.0	Religious	
FRANCE (50.1 million)				
Bretons (Brittany)	3,200,000	6.4	Linguistic	Celtic
Alsatians (Alsace)	1,500,000	2.9	Linguistic	Germanic (German)
Flemish	400,000	0.8	Linguistic	Germanic (Dutch)
Occitanes	10,000,000	19.9	Linguistic	French/Latin
Basques	200,000	0.4	Linguistic	Unique: cf. Spain
ITALY (53 million)				
S. Tyroleans (Bozen/Bolzano)	250,000	0.47	Linguistic	Germanic (Austrian)
Valdotaines (Val d'Aosta)	150,000	0.28	Linguistic	French

			Linguistic/religious	French
SWITZERLAND (6.2 million)				
Jurassiens (Bernese Jura)	130,000	0.02ª	Linguistic/religious	French
German-speakers		69.0		
French-speakers		19.0		
Italian-speakers		10.0		
Romansch-speakers		1.0		
SPAIN (32.5 million)				
Catalans (Cataluna)	6,750,000	20.8	Linguistic	Latin
Basques ("Euzkadi")	1,750,000	5.4	Linguistic/cultural	Unique
Galician (Galicia)	3,000,000	9.2	Cultural	Celtic w/Latin lang.
AUSTRIA (7.4 million)				
Croatians	50,000	0.66	Linguistic	Slavic
Slovenians	40,000	0.053	Linguistic	Slavic
Magyars	2,500	0.003	Linguistic	Hungarian
BELGIUM (9.8 million)				
Walloons (Wallonie)		44.0	Linguistic	French
Flemish (Flanders)		55.0	Linguistic	Germanic (Dutch)
Germans	75,000	1.0	Linguistic	Germanic (German)

ª15.4 percent of Bern.

voted for their adoption; they are binding only on those states which have specifically ratified them.[2] Although the content of these two Covenants has some bearing on the issue of minority civil rights, the actual text of the relevant passages is distressingly vague in import.

On the other hand, the initiative which the United Nations took in drafting and proposing conventions of this sort led to the movement in Europe to create a specifically European document for similar purposes. This convention, the most important of the postwar international agreements for purposes of this paper, is the European Convention for the Protection of Human Rights and Fundamental Freedoms (termed the European Convention), signed in 1950.[3] Part 1 of the convention sets out twelve rights and freedoms which are specifically guaranteed; two protocols since that time (the first in 1952, the second in 1963) increase the list of rights by three and four rights respectively.

Strikingly, not one of the enumerated rights and freedoms is designed specifically to protect the collective rights of ethnic minorities, nor is there any specific guarantee made with regard to the use of minority languages. Although article 6 contains certain provisions concerning the determination of civil rights and obligations when criminal charges have been lodged against an individual, the relevant portions have been interpreted by the Commission responsible for the implementation and enforcement of the Convention in such a manner as to preclude any general right on the part of the accused to insist upon being tried in a particular language. Article 14 reads: "The enjoyment of the rights and freedoms set forth in this Convention shall be secured without discrimination on any ground such as sex, colour, language, religion, political or other opinion, national or social origin, *association with a national minority* [italics added] property, birth or other status."[4] This provision appears to grant rights not specifically enumerated in that section of the Convention. Nevertheless, the Commission has ruled that this article applies only to the enumerated rights and freedoms and therefore does not forbid discrimination with regard to the enjoyment of rights and freedoms which have *not* been specifically enumerated.[5] Thus legal realities have not lived up to earlier hopes.

Many authors concerned with the problem of minority rights interpret the change in purpose and content of such agreements as due, in part, to the ideological principles associated with the two dominant political philosophies of the postwar era: democratic liberalism and Marxism. Both of these ideologies are essentially hostile to the political reality of ethnic identification although they are frequently concerned with minority identification and political activity for reasons of political strategy.

In liberal democratic ideology, individual opportunity and personal development and fulfillment are the legitimate ends of the "good polity." That is, cooperation and public spiritedness stem from individual interests and actions. Although various ethnic collectives may be wooed or manipulated for short-term political benefit, it is primarily with voluntary associations and groups—the product of individual initiative—that the polity should be and is concerned. Public bodies, citizens, and officeholders all believe that justice is served when people are treated and promoted based upon individual merit. A dilemma arises, however, when the reality of ethnic groups is denied theoretically while political strategies for electoral victory frequently display an inordinate concern with such groups and their (real or assumed) "bloc-voting" patterns. Cynthia Enloe comments: "Democratic ideology goes undisturbed as long as ethnic communities are intent upon assimilation or as long as they are too politically underdeveloped to make their existence forcefully known to the oblivious majority. . . . [thus enabling democracies to] sing the praises of individualism and pluralism simultaneously. The conceptual trick is to acknowledge diversity of cultures within the society but assume that culture deals mainly with styles and cooking recipes and has relatively little impact on ambitions, moral judgments, and public goals. . . . In other words, the discrepancy between democratic ideology and ethnic reality is resolved by reducing ethnicity to [questions] of style."[6]

In modern Marxism, opposition to particularistic sentiments is in some respects quite similar to that of the democratic ideology; that is, such sentiments delay or prevent national liberation and development. In fact, peoples have to be "deliver[ed] . . . from age-old religious and nationalist prejudices."[7] At the same time, however, Marxist theoreticians and practitioners have frequently argued for the functional value of alliances between ethnic communalism and the Communist party (CP) for the purposes of effecting the necessary revolution to socialism. When, however, ethnic communalism competes with or resists CP ideology, it is condemned as intolerable and bourgeois. The most common Marxist view of such ethnic or particularistic sentiments is that they are the product of, promoted by, and manipulated for the interests of the middle class, especially in developed societies.

Although both ideologies essentially agree that a commitment to ethnic particularism in the modern world is an anomaly and a characteristic of those portions of the population who have not discarded or outgrown their primitive myths and beliefs, the manner in which these two systems have attempted to provide some measure of human rights to minorities is substantially different. The liberal democratic societies—of North America and Western Europe—have, until very recently, guaranteed on an individual basis whatever human rights have been considered important enough to specify and to elaborate. In contrast, Marxian societies (the Eastern European states and the Soviet Union, as well as China) have tended to guarantee human rights on the collective level. It is easy, of course, to argue that this difference in emphasis is a reflection of different conceptions of which unit—the individual or the collective—is the focus of the "good polity." What is of interest here is what kinds of individual and collective rights have been guaranteed by some representative Western European nations; whether or not such guarantees are effective or meaningful; and what the possible social correlates of developments in this area are.

Human rights issues in postwar Europe. Any analysis of the rights which have become social issues in Western Europe today must be prefaced by making an essential distinction between different types of minorities. This is the distinction between minorities which have a "territorial" base (an ethnic group which occupies a relatively clearly-demarcated area within some given political unit) and minorities which are "dispersed" (do not lay claim to or occupy any specific piece of territory). Examples of the former are the Welsh, resident in Wales in Great Britain; the Bretons, resident in *Bretagne* ("Brittany") in France; the Basques in Spain and France, and the South Tyroleans in Italy. Examples of the latter are the Gypsies (*Rom*), hundreds of thousands of whom are found in the western European countries, and the so called guest workers, the foreign immigrant population temporarily employed in the industries of the economically advanced western European nations.[8] The latter category includes the East Indians, Pakistanis, West Indians, Turks, Spaniards, Greeks, North Africans, Italians and others in, primarily, Great Britain, France, Germany, and Switzerland.[9]

It is with the territorially based minorities within the western European nations that we are most concerned in this essay, because these minority groups are, at least in theory, considered to be full citizens. There is an increasing concern by many western European minorities about their current and future status—political, economic, and social. Even a cursory review of significant news stories since the end of World War II is sufficient to demonstrate that the Welsh and the Scots in Great Britain, the Jurassiens in Switzerland, the Bretons in France, the Basques in Spain, and the Flemish in Belgium all have become increasingly militant and vociferous in defense of their alleged rights. They have frequently agitated for some more meaningful recognition of their separateness within the political unit of which they form a part.

Why are ethnic minorities in western Europe at present becoming more militant in their demands for additional human rights? One explanation focuses on the policies adopted by governments and the pan-European organizations (such as the European Economic Community—the Common Market) concerning the general issues which have been raised. Some of the European minorities mentioned above began their protests against what they considered unfair, unjust, or illegitimate governmental policies decades ago; some launched their protests in the immediate postwar period. (The Jurassiens in Switzerland revived their separatist movement in 1947.) However, many of the currently active minorities began stressing their claims and escalating their militancy after the formation of the European Common Market (EEC). The latter development suggests that, as more and more decisions affecting the national economies of the member states were transferred to Brussels, some minorities lost comparative influence at the national decision-making level. This decline in the ability of some minorities to affect public policy regarding their own interests (in many instances, primarily agricultural ones) led to both an increasing militancy at home and demands for modifications in the processes and goals which formed part of the proposed pattern for European political and economic cooperation.[10] In fact, the leadership groups of many of the affected minorities have begun to suggest that the pattern for Europe's future ought to be not a federal state of Europe with the existing states as the membership units, but rather a Europe that is a federation of *peoples,* that is, the various ethnic groups in Europe today ought to be the constituent units. In this way, the various minorities would be able to retain or regain some measure of control over decisions which most affect their particular territorial base and its economic interests.[11]

A second possible explanation for ethnic militancy may be deduced from a review of the socioeconomic positions of the various western European minorities which indicates that many inhabit areas which are considerably below the European or national average in per capita income, access to public services, level of economic (especially industrial) development, and a host of other commonly accepted criteria of politico-economic development. It may be suggested, therefore, that as pan-European communications (both transportation facilities and media) have become more highly developed, these minorities have become more aware of their less developed status. They have begun to participate in the "revolution of rising expectations" and more vigorously and effectively to present their demands for achieving equal status and an equal standard of living.

A third explanation suggests that when assimilation rates rise, minorities inevitably become a less significant portion of the total population mix within a country. As viewed by the minorities, they become a less significant portion of that part of the total which they consider to be their "homeland." Consequently, there has appeared among the nonassimilated, remaining portion of the minority an increased awareness of their relative and absolute decline, which has, in turn, stimulated an increased self-awareness and desire to retain a measure of distinctiveness in the face of an ever-increasing tendency toward a homogeneous Europe. For whatever cause, increasingly militant minorities are demanding an expansion of their influence in the policy-making processes, and more explicit recognition of their distinctiveness from the governments of their respective countries.

Among the minorities which have been the most vociferous in recent years, a significant pattern is clear: all have, as a major factor in their demands, stressed *linguistic* differentiation from the majority. All of the currently active minorities have in common that at least part of their culture is based upon a language which is different from that of the dominant or majority group. The following analysis focuses on public policy that has developed in some of these countries in response to demands based on linguistic differences. The issue of linguistic civil rights is used to clarify the broader and more complex problem of minority civil rights.

Although homogeneity of language is not a necessary or sufficient condition for political cohesiveness among diverse people, it frequently acts as the most effective basis for some sort of social bond, if only because it makes meaningful communication possible. This, in turn, makes social and economic interaction possible, leading to cooperation and specialization. Many, if not most, persons and groups use language as an easy, immediate, and clear means of identifying the members of their own groups as opposed to persons belonging to other groups. Common language makes possible a relatively clear in-group and out-group differentiation.[12]

Conversely, a situation in which portions of the citizenry are not part of the majority language community can present substantial social, economic, and political difficulties for the authorities. Clearly, whether such a situation becomes fraught with political dangers depends upon a number of factors. Among these are: (1) the size or proportion of the population which is not part of the majority language community; (2) the degree of political awareness or political development which exists among the speakers of the minority language; (3) the degree to which the minority-language group seeks or avoids assimilation with the majority; and (4) the degree of group consciousness, the extent to which the members of the minority language community feel committed to their language as evidence of either their distinctiveness or their cultural identity.

In the United States, it was only when linguistic minorities chose publicly to promote and to work for separate rather than assimilated status that public policy decisions began to recognize the existence of those minorities as collectives. Political and social demands have led to bilingual instruction in some minority school districts; to the publication of certain government forms, applications, and regulations in minority languages; to the printing of bilingual ballots; and to acceptance of testimony in a court of law in the language of the minority (with the cost of an interpreter borne by the court). For minorities in other countries who view their language as the primary means of defining their distinctiveness, rights associated with that language are considered essential. The right to use and perpetuate a language is the basic criteria by which the attitudes, policies, and activities of a government are judged. In many instances, the continued separate existence of the minority is seen as a function of the right to continue to use the language.

LINGUISTIC RIGHTS IN EUROPE

In political societies which are essentially or totally monolingual, it often is difficult to conceive of the various ways in which a committed or self-conscious minority which is linguistically differentiated from the majority or dominant group may seek to press its demands for this particular human or civil right. Table 2 provides some indication of the multitudinous ways in which language use may be of sociopolitical relevance to such a minority. It is difficult to conceive of a right to education which does not, if it is to be meaningful, permit

Table 2. LINGUISTIC RIGHTS: "THE RIGHT TO USE ONE'S OWN LANGUAGE"

1. Individual use

   a) the right to use the language at home
   b) the right to use the language "in the street"
   c) the right to use the language for personal names (both first and family names)

2. Individual and collective uses

   a) the right to use the language in personal communications (letters, telephone conversations, telegrams)
   b) the right to use the language in activities designed to perpetuate its use in:
      (1) schools
      (2) newspapers, journals, magazines, books, etc.
      (3) radio and television broadcasting
      (4) movies
   c) the right to use the language in private economic activities in:
      (1) business or manufacturing enterprise between workers
      (2) advertising (storefront, media, etc.)
      (3) record-keeping (order, invoices, inventories, and the like.)
      (4) other communications (letterheads, etc.)
   d) the right to use the language in private associations in:
      (1) clubs of all types (social, sport, cultural)
      (2) churches and religious organizations
   e) the right to use the language in public meetings

3. Individual and collective uses vis-à-vis the government

   a) in courts of law (with or without an interpreter supplied at government expense)
   b) in communications with the government, such as license forms, filing required affidavits, tax forms, and applications for governmental services
   c) in public notices (street signs, public information signs, and the like)
   d) in campaigning and running for public office
   e) in government reports, documents, hearings, transcripts, and other official publications for public distribution
   f) in the national legislature (in debates), the national judiciary, and the national administrative agencies, bureaus, and departments

members of a linguistic minority to educate their offspring in their own language. To examine such issues, we must make our focus comparative. Given the relatively ineffectual impact of international agreements concerning minority rights, the civil and political rights of linguistically differentiated minorities in western Europe must be analyzed in terms of *national* policies.

The analysis must take into account the considerable variation in the amount of local autonomy over certain aspects of daily life which is permitted in western Europe. The British government, although it is frequently cited as an example of a highly centralized democratic government, permits some of its constituent parts (Scotland, Wales, and Northern Ireland) substantial degrees of control over local affairs. Northern Ireland has long had its own parliament (the Stormont), while the Scottish Office, although not legally the equivalent of the Stormont, has had considerable power in determining separate legislation for Scotland. The latter has, in addition, its own educational system and a separate state church. In France, on the other hand, no local decision making on any such matters as education and public policy for areas of the country which are dominated by a specific minority, such as the Bretons in Brittany, has been permitted since Napoleon Bonaparte. France, among the democratic states of Western Europe, has been the most reluctant to grant or implement extensive minority rights.

Language minorities in France. Contemporary writers who describe the demographic characteristics of France at present generally acknowledge the presence of the following ethnic groups: (1) the Flemish population, concentrated along the Atlantic coast near the border with Belgium; (2) the Breton population, concentrated in the Brittany Peninsula on the northwestern Atlantic coastline; (3) the Basques, located in the southwestern corner on the Bay of Biscay along the Spanish frontier; (4) the Catalans, located on the Spanish frontier on the Mediterranean coast around the city of Perpignan; (5) the Occitanes, comprising most of the population of the south below a rough line from Bordeaux in the west, through Clermont-Ferrand in the center, to Lyon in the east; (6) the Corsicans, on the island of Corsica in the Mediterranean; and (7) the German-speaking population of the east along the Rhine, in Alsace, and in part of Lorraine.[13]

All of these ethnic groups were part of France at the time of the Revolution of 1789. And much of the legislation and contemporary French governmental policy toward displays of ethnic distinctiveness has its origins in the Revolutionary and Napoleonic eras. In a series of decrees issued by the Committee of Public Safety in 1793, it was stated that "the diversity of local idioms and jargons" inhibited the growth and development of "reason" and unnaturally prolonged the life of prejudices and old attitudes; as a result, it was necessary to "extirpate all of them" and require that "in all parts of the Republic instruction would not be given in any other language than French."[14] In fact, in the minds of nearly all Revolutionary leaders, everything evil and reactionary was associated with the minorities: "federalism and superstition spoke Breton; emigration and hatred of the Republic spoke German; counter-revolution spoke Italian; fanaticism spoke Basque," and the like. Despite many efforts since that time by both public officials and organized groups representing the minorities to permit some official recognition of these other languages, official French government policy has continued essentially unchanged to the present. It was still possible for the French Minister of Education to state publicly in 1925, for example, that "the unity of France requires that the Breton language disappear." In 1973, as in 1793, official French public policy was that minority languages in France cannot be part of the regular school curriculum.[15]

The most significant change in French public policy in this connection was the *Loi Deixonne* of 1951 according to which, *optional* instruction in the minority languages (with the exception of Flemish, which is not covered) is permitted for both teachers and families *if* such optional instruction takes place *after,* and not as part of, the regular public and private school curricula and hours schedules.[16] Although there is no doubt that the organized efforts of some of the minorities were responsible for this relatively slight change, it has not been sufficient to quell or satisfy even the most moderate champions of increased civil liberties for the linguistic minorities. In fact, citing both the evidence of modern psychology and the ideals associated with a "new Europe,"[17] advocates of greater minority rights have succeeded in small ways: the number of hours per week of permitted instruction has, in nearly all instances, been increased and local radio and television have been allowed to broadcast in the minority language. Among other concessions, the printing and distribution of publications in minority languages has been almost entirely freed from constraints. On the other hand, some of these concessions appear pitifully small; for example, the Bretons are permitted only one hour per week of optional instruction, while the local radio station is now permitted to broadcast forty minutes per week in the Breton language and the regional television one and one-half minutes per week![18]

Regional ethnic minorities in France are not treated equally. In fact, there are substantial differences in the liberties which they have been permitted to exercise and in the public policies which have been adopted by successive postwar governments with respect to the different minorities. For example, while the Bretons are not permitted to make use of the Breton language in the naming of children or families, no such restrictions ever have been imposed on or attempted among the German-speaking minority. Attempts by Breton nationalists in recent years to challenge these restrictions has led to denial of all public assistance funds, government grants, and other government payments to which their families are entitled. In addition, children of families which have been given or use Breton names have been denied legal existence, thereby making it impossible for them to attend public educational facilities. Similarly, as late as 1960, the use by children in primary schools of the Breton language was so stringently forbidden that children were encouraged to report to the authorities any of their classmates who did indeed converse in Breton.[19]

On the other hand, although the German language was "provisionally" eliminated in Alsace and part of Lorraine after World War II, by 1950 the demand for public recognition that German was *the* language of daily communication for far more than 50 percent of the population of these areas led to its introduction, in 1952, into the public school curriculum as an optional language. By 1960, three hours per week of German instruction for the last three years of the basic curriculum (after age twelve) was permitted. It should be noted, however, that this instruction could be waived by either the local instructors or the family of the child, and, in any event, was to be offered only in accord with the limitations established by the *Loi Deixonne.*[20] In addition, no restrictions upon the use of the German language were imposed in public: street signs in the minority language were permitted (this was not and is not the case in Brittany); names were never regulated in any way; nor was there any overt governmentally supported or directed campaign to punish German speakers. The publication of both bilingual newspapers and journals has never been restricted, and considerably more time on local radio and television stations is permitted in the local language.

Why does such differential treatment exist? Inasmuch as the Bretons outnumber the German-speakers in France, we may dismiss the simplistic explanation that the more numerous minority enjoys the greater privileges and rights. On the other hand, as a partial explanation of how much political influence and pressure an ethnic group is able to bring to bear upon the dominant or majority group, this line of reasoning cannot be wholly eliminated from consideration. For example, there is evidence which suggests that the Basques and the Flemish minorities, which together constitute less than 1 percent of the total, have not been able materially to affect public policy precisely because they consistently fail to elect members of their own group as deputies to the National Assembly where they might be able to have some significant and relevant influence on matters of public policy which affect them. Although national parties are the only ones which regularly offer candidates for public office in the minority regions, it is frequently so that the local candidate belongs to the ethnic group and may even campaign in the local language.

A persuasive historical explanation of the observed differences in treatment can be made by going back briefly to World War II. Many French perceive a distinction between the level of loyalty to France as a whole demonstrated by the Bretons and that of the German-speaking population of Alsace and Lorraine. The Vichy Government was sympathetic to Breton aspirations, and it permitted substantially greater degrees of regional decision-making than the Third Republic had done.[21] Prominent Breton nationalists do not deny their distaste for French "cultural imperialism," but they cite that distaste as an indication of their commitment to the ideal of Breton autonomy *within* a federal France. Therefore, they vociferously deny the implied charge that they collaborated with the Germans, pointing out that their casualty rate in World War II exceeded that of the French by a factor of nearly three. In addition, they explain the rather high rate of executions of Bretons in the French army—for a variety of military offenses—as being due to the demonstrated inability of many Breton draftees to understand military commands in the French language.[22]

On the other hand, the loyalty to France demonstrated by the German-speaking population of Alsace and Lorraine has been cited frequently by French historians and writers on World War II. Although many French apparently expected that this minority would be openly pro-German in its war sympathies, and perhaps even participate in acts of sabotage and other acts which would benefit the German occupation forces, this rarely, if ever, happened. In other words, the German-speaking minority today is able to draw upon a considerable fund of good will generated during a traumatic period in modern French history—something the Breton minority cannot do.[23] This World War II experience, however, cannot serve to explain the observed differences. In fact, the behavior of the Bretons shows that there already had been a pattern of discriminatory treatment on the part of the French *prior* to the war. The Bretons simply exploited it for their own purposes.

For another possible explanation, we may turn to the level of political activism since the war. The levels and types of political activity designed and used to effect a change in the status of the Breton population differ markedly from those found among the German-speakers. In fact, the Breton example provides some evidence that there is a deep-seated fear on the part of the French authorities that the minorities harbor secret desires to dismember the country. For example, in the first decade of the twentieth century, the government attempted to justify its policies forbidding the teaching and speaking of Breton by the argument that such activities would provide support for and strengthen separatist sentiment among the Bretons. This rather rigid assimilationist policy brought into being a nationalist party (*Parti Nationaliste Breton*) which began to suggest separatism as a solution. Government policies produced precisely those sentiments among the Bretons which they had been calculated to destroy.[24]

Ever since that time, Breton efforts toward change in government policy have intensified. After World War I, petitions were sent to President Wilson; new political parties were created in the 1920s and 1930s; numerous periodicals dedicated to the cause of Brittany appeared; and, perhaps most important, political violence against the government broke out, usually consisting of bomb and arson attacks against public buildings and French monuments.[25]

The Vichy government permitted the establishment of a Consultative Committee for Bretagne, and permitted the teaching of Breton. The postwar era has seen the founding of additional political parties and associations, as well as cultural, social, and folkloric organizations designed to perpetuate and spread Breton self-consciousness among the population. Moreover, there now exist a *Front de Libération Breton* and an *Armée Républicaine Bretonne*. Apparently both are committed to the practice of political violence against the French government, although neither appears to have garnered much support and sympathy among the Breton population. Nevertheless, from the point of view of a Jacobin Frenchman, an active campaign is being waged in pursuit of the goal of autonomy. There is certainly a substantial body of literature which favors the separatist goal and ideology.[26]

These conditions do not prevail among the German-speaking population. There are, for example, no comparable politically active organizations in Alsace and Lorraine, although there is no lack of cultural and social organizations. What is more important, the population of Alsace and Lorraine produced the largest majorities in favor of Charles DeGaulle and his policies in the referendums of 1959, 1961, and 1962.[27] Thus, for the relevant elites of France, it appears clear that the Bretons today present a significant threat to the unity of France (just as they did in World War II); the German-speaking minority does not. It seems legitimate, therefore, to suggest that at least part of the explanation of the differential treatment which the Breton and German minorities receive is due precisely to this factor: the more threatening and activist the minority is perceived to be in seeking change, the less likely it is to have its demands met. Recent events seem to support this contention: on January 10, 1974, the government summarily decided to ban the activities of the most avowedly separatist minority political organizations.[28]

There remains the question of whether or not certain socioeconomic indicators may be related to the level of dissatisfaction, support for separatist organizations, and degree of activism among the minorities. Since the French government does not provide statistical data on minorities as such, it is necessary to consider the data that are available for the administrative subdivisions in which the minorities are found. Although not sufficient to warrant any far-reaching conclusions, the results of table 3 are nevertheless instructive. Bearing in mind the sizable margin of error which results from lack of a complete correspondence between the regions and the minorities (with the least disparity in the case of the Bretons and the Germans), it is nevertheless interesting that the most favorable socioeconomic characteristics are associated with the Germans. They have the lowest unemployment rate, the highest per capita consumption rate, and the second highest rate of modernization (as measured by the proportion of the population engaged in industry and services, rather than agricultural production).[29] Conversely, the Bretons show the greatest dependence on agriculture, a higher unemployment rate than the national average, and the second lowest per capita consumption rate. Thus, while it would seem there is some preliminary evidence for a possible relationship between socioeconomic indicators and the strength of commitment to separatist ideologies, there is certainly not enough information (in view of the comparable position of the Occitanes, for example) to warrant any general statement. The necessary data are not available at this time to support more precise statements.

In conclusion, it appears that a minority of substantial proportions in France (such as the Bretons, the Germans, and the Occitanes) is generally in a better position to obtain some limited measure of recognition from the highly centralized and essentially Jacobin French administrative and governmental organs. This is, in turn, a function of the fact that they dominate one or more of the administrative subdivisions which were made at the time of Napoleon Bonaparte, the prefectures and electoral districts.

On the other hand, it appears even clearer that the greater the amount of apparently threatening political and extralegal activity which the minority employs in the attempt to expand its rights, the less are the chances that any devolution, supplementary rights, or special privileges will be granted or permitted. The actions of the government in January of 1974 provide the best

Table 3. STATISTICAL INDICATORS OF FRENCH REGIONS

	Population	Percent	Area Percent	Percent GDP	Percent Unempl.	Percent in Agric.	Percent in Indust.	Percent in Services	Consumption per Inhabitant as Percent of Paris Region
France	51,030,000	100.0	100.0	100.0	1.5				100
Bretagne	2,503,000	4.9	5.0	3.9	1.6	25.7	30.6	43.7	63
(Bretons)	(3,200,000)	(6.4)							
Alsace	1,454,000	2.8	1.5	2.7	0.3	9.7	48.3	41.9	69
(Germans)[a]	(1,500,000)	(2.9)							
Nord	3,864,000	7.6	2.3	2.3	1.6	5.6	53.2	41.2	65
(Flemish)[b]	(400,000)	(0.8)							
Acquitaine	2,492,000	4.9	7.6	7.6	2.0	21.1	35.2	43.6	61
(Basques)[c]	(200,000)	(0.4)							
Occitanie	8,687,000	17.0	24.0	15.8	2.0	17.7	33.5	48.8	65
(Occitanes)	10,000,000	(20.0)							

Source: Regional Statistics 1972 ed. (Luxemburg: Statistical Office of the European Communities, 1973).
Occitanie has been artificially created by combining (and in certain instances averaging) the data from the following French regions: Midi-Pyrenees, Auvergne, Languedoc-Roussillon, and Provence-Cote d'Azur. While, in the view of the Occitanes, this is not a completely accurate reflection of what constitutes Occitanie, it is as close as French statistical data permit at present.

[a] A small number of Germans are also found in Lorraine.
[b] The Flemish percentage of Nord would be 10.4.
[c] The Basque percentage of Acquitaine would be 8.

evidence for this contention: those movements and organizations which are committed to an expansion of rights for the Corsicans, the Basques, the Bretons, and the Occitanes and which have elected to follow a comparatively extreme path have been completely prohibited from any further activity.

Language minorities in Great Britain. Great Britain also has a number of constituent peoples within the polity which are ethnically different from the dominant English majority. These are primarily the Welsh, the Scots, and the Northern Irish, although for the sake of completeness, table 1 includes a few smaller groups as well. For the limited purposes of this paper, only the Welsh and to a lesser extent the Scots will be used as examples to illustrate British policies toward minorities.

England and Great Britain are not the same.[30] Richard Rose comments on the political importance of this point: "Today, the institutions of the regime reflect both the diversity of the peoples of the United Kingdom, and the confusion of things English with things British. Formally, the regime is a unitary state. Yet, Northern Ireland has a separate Constitution, Parliament and Cabinet at Stormont with very substantial powers granted to it. Scotland lacks a separate Parliament, but there is concentrated in the Scottish Office much of the de facto responsibility for governing Scotland. . . . To a lesser extent, special provision is also made for Wales.[31] Until recently, Wales was considered an appendage of England. It was not until the 1950s and 1960s that devolution began to affect Wales; for example, it was not until 1964 that a Welsh Office with powers roughly comparable to those of the Scottish Office was established. These offices (with seats in Edinburgh and Cardiff respectively) have accumulated an impressive series of responsibilities, which include roads, housing and local government, town and country planning, water, sewerage, health and welfare services, tourist affairs, agriculture, among other matters. And significantly, it is precisely in some of these policy areas that many minorities see essential rights involved.[32]

In Great Britain, there is no specific guarantee which protects the continued existence of minority languages. Strictly speaking, Great Britain does not have the equivalent of a *Loi Deixonne* to permit instruction in Welsh, Gaelic, Manx, and the like. Welsh nationalists are quick to point out that as a result of various English policies, the percentage of Welsh-speakers declined from 54.4 percent in 1891 to 26 percent in 1961.[33] The Act of Union of 1536, which annexed Wales to England, stated: "Henceforth no person that uses the Welsh language shall have or enjoy any manner of office or fees from within this realm of England." Furthermore, the 1870 Education Act banned the use of Welsh in schools, providing punishments reminiscent of those imposed on the Bretons in France.[34] Clearly, however, the attachment to the language survived these and other attempts to limit its use. In the view of many Welsh, however, it was not these Acts so much as a combination of industrialization, certain democratizing educational acts (such as the Intermediate Education Act of 1889), and the premium placed on English for greater opportunity and social mobility which were the prime factors in the decline of the Welsh language.[35]

Nevertheless, as historians and Welsh publicists can show, Welsh patriotism (nationalism) never disappeared—either after the amalgamation with England, or as a result of the industrialization of Wales. There are numerous Welsh organizations, including some primarily political ones, which trace their histories into the nineteenth century, the period of nationalist fervor among the other European peoples. Even so, it seems clear that the precipitous decline in the percentage of the population able to speak Welsh brought about a renewed interest in, and concern with, the role which the Welsh language plays for the Welsh.

Since the 1950s, important devolutionary measures with regard to Wales have been implemented. The most important is the Welsh Language Act, passed in 1967 by the Labour Government (which, it should be noted, depends heavily upon Wales for its British successes). This Act was the first legal action, comparable to the *Loi Deixonne* in France, which provided the Welsh minority with certain stipulated linguistic rights. In effect, it permitted the use of the Welsh language in connection with certain official activities of the British government in governmental offices, law courts, and the like.[36] For some of the Welsh nationalists, it was regarded as the first step in the creation of a bilingual society; for others, it was a demonstration of essential British fairness.

"It has shown itself a sham" is, however, the view of many Welshmen since that time. Attempts to erect bilingual road signs in Wales have resulted in prison sentences for the individuals involved; attempts fully to implement its promise in Welsh courts have resulted in the raising of almost insuperable obstacles by English judges serving in Wales.[37] On the other hand, this Act has in fact resulted in an increase in the number of cases tried in the Welsh language and, at the same time, has encouraged other Welshmen to persist in their conflicts with the English language. For example, it appears that an increasing number of Welsh have refused to pay their BBC-TV license fees because the BBC does not provide sufficient programming in Welsh to warrant the amounts collected; (a maximum of twelve hours per week is broadcast). The most interesting development along these lines has been the refusal by Welsh judges to invoke the mandatory penalties set by British law against such nonpayers, resulting in an ongoing and increasingly serious dispute within the British court system concerning the implementation of the Act and the rights of Welshmen.[38]

The issue of language is not nearly as important in Scotland. The nationalists have not emphasized language distinctiveness to any significant degree, because the Scottish form of Gaelic is spoken only in isolated rural areas. Nevertheless, the Scottish dialect of English differs substantially from that spoken in England (due to its Gaelic and Germanic elements), and it is likely that the nationalists in the future will make an issue out of public education in Gaelic and the Scottish dialect.[39]

Although it would seem legitimate to suggest that, in the past, the British

Government was just as prepared to insist upon the primacy of the English language in the country as the French were (and are) prepared to insist upon theirs, British attitudes during the past forty years do seem to have undergone a marked change. It is, of course, impossible to find any real devolutionary actions in France (despite the formidable promises made under the proposed regionalization schemes) and, despite whatever demurrers the Welsh and the Scots are able to cite, current evidence indicates a more pragmatic and, indeed, open attitude toward the miscellaneous demands of the regional minorities in Great Britain. Perhaps the best evidence of the altered English attitude is the recent announcement that the government is considering some form of limited self-government for Wales and Scotland including, possibly, separate elected assemblies which would, nevertheless, be ultimately responsible to Parliament.[40]

In the review of French minorities and their demands for greater rights, it has been suggested that social scientists have tended to consider three variables as most important in explaining situations of the kind under review: (1) the relative percentage and absolute numbers of the minority, (2) the level of activism, and (3) socioeconomic indicators. In the British case, we have further evidence that size is a significant variable: since the Scots and the Welsh make up 10 percent and 5 percent, respectively, of the population of Great Britain, it seems possible to argue that it could have been predicted that the English would in time be faced with increasing demands for minority rights from these two peoples. And, the Scots, who make up the largest minority percentage of the total population of any country considered here, have, in fact, been making such demands and objecting to English "domination" longer than any of the others. However, the demands for increased recognition on the part of the Cornish population in Britain have been overwhelmingly treated with ridicule in the English press—in clear contrast to recent coverage of the Scots and Welsh.[41] A review of the "level of activism" variable shows, on the other hand, significant differences between the two countries. In twentieth century Great Britain, the higher the level of commitment and activism, the larger the number of concessions (either symbolic or real) which the British government apparently is prepared to make.

Although the publicists for both the Scots and the Welsh point to grievances and attempts to obtain greater rights in past centuries, the greatest efforts in this direction clearly have occurred since World War I. And, it is relatively easy to show that, as complaints and demands have increased, especially since the 1930s, so, in turn, have the administrative actions of the British government directed at accommodating them. Examples are the establishment of both the Scottish and the Welsh Offices; more recent Parliamentary Acts, including the Welsh Language Act; and the rather substantial responsibilities for various local affairs already listed.

Finally, there is the question of whether or not accepted socioeconomic indicators may be related to the level of dissatisfaction, support for separatist organizations, and the degree of activism among the Welsh and the Scots. A review of the literature published by the Welsh and Scottish separatists highlights an important difference between them and the publicists for the French minorities: a substantially greater emphasis upon economic factors on the part of the former. Both the Welsh and the Scots tend to regard their economic inferiority with respect to the English as, at least in part, responsible for their having been denied certain rights which they have come to view with special concern. Whereas the Welsh voice concern over their inequitable contribution to English economic development (through exploitation of their coal and water resources), the Scots at first complained about their unequal rate of economic development and substantially higher unemployment rate (due to a drastic decline in such Scottish industries as shipbuilding and textiles). More recently, their emphasis has shifted to the potential for sharply increased separate development through solely Scottish exploitation of "their" North Sea oil and gas deposits.

Table 4 provides an overview of some often-cited indicators on a regional basis.

COMPARATIVE MINORITY RIGHTS

We may now consider the following questions: (1) Are there any clear socioeconomic or political correlates to the heightened demand for minority rights at the present time? (2) What general statements concerning the protection afforded minorities in the western European countries today are warranted? (3) What changes may we expect to see in the future with regard to such minority demands for additional rights?

The answer to the first question is that there do not appear to be any patently evident socioeconomic and political correlates. In the first place, it is possible to identify minorities within the western European countries whose standard of living and characteristics of social and economic well-being (such as literacy, access to services, income, contribution to GDP and the like) are *above* those of the majority of the country in which they reside. Examples would include the Catalans, the South Tyroleans, and, generally speaking, the German population in France. This is, of course, not meant to deny the relative deprivation levels which do exist, nor the actual low rank in such characteristics which is found among others, such as the Bretons and the Corsicans in France.

The question of political correlates is considerably more difficult to answer. Without attempting an elaborate analysis (including the establishment of a complete array of quantitative criteria) of the relative levels of political freedom and political participation in the western European countries, it may be argued that Great Britain and Spain are at opposite ends of such a continuum, with France and Italy, for example, somewhere in between. Yet, in all of these countries, especially during the past three decades, there are minorities which have vigorously expressed demands for greater political and human rights. Thus, while the type of political system is a salient variable in any analysis of how

Table 4. STATISTICAL INDICATORS OF BRITISH REGIONS[a]

Region	Population (mil.)	Percent Population	Percent Area	Percent Unempl.	Percent in Agriculture	Percent in Industry	Percent in Serv.	Percent of GDP	Personal Wealth
England	45.8	85.0	54.8	1.9	3.7	38.5	57.6	87.1	100[d]
Scotland[f]	5.2	10.0	36.4	3.4[c]	6.6	35.3	58.1	8.7[h]	88
Wales[g]	2.7	5.0	8.8	3.3[e]	7.9	38.2	56.5	4.2	84
(N. Ireland)	(1.5[b])								

Sources: Richard Rose, *The United Kingdom as a Multi-National State* (Survey Research Center, University of Strathclyde, 1970). James G. Kellas, *The Scottish Political System* (Cambridge University Press, 1973).

[a]Comparable data to that given in table 3 on French regions are not available. It would appear, however, that the contribution to GDP made by each of the regions is roughly proportionate to population percentage; though both Scottish and Welsh nationalists have argued that they have been exploited by English domination, opponents of this view have been able to marshall some figures to counter the validity of this view. See, for example, Neil MacCormick, *The Scottish Debate* (London: Oxford University Press, 1970), especially the essays by David Simpson and K. J. W. Alexander.

[b]The percentage figures do not include Northern Ireland. They are for Great Britain alone, and not the United Kingdom.

[c]This figure is representative: unemployment in recent years in Scotland has been 50 to 80 percent higher than the British average, and would be far greater were it not for an emigration rate in excess of 40,000 persons per year during the 1960s (Kellas, ibid, pp. 13–14).

[d]While the rest of the table is based upon 1971 British Census figures, this datum is calculated as of 1964–65 (Rose, ibid, p. 16), though more recent work seems to indicate there has been no appreciable change (Kellas, ibid, p. 13).

[e]In 1972, this rate was 5% although in the mining areas the figure was 6.6% ("A Survey of Wales," in *The Economist,* July 15, 1972.)

[f]Douglas Young, *Scotland* (London: Cassell, 1971), p. 14.

[g]R. Brinley Jones, *Anatomy of Wales* (Glamorgan, Wales: Gwerin Publications, 1972), pp. 67, 77.

[h]James Kellas, *Modern Scotland* (New York: Praeger, 1968), p. 227.

these demands will be processed, what types of gratifications will be provided, and how intensely and in what way the demands will be made, it does not appear that it will contribute much to an explanation of whether or not such demands will be made.

Based upon the limited evidence presented here, it seems possible to suggest that the political characteristics of specific countries help to explain the kinds of actions that are taken to meet minority demands for expanded human rights. While it is conceivable that quantitative measures for such an explanation may be devised, there are no generally recognized criteria to date. Standard comparisons, as, for example, with the type of electoral system or the party system, do not appear to contribute much to any explanation of the differences reviewed here, although they may be important in explaining why certain governments, (such as the Labor government in Great Britain) may decide to grant greater local autonomy.

The historian, by contrast, may conclude that the differing national experiences of France and Great Britain need to be taken into account. Certainly, the Jacobin traditions of the French Revolution appear to remain as a significant strain in the political thought of the French elite. By contrast, the fact that the United Kingdom was formed by a series of amalgamations and expedient political alliances between the dominant English and the other peoples of the British Isles may explain why the English elite has, in the twentieth century, permitted some devolution and is willing to consider more.

Three widely accepted political variables are considered in the analysis: (1) the number and relative percentage of minority group members; (2) the level of minority aggressiveness in seeking greater rights and privileges; and (3) some standard socioeconomic indicators for evaluating the argument that the minority is, generally speaking, either less well off than the majority, or makes a significantly different contribution to GDP and other economic characteristics of the country.

With respect to the first variable, we find that minorities of very different actual and proportional sizes press demands for expanded rights; that size appears not to be a relevant variable in the *demand* for expanded rights. Yet, larger minorities are more likely to be visible, emphatic, and even successful in attempts at improving their relative and absolute status.

In the case of the third variable, although some of the minorities do not equal the majority in their relative contributions to GDP or relative employment patterns within the total economy, and the publicists for the minority often stress their economic disadvantage, these differences—while important—are not so gross as to warrant the facile assumption that economic grievances account for increased activism.

It is in the second variable that we find the largest difference between the two countries. In France, increased levels of activism produce little, if any, appreciable improvement in the minority's relative position in the society. In Great

Britain, increased activism appears to produce an obvious improvement in the rights and privileges which the minority enjoys, and even in those it may be expected to gain in the near future.

The significant question, then, is: what characteristic or characteristics account for the two very different reactions on the part of public policy makers in these two countries to the minority situations they face?

It is, of course, possible that a more intensive use of demographic, economic, and sociocultural data would more effectively determine the answer. For example, it may be that some as yet undetected curvilinear relationship exists; that in one or more of these (or other undetermined) variables a specific threshold exists beyond which behavior patterns of both minority members and public policy makers alter appreciably; that other variables which have not so far been considered are more relevant in the final analysis than those which have been used; and that multiple variables have supplemental or contradictory effects.

For the time being, therefore, it may be preferable to use such hoary concepts as historical tradition or political culture. For example, it is of more than passing interest that the policies of these two countries with regard to their own minority situations bear a notable resemblance to their postwar colonial policies. France's policy of decolonialization was characterized by a seeming inability, or unwillingness, to accept or to accede to nationalist demands of the indigenous population for greater rights, much less a greater voice in decision making. In nearly all of France's former colonies and territories, it took a substantial level of violence on the part of the indigenous nationalist movements to gain any substantial increase in political and human rights. Algeria, of course, is the outstanding example, although Syria, Lebanon, Morocco, Indo-China, Guinea, and Madagascar also are notable.

Britain's decolonialization, on the other hand, was marked by a seemingly greater ability, or willingness, to accept or to accede to the demands of nationalist groups; perhaps, indeed, by a greater ability to understand exactly what was at stake. In the overwhelming number of cases, the British departure was marked by a prior series of slow steps which granted an increasing measure of self-rule to the indigenous political forces. There was a simultaneous slow, but relatively consistent, increase in the number and variety of human and political rights which the indigenous population began to enjoy. Overall, although this departure was in some instances accompanied by violence, it is difficult to argue that the level and duration of such violence (e.g., in Egypt, Iraq, Jordan, India, Ghana, and Kenya) approached that in most French colonies. Indeed, in only one instance, in Aden—which may be explained by a uniquely gross disparity between levels of political sophistication and economic development in the urban center and the hinterland—was there any long-term and concerted campaign of violence against the British presence. Is it possible that there exists an essentially similar dichotomous approach to minority and colonial issues? Social scientists have collected conflicting evidence in their analyses of other minority situations. There are studies which support the popular contention that to know them is to love them, while simultaneously there is evidence for the folk contention that familiarity breeds contempt. Although these studies are primarily of black-white relationships in the United States, this may be significant: both attitudes exist within the same cultural milieu. Possibly these two patterns represent a basic, and so far unexplained, dichotomy in the reaction of human beings to the issues and problems represented by the presence of two kinds of human beings in the same time-space.

The political scientist might insist that the political cultures of the two societies differ substantially. However, inasmuch as the political culture of any society is simply the collection of historical precedents and traditions which make up the impedimenta of current attitudes, beliefs, and values, this does not contribute much. In any event, current attitudes, beliefs, and values are the result of interactions between the individuals who hold them at any given point in time, and the results of their being held in real situations, that is, their implementation. Which is to say that such attitudes are likely to be held and transmitted only as long as they have some intrinsic psychological, political, or economic worth. Thus, the individual member of any ethnic minority in societies such as the French or British is both affected by these attitudes and contributes to their modification and continuation.

It is not enough to seek out correlates of increased ethnic group demands for rights only in the actions of the larger society. These factors, in addition, must be sought in the minority itself. It is conceivable that increased awareness of separateness, and consequent demand for differential treatment (which can include an expanded demand for human rights of various kinds), is due to the activities of political entrepreneurs, individuals who seek to expand their own social, economic, or political positions and see their ethnic affiliations as the most effective or shortest way toward that goal. There are illustrations in the cases associated with the names of prominent nationalist leaders who have provided much of the impetus for increased group awareness and such expanded demands for rights, Gwynfor Evans in Wales and Yann Fouéré in Bretagne.[42]

An additional partial explanation for increased demands may be found in similar demands which have been voiced elsewhere, particularly those which have met with some success. For example, it seems quite likely that the anticolonialist successes of various peoples in the former French and British empires at least contributed to a heightened awareness of ethnic distinctiveness and, consequently, to an accelerated demand for human rights which, it was felt, should be guaranteed at home. No doubt the vast expansion of the mass media since World War II has effectively contributed to this contagion. That contagion exists is demonstrated by the fact that many of the leaders of the civil rights demonstrations and movements in western Europe in the late 1960s first gained increased awareness and expertise as participants in the American civil rights demonstrations of the early 1960s.

The second question, which concerns protection, can be answered only in relative terms: most political observers would agree that the average citizen of a Western European democracy at this time enjoys substantially greater rights of all varieties than the citizen of countries in Africa, Asia, and Latin America. However, members of distinctive ethno-linguistic minority groups clearly do *not* enjoy any special privileges, rights, or status in the political or judicial systems (with certain limited exceptions), whereas such special arrangements do, in fact, make their appearance in some countries in the third world, such as Cyprus, Burma, and Iraq. Based on the limited evidence available, however, it appears possible that some expansion of such special arrangements within the European countries may be expected.

This brings us to the third question: the future. The prevailing belief, which only recently has been called into question by a small number of writers, is that the nation-state is the apogee of modern political development: either (1) there existed a "nation," in the sense of a relatively homogeneous group which created a state for itself, or (2) there exists a state (for instance, Nigeria) which has diverse peoples, or "nations", within its frontiers and is seeking to create a nation, that is, an integrated population committed to the existing state. This process is commonly termed national integration.

However, Europe, which is considered the outstanding example of the modern nation-state system, and which, as a result, has become a tacit model of political development for others, has a far from consistent record. Within the 150-year span between 1815 and 1965, Europe was the scene of 27 state "births" and 23 state "deaths," an average of one every 27 months. In brief, then, there is no reason to believe that alternatives are not possible. In fact, such alternatives have been explored or implemented in both Europe and other areas. It is conceivable that more extensive devolutionary measures may come into existence in the near future in western Europe. Within the last decade, proposals for the federalization of France, Italy, and Great Britain have been broached and discussed. And the important feature of these federalization proposals is that areas in which ethno-linguistic minorities are dominant be allowed a substantially greater measure of self-government.

Whatever the fate of these proposals, the public discussion of the devolution alternative is an indirect indicator that current methods of minority governance in such areas have not been fully satisfactory, and that there continue to be insistent demands by their residents for expanded human rights. Presumably, alternative governmental frameworks have been suggested as one possible method by which it may be easier to implement and guarantee such expanded rights.

In this light, it is instructive to contrast developments in France and Great Britain with the attempt of another European minority, the Jurassiens of Switzerland, to achieve altered political status. Within the canton of Bern, the largest of the twenty-five states which make up Switzerland, there are seven districts collectively known as the Jura, or the Jura districts. The population of these districts is overwhelmingly French-speaking (an average of 73 percent) and Roman Catholic (an average of 75 percent), in contrast to the German-speaking and Protestant majority in the canton as a whole. Although the overlap between French speakers and Roman Catholics is partial, the separatist sentiment which exists among the population of these districts is in large part based upon this overlap.

In 1947, after a period of quiescence, demands for change in the political status of these districts reappeared. Through the efforts of a number of political and cultural organizations, separatist sentiment continued to grow. Although these efforts consisted primarily of legitimate political activity and extensive propaganda campaigns, they also included a relatively low level of political violence of the type which has characterized many other European minorities' attempts to produce change: arson, bombings, and similar acts. By 1959, it appeared that there was sufficient support for change for the cantonal government to agree to hold a referendum which was widely interpreted as an assessment of the level of separatist sentiment. Although the antiseparatists within the Jura districts themselves outpolled the separatists, the latter raised a number of objections concerning the referendum itself and continued their agitation. As a result, the federal and cantonal governments began a series of investigations into the bases of the movement and its claims of prejudicial cantonal policies. By the early 1970s, a number of proposals by both sides had been widely publicized and the Bern government again agreed to hold a special referendum to assess the level of support for an alternative political status for these districts. On June 23, 1974, the separatists obtained a majority, with the result that a new and separate canton could legally be carved out of Bern to become the twenty-sixth constituent state of Switzerland.[43]

This summary of another linguistic minority's successful campaign for expanded human rights (civil and political) in association with an altered political status is a *potential* pattern for similar changes elsewhere. Among its advantages are the fact that the change took place in accordance with democratic principles; that it took place with a minimum of violence; that it provided a legally recognized "home" within which the minority could implement certain distinctive policies; and that it retained within the original polity whatever social and economic contributions the minority previously had made to the whole.

Nevertheless, because the political context in which the demands were made, and the conditions associated with them, are substantially different from those prevailing in, for example, France and Great Britain, generalizations must be cautiously made. For example, the fact that Switzerland is a federal state means that there is already a tradition of permitting territorial subdivisions of the state a measure of distinctive political development. Second, the fact that the official language of the new canton is already an official language of the entire country greatly eases acceptance of a new political subdivision which also uses the minority language officially. Third, and probably most important, a division of constituent states within Switzerland organized to resolve persistent conflicts has taken place twice in the past (in Basel and in Appenzell). Thus, this solution does not constitute a radical break with past tradition.

Such a solution is relatively easy to implement within a system that is already federal in theory and practice. On the other hand, the discussion in this paper has shown that current arrangements for ethno-linguistic minorities within the western European democracies are not sufficient to assuage the minorities themselves. Most of them feel that they still are subjected to various degrees of differential or discriminatory treatment by the national majority, and for this reason seek some change in current arrangements.

The transformation of such unitary systems as France or Great Britain, although not inconceivable, would indeed be a radical break with the past. It may nevertheless still be argued that states with territorial minorities may have something to learn from the case of Switzerland: when a minority is sufficiently mobilized and committed to substantial change in its current political status, only the creation of a distinct subnational unit may prove sufficient to satisfy the minority's demands for expanded human rights and for some guarantee of its continued distinctiveness.

NOTES*

* In references to legal periodical literature, the number of the *initial* page of the work cited immediately follows the volume title. Page references to material specifically referred to in the text, if any, follow the initial page citation. Legal case citations correspond to *A Uniform System of Citation,* 11th ed. (Cambridge: The Harvard Law Review Association, 1974).

1. The field of comparative linguistic rights does not have a well-developed scholarly literature. Among the related general works on minorities, see Benjamin Akzin, *State and Nation* (London: Hutchinson University Library, 1964); Karl W. Deutsch, *Nationalism and Social Communication* (Cambridge: M.I.T. Press, 1966); Cynthia Enloe, *Ethnic Conflict and Political Development* (Boston: Little, Brown, 1974); Heinz Kloss, *Grundfragen der Ethnopolitik im 20, Jahrhundert* (Vienna: W. Braumüller, 1969); Alvin Rabushka and Kenneth Shepsle, *Politics in Plural Societies* (Columbus, Ohio: Charles Merrill, 1972); Anthony D. Smith, *Theories of Nationalism* (London: G. Duckworth Co., 1971). For reliable reference works on European minorities, see Guy Héraud, *Die Völker als Träger Europas* (Vienna: W. Braumüller, 1967); Manfred Straka, *Handbuch der Europäischen Volksgruppen* (Vienna: W. Braumüller, 1970); and Albert Verdoodt, *La protection des droits de l'homme dans les Etats plurilingues* (Brussels: Editions Labor, 1973). Reliable and basic current information on European minorities is available weekly in *The Economist* (London) and *Keesings Contemporary Archives* (London); and quarterly in *Europa Ethnica* (Vienna). On recent developments in the United States, see Heinz Kloss, *Les droits linguistiques des Franco-Américains aux Etats-Unis* (Quebec: Les Presses de l'Université Laval, 1970). See also U.S. Commission on Civil Rights, *A Better Chance to Learn: Bilingual-Bicultural Education* (Washington, D.C.: Government Printing Office, 1975). See also the related Supreme Court decision in *Lau* v. *Nichols,* 414 U.S. 563 (1974).

2. For full discussion, see Vernon Van Dyke, *Human Rights, the United States and World Community* (New York: Oxford University Press, 1970). The United Nations and its

subsidiary and affiliated organizations have been responsible for the promulgation of a large number of specialized conventions designed to protect the rights of both individuals and collectivities. Most of these have been developed by the International Labor Organization (ILO) and the Educational, Scientific and Cultural Organization (UNESCO). No doubt the best known of these is the Convention on the Prevention and Punishment of the Crime of Genocide (the Genocide Convention, 1948). Clearly, the cause and purpose of the latter was to lessen, if not eliminate, the possibility that policies such as those of Germany under the NSDAP with respect to the Jews would not be repeated. Since the Convention deals with collectives and was designed to cover the destruction of an ethnic culture through deportation or forced assimilation, it would appear relevant to our subject. However, it has been sharply criticized (even by those sympathetic to its purposes) because of its imprecision in the definition and consequences of presumed genocidal activities, and it has not been used even in those circumstances where it appeared relevant, for example, in Indonesia, Bangla Desh, and Brazil.

3. Gordon L. Weil, *The European Convention on Human Rights* (Leyden: A. W. Sythoff, 1963).

4. J. E. S. Fawcett, *The Application of the European Convention on Human Rights* (London: Oxford University Press, 1969), p. 232.

5. Ibid., pp. 235–37 and the sources cited there, and p. 177, where the application of the provision is outlined.

6. Cynthia Enloe, *Ethnic Conflict and Political Development* (Boston: Little, Brown, 1973), pp. 60–61.

7. B. Lunin, *Lenin and the Peoples of the East* (Moscow: Novosti Press, 1970), p. 29; cited in Enloe, *Ethnic Conflict.*

8. Donald Kenric and Grattan Puxon, *The Destiny of Europe's Gypsies* (New York: Basic Books, 1972) is the best of the recent books on the subject.

9. The literature on this problem has grown to immense proportions in recent years; see especially Robert Descloitres, *The Foreign Worker* (Paris: Organization for Economic Cooperation and Development, 1968); Ian M. Hume, "Migrant Workers in Europe," *Finance and Development* 10, no. 1 (March 1973): 2–6; and for a good account of the human problems, Anthony Sampson, *Anatomy of Europe* (New York: Harper and Row, 1968). Since the guest workers are not seen as permanent residents or citizens of the affected countries, there have been relatively few attempts in these countries effectively to guarantee all the human rights which are generally considered an essential part of citizenship. Indeed, there is substantial evidence of the denial of such rights as freedom of movement, housing, education, etc. Relevant reports appear regularly in *Race,* The Journal of the Institute of Race Relations (London).

10. *Times* (London), March 16, 1967, May 27, 1968, January 10 and 17, 1971; and March 23, 24, and 25, 1971, for an especially good illustration, the demonstrations in March 1971 by farmers from all the EEC countries against the Commission's Headquarters in Brussels.

11. The most vigorous defense of this alternative is found in the pages of *Europa Ethnica,* published quarterly in Vienna, which carries essays, reports, and reviews on the literature and activities of the various European minorities.

12. On the significance of language as a criterion of individual and group identification, and the political consequences thereof, the literature is enormous. An important older work is the article "Language" by Edward Sapir in the old edition of the *Encyclopedia of the Social Sciences* (1933). More recent are: Karl W. Deutsch, "The Trend of European Nationalism–the Language Aspect," *Readings in the Sociology of Language* ed. J. A. Fishman, (The Hague: Mouton, 1968), pp. 598–606, and *idem, Nationalism and Social Communication* (2nd ed.) (Cambridge, Mass.: M.I.T. Press, 1966) and the works cited therein.

13. Paul Sérant, *La France des Minorités* (Paris: Robert Laffont, 1965); Guy Héraud, *Die Völker als Träger Europas* (Vienna: W. Braumüller, 1967); and Manfred Straka, ed., *Handbuch der Europäischen Volksgruppen* (Vienna: W. Braumüller, 1970).

14. Sérant, *La France,* p. 30.

15. Ibid., pp. 31, 106, 87–155.

16. *Journal Officiel* 13 (January 1951): 483 (loi 51–46).

17. Héraud, *Die Völker*, p. 47; and, Heinz Kloss, *Grundfragen der Ethnopolitik im 20, Jahrhundert* (Vienna: W. Braumüller, 1969), pp. 133–34. The term, new Europe, is taken from Stephen Graudbard, ed., *A New Europe?* (Boston: Beacon Press, 1968), the tenor of which shows that Europe is open to new ideas and ways of doing things.

18. Surveys of the rights and status of the Bretons may be found in Héraud, *Die Völker*, pp. 124–28; Straka, *Handbuch der Volksgruppen*, pp. 73–90; and Sérant, *La France*, pp. 87–155. See, however, the works of the Breton authors cited by these authors.

19. Straka, *Handbuch der Volksgruppen*, pp. 85–86.

20. On the German-speaking population of Alsace and Lorraine, see: Héraud, *Die Völker*, pp. 118–23; Straka, ibid., pp. 338–54; Sérant, *La France*, pp. 255–353; and, Fritz-René Allemann, *Die Elsässer* (Mulhouse: Rugé Frères, 1969).

21. Sérant, La France, pp. 127–31, and sources cited there.

22. Ibid.

23. Ibid., pp. 276–79, 299–308.

24. Ibid., pp. 108.

25. Straka, *Handbuch der Volksgruppen*, p. 76.

26. For a good selection of relevant Breton literature, especially on its separatist elements, see bibliography in "The National Minorities in France," *Les Temps Modernes* (special issue) 29, nos. 324, 325, 326 (1973).

27. Sérant, *La France*, pp. 315–16.

28. *Keesings Contemporary Archives*, March, 18–24, 1974, pp. 26414–15.

29. On the other hand, the very substantial rate of daily emigration of labor from Alsace to the German side of the Rhine lends credence to the arguments of some German-speaking activists that the French government has indeed neglected the economic development of Alsace. See: J. N. Tuppen, "Alsace: Poor Relation in a Prosperous Region," *The Geographical Magazine* 44 (November 1973):96–103.

30. Any of the current textbooks on comparative government illustrate this point, although the most grotesque example is doubtless Richard Rose, *Politics in England* (Boston: Little, Brown, 1968).

31. Richard Rose, *The United Kingdom as a Multi-National State* (Glasgow: University of Strathclyde, 1970), p. 8.

32. Felicity Bryan, "Out of the Valley: A Survey of Wales," *The Economist*, July 15, 1972, p. 24; Gordon Lee, Bob Brown, and Ian Coulter, "Scotland: A Sense of Change," *The Economist*, February 21, 1970, p. 48; see also James G. Kellas, *The Scottish Political System* (Cambridge: Cambridge University Press, 1973) and Ned Thomas, *The Welsh Extremist* (London: V. Gollancz, 1971).

33. Glanmor Williams, "Language, Literacy and Nationality in Wales," *History* 56 (February 1971):1–16 at 15.

34. Hywel Roberts, "The Welsh Struggle for Survival," *Race Today* 4 (April 1972):115–16.

35. Kenneth O. Morgan, "Welsh Nationalism: the Historical Background," *Contemporary History* 6 (1971):135–72.

36. Trevor Fishlock, *Wales and the Welsh* (London: Cassell, 1972), pp. 85–86.

37. Roberts, "The Welsh Struggle."

38. Ann Clwyd, "The Welsh Way of Justice," *New Statesman*, July 21, 1972, pp. 82–83.

39. According to the 1971 British Census, only 1.5 percent of the population regularly speak Gaelic (Scottish form); see, Kellas, *Scottish Political System* p. 11.

40. *New York Times*, June 4, 1974, p. 3.

41. Straka, *Handbuch der Volksgruppen*, p. 93. It should be noted, however, that such respected journals as the *New Statesman* and the *Times* (London) have carried reports which speak of the nationalists (Welsh, Scottish, Cornish, and the like) in disparaging terms. Apparently only the *Guardian* has made it a point to report dispassionately on nationalist sentiments and movements in these regions of Great Britain.

42. Rabushka and Shepsle, *Politics in Plural Societies*, pp. 63–65 and esp. fn. 27, p. 77;

and *idem,* "Political Entrepreurship and Patterns of Democratic Instability in Plural Societies," *Race* 12 (April 1974): 461–75.

43. The literature on the Jurassiens is now rather large, but among the more relevant works, one should consult: Gonzague de Reynold, *Destin du Jura* (Lausanne: Editions Recontre, 1968); Roland Béguelin, ed. *La question jurassienne* (Delémont: Imprimerie Boéchat, 1970); Marcel Schwander, *Jura–Ärgernis der Schweiz* (Basel: Pharos Verlag); Kurt B. Mayer, "The Jura Problem: Ethnic Conflict in Switzerland," *Social Research* 35 (Winter 1968): 707–41; Kommission der 24, *Bericht zur Jurafrage* (Biel: Graphische Anstalt Schüler, 1968); and, *Vortrag des Regierungsrates an den Grossen Rat über die Bildung von Regionen und die Ausgestaltung des Jurastatuts* (Biel: Graphische Anstalt Schüler, n.d.).

Chapter **8** RACIAL DISCRIMINATION
AND THE LAW: RECENT
LEGISLATION IN GREAT
BRITAIN, CANADA,
AND THE UNITED STATES

Ved P. Nanda

A wide variety of social and legislative measures are being taken at present to regulate and combat racial discrimination.[1] Three such efforts are singled out here for comparative analysis. All three take the form of national legislation which seeks to prohibit discrimination in certain specific areas based on: "colour, race or ethnic or national origins" under the 1968 Race Relations Act, of Britain;[2] "race, creed, color, nationality, ancestry or place of origin" under the 1962 Ontario Human Rights Code,[3] which is the most comprehensive legislative effort in Canada; and "race, color, religion, sex, or national origin" under the 1964 Civil Rights Act in the United States,[4] and the Model Anti-Discrimination Act proposed by the U.S. National Conference of Commissioners on Uniform State Laws.[5]

Racial discrimination is hard to define in precise legal terms. However, the definition accorded to it in the International Convention on the Elimination of All Forms of Racial Discrimination[6] (Racial Discrimination Convention) is broad and precise enough to provide an adequate basis for the comparative study that follows. According to this definition, racial discrimination involves "any distinction, exclusion, restriction, or preference based on race, colour, descent, or national or ethnic origin which has the purpose or effect of nullifying or impairing" equality of opportunity or treatment.[7] Under the Racial Discrimination Convention, certain special measures taken "for the sole purpose of securing adequate advancement of certain racial or ethnic groups or individuals" requiring special protection and "more favorable" treatment are not deemed racial discrimination, provided that these measures are not continued indefinitely and that they do not "lead to the maintenance of separate rights for different racial groups."[8] Accordingly, such measures will be considered nondiscriminatory for the purposes of the discussion in this paper.

THE PROBLEM

Problems and policy. Racial prejudice and discrimination against individuals and groups on racial and ethnic grounds are by no means novel phenomena in human history; however, the intensity of racial tension manifested in recent violent outbreaks in many countries, including the three studied here, is currently a matter of considerable concern both in national and international arenas.[9] The discussion shows that national concern in Britain, Canada, and the United States has helped to bring about the adoption of legislation and implementing measures to prevent and punish discriminatory practices. However, a few significant international measures reflecting the global concern can be noted: The Racial Discrimination Convention and the International Covenant on Civil and Political Rights adopted in December, 1966, are the cornerstones of international efforts to eliminate discrimination.[10] Global concern was reflected in the designation by the United Nations General Assembly of 1971 as the Year for Action to Combat Racism and Racial Discrimination, and the decision of the General Assembly to launch the Decade for Struggle against Racism and Racial Discrimination as part of the observance of the twenty-fifth anniversary of the Universal Declaration of Human Rights.[11] Similarly, the 1960 UNESCO Convention against Discrimination in Education,[12] the draft Convention on the Elimination of All Forms of Religious Intolerance,[13] various United Nations studies, advisory services, and seminars,[14] including the 1971 seminar on the "Dangers of a Recrudescence of Intolerance in all Its Forms,"[15] are some of the recent efforts in the continuing search for ways to prevent and combat racial discrimination.

It should be mentioned that, although the blatantly visible, universally condemned policies of apartheid in South Africa offer the extreme example of racial discrimination, covert forms of discriminatory practices in North America and Great Britain are also invidious and harmful in outcome. Even a cursory review of the recent official reports from the countries studied here, for instance, the 1967 report of Political and Economic Planning on racial discrimination in England,[16] the reports of the Royal Commission Inquiry into Canadian civil rights,[17] and the reports of the United States Commission on Civil Rights,[18] show the extent, enormity, and seriousness of a problem which is both deep rooted and immensely complicated.

Since the purported role of the law is to regulate human relations, its use to influence human behavior in different settings is taken for granted. For instance, all broad categories of law (such as the law of contracts, criminal law, torts, family law, and property law,) have prescriptive elements which serve this purpose. The basic question obviously is how important a society must consider a specific setting to be before it provides an authoritative process of decision making to regulate interactions and relationships within that setting. To illustrate, if the society tolerates discriminatory practices based on race, failing to provide adequate legal protection to the victims because either there is no law on the subject or the law is not used to promote equality of opportunity and treatment regardless of race, a tentative conclusion could be reached that the society does not consider the subject important or suitable enough for active legal intervention. The following discussion shows that in all the countries studied here the subject is considered both important and suitable for legal intervention. Nonetheless, they all face hard choices in dealing with racial and minority problems. The discussion focuses on the measures taken by each country to prevent and combat racial discrimination and evaluates the effectiveness of these measures in accomplishing that objective.

Racial discrimination and the common law. English Common Law which lies at the basis of modern legal development in all the countries studied here does not provide adequate protection against racial discrimination. Lord Davey's observations in a case decided by the House of Lords in 1897 accurately reflect the state of common law as to employment practices: "An employer may discharge a workman (with whom he has no contract), or may refuse to employ one from the most mistaken, capricious, malicious, or morally reprehensible motives that can be conceived, but the workman has no right of action against him. . . . A man has no right to be employed by any particular employer, and has no right to any particular employment if it depends on the will of another."[19] Similarly, the common law offers no meaningful remedy against racial discrimination in transactions involving housing (including the services of a real estate agent), trusts and wills, insurance, mortgages, and the hire of goods.[20] The basic reason for the apparent indifference of the common law actively to seek to promote social justice lies in the nature of common law under which property rights and freedom of contract are sacrosanct, and there is no duty to do business with any one.

An observer has recently asserted that "no English case has expressly declared racial discrimination on a contract or deed to be contrary to public policy," and that despite the admitted prevalence of racial discrimination in England "there has been no reported case since 1943 in which a victim of this kind of discrimination has sought a remedy in the courts."[21]

The common law did, however, offer some protection insofar as it prohibited racial discrimination by private citizens in certain public fields: for instance, the duty of a common carrier (but not of a private hauler) to carry any person or goods; of a person carrying on a monopolistic business to give service to everyone; and of an innkeeper under the custom of the realm to accept any traveler. While a breach of any of these duties could result in legal sanctions, the primary objective in offering protection against racial discrimination in these cases seems to be the facilitation of travel and commerce rather than the recognition of equal treatment. A case in point involved the late Sir Learie Constantine, a popular West Indian cricketer who was subsequently knighted and became a member of the British Race Relations Board. His challenge of discriminatory treatment suggested that even the duty of an innkeeper was not generally to be taken seriously. The defendant, Imperial Hotels in London, had denied Constantine accommodations because of the color of his skin, but consequently was asked to pay the latter nominal damages of twelve dollars (five guineas).[22] Moreover, related litigation shows that the innkeeper's duty is of limited practical utility, for the courts have held that a lodging house, a restaurant, an alehouse, a motel which does not offer food, or a public house is not to be defined as an inn so as to be compelled to comply with the traditional obligation to treat people equally.[23]

Limited protection under the common law was also available to one facing discrimination because of racially restrictive covenants enuring to freehold land limiting alienability to specific classes of purchasers, or restrictions on lettings and assignments of leases providing that only "persons of the white or Caucasian race" could use or occupy the premises.[24] Also, the common law misdemeanor of sedition could be used against one who attempted to stir up racial hatred.[25] However, it was not a meaningful remedy. To secure a conviction under the law one would have to prove a clear incitement to violence. Similarly, other misdemeanors such as public mischief and criminal libel had limited utility. In short, remedies under these common law rules have been of nominal value to a victim of racial discrimination.

In an incisive survey of the limits of the common law to provide meaningful remedies against racial discrimination, Anthony Lester and Geoffrey Bindman have recently analyzed "judicial reluctance to adapt concepts of public policy." They amply substantiate their statement that the "limits of the Common Law must be remembered because the judges are imprisoned within them, but a survey of the decided cases suggests that the judges have made their prison more confining than it need have been; they have grown to love their chains."[26] The inadequacy of common law remedies has led the three countries studied here to adopt legislative measures, which are discussed in this study.

LEGISLATION AND IMPLEMENTATION IN GREAT BRITAIN

The common law regulation of human relationships in society reflected the traditionally British approach of economic and social laissez-faire. In dealing with questions of human rights, including racial discrimination, the emphasis was on freedom of choice and contract and on private and property rights, and discrimination was permitted, with the few exceptions which have been mentioned. At the same time, equality before the law was known as a kind of British trademark, and so it was felt that nothing more was needed to protect the rights of the individual.

Furthermore, there were other peculiarly British characteristics of English society, both factual and perceived, which contributed to the manifestly inadequate nature of British legislation on racial inequality until as late as the middle

1960s. For example, it is a fact that the racial problem in Britain initially surfaced and became intense primarily because of a large influx of immigrants into Britain—British subjects from the West Indies and former British subjects from the Commonwealth Territories—during the last two decades.[27] And as to perceptions, until recently a widely shared view was that color in Britain has never been a serious social or legal problem and that, even in contemporary Britain, the problem is not racial, but one of immigration.[28] Thus, the myth was perpetuated that it was only the fact of being foreign and unaccustomed to the English language, culture, and way of life that caused unequal treatment in society, something unfortunate and perhaps inevitable, but which was transitional and likely to disappear with time.

The racial nature of the problem became clearer, however, with the emergence of a pattern of unequal treatment of second generation immigrants;[29] and the prospect increased that matters would worsen if effective legislative and implementing measures were not taken to combat racial discrimination in areas such as employment and housing. These fears were confirmed by the findings of a research organization, Political and Economic Planning (PEP), which were made public in April, 1967.[30] Some of its conclusions were startling. For example, the longer people had been in Britain, the more discrimination they had faced. Also, experience of discrimination was highest among people who had the highest qualifications, who had spoken only English as a child, and who had been in full employment before they came to Britain.

The efficacy of legislation to bring about attitudinal and behavioral changes was seriously questioned by those opposing antidiscrimination legislation,[31] but in 1965 and in 1968, Britain opted for major antidiscrimination legislation—the Race Relations Acts. Earlier there had been attempts to enact such legislation, but without success. In 1950, a bill was introduced in the Parliament prohibiting racial discrimination by those providing services and facilities in public places and in advertising and displaying notices. Any violation would have constituted a criminal offense punishable by fine, but "The Colour Bar Bill" was not debated by the House of Commons. Similar bills introduced in the 1950s and the early 1960s were either not debated or lacked sufficient numbers of supporters to be taken seriously. However, in 1964, racial discrimination became an election issue, and in November, 1965, the first Race Relations Act came into force. The Act, limited in scope, was extended three years later.

The Race Relations Act 1965. The statute of 1965 prohibited discrimination "on the ground of colour, race, or ethnic or national origins" concerning access, services or facilities in places of public resort.[32] Such places were specified as hotels, restaurants, cafes, public houses and public transport or places such as theatres, cinemas, dance halls, sports grounds, swimming pools or places of public entertainment or recreation where food or drink was supplied for consumption. (sec. 1(2)) Discriminatory restrictions on the disposal of tenancies were also prohibited. (sec. 5) The provisions concerning access, services or facilities in places of public resort constituted an extension of the common law duty of innkeepers and common carriers but fell far short of the expectations of those who would have preferred the inclusion of a much broader definition of "places of public resort." Also, hotels were given the same restrictive definition as in the earlier Hotel Proprietors Act, which exempted private and residential hotels, boarding houses, landlords and "bed and breakfast" places from the purview of the Act. (sec. 1[5]) And since the prohibited conduct was that of practicing discrimination (sec. 1[1]), a single act of discrimination would not be prohibited.

Under the original proposal the offenses already noted were to be treated as criminal in nature, were punishable by a maximum fine of $100, and proceedings were to be initiated against the alleged offenders only with the consent of the Attorney General. The Bill provided for no civil remedy to the victims of discrimination, and no conciliation machinery to settle differences. Under the legislation finally adopted, incitement to racial hatred was illegal and punishable by a maximum fine of $1000 or up to 2 years imprisonment. (sec. 6[3]) Also, the scope of the Public Order Act of 1936 was extended to include threatening, insulting or abusive words or behavior, likely to cause a breach of the peace.[33]

Within two years of enactment of the Race Relations Act, disappointment developed at its lack of effectiveness. Criticism focused on the excessively narrow scope of the law and the absence of sufficiently strong enforcement machinery. Reform efforts gathered momentum with discussion, reports, and studies on the need to amend the Act. One such report, the Street Report, cosponsored by the Race Relations Board and published in October, 1967, included a comparative study of such laws in other countries.[34] It analyzed their effectiveness and offered various alternatives to Parliament, recommending that the scope of the existing law be considerably extended and that strong administrative machinery be established to implement the law. Although some of the Committee's major recommendations were not adopted by Parliament, the Report was nevertheless instrumental in shaping the 1968 Act.

The Race Relations Act 1968. In April, 1968, the Race Relations Bill was published. In the words of the Home Secretary, the purpose of the Bill was "to protect society as a whole against actions which will lead to social disruption, and to prevent the emergence of second-grade citizens."[35] After six months of debate in Parliament, it was passed by both Houses, and came into force in November, 1968, as the Race Relations Act 1968.[36] It extended the scope of the 1965 Act by prohibiting discrimination "on the ground of colour, race, or ethnic or national origins," in employment, housing, advertising, and the provision of goods, facilities, and commercial services such as insurance and credit.

Under the Act a person is deemed to have discriminated against another if, on any of the racial and similar grounds already mentioned, "he treats that other, in any situation (in which the Act applies), less favourably than he treats or would treat other persons." (sec. 1[1]) The grounds of discrimination are admittedly ambiguous, as is the term less favourably. The legislation, however, is based on the requirement of equal treatment, because segregating a person on any of these grounds is considered under the Act as treating him "less favourably." (sec. 1[2]) The law is applicable to even a single act of discrimination, inasmuch as it omits any references to the *practising* of discrimination, a prerequisite to the applicability of the 1965 Act.

Section 2 prohibits discrimination in the provision of goods, facilities, or services "to the public or a section of the public." The Act does not define facilities or services, but gives examples of the kind of activities they refer to: "access to and use of any place which members of the public are permitted to enter; accommodation in a hotel, boarding house or other similar establishment; facilities by way of banking or insurance or for grants, loans, credit or finance; facilities for education, instruction or training; facilities for entertainment, recreation or refreshment; facilities for transport or travel; the services of any business, profession or trade or local or other public authority." (sec. 2[2]) Unlike the 1965 Act, which was applicable only to "places of public resort," the 1968 Act applies to places "which members of the public are permitted to enter," thus considerably extending the scope of the earlier Act. Also, unlike the 1965 Act, the 1968 Act does not define hotel in the narrow sense in which the Hotel Proprietors Act of 1956 had earlier defined it. Thus a private hotel would now be covered under the Act.

One exemption that applies to all prohibitions should perhaps be noted at the outset. Any discriminatory act, otherwise prohibited under the Act, would be lawful if "done for the purpose of safeguarding national security." (sec. 10[1]) A certificate, by or on behalf of a Minister, certifying that an act was done for such purposes is conclusive evidence. Among other exemptions, under section 11 (1)(a)(*ii*), any refusal or omission "to provide any banking, financial or insurance facilities for a purpose to be carried out, or in connection with risks wholly or mainly arising, outside Great Britain" is not unlawful. In the educational field, exemptions include (1) discrimination on religious grounds, which is not covered under the Act and (2) discrimination done to comply with the provisions of any charitable instrument conferring benefits on racial or ethnic grounds. (sec. 9[1] [a] and [b]) While the prohibition concerning facilities for entertainment, recreation, or refreshment extends to clubs which are open to the public or are run as business establishments, the scope of the prohibiiton to other clubs which restrict the provision of their facilities and service to their members and guests is to be determined in a contextual setting.

General exemptions on the prohibition concerning transport and travel would permit discrimination: (1) in providing sleeping cabins for passengers on a ship if such prohibition would otherwise result in persons of different "colour, race or ethnic or national origins" being compelled to share any such cabin (sec. 7[6]); (2) in providing "goods, services or facilities, other than travel facilities", outside Britain on a foreign ship or aircraft (sec. 11[1] [a] [i]); and (3) on a British ship or aircraft, if the act is in compliance with the laws of a foreign country while such ship or aircraft is in or over the territory of that country. (sec. 11[2]) The prohibition concerning the services of business, profession, or trade or local or other public authority, coupled with the prohibition concerning membership of trade, business, professional or occupational organizations contained in section 4, is fairly broad. It also binds the crown now, unlike the 1965 Act.

Section 3 prohibits racial discrimination in employment and employment practices. Thus, it is unlawful for an employer, and his servants and agents, (sec. 13[1]), to discriminate on racial grounds in recruiting, training, and promoting employees, or in dismissing them, and in the terms and conditions of employment. Section 4 makes the Act applicable to trade unions and employers' organizations. However, there are several exceptions, such as: section 3(2), which exempts provisions of other enactments "relating to the employment or qualification of employment;" section 27(9)(a), which exempts restrictions in "employment in the service of the Crown" and specified public bodies; and section 6(2) which permits the publication or display of advertisements or notices which indicate that "Commonwealth citizens or any class of such citizens" are required for employment outside Britain or that non-Commonwealth citizens are required for employment in Britain.

During the first four years of the operation of the Act, its scope was limited—it applied only to employers employing more than twenty-five people until November 26, 1972. At present, it is applicable to all employers. Racial discrimination in recruitment or the selection for work in an undertaking or part of an undertaking is not unlawful, "if the act is done in good faith for the purpose of securing or preserving a reasonable balance of persons of different racial groups" employed in the undertaking or part of the undertaking. (sec. 8[2]) By racial group is meant here "a group of persons defined by reference to colour, race or ethnic and national origins," and persons wholly or mainly educated in Great Britain shall be treated as members of the same racial group. (sec. 8[4]) The employment of any person in a private household is not covered under the Act, nor are employment or applications for employment wholly or mainly in a foreign country. (sec. 8[6,7])

In Britain, as elsewhere, interest group politics affect the legislative process, even where civil rights are concerned. For example, the British ship industry succeeded in securing several exemptions to the 1968 Act. Discrimination covering the following situations pertaining to ships and aircraft is not covered: employment or applications for employment on a British or foreign ship or aircraft outside Britain (sec. 8[7] [b,c]), and on a ship or aircraft anywhere if such employment or application for employment took place outside Britain. (sec. 8[8]) Also, discrimination in respect of employment on a ship is not unlawful if the compliance with the prohibitions contained in the Act "would result in persons of different colour, race or ethnic or national origins being compelled to share sleeping rooms, mess rooms or sanitary accommodation."

(sec. 8[10]) Another exception provides that racial discrimination is not unlawful in "the selection of a person of a particular nationality or particular descent for employment requiring attributes especially possessed by persons of that nationality or descent." (sec. 8[11])

Section 5 prohibits racial discrimination in transactions involving housing accommodations, business premises, and other land, and applies to any person having power to dispose, or being otherwise concerned with, their disposal. Thus, in addition to the owners of a freehold or leasehold interest in property, tenants, estate agents and housing managers are also governed under the Act. The refusal or deliberate omission to dispose of housing accommodation, premises or other land to a person seeking to acquire it, "or to dispose of it to him on the like terms and in the like circumstances as in the case of other persons," is unlawful. (sec. 5[a]) It is also unlawful deliberately to treat an occupier differently because of racial grounds (sec. 5[b]), or deliberately to treat a person in need of any such accommodation, and the like, differently "from others in respect of any list of persons in need of it," on racial grounds. (sec. 5[c]) The provisions of the 1965 Act (sec. 5) prohibiting racial restrictions in leases and tenancy agreements are still operative inasmuch as the 1968 Act does not repeal those provisions. The landlord is not to withhold unreasonably his consent or license in the transfer of a tenancy where such restrictive covenants exist, and if such consent is withheld on racial grounds, it is to be construed as unreasonably withheld. (sec 5[1] 1965 Act) However, there is an exemption for the landlord or the person whose consent or license is required if he lives on the premises and shares more than just the means of access to the premises with his tenant. The Act does not prohibit the insertion of racial restrictions into leases and tenancy agreements, nor does it cover restrictive covenants on racial grounds concerning the resale of a freehold property.

Housing and land sale exemptions are spelled out by the statute. Major exemptions concerning the housing legislation include the provision or disposal of "small premises." This term is used in the Act to refer to that part of the premises occupied by the landlord or a member of his family, and (1) under separate rental arrangement where there is accommodation for two other households; and (2) without "separate letting" the rest, there is residential accommodation for not more than "six persons in addition to the landlord and any members of his household."[37] The refusal or omission on racial grounds to dispose of land outside Britain is not prohibited under the Act, even when the refusal or omission occurred or the contract was made in Britain. (sec. 11[1])[38]

Finally, the Act provides that any person "who deliberately aids, induces or incites another person to do an act" prohibited under the Act shall be treated as if he did that act. (sec. 12)

Conciliation machinery and enforcement. The 1965 Act established a Race Relations Board which was to appoint local conciliation committees with investigatory powers after receiving a complaint of discrimination; the main task of conciliation committees was to settle disputes. A local committee reported to the Board when it could not effect a settlement and the Board then notified the Attorney General who could seek an injunction to restrain the defendant from committing acts of discrimination. (sec. 2 [1,2,3] 1965 Act) In a case of noncompliance with the injunction, fines or imprisonment for the contempt of court are provided for. Racial incitement would still be subject to criminal sanctions. The 1968 Act continued the existing Race Relations Board, entrusting it with the task of securing compliance with the Act and the resolution of differences arising out of the Act's application. (sec. 14[1] 1968 Act) However, the 1968 Act restructured the Board, considerably extending its functions.

The Board is to appoint conciliation committees in different areas, as it considers necessary, to assist it in the discharge of its functions. The committees are to make periodic reports to the Board, which in turn is to make annual reports to the Secretary of State, who is required to present to Parliament such reports of the Boards. It will be recalled that these provisions are similar to the ones contained in the 1965 Act. However, unlike the procedure in the 1965 Act, where initially all complaints were to be investigated by local committees, the Board is now authorized to decide which complaints are to be referred to the committees and which complaints are to be investigated by the Board.[39] Even in the absence of a formal complaint, the Board is now empowered to investigate a matter on its own initiative where it has "reason to suspect" that discrimination has occurred in violation of the Act. (sec. 17[1]) Also, instead of the Board asking the Attorney General to bring proceedings in the courts, as provided in the 1965 Act, it is within the Board's powers to decide whether to institute such proceedings (sec. 15[5]) and whether to conduct those proceedings. (sec. 19[1]) The Board is also authorized to appoint persons who "have special knowledge and experience of . . . circumstances appearing to the Board to be relevant" in investigations, as assessors to assist the Board and the conciliation committees. (sec. 18)

A special procedure has been devised to handle complaints pertaining to employment, trade union, or employers associations: they are to be initially referred to the Secretary of State for Employment and Productivity (sec. 16[1] and schedule 2) and through him to a "body of persons suitable to consider that complaint." (schedule 2, para. 2[a]) If the Secretary decides that there is no such suitable voluntary machinery in an industry to investigate the complaint, the complaint is referred back to the Board for investigation. (schedule 2, para. 2[b]) However, the Board is not required to refer to the Minister a complaint pertaining to an act done in breach of a prior assurance, which the Board might either investigate itself or refer to suitable industrial machinery. (schedule 2, para. 13, 14) Where the Minister has referred the complaint to suitable voluntary machinery, the latter is to make a report to the Minister in four weeks time unless the Minister grants it extension to pursue its investigation. (schedule 2, para. 4, 5) Appeal is available to the Board within a week of the notification of decision. (schedule 2, para. 9, 10) The procedure, similar to the one used for handling industrial grievances, was instituted to promote the effective implementation of the Act by using the established industrial procedures.

Complaint procedures before the Race Relations Board are not complex.[40] Remedy patterns stress flexibility. In cases where there is a particular victim of discrimination, the Board or the conciliation committee investigating the complaint "shall use their best endeavours by communication with the parties concerned or otherwise to secure a settlement of any difference between them and, where appropriate, a satisfactory written assurance against any repetition of the act considered to be unlawful or the doing of further acts of a similar kind by the party against whom the complaint is made." (sec. 15[3][b]) In other complaints, such as those concerning discriminatory advertisements or notices, or inducement or incitement of a discriminatory act, "best endeavours to secure such an assurance" are to be used. (sec. 15[3][c]) However, if the Board forms an opinion that a violation has occurred and is unable to secure a settlement, such as an apology, assurance or compensation, or if the act seems to be done in breach of a relevant assurance, it is up to the Board to decide whether or not to bring court proceedings.[41] Similarly, if the committee forms such an opinion and is unable to secure a settlement and assurance, it makes a report to the Board which may itself investigate the complaint, or based on the report, make a decision whether or not to proceed in a court. There is no judicial review of the Board's determination at this stage and if the Board decides to reject a complaint, there is no recourse left to the complainant but to fall back on his common law remedies, for he cannot himself initiate court proceedings. However, once the investigation is completed, both parties are notified by the Board in writing whether it has formed an opinion, whether a settlement or assurance has been secured, and what future action is anticipated. (sec. 15[6])

As has been noted, the Board is now empowered to initiate investigation on its own without receiving any formal complaint. This is a welcome power but its scope is limited because in suspected violations pertaining to employment the matter has to be referred to the Secretary of State for Employment and Productivity.[42] Also, unless the Board suspects that a particular person has been discriminated against, it cannot initiate an inquiry into suspected discriminatory conduct or practices on its own.

The Act specifies county courts in which proceedings can be brought if the Board so decides.[43] The Act specifically provides, however, that communications made to the conciliation machinery are privileged and so the Board cannot produce in evidence any communication made to the Board or its committees, or to the Secretary of State for Employment and Productivity, and the voluntary machinery set up to deal with employment complaints, "except with the consent of the person" who made the communication. (Sec. 24) The court decision can be appealed to the Court of Appeal on questions both of fact and law. (sec. 19[9]) The judge is assisted by two assessors "appointed from a list of persons, prepared and maintained by the Lord Chancellor." The assessors include those who appear "to the Lord Chancellor to have special knowledge and experience of problems connected with race and community relations." (sec. 19[7])

The remedies the Board can claim under the Act are injunctions, damages, and declarations that the act complained of is unlawful. (sec. 19[1]) In the proceedings before the court the Board may also, on behalf of a party to a contract which contravenes the antidiscrimination provisions of the Act, ask that the contract or a term in it be revised. (sec. 23[2]) A defendant can also make such an application. Before the Court grants an injunction "restraining the defendant from engaging in, or causing or permitting others to engage in, conduct of the same kind as [the allegedly unlawful] act, or conduct of any similar kind specified in an order of the court," it has to be satisfied that (1) the act was done by the defendant and was unlawful under the statute; (2) the defendant had previously engaged in conduct which was of the same kind as, or similar kind to, that act and was unlawful under the law; and that (3) he is likely to engage in such conduct in the future, unless a court order restrains him. (sec. 21[1]) The second requirement, that the defendant had previously engaged in the same or similar conduct, is a new addition to the court's usual practice of granting injunction and has been criticized as a "completely unjustifiable" restriction.[44] For breach of an injunction a defendant may be considered in contempt of court, which is punishable by prison sentence. The court could award special damages and "such damages as the court thinks just in all the circumstances for loss of opportunity, that is to say, loss of any benefit which that person might be reasonably expected to have had but for [the unlawful] act." (sec. 22[1]) The normal rules under common law concerning mitigation of damages also apply. The Board is to account for damages recovered by the victim of discrimination. (sec. 22[3]) The Act does not provide for damages in claims for anguish, mental suffering, and humiliation.[45]

Interpretation. During the first five years of its operation, the 1968 Act has come before the House of Lords for interpretation in two cases. In *London Borough of Ealing* v. *Race Relations Board,* a decision by the Ealing Borough Council was scrutinized.[46] It had refused to place Zesko, a Polish national, on the waiting list for council housing (public accommodation). Nevertheless, a majority of the House of Lords decided that the term national origins contained in the Act did not cover nationality. After receiving a complaint from the Anglo-Polish Conservative Society on behalf of Zesko alleging that such a Council practice constituted treating Zesko "less favourably" on ground of national origins, the Board had sought a settlement of the parties' difference and an assurance from the Council against repetition of such an act. The Council sought declaration from the court that their practice was not unlawful under the Act. The court decided against the Council, refusing the declaration sought and suggesting that, in effect, the allegedly less favorable treatment on the ground of nationality would be the same as that of national origins.[47] However, on appeal, the Lords reversed the lower court, rejecting the argument that national origins covered nationality. The dissent would have interpreted the phrase in a contextual setting, in view of the nature of the statute in question "designed to remedy social grievance by assuring large groups of citizens of the protection of the law." Now that Britain has entered the European Common Market, article 48 of the Treaty of Rome, which provides for workers to have freedom of movement within the community, would have a bearing on the question and perhaps act as a catalyst to amend the Act to include nationality and residence in section 1(1) of the Act.[48] Discrimination on the ground of sex or of religion should also be included.

In the second case decided by the House of Lords, *Race Relations Board* v. *Charter*,[49] a majority of four to one overruled a unanimous Court of Appeal decision. The case concerned the application of the Act to clubs. The club in question, East Ham South Conservative Club, had allegedly denied admission to the complainant on racial grounds. The complainant, a foreign born resident of England for nine years, was otherwise qualified, being over eighteen years of age, male, and a Conservative. The Board, having failed to settle differences between the parties, initiated court proceedings seeking damages and a declaration that the rejection of membership in clubs on the basis of color was unlawful. From an adverse decision the Board appealed to the Court of Appeal. The judges unanimously held that since the club provided goods, facilities and services to its members and guests, it was covered under section 2(1) which refers to the provision of such goods, facilities, and services to "the public or a section of the public." The Court distinguished between personal and impersonal characteristics of a group, and it noted that the reach of the decision did not extend to interference with private freedom of action and domestic lives of the people. Thus, the case was differentiated from an earlier ruling involving a complaint that admission to a club function was denied on racial basis;[50] the Race Relations Board lost on the ground that a genuinely private club was not covered by the Act.

In another recent case eventually decided by the Court of Appeal, the Race Relations Board initiated proceedings alleging that the defendants had violated the Act by deliberately inducing or inciting a couple to accept only white children in their home as foster children.[51] Mr. and Mrs. Watson had acted as foster parents for over two decades for children in need of a temporary home. They had been registered with local authorities and usually took four or five children at a time with about 60 percent of these children being colored. The defendants, who were officers of an organization whose aim was to "make Britain white," pressured the Watsons not to accept colored children. The pressure took the form of writing letters to the Watsons, sending a circular to the residents of the area where the Watsons had moved accusing the Watsons of maliciously and disgracefully attacking their neighbors, and organizing public meetings criticizing the Watsons' fostering of colored children. The Board sought a declaration that the defendants were in violation of the Act, but lost in the lower court which held that the Watsons did not provide facilities for a "section of the public" under section 2 of the Act. On appeal, the Court of Appeal held that the defendants had violated section 12 of the Act and that, if the Watsons had succumbed to the defendants' pressure, they would have been in breach of section 2 of the Act. Lord Denning equated the facilities provided by the Watsons with those provided by a hotel or a boarding house. A declaration was granted but an injunction refused inasmuch as there was no repetition of the act and the defendants no longer were even members of the organization in question.[52]

Appraisal. The two decisions of the House of Lords briefly discussed above went against the Race Relations Board. Although it is possible to explain the decisions on the restrictive interpretations given by the Lords, it appears that the Act needs to be amended in certain areas. For example, section 1, which defines discrimination, should be broadened to include nationality, residence, sex, and religion; the scope of the Act concerning public housing and clubs should be clarified; various exemptions such as those applicable in overseas employment, and on British and foreign ships and aircraft; those on national security and on special national attributes also seem unnecessary and should be reexamined. Also, the provision concerning the power of the courts to revise discriminatory contractual terms should be replaced by one stating that a racially discriminatory contract is void and unenforceable.

The implementation provisions of the Act should be made effective by giving broader powers to the Race Relations Board. For example, the Board should be authorized to: (1) inquire into allegedly discriminatory situations without the current restrictions; (2) compel the attendance of witnesses, and the disclosure of documents; and (3) refuse to investigate a complaint which it considers to be vexatious or frivolous. The court should be authorized to give damages for distress and mental suffering. Also, the complainant should be permitted to initiate legal proceedings on his own if the Board decides not to proceed with court litigation. The Act should prohibit threats, penalties, intimidation, or coercion of a person who has made or may make a complaint, or who testifies or participates in a proceeding under the Act. Additionally, affirmative action is needed to promote equal employment opportunities.

CANADIAN POLICY

Legislation. Legislative authority to prescribe norms on basic human rights, including freedom from discrimination, is shared in Canada between federal government and provinces.[53] One might conclude from a reading of sections 91 and 92 of the British North American Act of 1867 (BNA Act), and of the pertinent judicial precedents, that perhaps the federal government has now assumed exclusive authority over traditional political rights.[54] However, whereas the authority of the federal government concerning antidiscrimination legislation extends to specific fields because of its legislative competence in these areas (such as transportation, federally incorporated companies, and banks), provincial authority to adopt antidiscriminatory legislation concerning employment and housing is similarly derived from provincial legislative competence in property and civil rights areas under section 92 (13) of the BNA Act.[55] The authority of the federal government does extend to all labor situations under the legislative competence of the federal government. On this basis, it has forbidden employers' discriminatory hiring practices.[56]

Heretofore, the major federal legislation on the subject of nondiscrimination has been the Canadian Bill of Rights enacted by the Parliament of Canada in 1960.[57] Section 1 declares the existence of "human rights and fundamental freedoms" in Canada, which "shall continue to exist without discrimination by reason of race, national origin, colour, religion or sex." These rights and freedoms are largely equated with the traditional political rights—freedom of speech, of the press, and of assembly, etc. Provisions of the Bill of Rights are applicable in the interpretation of federal statutes. In the late 1960s, the federal government proposed the entrenchment of a Bill of Rights in the constitutive law of the federation.[58] More recently, in 1974, the Trudeau government proposed establishment of a Human Rights Commission at the federal level. It would handle job and other discrimination cases that are not covered by provincial laws, and it would also serve as a national ombudsman.

The role of the federal government in support of fundamental rights and freedoms is important, especially in the prescription of norms to prevent discrimination.[59] Nevertheless, the major initiative for the protection of human rights has come from provincial legislatures. While the first legislative assembly of the province of Upper Canada in 1793 passed an Act "to prevent the further introduction of slaves and to limit the term of contracts for servitude within this province," it should be noted that modern provincial legislative efforts in Canada to secure human rights began only with the passage in 1944 of a Racial Discrimination Act in Ontario.[60] The 1944 Ontario Act prohibited the publication or display of any signs, symbols, or notices expressing racial or religious discrimination. Saskatchewan followed suit in 1947 by enacting a fairly comprehensive Bill of Rights.[61] Enforcement of these Acts was to be through penal sanctions. In 1950, Ontario adopted legislation to prohibit discrimination in restrictive property covenants[62] and in collective agreements.[63]

During the 1950s, the focus of legislation in several Canadian provinces shifted from the prescription of criminal sanctions to a search for procedures which would effectuate conciliation and settlement and would seek the application of sanctions only as a last resort. Fair Employment Practices Acts, the first of which was adopted in Ontario in 1951, and Fair Accommodation Practices

Acts, and Equal Pay Acts, the first of which were again adopted in Ontario, fall in this category.[64]

During the 1960s several provinces enacted human rights codes.[65] The initiative was again taken by Ontario which consolidated its existing antidiscrimination statutes into a Human Rights Code; the administering function was to be exercised by the Ontario Human Rights Commission, which was established in 1961 to replace the Anti-Discrimination Commission, which had been in existence since 1958.[66] These codes avoid a piecemeal approach by covering several areas such as employment, housing, public accommodation, and advertising; they also strengthen the existing enforcement procedures, primarily by entrusting the responsibility of implementation to persons who are independent and specialized in carrying out administrative and supervisory tasks instead of relying upon bureaucrats to perform a function which would be ancillary to their regular jobs.[67]

The Ontario Human Rights Code and the Ontario Human Rights Commission are singled out for further inquiry for two reasons: these institutions have been in existence longer than other similar codes and commissions; moreover, they have been more active than others and have accumulated extensive experience which can be usefully examined for comparative purposes.

The Ontario Human Rights Code. The Ontario Human Rights Code was proclaimed in 1962.[68] The preamble of the code refers to the Universal Declaration of Human Rights, to Ontario's public policy "that every person is free and equal in dignity and rights without regard to race, creed, colour, nationality, ancestry or place of origin," and to the desirability of enacting a measure to "codify and extend" prior enactments of the Ontario legislature on fundamental rights and freedoms and to "simplify their administration." The Act seeks to prevent discrimination in specific fields. Among its substantive provisions (some of which have been subsequently amended), section 1 prohibits discrimination in notices, signs, symbols, and the like. Section 2 forbids discrimination in places to which the public is customarily admitted "with respect to the accommodation, services, or facilities available" there. Section 3, which banned discrimination with respect to occupancy in apartment buildings containing more than six self-contained dwelling units, is now applicable to "any commercial unit or any housing accommodation."[69] Section 4 outlaws discrimination in employment practices, such as by an employer "with regard to employment or any form of condition of employment," in membership requirements for trade unions, and in advertisements for employment and in employment applications. Exemptions are set up for certain categories: an employer with less than five employees, a domestic employed in a private home, and exclusively religious, philanthropic, educational, fraternal or social nonprofit organizations or any nonprofit organization operated primarily to foster the welfare of a religious group or ethnic groups.

During the first decade of its existence, the substantive provisions of the code have been amended in several important respects. For example, in 1967, one of the exceptions to section 4, that of an employer employing less than five employees, was repealed (S.O. 1967, ch. 66, sec. 2) thereby obligating every employer to comply with the directive of the section which prohibits discrimination in employment practices. In 1968, the exemption concerning special organizations was narrowed by adding a caveat that such exemptions applied only in cases where "race, colour, creed, nationality, ancestry or place of origin is a reasonable occupational qualification."[70] Since the term "reasonable occupational qualification" can be defined only in a contextual setting, the application of amended section 4 is likely to cause considerable confusion. For example, is citizenship a "reasonable occupational qualification" for faculty appointments in Canadian universities?[71] As has been noted, the amended section 3 prohibits discrimination in housing in all commercial units and housing accommodations.

It should be noted also that there is no substantive ban on the discriminatory membership practices of private clubs. For example, a prospective member of the Loyal Order of Moose, a fraternal organization, must certify that he is "of sound mind and body, being a member of the Caucasian, white race, and not married to one of any other race, and a believer in a Supreme Being." The Commission obviously has no statutory jurisdiction in such cases. Another unsettled issue is whether or not a private club which frequently admits the public to social events on the club's premises must comply with section 2 of the Code. However, in 1969, a board of inquiry rejected the defense of "private property" in a case concerning rental of a summer cottage to a Jewish couple.[72]

Implementation. The Ontario Human Rights Commission is authorized to inquire into complaints concerning the violation of the Act. The complaint, which "shall be in writing," has to allege that a person "has been discriminated against contrary to this Act," and the Commission's task is to "endeavor to effect a settlement of the matter complained of" (sec. 12; R.S.O. 1970, ch. 318, sec. 13). If the Commission is unable to effect a settlement, the Minister of Labor is authorized to appoint a board of inquiry upon the Commission's recommendation. The board, whose function is investigatory in nature, has all the powers of a conciliation board under section 28 of the Labor Relations Act, such as the power to compel the attendance of witnesses, the giving of evidence, and the production of documents which are necessary to insure a genuine opportunity to be heard. The board is to give the parties "full opportunity to present evidence and to make submissions and, if it finds that the complaint is supported by the evidence, it shall recommend to the Commission the course that ought to be taken with respect to the complaint." (sec. 13[3]; R.S.O. 1970, ch. 318, sec. 14 [3]) The Commission, in turn, may make recommendations to the Minister of Labor, who on such recommendation "may issue whatever order he deems necessary" to carry the board's recommendations into effect. (sec. 13 (6); R.S.O. 1970, ch. 318, sec. 14 [6]) Penalties for the violation of the Act are at present a fine of not more than $1000 in the case of an individual, or $5000 in the case of an organization; no prosecution shall be instituted except with the consent of the Minister of Labor.[73]

The Commission has also undertaken extensive educational and research projects pursuant to the specific promotional and educational functions it is assigned under the Code. (sec. 8; R.S.O. 1970, ch. 318, sec. 9)

For instance, the Commission was instrumental in conducting a study of the text books used in Canadian schools which showed excessive racial bias.[74] In the first 7 years of its existence the Commission had "investigated, settled, dismissed or referred over 12,000 formal, informal and miscellaneous complaints and inquiries," and had investigated 2,000 formal cases. It was necessary to set up boards of inquiry in only about 50 cases.

Interpretation. Section 1 on signs and notices is a reminder of a past time when signs such as "Whites Only" were commonplace. Although such forms of discrimination have now disappeared, other more subtle forms persist. For example, advertisements in newspapers concerning mortgages for sale might still list the ethnic nationality of the mortgagor. The Commission considers this practice undesirable inasmuch as it is likely to encourage discrimination against other nationalities. The Commission has also applied this section in attempting to find informal resolutions of complaints alleging the stereotyping or portrayal of a prejudiced point of view of a minority group in films, articles, and books.

The prohibition on discrimination in places "to which the public is customarily admitted" contained in section 2 was formerly contained in section 2 of the Fair Accommodation Practices Act, and was restrictively interpreted in a 1956 case, *Forbes* v. *Shields.*[75] A black salesman was denied accommodation in a large apartment building because of his color. Judge Thomas dismissed the complaint on the ground that the common type of apartment house could not be considered to be a place to which the public is customarily admitted. Such a restrictive interpretation seems unwarranted since the Fair Accommodation Practices Act was obviously enacted to rectify the situation under common law which obligated only hotels and innkeepers to provide accommodation to all persons. And if the term accommodation (sec. 2) does not include apartment houses and homes, the only places covered by the Act would be hotels and inns which were already covered under common law. In the light of the reference to the Universal Declaration of Human Rights in the Preamble of the Act and with a view to interpreting the Act in the light of its broad purposes, it is almost impossible to find a reasonable justification for Judge Thomas's interpretation. However, section 3 is sufficiently broad inasmuch as it now covers any housing accommodation. Formerly it referred to any self-contained dwelling unit.

The term self-contained dwelling unit was given a broad interpretation by a board of inquiry in a 1968 case.[76] A third-floor, two-room flat with a balcony requiring a tenant to share a common entrance hall, stairway, and bathroom with other tenants was considered a self-contained unit. The board decided the question with reference to the legislative intent, saying that if a tenant lived as part of the landlord's family, "i.e., perhaps sharing meals, perhaps having a room or rooms occupied by the landlord and his family," the accommodation in question would not be covered by the phrase self-contained. During the next year other boards of inquiry reached similar conclusions in similar cases, one suggesting that the legislative intent was to exclude only such accommodation which necessitated the tenant to intrude "into the landlord's routine family life."[77] By way of clarification, the board noted that "the modifier 'self-contained' relates more to 'dwelling' than to 'unit'." In another case, the board found the premises to meet the requirements of the Act, since the flat was "as independent as it could be in a home such as that of (the defendant) Mr. Domokos."[78] The latter approach seems especially helpful in interpreting self-contained, for it seeks a balancing of the claims made in a contextual setting. Thus, the reasons given for refusing accommodation could be tested by reference to factual and constructional considerations, such as, the layout of a particular building, the nature of the flat in question, and the degree of independence to be enjoyed by the prospective tenant.

However, in Bell v. *Ontario Human Rights Commission*, a case decided by the Supreme Court of Canada in 1971, the term self-contained was given a restrictive construction.[79] The layout of premises in question would have required the prospective tenant, a black Jamaican, to share the entrance and hallway to the stairs with the owner of the house, even though the three-room flat, situated on the second and third floors of the house, had a separate bathroom, kitchen, living room, and bedrooms. McKay filed a complaint with the Commission alleging that his "failure to obtain accommodation was determined by factors of race, colour and place of origin." A majority of the Supreme Court found that the flat was not a self-contained dwelling, since, in Judge Martland's words, "it would appear to me that (the phrase) includes now either a self-contained house, or self-contained premises similar to an apartment in an apartment house."[80] The decision has been criticized as unsound on two major grounds. One, the court's conclusion that a self-contained dwelling unit is to be equated with a self-contained house, or self-contained premises similar to an apartment in an apartment house, "in the light of the past history of the legislation," is unsupportable, for the legislative history of section 3 shows that the legislature has continuously expanded the scope of the section, and has even dropped any reference to apartments. Furthermore, the court conveniently ignored prior decisions of boards of inquiry. Two, the court gave no reason to justify its conclusions that the premises in question were not "similar to an apartment in an apartment house."

The Commission's authority and procedures were also under attack in *Bell*. After investigation, the Commission had found "sufficient evidence supporting Mr. McKay's allegations of discrimination to warrant further involvement of the commission in this matter." It invited Bell to discuss "possible terms of settlement and conciliation," which subsequently it elaborated in correspondence with Bell's solicitor: "Typical terms of settlement would include a written expression of apology to the complainant from Mr. Bell as well as an offer of the next available accommodation, and remunerations to the complainant for monies expended as a result of his failure to obtain" the said accommodation. The solicitor wrote back that Bell had not violated the Code and suggested that, since the Commission said that it had found sufficient evidence supporting McKay's allegations, it should proceed with Bell's prosecution in the courts instead of attempting to negotiate a settlement. The Commission thereupon sought appointment of a board of inquiry, and Walter Tarnopolsky, Dean of the University of Windsor Law School, was appointed to the board. Bell's solicitor had, in the meantime, objected to such an appointment and had requested the Minister of Labor to authorize a prosecution. The Minister refused the request for prosecution, noting that Ontario's human rights legislation "was not punitively-oriented but was basically educational and conciliatory, with prosecution as a last resort."[81] In his subsequent correspondence with the Commission, Bell's solicitor said that since the Commission had already investigated the matter and had indeed indicated that it had enough evidence to support a charge under section 3, the board had "forfeited any purported jurisdiction," the appropriate remedy now being in the courts.[82] The board was, however, convened and refused to find that it lacked a jurisdictional base on the grounds that the premises in question were not within section 3, a suggestion made by Bell's solicitor. At this stage Bell made an application for an order of prohibition. The trial judge granted prohibition, accepting Bell's contention that since the flat in question was not a "self-contained dwelling unit" within the meaning of section 3 of the Act, the board lacked jurisdiction. The Court of Appeal reversed, holding that "it is premature to seek to stall [the board's] proceedings at their inception on the ground of an apprehended error of law, i.e. misconstruction of a provision of the Code, which it is assumed the board will make."[83] The Supreme Court reversed the Court of Appeal, restoring the trial court's judgment. The board was prevented from inquiring into the complaint.

The major criticism leveled against the Commission's powers is that they are excessive and should not have been granted to administrative agencies and officials. The trial judge said: "The Commission and the Minister have always refused Mr. Bell access to any Court and, in spite of invitations to prosecute, refuse to allow a trial on the merits. The Minister's powers are so great, as will appear, and the Act generally so contrary to the principles set forth by the Honourable J. C. McRuer's advice in his learned and practical report concerning civil rights that the policy of not granting access to the Court is understandable."[84] The majority of the Supreme Court addressed itself to the question of the board's authority to inquire into the "scope of the operation of the Act," that is, whether the accommodation in question was covered under the Act. They declared, "The Act does not purport to place that issue within the exclusive jurisdiction of the board."[85] The trial judge, therefore, had jurisdiction to deal with the question.

At hearings before a board of inquiry concerning the application forms used by the City of Ottawa for municipal employment, the city solicitor admitted a breach of the Code under section 4 prohibiting the circulation of applications for employment which express preference as to the race, creed, color, nationality, or place of origin and promised to change the forms to comply with the Code.[86] The forms in question required an applicant to provide information regarding nationality, citizenship, place of birth, mother's and father's names, and place of birth.

In another hearing under section 4 before a board, a foreman's use of a racially derogatory epithet in addressing a Ford Motor Company employee was considered not to constitute discrimination by the employer "with regard to employment" for which the company would be liable.[87] The board's reasoning was that it was an isolated incident, and not a problem of conduct acquiesced in by the company.

Appraisal. The powers of the Ontario Human Rights Commission are fairly extensive and certainly broader than those of the Race Relations Board in Britain, and its procedures allow it sufficient flexibility. In Bell's case, the defendant's solicitor criticized the procedures of the Commission, contending that the board's procedure was "arbitrary, vicious and destructive of the role of the law," which ought to be prohibited by courts. Another criticism is that, under the Commission's procedures, the same individual is entrusted with both investigation and conciliation powers, which is not conducive to the effective functioning of the Commission. A persuasive case has been made by Dean Tarnopolsky for a functional separation of these roles.[88]

Those defending the Commission's powers and procedures rely mainly on the legislative purposes and intent in order to argue that in view of the nature of the subject matter, human rights, the emphasis on flexibility and informal settlement, on negotiation and conciliation is warranted. It is necessary, they say, to distinguish this type of legislation from criminal law or quasi-criminal law-oriented legislation and its implementing machinery, which usually are characterized by concepts such as retribution and guilt. It is contended that there are adequate safeguards provided under the Code. Examples cited are the appointment of boards of inquiry, who are drawn from the ranks of judges or deans of law schools, and the powers granted the Commission, the board, and the Minister of Labor, which are by no means excessive.

The recognition that the legislation, as construed by the Supreme Court, was deficient led the Ontario legislature to amend the Code in 1971 and 1972. Changes in section 3 have already been noted. The complaints procedure now permits any person to invoke the Act, subject to the consent of the person allegedly discriminated against. (S.O. 1971, ch. 50, sec. 63) The Commission may also initiate a complaint. (S.O. 1972, ch. 119, sec. 10) The board members

hearing a complaint "shall not have taken part in any investigation or consideration of the complaint prior to the hearing. . . ." (S.O. 1971, ch. 50, sec. 63) The
same section provides that the board's decision or order may be appealed to the
Supreme Court and prohibits discrimination on grounds of sex and marital
status. Inasmuch as codes in British Columbia and Manitoba have provisions
similar to section 3 of the Ontario Code, those provinces may follow the Ontario
example and amend their codes. Quebec still seems to have inadequate legislation,[89] and it has yet to consolidate its antidiscrimination statutes into one
code. Its two pertinent statutes are the Employment Discrimination Act and the
Hotels Act. The former still exempts both employers who employ less than five
persons and managerial positions from the purview of the Act. There is no
provision for the establishment of an independent commission to hear complaints under the Act and the maximum penalty for a violation is only a $100
fine. And the Hotels Act is merely a codification of the common law protection
that an innkeeper is obligated to serve every traveler. There is still no legislation
prohibiting discrimination in housing.

UNITED STATES POLICY

The two approaches which have been adopted in both Britain and Canada to
prevent and combat racial discrimination—laissez-faire and conciliation—also
have been tried in the United States at every level of government. However,
efforts in the United States to promote equal opportunity are now centered on
testing the next step beyond conciliation, that of affirmative action. Measures
adopted to legislate and implement the affirmative action approach are reviewed,
preceded by a brief recounting of the prior experimentation with laissez-faire
and conciliation.

The laissez-faire approach. The historical laissez-faire approach represents
the policy of the federal government from the end of the Civil War to the end of
World War II.[90] The Civil War had generated the thirteenth and fourteenth
Amendments to the Constitution and related civil rights legislation; but these
measures were accompanied by neither the mechanisms nor the desire to enforce
them. Even before this fragile structure of human rights laws had been completed, a judicial assault was under way, which eventually left the structure in
ruins.[91] The fatal blow came from the famous *Civil Rights Cases* in which a
congressional act banning discrimination in accommodations was declared
unconstitutional by the Supreme Court.[92]

The federal government finally created the first institutional structure to
implement civil rights legislation in 1939, when it established the Civil Rights
Section of the Department of Justice. Even then, a full commitment was not
made in terms of staff and updated legislation. Further attempts were made in
the Roosevelt and Truman administrations to create federal enforcement agencies, but each attempt died in congressional filibuster.

During the 1950s, however, the Civil Service began implementing certain policies of "simple nondiscrimination" which were instrumental in increasing the number of minorities employed by the federal government.[93] Although these policies were not successful in promoting advancement of minorities within the structure, they nonetheless constituted a necessary first step toward the formulation of a more active employment policy and other government programs as well.[94]

The laissez-faire approach in the United States has been characterized by (1) the existence of legislation which is either not enforced or is judicially unenforceable; (2) a lack of institutional structures; and (3) an unwarranted reliance on good faith and change in attitudes to achieve the legislative goals. Although the federal government has abandoned the approach, considering it ineffective, it still prevails among some state and local governments.

The conciliation approach. As discussed in this study in the British and Canadian context, the conciliation approach attempts to create nonenforcement mechanisms to receive and act upon complaints of discrimination in informal ways. Wherever the discriminatory practice is attributable to a government agency, conciliation has had its greatest success. A few state and local governments have established ombudsmen whose conciliation efforts have been successful in welfare, employment, and licensing cases.[95] Often a government official (primarily a lieutenant-governor) serves as the ombudsman. Since reliance on an ombudsman is better suited to a small administrative unit, the federal government and many states have adopted other more sophisticated mechanisms to implement conciliation.

The conciliation approach was adopted in the field of housing in 1962 by executive order.[96] Following years of government inaction, President Kennedy issued an order to all departments of the federal government to prevent discrimination in housing connected in any way with the government. This included residential property owned or operated by the federal government, purchased with the aid of loans or grants by the federal government, purchased with loans insured by the federal government, or purchased or leased from a government or agency receiving financial assistance from the federal government.

While the order gave the Federal Housing Authority (FHA) powers to take any "appropriate action permitted by law, including the institution of appropriate litigation," the FHA did not exercise that power until 1968. Instead, the implementation of the order was designated primarily as the responsibility of a Committee on Equal Opportunity in Housing. Essentially, this committee was given the duty to set guidelines, make recommendations, promote studies, confer with various interest groups, and encourage educational programs. It had many mandates, but few powers.

A similar approach was adopted concerning discrimination in employment. In 1965 the Equal Employment Opportunity Commission (EEOC) was created under Title VII of the Civil Rights Act of 1964.[97] Under the Act the Commission was composed of five members, no more than three of whom could be from the same political party. The Commission and its staff were given the power to cooperate with other agencies, furnish technical assistance, assist in conciliation, make technical studies, refer matters to the Attorney General, appear as amicus curiae in any civil suit, and carry on educational activities. The Commission could join proceedings instituted by other government agencies, but the only circumstances under which it could commence an action itself was in order to compel compliance with a court order in a previous civil action. Thus, if a complaint was filed before the EEOC, the Commission attempted to negotiate an agreement. If that failed, however, the burden was on the victim of the discrimination to seek an enforceable court order. This system was the creation of congressional compromise. Distinctive characteristics of the conciliation approach in the United States are the existence of laws against discrimination and mechanisms for receiving complaints for violation of those laws, but also, a lack of enforcement or litigation power within those mechanisms.

Affirmative action approach. The affirmative action approach in the United States involves empowering the machinery created under the conciliation approach to enforce the antidiscrimination laws by issuing orders, such as cease and desist and affirmative orders, in order to remedy a wrong. Moreover, in government contracts, the newer approach relies upon requirements that affirmative action plans for elimination of discrimination in employment be submitted before approval of any such contracts. Recent legislative developments concerning the EEOC illustrate the trend in the United States. In 1972 Congress amended the Civil Rights Act giving the EEOC broad new powers. The major innovation is that the Commission is now allowed to bring actions in Federal District Courts to force compliance with antidiscrimination laws. The results have been dramatic.[98]

Under the new law these procedures must be followed: (1) a charge alleging discrimination must be filed with the Commission within 180 days of the alleged discriminatory practice; (2) within ten days the Commission must serve notice of the charge upon the respondent employer, employment agency, or labor union; (3) an investigation must be conducted promptly and within 120 days it must be determined if there exists reasonable cause in the complaints; (4) if, upon preliminary investigation, the Commission determines that prompt judicial action is necessary to carry out the intentions of the Act, it may bring an action for immediate temporary relief, usually in the form of reinstatement of an employee, pending a final disposition of the charge; (5) if, after a full investigation, no reasonable cause is found, the complaint is dismissed; (6) if the Commission does find reasonable cause, it shall enter into secret negotiations with the respondent through informal methods of conference, conciliation, and persuasion to eliminate the unlawful employment practice; (7) if, within 30 days after the charge has been filed, the Commission has not been able to secure a conciliation agreement acceptable to the Commission, it may bring an action against the respondent in federal court to enforce the law.

There are two basic exceptions to these procedures. First, if the respondent employer is a government or governmental agency, the U.S. Attorney General must bring the charges. Secondly, when a complaint alleges discrimination in a state or locality where there exist applicable laws and an appropriate local enforcement agency, the EEOC must afford the local authorities a reasonable time (at least sixty days) to act under local law to remedy the alleged practice. This will often be the case because there are many state and local agencies which have responsibilities and powers as great or even greater than that of the federal Commission.

One instructive example is the Pennsylvania Human Relations Commission. While by no means unique, the Commission, created in 1955, is one of the oldest in the country. Its powers are some of the most farreaching of any agency on any level of government.[99] The Pennsylvania Commission is mandated to deal with discriminatory activities in employment, housing, and education. To fulfill this broad mandate, it has essentially the same conciliatory function and powers as the pre-1972 EEOC with one major addition. The Pennsylvania Commission has the power, on the basis of its own investigation, to issue court enforceable orders to cease and desist from unlawful discriminatory practice. Further, the Commission may order affirmative action to remedy any wrong, including reinstatement or employment with or without back pay. These powers are, of course, subject to judicial review. One problem, however, is that the penalty for violation of an order is a relatively light $500 fine or thirty days in jail or both.

The California Fair Employment Practice Commission supplies another interesting example.[100] The Commission can hold hearings, subpoena witnesses, examine witnesses under oath, and pass upon complaints. It can issue cease and desist orders comparable to those of the Pennsylvania Commission and, like the federal EEOC, it can seek temporary injunctions. Under a 1971 amendment, it has acquired the important power to investigate, approve, and certify equal opportunity programs which must be submitted by every contractor performing a public work contract of over $200,000 awarded by the state.[101]

This power is similar to that granted the Office of Federal Contract Compliance (OFCC) on the national level. By executive order, all federal government contracts must contain extensive provisions requiring affirmative compliance with nondiscriminatory employment practice by contractors, subcontractors, vendors, and labor unions.[102] For construction contracts, the government has developed plans to be implemented on a metropolitan-wide scope, the most celebrated of which is the Philadelphia Plan. In the metropolitan areas where the plan is in force, the OFCC has annually proposed a numerical range for minorities in each construction trade and required an affirmative action plan to meet these standards in all federally financed projects. While the plan suffered from strong union pressures against it in the 1972 election year, it still retains government support, and compliance has actually surpassed the minimum goals set in each year of its operation.[103]

For nonconstruction contracts with the federal government, standard affirmative action procedures have been implemented whereby all contractors and subcontractors with more than 50 employees must develop a written affirmative action program within 120 days after being awarded a government contract. If the plans are not acceptable to the agency, informal methods of conciliation must take place. Following any unsuccessful efforts, hearings may be held which eventually can lead to termination of the contract. This is, of course, a highly effective sanction.

A review of the various examples indicates that there are three basic types of affirmative action legislation in the United States. They have one similar important characteristic. The basis of each is the conciliation approach, a preference for negotiation and persuasion that is informal but is backed by strong enforcement sanctions.

The first type is that which grants litigative powers to the appropriate commission or agency. The prime example is the 1972 federal legislation granting such powers to the EEOC. Usually included is the right to ask for immediate temporary injunctive relief, the right to bring an action following an unsuccessful conciliation attempt, and the right to seek enforcement of court orders. The second type of affirmative action legislation gives commissions the right to issue cease and desist orders and prescribe court enforced means to eliminate discriminatory practices. The Pennsylvania Human Relations Commission is an example. That experience shows that this type of affirmative action program can extend into all fields of human rights. The final type of affirmative action legislation requires submission of affirmative plans for elimination of discrimination in employment before approval of government contracts. The California Fair Employment Commission and the Office of Federal Contract Compliance are the results of such legislation. The scope of OFCC enforcement powers extends beyond the contractor to subcontractors, vendors, and labor unions.

Interpretation. There has not yet emerged an unequivocal and stable pattern of decisions to indicate how affirmative action programs will be treated by American courts. While some courts have rather strictly interpreted affirmative action requirements, most have at least upheld the principle. Two of the most important decisions have been those upholding federal government construction contract affirmative action requirements in Newark and Philadelphia. In the important Newark case [104] the court upheld government quotas of between 30 and 37 percent minorities in the various construction trades. The court ruled that, if the quota were not met, the burden was on the contractor to make a showing of a good faith effort. In another case originating from a similar scheme in the State of Illinois, a federal court ruled that a preferential quota system for blacks was legal. [105] In these cases the reverse discrimination of affirmative action programs has been upheld. At the same time, courts have ruled that these acts do not require an employer to fill a position with someone not capable of doing the job. [106] Thus quotas can be filled only to the extent that qualified minority candidates exist.

The new powers of the EEOC have barely begun to be tested. In two of its very first cases the procedures of the Commission have been closely scrutinized by two southern courts, and in each case the EEOC action was dismissed. In the first, the court held that each step in the statutory scheme (charge, notice, investigation, reasonable cause, and conciliation) is "a condition precedent to the next succeeding step and ultimately legal action."[107] In this case, the EEOC failed to state each action taken by the Commission to satisfy the statute. The complaint was therefore dismissed. In the second case, the action was dismissed on the same grounds.[108] The court found that the EEOC had not stated sufficient affirmative allegations concerning attempts to secure a conciliation agreement. However, the significant point in both these cases is that the law has been upheld, although some courts have given it rather restrictive interpretation. In a more recent case in a northern court, the procedures of the EEOC were found adequate and in compliance with the statute.[109]

In states where agencies hold cease and desist powers, there have been criticisms that these commissions violate the principle of due process of law by combining investigative, prosecution, and adjudicatory powers in one body. In Ohio litigation, a state court upheld the powers of one such commission, adopting the prevailing view that so long as safeguards through judicial review are available, cease and desist powers will be upheld.[110]

Some of the most interesting litigation has involved state and citizen attempts to challenge the discriminatory practices of various fraternal organizations. The U.S. Supreme Court has ruled in *Moose Lodge* v. *Irvis* that membership policies could not be challenged simply on the grounds that the state granted the Lodge a liquor license.[111] The complainant, Irvis, was a non-Caucasian guest of a club member and was denied admission to the Lodge dining room, which had a state liquor license. He was barred from the Moose restaurant solely on the grounds that he was black. The court limited its ruling to a challenge of membership and not guest policies. Subsequently, however, lower courts have upheld narrower but equally intriguing attacks on discrimination policies. In a case arising out of the same factual situation as in the *Irvis* case, the Pennsylvania Human Relations Commission was affirmed in its ruling that the Lodge dining room fell into the category of public accommodations and, thus, it was not allowed to discriminate against non-Caucasians.[112] The court noted that any guest of any member could eat there with only one qualification—that he or she be Caucasian. This, then, was an unlawful standard in what was essentially a public eating place.

One of the more unusual attempts to influence membership policies has occurred in Oregon where a law was upheld allowing the state to lift the tax exempt status on organizations discriminating racially in their membership policies.[113] Noting the *Irvis* case, the court held that the tax status provided a much stronger link than a liquor license. A tax exemption is granted to benefit and encourage certain activities, and when public policy is contradicted by those activities the perpetrators are not entitled to public assistance.

Appraisal. Affirmative action legislation is so new in the United States that the relative effectiveness of each type of litigation is by no means clear. It can be safely concluded, however, that the affirmative action approach has been much more successful than the previous laissez-faire and conciliation approaches. In contrast to certain British and Canadian examples of restrictive statutory interpretation, the United States judiciary has interpreted the affirmative action legislation in ways which have not significantly reduced its efficacy. While in some areas, courts are insistent that the statutory procedures be strictly complied with, in most cases, the general principle of affirmative action has been upheld.

The granting of court enforcement powers to the EEOC in 1972 represented a defeat for its most enthusiastic supporters, who strongly felt that the commission should be given cease and desist authority.[114] After more than a year, however, the EEOC chairman and many others have expressed satisfaction with their new powers. They now argue that the cease and desist procedure can be cumbersome and time consuming because it often involves going through both long administrative and judicial procedures. Under the 1972 amendment, the EEOC can be in court within thirty days of receiving the complaint. It can obtain immediate temporary action through injunctive relief. In most cases, this streamlines the procedure, for respondents are stimulated to settle quickly before expensive litigation is begun.

It is worth noting that the recent EEOC successes and prestige should be attributed not so much to court activities, as to some very successful out-of-court settlements. The most notable settlement was reached with American Telephone and Telegraph in a case begun, ironically, before the EEOC was granted court enforcement powers. The EEOC had intervened in 1971 in a Federal Communications Commission rate case alleging discrimination on the basis of sex and race. A $38 million settlement was reached (including back pay and wage adjustments), which shocked the business community.[115] With this kind of precedent, fear has been the common word used to express the business community's new feelings about the EEOC. Now with its court enforcement powers, the Commission is rapidly reorganizing and expanding. In less than a year its staff of lawyers has jumped from 40 to well over 200. It has an astonishing backlog of 60,000 potential cases. The goal of the Commission is to file a limited number of actions (150 in fiscal year 1973 and 600 in fiscal year 1974) against a representative grouping of employers and labor unions and then to use the expected favorable results to strengthen its bargaining position with other respondents.[116]

While the members of the Commission and many observers have been highly enthusiastic about the new role of the EEOC, there is some basis for criticism. The main complaint is that the EEOC has neglected its conciliation functions by concentrating excessively on litigation. One case is illustrative. In July, 1972, the Commission under its new powers sought and was granted a preliminary injunction against Liberty Mutual Insurance Company ordering the reinstatement of a woman employee who allegedly suffered discrimination.[117] Back pay with interest was granted. According to the law, the preliminary injunction is a temporary measure to be taken pending the resolution of the complaint. But by the end of March, 1973, when the case reached the appellate level, the EEOC had still not resolved the matter administratively. The court was not lax in its criticism: ". . . nothing substantial has been accomplished by the Commission with respect to Mrs. Drew's complaint since the District Court entered its order. This case should receive immediate attention and the controversy should be brought to a proper conclusion. We do not approve the delay by the Commission which is evident in this case, especially in circumstances in which the relationship between employer and employee is seriously affected by the terms of an injunctive order. . . . [This] litigation [must] be brought to a conclusion without further undue delay."[118]

When properly exercised, the affirmative action powers of the EEOC have generally been promising. One indication of their effectiveness is marked by the sharp response from the business community. But whether the new powers will result in long-term compliance is problematic. At least it can be said confidently that the affirmative action programs for employment within the federal bureaucracy, which have been in existence over a decade, can now be evaluated with some perspective as highly successful. The previous policy of simple nondiscrimination was helpful in getting minorities hired. But only the affirmative action program has been instrumental in advancing many minority employees to intermediate and higher level positions.[119]

As far as the Philadelphia Plan is concerned, in spite of fairly serious political attacks, "in each year since the Plan was implemented, the minimum goal established . . . has been surpassed."[120] Under current government programs, the burden of proof for compliance with the government's guidelines has shifted to the contractors. They must set goals and time tables to correct deficiencies wherever they exist.

As for cease and desist powers, the Pennsylvania situation offers a good example. The key word here is flexibility. The Pennsylvania Commission has been able to adapt itself to newly perceived areas, such as sex discrimination and school desegregation, with little difficulty. Its powers give it the ability to order the development of acceptable affirmative action plans by the offending institution, the implementation of which plans can then be negotiated in informal ways. The Commission's broad mandate carries its activities into virtually every area of human rights.

In sum, recently adopted affirmative action programs in the United States seem to be highly effective, even though hard data are essentially unavailable to determine long term trends. This does not mean that there has been no criticism, even from those who support the goals of these programs. One recent criticism of the affirmative action programs of the Department of Health, Education and Welfare (HEW) is worth reviewing here.[121] HEW has recently required educational institutions which receive any kind of federal assistance to submit affirmative action plans for eliminating discrimination based on race and sex within their institutions. Critics of this program have two basic charges. One, the government is wrongly equating *equal* distribution with *normal* distribution. By insisting on equal distribution of races and sexes at all levels, the government is causing positions to be filled by people not yet qualified to fill them, thus causing the overall quality of the institutions to decline. The critics assert that the important first step is to concentrate on training, to equalize individuals first in ability, and then in opportunity. Two, the critics state that a minimum quota for one group implies a maximum quota for the rest. This, then, becomes reverse discrimination which, they argue, should be equally avoided.

Thus, in evaluating the effectiveness of various affirmative action programs in eliminating discrimination, pure statistical success may be deceptive. Factors such as the effectiveness of conciliation efforts and the quality of the ultimate results must be balanced against raw data. Nevertheless, even at this early date, it is clear that affirmative action programs of all types have produced far better concrete results in providing opportunities for minorities than have the earlier programs.

CONCLUSIONS

This discussion has demonstrated the need for effective legislation to eliminate racial discrimination, because the traditional laissez-faire approach has been unable to bring about the behavioral changes necessary to allow equality of opportunity. However, it is equally clear that the elimination of racial discrimination will not come about simply by the passage of laws, for no legislative effort will succeed without effective implementation measures. Also, various experiments with conciliation mechanisms in the countries studied here show that such mechanisms play a vital role in educating people and in breaking racial barriers. However, conciliation efforts can succeed only when they are backed up by legal sanctions which act as deterrents. Changed conditions and attitudes demand updated laws. It is startling to realize that, until the end of World War II, no major legislative effort was made anywhere to protect victims of racial discrimination.

Broad generalizations and conclusions concerning legislation and implementation summarized in these sections are equally applicable to other areas such as discrimination based on sex or on religion. They should also be valid regardless of the stage of economic development of a society, provided that there is consensus on the paramount role of the rule of law in governing and regulating human relationships. This is not to say that societal conditions and historical developments will play no part in affecting the outcome in a given case, but it is to say that the influence of various conditioning factors can be minimized, predicted, and counteracted by taking necessary legislative and implementing measures. For example, Britain is feeling the impact of the Race Relations Acts in spite of the widespread resentment and indignation felt and expressed by the English against legislating in the racial field.

It is evident that further studies on the role of law and its effectiveness in protecting human rights are needed. Empirical and comparative research is needed to collect hard data and to evaluate facts so as to identify trends and to suggest alternatives. However, even a brief survey of the experiment in the United States with the successful affirmative action approach, indicates that both Britain and Canada could benefit by adoption of similar measures, adapted to meet the special needs of the two countries. Affirmative action has much to recommend it: perhaps for the first time in human history the realization of the ideals of human dignity and equality of opportunity does not have to depend exclusively upon humane toleration; instead, it can be achieved by linking rights with effective remedies.

NOTES*

* In reference to legal periodical literature, the number of the *initial* page of the work cited immediately follows the volume title. Page references to material specifically referred to in the text, if any, follow the initial page citation. Legal case citations correspond to *A Uniform System of Citation,* 11th ed. (Cambridge: The Harvard Law Review Association, 1974).

1. The literature on the subject of racial discrimination is extensive, although the number of studies which focus on the subject in comparative terms is surprisingly modest. Among the more useful titles associated with comparative race relations are the following. Michael Banton, *Race Relations* (New York: Basic Books, 1968); Milton Barron, *Minorities in a Changing World* (New York: Knopf, 1967); Hubert Blalock, *Toward a Theory of Minority-Group Relations* (New York: John Wiley, 1967); Ralph Bunche, *A World View of Race* (New York: Kennikat Press, 1968); Yvan Debbasch, *Couleur et Liberté* (Paris: Dalloz, 1967); Manfred Halpern, *Applying a New Theory of Human Relations to the Comparative Study of Racism* (Denver: University of Denver, 1970); Ira Katznelson, ed., "The Politics of Race," *Race* 14 (1973): 365–480; Natran Lerner, *The Crime of Incitement to Group Hatred, A Survey of International and National Legislation* (New York: World Jewish Congress, 1965); Julius Lewin, ed., *The Struggle for Racial Equality* (London: Longmans, 1967); Phillip Mason, *Patterns of Dominance* (London: Oxford University Press, 1971); W. G. Runciman, ed., "Race and Social Stratification," *Race,* 13 (1972): 385–509. George W. Shepherd et al., ed., *Race Among Nations: A Conceptual Approach* (Lexington, Mass.: Heath, 1970); Melvin Tumin, ed., *Comparative Perspectives on Race Relations* (Boston: Little Brown, 1969); Pierre Van den Berghe, *Race and Racism: A Comparative Perspective* (New York: John Wiley, 1967).

2. *Race Relations Act, 1968,* 1 Elizabeth 2, ch. 71, sec. 1.

3. Ontario, *Human Rights Code, 1962,* Revised Statutes of Ontario, ch. 318, sec. 1 (1) (1970).

4. U.S., *Civil Rights Act, 1964,* See, e.g. 42 U.S.C. sec. 2000–02(a to d)(1970).

5. See National Conference of Commissioners on Uniform State Laws, "Model Anti-Discrimination Act," *Harvard Journal on Legislation* 4 (1967): 224–78.

6. The convention was unanimously adopted December 21, 1965. United Nations, General Assembly, *International Convention on the Elimination of All Forms of Racial*

Discrimination, Suppl. 14 (A/6014) (1966) p. 47. See generally, Egon Schwelb, "The International Convention on the Elimination of All Forms of Racial Discrimination," *International and Comparative Law Quarterly* 15 (1966):996–1068 and W. M. Reisman, "Responses to Crimes of Discrimination and Genocide: An Appraisal of the Convention on the Elimination of Racial Discrimination," *Denver Journal of International Law and Policy* 1 (1971):29–64.

7. Article 1 (1) of the Racial Discrimination Convention. The International Labor Organization has defined the term racial discrimination in a similar fashion. See *Fighting Discrimination in Employment and Occupation* (Geneva: International Labor Organization, 1968).

8. Article 1 (4) of the Racial Discrimination Convention.

9. For various perspectives on this question, see John H. Franklin, ed., *Color and Race* (Boston: Houghton Mifflin, 1968). But see, Ashley Montagu, *Statement on Race,* 3d ed. (New York: Oxford University Press, 1972), p. 190: "It comes as a distinct surprise to most people to learn that the origins of racism are quite recent. . . ." See also, United Nations, Economic and Social Council, *Racial Discrimination,* prepared by H. Santa Cruz E/CN.4/Sub.2/307/Rev. 1, 1971, pp. 1–20; Edgar G. Epps, ed., *Race Relations: Current Perspectives* (New York: Winthrop, 1973); "Dimensions of the Racial Situation," *International Social Science Journal* 23 (1971):505–625.

10. United Nations, General Assembly, *Human Rights: A Compilation of International Instruments of the United Nations,* (A/C.32/4) 1967, p. 8.

11. The "Year for Action" resolution was adopted unanimously on Dec. 11, 1969. See Res. 2544 (24) in 1969 *United Nations Yearbook* pp. 486–87. The "Decade for Struggle" resolution was adopted unanimously on Oct. 19, 1972. Res. 2906 (28). See *United Nations Monthly Chronicle* 9 (November 1972):38.

12. United Nations, Education and Social Council, *Convention Against Discrimination in Education,* 1960, 429 U.N.T.S. 31.

13. On Dec. 18, 1972, the General Assembly decided in resolution 3027 (27) to accord priority to the completion of the Declaration on the Elimination of All Forms of Religious Intolerance before resuming consideration of the convention on the subject. See United Nations, General Assembly (A7497) 1969.

14. See generally, *The United Nations and Human Rights* U.N., Division of Human Rights, (U.N. Office of Public Information, E. 67.2.29) pp. 78–84.

15. United Nations, Division of Human Rights in Cooperation with the Government of France, "Seminar on the Dangers of a Recrudescence of Intolerance in All Its Forms and the Search for Ways of Combating and Preventing." U.N. Doc. ST/SAO/HR/44 (1971).

16. Harry Street et al., *Antidiscrimination Legislation: The Street Report* (London: Political and Economic Planning, 1967). See also, Eliot J. Rose et al., *Colour and Citizenship* (New York: Oxford University Press, 1969); William W. Daniel, *Racial Discrimination in England* (Penguin: 1968).

17. The first report was released in 1968; since then several volumes of reports have been published. See *Report of the Royal Commission Inquiry Into Civil Rights* Hon. T. C. McRver, Commissioner (Toronto: Queen's Printer, 1968–). See also, D. A. Schmeiser, *Civil Liberties in Canada* (Oxford University Press, 1964).

18. U.S., Commission on Civil Rights, *Federal Civil Rights Enforcement Effort* (Washington, D.C.: Government Printing Office, 1970); *The Federal Civil Rights Enforcement Effort: One Year Later* (Washington, D.C.: Government Printing Office, 1971); *Law Enforcement: A Report on the Equal Protection in the South* (Washington, D.C.: Government Printing Office, 1965). *Report of the National Advisory Commission on Civil Disobedience* (Washington, D.C.: Government Printing Office, 1968). See also, annual reports of U.S. Equal Employment Opportunity Commission.

19. *Allen* v. *Flood* A.C.1, at 172–3 (1898).

20. Quinton Hogg, "Race Relations and Parliament," *Race* 12 (1970):1–13; Jeffrey Jowell, "The Administrative Enforcement of Laws Against Discrimination," 1965 *Public Law* 119, 171–76 (1965).

21. B. A. Hepple, "The British Race Relations Acts, 1965 and 1968," 19 *University of Toronto Law Journal* 248, 248 (1968).

22. *Constantine* v. *Imperial Hotels Ltd.*, 1 (1944). K. B. 693. See also, *Rothfield* v. *Northern British Railway Co.*, 57 Sc. L.R.661(1920). Steven J. Hartz, "Race Relations and the Law in Britain," 41 *Temple Law Quarterly* 429, 440 (1968) notes that "the action does not seem to have been used for this purpose in any decision reported since the *Constantine* case."

23. *Parker* v. *Flint*, 12 Mod. Rep.254 (1699); *Ultzen* v. *Nicols*, 1 Q.B. 92 (1894); *Pidgeon* v. *Legge*, 21 J.P. 743 (1857); *Webb* v. *Fagotti Brothers*, 79 L.T. 683 (1898); *King* v. *Barclay and Barclay's Motel*, 31 W.W.R. (N.S.) Canada 451 (1960).

24. See generally, J. F. Garner, "Racial Restrictive Covenants in England and the United States," 35 *Modern Law Review* 5 478 (1972). See also, *Schlegel* v. *Corcoran & Gross*, (1942) I.R. 19; *Adler* v. *Upper Grosvenor Street Investment Ltd.*, (1957) 1 W.L.R. 227.

25. See generally, D. G. T. Williams, "Racial Incitement and Public Order," 1966 *Criminal Law Review* 320 (1966).

26. Anthony Lester and Geoffrey Bindman, *Race and Law in Great Britain* (Cambridge: Harvard University Press, 1972), p. 26. In the present discussion I have frequently relied upon this study, which is thorough and incisive, and is by far the best available on the subject.

27. See, e.g., Dominik Lasok, "Some Legal Aspects of Race Relations in the United Kingdom and the United States," *Journal of Public Law* 16 (1967):326–44, at 327. ". . . the problem [in Britain] is rather new—a result of the influx of coloured immigrants after the last war."

28. Richard Plender, "Protection of Immigrant and Racial Minorities: A Survey in British Legal History," 13 *William and Mary Law Review* 338, 339–41 (1971).

29. See, e.g., Roy Jenkins, *Essays and Speeches* (London: Collins, 1967), p. 271.

30. Street, *Street Report*, n. 16.

31. See generally, Paul Foot, *Immigration and Race in British Politics* (Baltimore: Penguin, 1966); and Bill Smithies and Peter Fiddick, *Enoch Powell on Immigration* (London: Sphere, 1969). For a particularly thorough and incisive discussion of state human rights legislation in the United States which generated scholarly interest in pursuing further research and exploration in Britain, see Arthur E. Bonfield, "State Civil Right Statutes: Some Proposals," 49 *Iowa Law Review* 1067 (1964). See, e.g., Keith Hindell, "The Genesis of the Race Relations Bill," *Political Quarterly* 36 (1965):390–405, at 395.

32. *Race Relations Act 1965*, sec. 1 (1), chap. 73.

33. Section 7 of the Act substituted for section 5 of the *Public Order Act 1936*.

34. Street, *Street Report*, n. 16.

35. Lester and Bindman, *Race and Law*, p. 134.

36. Race Relations Act 1968, ch. 71.

37. See sec. 7 (2) (a,b) and 7 (4). The number specified in sec. 7 (3) before Nov. 27, 1970, was twelve. Where the second exemption noted in the text above is concerned, the Act specifically provides that residential accommodation include "accommodation in a hotel, boarding house or other similar establishment." (sec. 7[5]) In order to be covered under the exemption, the landlord or any member of his family resides and intends to continue to reside on the premises (sec. 7[1][b]), and shares relevant accommodation "with other persons residing on the premises who are not members of his household." (sec. 7[1][c]) The term "relevant accommodation" means any accommodation "other than storage accommodation and means of access." (sec. 7[5]) Another exemption is in favor of an owner-occupier who disposes his "interest in any premises owned and wholly occupied by him unless he uses the services of an estate agent for the purposes of the disposal, or publishes or displays, or causes the publication or display, of an advertisemenet or notice in connection with the disposal." (sec. 7[7]) An owner is one "if the fee simple or a lease of the premises is vested in him." (sec. 7[8])

38. Among general exemptions applicable alike to the provisions of goods and services, employment, and housing, that on national security has been noted. Another exemption applies to any charitable instrument which "confers benefits on persons of a particular race, particular descent or particular ethnic or national origin." Finally, section 23 awkwardly, but ingeniously, says that any contract or term in a contract that contravenes the Act may

be revised by the court, on application made by the Race Relations Board, if the court considers it feasible to do so without affecting the rights of third parties.

39. Section 2 of the 1965 Act is thus altered by sections 14 and 15 of the 1968 Act.

40. Under the Act, a complaint has to be made to the Board or its conciliation committees within two months of the alleged discrimination, unless the Board has waived this time requirement under "special circumstances." (sec. 15[2]) The complaint has to be "accompanied by the name and address of the person by whom it is made." The Board must receive and investigate complaints. The investigatory officer conducts interviews with the principals and witnesses and reports his findings to the Board or to the committee conducting the investigation. Since the Board has no subpoena power to compel the attendance of witnesses or the production of documents, it or the conciliation committee must "form an opinion" at this stage whether an unlawful act has been done. (sec. 15[3][a])

41. Sec. 15 (4) (5). For further discussion, see Lester and Bindman, *Race and Law,* p. 306.

42. Sec. 17 (1). Initiative may be taken "in consequence of an allegation made by any person that he has been discriminated against" in violation of the Act, "or for any other cause" the Board has "reason to suspect" that an unlawful act has been done within two months before the matter first comes to its notice, or longer if the time requirement is waived by the Board under "special circumstances." (sec. 17[1], schedule 3, part 2, para. 7)

43. Although the usual jurisdictional limits do not apply, according to sec. 19 (1,6), the normal court procedures concerning pleadings, witnesses, evidence, interlocutory injunction, and examination and cross examination do apply.

44. Lester and Bindman, *Race and Law,* 331.

45. The reader should be aware of three additional features of the British law against racial discrimination, discussion of which is beyond the scope of this essay. First, the 1968 Race Relations Act sets up a Community Relations Commission for purposes of promoting "harmonious community relations" and to advise the Secretary of State and make recommendations to him. (sec. 25(3)) Its functions are primarily educational. Second, discriminatory immigration laws are closely related to the issues discussed above; they are ably analyzed in Ian A. MacDonald, *Race Relations and Immigration Law* (London: Butterworths, 1969). Finally, the criminal offense of incitement to racial hatred, created under the 1965 Act remains in force; see Anthony F. Dickey, "English Law and Incitement to Racial Hatred," *Race* 9 (1968):311–29, and idem., "Prosecutions under the Race Relations Act 1965, s. 6," 1968 *Criminal Law Review,* 489 (1968).

46. *London Borough of Ealing* v. *Race Relations Board,* 1 All E. R. 105 (1972); 1 All E. R. 424 (1971).

47. *London Borough of Ealing* v. *Race Relations Board,* 1 All E. R. 434–35 (1971).

48. See generally, Winifred Holland, "Nationality and the Race Relations Act 1968," 122 *New Law Journal* 234, 235 (1972).

49. *Race Relations Board* v. *Charter,* 1 Q. B. 545 (1972); *Charter* v. *Race Relations Board,* 2 W.L.R. 299 (1973).

50. *Race Relations Board* v. *Bradmore Working Men's Club* (Plaint No. 69.51765, 1970). A private club rented a hall for a Christmas party, tickets for which were sold to employees of telephone exchange who were permitted to bring relatives and friends. It was held by a county court that it was unlawful to refuse admission to employee and friends on the ground of color.

51. *Race Relations Board* v. *Applin,* 2 W.L.R. 895 (1973).

52. For a discussion, see J. K. Bentil, "Interpreting the Race Relations Act," 1973 *Public Law* 157, 172 (1973). The decision was affirmed by the House of Lords (*Times* (London), March 28, 1974).

53. See generally, John Hucker and Bruce C. McDonald, "Securing Human Rights in Canada," 15 *McGill Law Journal* 220, 221–23 (1969).

54. See generally, Patricia J. Myhal, "Canada's Unjustified Ratification of the Race Convention," 30 *University of Toronto Faculty of Law Review* 31, 35, 36 (1972).

55. See *Canada Revised Statutes* (1970), appendices, *The British North America Act,* 1867, 30 and 31 Victoria, ch. 3, 191 at 217.

56. *Canada, Revised Statutes* (1970) ch. L–1. However, under the labor code, nonprofit charitable, social, fraternal or philanthropic organizations and organizations employing less than five persons, are exempted from the Act. Further, the criminal code amendments of 1970 include new provisions in sections 281.1 and 281.2 which respectively make it an offense to advocate genocide and to incite hatred against undentifiable groups. See Patricia J. Myhal, "Canada's Ratification," pp. 39–40.

57. Canada, *Bill of Rights* (1960), 8–9 Eliz. 2, S.C., vol. 1, ch. 44.

58. For discussion, see Hucker and McDonald, *Human Rights in Canada,* pp. 223–24.

59. See Walter Tarnopolsky, "The Canadian Bill of Rights From Diefenbaker to *Drybones,*" 17 *McGill Law Journal* 437 (1971); see also, 37 *Canadian Bar Review* 7 (1959).

60. *Revised Statutes of Upper Canada* (1793), ch. 7; *An Act to prevent the Publication of Discriminatory Matter Referring to Race or Creed* (1944), 8 Geo. 6, S.O., ch. 51.

61. *Ontario Act* (1944), 11 Geo. VI, S.S. ch. 35. The more extensive 1965 Act is R.S.S., ch. 378.

62. *An Act to Amend the Conveyancing and Law of Property* (1950), S.O., ch. 11.

63. *Labor Relations Act* (1950), S.O., ch. 34, sec. 34 (b).

64. *Fair Employment Practice Act* (1951 and 1954), S.O., ch. 24; S.O., ch. 28. Chapter 26 of S.O. 1951 set a model for other provinces.

65. See, e.g., S.O. 1961–62, ch. 93; S.N.S. 1963, ch. 5; S.N.S. 1967, ch. 12; R.S.S. 1968, ch. 378; S.A. 1966, ch. 39; S.N.B. 1967, ch. 13; P.E.I. Acts 1968, ch. 24.

66. S.O. 1961–62, ch. 93; S.O. 1960–61, ch. 63; S.O. 1958, ch. 70.

67. See generally, Walter S. Tarnopolsky, "The Iron Hand in the Velvet Glove: Administration and Enforcement of Human Rights Legislation in Canada," 46 *Canadian Bar Review* 565, 572–73 (1968).

68. Ontario, *Human Rights Code* (1962), S.O., chap. 93. The current legislation is contained in R.S.O., ch. 318 (1970), as amended in 1971. (ch. 50, sec. 63) and in 1972 (ch. 119)

69. Section 3 was amended in 1965 to apply to apartments in buildings containing more than three self-contained dwelling units (S.O. 1965, ch. 85, sec. 2); it was further amended two years later to apply to any self-contained dwelling unit (S.O. 1967, ch. 66, sec. 1) deleting the earlier reference to apartments. However, the marginal note to section 3 still reads "Discrimination prohibited in apartment buildings," a discrepancy which was responsible for confusion in interpreting the section. For example, see *Regina* v. *Tarnopolsky, Ex parte Bell,* (1969) 2 O.R. 609; *Bell* v. *Ontario Human Rights Commission,* (1971) S.C.R. 756. Section 3 was further amended in 1972, making it applicable to "any commercial unit or any housing accommodation." (S.O. 1972, chap. 119, sec. 4)

70. S.O. 1967, ch. 66, sec. 2 repealed the five-employee exception. S.O. 1968–69, ch. 83, sec. 1; the original section 5 requiring equal pay for equal work was repealed in 1968 and was subsequently incorporated in the Employment Standards Act. (S.O. 1968, ch. 35) A new section 5 bans threats, penalties, intimidation, or coercion of a person who has made or may make a complaint or disclosure concerning a complaint, or who has testified or may testify in a proceeding under the Act, or who has participated or may participate in any other way in a proceeding under the Act. (S.O. 1968–69, ch. 83, sec. 2; R.S.O. 1970, ch. 318, sec. 5)

71. See Ian A. Hunter, "The Development of the Ontario Human Rights Code: A Decade in Retrospect," 22 *University of Toronto Law Journal* 237, 241 (1972).

72. *Organ and Bernstein* v. *Fletcher,* Report of a board of inquiry, Aug. 4, 1966, cited in Hunter, *Ontario Human Rights Code,* 252 n. 92.

73. Sec. 14 of the Act as amended in 1968 (S.O. 1968–69, chap. 83, sec. 3) fixed the fine at $500 in the case of an individual and $2000 in the case of an organization. The present limits were enacted in 1972. [S.O. 1972, chap. 119, sec. 12]. The Minister's consent to prosecution is required under R.S.O. 1970, chap. 318, sec. 16.

74. See generally, Daniel G. Hill, "The Role of a Human Rights Commission: The Ontario Experience," 19 *University of Toronto Law Review* 390, 397–400 (1969).

75. *Forbes* v. *Shields,* Commission of inquiry decision, July 16, 1956, unreported.

76. *Michael* v. *O'Brien,* Report of a board of inquiry, July 11, 1968, cited in Hunter, *Ontario Human Rights Code,* p. 253 and n. 92.

77. *Duncan* v. *Szoldaritis,* Report of a board of inquiry, Jan. 3, 1969, cited in Hunter, *Ontario Human Rights Code,* p. 254 and n. 102.

78. *Laws* v. *Domokos,* Report of a board of inquiry, Jan. 3, 1969, cited in Hunter, *Ontario Human Rights Code,* p. 254 and n. 105.

79. *Bell* v. *Ontario Human Rights Commission,* (1971) S.C.R. 756.

80. Id., at 767–68.

81. *Bell,* quoted in 11 D.L.R. (3d) 658 at 664 (1970).

82. *Bell,* cited in (1971) S.C.R. 756 at 764.

83. *Bell,* at 770.

84. *Bell,* (1969) 2 O.R., 709 at 714.

85. *Bell* S.C.R. (1971) 756 at 775.

86. *Lomer and Borovoy* v. *Corporation of the City of Ottawa,* Report of a board of inquiry, Feb. 28, 1964, cited in Hunter, *Ontario Human Rights Code,* p. 257 and n. 11.

87. Report of a board of inquiry, June 4, 1970, cited in Hunter, *Ontario Human Rights Code,* p. 257.

88. See Tarnopolsky, "Iron Hand," p. 577; and T. M. Eberlee and D. G. Hill, "The Ontario Human Rights Code," 15 *University of Toronto Law Journal* 448, 449–50 (1963) for arguments on both sides.

89. See "Projet collectif québecois pour une charte et une Commission des Droits de l'Homme au Quebec," *Justice S'il Vous Plait!* 1 (October 1973):37.

90. George P. Sape and Thomas J. Hart, "Title VII Reconsidered: The Equal Employment Opportunity Act of 1972," 40 *George Washington Law Review* 824 (1972).

91. Eugene Gressman, "The Unhappy History of Civil Rights Legislation," 50 *Michigan Law Review* 1323, 1336 (1952).

92. *The Civil Rights Cases,* 109 U.S. 3 (1883).

93. Samuel Krislov, *The Negro in Federal Employment* (Minneapolis: University of Minnesota Press, 1967).

94. L. E. Short, "Nondiscrimination Policies: Are They Effective?" *Personnel Journal* 52 (1973):786–92, at 790.

95. Victor G. Rosenblum, "On *Davis* on Confining, Structuring, and Checking Administrative Discretion," *Law and Contemporary Problems* 37:(1972) 49–62.

96. Executive Order No. 11063, 27 F.R. 11527 (1962). See generally, Nancy LeBlanc, "Race, Housing, and the Government," 26 *Vanderbilt Law Review* 487 (1973).

97. U.S., *Civil Rights Act* (1964), 42 U.S.C. sec. 2000e–4. For a general background, see Sape and Hart, *Title VII Reconsidered,* p. 829; and Gopal C. Pati and Patrick E. Fahey, "Affirmative Action Program: Its Realities and Challenges," *Labor Law Journal* 24 (1973):351–61.

98. For an excellent summary, see Karen DeWitt, "Strengthened EEOC Accelerates Action against Business, Labor, Employee Discrimination," *National Journal* 5 (1973):913–21.

99. 43 Pa. Stat. 956–63 (1964). See Comment, "Survey: The Pennsylvania Human Relations Commission," 77 *Dickinson Law Review* 522 (1973). See *Mayor of Philadelphia* v. *Educational Equality League,* 415 U.S. 605 (1974).

100. Cal., *Labor Code,* Sec. 1414 (1971).

101. Cal., *Labor Code,* secs. 1419 and 1431 (1971), as amended by stats. ch. 1814, secs. 1 and 2.

102. Executive Order No. 11246, 3 C.F.R. 169 (1974).

103. Arthur Fletcher, "Whatever Happened to the Philadelphia Plan?" *Business and Society Review* 5 (Spring 1973):24–28, p. 25. See also, Peter G. Nash, "Affirmative Action Under Executive Order 11246," 46 *New York University Law Review* 225 (1971).

104. *Joyce* v. *McCrane,* 320 F. Supp. 1284 (D.N.J. 1970).

105. *Southern Illinois Builders Association* v. *Ogilvie,* 471 F. 2d 680 (7th Cir. 1972).

106. *United States* v. *Chesapeake and Ohio Railway Co.,* 471 F.2d 582 (4th Cir. 1972).

107. *E.E.O.C.* v. *Container Corporation of America,* 352 F. Supp. 262, 265 (M.D. Fla. 1972).

108. *E.E.O.C.* v. *Griffin Wheel Company,* 360 F. Supp. 424 (S.D. Ala. 1973).

109. *E.E.O.C.* v. *Mobil Oil Corp.,* 362 F. Supp. 786 (W.D.Mo. 1973).

110. *Miller Properties* v. *Ohio Civil Rights Commission,* 296 N.E. 2d 300 (Ohio Ct. App. 1972).

111. *Moose Lodge No. 107* v. *Irvis,* 407 U.S. 163 (1971).

112. *Commonwealth, Human Relations Commission* v. *Loyal Order of Moose,* 294 A.2d 594 (Pa., 1972).

113. *Falkenstein* v. *Dept. of Revenue, State of Oregon,* 350 F. Supp. 887 (D. Ore., 1972).

114. See Recent Developments, "In America, What You Do Is What You Are: The Equal Employment Opportunity Act of 1972," 22 *Catholic University Law Rev.* 455, 460 (1973).

115. DeWitt, "E.E.O.C. Accelerates Action," pp. 913–14.

116. Ibid., 916–18.

117. *E.E.O.C.* v. *Liberty Mutual Insurance Company,* 346 F. Supp. 675 (N.D. Ga. 1972).

118. *E.E.O.C.* v. *Liberty Mutual Insurance Company,* 475 F. 2d 579 at 580 (5th Cir. 1973).

119. See Short, "Nondiscrimination Policies," pp. 790–91, and comparative tables. See also Executive Order 11478, 3 C.F.R. 207 (1974).

120. Fletcher, *"Philadelphia Plan,"* p. 27.

121. See, e.g., Abba P. Lerner, "The Deformation of Affirmative Action," *Midstream* 19 (April 1973): 33–38. See also *De Funis* v. *Odegaard,* 416 U.S. 312 (1974).

Chapter 9 THE STATUS OF WOMEN IN THE UNITED STATES AND THE SCANDINAVIAN COUNTRIES

Anna P. Schreiber

Scandinavia and the United States are commonly looked to as leaders in attempts to promote the equality of women and, to a great extent, this reputation is comparatively well deserved. In both systems, however, a considerable gap still exists between acceptance of the principles of equal rights and the concrete application of such principles in the day-to-day life of most women. A comparison of American and Scandinavian experiences regarding the changing status of women may help to pinpoint some common roots of sex inequality and help to explain the persistence of traditional patterns within these societies.[1]

After the suffragette movement of the early twentieth century, women in both Scandinavia and the United States made steady gains in education and professional attainment. These early strides did not lead to basic changes in the lifestyles of most women, however. Traditional patterns continued to define most women's societal roles. In both societies, the 1960s and 1970s saw renewed vigorous efforts on behalf of equal rights for women which stimulated widespread debate and contributed to a more thoroughgoing evolution of ideas, laws, and practices than heretofore.

THE GOAL AND REALITY OF EQUALITY

Equality before the law. By the 1970s few legal distinctions remained between the rights and duties of men and women in Scandinavia, and those areas in which different treatment existed were being reviewed for possible revision.[2]

In Norway and Sweden the same age requirements for marriage apply to both men and women. In both countries women have a right to retain the maiden name after marriage and children may petition to take the surname of the other parent. The general rule of equal rights in inheritance is limited in Norway by the two very old legal institutions of *aasetesrett* and *odelsrett* which give preference to sons in inheriting or buying back family farmland.

Husband and wife may agree to hold property independently, but joint ownership, operative at the termination of a marriage, is the most common rule in Sweden and Norway. During the marriage, each spouse owns what that person brought into the marriage or later acquires, but upon death or divorce the property is divided equally after debts are paid. During the marriage, both partners must agree to any sale or mortgaging of their residence or other property on which the maintenance or livelihood of one or both may depend.

In Norway and Sweden few distinctions exist between men and women in the law governing divorce and separation. In Sweden, the law states that both husband and wife have a duty to contribute to maintenance during separation and divorce, but, in practice, it is the husband who makes most payments because he is usually the principal breadwinner. Norwegian law recognizes a right to alimony provided it is needed for maintenance due to a reduction in the spouse's ability to earn a livelihood as a consequence of marriage or child care. In determining child custody, the prime criterion is the child's best interest. Before 1969, Norwegian law gave a strong preference to the mother, and a father had to prove that the mother was unfit before he could gain custody.

Family law is at present under review in both Norway and Sweden. In Sweden, the question now being debated is the extent to which social benefits and insurance schemes can be extended to reduce the legal and economic obligations of family members toward one another. It will be many years, however, before a system can come into effect which would permit both spouses to be treated legally as economically independent individuals.

The Norwegian law of nationality draws distinctions between the rights of men and women. The child of a Norwegian man and a foreign woman acquires Norwegian nationality upon birth, but the child of a Norwegian woman and a foreign man does not. Norwegian nationality is not automatically acquired by a foreigner marrying a Norwegian citizen. In practice, foreign brides find it easier to gain Norwegian nationality than foreign men married to Norwegian women.[3]

Many legal distinctions between men and women existed in the United States until the early 1970s, when efforts to eliminate them began to bear fruit. Attempts to achieve equality before the law for men and women in America are complicated by the federal system of government which divides authority between the federal government and the governments of each of the fifty states. In 1972, it was estimated that there still were more than 1,000 state laws which treated men and women differently.[4]

In March, 1972, the United States Congress voted approval of a proposed equal rights amendment to the Constitution. Thirty-eight states must ratify the amendment before it can go into effect. It states that "equality of rights under the law shall not be denied or abridged by the United States or by any state on account of sex." Its supporters argue that such an amendment is necessary because of the number of discriminatory laws and practices in existence which otherwise could be changed only through an uncertain, slow, and expensive case-by-case procedure.

One effect of the equal rights amendment would be to require state authorities to prove the reasonableness of disparate treatment of men and women rather than, as at present, requiring an aggrieved individual to prove the unreasonableness of the law or practice in question. This may be the major impact of the amendment: to create a presumption against the validity of all sex-based legislation.

The equal rights amendment would affect federal, state, and local laws, governmental activities, and judicial decisions. In family relations, some state courts are already reflecting the philosophy of the proposed equal rights amendment in divorce proceedings. Increasingly, young able ex-wives are awarded support for only a fixed period of time during which they are expected to prepare themselves for self-support. The equal rights amendment should lead more courts to decide alimony based on individual circumstances and not on sex alone.[5]

In employment, the equal rights amendment would invalidate most state "protective" laws regulating the hours, conditions, and type of work open to women. In recent years, the impact of such laws has been to bar women from competing for better jobs. Job applicants would be screened not by sex but through tests of ability. Minimum wage rules, rest period regulations, and lunch break privileges would apply equally to men and women. The amendment would invalidate state laws which require married women, in order to engage in business, to comply with legal procedures which are not required of men.

The amendment would end different age stipulations for men and women for marriage, work, parental support, and in the jurisdiction of juvenile courts. It would invalidate laws which set different criminal penalties for men and women who commit the same offense. It would affect exemptions from jury duty which at present are open to women but not to men. In the armed forces, the amendment would open the way to greater participation by women. Steps in this direction already have been taken. In 1972, the U. S. Navy for the first time allowed women recruits to go to sea with men. By 1972, the U. S. Army had opened all but 48 of 482 occupational specialties to Women's Army Corps members. Previously, women tended to train for clerical chores.

The amendment would serve as the constitutional basis for efforts to open public school admissions to both sexes. At present, some technical and professional public schools are restricted to one sex. In addition, the equal rights amendment would permit, but not require, special maternity benefits for women. Some feminist groups argue strongly against such benefits if they would have the effect of putting women into a special category. They argue that the costs of childbirth and maternity leave should be treated in the same category as other medical disabilities which temporarily prevent workers from performing their duties.

Some supporters of the equal rights amendment hope that it will begin a process leading to a fundamental restructuring of the present condition of women in American society. Formal equality before the law, however, is not in itself an accurate description of woman's status in a society. The attainment of legal equality cannot, by itself, bring about a basic reordering of the condition of women. In both Scandinavia and the United States, it is recognized that the status of women is determined as much by patterns of education and employment as by law.

Educational patterns. In Scandinavia, girls and women have a lower level of educational attainment than boys and men despite equal access to schools and the availability of scholarships and loans to students of both sexes. Governmental efforts to change this situation have not yet succeeded.[6]

In elementary school and until children reach their early teenage years, girls and boys receive the same general educational content. Thereafter, girls tend to choose training for jobs in teaching, health services, social work, office work, food industries, and personal services. Few choose technical subjects or natural sciences. Boys choose a wide variety of industrial and technical vocational courses. More boys than girls go to secondary schools leading to university. Except in a few traditional feminine fields, there are fewer women studying at each successively higher level in the educational system.

Recently, Sweden moved toward a comprehensive system of education in which all students are exposed to a common core of material. For several years boys have had to take courses in handicraft, domestic science and child care, and girls must study woodwork, metal work, and similar masculine crafts. Sweden has made an effort to eliminate school books containing sex-typed attitudes and to discourage school curricula that portray women primarily in roles as housekeepers and mothers.

The creation of comprehensive schools has not yet eroded the tendency of girls and boys to make traditional, sex-linked vocational choices. Although the comprehensive schools delay specialization until later grades, studies show that when the choices finally are made, girls still tend to choose training in traditionally feminine fields. The Swedish government hopes that new vocational guidance programs will help expand children's perceptions of their future roles.[7]

The administration of education in the United States is more decentralized than in most of Scandinavia. There are side differences in school policy, curriculum, and quality among states and between school districts within each state. In many schools, boys and girls continue to receive different types of instruction, with boys studying carpentry while girls learn cooking. Change is occurring on a piecemeal basis. In New York state, for example, it has been illegal since 1972 to bar a student from a course solely on the basis of sex. Vocational guidance programs, which might be one method of counteracting traditional concepts of boys' and girls' roles in society, vary in content and quality among the states. Grants from the federal government might have some impact in improving existing state programs.

Except in Finland, the proportion of Scandinavian women completing higher education is significantly lower than the proportion of men.[8] In Finland in the late 1960s, 40 percent of university students were women. In Norway in 1967, only 24.9 percent of students at universities or institutions of higher learning were women. According to the 1960 census, 23 percent of Norwegian women and 38 percent of men between 25 and 29 years of age had completed specialized training beyond the elementary and basic secondary school level.

In Sweden in 1965, approximately one-third of university graduates were women. Most earned general liberal arts degrees or bachelor's degrees leading to teaching credentials. Women earned only 50 out of 273 law degrees awarded in 1965. In the period 1958–1970, only four Swedish women earned the Doctor of Laws degree. In 1965, of 963 students who received engineering degrees, only 49 were women. The tendency for women to choose a narrower range of subjects than men at a university also is present in Norway, where comparatively few women students are found in law, business administration, or engineering. In 1967 only about 18 percent of the medical students in Norway were women.[9]

Research conducted at the University of Lund in Sweden attempted to isolate factors which discourage women from studying theoretical sciences. It was found that lingering traditional views of science as a masculine profession and negative attitudes about women in intellectual pursuits cause enough anxiety to discourage and impede the development of women scientists.[10]

In the United States, some public and private schools deny admission to women solely on the basis of sex. In recent years through voluntary action and court challenge, the number of single sex schools has diminished. In many coeducational schools, however, higher admissions standards for women than for men persist. As a result, women do not yet form as large a percentage of the student body of professional schools as their qualifications might suggest. In July, 1972, sex discrimination was prohibited by law in some federally assisted schools. To receive federal funds, these institutions are required to make all benefits and services available to students without discrimination. The law requires private vocational schools, professional schools, and graduate institutions to open their admissions equally to both sexes.[11]

The number of women receiving higher degrees in the United States is increasing, but women still lag behind men. In 1968, of every 100 men, 26 received bachelor's degrees, compared to 19 out of every 100 women. In 1970, 3.5 million women were enrolled in college. They represented 41 percent of all college students. Women students are still comparatively rare in fields such as engineering, medicine, sciences, and architecture.

Many factors contribute to the differences in educational patterns between men and women in Scandinavia and in the United States. Historically, parents gave preference to boys in providing education because school was costly and men were the traditional breadwinners. In present day Scandinavia, the cost factor is less important due to generous state scholarships and loans. In Sweden, married students may both receive study grants and they also are eligible for family allowances if they have children. In the United States the high cost of education is still a limiting factor, although the number of scholarships and loans is increasing.

Perhaps the primary factor which affects the educational choices made by boys and girls in both Scandinavia and the United States is their perception of the persistence of traditional life patterns. Most women marry, care for children, and receive their primary support from a husband for a substantial portion of their adult lives. Girls grow up not expecting to pursue life-long uninterrupted careers. The wife-mother expectation is instilled in girls at an early age by a combination of family and societal pressures and influences, just as the importance of work is instilled in boys. The expectation that they will be supported by a husband gives girls less drive to prepare for and pursue careers persistently. In the United States, most young girls do not view the pursuit of a career as a task vital to their future security. Whereas boys expect to attain money, status, and security through success in their employment, most girls expect to attain these primarily through marriage.

A survey undertaken in Norway in the mid-1960s indicated that only 50 percent of a group of mothers interviewed believed that children of both sexes should receive an equally high quality education. If a choice had to be made between sexes, the majority thought that boys should have the better education. No mother thought that girls should have a better education than boys.[12] Such parental attitudes must affect children's perceptions of appropriate educational choices and life goals.

Both Scandinavian and American parents raise boys and girls differently. Girls are taught order, obedience, care, and helpfulness more often than are boys, who are encouraged to be daring, resourceful, and independent. Although more mothers are now working in both Scandinavia and the United States, children perceive that fathers inevitably go off to work while mothers often may remain at home. American and Scandinavian parents differentiate between boys and girls far less than do other cultures, however. The child-raising practices of Mediterranean cultures, for example, put far greater stress on the differences between the masculine and feminine roles.

During the last decade there has been some increased recognition of the special educational and training needs of mature women in both the United States and Scandinavia. Large numbers of mature women reenter the labor force after their children have grown, and many more would like to do so. Yet inadequate education and training confine such women to low paying, low status positions in most cases. A survey taken in 1966 in the United States revealed that such women did not advance beyond the level of the jobs they held before they married, and one-fifth of those questioned had to take jobs of lower status than those they had once held.[13]

In 1967, new efforts were begun in Sweden to encourage mature women to reenter the labor market and to train for occupations traditionally considered to be men's work. Evening secondary schools, part-time vocational colleges, and adult evening schools run primarily on a correspondence basis try to shape their schedules to meet the needs of housewives. Retraining courses organized by the Labor Market Board are open to housewives on the same basis as to unemployed men. Through such courses, women train as bus drivers and crane operators. Some retraining courses exist in the United States, but they reach a very small percentage of mature women attempting to return to the work force. With as many as twenty-five potential work years ahead of them, mature women are an important sector of the economy. Specialized refresher courses in the professions might encourage girls to make broader initial career choices. Thus, medical refresher programs might lead more girls to study medicine if they could perceive that it would be possible to pursue a few years of child-raising and then return to a professional career.

Patterns of employment. One measure of the status of women in society is the nature of the jobs they hold. In Scandinavia and the United States, women tend to hold low paid jobs and to cluster within a narrow range of activities.

Women are a sizeable segment of the work force in Scandinavia.[14] In Sweden in 1971, there were 1.4 million women in a work force of 3.5 million. In Finland in 1966, 43.3 percent of the total economically active population consisted of women. Women in Scandinavia tend to hold jobs in retail trade, banking, insurance, domestic work, hotel and restaurant work, education, medical services, clothing and textile industries, and the public services. In Sweden, 44 percent of the entire female labor force was employed in public administration. Although the majority of Finnish pharmacists and dentists are women, most working women fall into traditional categories.

In 1967, Swedish authorities noted that "women have by no means attained real parity with men on the Swedish labor market." In a 1968 report to the United Nations, the Finnish government pointed to a need to train more women as skilled workers and to bring more women into higher level posts in administration, science, and technology. Shortages of services designed to free women from home duties and prevailing attitudes toward women were cited as factors blocking improvement in women's position in the labor market.

The pay received by Scandinavian women has tended to be lower than pay received by men in the same industry. In Norway in 1967, women received wages which were 67 percent of men's wages in banking and 55 percent in insurance. Inequity in pay scales was publicly recognized by the government in Denmark in the 1960s. Equal pay regulations now apply in public sector jobs, and the government is encouraging employers in the private sector to eliminate different pay scales based on sex. In 1970, the Danish women's movement reported that the level of salaries received by unskilled female workers was still only 80 percent of that of unskilled male workers.

In Sweden, it was clear by 1966 that most women received lower wages than men.[15] In industry the average woman's wage was 76.6 percent of men's. The

Swedish government introduced equal pay regulations in public sector jobs and made efforts to achieve this goal in the private sector as well. It struck out differing pay scales written into collective bargaining agreements in the engineering, printing, and steel industries. The Scandinavian governments are recognizing that the problem of equal pay cannot be fully solved until the majority of women no longer hold low level jobs, and Scandinavian governments are actively trying to alter the status of women in employment. In the last few years, the Swedish Labor Market Board has made efforts to recruit women for jobs traditionally held by men.

The proportion of married women at work differs from one Scandinavian country to another. In Finland, Sweden, and Denmark in the early 1960s, between 23 and 30 percent of the total number of married women were employed. In Norway, only 9.5 percent of married women worked in 1960. In Oslo, 21 percent of Norwegian married women worked compared to 37 percent in Stockholm. A shortage of child care facilities contributed to Norway's low percentage working of married women. Half of all nursery schools, kindergartens, and other day care facilities were concentrated in Oslo. Day care is more readily available in Sweden, but the demand still exceeds the supply. Norway's dispersed population limits the variety of jobs available to women in rural areas. However, Finland, which also has a dispersed population, has three times as many working married women as Norway. Most married working women carry a double burden since many continue to cope fully with household duties.[16]

Traditional attitudes about woman's role appear to be stronger in Norway than elsewhere in Scandinavia. Surveys taken during the 1960s found negative attitudes toward working mothers, especially on the part of nonworking mothers. Attitudes are changing among the young, however. In the United States, negative attitudes concerning working mothers also persist. A survey in 1966 revealed that less than 25 percent of married white women believed that it was either definitely or probably appropriate for mothers to work. Among black married women, only slightly more than one-third thought that it was suitable for mothers to work.[17]

In both Scandinavia and the United States, one deterrent to mothers returning to work is their inability to secure satisfying jobs. By the time children are grown and wives are prepared to return to work, the skills acquired at school or through previous work experience may have faded. Unless they have had specialized higher education, the jobs available are usually poorly paid and unskilled, and staying at home may appear more desirable. As has been noted, Scandinavian countries have begun to combat this problem through adult education, whereas in the United States, efforts in this direction are still small.

In many countries, taxation policy deters married women from working. In Norway until 1960, the incomes of working husbands and wives were added together and taxed as a single income. The working wife was allowed a deduction for the expenses of child care and household help, but the actual expenses usually far exceeded the allowed deduction. The Norwegian income tax is sharply graduated, and the wife's income, added to the top of that of her husband was much more heavily taxed than if she were unmarried. In 1960, the tax regulations were revised to permit couples to file separately. Various conditions make it more advantageous to file jointly if the wife's income is small. Separate taxation is advantageous where there are few dependents and both incomes are moderately high.

Until recently, Sweden also applied a system of joint taxation which was thought to deter married women from working. In 1971, the Swedish tax system was revised to make the basis of taxation no longer the family unit but the individual. Different tax scales for married and unmarried persons were abolished. Single wage earners no longer pay a higher rate of tax than married persons. Under the new system, taxes are expected to increase for families with only one wage earner, thus encouraging more wives to work.

Income tax provisions in the United States at the federal and state level have been reasonably flexible in allowing couples to file either jointly or separately, whichever is most advantageous in a specific case. The regulations on child care and household expense deductions were restrictive until 1972, when a deduction from federal income tax for such expenses began to be allowed if combined income does not exceed $27,500.

Both in Scandinavia and the United States, women form a large segment of the work force, but hold low paid, low status jobs. In the U.S., there were 33 million women in the labor force in 1972. There were 12.2 million working mothers in 1971. Of these, 4.3 million had children under 6 years old and almost 2 out of every 5 working women had children under 18. Forty-two percent of all U.S. mothers worked in 1970. A much larger percentage of black women with children under 6 years old worked than white women with children under 6.

As in Scandinavia, working women in the United States are found in a comparatively narrow range of jobs. In 1969, one-fourth of all working women were secretaries, stenographers, household workers, bookkeepers, elementary school teachers, and waitresses. Only 1 out of every 6 working women held a blue collar job and few were skilled workers. In 1970, only 7 percent of doctors, 3 percent of lawyers, and 1 percent of engineers were women. In the field of law, these figures were changing rapidly in the 1970s when the number of women admitted to law school began to expand. In 1966, the vast majority of elementary school teachers were women, but 75 percent of elementary school principals were men. In private business and industry, only 10 percent of officers and managers were women.

In the 1970s women began to seek and find jobs in traditionally masculine fields, for example, as telephone pole climbers, welders, electricians, and airline pilots. However, the number of women in such positions was very small. American women still act upon ingrained attitudes about themselves which restrict their role in the labor market. Concepts of femininity lead women to shape their actions along certain lines to avoid being considered unfeminine. Most American women are still not career minded. They believe that their status, security, and achievement will be determined by whom they marry and by their husbands' successes or failures, rather than their own efforts in jobs outside the home. In the late 1960s and early 1970s, these attitudes began to weaken, especially among the young.

Federal efforts to combat discrimination against women in employment began when the Civil Rights Act of 1964 prohibited discrimination in hiring, advancement, and all other conditions of employment on grounds of race, color, religion, national origin, and sex. The Equal Employment Opportunity Commission (EEOC) receives and investigates charges and promotes affirmative action programs by employers, trade unions, and employment agencies. In 1968, the Commission found "a dismal picture (of discrimination against women in employment) throughout American industry as a whole."[18] Women had a higher unemployment rate than men and held jobs below their talents and training much more frequently than men. According to the Department of Labor, the median earnings in 1970 of year round, full-time workers were $8,966 for men and $5,323 for women. Only 7 percent of women working full-time the year round earned more than $10,000 per year compared to 40 percent of men. The average salary of employees who were high school graduates was $9,567 per year for men and $4,480 for women. This trend carried over to college graduates as well, with men receiving $13,264 per year and women earning $8,156.[19]

Because of its limited enforcement powers the EEOC at first made little impact on the number of actual cases of job discrimination. The Commission stimulated discussion and attempted to dispel myths and stereotypes about women in employment. It also attempted to settle complaints through conciliation. The EEOC now has the power to bring suit in Federal Court to win compliance once conciliation fails. In January, 1973, the EEOC negotiated what then was the largest single complaint settlement when American Telephone and Telegraph Company agreed to give $15 million in back pay and $25 million per year in raises to women and minority groups. Approximately 15,000 employees were affected.

American courts are gradually striking down laws barring women from certain jobs. In 1969, for example, one case held that women could not be prevented from taking jobs requiring weight lifting. The court called for individual testing of applicants. Through the courts, the EEOC and private groups have begun to establish the principle that all jobs should be open to both sexes except those in which sex is a bona fide occupational qualification. In the past, state laws banned women from jobs as railroad crossing guards, gas or electric meter readers, freight or baggage elevator operators, and drivers of delivery vehicles of over one ton capacity. Several states have laws prohibiting women from mixing, selling, or dispensing alcoholic beverages for on-premise consumption. In 1963, forty states had laws regulating the maximum hours which women could work. This had dropped to ten by 1971.[20]

Federal efforts to end sex discrimination in employment were strengthened through presidential executive orders prohibiting job discrimination against women by employers holding federal contracts or subcontracts. In December, 1971, the Office of Federal Contract Compliance ordered contractors to set timetables and establish affirmative action programs designed to meet goals set forth in federal guidelines.

POLICY FOR WOMEN AND WOMEN IN POLITICS

The impact on women of social welfare programs. The Scandinavian countries have well developed social services which lessen the constraints which have operated to keep mothers at home, and which help them compete more effectively in the labor market. The basic aim of the system is to prevent distress rather than simply to cure it after it has arisen.

Scandinavian countries pay family allowances to parents of children under sixteen regardless of income. Unmarried mothers also receive such payments. In the United States, family allowances as such do not exist, but indigent families may receive welfare payments.[21] Pregnant women in Scandinavia may receive free or inexpensive prenatal and postnatal care under national insurance programs. These schemes also cover most of the costs of giving birth, including hospitalization, the fees of midwives and doctors, and medication. In some cases, even the costs of transportation to and from the hospital may be reimbursed. Postnatal care for mother and infant, including innoculations and vitamins, are also made available at minimal cost. In the United States, such services are available without cost only to low income women.

In Scandinavia, pregnant women also receive cash grants to help cover the many incidental expenses of childbearing. Working women may receive payments to compensate for lost income if they have paid insurance premiums for this purpose for nine months prior to giving birth. Low-income pregnant women also are eligible for additional aid under other categories of social legislation.

Despite the very high costs of medical care in the United States, there is as yet no nationwide insurance program to cover the medical needs of most American families. Some states have programs which benefit low income families. Federal social security provisions provide medical coverage to people over sixty-five years of age. Most Americans subscribe to private insurance programs and many of these are partially funded by employers.

In Scandinavia, other forms of aid reflect the view that government should help to ease the burden of parenthood. For example, Sweden pays subsidies to families for housing based on, among other factors, family size. In Scandinavia, the public authorities may advance the costs of child maintenance to unwed, divorced, or separated mothers if the father fails to make support payments for which he is responsible. The government may then proceed against the delinquent parent to reclaim the payments. Widows and unwed mothers with small children are eligible for cash allowances while they look for work and make child care arrangements. Free school meals, inexpensive health and dental care for children, and domestic help for families in time of emergency are other facilities which help ease burdens on parents.

In Norway, contraceptive information and instructions are available at clinics, hospitals, and from doctors. No coordinated, widespread contraceptive education and distribution effort exists in the United States on a nationwide basis. Until recently, several states in the United States prohibited the sale of contraceptives. There still are restrictions on the manner in which they may be displayed, advertised, and sold. The results in Scandinavia have not been perfect. The Norwegian government has acknowledged that greater efforts in family planning are required if its publicly declared policy favoring the minimizing of abortions is to be achieved.

Abortion has been available in Norway since 1964 on broadly interpreted medical grounds. Women seeking abortions are informed of the financial aid which they can receive if they decide to keep the child. In the investigation of the application for abortion, the woman's social and economic condition is taken into account. In Sweden, abortion on medical, humanitarian, and eugenic grounds has been legal since 1938. In Finland and Denmark laws permitting nontherapeutic abortion were passed in 1970.

In the United States, a Supreme Court decision on January 23, 1973, seemed to end a long, bitter debate on the right of abortion.[22] Until then, the laws concerning abortion in most of the fifty states were very restrictive. Many states permitted abortion only to save the life of the mother. Others permitted abortion in cases of rape, incest, fetal deformity, or due to the physical or mental health of the mother. In 1970, New York became the first state to adopt a liberal abortion law. It permits abortion on request until the end of the sixth month of pregnancy and does not impose a residence requirement. Passed over strong opposition, it was saved from repeal in 1972 only by the governor's veto. The Supreme Court decision of January, 1973, overruled all state laws that prohibited and restricted a woman's right to obtain an abortion during the first three months of pregnancy. It also provided that state laws may ban abortion only during the last ten weeks of pregnancy. In the intermediate period, state laws may intervene only to establish requirements as to who can perform the abortion and where.

The existence of child care facilities is important to a mother's ability to pursue a career. In 1966, the Swedish government acknowledged a shortage of such facilities and launched a program to expand the number of child care centers by providing subsidies to local authorities to create new institutions. By 1970, the number of places in government-supported day nurseries was 35,000.

Simultaneously, efforts were made to increase the number of nursery school teachers. In Norway, only an estimated 10,000 places existed in child care institutions in 1968 and half of these were in Oslo. The government recognized the need to develop additional places and began a program of subsidies. The need is expected to continue to expand as more married women seek work. In the late 1960s there were 260 day nurseries in Denmark with room for 9,500 children, and an additional 1,250 nursery schools with room for 56,000 children. These places could accommodate only a small percentage of the total number of children in the affected age groups.[23] In Finland in 1965, there were 139,000 children of working mothers or of university students who needed child care. To accommodate them, there were only 12,000 full-day places and 17,000 half-day places.[24]

There is a great shortage of child care facilities in the United States, as well. This constitutes a serious barrier to low income mothers who need job training and steady employment to escape from poverty. Many working mothers must leave children with relatives, with poorly paid neighborhood women, or alone. Private nursery schools can be expensive and they are used primarily by middle class parents. An expansion of federal grants to state and local authorities and to private groups is needed to stimulate more quality child care facilities.

Women in politics. Although women in Scandinavia and the United States gained the right to vote early in this century, they play a relatively minor role in politics today. In both societies, few women sought political office until the 1960s or thought it appropriate to do so. Societal norms held that the nature of political life was in conflict with behavior thought to be appropriate for women.

In 1965, less than 10 percent of the Norwegian parliament was composed of women. Women were also poorly represented in the executive councils of the communes until 1971. In that year, through a successful write-in campaign which circumvented the usual nomination process of the political parties, Norwegian women captured forty-eight out of eighty-five seats in Oslo and forty-six out of eighty-five in Trondheim. Political parties habitually placed women candidates low on the electoral lists. Party lists still dominate elections at the national level.[25]

In Sweden, the traditional attitudes which hold that politics are more men's business than women's have continued among both men and women. In 1971, the proportion of women in the directly elected second chamber of parliament reached 15 percent, and out of eighteen Cabinet ministers two were women. Only 20 percent of municipal councillors were women.

Few women hold public office in the United States, although by 1974 more and more were seeking office. The largest number of women in Congress at any one time has, up to the present time, been 18. Modest gains were made in recent years in the election of women to state legislatures. Nationwide, women comprise 459 out of 7,300 state legislators. A mere 14 out of 9,343 mayors were women in 1974. Women made some gains in high level appointments in the federal government, but the most powerful posts remained in the hands of men.[26]

Efforts to expand the role of women in politics were well underway in the United States and Scandinavia in the 1970s. Many groups were attempting to encourage more women toward greater participation in politics and to counteract traditional attitudes about politics as an unfeminine occupation.[27] There were many signs that these efforts were beginning to alter traditional patterns.

CONCLUSION

Differences in the status of women in Scandinavia and the United States have roots in numerous political, economic, and social difference between the two societies. Among the more important of these are the diversity of the United States population contrasted with the relative homogeneity of Scandinavia and the federal system of American government compared to the more centralized forms in Scandinavia, especially in Sweden.

A comparison of societies is a fruitful exercise if, in addition to highlighting differences, it can reveal common roots to shared problems. In Scandinavia and the United States it would appear that one common root which affects the status of women is the persistence of traditional life styles for men and women in which marriage and childraising are perceived to be the woman's central role and work is seen to be the man's. The persistence of such views in Scandinavia, a society deemed to be most in advance in securing the rights of women, suggests that a basic change in the status of women cannot occur on a large scale without thoroughgoing change in traditional definitions of appropriate behavior for men and women. In this sense the problem of the rights of women is much more than a legal question. It involves the entire fabric of a society and the psychology of its people.

NOTES*

* In references to legal periodical literature, the number of the *initial* page of the work cited immediately follows the volume title. Page references to material specifically referred to in the text, if any, follow the initial page citation. Legal case citations correspond to *A Uniform System of Citation,* 11th ed. (Cambridge: The Harvard Law Review Association, 1974).

1. Comparative material is still relatively rare in the field of women's rights despite the current vogue for this subject. The following citations represent a cross-section of the type of material presently available: Ruth Bader Ginsburg, "The Status of Women," 20 *The American Journal of Comparative Law* (Fall 1972). This symposium focuses on Great Britain, Sweden, Norway, France, The Soviet Union, Israel, and Senegal. On Great Britain, see Anna Coote, *Women's Rights* (Harmondsworth: Penguin Books, 1974). See also, Katherine Anthony, *Feminism in Germany and Scandinavia* (London: Constable and Co.,

1966). In "Recent Developments in the Status of Married Women in Law and Fact," in *Proceedings of the Ninth International Symposium on Comparative Law* 9 (1971):181–298 comparisons are drawn between Eastern Europe, the United States, Scandinavia, and Canada. On South and Central America see I. A. de Garcia Garza, "Derechos de la mujer en America latina," 28 *La Justicia* 51 (August 1968). Interesting two-country comparisons are given in Judith Bardwich, *Psychology of Women; A Study of Bi-cultural Conflicts* (New York: MacMillan and Co., 1968). Florence Dodge, "Women in the Professions: Russia and the United States," 58 *Women Lawyers Journal* 48 (Spring 1972); and Gail M. Beckman, "Comparison of Women in the Legal Profession in Scotland and America," 42 *New York State Bar Journal* 20 (January 1970). "Sexism in Europe", in *Agenor*, no. 35 (May-June 1973) contains viewpoints of the left and new left. More analytical is T. E. Polson, "Rights of Working Women," 15 *Virginia International Law Review* 729 (1974).

2. Gunvor Wallin, "The Status of Women in Sweden," and Karin Bruzelius Heffermehl, "The Status of Women in Norway," in Ginsburg, *Status of Women,* 620–46.

3. K. B. Heffermehl, "The Status of Women in Norway," 20 *American Journal of Comparative Law* 630 (1972).

4. "The Equal Rights Amendment," *The Record of the Association of the Bar of the City of New York,* March 1972, pp. 172–87.

5. "A Simple Matter of Justice," Report of the President's Task Force on Women's Rights and Responsibilities (Washington, D.C.: Government Printing Office, 1970).

6. *The Status of Women in Sweden: Report to the United Nations* (Stockholm: The Swedish Institute, 1968). Betty Selid, *Women in Norway* (Oslo: Norwegian Joint Committee on International Social Policy, 1970). United Nations, Economic and Social Council, *Report on the Role of Women in the Economic and Social Life of Countries* (E/CN. 6/493/add. 1), January 22, 1968.

7. Ingrid Fredrickkson, "Sex Roles and Education in Sweden," *New York Press Quarterly* 3 (Winter 1972):17–25.

8. Torgim Gjesnc, "Sex Differences in Scandinavia and School Performance," *Journal of Applied Psychology* 58 (1973):270–72.

9. Harry K. Schwarzweller, "Regional Variation in the Education of Youth: Norway, Germany, and the United States," *Rural Sociology* 38 (1973):139–58.

10. "Women Scientists in Sweden," paper prepared for the Research Policy Program, University of Lund, Sweden, 1967.

11. Department of Health, Education, and Welfare, "Memorandum to Presidents of Institutions of Higher Education Participating in Federal Assistance Programs," August 1972.

12. Selid, *Women in Norway* pp. 46–47. See also, *Report to the Nordic Council of Ministers* Committee for Investigating Sex Roles in Education (Stockholm: Womens' History Collection, Goteburg University, 1972).

13. Patricia Marshall, "Women at Work," *Manpower,* June 1972, p. 5. Cf. Olaf Palme, "The Emancipation of Man," *Journal of Social Issues* 28 (1972):237–46.

14. Hans Rudolph Briner, *Die Wirtschaftsbeziehungen Schweiz-Skandinavien* (Zurich: Juris-Verlog, 1970).

15. Nancy S. Banet, "Have Swedish Women Achieved Equality?" *Challenge* (1973): 14–20.

16. E. Haavio-Mannila, "Sex Role Attitudes in Finland, 1966–1970," *Journal of Social Issues* 28 (1972): 93–110.

17. Marshall, "Women at Work," p. 5. See generally, Barbara Babcock et al., *Sex Discrimination and the Law* (Washington, D.C.: American Enterprise Institute, 1975).

18. U.S. Department of Labor, "Laws on Sex Discrimination in Employment," (Washington, D.C.: Government Printing Office, 1970). See generally, K. Davidson, R. B. Ginsburg and Herma Hill, *Sex-Based Discrimination* (St. Paul: West Publishing, 1974).

19. U.S. Department of Labor, "Fact Sheet on the Earnings Gap," (Washington, D.C.: Government Printing Office, 1970). Clarification of the Equal Pay Act of 1963 may be found in *Corning Glass Works* v. *Brennan,* 417 U.S. 188 (1974).

20. U.S. Department of Labor, "Status of State Hours Laws for Women," (Washington, D.C.: Government Printing Office, 1971).

21. U.S., Department of Health, Education and Welfare, *Social Security Programs Throughout the World* (Washington, D.C.: Government Printing Office, 1974).

22. *Roe* v. *Wade,* 410 U.S. 113 (1973); *Doe* v. *Bolton,* 410 U.S. 179 (1973).

23. Alfred Toft, "Care of Children and Young People," in *Social Conditions in Denmark* (1967), pp. 25–28. See also Astrid Webster, *The Swedish Child: A Survey of the Legal, Economic, Educational, Medical, and Social Situation of Children and Young People in Sweden,* (Stockholm: Sweden Institute, 1970).

24. United Nations, Economic and Social Council, *Women Worldwide* (E/CN, 6/493/Add. 1), 1965, p. 87.

25. K. B. Heffermehl, *Status of Women,* p. 638. See also I. Nordeuval Means, "Political Recruitment of Women in Norway," *Western Political Quarterly* 25 (1972):491–521. J. Conad, "Women in Local Politics: The Norwegian Experience," *Political Science,* September 1972, 365–68.

26. Jean Kirkpatrick, *Political Woman* (New York: Basic Books, 1974); C. S. Bourque and J. S. Grossholtz, "Politics, an Unnatural Practice: Political Science Looks at Female Participation," *Politics and Society* 4 (1974):225–66.

27. See generally, *Women and American Politics: A Selected Bibliography,* Center for American Women and Politics (New Brunswick: Rutgers, The State University, 1973). Not until 1975 was sex discrimination in jury duty unequivocally struck down in the United States; *Taylor* v. *Louisiana,* 419 U.S. 522 (1975).

Chapter **10** THE RIGHTS OF CHILDREN
IN THE UNITED STATES AND
THE SCANDINAVIAN
COUNTRIES

Linda Breeden

While equality under the law may provide the underlying value appropriate to the analysis of women's rights, it is not an adequate standard for the rights of children. The child's welfare is the value at stake in the newly emerging field of children's rights. This concept of welfare (as distinguished from equality and nondiscrimination) is examined in this study in very specific terms. It is the thesis of this chapter that establishment of the rights of children should assure to each child the right to fair treatment in his relations with the state, with his family, and with other members of society. The paper explores specific examples of the treatment of each child by the state, family, and other individuals in the United States and Scandinavia.

Approximately one-half of all Americans are under the age of twenty-one. Much is written about America's youth-oriented society and its youth culture. Yet, curiously, little is written seeking to explain or define the rights of America's children.[1] It was not until 1967 that children were expressly guaranteed some of the constitutional rights long accorded to adults.

With a youth population proportionately less than one-half of that of the United States, one could expect less emphasis on the rights of children in Scandinavia. However, as early as 1935, Sweden, for example, faced a crisis of declining population. The Swedish Population Commission was asked to study the problem. In her book *Nation and Family,* Alva Myrdal details the background which led to the development of a comprehensive social insurance system with family incentives, child allowances, and day care.[2] Thus, the Swedish national government established governmental policies which emphasized the child's importance within the nation and also within the family.

In the United States, no periodical such as *Ms.* espouses the issue of children's rights. However, public attention occasionally focuses on issues which could be called children's issues. For example, child abuse has received much current public attention. The twenty-sixth amendment, ratified in 1970, lowered the voting age in state and federal elections from twenty-one to eighteen. Ratification of that amendment indicated a strong desire by those individuals over twenty-one to equalize a young person's right to vote with that young person's duty to fulfill military obligations. However, at the same time, Americans exhibit much resentment towards young people. A sufficiently strong and unified disapproval of the communal life style of youths motivated Congress to deny them food stamps. This attempt was recently invalidated by the U.S. Supreme Court because the legislation was deemed to deny fundamental constitutional rights.[3]

Sweden has undertaken a comprehensive examination of the individual's role within the state welfare system. That examination has prompted discussion of the treatment of children. Children receive child allowances, medical care, day care, and other benefits from the state welfare system. Such an examination may well result in more state services which will reduce the financial obligation of parents toward their children.

On the other hand, much Scandinavian literature dramatically describes the dehumanizing effects of the welfare state on Scandinavian citizens, including Scandinavian children. Dr. Hans Lohman, a psychiatrist, reported to the Swedish Parliament that he had observed undercurrents of a "human-crushing process" in Swedish society. This process particularly affects children. He notes that "What we have managed to put together for our children is an extremely cold and anti-child society."[4]

For purposes of this paper, the term Scandinavian refers to those countries grouped together as Norden: Denmark, Finland, Iceland, Norway, and Sweden. A close examination of the laws and practices of these countries reveals many distinctions. However, since 1954, these countries have met as the Nordic Council to work out problems of common interest. As a unit, they can be compared to the United States. A similar warning must be made about the states of the United States. Each state operates relatively independently of the other states. There are, however, similarities which can be compared to Scandinavian practices.

THE CHILD AND THE STATE

Juvenile delinquency. As an example of the child's treatment by the state, a comparison is made of the American juvenile court system and the Scandinavian Child Welfare Board. Few children ever have direct contact with either of these governmental institutions; but, for those who do, the right to fair treatment is essential. The institutions may represent the youth's first contact with the authority of the state.

All states within the United States provide for specialized treatment of youths who get into trouble with the law. In every state, specialized treatment is handled by a juvenile court system, which is separate from the courts of adults.[5] The present juvenile court system evolved from reformist activities begun in the latter part of the nineteenth century. The reformers, shocked at harsh procedures in adult criminal courts, proposed a separate juvenile court system. They envisioned that the juvenile court judge, representing the state, would apply procedures developed from civil cases in lieu of those developed from adult criminal cases. The judge was not to wield the power of the state for purposes of punishment. The judge was to help the youth in a nonpunitive atmosphere. The system is predicated on the existence of adequate state resources to rehabilitate the juvenile. The system is called *parens patriae,* because it was intended to place the judge in a paternalistic relationship to the youth.[6]

The Scandinavian system for the treatment of juvenile offenders evolved from the poor laws, not from the adult court system.[7] As such, it is not a legal system with specialized juvenile courts. Rather, an administrative agency handles the cases. People who work within the agency are trained in disciplines other than law such as social work and psychology. Each unit of local government elects a Child Welfare Board of five members for four-year terms. The Board in turn hires a staff which handles a wide variety of juvenile issues only one of which involves juvenile delinquency. The use of such boards originated in 1892, at the same time that the U.S. established juvenile courts.

Evolution in the United States from a court system has caused the juvenile courts to take on a legal aspect. Juveniles brought before the judge must be charged with "offenses." State laws define the offenses. For example, the juvenile court considers an act of "juvenile delinquency" to be an offense punishable as a criminal offense if committed by an adult. Other such offenses handled by the juvenile courts may have no adult counterpart. For example, "habitual truancy," "unruliness" and others are handled by the juvenile courts. Sometimes, these latter offenses can be very puzzling. For example, a California law provides that a juvenile ". . . who from any cause is in danger of leading an idle, dissolute, lewd or immoral life" can be brought before a juvenile court.[8] Recently, the Massachusetts State Supreme Court upheld the constitutionality of a law which provided for reform school commitment of "stubborn children."[9] As a response to the harshness of that decision, all state reform schools in Massachusetts have been closed.

Inasmuch as the Scandinavian method of treating juveniles did not evolve from a legal system, Scandinavian law does not precisely define the offenses to be dealt with by the Child Welfare Board. Obviously the Child Welfare Board deals with all offenses as they are defined by American laws, but they are handled by psychologists or social workers, not judges. The Child Welfare Board also considers many other issues. For example, if parents oppose medical treatment of their child on religious grounds, the Child Welfare Board considers whether the best interests of the child require intervention. Thus, the Child Welfare Board handles a wide assortment of issues relating to children. It also has a far greater responsibility for taking preventive action than American juvenile courts.[10]

The two systems differ as to the age an individual is considered a juvenile subject to juvenile court jurisdiction or Child Welfare Board authority. Approximately two-thirds of the states in the United States provide that the juvenile court's jurisdiction can extend up to the age of eighteen. In recent years the age has been lowered from twenty-one to eighteen.[11] The lowering of the age threshold for criminal responsibility possibly corresponds to the lowering of the age of the right to vote.

The Child Welfare Board's authority over minors of different ages varies with the issue involved. If the Board provides for care such as lodging or food, its authority can last up to the age of twenty-four. Usually, however, the authority of the Board ends at the age of eighteen. The Scandinavian principles regarding age are far more flexible in considering both individual needs and development. An example illustrates this flexibility.

In Norway, parents generally have an obligation to support their children up to the age of eighteen. However, parental duty may extend beyond that date, if reasonable, according to the abilities and wishes of the child, economic capacity of the parents, and various other factors. If disagreement arises, such factors are considered by the Child Welfare Board. In the United States, several states have recently lowered the age of parental obligation to children. For example, parental support extends up to the age of eighteen in California.[12] Beyond that age parents are not obligated to provide further financial aid, regardless of circumstances. No impartial authority, such as the Child Welfare Board, intervenes on behalf of the child if parents choose to cut off support at age eighteen. Such arbitrariness displays a glaring antichild bias on the part of the state which was not remedied until 1975. At that time, the U.S. Supreme Court ruled in *Stanton* v. *Stanton* that (at least in the context of a parent's obligation for child support) state laws specifying a greater age of majority for males than for females deny the equal protection of the laws.[13]

Juvenile courts in the United States may turn over certain serious offenses to adult criminal authorities, even though the juvenile suspect qualifies for juvenile court treatment. The youth is treated as an adult. The minimum age for trial as an adult is somewhat lower in large cities where the sophisitication of youth is expected to be higher. Nevertheless, in *Dorszynski* v. *United States,* the Supreme Court held that the sentencing of a youth offender as an adult requires an explicit finding by the trial judge that the offender would not benefit from treatment under the Youth Corrections Act with its rehabilitation provisions.[14]

In most Scandinavian countries juveniles who are suspected of violating certain "adult" laws may be subject to adult courts at the age of fifteen. In Norway the age is fourteen. As in the United States, the decision for adult prosecution is discretionary. Between 80 and 90 percent of the Danish criminal cases with defendants aged fifteen to eighteen are handled by the Child Welfare Board instead of adult courts.[15] Thus, most Scandinavian juvenile delinquents rarely come into contact with any court at all.

Criticism of the juvenile court system in the United States reached its peak during the 1960s. The stated purposes of the system appeared patently inconsistent with reality. It became apparent that juvenile courts punished the youth who came before them without guaranteeing procedural protections which had long been guaranteed to adults. Furthermore, it became obvious that rehabilitation could be achieved only in an atmosphere of fairness. Institutionalization did not rehabilitate, but instead it restricted access to employment and education.

As has been noted, juvenile courts are administered by the states within the United States. Thus, response to the mounting criticism must be made in each of the fifty states unless the federal government steps in. The federal government could become involved in two ways. First, the Congress could pass legislation granting federal funds to state juvenile court systems meeting certain standards. Alternately, the federal courts could cause a state reform of the system if an individual claimed a violation of some federally protected constitutional right under the Bill of Rights.

As is characteristic of the federal system, Congress up to the 1960s had not chosen to intervene in the state juvenile court systems. The lack of interference may have been due to several factors, not the least of which is the reactionary nature of Congress, which reacts to its constitutents or to lobby groups. Without organized efforts for reform, Congress would be unlikely to act.

It has been seen that the Scandinavian Child Welfare Board is composed of locally elected members. Obviously, it is hoped that these members have close local contact with the community, its needs, problems, and resources for juveniles. Yet, on the other hand, the Child Welfare Board retains a close connection with the national government. For example, the Act creating the Child Welfare Board is a national act. Both the Board and other social welfare agencies are subject to supervision at the cabinet level. Thus, the Scandinavian juvenile system has always had a national focus.

In the United States national attention focused on the juvenile court system after individuals contested the fairness of the system in the federal courts. When the individual claims finally reached the U. S. Supreme Court, they were brought against the backdrop of landmark judicial decisions emphasizing individual rights. This emphasis had resulted in the extension of the constitutional protections to adults accused of crimes in such matters as the right to counsel and the right against self-incrimination. Landmark judicial decisions also emphasized the rights of minority individuals to protection from racial discrimination. Such a climate appeared favorable to those working for reforms of the juvenile court system. Juveniles had been guaranteed none of the procedural rights extended to adults. Sociological evidence on racial discrimination indicated that the juvenile court system had tended to discriminate both racially and economically.[16]

In 1967, the U. S. Supreme Court decided a landmark case concerning the rights of juveniles, *In re Gault*.[17] It is summarized in some detail because of its immense importance to the juvenile's relation to the state. The facts of the case appeared to be typical of juvenile court procedure at that time. Gerald Gault was on probation for accompanying a youth who had stolen a wallet. As a result of a neighbor's verbal complaint about a lewd phone call, Gerald was detained for three days by authorities during which his parents received no actual notice as to his whereabouts. Two months later an informal hearing was held in the judge's chambers. The judge did not at any time question the neighbor, nor did he show to Gerald's parents the police report upon which his decision was based. He decided to commit Gerald to the State Industrial School for an indefinite period which could have extended up to six years. The U.S. Supreme Court concluded that the procedures employed were too informal to guarantee Gerald his right to procedural due process of law under the Fifth Amendment to the United States Constitution. At a minimum, Gerald was entitled to adequate and timely notice in order to prepare a defense, advice as to his right to counsel, and advice as to his right to confront and cross-examine witnesses against him. He was also guaranteed the privilege against self-incrimination. The Court concluded that due process rights do not endanger the juvenile court's desirable features of informality and rehabilitation. Furthermore, the Court was not impressed with the industrial school's effectiveness as an institution for rehabilitation. "The fact of the matter is that, however euphemistically applied, the title, a 'receiving home' or an 'industrial school' for juveniles is an institution of confinement in which the child is incarcerated for a greater or lesser time."[18] A later decision additionally required juvenile courts to apply the criminal standard of proof to the evidence submitted against the juvenile.[19] Evidence used to convict a juvenile must now be equal to the evidence used to convict an adult. However, a juvenile has not been granted a jury trial.[20]

The Scandinavian system has also recently been examined and is undergoing modification, although less fundamentally than in the United States. The 1960 Child Welfare Act of Sweden required the Child Welfare Board to consult with a lawyer whenever possible in matters which were deemed to involve legal rights of a juvenile.

In Norway, the institutions of confinement have undergone much criticism. If a juvenile is prosecuted by an ordinary court, he can be sentenced to a special youth prison, originally called a borstal institution. Norway first established them in 1952. It was hoped that a borstal institution would isolate juveniles from adult criminals and thereby render special education and guidance services not available in adult prisons. However, in practice, Norwegian courts showed much reluctance to sentence juveniles to the crowded institutions. Confinement in these institutions could exceed the confinement of an adult in an adult prison for the same offense. Reforms of these institutions, which are now called youth prisons, permit the juvenile to become eligible for parole within nine months of confinement.

Detention centers were introduced in Norway by legislation in 1965. However, no such centers have as yet been built. They have received much criticism by criminologists there.[21] United States detention centers confine thousands of youths and have been the target of much criticism. They have been in operation for years.

Reform of the Child Welfare Act of Sweden and the confinement institutions of Norway was not the result of court action, but of legislative efforts. The amended Child Welfare Act, passed in various forms in other Scandinavian countries, now guarantees fundamental legal rights to Scandinavian youths. For instance, a provision was inserted providing that the Child Welfare Board should include a judge, if at all possible. Also, the child has a right to a hearing, to bring counsel, to inspect data used against him, and to receive information about his right to appeal a Board decision. Since these rights apply in all Child Welfare Board proceedings, including matters other than juvenile delinquency, the legislation has potentiality for broader impact on children's rights than the Court decision in *Gault*.

In the United States, it is evident that the concept of *parens patriae* justice toward juveniles will be replaced with a concept more closely corresponding to the rights accorded to adults charged with comparable offenses. The *Gault* decision may spell the end of the juvenile court's handling of less serious matters relating to juveniles, such as the so-called stubborn child offenses described earlier. These matters are not even defined in Scandinavian law and are handled by the Social Welfare Board as a counseling matter.

A recent *New York Times* survey indicates that juveniles in New York City are being diverted from the juvenile court system.[22] Misbehavior problems are beginning to be treated through preventive and family services. Detention center population has dropped and there appears to be a trend towards less severe disposition of cases that eventually do reach juvenile court.[23] Such results are predictable following the *Gault* case because juvenile courts could not handle their pre-*Gault* volume in the manner now constitutionally required. The states may now begin to explore nonlegal ways of dealing with juveniles. States may develop some sort of Youth Services Bureau[24] patterned after the Scandinavian Child Welfare Board.

We have seen that Scandinavia has traditionally approached the treatment of juveniles from a social welfare point of view. This has probably resulted in reducing the stigma attached to youth encounters with the state. However, the recent reforms indicate a certain borrowing from the American system by their emphasis on legal rights of the juvenile when he deals with the Child Welfare Board. Both systems thus display a varying blend of legal and social welfare characteristics.

THE CHILD AND THE FAMILY

The child's role within the family has been extensively explored in matters relating to adoption, divorce, inheritance, child abuse, and illegitimacy. This paper in no way treats such matters comprehensively. A few examples of the child's role within the family are discussed merely in order to compare the attitudes of Scandinavians and Americans toward children's rights. The examples chosen deal with those areas in which the rights of children probably suffer vis-à-vis the authority of parents.

American attitudes toward the child evolved from the common law concept of the child as property of the family. In that context, the child is considered a chattel, historically similar to a slave or a woman. An old truism of common law says that "the husband and wife are one, and that one is the husband." It probably is possible to substitute the word child for wife and accurately describe the rights of the child within the family. In Scandinavia the child has also historically been considered as property of the family, especially of the father. In both Scandinavia and the United States, attention focused on better treatment of the child towards the end of the nineteenth century. Many states within the United States began to enact laws which prohibited the exploitation of a child's labor. Some Scandinavian countries at the same time passed laws substantially increasing the rights of illegitimate children.

Turning from the past to the present, startling and sensational news accounts in the United States now draw the public's attention to the problem of child abuse within the family. Estimates of instances of child abuse vary tremendously because of the difficulty of diagnosing its occurrence, the absence of witnesses, and the type of reporting provisions within each state. Congress has discussed ways to combat child abuse on a national level and all states have laws on child abuse. But the discussion and the present laws focus on procedures for reporting child abuse to authorities.

Little attention is given to establishing facilities for family counseling. Americans display much reluctance to deal on a collective level with social problems.[25] Intervention occurs only in the most extreme instances of abuse. When authorities do intervene on behalf of the child, they must use the courts. Experts on child abuse question whether such a problem belongs in courts at all. Many suggest that multidisciplinary panels could handle child abuse problems more informally. The present reluctance to interfere with the parent-child relationship, except in the extreme cases of abuse, ignores the child's physical and mental welfare. It operates with a built-in bias in favor of child-abusing parents.

Scandinavia does not appear to experience a problem of comparable magnitude. A recent search of the records of the Child Welfare Board of Reykjavik, Iceland, revealed four cases of "willful pre-meditated trauma", child abuse, during the period 1960–69.[26] The very low frequency of reported physical abuse is attributed to the organization of Icelandic society. Iceland still possesses the unique characteristics of a small society, such as close ties to relatives, friends, and neighbors. Also, no well-defined economic class structure operates to frustrate the economically disadvantaged. It is very likely that Iceland represents one extreme of the Scandinavian spectrum. At the opposite end of the spectrum, Sweden has noted a marked increase in instances of child abuse which began in 1960.[27]

A child also needs special attention if his parents decide upon divorce. Both Scandinavia and the United States record high divorce rates. Parents often dispute custody. Laws of the states provide that the best interests of the child will be controlling in custody matters. However, the statements often are pious expressions, because procedures for the granting of divorce do not guarantee that a child's best interests are protected. Children usually are unrepresented when parents seek divorce. If parents agree to an uncontested divorce, the lawyers for both parents draw up the necessary papers and submit them to the court for pro forma approval. If the divorce is contested, the court will become involved. However, the child still does not have an attorney or other disinterested party to represent him. The judge may discuss the divorce with the child, but often he is not required to do so.

Children should have legal counsel to represent them in divorce proceedings. Counsel for the parent owes allegiance to his client. He cannot adequately look after the child's interests. But even newly reformed divorce procedures do not safeguard the best interests of the child. The new California law, considered to be unusually progressive, provides that issues of parental fault may be considered in determining the child's best interests.[28] The degree of fault in relation to a spouse may have little relevance to the child's best interests. The spouse at fault may well be the parent best suited to be given custody of the child.

A comparable situation exists in Scandinavian countries. In Norway, the parents may reach an agreement on custody without official interference. If they do not reach an agreement, the question of custody may be decided in court or by an official. He is to act primarily in the child's interest, but, if the child is young, the mother is preferred by law. A parent or an official may (but this is not required) ask for the advice of the Child Welfare Board concerning the child. Thus, as in the United States, the parents can determine the best interests of the child in an uncontested divorce. There is no impartial determination of that interest. Thus, it is entirely possible for a settlement to be detrimental to the child.

The rights accorded to an illegitimate child are another illuminating example of a child's rights in relation to his parents (particularly his father) and in relation to other family members (particularly legitimate children). Furthermore, the rights of the illegitimate child affect all of society. If a child has no right to support from the parent, then that responsibility will ultimately fall on society.

In most western societies, social stigma customarily applies to the illegitimate child until he establishes his legal relation to his father. In the United States, the states generally provide procedures to establish paternity, but they are irregularly used. They also vary from state to state. Some states consider paternity suits as criminal actions used solely for punishment of the father. Other states treat them as civil actions for support. However, a father who is civilly obligated to support his illegitimate child will incur less financial obligation toward that child than toward a legitimate child.

State courts will not admit serological evidence and other scientific tests as evidence of paternity. The father can claim that such tests invade his right of privacy. Also, the mother need not cooperate in locating or identifying the father. She can claim that such a requirement of cooperation invades her right of privacy. The right of privacy is discussed in another chapter of this book. In this instance, the parents' right of privacy operates to the detriment of the child's right to support and legitimacy.

Establishment of paternity will not affect the child's right to a legally recognized role within the family. Thus, paternity is independent of the illegitimate child's right to inherit from his father. In recent years many individuals have challenged provisions barring an acknowledged illegitimate child from inheriting from his father. They charge that such provisions violate the child's fundamental constitutional right to equal protection of the law. That is, the child deserves as equal treatment as does a legitimate child. State laws which treat him differently unconstitutionally discriminate against him. To date, no farreaching principles have defined the constitutional rights of illegitimate children.

No constitutional objection was found to a state inheritance law which preferred the brothers and sisters of a decedent over an acknowledged illegitimate child.[29] Yet a law precluding an illegitimate child from recovering damages in the wrongful death of his mother has been invalidated.[30] In the latter situation, reliance on the legal formality of marriage was deemed insufficient justification for the state law denying the child compensation for his mother's death as a consequence of another person's wrongdoing. It is equally possible to apply that reasoning to the child's right to inherit from his father.

In the latest consideration of the constitutional rights of illegitimate children, a father of illegitimate children challenged a state law which treated him as a stranger for the purposes of adoption of his children.[31] Prior to the mother's death, he and she had lived together with the children. After the mother's death, the law required a hearing on the father's fitness as the guardian. It would have required no such hearing for the mother. That scheme was held to discriminate against the father vis-à-vis the mother. There was no discussion of the best interests of the child.

Such examples indicate that there is no national policy concerning the rights and status of illegitimate children. Laws discriminate against the illegitimate child by denying him the rights accorded to legitimate children. These laws are justified by the theory that they encourage marriage and stable family relationships. Apparently, it is believed that the mother will be so concerned with the future harsh treatment of an unborn child that she will be discouraged from an illicit relationship with a man. For those mothers not so deterred, such disabilities should not have to be borne by children. Furthermore, the argument is offered that the threat of support liability from the father would have far greater deterrent effect.

Scandinavia has been the leader in recognition of the rights of the illegitimate child. As early as 1915, Norway equalized the obligations of both the mother and father toward their illegitimate child. If the identity of the father was definitely ascertainable, a complete family relationship was deemed to exist, including a right to inheritance and support. Procedures were established at that time for ascertaining the identity of the father and collecting support from him. The 1915 law was superseded by a 1956 Norwegian law which abolished nearly all the remaining differences between illegitimate and legitimate children.

Both the 1915 and 1956 Norwegian laws established detailed procedures for the determination of paternity. Under the 1915 law, if paternity could not be determined precisely by scientific evidence, the possible fathers all contributed partially to the support of the child. None of the other rights such as inheritance accrued however. This system came under attack as degrading to the child and was abandoned in the 1956 Children's Acts.

Detailed procedures for the determination of paternity are closely tied to state health care programs in Scandinavia. A mandatory procedure begins with the mother's prenatal clinic visits. She is required to give a statement concerning the identity of the father. If he agrees, he is considered the father without further official action. If he does not agree, then a court determines the answer. If the mother names several possible fathers, the court will then determine, on the basis of scientific evidence, whether or not any one of the named men is the father. Court action occurs in less than 20 percent of the cases in Sweden.[32]

If the father falls behind in child support payments, the money can be claimed out of public funds. This assures the child of the money. It also puts the government in a position to make sure that the father pays.

Not all Scandinavian countries have laws that are as farreaching as that of Norway. Finland, for example, has not set up comprehensive procedures to establish a relationship between the father and the illegitimate child. Many reasons can be offered for this. For example, at the beginning of the twentieth century, when such ideas were spreading in Scandinavia, Finland was united with the Russian empire. That union meant strong influence by the Orthodox Church. Organized religion has historically opposed recognition of the rights of illegitimate children.[33] Apparently, organized religion viewed such rights as a discouragement to the sacrament of marriage.

As was noted earlier, illegitimacy in both the United States and Scandinavia is closely tied to the welfare system. If the child is not supported by his parents, the state bears the cost. However, the welfare systems differ greatly. Children in Scandinavia receive a child allowance without regard to need. Additional allowances are paid to children of unmarried mothers. The United States has no direct child allowance. Parents are reimbursed through tax deductions indirectly for the costs of children. Children, however, are clearly a greater economic burden in America than in Scandinavia.

Welfare in the United States reaches the children of the very poor. Aid to Families with Dependent Children (AFDC) is federally funded under the Social Security Act administered by state and local governments jointly. Payments under that program are based on complex computations of need. Some of the factors used in determining need have no relation to the child. For example, one requirement states that adult members of the family must attempt to find work. If that requirement is not met, the state cuts off aid to the entire family. The parents' conduct may operate to deny aid to needy children. The program also has been criticized for handing out money to parents without supervising how they spend the money.[34] In 1975, Aid to Families with Dependent Children was restrictively interpreted by the Supreme Court. In *Burns v. Alcala*, Justice Powell ruled that the statute did not include unborn children, and thus, that, the states were not required to offer welfare benefits to pregnant women for their unborn children.[35]

The Scandinavians supervise their welfare programs more closely. The Child Welfare Board can take steps to assure that any money provided is actually spent for the child's food, clothing, and other necessities. Scandinavians also enforce the father's financial responsibility for his illegitimate child. Professor Harry D. Krause, a leading United States expert on illegitimacy, has observed that the comprehensive child welfare system in Scandinavia may require vigorous parental responsibility. The state could not bear the full cost of the welfare program.[36] The child tends to suffer if the state takes a laissez-faire attitude towards the family. In the examples discussed, Americans adopt that attitude more frequently than Scandinavians.

THE CHILD AND THIRD PARTIES

School and employment. A child's major encounters with the world outside his family is likely to be at school or at a job. His relations to an employer are closely linked to compulsory school attendance requirements, inasmuch as the latter restrict access to full-time employment. Therefore, the child's rights in employment and at school are considered together.

The use of child labor persisted in the industrialized countries of Scandinavia and the United States up to the twentieth century. Most discussions of the development of the rights of children concentrate on the great strides achieved by the abolition of child labor. Yet, the International Labor Organization (ILO), a specialized agency of the United Nations, reported in 1972 that 43 million children were still employed, though 90 percent of the children lived in developing countries. The United States and Scandinavia have both mitigated the effects of child labor found in the sweat shops of the early part of this century. This paper concentrates on the various protective measures now in force with reference to how they actually affect the rights of children.

Within Scandinavia and the United States, many protective measures regulate child labor. Often such measures regulate both minimum wages and maximum hours of employed children. In many states within the United States the wages and hours of children are regulated under the same laws that prescribe minimum wages and maximum hours for women. (See chapter nine on the rights of women.) It has been noted that such laws are currently being reexamined by state legislatures because the courts have held that many of the laws discriminate against women. Such laws also need to be reexamined with respect to children. However, the "protective" aspects concerning children have not, up to the present time, undergone critical court or legislative examination. It has been noted that the *Gault* decision exposed the fallacy of the so called protective features of the juvenile court system. Analogously, the protective features regulating child employment may well operate to the detriment of the child.

At common law, women and children had no right to keep their earnings from work. The family as one, earned its salary as a unit. In most states children are not entitled to keep their own earnings. Such a situation does not reflect reality, because few parents of working children would insist on parental assignment of the child's earnings. Furthermore, denial of the right to keep one's earnings amounts to a disregard for the child's status as a person apart from the family unit.

Scandinavian countries have similar so called protective measures. For example, a child under the age of fifteen in Norway does not have a right to keep his own earnings. In view of current Scandinavian efforts to reduce the obligations of family members toward one another, such protective measures appear anachronistic.

Both the states and the Scandinavian countries have recognized that the protective measures are often inappropriate. In the states, oftentimes a child can conclude a contract if he is a special child, such as a movie star. In Norway, a child between the ages of fifteen and eighteen who is working at a job at which he can provide a living for himself may terminate a working contract. Thus, both jurisdictions recognize the child's capacity to contract if he provides his own living. A better rule would state that a child old enough to work is old enough to keep his earnings. That rule, hardly revolutionary, would assure the child of the respect due to any other working individual.[37]

Turning to the wages paid to working children, the United States first enacted a federal minimum wage law in 1934. That law was designed as a protective law, but it did not guarantee that a minimum wage would be paid to children until 1966.[38] Even after 1966, several key occupations which customarily employ youths remained exempt from the federal minimum wage provisions. These include recreational establishments, agricultural labor, newspaper delivery service, and housework. In addition, a subminimum wage applies to part-time employment of students in retail or service establishments or in agriculture. The rate paid to students is 85 percent of the present minimum wage paid to adults in comparable employment. In the last few years, congressional debate has arisen over the subminimum wage. In 1972, the House of Representatives refused to confer with Senate representatives on minimum wage amendments in large part because they feared that a compromise bill would delete the subminimum wage provision. However, amendments to the Fair Labor Standards Law, which were passed on April 8, 1974, retained the subminimum wage.[39] Exclusion of such employment as household chores from the coverage of minimum wage probably encourages employment of youth by employers who could not otherwise afford to do so. However, payment of a subminimum wage to students who work in retail and service establishments smacks of legislative accommodation to large businesses which hire thousands of youth. If such corporations then contribute to political campaigns, one might fairly wonder about the contrast between the poverty of the young and the privilege of the political elite.

Wages in Scandinavia are not regulated by law. Scandinavia, like other European countries, has relied on strong trade unions to negotiate wages. The state does regulate the type of work available to children. For example, Norway's Worker Protection Action of 1956 prescribes a minimum age for employment which varies with the nature of the work performed.

Turning to compulsory school attendance, children in the United States have very little choice other than high school attendance. For example, with few exceptions, children between the ages of six and sixteen in New York are required to attend school.[40] Many children would probably prefer job training programs to school attendance. But compulsory attendance laws do not provide an alternative. If children do drop out of school, they qualify for meaningless jobs often not protected by minimum wage and maximum hours provisions. [41]

Scandinavian countries offer apprenticeship programs as an alternative to high school. In Denmark, the programs operate in conjunction with the schools and offer a flexible alternative to compulsory education. Apprenticeship may be negotiated at the age of fourteen, after completion of nine years of compulsory education. The apprenticeship program is conducted by private employers. The Ministry of Education grants approval of these programs.[42]

Other Scandinavian countries have expressed dissatisfaction with certain aspects of apprenticeship programs. In 1962, Sweden began revision of its national education policy. The revision concluded that apprenticeship programs tend to channel children into college or vocational programs at too early an age. Actually, parents made the decision for the child since they negotiated the apprenticeship contracts. Sweden's revisions postpone choice to the age of sixteen. Even after that age, the choice can be reversed.

Sweden's reform of the apprenticeship program attempted to further the rights of children in three ways.[43] First, the reform aimed to provide all children with equal access to the educational system. Second, the revision attempted to assure that the child's future would not be unduly molded by the desires of his parents. Third, inasmuch as the child was treated unfairly in the old education system because it operated arbitrarily, the revision was intended to provide a chance for equal access to education, to mitigate the undue influence of parents on educational choice, and to treat the child fairly within the system. There are other examples of these three laudable goals.

The goal of equal access to education has been discussed in considering school financing in the United States. Local property taxes in the United States provide much of the resources for school finance. The system deprives children from poor communities with low property tax bases of access to equal educational opportunity. Thus, schools reflect and foster economic disparity. Various challenges have been brought against school financing with some success.[44] Such efforts have not been encouraged nationally. The U.S. Supreme Court has expressly refused to give national impetus to school financing reforms.[45]

Sweden's educational system has been termed "free-wheeling."[46] Educators speak of it as a bold system designed to erase social differences and to promote equality. Financial aid is available for all who desire to attend college. Local schools come under national financing policies. Yet, studies of college student bodies still reveal that the Swedish student population does not contain students of working class origin.[47]

Parents in both Scandinavia and the United States exert great influence over a child's beliefs and his educational opportunities. When is this influence undesirable? That question will be raised but not answered in two examples from the United States and Scandinavia. An Amish father in the United States claimed that his own religious beliefs precluded him from sending his children to ninth and tenth grades at public school. The U.S. Supreme Court held that the father's way of life and religious beliefs permitted him to withdraw his children from public school.[48] His beliefs were held to override the state's interest in compulsory education. Did the children's beliefs and desires deserve the greatest attention? The dissenting opinion thought so. Similar examples exist in Scandinavia. Scandinavian countries recognize state religion. If parents profess membership in the state church, their children are required to take religious education in school. It is not until children reach the age of fifteen that they are entitled to express religious thoughts contrary to that of their parents. At that age they may withdraw from compulsory religious instruction.

Fair treatment of the child within the educational system itself is an easier goal to achieve than a resolution of philosophic problems. Treatment within the compulsory school system has changed drastically within the past few years in the United States. School authorities traditionally exercised an iron hand in school disciplinary procedures. However, the past few years have brought significant reform of those procedures. New school regulations concerning dress and hair length have been enacted in several states as a result of court challenges.[49]

Such matters may seem trivial but, if appearance is viewed as a form of expression of individuality, interference with personal choice is seen as particularly degrading. School administrators have begrudgingly recognized that school regulations on dress and hair length must be reasonable. School disciplinary proceedings have been reformed since the *Gault* decision. They must now meet certain minimum procedural requirements such as a right to a hearing, a right to appeal from a principal's decision, and a right to inspect school records.[50] These requirements appear essential in a compulsory system. If children are required to attend school, they are at least entitled to some assurances that the institution is operated in a fair manner.

It has been seen that Sweden began revision of the school system in 1962. Student reforms in Sweden are carried out by powerful group organizations. The Central Organization of Swedish High School Students (SECO) is the official representative of Swedish junior and senior high school students.[51] It is government-subsidized and has a small paid full-time staff. It is organized as a trade union. Recently, its efforts as a pressure group to prevent the building of larger schools were successful.

CONCLUSION

Scandinavian parents, like those in other countries, often note that this is the age of youth. In their own day, things were different: young people were schooled in obedience to their elders. Those beginning a job received only a minimum wage; young people early in this century had to pay dearly for their training. Certainly, things have changed radically on all of these scores over the past fifty years. In Sweden, for example, society has come to realize its obligations to its citizens from the moment of their birth. Solicitous child welfare laws are understandable in a country of only eight million inhabitants and with a current birthrate of 1.7 children per family. In the United States, with its population of over 200 million, children may be regarded as equally precious, but the position of the state in terms of acknowledged children's rights reflects a policy which, by comparison, must be described as laissez-faire.

Attitudes toward children in Scandinavia and in the United States developed from different historical perspectives. Scandinavia has faced a declining population since the 1930s. Survival necessitated measures which increased the status and welfare of children within society. The measures lessened the financial burden of children upon parents.

The United States, until recently, has experienced fast population growth and, thus, has had little incentive to encourage or enhance the status and welfare of children. Furthermore, child-oriented issues have been linked to problems many Americans would rather forget or ignore, the problems of poverty and race. Juvenile delinquency and illegitimacy are two examples of issues which particularly affect poor and black children.

This chapter discusses instances of reform efforts which seek to extend adult rights to children—most notably in juvenile delinquency proceedings. In other instances, the unique needs of children should be recognized. Children have interests apart from those of their parents which merit special attention. The discussion of the divorce procedures in both Scandinavia and the United States shows that these unique needs are often not protected.

NOTES*

* In references to legal periodical literature, the number of the *initial* page of the work cited immediately follows the volume title. Page references to material specifically referred to in the text, if any, follow the initial page citation. Legal case citations correspond to *A Uniform System of Citation*, 11th ed. (Cambridge: The Harvard Law Review Association, 1974).

1. Scholarly analysis in the field of children's rights is rapidly developing, but systematic comparative research is relatively rare. The student of comparative children's rights should be aware of the following titles: Paul Adams, et al., *Children's Rights: Toward the Liberation of the Child* (New York: Praeger, 1971). In this book, many disciplines, including law, psychiatry, and education are represented. Articles concerning the treatment of children in Great Britain predominate. An invaluable study of the history of the status of children in the United States is Robert Bremner, ed., *Children and Youth in America: A Documentary History,* vol. 1, 1600–1865, vol. 2, 1866–1932 (Cambridge: Harvard University Press, 1970 and 1973). On the program of Aid to Families with Dependent Children, see Helen L. Buttenweiser, "Children's Rights: Children Aren't Chattels," *Popular Government* 38 (February 1972):1–3. The author notes that the concern about the family as an entity tends to lessen the status and protection of the children in relation to their parents. Lois G. Fisher states that the rights of children are "in their infancy." Rights of Children: The Legal Vacuum" 55 *American Bar Association Journal* 1151 (1969). She notes that in American society today, children are an economic liability and adults display ambivalent feelings toward them. The author proposes four basic rights for children: the right to life, to a home, to an education, and to liberty. A bill of rights is also proposed by Henry H. Foster, Jr., and Doris Jonas Freed in "A Bill of Rights for Children," 6 *Family Law Quarterly* 343 (1972). They discuss how such a bill of rights would necessitate reforms in present United States law. Related discussion is presented by Patricia Wald, "Making Sense Out of the Rights of Youth," *Human Rights* (Fall 1974):4 13–29. For research and analysis that is explicitly comparative include the following titles: Remi Clignet, *Liberty and Equality in the Educational Process,* (New York: John Wiley and Sons, 1974) in which the author examines the sociology of education in Europe, Africa and the United States. Another sociologist has studied family life in contiguous villages in Sweden and Finland. See, Elina Haavio-Mannila, "Cross-National Differences in Adoption of New Ideologies and Practices in Family Life," *Journal of Marriage and the Family* 34 (1972):525–37. She hypothesizes that new ideas about roles within the family have been accepted more readily in Sweden than in Finland, and she offers some explanations. Comparative references are scattered throughout the two issues of the *Harvard Educational Review* devoted to "The Rights of Children," vol. 43, part 1 (1973):pp. 481–668 and vol. 44, part 2 (1974):pp. 6–157. A comprehensive text on the law of illegitimacy has been written by Harry D. Krause, *Illegitimacy: Law and Social Policy* (Indianapolis: Bobbs–Merrill, 1971). It includes discussion of the laws relating to illegitimacy in Norway, France, and West Germany. A very useful, but now rather dated, comparative study of Scandinavian and American juvenile justice systems can be found in Ola Nyquist, *Juvenile Justice: A Comparative Study* (New York: St. Martin's Press, 1960).

2. Alva Myrdal, *Nation and Family, the Swedish Experiment in Democratic Family and Population Policy* (Cambridge: MIT Press, 1968).

3. *United States Department of Agriculture* v. *Murry,* 413 U.S. 508 (1973); *United States Department of Agriculture* v. *Moreno,* 413 U.S. 528 (1973).

4. Bernard Weinrub, "Sweden Discusses the Impact of the Welfare System on Freedom," *The New York Times,* Nov. 12, 1972, p. 28.

5. This statement is an over-simplification since many states do not have a "court" but have judges from the regular courts who sit on juvenile matters. See Hon. Justine Wise Polier, "Myths and Realities in Search for Juvenile Justice," *Harvard Educational Review* 44 (February 1974):114. See also, *Davis* v. *Alaska,* 415 U.S. 308 (1974).

6. For a discussion of the concept, the reader is referred to Gilbert T. Venable, "The Parens Patriae Theory and its Effect on the Constitutional Limits of Juvenile Court Powers," 27 *Univ. Pittsburgh Law Rev.* 894 (1966).

7. Holger Romander, "Introduction," in *The Child Welfare Act of Sweden* trans. Thorsten Sellin (Stockholm: Ministry of Justice, 1965).

8. *California Welfare and Inst'ns. Code* sec. 602. (West 1962).

9. *Commonwealth* v. *Brasher,* 270 N.E. 2d 389 (1971). See L. E. Ohlin et al, "Radical Correctional Reform: A Case Study of the Massachusetts Youth Correctional System," *Harvard Educational Review* 44 (February 1974):74.

10. Hans Grobe, "Juvenile Delinquency in Sweden," 53 *Ky. Law Journal* 247 (1965).

11. U.S., President's Commission on Law Enforcement and Administration of Justice, *Task Force on Juvenile Delinquency,* (Washington, D.C.: Government Printing Office, 1967), p. 7.

12. *California Civ. Code* sec. 4700 and *California Civ. Code* sec. 25. These sections do not modify preexisting child support agreements.

13. *Stanton* v. *Stanton,* 421 U.S. 7 (1974).

14. *Dorszynski* v. *United States,* 41 L.Ed.2d 855 (1974).

15. Based on statistical tables in Holger Horsten, *Borne-og Ungdomsforsorgen i Danmark ("Child Welfare in Denmark")* 7th ed. (Copenhagen: Nyt Nordisk Forlag, Arnold Busch, 1969), p. 534. The data are interpreted and discussed by Dr. Finn Henriksen, Senior Legal Specialist, European Law Division, Library of Congress.

16. Terence P. Thornberry, "Race, Socioeconomic Status and Sentencing in the Juvenile Justice System," 64 *The Journal of Criminal Law and Criminology* 90 (1973).

17. *In re Gault,* 387 U.S. 1 (1967).

18. *Id.* at p. 27.

19. *In re Winship,* 397 U.S. 358 (1970).

20. *McKeiver* v. *Pa.* 403 U.S. 528 (1970).

21. R. Goral, "Norwegian Legislation in Respect of Juvenile Delinquency," 28 *Nowe Prawo* 626 (1972).

22. Lesley Oelsner, "Juvenile Justice," in 4 pts., pt. 1 *New York Times,* April 2, 1973, p. 1. Also, Ohlin et al, "Radical Correctional Reform", p. 77.

23. Charles E. Reasons, "Gault: Procedural Change and Substantive Effect," *Crime and Delinquency* 16 (1970):165.

24. *e.g.,* Note, "A Proposal for the More Effective Treatment of the 'Unruly' Child in Ohio: The Youth Services Bureau," 39 *Univ. Cincinnati Law Rev.* 275 (1970).

25. *Cf.* Harry D. Krause, "Child Welfare, Parental Responsibility and the State," 6 *Family Law Quarterly* 382 (1972).

26. Asgeir Karlsson, "The Battered Child Syndrome in Iceland," *Nordisk Psykiatrisk Tidsskrift* 25 (1971):112–18. Iceland's present population is approximately 200,000. An article in a publication of the American Medical Association states that America's national average of child abuse is 30 cases per 100,000 population: James H. Ryan, M.D., "The Battered Child Deserves a Better Deal," *Prism* Amer. Med. Association, August, 1973, p. 40.

27. Karlsson, "Battered Child Syndrome."

28. *California Civ. Code* Sec. 4509, discussed by Wendell H. Goddard, "A Report on California's New Divorce Law: Progress and Problems," 6 *Family Law Quarterly* 405, 417 (1972).

29. *Labine* v. *Vincent,* 401 U.S. 532 (1971).

30. *Levy* v. *Louisiana,* 391 U.S. 68 (1968).

31. *Stanley* v. *Illinois,* 405 U.S. 645 (1972).

32. Krause, "Child Welfare."

33. O. M. Stone, "Illegitimacy: A Comparative Survey," 15 *International and Comparative Law Quarterly* 505 (1966).

34. Helen L. Buttenweiser, "Children's Rights: Children Aren't Chattels," *Popular Government* 38 (February 1972):1.

35. *Burns* v. *Alcala,* 420 U.S. 575 (1975).

36. Krause, "Child Welfare."

37. *Norwegian Social and Labour Legislation,* 3d ed. (Oslo: Joint Committee on International Social Policy, 1954-)

38. 29 U.S.C. Secs. 201 to 219.

39. *Fair Labor Standards Amendments,* Apr. 8, 1974, P.L. 93-259, sec. 24 (a), (b); Stat. 69, 72; 29 U.S.C. 214.

40. But see *Wisconsin* v. *Yoder,* 406 U.S. 205 (1972), exempting on first amendment religious grounds the application of compulsory education laws where Amish children are concerned.

41. Henry H. Foster, Jr., and Doris Jonas Freed, "A Bill of Rights for Children," 6 *Family Law Quarterly* 343, 369 (1972).

42. Denmark, Information Service, *School-Systems—A Guide, Denmark* (Copenhagen: Danish Information Service, 1971).

43. Verne Moberg, "The Great Swedish School Reform," *Saturday Review* February 10, 1973, pp. 55–58. See generally, Abe Holmbäck, *Scholarly Freedom in Sweden* (Uppsala: Lundequistka bokhandeln, 1954).

44. *Serrano* v. *Priest,* 5 Cal. 3d 584 (1971).

45. *San Antonio Independent School District* v. *Rodriguez,* 441 U.S.1, (1973).

46. Bernard Weinraub, "Sweden Discusses the Impact of Welfare System on Freedom," *New York Times,* November 12, 1972, p. 28.

47. Moberg, "School Reform," p. 56.

48. *Wisconsin* v. *Yoder,* 406 U.S. 205 (1972).

49. Runkel and Bettis, "Public Schools and Personal Appearance: Some Theories," 7 *Willamette Law Journal* 419 (1971).

50. Goldstein, "The Scope and Sources of School Board Authority to Regulate Student Conduct and Status: A Nonconstitutional Analysis," 117 *Univ. of Pennsylvania Law Rev.* 373 (1969). See also, "An Interview with Marian Wright Edelman, *Harvard Educational Review* 44 (1974):53–73.

51. Steve Kelman, "Swedish Student Group Presses for School Revisions," *Chicago Tribune,* November 15, 1970 p. 14. See also Knut Akerlund as told to Floyd L. Bergman, "Schools, Strikes, and Students: Swedish Style," *Phi Delta Kappan* 51 (1970):430–32.

Chapter 11 RESEARCH RESOURCES ON COMPARATIVE RIGHTS POLICIES

Jay Adrian Sigler

Legal philosophers, jurists, and law professors have consumed reams of paper debating whether comparative law is a method or a science. The argument centers around the question of whether or not comparative law represents an autonomous body of knowledge comparable to a self-contained science. The less ambitious are satisfied to use a comparative method in order to illuminate a particular problem of concern to them. As is suggested by some of the essays in this volume on the rights of children, the status of women, racial discrimination, equal access to the courts, and issues of privacy, the comparative approach can usefully form the basis for reform proposals. Eschewing scientific pretension, the second approach, which sees comparative law as a method, is altogether appropriate to the study of comparative rights policies. Furthermore, the student of comparative rights need not, and usually cannot, claim to be universal in the scope of his descriptive and analytical coverage. Comparisons within a grouping, such as among common-law nations or among French, Spanish, and Italian principles are obviously useful to undertake. Certainly at present, it must be said that comparative rights is not a discipline, but is an approach—a way of expanding and extending our understanding of emerging human rights.

The comparative study of rights policies is made more difficult by both the lack of any single source of material and the wealth of primary and secondary material on aspects of human rights. There is no easy path towards enlightenment and the student of comparative rights must be more skilled at finding and evaluating sources than many other scholars. There is one hopeful sign. The International Association of Legal Science is at present compiling a massive *International Encyclopedia of Comparative Law,* embracing every nation of any significance. This could be a good point of departure for future work in comparative law, although rights subjects are not always treated in detail. Professor Ian Brownlie has produced the best single-volume compilation of rights documents, *Basic Documents on Human Rights.*[1]

Major sources of information about comparative rights policies are the various international organizations, most notably the United Nations. The United Nations Charter calls for "respect for the principle of equal rights and fundamental freedoms for all without distinction as to race, sex, language or religion."[2] The United Nations is required to promote respect for and observance of human rights and its members, as well as the General Assembly and the Economic and Social Council, are all responsible for assisting in the realization of human rights.[3] Accordingly, in 1946, the Economic and Social Council established the Human Rights Commission and this body produced, among other things, a major piece of international rights legislation, the Universal Declaration of Human Rights, which sets a common standard of achievement in rights policymaking. This Declaration has been incorporated into the substantive law and constitutions of many nations. It provides a useful benchmark for making comparisons among nations, although the Declaration is by no means self-enforcing and is, in many instances, merely an idealistic symbol, rather than an operative policy foundation.

There are other important United Nations documents such as the International Covenant on Economic, Social, and Cultural Rights and the International Covenant on Civil and Political Rights. Both documents can be found in volume 61 of the *American Journal of International Law,* or they may be obtained directly from the United Nations. Neither has been ratified by a sufficient number of countries to form a viable basis for comparing human rights policies, although the rights mentioned are sometimes (as with the right to an adequate standard of living) very progressive indeed.

The United Nations also has adopted conventions on detailed rights issues. The Abolition of Slavery Convention was adopted in 1957. The Abolition of Forced Labor Convention was adopted in 1959. In 1950, a Convention on Freedom of Association and Protection of the Right to Organize was adopted, and many other conventions, which may be found in the United Nations Treaties Series, have some potential significance as a source of comparative rights ideals. Other United Nations agencies, such as the International Labour Organization; the Food and Agriculture Organization; The Educational, Scientific, and Cultural Organization; the World Health Organization; and the Children's Fund are concerned directly or indirectly with the promotion of rights policies across national borders. Each agency has produced suggestive studies which may be obtained directly from that organization.

The most accessible United Nations publication in this area was published in 1967 and is entitled *Human Rights: A Compilation of International Instruments of the United Nations;*[4] it includes more than United Nations materials. In 1968, a summary of United Nations action for human rights was developed as a part of Human Rights Year. The results of an international conference devoted to a review of United Nations progress in the field of human rights up until 1968 may be found in the *International Yearbook of Human Rights.*[5]

There are other regional sources of international quasi-legislation in the field of human rights. The European Convention for the Protection of Human Rights was signed in 1950, and it closely follows the provisions of the Universal Declaration of Human Rights. The decisions of the European Commission on Human Rights and the European Court of Human Rights may be found in the *Yearbook of the European Convention.*[6] The American Declaration of the Rights and Duties of Man, adopted at a conference at Bogota in 1948, is more similar to the American Bill of Rights than to the United Nations Declaration, but it contains many social and economic rights not found in the United States document. The Organization of American States (OAS) is responsible for any action under this Convention, but enforcement is nominal.

Two major private organizations publish materials which contribute to the international rights movement. They are the World Peace Through World Law Center, located in Geneva and the International Commission of Jurists, whose journal is exceedingly valuable as a source. A quasi-private group, the International Institute of Human Rights at Strasbourg, now seeks to stimulate comparative rights research and will probably be a contributor to all sorts of human rights projects. For OAS material, the quasi-public Inter-American Commission on Human Rights in Washington is a valuable respository of information. Amnesty International, a private (sometimes propagandistic) group issues many interesting reports on subjects such as politically motivated torture and press suppression.

For those interested in the important field of human rights on the international level, there is a large and growing literature. The protection of individuals against the deprivation of rights by national authorities is still a fairly new phenomenon, but the activities of the United Nations, the European Convention of Human Rights, and various other treaty arrangements have given rise to whole new areas of rights policies. While not strictly comparative, they are potentially of great importance for all nations. For most students and scholars the best starting point is *International Protection of Human Rights* by Louis B. Sohn and Thomas Buergenthal.[7] This compilation of treaties, cases, treatises, diplomatic notes, and essays is a rich source of basic materials, and the bibliographies supplied will lead the researcher onward. One of the most unusual and interesting works on comparative rights is by Josef Lador-Laderer and is entitled *International Group Protection.*[8] The book addresses itself to the problem of protection of minority groups against rights deprivations by national majorities.

There are some useful bibliographical sources which can lead scholars further into more specific areas. Among the best of these surveys are David Bayley's, *Public Liberties in the New States,* Armin Rusis's, "Human Rights: A Selective Bibliography,"[9] and the Council of Europe's, *Bibliography Relating to the European Convention on Human Rights.*[10] The United Nations has sponsored some major bibliographies in the human rights area. For these, it is advised that the scholar consult the latest lists of United Nations publications. Among these, the UNESCO publication, *Birthright of Man,* edited by Jeanne Hersch, is very useful.

The study of national rights policies is most advanced in America, where scholars have penetrated below the surface of constitutional pronouncements and radical interpretations to reveal the springs of American rights policies. For most nations the primary source and, sometimes, the only source is the national constitution. The classic collection is by Amos J. Peaslee, *Constitutions of the Nations.*[11] This has been improved upon by the fourteen-volume collection edited by Albert P. Blaustein and Gilbert H. Flanz, *Constitutions of the Countries of the World.*[12] The advantage of the Blaustein-Flanz collection is that it is a loose-leaf service prepared by experts on each nation. The comments of the experts are often illuminating and suggestive for rights research. There are innumerable other lesser collections of national constitutions, most of which are now quite dated. The best of these is the British Foreign Office publication *Constitutions of All Countries,* which is incomplete.[13] *Les Constitutions Européenes,* edited by B. Mirkine-Guetzevich, is excellent in spite of the limitations in coverage of time and place.[14] The best collection of communist constitutions, also dated, is edited by Jan Triska, *Constitutions of the Communist Party States.*[15] As a last resort scholars can write to a consulate or the embassy of the nation under study. This should be a first resort if there is a possibility that the national constitution is undergoing revision.

At one level of comparison, constitutional rights and liberties can be examined simply by placing constitutional provisions side by side. For example, the Japanese 1946 Constitution, the Russian 1936 Constitution, the West German 1949 Basic Law, and the Mauretanian Constitution all refer to equality of human rights in one way or another. This form of comparison may be useful for tracing historical roots of national rights policies or for showing certain generally accepted views of rights. Many newly independent African states have chosen to retain some association with French culture and have absorbed the French Declaration of 1789 into their own constitutions. Similarly, the influence of the British and American constitutional conceptions of rights may also be related in this way, as can the Russian and Chinese Constitutions, which bear a strong family resemblance to one another.

Comparisons of constitutional principles and rights tend to be superficial, but they can be instructive. There is a strong contrast between eighteenth, nineteenth, and twentieth century constitutional rights statements. Most early constitutions, such as the American, are essentially negative in form, placing prohibitions upon Congress or the states or government generally. Twentieth century constitutions, reflecting more generous political philosophies, usually add lists of economic and social rights to be provided by the state. These so called positive rights include health, education, work, public assistance, rest and leisure, and other rights which vary somewhat from country to country. The modern constitutions were derived, in part, from socialist doctrines or even from religious doctrines rather than from John Locke or Jean-Jacques Rousseau, who inspired most eighteenth and nineteenth century bills of rights. Whether the newer positive statist declarations of rights necessarily operate differently from the negativist earlier declarations is an interesting and challenging issue for future research. On this issue, see Carl J. Friedrich in *Constitutions and Constitutional Trends Since World War II.*[16]

One fruitful method of comparative inquiry is to take particular aspects of rights policies and contrast them from one nation to another. This approach permits in-depth analysis below the level of constitutional documents. Selection of an appropriate category of comparison is difficult. Possible choices for comparison are minority rights, the rights of privacy, education, religion, speech, assembly, voting, or various specific rights of accused persons. Inevitably, such comparisons run severe risks of bias on the part of the investigator. Furthermore, documentation is sometimes spotty and multilingual competence is essential, because the scholar must consider original court cases, legal commentaries, speeches, newspapers, journal articles, and quite possibly conduct interviews, all of which require some competence in a foreign language unless the researcher is willing to limit his investigations to publications in his native language. Because of the wealth of material available, the books mentioned below are intended merely as illustrations of comparative rights studies.

Surprisingly, there are few major works in comparative rights which use a topical approach. Among the best is Luis Kutner's *The Human Right to Individual Freedom,* which is a symposium on habeas corpus.[17] M. L. Friedland's *Double Jeopardy* is a fine Anglo-American comparison in this vital area of criminal rights.[18] Sir Ernest Barker's, *Church, State, and Education* is a valuable and suggestive work.[19] David Bayley's *Public Liberties in the New States* is comparatively ambitious and exceeds a single topic, but it is well done.[20] There are numerous works on the subject of minority group rights and this is the best researched area of comparative rights study.[21]

Those seeking a model for work in comparative rights should consider Frede Castberg's, *Freedom of Speech in the West: A Comparative Study of Public Law in France, The United States, and Germany.*[22] The treatment crosses cultural and linguistic barriers and defines the topic skillfully. Otto Kirchheimer's *Political Justice* is another example of a thorough, in-depth comparative rights problem although it is rather less well defined.[23] On a more empirical level, a useful model is Douglas Rae's *The Political Consequences of Electoral Laws,* a limited, but highly successful, effort to describe the operational effects of suffrage limitations and representation rules.[24]

Beyond the level of constitutional analysis, the best starting point for the comparative analysis of rights is the list of various broad national studies by American scholars. There is no foreign counterpart to Emerson, Haber, and Dorsen's, *Political and Civil Rights in the United States;* D. A. Schmeiser's *Civil*

Liberties in Canada is much less ambitious. Professor Albie Sachs's *Justice in South Africa* is one of many useful surveys for that country, perhaps the best.[25] The literature on Great Britain is enormous, but much of it is historical or technically legalistic. David Fellman, an American scholar, has written the most accessible general work, *The Defendant's Rights Under English Law.* Harry Street, in *Freedom, The Individual and the Law,* provides a good survey of British civil liberties policies as does Anne Coote and Lawrence Grant, *Civil Liberty.*[26] There are also numerous works on the subject of racial discrimination.

For Australia, consult Enid Campbell, *Freedom in Australia.* The British Commonwealth, generally, is treated by Gaius Ezejiofor, *Protection of Human Rights Under the Law* and the bibliography is very helpful. Ireland is available through John M. Kelly, *Fundamental Rights in the Irish Law and Constitution.*[27]

Materials on the Soviet Union are abundant, but few are reliable. Harold J. Berman has contributed importantly to this field, and Robert Conquest's *Justice and the Legal System in the U.S.S.R.* is also very good.[28] Extensive reports of civil liberties violations in the USSR can be found in the English language, *Chronicle of Human Rights in the U.S.S.R.,* an emigré publication.[29] There are other writings on rights in communist states but not much hard information outside of journalistic accounts. The situation is much better for noncommunist states, but even France and Italy lack a single reliable English-language book describing rights policies for those nations. In general, there are few works describing national rights policies for nations outside the English-speaking orbit. Curiously, there are few books in non-English languages which describe national rights policies, except as aspects of other, usually legal, descriptions.

The actual implementation of civil rights policies has rarely been studied outside the United States. The machinery of human rights protection within the Council of Europe is described in Ralph Beddard, *Human Rights and Europe.*[30]

There has been little comparative rights research which has penetrated below the level of constitutional statements and official pronouncements. The best attempt to deal with political limitations upon the actual enjoyment of rights is in Ivo Duchacek, *Rights and Liberties in the World Today.*[31] This is a pioneering study and should be consulted by any serious student in this field. Duchacek uses political science and other social science materials much more than legal documents, but this may be a healthy corrective to the older formalistic approach. Still, the author scratches only a little below the surface and there is much more thorough work to be done.

Because many civil rights problems involve aspects of the administration of criminal justice, one useful starting point for research is the criminal procedure codes of particular nations. Frederick B. Rothman of South Hackensack, New Jersey has published many of these in English. Examine, for example, G. O. W. Mueller's, *The German Criminal Procedure Code (1965)* to gain insight into the limitations upon the power of police and prosecutors on behalf of individual rights.[32] For France the best single source is G. Stefani and G. Levasseur, *Procédure Pénale,* for very useful notes and historical material.[33] Criminal procedure codes for other nations may sometimes be obtained from the appropriate embassy.

For nonlawyers who choose to study comparative rights policy, some introduction to legal research is indispensable. Necessarily, locating cases, statutes, and rules is preliminary to their interpretation. The outstanding work in this field is Miles O. Price and Harry Bitner, *Effective Legal Research,* which permits access to American, British, and Canadian materials. For Belgium, Luxembourg and the Netherlands, see Paul Graulich, *Guide to Foreign Legal Materials.*[34] For other countries there are some useful guides, but they must be sought out with care from experts in comparative law or law librarians.

Inevitably the investigator and scholar of comparative rights must turn to the masterful bibliography by Charles Szladits, a thorough listing of foreign and comparative law materials in English in four volumes entitled *A Bibliography on Foreign and Comparative Law.*[35] This is supplemented by his frequent contributions to the *American Journal of Comparative Law.* There is a partial subheading for human rights which leads the scholar into books, articles, and some official documents in the field. If all these efforts prove fruitless, resort to the Library of Congress is suggested, inasmuch as it has the best comparative law collection in North America. However, it is quite possible that for some nations there are insufficient data upon which to base serious comparative research.

There is an abundance of journal material available to the comparative rights scholar. Much of it is scattered and difficult of access. Aside from the *Index to Foreign Legal Periodicals,* there is no convenient guide to each of these journals. Certainly the Szladits bibliographies already mentioned are invaluable. I list some of the prominent journals in which comparative rights policies are likely to be, or have recently been, examined. Although this list is personal, it is probable that it will save scholars hours of research:

African Legal Studies; Archiv für Rechts and Sozialophilosphie; American Journal of Comparative Law; American Journal of International Law; Bulletin Mexicano de derecho comparado; Chronicle of Human Rights in the U.S.S.R.; Civil Liberties Review; Columbia Human Rights Law Review; Georgia Journal of International and Comparative Law; Harvard Civil Rights and Civil Liberties Law Review; Human Rights Journal; International and Comparative Law Quarterly; International Legal Materials; Jewish Social Studies; Journal of Church and State; Journal of Developing Areas; N.Y.U. Journal of International Law and Politics; Philippine International Law Journal; Race; Review of the International Commission of Jurists; Rivista di diritto europeo; Revue asienne de droit comparé; Revue de droit internationale et de droit comparé; Revue des droits de l'homme, Human Rights Journal; Revue internationale de droit comparé; Revue juridique et politique; Search and Seizure Law Report; Soviet Yearbook of International Law; Texas International Law Journal; Virginia Journal of International Law; Yearbook of the European Convention on Human Rights; and Zeitshrift fur Auslandisches Öffenttliches Recht und Volkerrecht.

Empirical work in comparative rights research is sorely needed. Survey research data are sparse. Interview-based work is rarely available outside of England, America and, for some matters, France and Germany. Analysis of judicial and other official attitudes towards rights policies is largely confined to the United States. In America we have learned that civil liberties are constantly undergoing expansion and contraction, responding somewhat to the political and social environment. Moreover, we have come to appreciate the fact that the implementation of rights policies depends upon the knowledge and understanding of bureaucrats, as well as on the police. In the future, successful studies of comparative rights will have to take into account the attitudes and practices of public officials whose task it is to discover and implement our rights. Clearly, the range of research possibilities in the field of comparative human rights is enormous.

NOTES

1. Ian Brownlie, *Basic Documents on Human Rights* (Oxford: Clarendon Press, 1971).
2. United Nations, *Charter,* art. 1.
3. Ibid., art. 55. See also, Moses Moskowitz, *International Concern with Human Rights* (Dobbs Ferry, New York: Oceana Publications, 1974), pp. 106–33.
4. United Nations, General Assembly, *Human Rights: A Compilation of International Instruments of the United Nations* (A/C 32/4), 1967.
5. United Nations, Commission on Human Rights, *International Yearbook of Human Rights* (A/C 32/41), 1968.
6. Directorate of Human Rights of the Council of Europe, *Yearbook of the European Convention on Human Rights* (Heule, Belgium: Editions administratives, 1970).
7. Louis B. Sohn and Thomas Buergenthal, *International Protection of Human Rights* (Indianapolis: Bobbs-Merrill Company, 1973).
8. Josef Lador-Laderer, *International Group Protection* (Leyden: A. W. Sijthoff, 1968).
9. David Bayley, *Public Liberties: The New States* (New York: Rand McNally, 1964); Armin Rusis, "Human Rights: A Selective Bibliography," *Bulletin,* International Association of Law Libraries, June 1969, pp. 4–20.
10. Council of Europe, *Bibliography Relating to the European Convention on Human Rights* (Strasbourg: Secretariat of the Commission, 1970).
11. Amos J. Peaslee, *Constitution of the Nations* (New York: Justice House, 1956–1967).
12. Albert P. Blaustein and Gilbert H. Flanz, *Constitutions of the Countries of the World* (Dobbs Ferry, N.Y.: Oceana Publications, 1973–1976).
13. Great Britain, Foreign Office, *Constitutions of all Countries* (London: H. M. Stationary Office, 1938).
14 B. Mirkine-Guetzevich, ed., *Les Constitutions Européenes* (Paris: Presses Universitaires de France, 1951).

294 / Policy Problems in Comparative Perspective

15. Jan Triska, *Constitutions of the Communist Party States* (Stanford: Stanford University Press, 1968).

16. Carl J. Friedrich, *Constitutions and Constitutional Trends since World War II*, ed. Arnold J. Zurcher (New York: N.Y.U. Press, 1955). See also Robert Martin, *Personal Freedom and the Law in Tanzania* (Nairobi, Kenya: Oxford University Press, 1974), pp. 1–36.

17. Luis Kutner, *The Human Right to Individual Freedom* (Miami: University of Miami Press, 1970).

18. M. L. Friedland, *Double Jeopardy* (Oxford: Oxford University Press, 1969).

19. Ernest Barker, *Church, States and Education* (Ann Arbor, Mich.: University of Michigan Press, 1957).

20. David Bayley, *Public Liberties in the New States* (New York: Rand McNally, 1964).

21. Vernon Van Dyke, "Human Rights and the Rights of Groups," *American Journal of Political Science* 18 (1974):725–42.

22. Frede Castberg, *Freedom of Speech in the West: a Comparative Study of Public Law in France, the United States, and Germany* (London: Allen and Unwin, 1961).

23. Otto Kirchheimer, *Political Justice* (Princeton: Princeton University Press, 1961).

24. Douglas Rae, *The Political Consequences of Electoral Laws* (New Haven: Yale University Press, 1967).

25. Thomas Emerson, David Haber, and Norman Dorsen, *Political and Civil Rights in the United States* (Boston: Little, Brown and Co., 1967); D. A. Schmeiser, *Civil Liberties in Canada* (Oxford: Oxford University Press, 1964); Albie Sachs, *Justice in South Africa* (Berkeley: University of California Press, 1974).

26. David Fellman, *The Defendant's Rights under English Law* (Madison: University of Wisconsin Press, 1966); Harry Street, *Freedom, the Individual and the Law* (London: Penguin Books, 1963); and Anne Coote and Lawrence Grant, *Civil Liberty* (London: Penguin Books, 1973).

27. Enid Campbell, *Freedom in Australia* (London: Methuen, 1966); Gaius Ezejiofor, *Protection of Human Rights under the Law* (London: Butterworths, 1964); and John M. Kelly, *Fundamental Rights in the Irish Law and Constitution* (Dobbs Ferry, N.Y.: Oceana Publications, 1961).

28. Harold J. Berman, *Soviet Criminal Code and Procedure* (Cambridge: Harvard University Press, 1966); Robert Conquest, *Justice and the Legal System in the U.S.S.R.* (New York: Praeger Publishers, 1968).

29. *A Chronicle of Human Rights in the U.S.S.R.* (New York: Khronika Press, 1973–).

30. Ralph Beddard, *Human Rights and Europe* (London: Sweet and Maxwell, 1973).

31. Ivo Duchacek, *Rights and Liberties in the World Today* (Santa Barbara, Cal.: ABC-Clio, 1973).

32. G. O. W. Mueller, *The German Criminal Procedure Code, 1965* (Hackensack, N.J.: Rothman Reprints, 1969).

33. G. Stefani and G. Levasseur, *Procédure Pénale*, 7th ed. (Paris: Dalloz, 1973).

34. Miles O. Price and Harry Bitner, *Effective Legal Research* (Hackensack, N.J.: Rothman Reprints, 1969); Paul Graulich, *Guide to Foreign Legal Materials* (Dobbs Ferry, N.Y.: Oceana Publications, 1968).

35. Charles Szladits, *A Bibliography on Foreign and Comparative Law* (Dobbs Ferry, N.Y.: Oceana Publications, 1955–1975).

PART III NEW DIRECTIONS IN BEHAVIORAL RESEARCH

EDITOR'S INTRODUCTION

Talk about individual rights and human dignity affects ever broader areas of public policy among liberal democracies. Indeed, it increasingly influences the thought and expectations of people all over the world, including citizens of the numerous developing countries and of socialist people's democracies. There is almost no place in the world where the awareness of human rights has not penetrated.

The diffusion of heightened human rights aspirations has had two healthful effects on scholarship. First, it has spurred academic interest in developing conceptual clarity in the use of such terms as rights. Second, it has created a demand for interdisciplinary inquiry because of a new understanding that the subject matter involved in the study of human rights is too important to be consigned exclusively to research and administration by lawyers. The behavioral and social sciences must become involved as well. Inasmuch as the topic of rights has been the traditional professional preserve of lawyers, it is not surprising that legal literature has contributed substantially to the categories of analysis used in related research, including research in the social sciences.

The terms rights, duties, privileges, and liberties have stimulated extensive analytical literature in the fields of philosophy and law. The quest for conceptual clarity in the use of these terms has exercised some of the best minds particularly among English, Scandinavian, American, and other students of jurisprudence. Among American scholars, the work of Wesley Hohfeld has been of seminal importance. In *Fundamental Legal Conceptions as Applied in Judicial Reasoning,* he defines a right as one's affirmative claim against another, and a privilege as one's freedom from the right or claim of another. Similarly, a power is one's affirmative control over a given legal relation as against another; whereas an immunity is one's freedom from the legal power or control of another as regards some legal relation.[1] In Karl Llewellyn's condemnation of doctrinal formalism, *The Bramble Bush,* Hohfeld's scheme of jural relations is considered from the American "legal realist" point of view, and the reaction of a court is

297

made the determining factor in the effectuation of rights.[2] In *On Law and Justice,* the Danish scholar and "legal realist" Alf Ross presents a detailed analysis of rights, describing them as technical language tools to create duties and present claims. In practical terms, he argues, they must be interpreted as directives to judges and other enforcement officials.[3] Attitudes and behavior of decision makers, no less than the professional standards which they proclaim, must be examined to see whether a claim asserted as a right will or will not be honored and enforced. The law is as the law does—has become the watchword of the school of "legal realism."

The attitudinal components of various rights are important, not only where decision makers are concerned, but also for the average citizen and the public. An influential indication of this appears in the analysis of the Swedish legal scholar, Axel Hägerstrom. In his *Inquiries into the Nature of Law and Morals,* Hägerstrom argues that the term right is a hollow word, that is, one can appreciate the advantage of the right, but not the right itself. A right is not a tangible thing that can be touched, grasped, or measured.[4] Psychological and historical explanations are given by Hägerstrom for the continued talk of rights: mental constructs about rights are used to awaken patterns of conduct in the minds of people. How people learn about rights, how they talk and feel about them, have an important bearing on how they behave in relation to one another.

Where the legal realism of the 1930s and 1950s beckoned, social science of the 1960s and 1970s has begun to follow. The insights from analytical literature in the field of the philosophy of law are beginning to influence research on the topic of rights in the behavioral and social sciences. It is now recognized that the human rights situation in any given political system is made up of many socioeconomic and cultural elements and that the legal guarantee of rights is only one such element.

An important dimension of any right is its legal definition, a central consideration in many of the essays in part II of this volume. Part 3 turns from the problem of comparing the legal definition of diverse human rights in different systems (along with some of the sociopolitical and legal influences upon the resolution of definitional difficulties) to the problem of the function of various rights.

Talk about rights may serve one of four functions. First, as has been shown, statements about rights have a *technical function,* such as in the formulation of a constitution, statute, or ordinance stipulating a right in legal terms. For example, article 37 of the Venezuelan Constitution of 1961 states, "The Nation guarantees the liberty of thought manifested by word, by writing, by means of print, by radio, or other systems of publicity, as to which previous censorship cannot be established." Second, statements that might be made by a court such as that "Miss Doe is entitled to decide for herself whether or not she will have a therapeutic abortion" have a *directive function.* Such a statement effectively prevents others from interfering with Doe; her decision becomes recognized as reserved for her judgment in consultation with her physician. A directive statement of a right is typically expected as the solution of legal disputes with res judicata effect, using a procedure granting specific guarantees to the parties. Third, statements about rights may have an *informative function.* The listener acquires a certain piece of information by coming to know, for instance, that a young man may be exempt from military conscription because he is a conscientious objector, or that, a citizen is entitled to social security benefits at the age of sixty-five. Fourth, statements such as "since this is a free country, I can say what I want" have a *legitimizing effect.* Whether or not the statement, if applied to a specific situation, would be found legally acceptable by a police officer or judge, it is designed to make an action done seem rightful and appropriate in terms of accepted norms and standards of opinion. H. L. A. Hart remarks, "Men speak of their moral rights mainly when advocating their incorporation in a legal system."[5]

Most legal analysis of public policy, such as the comparative essays in the preceding sections, discuss rights in terms of their evolving definitions and in terms of their technical and directive functions. Social science inquiry is better equipped to explore the legitimizing and informative functions served by talk about rights. Breeden's analysis of the rights of children has explored these rights in terms of their technical functions (changing statutory policy) and directive functions (how administrators and parents must act toward children according to courts and administrative boards in Scandinavian countries and the United States). But in this section, Judith Gallatin is concerned not with clarifying what rights children legally have, but with exploring how adolescents evaluate and learn about various human rights. Her comparative data on "political socialization" to human rights norms is drawn from Great Britain, West Germany, and the United States. A questionnaire, similar to that used in psychological research, was given to school children in these countries. The responses brought out differences among them regarding informative and legitimizing statements about various rights: what was the level of information possessed by the respondents regarding various rights and by what criteria (utilitarian, pragmatic, public welfare) did they appraise the legitimacy of various rights? In her conclusion, Gallatin emphasizes that the processes of psychological development associated with age appear to explain more satisfactorily differences among the children regarding what they think their rights are and should be than do nationality differences among the children.

William B. Devall's essay, "Social Science Research on Support of Human Rights," supplies an extensive literature review of the political sociology of support in public opinion for various human rights. He reviews comparative research that identifies the salient variables associated with high and low levels of information about various rights and with high and low levels of tolerance toward the legitimacy of asserting various claims to human rights. He explores the methodological difficulties in cross-national opinion-surveying by political science and sociology scholars, and he particularly notes some of the pitfalls of such inquiry as it focuses on information and opinion about human rights.

Directive statements about human rights have a peculiarly political dimension that is open to social science inquiry. "Who decides?" is a question of perennial interest to political science. When an authoritative finding is made by a court that X's rights of conscience have been infringed on by conditioning public employment upon an affirmation of a belief in God, then we may fairly ask, who decides and with what effect? In comparative research, such questions take on added interest as we range from religiously pluralistic to more homogeneous societies and from religiously pluralistic to denominationally more uniform decision-making bodies. The way having been cleared years ago by such comparative institutionalists as Sir Carleton K. Allen and René David, recent forays in comparative decision making have successfully been made by Theodore Becker, David Danelski, Glendon Schubert, and others.[6] However, such research in comparative behavior has not been launched without inviting the criticism that it is affected by an American bias which overemphasizes judicial behavior. In this regard, Carl Baar's comparison of Canada and the United States is instructive. He emphasizes that judicial behavior is by no means the only relevant decisional behavior of importance in policy fields related to rights and liberties. Systematic comparative study of decisional behavior and policy among boards, commissions, tribunals, and other parajudicial bodies has yet to be initiated by political scientists, although in institutional terms it is familiar territory for students of comparative law. Baar's essay is valuable also because, relying on an original developmental perspective, he offers a partial theory about judicial activism in federal systems that can be tested elsewhere.

The concluding essay, by the editor, presents some observations on the scope of human rights research and notes some of the difficulties that must be overcome in order to promote interdisciplinary work. The division of labor that has characterized human rights inquiry among legal scholars and social scientists is analyzed critically. The discussion in this chapter constitutes an appeal to scholars to surmount the artificial academic boundaries which have heretofore stood in the way of systematic research in the field of comparative human rights.

NOTES

1. Wesley Hohfeld, *Fundamental Legal Conceptions as Applied in Judicial Reasoning* (New Haven: Yale University Press, 1923).

2. Karl Llewellyn, *The Bramble Bush* (New York: Knopf, 1930).

3. Alf Ross, *On Law and Justice* (Berkeley: University of California Press, 1959). Two recent and valuable efforts to examine various rights and liberties from realistic points of view should be noted. Stuart A. Scheingold, *The Politics of Rights: Lawyers, Public Policy*

and Political Change (New Haven: Yale University Press, 1974). Jay A. Sigler, *American Rights Policies* (Homewood, Illinois: The Dorsey Press, 1975).

4. Axel Hägerstrom, *Inquiries into the Nature of Law and Morals* (Oxford: Clarendon Press, 1931).

5. H. L. A. Hart, "Are There Any Natural Rights?" in *Human Rights,* ed. A. I. Melden (Belmont, California: Wadsworth Publishing Co. 1970), pp. 61–75 at 63.

6. Theodore L. Becker, ed., *Comparative Judicial Politics* (Chicago: Rand McNally, 1970). Glendon Schubert and David J. Danelski, eds., *Comparative Judicial Behavior* (New York: Oxford University Press, 1969). See also, relevant comparative studies in Joel B. Grossman and Joseph Tanenhaus, eds., *Frontiers of Judicial Research* (New York: John Wiley and Sons, 1969). Useful for comparative theory, although short on cases (principally focusing on the United States) is Walter F. Murphy, Joseph Tanenhaus, and Daniel Kastner, *Public Evaluations of Constitutional Courts: Alternative Explanations,* Comparative Politics Series no. 4 (Beverly Hills: Sage Publications, 1973). See also Austin Sarat and Joel Grossman, "Courts and Conflict Resolution," *American Political Science Review* 69 (1975): 1200–17.

Chapter 12 THE CONCEPTUALIZATION OF RIGHTS: PSYCHOLOGICAL DEVELOPMENT AND CROSS-NATIONAL PERSPECTIVES

Judith Gallatin

Although the situation has altered in recent years, social scientists have generally avoided empirical investigation of the development of normative concepts such as justice and rights.[1] A handful of investigators have explored related topics such as moral development and the process and content of political socialization,[2] but there have been few attempts to trace the growth of political ideas per se. Well over a decade ago, the eminent political scientist Herbert Hyman remarked:

What a strange imbalance we find today! Political behavior is seen as determined by all sorts of motivational and emotional factors operating through complicated psychodynamic processes. Certainly such behavior is full of purpose and direction, but it is guided, if only imperfectly, by reason, knowledge, judgment, intelligence. Men are urged to certain ends but the political scene in which they act is perceived and given meaning. Some cognitive map accompanies their movements toward their ends. The role of cognitive processes must be reinstated as a necessary counterbalance to the distorted analyses of political behavior.[3]

Yet political scientists and psychologists alike still incline much more toward the psychodynamic than the cognitive. Lane's well-known work on ideology has concentrated primarily on personality variables, and a recent book by Knutson contains an elaborate discussion of possible *motives* which might exert an influence on political thinking, although she makes little mention of relevant cognitive factors.[4] Investigators who adopt this orientation seem to assume that people who endorse a particular political philosophy do so because it suits their characters: the rigid, anxious person, for instance, holding tenaciously to authoritarian beliefs; the self-actualizing, open individual, permitting himself a democratic-humanitarian stance. No doubt, a case may be made for this point of view.

However, when we turn to cross-cultural and comparative research, the need to consider other influences becomes evident. Human motives are presumably

302

quite similar in every country of the world, but political systems vary widely. And even in countries with a more-or-less common political heritage, for instance, western democracies such as Britain, Germany and America, researchers have detected some fairly marked differences in attitude.[5] Patrice Gélard appears to suggest that political traditions and historical forces have more impact on ideology than personality variables:

Each nation remains marked by its traditions, its culture, its language, its history, sometimes its dominant religion. We are still in a multistate society, and so we will stay, as long as a supranational organization capable of imposing its decisions and of chastising members of the international collective has not been established. And even in such a framework, the collective traditions of the peoples will retain differences which may be only minor, but which will subsist in the legal system.

Therefore, the study of systems of law and comparisons between them—that is to say comparative law—is still of primary importance to the comprehension of social psychology. This becomes evident when one reflects that the law mirrors a nation's collective morality. Thus at the outset comparative law enables one to grasp the mentality of a nation, to see which are the outstanding general principles and which are the rules that the society has progressively abandoned. It also provides a basis for measuring differences in mentality between societies and nations.[6]

My own work—a cross-cultural study of the development of the concept of rights during adolescence—leads me to agree with Gélard about the possible influence of differing political systems upon the collective mentality of a nation.[7] In this study, 330 interviews were conducted with schoolchildren in America, Britain, and Germany. One-third of the sample was of superior intelligence (125+) and the remaining two-thirds were of average intelligence (95–110). An equal number of boys and girls were included, and there was a not entirely successful attempt to control for social class.[8] Although the school systems in the three countries differ considerably (a point which will be taken up in greater detail later on), the subjects were drawn from settings which were, at least, comparable.[9]

Each subject was approached individually and asked to imagine the following situation: A thousand people, dissatisfied with their government had moved to an island in the Pacific. Once there, they were confronted with the task of establishing a new political order. The interviewer then posed a series of standard questions ranging over a wide array of topics: law and government, crime and punishment, political parties, conflicts of interests, and the like. All of the items which were chosen for analysis from this questionnaire dealt more-or-less with the concept of rights.

For the most part, the pattern of political thinking which emerged among adolescents in the three countries was similar, but there were some systematic differences. With increasing age, youngsters in all three western democracies exhibited an increasing commitment both to the rights of the community *and* the rights of the individual—what might be called a kind of "social contract" mentality. But the actual terms of the contract seemed to differ from country to country.

In interpreting these results, it is useful to consider the philosophical traditions and assumptions which underlie the concept of rights, traditions, and assumptions which are common to all liberal democracies.[10]

PHILOSOPHICAL CONCEPTS

Negative rights. In any discussion of rights, one fact becomes apparent almost immediately: they usually are defined in terms of some sort of social relationship. As Benn and Peters have put it: "Since rights imply duties, they imply someone in a social relationship with their subject upon whom the duties can rest. Robinson Crusoe had no rights until he met Man Friday."[11]

Once this social relationship has been established, that is, once two or more individuals are faced with the necessity of interacting, the rights of one person impose certain obligations on the other, a principle which is known as the correlative theory. But what sort of duties do an individual's rights impose upon other people? And by what agreement or authority?

One of the simplest and clearest cases of a right being correlated with a duty is the situation in which one individual has loaned money to another. If A has loaned B ten dollars, one cay say that A has a right to the ten dollars and that it is B's duty to pay it back. Although it may not be written out, A and B may be said to have a contract. Matters become somewhat more complex when more than two people are involved.

When a man buys a house, he is also described as having a right to it, but in this instance, the correlation is less direct, the contract less specific. Assuming the absence of relevant zoning regulations, the owner of a house has the privilege of doing as he pleases with it—painting it fuchsia, knocking out all its windows, or building a concrete wall around it (providing that it does not impinge on another's property). Just as long as he does not violate another's rights he is entirely within his own. His neighbors may deplore the hue of his house, but they have no *legal* claim on him to change it. Their duty, then, is one of not interfering with him.

The principle of noninterference. Like the correlative principle, the principle of noninterference, is central to the whole concept of rights. Indeed, one could characterize noninterference as a more general statement of the contract which is always implicit in the concept of rights. In addition to the specific rights one individual may have with respect to another (such as the right to have money which is owed him paid back), every individual has certain claims on all the other members of the society in which he lives. As long as he treats them with equal respect, they must not interfere with the way he conducts his life or disposes of his property. An individual is entitled to such prerogatives not so much because of anything he might do (such as lending money) but simply by virtue of having been born a human being. The reader will readily recognize this as part of the theory of natural rights, a doctrine first advanced by Locke and considerably refined two centuries later by John Stuart Mill.

Positive freedom. Not being interfered with has been designated as a "negative freedom" but the theory of natural rights guarantees the individual certain opportunities or positive freedoms as well, education and the pursuit of happiness being two rather well-known examples.[12] Applying the correlative principle to these kind of rights, however, raises some perplexing questions. Upon whom does the right to education confer a duty? Certainly no single individual is obliged to provide schooling for anyone else in the same sense that a debtor is required to pay back his creditors. The contract is not that explicit. Consequently, an uncle who refuses his nephew the money to attend college is not infringing on his nephew's right to an education.

On the other hand, a father who keeps his twelve-year-son home on the pretext that he will get more out of joining the family business than going to school *is* generally considered to be abridging his son's rights. Indeed, such parents can be formally charged with child neglect. In most western countries—certainly the three which are under scrutiny in this paper—education is compulsory up to the age of at least fourteen. This hypothetical contrast between the stingy uncle and the business-minded father may serve to illuminate the nature of positive rights. An individual's right to an education usually implies some sort of *minimum* standard, a minimum opportunity for each person to learn, to prepare himself for an occupation, and to develop his talents.

Hence, positive rights are more nebulously defined than are negative rights. Adapting Erich Fromm's terminology, negative rights are more-or-less synonymous with "freedom-from" and positive rights with "freedom-for."[13] The right to free speech (a negative right) is quite specific. As long as an individual's views do not injure anyone else, no other person or group can keep him from expressing them. Liberal democratic regimes insure their citizens (at least in theory) a certain freedom-from censorship or oppression. An education, on the other hand, permits the individual opportunities which he might otherwise have been denied. It represents a kind of freedom-for, a means by which a person may enhance his standing in the community and better satisfy his wants. But what he actually *does* with this freedom—whether he drops out of school in his teens to become a factory worker or labors through the university to become a college professor—is left unspecified. And in any case, the state is legally bound to provide him only with a certain minimum.

Prima facie considerations and the nature of the social contract. One question which inevitably arises is whether natural rights—either positive or negative—are absolute, whether they must be respected regardless of the circumstances. As has already been noted, in the case of negative rights there is at least one restriction. If Jones sprays paint on Smith's house while painting his own fuchsia, Jones is no longer within his rights. But this sort of limitation is implicit in the definition. Without mutual respect, the contract upon which rights are based would fall apart.

In practice, there are other restrictions as well. The social contract which governs a democratic community turns out to be considerably more complicated than the contract of mutual respect which regulates the relations of any two individuals. Every individual may possess his set of inalienable rights, but the community as a whole has certain collective rights as well. Consequently, the two may come into conflict, and in some cases, the rights of the individual may be sacrificed to the public good. Ordinarily, a farmer may not be forced to give up his land. However, if his property lies in the projected path of a freeway, he may be compelled to sell his holdings to the state "for a fair price." Similarly, though a communist may be free to express "subversive" ideas in peacetime, the same views publicly aired may bring about his imprisonment during a national emergency. Hence, the rights of any given individual are prima facie rather than absolute. A man has the privilege of owning a certain piece of property or saying what he pleases in the absence of a good reason for denying him this privilege. As a practical matter, his negative and positive rights must always be weighed against the negative and positive rights of the community.

To complicate matters even further—and this is a particularly critical point for any cross-national study—the social contract may vary from one community to another. In some democracies, the individual citizens may be particularly insistent upon having the state provide them with certain positive rights— education, housing, health care, pensions—and at the same time may adopt a rather cavalier attitude toward "negative rights." By contrast, in other societies more emphasis may be placed on the formal guarantee of certain negative rights—freedom of speech, the right to bear arms, the separation of church from state—and positive rights may be slighted.

PSYCHOLOGICAL PERSPECTIVES ON THE CONCEPT OF RIGHTS

Of course, the important question at this point is how these principles, drawn from political philosophy, might apply to research on the concept of rights. A nodding acquaintance with political philosophy on the part of this researcher supplied a workable framework, and I analyzed the items on my questionnaire under the headings: "Positive rights," "Negative rights," and "Conflicts over rights."

Positive rights from a psychological point of view. Space limitations prevent the inclusion of more than a single example under each heading.[14] However, the item on education, one of the most firmly established positive rights in most western democracies, can be used to illustrate some rather consistent developmental and cross-national trends. The question read: "To begin with, some people suggested a law which would require children to go to school until they were 16 years old. What would be the purpose of law like that?" The response, summarized by age and country, is presented in table 1.

Taking up the developmental results first, it is apparent that the younger subjects are, for the most part, oblivious to the broader implications of the question. A sizable percentage simply parrot back the obvious: You go to school to learn something. Those who are able to address themselves to the issue stress the more tangible benefits of having an education, such as getting a better job. Schooling is simply the means to an end, a way for the individual to insure that his material wants will be satisfied. It is only with the older subjects that we begin to see anything like a true concept of positive rights. With this group—especially the eighteen-year-olds—education becomes an ideal and an abstraction. It is justified either in terms of its effect on the public good: Well, the community couldn't continue to progress if the people weren't educated—or the way in which it enhances an individual's opportunities for self-actualization: Going to school helps you to decide what you are going to do with your life. The older subjects, in other words, display a kind of social-contract mentality while the younger subjects remain concrete and personalized. For the older subjects education is viewed as promoting life, liberty, and the pursuit of happiness. As far as the younger subjects are concerned, education serves no particular purpose or is simply a requirement for achieving occupational success.

On this particular item, the cross-national results are equally striking.[15]

Table 1. PERCENT OF RESPONDENTS SELECTING VARIOUS ARGUMENTS FOR EDUCATION LAWS, BY AGE AND NATIONALITY (Question 14)

	Age				Nationality		
	11	13	15	18	American	British	German
1. Unreflective: "You go to school to learn something."	44	38	28	21	26	20	42
2. Increase economic opportunities	33	39	32	17	26	42	18
3. Preparation for life: self actuali-zation	0	7	13	18	4	9	25
4. Benefit to com-munity: progress, survival, etc.	23	16	27	44	44	29	15
N	(54)	(89)	(84)	(88)	(89)	(85)	(84)

Age: $X = 38.08$ (9), $p = <.001$
Nationality: $X = 43.71$ (6), $p = <.001$

Inspection reveals that the justification for a positive right such as education differs considerably from country to country. Relatively unconcerned about possible benefits to the individual, the American subjects stress the impact of education on the community as a whole. The British subjects have a tendency to adopt a utilitarian stance, emphasizing the financial gains which are likely to accompany a good education. And the German subjects display an interesting split. A disproportionate number of them are unable to articulate any higher purpose whatsoever for schooling while a lesser, but still substantial number, point up the opportunities for self-actualization.

Negative Rights. The questions included under the heading negative rights yielded some equally interesting developmental and cross-national differences. Barry defines negative rights as: ". . . contrasted with interference, censorship, control, regulation, restriction, constraint, etc. Examples are freedom of speech, freedom of worship, freedom of travel, freedom to paint one's house any colour one chooses."[16] The following items of the interview were the two which touched upon this issue most directly:

Q. 29. After a great deal of discussion the people of the island developed a fairly complete system of principles and laws. At this point another issue arose. There were some who felt that certain laws, guaranteeing freedom of speech were so important that they should never be changed, and that it should be agreed that no future government would ever be able to change those laws. On the other hand, there were those who felt that as times change then laws must change and that there ought to be no laws which future governments could not change if they wanted to. What do you think of those arguments?

Q. 30. Could you give me some examples of the kinds of laws that should be permanent and unchangeable?

The response to the second of these two questions was especially illuminating. It is reported in table 2. Once again, taking up the developmental results first, the younger subjects displayed markedly little interest in safeguarding individual liberties. They exhibited two distinct tendencies. They were either preoccupied with relatively minor infractions, stating, for example, that ordinances like traffic laws ought to be permanent and unchangeable, or they displayed a kind of law and order orientation, declaring, for example, that the death penalty ought to prevail for all time. In sharp contrast, the older subjects tended to ignore misdemeanors and criminal statutes, advocating instead that the laws protecting freedom of speech, freedom of religion, and the like be unalterable. The younger subjects, in short, had no conception of negative rights. They apparently could not see the necessity of protecting civil liberties. A majority of the older subjects, on the other hand, declared their dedication to this principle.

In this instance, the cross-national differences were less striking than those shown in table 1, but they were, nevertheless, still in evidence. The American subjects proved to be the most concerned with safeguarding individual freedoms,

Table 2. PERCENT OF RESPONDENTS NAMING VARIOUS LAWS WHICH SHOULD BE PERMANENT, BY AGE AND NATIONALITY (Question 30)

	Age				Nationality		
	11	13	15	18	American	British	German
1. Misdemeanor: traffic laws, disturbance of peace	41	26	14	18	14	22	22
2. Criminal: murder, robbery	47	45	26	17	15	44	28
3. Individual freedom: freedom of speech, religion	12	29	60	65	71	34	50
N	(51)	(78)	(78)	(77)	(78)	(77)	(78)

Age: X^2 = 57.747 (6), p = <.001
Nationality: X^2 = 22.890 (4), p = <.001

the British most preoccupied with criminal penalties, and the Germans somewhere in between.

Conflicts over rights. There were also several items in the group analyzed which appeared to address themselves to the prima facie aspect of rights (either positive or negative). The subjects were presented with a number of situations in which the rights of the individual might be at variance with the rights of the community at large, where "personal freedom," so to speak, was pitted against "public good." Among these was the following question:

Q. 20. A law was suggested which required all children to be vaccinated against smallpox and polio. There was a religion which was opposed to vaccination. They said their religious beliefs disapproved of vaccination. What would you do in a case like that?

Of course in this case, the actual threat to the community would have been more apparent than real. If all the islanders *other* than the dissenting religious group were immunized, the only risk would have been to the dissenters themselves. Nonetheless, as the results in table 3 reveal, the younger children were considerably more likely to declare outright that the conscientious objectors ought to be coerced in some respect: forced to comply, exiled, or be segregated. The fifth and seventh graders who did not insist on compliance were more likely to advance a laissez-faire argument: Well, if they get sick they have only themselves to blame.—than to display a commitment to religious freedom. The older subjects, by contrast, were far more likely to articulate some political ideal in grappling with the dilemma which had been posed. Of those who did appeal to

Table 3. PERCENTAGE SELECTING VARIOUS RESPONSES TO QUESTION ABOUT
COMPULSORY VACCINATION, BY AGE AND NATIONALITY (Question 20)

	Age					Nationality		
	11	13	15	18		American	British	German
1. Coercion: conscientious objector group should be forced, exiled, or segregated.	38	30	27	14		14	25	31
2. Religious tolerance: conscientious objector group should be free to worship as it pleases.	4	23	23	31		44	21	11
3. Laissez-faire: conscientious objector group should be left to its fate.	31	23	17	11		9	27	15
4. Community welfare: conscientious objector group should be vaccinated for public welfare.	2	5	10	15		15	10	6
5. Persuasion: conscientious objector group should be reasoned with.	25	19	23	29		18	17	36
N	(56)	(78)	(86)	(81)		(81)	(84)	(80)

Age: $X^2 = 36.52$ (12), $p < .001$
Nationality: $X^2 = 46.49$ (8), $p < .001$

principle, most declared that the religious beliefs of the dissenters ought to be respected. However, a smaller proportion of the older subjects recommended that they be vaccinated anyway "for the good of the island." The important point is that, once again, whichever side of the argument they favored, the older subjects displayed much more comprehension of the issues at hand than the younger ones—and far more appreciation of certain political ideals.

The cross-national differences on this question were also consistent with the other data presented. Forced to choose between religious freedom, a negative right, and health, a positive right, a disproportionate number of Americans declared themselves to be civil libertarians, and a smaller, though still disproportionate number, came down on the side of public welfare. The British (as in the question on positive rights) exhibited a certain utilitarianism, unclouded by extraneous principle. They were more likely than either the Americans or the Germans to adopt a laissez-faire stance, stating rather matter-of-factly that, if the conscientious objectors chose to take the risk of becoming ill, it was entirely their own affair. And finally the Germans (again, as in the first example on positive rights) split into opposing camps, one side advocating the use of force, the other side eschewing force in favor of reason and persuasion.

DEVELOPMENTAL AND CROSS-NATIONAL PATTERNING

Only three of the items, out of a total of twenty on which the research was based have been presented here, but they exemplify the results which emerged.[17] It should be said that this presentation has exaggerated the cross-national differences to some extent. In general, whether the issue was positive rights, negative rights, or some conflict between the two, the age differences were more numerous and more striking. However, when a question *did* elicit significant cross-national differences, they tended to fall into the patterns which are evident in tables 1, 2, and 3.

Developmental patterns. Because they appeared more consistently, the developmental results can probably be summarized more readily. It is quite clear that younger children in the study under consideration have no real grasp of the concept of rights. For the most part they do not comprehend the purpose of supplying people with certain positive rights such as education and health or insuring them certain negative rights such as freedom of speech and freedom or worship. And when asked to resolve conflicts over rights, for instance, a religious group's right to religious freedom vs. the community's right to preserve health, they simplistically adopt one side or the other in the argument without being able to justify their positions. By contrast, the older subjects' responses seem to be characterized much more by what might be called an "appeal to principle." It is probable that very few, if any, are versed in political philosophy. Nonetheless, they appear to be much more aware than the younger subjects of certain ideals and much more attached to those ideals. They characterize the political system in terms of such concepts as individual freedom and public welfare. And when pressed to resolve an apparent conflict between the two, they weigh the merits of the case and come to a decision on that basis rather than by fiat. In short, what seems to develop during adolescence is an appreciation of the social contract. Just as each individual citizen is viewed as having certain inalienable rights, so is society as a whole, and there is also the recognition that some sort of balance ought to be maintained.

What distinguishes the political judgment of the older adolescent from that of the younger adolescent or preadolescent is chiefly the ability to differentiate. As has been noted, only with the older subject does one begin to see anything like a concept of rights. And it is also only with the older subject that one finds an appreciation for some of the complexities of the concept. The eighteen-year-old would be capable of understanding Benn and Peters' dictum that rights cannot exist *in vacuo,* that they derive their meaning from some sort of social relationship. For this is precisely what the older adolescent tends to refer to when arbitrating disputes over rights. As examples, consider the following responses to an item which pitted the negative rights of an individual property owner against the positive rights of the community at large. It is the item cited at the beginning of this paper concerning the farmer who refuses to move in order to accommodate a superhighway:

Well, if this man is directly in the way of the road and it is necessary that the road go through his land, I think that he should yield to the desires of the people. Yet if the government could build the road without having to go through his property, then I think that the government has an obligation to do it—to build the road and get a way that would be . . . that would bother its inhabitants least. [Eighteen-year-old boy]
Technically he was in the right. There are some things that people have to realize are kind of holding up production in a sense. Well I think our state road commissioners have faced this problem many a time whereas. . . . Well I could honestly see . . . I know we have quite a lot of families in Flint and when the new [route] 23 was going in there a lot of times the road was held up because the people didn't want to sell their land. . . . Well, some may be attached or something. I can really see this, but if you've been given a reasonable amount of money . . . I can see if it's something you really like, you don't want to get rid of it no matter how much money you get, but it's something that's a problem that comes up in life that has to be solved the best way known . . . [Eighteen-year-old boy]

These answers are essentially democratic in tone. They describe the individual as a member of a larger, more encompassing group, and they weigh his rights against those of the society as a whole. Although the two subjects reach somewhat different conclusions, each attempts to maintain a balanced perspective on the issue and arrive at a solution which will represent "the greatest good for the greatest number." Although it is unlikely that either of these adolescents could write a treatise on the subject of rights, the rhetoric—"the desires of the people," "obligation," "technically he was in the right," "if it is necessary," "a reasonable amount of money"—is basically that of the political philosopher.

In contrast, consider the responses of two younger subjects to the same question:

Well I think that he or they shouldn't be able to take him off his land because he didn't want to sell. I think they should make the road go around his land even though it would cost more money. [Thirteen-year-old boy]

Well I don't think he was selfish, because it's his land and he doesn't want to pack up and leave. He likes the spot he's living on and doesn't want to leave. [Thirteen-year-old boy]

Here there is no attempt to balance one set of interests against another nor to appeal to principle. These early adolescents appear limited to expressing their views without being able to support them. Perhaps most striking is the virtual absence of any larger social awareness. Eighteen-year-olds are capable of describing the interplay of societal forces with abstractions like the people, government, state road commission, and holding up production. But such conceptualizations are beyond the thirteen year old. He refers instead to an impersonal and monolithic "they."

And without this larger view, the early adolescent is incapable of true respect for human dignity or the basic tenets of democracy. No wonder, then, that he is unable to appreciate the long-range benefits of education, that he rides roughshod over the rights of a dissenting religious group, and is unconcerned about the legal guarantee of certain freedoms.

Characterizing the cross-national differences. The precise manner in which the social contract is defined appears to differ from country to country. Although adolescents from all three nations included in this study exhibit a tendency to become increasingly democratic with increasing age, there are, as noted, some interesting variations.

The Americans. In their attempts to characterize the relationship between individual and state, the American subjects are more likely than either of the other two groups to articulate a number of ideals. It is not difficult to recognize these as the same ideals which have long been identified with liberal democracy: the insistence on a certain standard of education "to insure progress," the requirement that certain individual freedoms be guaranteed by law, the explicit tolerance for differing religious faiths. In short, there is a strong "civil libertarian" flavor to the American responses. Thus, on the whole, it is the Americans who seem most imbued with the political philosophy of Locke and Mill. For example, they defend a positive freedom like education in the following terms:

Basically the purpose [of the education law] would be for every individual to have a sort of limited education. I feel this is a good law and as we do have it in the state of Michigan. Everyone would be subject to some sort of education in a school system. Education really never stops but a limited education is certainly necessary for the betterment of people in society. [Eighteen-year-old boy]

Well so they can get everyone in the U.S. who needs to know something of history and mathematics, and be able to read and write in order to get along, because I think our society is based on this. I mean you couldn't even read a street sign unless you had some education, and if you want to vote you have to know something about the way our government is run. [Eighteen-year-old girl]

And the defense of a "negative right" provokes the same sort of idealistic fervor. In response to the question of whether or not freedom of speech should be restricted during an emergency, a fifteen-year-old girl replies:

Well in time of war I think maybe those should be disregarded maybe, but not all of them like the dentist and stuff like that, but freedom of speech maybe, because not all the people agree with the government . . . because if they didn't have freedom of speech, then they shouldn't talk against the government and well . . . maybe someone on this island believes that the other people are right and I think they should make speeches and stuff like that maybe to . . . [Even against the government?] Yes.

And though he obviously feels some ambivalence about the whole matter, an eighteen-year-old boy upholds the rights of religious dissenters:

Another case in point is Jehovah's Witnesses which I believe don't allow transfusions and lots of times it happens and it's some little kid in the hospital and he needs transfusions to stay alive, they generally get a court order to force it. Somehow I think that's right because I think it's sort of ridiculous not to take blood, but that's their religious belief and that gets very touchy when you start involving church and state.

The British. British adolescents, by contrast, appear to be more pragmatic than idealistic. The contract between the individual and the state is basically a utilitarian business arrangement. The government is to satisfy the material wants of its citizens and otherwise leave them alone. It stipulates a certain minimum level of education "to make sure people get good jobs." Its permanent statutes are supposed to deter criminals who might threaten life and property. And other than that it ought to leave people to their own devices. If a dissenting religious group wants to oppose vaccination, let them. It will simply be their own fault if they fall ill. In sum, the British orientation toward the whole issue of rights is considerably more laissez-faire than that of either of the other two nationalities.

It is a cost-benefit analysis of relative utilities rather than an appeal to principle which determines whether a policy will be defended or opposed. Compulsory education is defended in the following terms by two fifteen year old British boys:

Well, then there wouldn't really be any people backward because they'd have a good education and most probably get a good job. They've no need to go against any laws that are made.

Well, a law like that would be needed like that because if, when the boys, you know, have grown into men, say, might want to leave the island. They might want to go out into the world to get some better job. Well, then they'd need their education to help get that job.

Similarly, a law which requires universal vaccination may be objectionable not because it infringes on the rights of the individual but simply because it is impractical to force the dissenters to comply:

That is a problem, isn't it? I don't think there would really be much you could do. You could try to persuade them that it was necessary, but if they didn't move, it would be difficult, really. You can't risk the chance of an epidemic caused by them. But if there was an epidemic and everyone else was vaccinated, only they could be affected. [Eighteen-year-old boy]
Well, if they refused, there's nothing really you could do about it. You couldn't force them to have it if they didn't want it. [Fifteen-year-old girl]

At times this inherent pragmatism shades off into a kind of cynicism. Perhaps because the British are more "materially minded" than either of the other two groups—and more aware of "what counts" in society—they are also inclined to be more bitter about status distinctions. In any case, while the following type of response was not necessarily common, it was a uniquely British phenomenon. In reply to the question of whether the subject would vote for a more qualified candidate whose beliefs did not coincide with his own or for a less qualified candidate who agreed with him, an eighteen-year-old boy answered:

You mean a chap with a degree and a nice accent and perhaps had better knowledge. It depends on what he is going to do, you see, you must qualify this. If the fellow for whom you are voting is probably a Cabinet Minister, and a likely choice for a Foreign Minister I should perhaps pick the better diplomat—if I knew that it was going to be somebody who could speak French or something. I think that the local parties see their candidates are tailored to what they need, and if it were merely an ordinary back-bencher then I don't think it would make this much difference, whether he had a degree in economics or something like this, because, even if he does have a degree in economics and he is a Conservative, it obviously hasn't done him much good.

The Germans The Germans, by comparison, are an intriguingly mixed group. At first glance, their version of the social contract strikes a somewhat authoritarian note. Judging from their response to the question on positive rights, a considerable proportion of them believe that the requirements of the state do not have to be justified. A person goes to school to learn something and for no other purpose. Nor are they particularly concerned about respecting the rights of a nonconforming religious sect. By fair means or foul, the vast majority of them wish to insure compliance. One might conclude, then, that the German subjects view the relationship between state and individual in much the same way as the relationship between parent and child, but this would be an over-simplification. When asked whether certain rights of the individual (employing Barry's terminology, certain "negative freedoms,") ought to be guaranteed by law, the Germans are less likely than the Americans, but more likely than the British, to reply in the affirmative. They are also more likely than either of the other two groups to defend compulsory education in terms of its less tangible benefits to the individual. So there is an element of authoritarian submission in the German responses, but it is not uniform.

However, one *can* say that in their version of the social contract, the Germans emphasize the importance of protection. The government exists not so much to insure certain freedoms nor to provide certain services but to take care of its citizens. To question the policies of such an agency is a breach of trust, an act of disobedience. Hence, when asked to give arguments *against* the compulsory education law, many German youngsters replied as follows:

I wouldn't know any objection to this law. There would be ones that I've said speak in favor in any case of such a law. In any case, I'm in favor of it. [Eighteen-year-old girl]

In any case they'd learn more if they went to school up to the age of sixteen. Today people go to school only up until the age of fourteen or fifteen: there are only reasons in favor of it. Why should there be reasons against it? I personally wouldn't have anything against it. [Eighteen-year-old boy]

The emphasis on obedience and protection is compelling—so much so that in a conflict between public welfare and personal freedom, the rights of the individual may be sacrificed. In response to the question on religious dissent, two German youngsters replied:

You should convince the people that it would be better for the children to be vaccinated. [If they couldn't be persuaded?] Well, if the law prescribes it then all the people on the island must certainly have themselves vaccinated, all the children and also those who don't believe that its good. You have to for them anyway. That just won't do, because then later maybe they'd catch smallpox and polio. [Fifteen-year-old girl]
Well, they have to go to another island, because it doesn't make any sense to have one part vaccinated and the other out of some Christian persuasion or whatever, be against it, so that they're not vaccinated and live on the same island. Then vaccination wouldn't have any purpose if—then all or if only half, than better none at all. The solution would probably be this: The one half who have themselves vaccinated stay on island A and the other go to island B. [Eighteen-year-old boy]

But there are various kinds of security. While the Germans are usually more interested in having the government provide them with a measure of physical comfort, they are not always so eager to write off civil liberties. Indeed, in addition to protection *by* the state, a surprisingly large number of these youngsters expressed the wish for protection *from* the state as well. The question as to whether laws guaranteeing freedom of speech should be permanent commonly drew this sort of response:

There are some laws that should not be allowed to change. Surely, as has been mentioned, freedom of speech, or freedom of the press and human rights. [Eighteen-year-old boy]

Well, I'd say the right to freedom, freedom of opinion, and also privacy of the mail, that nobody in his home can—how do you say that? I don't know any more at the moment (Conduct a search?) Yes. And freedom of religion. [Eighteen-year-old girl]

Laws for freedom of speech, in short, all laws that don't have anything to do with the times. [Fifteen-year-old boy]

For instance that each voting citizen can freely choose. Is that what you're talking about? [Yes.] That he could choose freely which party he wants to elect. And then he can live in his country, so that he's not thrown out. There are some, where people can be thrown out, where they can be exiled. [Fifteen-year-old girl]

So the German adolescents are a curious amalgam, not much inclined when specific conflicts arise to question the dictates of the state, but, at the same time, not altogether unaware of the possible abuses of power.

DISCUSSION

This empirical exploration of the concept of rights demonstrates, I believe, that there are some distinctive developmental and cross-national variations. However, the problem which remains is how to account for them. Why, one might ask, are the younger subjects oblivious to the larger social issues, comparatively unconcerned about either public welfare or individual freedom? And why are the Americans inclined to be libertarian, the British utilitarian, and the Germans a curious blend of authoritarian and idealistic?

Asking why the concept of rights develops as it does during adolescence is tantamount to asking why the intellect develops as it does during adolescence. Presumably, the evolution of political thought is similar to the evolution of thought in general. Very likely, then, the emergence of the concept of rights during adolescence is part and parcel of a larger developmental process. Unfortunately, it is easier to describe this process than to explain it. The possible influences on intelligence are myriad—prenatal environment, heredity, nutrition, upbringing, and education—to mention only a few, and who knows how they may all interact? The complexity of the problem very likely accounts for the fact that the most eminent scholar in the field, Piaget, has devoted more of his efforts to description than to causation. However, Piaget does provide us with some plausible clues about causation. First of all, he emphasizes the role that social interaction plays in shaping intellect. "It is only vis-à-vis others," he remarks, "that we are led to seek evidence for our statements. We always believe ourselves without further ado until we learn to consider the objections of others and to internalize such discussion in the form of reflection." He elaborates on this point: "At about the age of seven the child becomes capable of cooperation because he no longer confuses his own point of view with that of others. He is able both to dissociate his point of view from that of others and to coordinate these different points of view. This is apparent from conversations among children. True discussions are now possible in that the children show comprehension with respect to the other's point of view and a search for justification or proof with respect to their own statements. Explanations between children develop on the plane of thought and not just on the level of material action." Although he does not identify social interaction as the only influence on intelligence, Piaget obviously believes that the child's dealings with other people and his discovery that their own views do not always coincide with his compel him to become less egocentric and more logical. Indeed, logic itself "constitutes the system of relationships which permit the coordination of points of view corresponding to different individuals, as well as those which correspond to the successive percepts or intuitions of the same individual."[18]

The concept of rights is, of course, part of this more general system and hence presumably develops in much the same way as any other idea. In fact, since rights themselves represent a set of rules for regulating interpersonal conduct, the child's own social experiences very likely have an especially strong impact on the development of this concept.

In my initial encounter with the subject, I speculated on what some of these experiences might be and also attempted to explain why the concept of rights appears comparatively late in adolescence:

It is my contention that the older adolescent's view of rights as a kind of contract between individual and state is an outgrowth of his developing sense of identity. Erikson implies in the "Eight Ages of Man" that as the individual learns who he is and what he can do (identify), as he defines himself through his close relationships with others (intimacy), he becomes increasingly committed to enhancing the culture in which he lives (generativity). Of course, this leaves us with another "why," one for which there is no ready answer. Whether for purposes of survival or as a matter of custom, the culture expects individuals to assume adult responsibilities and to participate more directly in the community as they become older. As the adolescent approaches adulthood he experiences such pressures more acutely. He takes marriage and family-living courses in school, people ask him what he is going to do for a living, and his parents leave more and more decisions to his discretion.[19]

But along with the increase in one type of constraint, there is an increase in another type of freedom. Society expects the adult to share in its purposes and it also gives him the opportunity to do so. Society expects the adult to be autonomous and it also allows him to be so. I maintain that the adolescent owes his comprehension of the social contract to an analogous combination of pressure and opportunity. The expectation that he will choose an occupation makes him aware of a larger social reality. He will have to interact with people outside his immediate family or friendship groups. He will achieve a certain status in the community, being designated a doctor, factory worker, or plumber. At the same time, his opportunity to participate in the community will increase. He may own property. He may approve or vote down millage increases. He may write the mayor deploring the parking situation (or the President deploring the Vietnam War). The eighteen-year-old's actual participation in this larger social reality may be limited, but informally, he is in a better position to prosecute his rights. Unlike the eleven-year-old, his decisions are frequently not subject to parental approval and he may broaden his horizons by actually leaving home in search of education or employment. Hence, his appreciation of something like individual liberties is increased.

A concern with freedom in a more personal sense may, of course, exist well before the age of eighteen. While he has little awareness of the Bill of Rights, the eleven or thirteen-year-old may protest at times that he wants to make his own decisions. He may also complain about a "bossy" teacher. But his horizons are still too limited and his intellectual capacities too restricted for him to be preoccupied with rights in a more formal sense.

In this rather anecdotal account, however, I have neglected to consider the probable contributions of the educational system, an omission which should now be corrected. Beyond the age of six and generally into his middle or late teens, the child spends a sizable portion of his waking hours in school, and, consequently, it becomes the setting for much of his social interaction. Equally (and perhaps more) important, it is in school that he begins to become acquainted with the culture in which he resides, learning something about its history, customs, and traditions. He also receives, particularly if he experiences adolescence in a culture of liberal democracy, a formal introduction to politics—and hence to the concept of rights. This is especially true of the American educational system which makes courses in civics and American history a mandatory part of the high school curriculum.

A more recent study provides some indirect but compelling evidence that the American system performs its task of political socialization quite effectively.[20] The research is similar in format to the work I have reviewed here, except that the sample is drawn exclusively from the United States and includes black and white youngsters in one metropolitan and one suburban community. Although there are some regional and racial variations, they pale in significance compared to the vast number of age differences, differences which crop up on practically every item of the revised questionnaire. The pattern is much the same as the one which emerged in the initial study: a startling increase in political sophistication between the sixth and twelfth grades. The comparative absence of regional and racial differences suggests that the system has managed to wash out any very significant variations which might have existed by requiring its students to take the same core curriculum (that is, courses in civics and American history).

This brings us quite naturally back to my first venture, an exploration of the concept of rights, and provides us with a possible explanation for the cross-national differences. I suspect that the American, British, and German subjects expressed somewhat different views regarding rights because they were enrolled in three different school systems, each with its own distinct traditions and customs, each reflecting a different national heritage.

It is not unreasonable to assume that the American youngsters demonstrated a strong concern for individual liberties because they had received formal instruction to this effect. The Constitution, the Bill of Rights, the Declaration of Independence (with its life, liberty, and the pursuit of happiness)—these are the staples of any American government course. They are even present to some extent in the junior high school curriculum as part of the general social studies program. Indeed, the educational system in the United States probably owes its distinctive character to these very same documents. Since its inception, America has prided itself on being the land of freedom and equal opportunity. Consequently, it has attempted to develop a mass educational system which will furnish all of its citizens with a fair chance. (Unfortunately, it has proved impossible to deliver on this promise—which may help to explain why American schools have been so much maligned as of late.)

In any case, neither the British nor the German system makes such a pledge. Education in Britain is essentially elitist in character. Although they are provided with a certain minimum of schooling, students may drop out at the age of fourteen (two years earlier than in the American system), and the tracking system is such that the vast majority of them are not permitted to prepare themselves for a university. Consequently, only a tiny fraction of the college-age population actually enrolls in college (again in sharp contrast to the American system where almost three-quarters of all high school graduates receive at least some education beyond high school). And the few British youngsters who make it through the university, quite naturally, get the best jobs. To be sure, the British adolescents I studied were in a comprehensive school, an alternative to the traditionally rigid tracking system which has emerged rather recently. Nonetheless, they could not have been totally ignorant about the workings of that system.

Although it may be hazardous to extrapolate in such a manner, I wonder if this does not help to explain the cynicism which some of the British adolescents displayed and why they took a stance toward education which was more pragmatic than equalitarian. In terms of their own experience, they might well be expected to conclude as they do that the purpose of education was to secure "good jobs" rather than to "make sure that people would know how to run the government."

And finally, the British educational establishment, like its American counterpart, presumably reflects a particular set of national values. As Richard Rose has observed: "Implicitly, the English educational system transmits and emphasizes cultural norms concerning inequality. Inequality is presented as natural and often desirable. If the melting pot has been the symbol of American education, then the cream separator is appropriate for England. English governments have repeatedly held the belief that the great majority of the population is fit only for the most rudimentary sort of education."[21] In short, the British system is imbedded in a highly stratified society, one which, as a welfare state, provides basic services for its citizens but does not attempt to insure equality of opportunity. It should be noted that there is no equivalent of the American Constitution in Great Britain. The nation itself has enjoyed a long history of tolerance and personal freedom (Locke, after all, was an Englishman), but there is not the same emphasis on formal guarantees. Hence, adolescents brought up in such a society might well evince less concern for such guarantees than those schooled in the formalistic guarantees of the Bill of Rights.

A similar sort of explanation might be advanced to account for the German adolescent's stance regarding rights. Germany's recent political history has been characterized by abrupt shifts in government and upheaval—a deposed monarchy following World War I, a democratic but weak regime prior to Hitler, the fascist horrors of the Nazi era, a devastating second World War, and finally, a stable, strong democracy with socialist programs clearly in evidence. Within this historical context, the educational system has traditionally been authoritarian, and like its British counterpart, somewhat elitist. However, there is at present more interest in promoting equality of opportunity than in the British system. In Hamburg (where the German sample was obtained), adolescents must attend school, at least part-time, until they are eighteen. Although German universities are quite selective, they are not as restrictive as British universities, even though political restrictions have lately developed.

I suspect that the German youngsters in my study were aware—at least to some extent—of their nation's history, and it is reasonable to assume that they had also been lectured to in school about the importance of preserving civil liberties. (The girl who exclaimed that there were some countries "where people can be thrown out, where they can be exiled" provides some indirect support for this hypothesis.) However, they were both pupils in a system which stresses obedience, deference, and uniformity and future citizens of a nation which has tended to regard such qualities as virtues.[22] This may help to explain their intriguingly mixed approach to the concept of rights, the unquestioning acceptance of certain policies, the disregard for personal freedom in a concrete situation, and yet the surprisingly strong insistence on legal protection for individual freedoms.

These findings and their interpretation correspond to those of other investigators. In their study of five nations, including America, Britain, and Germany, Almond and Verba assert that democracies are characterized by two kinds of "political competence," citizen and subject. The competent citizen believes himself to be capable of influencing policy and decisions by writing his representatives, petitioning, demonstrating, and the like. "He participates by using explicit or implicit threats of some form of deprivation if the official does not comply with his demand. The role of competent subject is less active than that of competent citizen. The subject's competence stems from his awareness of his rights under the rules rather than his readiness to apply pressure. If he wishes to influence a government official, he appeals to those rules or to the official's good will.[23]

Some democracies, Almond and Verba note, have a strong tradition of citizen competence; others tend to emphasize subject competence. The differences that they observed in this respect among their American, British, and German adults parallel those which I discovered among teenagers of the same nationalities. Almond and Verba report that although their American respondents were somewhat low on subject competence (only 37% felt that they could expect polite treatment at the hands of government officials), two-thirds were satisfied with their participant role (they felt confident that they could exert influence on government officials). British respondents, on the other hand, exhibited a higher level of subject competence (50 percent) but a lower level of citizen competence (56 percent). And the Germans were much lower than the Americans on citizen competence (33 percent) but a little higher on subject competence (43 percent).

It is not unreasonable to assume that these differences—like the differences in my own study—reflect differences in political culture, tradition, and history. Whether or not all Americans care to exercise their rights (the percentage turnout in national elections has led to complaints of voter apathy), the ethic of participation has long been strong in the United States—and so has the fear of government interference. The British and the Germans, particularly the British, have had more experience as loyal and satisfied subjects. This may perhaps explain their seemingly greater tolerance for government intervention. As Edward Banfield puts it in contrasting the difference between the American and British approach to politics: "The British still believe that the government should govern. And we still believe that everyone has a right to 'get in the act' and make his influence felt.[24] In any case, both England and Germany have adopted social welfare policies which would be denounced as socialism or communism in the United States.

In addition, Almond and Verba reinforce my conclusion that the educational systems in all three countries enhance whatever differences there are in political tradition and efficacy. They asked their subjects, for instance, whether they remembered being free to participate in discussions at school. An impressive 55 percent of the Americans reported that they had been afforded this opportunity; 68 percent of the British and Germans replied that they had *not*.[25]

I should emphasize that, interesting as are the cross-cultural differences apparent in my study, the developmental differences appeared, on the whole, to be more impressive. In all three national groups, despite the variations noted, a similar orientation to the concept of rights emerged with increasing age. Although this trend was most marked for the American sample, older subjects from all three countries demonstrated far more understanding of the concept and commitment to the ideal than younger subjects.

Nor is it surprising to discover that children in three Western democracies come to resemble each other in their regard for human rights. Whatever their differences, these three nations share, at least in recent history, a common political philosophy. The underlying theory of liberal democracy rests upon certain assumptions about the proper relationship between the individual and the state. This theory stipulates that rulers serve the ruled and that the government is obligated to furnish certain basic services for its citizens and grant them a set of inalienable rights. Although the actual systems differ considerably, Germany, England, and America all insist that their citizens receive a certain minimum of instruction, and all three prohibit interference with individual prerogatives such as freedom of speech by law. (In England the guarantee of such freedoms is less formal, but it is firm nonetheless.)

To sum up, the institutions and customs of these three western nations, whatever their differences in social structure, reflect a fundamental respect for human dignity. My work provides evidence, I think, that such respect is gradually inculcated in their young as well.

NOTES

1. For the comparative research most directly related to this essay, see J. Adelson and L. Beall, "Adolescent Perspectives on Law and Government," *Law and Society Review* 11 (1970):495–504; J. Gallatin and J. Adelson, "Individual Rights and the Public Good," *Comparative Political Studies* 3 (1970):226–42; J. Gallatin and J. Adelson, "Legal Guarantees of Individual Freedom," *Journal of Social Issues* 27 (1971):93–108; and J. Adelson, "The Political Imagination of the Young Adolescent," in *Twelve to Sixteen: Early Adolescence,* ed. Jerome Kagan and Robert Coles (New York: W. W. Norton, 1971). For research similar in format, see Fred Greenstein and Sidney G. Tarrow, *Political Orientations of Children: The Use of a Semi-Projective Technique in Three Nations,* Professional Papers in Comparative Politics, no. 01-009 vol. 1 (Beverly Hills: Sage Publications, 1970). There is also a considerable body of comparative research in the related area of moral development. These studies are summarized in: L. Kohlberg, "Development of Moral Character and Moral Ideology," in *Review of Child Development Research,* vol. 1, eds. Martin L. Hoffman and

Lois Wladis Hoffman (New York: Russell Sage Foundation, 1964) pp. 383–431. See also, L. Kohlberg, "The Adolescent as Philosopher," in Kagan and Coles *Twelve to Sixteen.* J. Tapp and L. Kohlberg, "Developing Senses of Law and Legal Justice," *Journal of Social Issues* 27 (1971):65–92. On problems of measurement, see A. K. Korman, "Disguised Measures of Civil Rights Attitudes," *Journal of Applied Psychology* 59 (April 1974):239–40. On problems of philosophy, see A. J. M. Milne, "Philosophy and Political Action: the Case of Civil Rights," *Political Studies* 21 (December 1973) 453–66. And finally, although he has not carried out any comparative studies, the Australian political scientist, Robert Connell provides a valuable critique of this type of work in a forthcoming publication: Robert W. Connell and M. Goot, "Science and Ideology in American 'Political Socialization' Research," (n.p.). See also, Fred I. Greenstein, "The Benevolent Leader Revisited: Children's Images of Political Leaders in Three Democracies," *American Political Science Review* 69 (1975): 1371–98.

2. Jean Piaget, *Six Psychological Studies* (New York: Vintage Books, 1967); David Easton and Robert D. Hess, "The Child's Political World," *Midwest Journal of Political Science* 6 (1962):pp. 229–42; Robert D. Hess and Judith V. Torney, *The Development of Political Attitudes in Children* (Chicago: Aldine, 1967).

3. Herbert Hyman, *Political Socialization: A Study in the Psychology of Political Behavior* (Glencoe, Illinois: The Free Press, 1959), pp. 18–19.

4. Robert Lane, *Political Thinking and Consciousness: The Private Life of the Political Mind* (Chicago: Markham, 1969), and idem., *Political Ideology* (Glencoe: The Free Press, 1962); Jeanne N. Knutson, *The Human Basis of Polity* (New York: Aldine, 1972).

5. Gabriel Almond and Sidney Verba, *The Civic Culture* (Boston: Little, Brown, 1963).

6. Patrice Gélard, "Droit comparé et psychologie des peuples," *Revue de Psychologie des Peuples* 25 (1970):pp. 18–45.

7. Gallatin and Adelson, "Individual Rights;" Gallatin and Adelson, "Legal Guarantees of Individual Freedom."

8. Despite determined attempts to control for social class, the British sample contained a disproportionate number of lower-class adolescents. However, since there were few statistically significant differences which could be attributed to social class, this did not turn out to be a serious problem.

9. The American subjects were drawn from a more-or-less typical midwestern high school. The German subjects resided in Hamburg where they were required to attend school at least part-time up to the age of eighteen. And the British youngsters were all enrolled in comprehensive schools which permit their pupils to continue up to the age of seventeen or eighteen.

10. I would like to acknowledge the very significant contribution which the late Arnold Kaufman made to my own thinking about the concept of rights.

11. Stanley I. Benn and Richard S. Peters, *The Principles of Political Thought* (New York: The Free Press, 1959), p. 111.

12. Brian Barry, *Political Argument* (New York: Humanities Press, 1965); and idem., *The Liberal Theory of Justice* (Oxford at the Clarendon Press, 1973). See also, Benn and Peters, *Political Thought.*

13. Erich Fromm, *Escape from Freedom* (New York: Rinehart and Winston, 1941).

14. In the set of questions analyzed, there were three age comparisons significant at the .05 level and sixteen age comparisons significant at the .01 level or below. For the cross-national differences, the corresponding figures were five significant at the .05 level and nine significant at the .01 level or below. Interestingly enough, there was only a handful of social class, intelligence, and sex differences.

15. It ought to be borne in mind that this was not usually the case. For most of the items I analyzed, the age differences were more marked than the cross-national differences.

16. Barry, *Political Argument,* p. 141.

17. Gallatin and Adelson, "Individual Rights."

18. Piaget, *Psychological Studies,* pp. 29, 39, and 41.

19. Judith Gallatin, "The Development of the Concept of Rights in Adolescence," doctoral dissertation, University of Michigan, 1967. Cf. Erik H. Erikson, *Childhood and Society* (New York: W. W. Norton, 1950), pp. 247–74.

20. Judith Gallatin, "The Development of Political Thinking in Urban Adolescence," National Institute of Education (Grant 0-0554), 1972.

21. Richard Rose, *Politics in England* (Boston: Little, Brown, 1964), p. 85.

22. Koppel S. Pinson, *Modern Germany: History and Civilization,* 2d. ed. (New York: Macmillan, 1966); David Rodnick, *Postwar Germans* (New Haven: Yale University Press, 1948).

23. Almond and Verba, *Civic Culture,* pp. 214–229.

24. Edward Banfield, "The Political Implications of Metropolitan Growth," *Daedalus* 90 (1960):pp. 61–78, at p. 67.

25. Almond and Verba, *Civil Culture,* pp. 115–27.

Chapter 13 SOCIAL SCIENCE RESEARCH ON SUPPORT OF HUMAN RIGHTS

William B. Devall

What kinds of people express support for civil liberties and human rights and what kinds of people oppose them? Why do some people give verbal support to the abstract principle of civil liberties for everyone and, at the same time, advocate destroying the rights of their fellow citizens? What structural factors in a nation or community encourage and sustain civil liberties and human rights? A growing body of studies conducted in North America, in some western European countries, and elsewhere has explored these questions. Research results are discussed in this chapter, and a model is developed in an attempt to explain the social bases of support for human rights.

In this review essay, the behavioral approach to social research is emphasized. David Danelski summarizes the use of a behavioral approach to human rights:[1]

One of the more fruitful aspects of a behavioral conception of human rights is that it can be used in scientific research. Each of the component behaviors of human rights can be specified empirically, and survey-research methods can be used for that purpose. World wide inventories of man's perceptions of man, of his acknowledgements of the kind of treatment man is entitled to as man, and of rights in action would be a beginning. A comparative study of man's differing acknowledgements would be as revealing as would a comparison of acknowledgements and rights in action. With such data, men's perceptions of other men could be explored more fully and profoundly than they have ever been before, and hypotheses concerning man's failure to perceive some of his fellow men as fully human could be tested. The whole acknowledgement process could be explored in terms of learning theory and other psychological theories. And finally hypotheses could be tested concerning the conditions under which they do not. These cursory comments about possible research paths in regard to the study of human rights are at best suggestive. The only point being made here is that once human rights are defined in terms of observable behavior, such research can be carried on.

In this essay, only the behavioral approach to civil liberties is considered, but it is recognized that the sociology of civil liberties and the political philosophy of civil liberties are, in the words of W.G. Runciman, "inextricably linked."[2] Behaviorism predicts the probable outcome of actions, but it does not tell us which actions to take. It is important to ask how men *do* behave, as well as how they *ought* to behave.

There is much documentary literature on the legal basis of human rights,[3] on the historical development of civil liberties and human rights in specific countries,[4] on specific court decisions,[5] on the role of the United Nations in the area of human rights,[6] and on the relationship of political philosophy and human rights.[7] There is less information on organizations (other than courts) which may protect or impede the protection of specific human rights.[8]

PROBLEMS OF SURVEY RESEARCH

There are very few international comparative studies of attitudes and opinions in the field of human rights that cover various population segments (that is, social classes, religious groups). There is also a lack of consensus among social scientists as to what methodological approach should be taken in comparative research.[9] Gabriel Almond and Sidney Verba's study of the political cultures of five nations is widely viewed as a model of comparative analysis using survey research techniques.[10] Almond and Verba sampled households in the United States, Mexico, Italy, Germany, and Great Britain. Employing the concept of "political culture," they inquired into the political orientation of citizens of these five nations. Their research is developed in terms of (1) cognitive orientation, or the "knowledge of and belief about the political system, its roles and incumbents of these roles, its inputs and its outputs"; (2) affective orientation, or "feelings about the political system, its roles, personnel, and performance"; and (3) evaluational orientation, or "the judgments and opinions about political objects that typically involve the combination of value standards and criteria with information and feelings."[11]

Almond and Verba apply the methods of systematic survey research to the study of comparative politics, and they acknowledge the influence of voting studies on their procedures.[12] They note the great expense, labor, advance planning, coordination, and substantial risks involved in cross-national surveys and, at the same time list several of their advantages. First, "a direct look at political attitudes . . . is useful in order to validate the inferences we have made about them from other material, and to develop independent measures that can be used to explain other phenomena."[13] A second advantage is that quantitative meaning can be given to typically vague analytical terms such as "characteristic" of country A or the "usual" attitude of workers in country B. Comparative analysis of answers to the same question can show variations within and between nations. Third, for the comparative analysis of political behavior, the use of crossnational surveys seems quite apt, because "the statistical methods by which one analyses the results of survey research are essentially comparative."[14] A fourth advantage of cross-national surveys is that one must undertake "a very important task for comparative analysis: the development of a means of conceptualizing politics in ways that have wide applicability."[15]

The scarcity of effective comparative opinion research is understandable in view of the large costs invoived. Thus, when crossnational surveys or, in particular, panel surveys, are too expensive or difficult, the researcher may utilize polls conducted for different purposes based on different types of samples in several countries. This is the approach of Seymour Martin Lipset in his analysis of "working class authoritarianism," which utilizes a secondary analysis of opinion data from several western European countries, and from Mexico, Japan, and the United States.[16]

Pursuit of comparative research may involve not only financial cost but also some political risk. Some regimes, such as those in Spain and the Soviet Union, forbid social research which may reveal dissatisfaction or revisionist attitudes among their citizens. Both crossnational surveys and comparative analyses of polls taken in different countries are few in number. Research interest in civil liberties or human rights is a reflection of preoccupations or restraints on social scientists during certain periods in the history of a given country. In the United States, for example, some social scientists during the 1950s felt personally threatened by the attack of government agents on their civil rights.[17] Still, important research on civil liberties was undertaken at that time.

Survey research faces other practical obstacles. It may prove abortive as the investigator comes to appreciate the effect of political culture on his own research design. For example, political controversy, which in the United States may be phrased in terms of battles over human rights, may be phrased in other countries in terms of class warfare, class rivalry, or some other referrent.[18] Absence of research models further explains the scarcity of cumulative research on support for civil liberties.[19] Among the social surveys utilizing nationwide samples concerning attitudes toward civil liberties, Samuel Stouffer's *Communism, Conformity, and Civil Liberties* is preeminent in the literature.[20] In the spring of 1954, over six thousand respondents were polled by two of the foremost public opinion research organizations in the United States. Topics covered in this survey included: What are the attitudes of civic leaders as compared with the rank and file within a community? Do attitudes towards civil liberties differ in different regions of the country? When urban areas are compared with rural areas? Among men as compared with women? What role does religion play? How important are agencies of mass communications? What can be accomplished by responsible citizens in their local communities?[21] This survey pioneered the effective use of so called "free answer" or "open-ended" questions, in which the respondent answers questions in his own words rather than in terms of a precoded set of responses. Furthermore, a series of questions is asked rather than relying on a single question to summarize a given opinion. Stouffer tied his research to previous surveys on the subject and many later researchers profitably followed his example of pursuing cumulative research strategies.[22]

PROBLEMS OF CONCEPTUALIZING HUMAN RIGHTS

Attempts to provide nominal and operational definitions of *rights* and *freedoms* have a long history.[23] The doctrine of "natural rights" or "the rights of man" was codified in writings of eighteenth century philosophers. The documents of the American Revolution, including the Declaration of Independence and the Bill of Rights, along with the French Declaration of the Rights of Man of 1789, are of particular importance in the history of human rights, for they stated in formal terms the universal conception of *rights*—that *all* men have rights vis-à-vis the government of a state.[24] It remains to be seen whether the United Nations Universal Declaration of Human Rights of 1948 will be equally important in the development of the concepts of human rights.

Recently, there has been expansion of the scope of topics considered under the heading of human rights. In an anthology honoring the fiftieth anniversary of the American Civil Liberties Union, separate chapters are devoted to a long list of rights never explicitly mentioned in eighteenth century documents. They include equal educational opportunity, equal employment, housing, welfare, legal services, suffrage, participation in politics, protest, free association, publishing, access to mass media, property, religious liberty, control of the use of one's body, and travel.[25] This list is by no means complete, however, especially for industrialized countries with democratic forms of government. For example, the right to decent environmental quality and the right to privacy are omitted, yet court cases and legislation designed to protect these rights are rapidly developing, at least in the United States and Canada.

Even when identified and guaranteed by laws, constitutions, or creeds, and reaffirmed by court decisions in test cases, rights (which often conflict with one another) are difficult to define in actual practice and more difficult to implement.[26] The articulation of human rights on a worldwide basis has barely begun. The 1948 United Nations declaration is not universally accepted by member nations as a program of rights, and even those rights upon which there is wide constitutional consensus are not universally implemented.

For systematic comparative analysis, a careful conceptualization of rights needs to be undertaken. Consistent with usage throughout this volume, the distinction is between *civil liberties, civil rights,* and *human rights. Civil liberties* refers to rights of persons vis-à-vis government. These include freedom of speech, freedom of association and assembly, freedom of religion, rights of conscience, and rights to due process under law. *Civil rights* in the United States is identified with the struggles of blacks and other ethnic minorities for equal participation in the political and social life of the country. In early writings (before 1960) and in some comparative work, civil liberties and civil rights are used interchangeably. *Human rights* refers broadly to civil rights and to civil liberties, but also to a wide range of emerging rights that include housing, jobs, and health services.

Conceptual definition has its corollary in the area of *operational definition.*

Various social researchers have used a wide variety of operational definitions and different indices or scales, to define the abstract concepts of human rights. [27] Gerhard Lenski in his 1961 survey of Detroit, Michigan, used four questions concerning freedom of speech as part of a long interview.[28] Lenski also asked respondents whether they felt the government should make laws forbidding gambling, or moderate drinking, birth control, and Sunday business. In 1954, Samuel Stouffer relied on open-ended questions to summarize given opinions. Stouffer combined the answers to obtain scales of attitudes towards civil liberties.[29]

Much of the research conducted in the United States has focused on the subject of support for the principles of the American Bill of Rights. Historical analysis of advocacy for the first ten amendments to the Constitution has shown some relation between social class in America in the postrevolutionary era and desire for strong or limited government, depending upon the perceived self-interest of different social classes.[30] There has been some discussion of whether attitudes upholding the principles of the Bill of Rights have ever been held by a majority of American citizens and whether or not such support has been declining since the 1930s. A 1970 television presentation, reported the results of a national sample survey commissioned by CBS news was entitled "Would It [the Bill of Rights] Pass Today?" In this survey of 1,136 randomly selected American adults, a number of findings seemed startling. For example, 76 percent believed that protest demonstrations should not be allowed.[31]

In 1957, in a study of students at the University of California at Berkeley, Hanan Selvin and Warren Hagstrom constructed a unidimensional scale embodying principles derived from the American Bill of Rights. In their words:

It is easy enough to support liberty as an abstract idea or even a set of specific privileges such as are embodied in the Bill of Rights. But this support may be meaningless if it disappears whenever the values of individual liberty come into conflict with other values, as they inevitably do. We therefore measured students' support for the Bill of Rights by a series of fifteen statements, each embodying an implicit conflict of values.[32]

Selvin and Hagstrom point out the methodological problems involved in their approach:

The libertarianism index is admittedly crude. For one thing, it attributed equal importance to all fifteen questions, where a more refined analysis would be able to take into account the varying importance of the items. And, unlike the cumulative scales now coming into wide use, knowing how many questions a person answers in a libertarian way does not identify the particular questions involved; for example a score of 14 could be acquired in fifteen different ways. A very low score is even more ambiguous, for we have counted "don't know enough about it to decide" as equivalent to an anti-libertarian response. . . . Finally this index is not unidimensional. The fifteen items may be considered as manifestations of several more basic concepts, much as questions on an intelligence test yield scores on different mental abilities.[33]

Social science methodologists warn that problems such as those noted above are compounded by the perils of comparative research.[34] Important variables to consider in comparative cross-national surveys are: (1) phrasing of the question and comparability of phrases in different languages; (2) the milieu in which the questions are asked (for example, a repressive versus an open society); and (3) the number and complexity of questions asked. The point that Almond and Verba make should also be reemphasized: opinions are formed and behavior occurs within the context of a political culture. Cross-national comparison of attitudes has meaning only if the social scientist conceptualizes his study within an international framework.

Moreover, the international framework must include a time orientation. Most of the surveys cited are admittedly time-bound as well as culture-bound. They are conducted at a specific time and place, and any attempt to use the data in a developmental model is fraught with methodological difficulties.[35] The studies reflect the controversies of the period in which the data were collected, as well as the cultural biases of the respondents at a particular time. In America, for example, there was at certain periods an almost paranoid concern with the threat of communism; in the 1950s, Americans were most unwilling to guarantee freedom of speech, assembly, due process, or the right to publish, to anyone labeled "communist" or "Communist sympathizer."[36] Frede Castberg describes similar problems in France and Germany.[37] In both of these countries, heated debates occurred and bills were introduced in the legislatures to exclude the Communist Party, as an enemy of freedom, from the constitutional protection of free speech and freedom of association.

Polls reflect a climate of opinion, but long-term trends are rarely tapped by national polls, and research on cross-cultural trends has barely begun. Because polling was developed as a methodology in the United States in the 1930s, some studies of trends do exist. Herbert Hyman and Paul Sheatsley find that in America, beginning in 1937, when the first Gallup polls were conducted, and through World War II and the Cold War until about 1950, support for restrictions on freedom of speech, assembly, and academic freedom was increasing.[38] In a review of polls concerning freedom of the press, Hazel Erskine finds tentative evidence that few Americans would accord complete freedom of speech to political extremists, and that permissiveness towards radicals has been decreasing in the United States since the 1930s.[39] Comparative studies of support for human rights cannot ignore the bias which was created by feelings and beliefs during certain historical periods.

A further pitfall of survey research is the assumption that all opinions of all persons are equal to one another.[40] The intensity with which a person holds a belief or opinion and the clarity with which persons perceive issues vary greatly.

Education and other social factors, along with individual intelligence and personal life experiences, mold opinion. When both citizen A and citizen B say that they oppose granting voting rights to eighteen-year-olds, A may express stronger ideological opposition than B. Of course, A and B may also vary greatly in their ability to act upon their beliefs. That is why a comparison of community leaders and followers is important. Community leaders have more power and resources to implement human rights than do followers; at the same time they will be somewhat sensitive to their opinions.

There is also considerable controversy over the relation between attitudes and behavior. It would be naive to assume there is always a one-to-one correlation between opinions and behavior in a real situation. It is difficult, however, to discern the effects of attitudes, opinions, and situational factors on behavior.[41] Whereas it is frequently said that changing attitudes lead to changing behavior, the reverse may also be true. Thomas Pettigrew makes the point that changing behavior which leads to changing attitudes may be, in fact, more common. He writes: "After the fact, individuals modify their ideas to fit their new act, often proving amazingly adaptable in doing so. Indeed, considerable research suggests that this behavior-to-attitude cycle of change is generally easier and more effective than the attitude-to-behavior cycle."[42] Too much reliance must not be placed on cross-sectional studies in attempting to understand the development of attitudes towards human rights. There is, for example, a great deficiency of panel or other longitudinal studies which employ the same sample of people to see how or whether or not opinions change over time. In nearly all the cross-sectional surveys, persons over fifty years of age are much less tolerant of political deviants than are people under thirty. What is the effect of aging on political opinions when aging is separated from the effects of education, religion, and social class? Do generations share similar experiences which mold attitudes, although they develop different attitudes towards human rights? These are the types of intriguing questions about which there is as yet little information. Clearly, where the topic of survey research is complex, the methodology is correspondingly complicated.

Cross-national research on human rights is also made complex by the historical dimension of time. An historicist might argue that the unique rights developed in each separate nation defy efforts to generalize about historical processes among nations.[43] But people do make decisions under certain historical circumstances, and it is possible to identify factors which are conducive to the development of human rights. People are not robots in history, but neither are they free from the influences of history and circumstances. Lipset, in analyzing the development and maintenance of two-party democracy in labor unions, discusses factors which resulted in a "favorable throw of the die," making it more likely that in the future a two-party system would be maintained.[44]

In summary, researchers who study support for the principles of human rights must deal with a number of complex, interacting variables. They include: (1) changing definitions of human rights and shifting priorities of rights during different periods in history; (2) the relation between attitudes verbally expressed by individuals and their actual behavior in specific social situations; (3) the reliability and validity of scales and indices of attitudes used in cross-national surveys; and (4) the specific historical conditions affecting such research factors as the possible fear of respondents in answering questions.

CORRELATES WITH SUPPORT FOR HUMAN RIGHTS

What favorable throw of the die sustains human rights in the different nations? What are the findings of survey research in America, Canada, and western Europe? Table 1 summarizes the most frequently mentioned variables which have a relationship to support for human rights. These are the effects of social class, education, leadership, religion, and personality. In the discussion, the relationships of these variables to support in different segments of the population, in the same country over a period of time, are compared. Cross-national comparisons also are made.

Economic roles and human rights support. High socioeconomic status is generally associated with a high degree of support for human rights. The converse is true for lower socioeconomic strata.[45] Lenski, writing about his Detroit survey, speaks for the body of this research: "The working class was less willing than the middle class to concede the right to criticize presidential action, attack religion, and speak in favor of Fascism and Communism. Similarly with respect to the issue of school integration, one finds a higher percentage of segregationists among the working class."[46]

Table 1. SUMMARY OF VARIABLES CORRELATED WITH SUPPORT FOR HUMAN RIGHTS

More Support	Less Support
College education	High school or less
Among college students	
Social science	Education majors
Humanities	Business
	Physical education
	Vocational studies
Jews	"Conservative" Catholics
White protestants	Black protestants
"Moderate" protestant churches	"Conservative" protestant churches
High socioeconomic classes	Low socioeconomic classes
Urban residence	Rural residence
Lower personal anxiety	Higher personal anxiety
Lower status anxiety	Higher status anxiety
Liberal personality	Authoritarian personality

In Robert Lane's study of the political ideology of the "common man," based on extensive and intensive interviews with a small sample of blue collar workers in America, two themes are documented on the respondent's conception of human rights, a fear of freedom and a "constricted attention."[47] With limited education and limited sophistication, blue collar workers restrict their interests to family, union, and sometimes the local community. This constricted attention, as a mode of adaptation, may also be common to western Europe, even though electronic media can increase many times the opportunities of this generation of workers over other generations with respect to new experiences, people, and ideas.

Lewis Feuer, an academic philosopher, expresses this theory of the antidemocratic nature of the lower classes in his introduction to the writings of Marx and Engels: "the masses have been the most consistently antiintellectual force in society."[48] But Lipset, more completely than other writers, expounds on the relations between working-class status and low support for civil liberties.[49] In his hypothesis about "working-class authoritarianism" he uses occupation as the primary index of social class. Lipset concludes, on the basis of his analysis of public opinion surveys in thirteen countries, that members of the lower class are less likely than those of higher class to support universalistic conceptions of civil liberties because of their *social condition.* That is, lower-class citizens are less likely to have college education, less likely than higher classes to participate in formal organizations, and take less interest in politics than do the middle classes.[50] Lipset argues, moreover, that the same conditions are associated with middle-class authoritarianism.[51] Is the liberalism of higher classes simply attributable to the likelihood that they have more years of education? This question is discussed elsewhere in this essay.

In a study conducted in Cuba in 1962, a year after the Bay of Pigs invasion and three years after the Cuban revolutionary regime came to power, Maurice Zeitlin tested the Lipset thesis that lower classes give little support to civil liberties.[52] He interviewed 210 workers in 21 industrial plants, and asked the workers: "What do you think should be done to an individual who publicly criticizes the government or the revolution?"[53] Although there were confounding variables (for instance, the revolutionary background), Zeitlin found that the revolutionary workers with the least education are the least likely to be "libertarian." Those with comparatively more education (some high school education, or better) were more likely to support civil liberties and were more interested in politics.[54]

Education and human rights support. Zeitlin's finding that support for civil liberties correlates with number of years of education has been supported by other studies. Surveys conducted in the United States after World War II indicate that people with college educations are much more likely to give verbal support to civil rights for minorities and political dissidents than are citizens with less than a college education.[55] This is true even with age and religion held constant.

Stouffer finds that older persons with college educations are less tolerant of nonconformists than are younger persons with college educations; but in all age brackets, college educated persons are more tolerant than those with less than a college education. Younger college-educated people of both black and white races are more likely than other respondents to support student protest in America, including civil rights protests and protests against objectionable foreign policy.[56]

These findings, which relate support for civil liberties and college education, have stimulated research on the attitudes and opinions of college students in America, Canada, and Britain towards various civil liberties.[57] Studies in Canada and the United States indicate that the longer students are in college, the more homogeneous are their opinions and the more likely they are to give verbal support to the principles of freedom of speech, assembly, religion, life style, and equal opportunity for minorities. The more secular the students, that is, the less church attendance and less affirmation of religious beliefs, the more likely they are to give verbal support to civil liberties. Students in the social sciences and humanities are more likely to score high on civil liberties scales than are students in business, education, or other professional schools. Men are more likely to give libertarian responses than women. There is some indication that the proportion of American college students giving "high libertarian" responses to principles of the Bill of Rights has remained constant over the last quarter of a century. Clyde Nunn, in a survey of University of Nebraska students in 1972, found almost identical proportions to those in Selvin and Hagstrom's study at Berkeley fifteen years earlier.[58]

Richard Flacks, in a study of American college political activists in the 1960s, concluded that many who demonstrated for civil rights for blacks and other minorities tended to come from more affluent homes, placed greater emphasis on involvement in intellectual and esthetic pursuits, and had more humanitarian considerations than did nonpolitical activists. The students whom Flacks interviewed tended to deemphasize conventional morality, religiosity, and personal achievement.[59]

These findings should not be applied to university students in different historical periods, or in different countries, unless a careful examination is made of the relationship between universities and other social institutions in the country being studied. Valid comparative studies of civil rights orientations and the behavior of college students are rare. Several anthologies of student politics have been published, but they do not include any attempt at comparative empirical research.[60]

In his introductory essay in an issue of *Daedalus* on the subject of politics, Lipset points out analytical problems associated with the effort to move beyond the case study approach.[61] Student politics are affected significantly by the social position and political values of the intellectual community. The position of English intellectuals vis-à-vis power differs notably from that of French or

American intellectuals. English intellectuals are included in effective political life, but French intellectuals are not. In the United States, intellectuals rank as experts, but there is no community of intellectuals such as in Great Britain. The nonexpert American intellectual may be compared with the French intellectual, who lacks pragmatic power, whereas the American academic expert compares favorably with the English intellectual in terms of status and his tendency to identify with the political decision maker.

Lipset comments upon statistically significant relationships between one country and another: "Disciples tend to be identified with student activism and leftist ideas in some countries, but not in others."[62] In another relevant qualification of research data, he notes that "there are even fewer reliable data concerning the attitudes of the adults of the intellectual classes than concerning students."[63]

Feuer, in an analysis of student movements between 1817 and 1962, ranging from Germany to Berkeley, California, implies that when college students take up the cry of civil liberties and freedom, they may be expressing a "conflict of generations." The struggle between generations, he argues, is little understood and little studied. Feuer argues further, that student movements show romantic idealism, intellectual elitism, alienation, and a "back-to-the-people" spirit. "Love of nation and mankind" and hatred of existing institutions are really an expression of revolution against fathers.[64] In conservative and backward countries, using Feuer's rationale, student revolts would be expressed in terms of freedom and civil liberties; but in liberal countries, student movements are just as likely to be fascist as liberal.

It should not be concluded that college students, per se, are always more liberal on civil liberties and human rights than other segments of the population. During the 1950s in the United States, one study finds that an average of 41 percent of college students surveyed agreed with the statement, "It's unwise to give people with dangerous social and economic viewpoints a chance to be elected." An average of 35 percent agreed that "steps should be taken right away to outlaw The Communist Party."[65]

Franklin Henry, using data from Canadian university students, develops the hypothesis that faculty and academically-inclined students are likely to sympathize with new social and political ideas, because of their "positive orientation to research and new ideas generally."[66] It is in their self-interest to support civil liberties, or at least freedom of speech and assembly, because they value new ideas and association with other scholars across national boundaries. New students exposed to these academic values as well as to the liberal disciplines tend toward learning and opinion change. Moreover, Henry observes that students in the social sciences and humanities are more likely to be made aware of the social and political opinions of faculty members than those in other fields such as the natural sciences.

Gertrude Selznick argues that if education inculcates a "sophisticated cognitive structure," graduates are likely to share democratic values. This is not the case if education relies on conformity, conventionalism, and "primitive cognitive structure."[67]

One important question, particularly for so called third world countries, the new nations of Africa and Asia, is whether or not college students—the future leaders of these nations—will sacrifice personal liberties in the name of national security and economic development. If support for human rights decreases with age, and if students currently in college do not exhibit strong support for human rights, then there may be little hope that rights will be sustained or advanced in these countries.

Elite groups in different countries place different priorities on rights. Because the intelligentsia in western European and North American countries has fought for freedom of speech, due process of law, and academic freedom does not necessarily mean that intellectual elite groups in developing countries will do likewise. Rights to employment, health services, housing, and education may take priority over rights which in America have been called civil liberties—freedom of speech, press, religion, petition, and assembly. T. C. van Boven alludes to some of these issues in his article, "Some Remarks on Special Problems Relating to Human Rights in Developing Countries."[68] He makes the valid point that assumptions for purposes of research concerning civil liberties derived from the "natural rights" doctrines of the Enlightenment and Anglo-Saxon common law traditions cannot be easily translated into the tribal law traditions, Islamic law, Hindu codes, and other legal traditions of developing countries in Africa and Asia.

Studies of college students in Canada and the United States indicate that students who are active in voluntary organizations are more tolerant of noncon-formists and willing to grant them rights than are students who are isolated from such associations. Selvin and Hagstrom's study of the University of California, and William Devall's study of English-speaking Canadian college students are in line with Lipset's observation that the sophisticated, active members of a community are more likely to support civil liberties for minorities than are the parochial, isolated members of a community.[69]

In contrast to the number of studies on college students, there are only a few studies of adolescents and their attitudes towards civil liberties and human rights. One such is Timothy Hennessey's study of 410 Italian adolescents conducted in 1967.[70] His main emphasis is on support for democratic norms, but he includes in his scale of support for democratic norms two items which relate to civil liberties. He finds that children of lower-class families are more supportive of democratic norms than are children of upper and middle-class families. He also finds that adolescents who identify with left-wing political parties are more likely to support democratic norms than are adolescents who identify with right-wing parties. Hennessey concludes that "The whole question of the process by which such attitudes are acquired is still an open one."[71]

Community leadership and human rights support. The opinions and attitudes of community leaders are a more important guarantee of civil liberties than the opinions of followers en masse in a community. This is because community leaders have many chances to influence political actions and because they hold economic and political positions of power. One important aspect of Stouffer's study is a comparison of a sample of community leaders with a random sample of community residents across the United States.[72] Stouffer finds that on such items as freedom of speech, or the rights of atheists, communists, and socialists to employment, community leaders are more tolerant than the cross-section sample of other respondents in the same community. This does not mean that all community leaders are extremely tolerant, but only that, in comparison with their fellow citizens who are nonleaders, they are more willing to tolerate political nonconformists.

Similar findings have been obtained for such disparate political constituencies as Puerto Rico and Denmark. Franklyn Haiman's analysis of students at the University of Copenhagen is of a random sample of 180 persons selected to represent a cross section of the total population by sex and urbanization variables.[73] He concludes that in Denmark, strong social norms exist in support of openmindedness and liberal belief, but that these norms may be sustained more by a powerful leadership elite than by any solid grassroots base. Public support of government policies on freedom of expression presented a mixed picture, depending on a variety of subgroup variables; but, by and large, it is more a matter of acquiescence than of positive conviction. E. Seda Bonilla, in his study of Puerto Rico, finds that large sectors of the population ignore the Constitution's guaranteed rights or possess attitudes contrary to those necessary for democratic coexistence in a society.[74] Higher-class respondents give more verbal support to civil liberties than do lower-class respondents; but Bonilla concludes that if the population is to demand and defend its civil rights within a democratic community, such rights must be converted into codified, existential experience on the level of everyday life, that is, the experiences of citizens with police and administrative agencies of the government.

Religion and personality and human rights support. One factor, reported in several surveys, which correlates with verbal support for civil liberties is religious affiliation. Lenski, in his exhaustive treatment of *The Religious Factor,* using data collected in Detroit, concludes that white Protestants are "generally more likely to adopt a liberal interpretation of the Bill of Rights; Negro Protestants the least likely."[75] Catholics stand between the two.

Lenski was interested in the relation between commitment or involvement with a church and support for freedom of speech (as indicated by his survey questions). Of Catholic involvement he writes:

In the area of civil rights, Catholic involvement in both the church and the subcommunity is linked with a strict (or narrow) interpretation of the principle of freedom of speech. On each of the four questions dealing with criticism of presidential actions, speeches attacking religion and speeches espousing Fascism or Communism, those Catholics who were more active in their church more often expressed doubt that the Bill of Rights permits these actions than did marginal members of the group. Similarly, those who were more involved in the Catholic subcommunity favored a strict interpretation of the Bill of Rights more often than those who had more extensive primary relations with members of other subcommunities.

Among Protestants, both negro and white, "involvement of the individual in the group tended to strengthen commitment to a liberal interpretation of the Bill of Rights."[76]

Lenski does not distinguish between moderate and conservative Protestant churches. Charles Glock and Rodney Stark, in their book, *Christian Beliefs and Anti-Semitism*, use a nationwide American sample to study this issue. They find that moderate Protestants are much less antisemitic, anti-Catholic, and anti-Negro than members of conservative Protestant churches.[77] In their index of religious libertarianism, 53 percent of the moderate Protestants (Congregational, Methodist, and Protestant Episcopal) would not allow, under any conditions, an atheist to hold public office, and 65 percent of the conservative Protestants (Lutheran, Baptist, and the like) would do the same. Fifty-seven percent of the moderate Protestants would not allow an atheist to teach in a public school, and 74 percent of the conservative Protestants likewise. Thirty-two percent of the moderate Protestants and 44 percent of the conservative Protestants scored high on the index of antisemitic beliefs. The above percentages are given as representative of the differences found in all of the survey questions.

Glock and Stark relate the antisemitism of conservative Protestants to the particularism of these churches. They point to the attention directed to the church by members and to the belief in ideological righteousness which is intolerant of deviants from the True Faith. When the commitment to traditional Christian ideology is combined with the belief that one is exclusively part of God's chosen people, a powerful stimulant exists for intolerance toward other groups.

Norbert Wiley reports similar findings for Catholics; Catholics who are religious liberals are more likely to be liberal regarding civil rights than are religious conservatives.[78] The commitment of religious liberals in the Catholic church to human rights is evidenced by the writers represented in *Human Rights and the Liberation of Man in the Americas*. This book, a collection of papers delivered at the Sixth Annual Catholic Inter-American Cooperation Program Conference in 1969, includes progress reports and philosophical papers dealing with political repression in Latin America. The preface asserts that "Christian social doctrine emphatically states that the advantaged owe the disadvantaged access to a more fully human life as a debt of justice and not as an act of mercy or paternalistic charity."[79]

The separation between liberal clergy and laymen and conservative clergy and laymen is evident in several studies. Jeffrey Hadden in "Clergy Involvement in Civil Rights" finds that in the Protestant churches surveyed there is deep schism between clergy working in the civil rights movement in America and parishioners who feel that black militants have been treated too leniently in the United States.[80]

While Protestants and Catholics evidence great splits concerning human rights, most studies of Jews indicate a high and continuing support for civil liberties. Daniel Snowman's study, "The Jewish Voter," finds Jews in Britain and the United States firmly committed to the cause of civil liberties.[81]

Much research on religion and attitudes towards civil liberties is summarized by Milton Rokeach in a 1970 article, "A Mighty Fortress, Faith, Hope and Bigotry."[82] He concludes:

Many research studies have shown that there are significant differences in beliefs and attitudes between Jews, Catholics, and Protestants, and even between various Protestant denominations. Most disturbing are findings that show that the religiously devout are on the average more bigoted, more authoritarian, more dogmatic, and more anti-humanitarian than the less devout. Such findings are disturbing from the religious standpoint because they point to a social institution that needs to be reformed. They are disturbing from an anti-religious standpoint because they point to a social institution that deserves to be destroyed.

Personality and human rights support. One variable we will mention but not discuss extensively is the effect of personality on attitudes toward human rights. Beginning with the work of T. W. Adorno and his associates, a large literature has developed on the authoritarian personality.[83] Although this concept has been criticized, research findings consistently find a strong correlation between high scores on Adorno's alienation F-scale and antisemitism, antiblack prejudice, and support for repression of political extremists.

Christian Bay and Patricia Richmond, in a northern California study of the Society of Friends, a very liberal religious group, give further support for relating personality and support for civil liberties. They say:

What we wanted to find out, above all, is whether within [the Friends Committee on Legislation in Northern California] an organization of people who think of themselves as liberals and who in most cases enjoy a high social status and exhibit relatively low levels of social anxiety compared to the general population, there is nevertheless a tendency for those who are the least anxious, consciously or unconsciously, to be more liberal in the sense of human rights liberalism.[84]

The "human rights liberalism scale" consists of four items. Those who were favorable to human rights agreed with the first two items and disagreed with the last two:

(1) Victims of flagrant racial discrimination should, if a practical way can be found, be entitled to sue the state for damages. (2) The right to express Communist beliefs needs better protection in this country. (3) Nobody should be allowed to disseminate anti-semitic literature through the mail. (4) No society should tolerate homosexuality as freely as it can tolerate heterosexual relationships.[85]

CITIZEN INFORMATION ABOUT HUMAN RIGHTS

Surveys in the United States and Puerto Rico demonstrate confusion and misinformation on the part of citizens about what their rights really are. Ramond Mack concludes from his analysis of the responses of college students to his civil rights survey that there has been "impressive ignorance of educated people regarding the constitutional provisions for civil liberties."[86] In polls conducted by the Harris organization in December, 1966, and July, 1967, in the United States, 40 percent of the respondents felt that citizens did not have the right "to engage in peaceful demonstrations against the war in Vietnam." Thus, it appears that these citizens were unaware that peaceful demonstrations have the same legal status in America as writing to a congressman or speaking up at a town meeting. Bonilla, in his study of Puerto Rico, reports the Harris poll figures and finds a similar lack of knowledge about rights which correlates with years of education. The more educated, the more likely the respondent is to identify correctly his constitutional rights.[87]

These findings suggest that cross-national research should investigate the degree to which citizens of different countries understand their rights as guaranteed by the constitutions of these countries. Such an understanding is a politically significant element of any national culture. Political cognition, which includes an awareness of legal rights and duties, is an essential feature of any behavioral pattern when judged by human rights standards. By contrast, there is little prospect for realizing such rights in a parochial culture wherein those affected are only dimly aware of their legal rights.

In summary, survey research in the United States, Canada, and a few western European countries conducted during the past thirty years indicates consistent variations in support among different population aggregates for specific rights, such as freedom of speech. Free expression rights are most consistently the object of attitudinal support, while the rights of criminal defendants are the least supported by citizens of these countries. There is lack of awareness of what these constitutionally protected rights are, even among highly educated segments of the population. Political deviants of any historical period—fascists in the 1930s, communists in the 1950s, and protesters in the 1960s—would be denied freedom of speech, assembly, and rights of due process for criminal defendants by over one-third of the respondents in most surveys.

THE PROBLEM OF THEORY CONSTRUCTION

The diverse empirical observations reported heretofore now position us to focus on problems of explanation, an effort which will be made in terms of an analytical model. Nevertheless, caution is called for. It now should be obvious that comparative research on human rights support is in its infancy. Many approaches have been taken to the study of individual rights and liberties, but few general theories exist as yet. William Spinrad, in his book *Civil Liberties,* presents one of the few analytical models of human rights.[88] Restricting himself to an attempt to explain changing opinions concerning freedom of expression and association in the United States, he sketches the beginnings of an analytical model based upon a multivariate, or "field," approach to the study of social situations. He emphasizes that decisions in the area of civil liberties are the "output" of a complex political decision-making process. In his model:

Particular political actors are involved in particular ways because of the particular values, roles, structures, and situations. Furthermore, the number of actors is generally rather small, much less than in many other political disputes, but with sufficient value support in many publics to permit a wide variety of decisions.[89]

We begin the sketch of our model with the assumption that people will work for goals which they perceive are in their self-interest. We assume that formal organizations develop among like-minded people who wish to pursue their similar interests in common. Within collectivities (social classes, ethnic, racial, age, and sex groupings) grow formal organizations (churches, interest and lobbying groups, cadre parties, and the like).

We hypothesize that people will want rights for themselves and their collectivity (other women, other homosexuals) if they perceive these rights as furthering their self-interest. Second, they will work for these rights (lobbying, protests,) if they see the political community as a viable arena in which to resolve their collective problem. Obviously a world-denying religious sect whose members do not believe in participating in political action and who believe the Biblical statement "resist not evil" would not utilize any channels in the political system to further their civil liberties.

This hypothesis can provide a theory of historical development of human rights. If a group of people (ethnic group, social class, status group) is able, through political struggle, to win rights for itself, these rights may be generalized to other groups. As Spinrad describes this process: ". . . those who demand their 'rights' are frequently making a claim for their own group exclusively, sometimes explicitly denying these rights to others. But the 'indivisibility of freedom' principle is usually operative, if not always immediately."[90] Under this principle, liberty (or suppression of liberty, as the case may be), tends to spread from one segment of society to another. For example, Robert Lane in his book, *Political Life,* describes in some detail the development of voting rights in America in the nineteenth century.[91]

Each time a new collectivity of people has attempted to win 'rights' in Britain, or the United States at least, it has been opposed by a large segment of public opinion and by members of the political elite. Usually a collectivity fighting for guaranteed rights will work for some form of institutionalization by means of legislation, litigation, or regulation by commissions or agencies. If they succeed in obtaining these changes in their self-interest, the attitudes of the general public, as measured by public opinion polls, begin to change in favor of the new right. This happened in the United States after the civil rights movement in the 1950s and 1960s. The national public polls indicated that more and more people, regardless of age, sex, or ethnic group, began to favor civil rights for Blacks.

In the 1960s and early 1970s, the case of homosexuals in America followed a similar pattern. In their civil rights movement, they formed alliances with some high-status liberal professionals (lawyers, psychologists, and the like) and attempted to penetrate political institutions through lobbying, protest demonstrations, and court cases. The opposition and inertia of police, politicians, and professional organizations (such as the American Sociological Association) was phrased in such terms as "law and order," "protect our children," "national security," and "homosexuality is a characteristic of decadent capitalism."[92]

Mary Sengstock tested the hypothesis of perceived self-interest and support for civil liberties with data obtained from a survey of American college students in Detroit.[93] She hypothesized that "Establishment types were likely to oppose the Bill of Rights, non-Establishment types to support it.... It would be expected that whites, high-income people, those with high status jobs, older people, and Protestants would be likely to exhibit low support for the Bill of Rights. Blacks, low-income persons, those with lower status jobs, the young, and members of other religious groups were expected to score higher." In her study, she utilized three scales embodying principles of the Bill of Rights. The hypothesis was supported on the "right to privacy" and "freedom of speech" index but not on the "criminal rights index." Many other studies cited previously in this chapter also show less support for criminal rights than other principles of the Bill of Rights. Sengstock suggests "it is likely that most people have difficulty visualizing themselves as criminal suspects and probably would also find it difficult to see themselves requiring the protection of the criminal safeguards."[94]

She concludes that, aside from criminal process rights, results were in the direction hypothesized. For example, "people whose livelihood depends on freedom of speech," in particular college students and "professionals" (such as physicians, and lawyers) were most likely of any groups to support the freedom of speech items in the survey.

The practical implication of this hypothesis is that "an increase in popular support for the Bill of Rights is not likely to be achieved by appeals to general liberal philosophy. Rather, it is necessary to convince Americans that their own goals in life are best secured by the protection of our system of Constitutional rights."[95]

In predicting support for various rights and liberties, the model sketched here relates perceived self-interest on the one hand and, on the other, political cognition and orientation toward politics. Certainly, the model does not account for the specific *content* of a *specific right,* or institutions which protect civil rights, or the *priority of rights* in a given political system.

An elaboration of the model can be developed by utilizing the particularism-universalism dimension. A particularistic conception of rights would see a specific right as the privilege of "my group," such as restriction of voting rights to white property holders in eighteenth century America. A universalistic conception of rights would see rights as viable for "all men everywhere." The Enlightenment conception of "natural rights" developed by European intellectuals in the eighteenth century and embodied in the Declaration of the Rights of Man and of the Citizen, written at the height of the French revolution, carries this connotation of universalistic conception of rights.

We would hypothesize that the ideology of universal human rights remains the property of western intellectuals. The high sophistication of western intellectuals and professionals, their agnosticism, tolerance for new ideas, and generally liberal political positions have sustained more support for universal conceptions of human rights than other segments of the population of Western European and North American countries. This does not mean, of course, that all intellectuals have supported civil liberties and human rights in a universalistic ideology, but that, all other variables held constant, they are more likely to do so than other citizens.

Jerome Skolnick, in his explanation of changing attitudes towards blacks by white Americans, utilizes the reverse of this universalistic conception of rights.[96] He specifically cites the particularistic dimension, or what he calls "dogmatic ethnocentrism" meaning prejudice towards anyone outside "my group" (whether religion, race, social class, or region) as a factor correlated with the extreme hostility expressed by respondents in many surveys towards civil rights for blacks.

An hypothesis derived from this part of the model explains the hostility of blue collar workers (less educated and more religious) towards civil liberties. We hypothesize that the "boundaries of political tolerance" for such people is apt to be very narrow. Christians of low socioeconomic status and who belong to fundamentalistic sects, for example, may see themselves as God's chosen people. While respecting government (render unto Caesar. . . .) they find it impossible to support government action to encourage development of "human rights" for such persons as atheists, communists, and homosexuals.

A final variable utilized in our model is "orientation toward the political system." We hypothesize that people will have a conception of civil liberties and human rights only if they see themselves as actors in a political system, only if political action is a viable part of their *Weltanschauung.*

The typology of political orientation we use is derived from Almond and Verba's previously cited study of *The Civic Culture*.[97] They define three political types: the parochial, subject, and participant:

(1) *The parochial.* The parochial expects nothing from the political system. He is dimly aware of the central government. His orientation is to traditional, community relationships. The central government does not guarantee "rights" and his feelings towards it are ambivalent or negative.

(2) *The subject.* The subject is aware of specialized governmental authority; he is affectively oriented to it, perhaps taking pride in it, perhaps disliking it; and he evaluates it either as legitimate or as not. But the relationship is toward the system on the general level, and toward the output, administrative, or "downward flow" side of the political system.

(3) *The participant.* The participant members of society tend to be explicitly oriented to the system as a whole and to both the political and administrative structures and processes: in other words, to both the input and output aspects of the political system. . . . They tend to be oriented toward an "activist" role of the self in the policy, although their feelings and evaluations of such a role may vary from acceptance to rejection.

In Max Weber's terminology, these categories may be considered "ideal types" of political cognition, against which an actual situation can be measured.[98] The mixture of these "political types" in a given nation may partly account for the variability in survey findings for different segments of the population of that nation. Comparison of surveys of different nations can show the different proportions of these types in different nations.

It is suggested that by utilizing these variables, political cognition (knowledge and consciousness about politics and human rights), political orientation (parochial, subject, participant), particularism-universalism ideology, and perceived self-interest, cross-national and longitudinal studies can be developed to explore the changing values of the nations studied.

Nicholas Rescher provides us with an example of this type of research effort. In his article, "What is Value Change? A Framework for Research," Rescher proposes a related model based on cost-benefit concepts in economics.[99] If we can map out the "major value orientations" of a nation, he suggests, we can show that value change occurs when a specific value is redistributed through society, when it gains or loses adherents. Certain changes in values are called "upgrading," and other changes "downgrading." Rescher applies part of his model to forecast the future, by asking a sample of "high level scientists and science administrators whose interests are significantly future-oriented" what changes they foresee in values during the next quarter of a century in the United States. The results of the questionnaire are reported in "A Questionnaire Study of American Values by 2000 *A.D.*"[100] The majority of the respondents foresee gains in the area of "equality and civil rights" (unspecified in the questionnaire) and view such changes as desirable.

Using surveys such as this of "style leaders," intellectuals, and technologists in different countries, and correlating the findings with technological changes which will affect human rights (for instance, computer use and sensor systems which may eliminate privacy), we should be able to predict more confidently the values associated with human rights support.

CONCLUSIONS

The overwhelming emphasis in the findings of the research reviewed in this essay is that verbal support for civil liberties and human rights is weak and limited. And recent research on behavior indicates that even if people state they "strongly believe" in rights for other people, they may systematically violate those rights in certain situations. Repeatedly we have witnessed the overnight loss by groups of people of the rights which have developed over hundreds of years with little protest from the "general population," or even from the intellectual community. Opinion leadership sometimes emerges to counter human rights violations, but its effectiveness depends upon the circumstances of political strength. Given the prevalence of these melancholy conditions, two valuational conclusions follow.

First, social science data on supportive opinion favorable to human rights supply substantial grounds for pessimism. Nevitt Sanford and his associates in a series of studies published in their book, *Sanctions for Evil,* demonstrate how easy it is to "dehumanize" some group or category of people and thereby place them outside the "community of tolerance."[101] They cite studies of U. S. servicemen who refer to Vietcong as "gooks" and South Vietnamese soldiers as "faggots." If people are defined as "not human," they "do not deserve liberties." Many examples of this process of removal of rights can be cited. Between 1870 and 1890, the Chinese in California and British Columbia had civil rights protections systematically removed from them.[102] Twenty years before, native Americans in California were dehumanized—hunted down, enslaved, and killed as animals. Sanford and his associates suggest a psychological hypothesis to explain dehumanization. They say it serves as an ego-defense for individuals called upon to brutalize other human beings. The ease with which ordinary people follow commands, if these commands come from "legitimate authority," is demonstrated by the experimental work of Stanley Milgram.[103] Abstract concepts such as human rights are easily ignored in concrete situations. In Milgram's experiments, those subjects who professed abhorrence of hurting other people still tended to follow orders and "torture" other humans on command. In Brazil and Chile in the mid-1970s, suppression of free expression and political torture are justified by military regimes on the ground that efficient economic development requires such extremes.

Second, the promotion of human rights efforts can receive significant impetus from official sources, and educational efforts to change opinion supplies some basis for optimism. Where courts, ombudsmen, study commissions, private groups, and educational institutions give leadership, a human rights ethic can be promoted. Louis Sohn and Thomas Buergenthal report that the United Nations Commission on Human Rights has sponsored studies on methods for promotion of human rights. Conferences conducted by the United Nations Sub-Commission on Prevention of Discrimination and Protection of Minorities were undertaken not only to supply a basis for making recommendations relevant to international law "but also with a view to educating world opinion."[104] Another widely noted example of opinion leadership by an official body is the United States Supreme Court in its racial discrimination rulings, most notably *Brown v. Board of Education.*[105] As to the effect of such efforts, scant empirical evidence is available.[106] Nevertheless, there is widespread appreciation for the proposition that human rights are without substance unless the actual behavior of officials— police officers, government bureaucrats, and judges—is in support of these rights. Alexis de Tocqueville argued in his theory of democracy that the "tyranny of the majority" and of government could be checked only if the courts were independent of the political regime and if they supported the rights of the people.[107] However much one may disagree on such institutional specifics, it remains true that only if officials of major public and private institutions, in their daily encounters with citizens, implement human rights will these rights be anything more than hollow rhetoric. True, if enforcement officials should prove solicitous of human rights, the pervasive power of public opinion still remains. No court, commission, or ombudsman can rectify human rights violations if public opinion is hellbent on intolerance. Nevertheless, the promotion of human rights, it is hoped, can reduce intolerance and point toward a better future. This analysis has been aptly developed by Karel Vasak of the Directorate of Human Rights of the Council of Europe. Dr. Vasak writes:

The promotion of human rights . . . implies action resolutely directed towards the future: the question of human rights is seen as containing a lacuna, because they are not all, or are only incompletely, guaranteed under national legislation or international law, or because they are not sufficiently understood by the persons entitled to them or by States and their subsidiary bodies which are bound to respect them. In these circumstances, a body for the promotion of human rights will attempt to determine inadequacies and even violations, not so much in order that they may be punished but that similar situations may be prevented from recurring in the future.[108]

Once public opinion has accepted the legitimacy of human rights, it becomes more feasible to adopt formal techniques of enforcement.

NOTES

1. David J. Danelski, "A Behavioral Conception of Human Rights," *Law in Transition Quarterly* 3 (Spring 1966):63–73.

2. W. G. Runciman, *Social Science and Political Theory*, 2d ed. (Cambridge: Cambridge University Press, 1971), pp. 156–76.

3. Many of these studies are referred to in other chapters of this volume. Representative works include: Peter Archer, *Human Rights* (London: Fabian Society, 1969); Ian Brownlie, ed., *Basic Documents on Human Rights* (Oxford: Clarendon Press, 1971); D. E. T. Luard, ed., *The International Protection of Human Rights* (New York: Thomas and Hudson, 1967); Egon Schwelb, "International Protection of Human Rights: A Survey of Recent Literature," *International Organization* 24 (Winter 1970), 74–92; Vernon Van Dyke, *Human Rights, The United States and the World Community* (New York: Oxford University Press, 1970).

4. See, for example, Frede Castberg, *Freedom of Speech in the West: A Comparative Study of Public Law in France, the United States and Germany* (Oslo: Oslo University Press, 1960); Irving Brant, *The Bill of Rights: Its Origin and Meaning* (New York: Bobbs–Merrill, 1965); F. Ayala, "Las garantías de la libertad en una sociedad de masas" ("Guarantees of Freedom in a Mass Society"), *Mexican Review of Sociology* 20 (1958):147–80.

5. See, for example, John M. Maki, *Court and Constitution in Japan: Selected Supreme Court Decisions, 1948–1960* (Seattle: University of Washington Press, 1964).

6. For a collection of essays on the role of the United Nations in preservation of human rights, see "Current Status of Human Rights—Essays in Honor of Erich Hula," *Social Research* 38 (Summer 1971), pp. 175–410; *Human Rights, Comments and Interpretations, a Symposium edited by UNESCO* (New York: Columbia University Press, 1949); United Nations, *Year Books on Human Rights,* 1946–present.

7. See, for example, Harold J. Laski, *Liberty in the Modern State* (New York: Viking Press, 1949; Clifton, New Jersey: Augustus M. Kelly, 1972); Milton R. Konvitz, *Fundamental Liberties of a Free People: Religion, Speech, Press, Assembly* (Ithaca, N.Y.: Cornell University Press, 1957).

8. Examples of such studies include E. Cray, *The Big Blue Line: Police Power versus Human Rights* (New York: Coward-McCann, 1967); L. H. Mayhew, *Law and Equal Opportunity: A Study of the Massachusetts Commission Against Discrimination* (Cambridge: Harvard University Press, 1968).

9. Robert T. Holt and John E. Turner, eds., *The Methodology of Comparative Research* (New York: The Free Press, 1970); Adam Przeworski and Henry Teune, *The Logic of Comparative Social Inquiry* (New York: John Wiley and Sons, 1970).

10. Gabriel Almond and Sidney Verba, *The Civic Culture: Political Attitudes and Democracy in Five Nations* (Princeton: Princeton University Press, 1963).

11. Ibid., p. 15.

12. Ibid., p. 45.

13. Ibid., p. 50.

14. Ibid., p. 53.

15. Ibid., p. 55.

16. Seymour Martin Lipset, *Political Man* (Garden City, N.Y.: Doubleday Anchor, 1962), p. 95. On the role of intellectuals in modern western history, see Georg B. deHuszar, *The Intellectuals: A Controversial Portrait* (Glencoe, Ill: The Free Press, 1960).

17. Paul Lazarsfeld and Wagner Thielens, *The Academic Mind: Social Scientists in a Time of Crisis* (Glencoe, Ill.: The Free Press, 1958).

18. Lipset, *Political Man,* pp. 285–309. Also David H. Bayley, *Public Liberties in the New States* (Chicago: Rand McNally, 1964).

19. One type of cross-national survey deals with political systems rather than individuals in a nation-state. See Arthur S. Banks and Robert B. Textor, *A Cross-Polity Survey* (Cambridge, Mass.: M.I.T. Press, 1963), p. 67.

20. Samuel Stouffer, *Communism, Conformity and Civil Liberties: A Cross-section of the Nation Speaks Its Mind* (Garden City, N.Y.: Doubleday and Co., 1955).

21. Ibid., p. 14.

22. Ibid., p. 274.

23. Carl J. Friedrich, "Rights, Liberties, Freedom: A Reappraisal," *American Political Science Review* 57:4 (1963), 841–54.

24. Castberg, *Freedom of Speech,* pp. 9–31.

25. Norman Dorsen, ed., *The Rights of Americans: What They Are–What They Should Be* (New York: Random House, 1970). For three important books on emerging human rights see Paul Adams, et al., *Children's Rights: Toward the Liberation of the Child* (New York: Praeger, 1971); Nicholas Kittrie, *The Right to Be Different: Deviance and Enforced Therapy* (Baltimore: Johns Hopkins Press, 1971); Alan Stone, *Mental Health and the Law* (Washington, D.C.: National Institute of Mental Health, 1975).

26. On the implementation of recent U.S. court decisions, see Norman Dorsen, *Frontiers of Civil Liberties* (New York: Pantheon Books, Random House, 1968); Theodore Becker and Malcolm Feeley, eds., *The Impact of Supreme Court Decisions,* 2d ed. (New York: Oxford Press, 1973); Stephen L. Wasby, *The Impact of the United States Supreme Court* (Homewood, Illinois: The Dorsey Press, 1970).

27. Julian L. Simon, *Basic Research Methods in Social Science* (New York: Random House, 1969), pp. 15–30. Also, Morris Rosenberg, *The Logic of Survey Analysis* (New York: Basic Books, 1968); Pauline Young and Calvin F. Schmid, *Scientific Social Surveys and Research,* 4th ed. (Englewood Cliffs, N.J.: Prentice-Hall, 1966), pp. 348–86. An empirical reference work on political attitudes toward civil liberties is by John P. Robinson, Jerrold G. Rusk, and Kendra B. Head, *Measures of Political Attitudes* (Ann Arbor, Michigan: Survey Research Center, 1968).

28. Gerhard Lenski, *The Religious Factor: A Sociological Study of Religion's Impact on Politics, Economics, and Family Life* (Garden City, N.Y.: Doubleday Anchor, 1963).

29. Stouffer, *Civil Liberties,* p. 19.

30. Samuel E. Morrison and Henry S. Commager, *The Growth of the American Republic* 4th ed. (New York: Oxford University Press, 1952), pp. 295–99.

31. "Sixty Minutes," CBS Broadcasting Corporation, April 14, 1970.

32. Hanan Selvin and Warren O. Hagstrom, "Determinants of Support for Civil Liberties," in *The Berkeley Student Revolt: Facts and Interpretations,* ed. Seymour Martin Lipset and Sheldon S. Wolin (Garden City, N.Y.: Doubleday Anchor, 1965), pp. 494–518.

33. Selvin and Hagstrom, "Support for Civil Liberties," pp. 599–600.

34. Holt and Turner, *Comparative Research.* Many problems of cross-cultural research are discussed in this book. Frederick Frey's article, "Cross-Cultural Survey Research in Political Science," pp. 173–294, is of particular interest for those planning cross-national surveys of support for human rights.

35. Leslie Kish, *Survey Sampling* (New York: John Wiley, 1965).

36. Richard Hofstadter, *The Paranoid Style in American Politics* (New York: Knopf, 1965).

37. Castberg, *Freedom of Speech,* pp. 107–31 and 378–90. Also, C. H. Sheldon, "Public Opinion and High Courts: Communist Party Cases in Four Constitutional Systems," *Western Political Quarterly* 20(1967):341–60.

38. Herbert H. Hyman and Paul B. Sheatsley, "Trends in Public Opinion on Civil Liberties," *Journal of Social Studies* 9:3 (1953):6–16.

39. Hazel Erskine, "The Polls: Freedom of Speech," *Public Opinion Quarterly* 34(1970), 483–96.

40. O. W. Redder and Ole Tonsgaard, "Saliency and Political Attitudes," *Scandinavian Political Studies* 7 (New York: Columbia University Press, 1971).

41. Stan Albrecht, M. DeFleur, and L. G. Warner, "Attitude-Behavior Relationships," *Pacific Sociological Review* 15(1972):149–68; Ernest Chaples and William Sedlacek, "Measuring Prejudicial Attitudes in a Situational Context: A Report on a Danish Experiment," *Scandinavian Political Studies* 8; Milton Rokeach, *Beliefs, Attitudes, and Values* (San Francisco: Jossey-Bass, 1970), pp. 132–55. Rokeach says "attitude is a relatively enduring organization of inter-related beliefs that describe, evaluate, and advocate action with respect to an object or situation, with each belief having cognitive, affective, and behavioral components. Each of these beliefs is a predisposition that, when suitably activated, results in some preferential response toward the attitude object or situation, or toward others who

take a position with respect to the attitude object or situation, or toward the maintenance or preservation of the attitude itself. Since an attitude object must always be encountered within some situation about which we also have an attitude, a minimum condition for social behavior is the activation of at least two interacting attitudes, one concerning the attitude object and the other concerning the situation."

42. Thomas Pettigrew, *Racially Separate or Together?* (New York: McGraw–Hill, 1971), pp. 191–93.

43. Karl Popper, *The Poverty of Historicism* (Boston: The Beacon Press, 1957).

44. Seymour Martin Lipset, Martin Trow, and James Coleman, *Union Democracy* (Garden City, N.Y.: Doubleday Anchor, 1962).

45. There are many indices of socioeconomic strata. The most frequently used is the occupation of the head of the household.

46. Lenski, *The Religious Factor,* p. 209.

47. Robert Lane, *Political Ideology: Why the American Common Man Believes What He Does* (New York: Free Press–Macmillan, 1972), pp. 17–25.

48. Karl Marx and Fredrich Engels, *Basic Writings on Politics and Philosophy,* ed. Lewis Feuer (Garden City, N.Y.: Doubleday, 1959), pp. *xv–xvi.*

49. Lipset, *Political Man,* pp. 97–130.

50. Ibid., p. 104.

51. Ibid., p. 105.

52. See Maurice Zeitlin, "Revolutionary Workers and Individual Liberties," *American Journal of Sociology* 72 (1967):619–32; also idem, *Revolutionary Politics and the Cuban Working Class* (Princeton: Princeton University Press, 1967). For another reevaluation of Lipset's "working class authoritarianism" see Lewis Lipsetz, "Working Class Authoritarianism: A Re-evaluation," *American Sociological Review* 30 (1965):103–9.

53. Zeitlin, "Revolutionary Workers," p. 621.

54. Ibid., p. 631.

55. Stouffer, *Civil Liberties,* p. 95.

56. Joseph Spaeth, "Public Reactions to College Student Protests," *Sociology of Education* 42 (1969):199–206.

57. Selvin and Hagstrom, *"Support for Civil Liberties."* See also A. A. Alonzo and J. W. Kinch, "Education Level and Support of Civil Liberties," *Pacific Sociological Review* 7 (Fall 1968):89–93; Wallace Dynes, "Education and Tolerance: An Analysis of Intervening Variables," *Social Forces* 46 (September 1967):22–33. Henry C. Finney, "Political Libertarianism at Berkeley: An Application of Perspectives of the Student New Left," *Journal of Social Issues* 27 (1971):35–61. Rose Goldsen et al., *What College Students Think* (Princeton: Van Nostrand, 1960). Raymond Mack, "Do We Really Believe in the Bill of Rights?", *Social Problems* 3 (1956):264–69; E. O. Melby and M. B. Smith, eds., "Academic Freedom in a Climate of Insecurity," *Journal of Social Issues,* 9:3 (1953):2–59; Philip Jacobs, *Changing Values in College* (New York: Harper, 1957); W. B. Devall, "Support for Civil Liberties Among English-Speaking Canadian University Students," *Canadian Journal of Political Science,* 3 (1970):433–49.

58. Clyde Z. Nunn, "Support for Civil Liberties among College Students," *Social Problems* 20 (1973):300–316.

59. Richard Flacks, "The Revolt of the Advantaged: An Exploration of the Roots of Student Protest," *Journal of Social Issues,* 23:3 (1967):52–75. Richard Flacks, *Youth and Social Change* (Chicago: Markham, 1971).

60. Seymour Martin Lipset, ed., *Student Politics* (New York: Basic Books, 1967). "Students and Politics," *Daedalus* 97:1 (1968); Georg Karlsson, "Political Attitudes Among Male Swedish Youth," *Acta Sociologie* 3 (1958):220–41; O. Albornoz, "Student Opposition in Latin America," *Government and Opposition* 2:1 (1966–67):105–18; Gosta Carlsson and Bengt Gesser, "Universities as Selecting and Socializing Agents: Some Recent Swedish Data," *Acta Sociologie* 9:1 (1965):25–39.

61. Seymour Martin Lipset, "Students and Politics in Comparative Perspective," *Daedalus* 97:1 (1968):14.

62. Ibid., p. 17.

63. Lipset, *Student Politics,* p. 35.

64. Lewis Feuer, *The Conflict of Generations* (New York: Basic Books, 1969), p. 7.

65. Jacobs, *Changing Values.*

66. Franklin Henry, "University Influence on Student Opinion," *Canadian Journal of Sociology and Anthropology* 8:1 (1971):18–31.

67. Gertrude Selznick and Stephen Steinberg, *The Tenacity of Prejudice* (New York: Harper and Row, 1969), pp. 16, 18.

68. T. C. van Boven, "Some Remarks on Special Problems Relating to Human Rights in Developing Countries," *Revue des Droits de l'Homme* 3 (March 1970):151–69.

69. Selvin and Hagstrom, "Support for Civil Liberties;" Devall, "Support for Civil Liberties among Students," p. 440.

70. Timothy M. Hennessey, "Democratic Attitudinal Configurations among Italian Youth," *Midwest Journal of Political Science* 13 (1969):167–93. For American data see Herman H. Remmers, ed., *Anti-Democratic Attitudes in American Schools* (Evanston, Illinois: Northwestern University Press, 1963).

71. Hennessey, "Democratic Italian Youth," p. 193.

72. Stouffer, *Civil Liberties,* pp. 26–57.

73. Franklyn S. Haiman, "Danish Attitudes toward Freedom of Expression," *Sociologiske Meddelelser,* 14:1 (1970):21–57.

74. Edwin Seda Bonilla, *Los derechos civiles en lan cultura puertoriqueña,* (Rio Piedras Puerto Rico: University of Puerto Rico, 1963).

75. Lenski, *The Religious Factor,* p. 160.

76. Ibid., p. 190.

77. Charles Glock and Rodney Stark, *Christian Beliefs and Anti-Semitism* (New York: Harper and Row, 1966); also Seymour Martin Lipset and Earl Raab, *The Politics of Unreason: Rightwing Extremism in America, 1790–1970* (New York: Harper and Row, 1970).

78. Norbert Wiley, "Religious and Political Liberalism among Catholics," *Sociological Analysis* 28:3 (1967):142–48; also Gary Maranell, "An Examination of Some Religious and Political Correlates of Bigotry," *Social Forces* 45 (1967):356–61; Peter Henriot, "The Coincidence of Political and Religious Attitudes," *Review of Religious Studies* 8:1 (1966): 50–57; Hart M. Nelsen and Raytha L. Yokley, "Civil Rights Attitudes of Rural and Urban Presbyterians," *Rural Sociology* 35 (1970), 161–74.

79. Louis M. Colonnese, ed., *Human Rights and the Liberation of Man in the Americas* (South Bend: University of Notre Dame Press, 1970).

80. Jeffrey Hadden, "Clergy Involvement in Civil Rights," *Annals of the American Academy of Political and Social Science* 387 (1970):188–227; Hazel Erskine, "The Polls: Demonstrations and Race Riots," *Public Opinion Quarterly* 31 (1967):655–77.

81. Daniel Snowman, "The Jewish Voter," *New Society* 7:173 (1966):13–16.

82. Milton Rokeach, "A Mighty Fortress, Faith, Hope and Bigotry," *Psychology Today,* 11:3 (1970), 33–37.

83. T. W. Adorno et al., *The Authoritarian Personality* (New York: Harper and Row, 1950); M. Brewster Smith, Jerome Bruner, and R. W. White, *Opinions and Personality* (New York: John Wiley and Sons, 1956); R. Christie and M. Jahoda, *Studies in the Scope and Methods of the Authoritarian Personality* (New York: The Free Press, 1954); Milton J. Rokeach, *Beliefs, Attitudes, and Values* (San Francisco: Jossey-Bass, Inc. 1968); Leonard D. Goodstein, "Intellectual Rigidity and Social Attitudes," *Journal of Abnormal Social Psychology* 48 (1953):345–53; Fred Greenstein, "Personality and Political Socialization: The Theories of Authoritarian and Democratic Character," *Annals of American Academy of Political and Social Sciences* 361 (1965), 81–95. For specific scales, see John P. Robinson and Phillip R. Shaver, *Measures of Political Attitudes* (Ann Arbor, Michigan: Survey Research Center, 1969), pp. 11–654.

84. Christian Bay and Patricia Richmond, "Some Variables of Liberal Experience," (Paper, Department of Political Science, University of Alberta, 1968).

85. Ibid.

86. Mack, "Bill of Rights."

87. Bonilla, "Los derechos civiles."

88. William Spinrad, *Civil Liberties* (Chicago: Quadrangle Books, 1970).

89. Ibid, pp. 84–100.

90. Ibid., p. 21.

91. Robert Lane, *Political Life* (Glencoe, Ill.: Free Press, 1966).

92. William Devall, "Gay Liberation: An Overview," *Journal of Voluntary Action Research* 2 (January 1973):24–35.

93. Mary Sengstock, "Self-interest and Civil Liberties," *Criminal Law Bulletin* 10 (1974):63–79.

94. Ibid., p. 75.

95. Ibid., p. 79.

96. Jerome Skolnick, *Justice Without Trial* (New York: John Wiley and Sons, 1966), p. 197.

97. Almond and Verba, *Civic Culture,* p. 97.

98. Roger E. Rolf, *Max Weber's Ideal Type Theory* (New York: Philosophical Library, 1969).

99. Nicholas Rescher, "What is a Value Change? A Framework for Research," in Kurt Baier and Nicholas Rescher, *Values and the Future* (New York: The Free Press, 1969), pp. 69–109.

100. Nicholas Rescher, "A Questionnaire Study of American Values by 2000 A.D.," ibid., pp. 133–47.

101. Nevitt Sanford et al., *Sanctions for Evil* (San Francisco: Jossey-Bass, 1971); Danelski, *Conception of Rights,* p. 64, for a similar conception: "There can be no human rights where men fail to perceive other men as human."

102. Herbert Hill, "Anti-Oriental Agitation and the Rise of Working-Class Racism," *Society* 10:2 (1973):43–54.

103. Stanley Milgram, *Obedience to Authority* (New York: Harper and Row, 1974).

104. Louis B. Sohn and Thomas Buergenthal, *International Protection of Human Rights* (Indianapolis: Bobbs–Merrill, 1972), pp. 543–52.

105. *Brown v. Board of Education,* 347 U.S. 483 (1954) and 349 U.S. 294 (1955).

106. Stephen L. Wasby, *The Impact of the United States Supreme Court* (Homewood, Illinois: The Dorsey Press, 1970), pp. 169–85.

107. Paul Eberts and Ronald Witton, "Recall from Anecdote: Alexis de Tocqueville and the Morphogenesis of America," *American Sociological Review* 351 (1970):1081–96.

108. Karel Vasak, "National, Regional and Universal Institutions for the Promotion and Protection of Human Rights," *Revue des Droits de l'Homme* 1 (1968):165–72.

Chapter 14 JUDICIAL BEHAVIOR AND COMPARATIVE RIGHTS POLICY

Carl Baar

American political science has been unable to deal effectively with human rights. The subject has aroused the interest of individual political scientists.[1] Two recent studies have examined the international dimensions of human rights policy-making and enforcement.[2] But the systematic comparative study of human rights in national political systems has remained out of the reach of the discipline.

The purpose of this essay is to bring the study of human rights and the discipline of political science as it is practiced in the United States closer together. This task requires a number of steps: assessing which elements of American political science can contribute to the systematic comparative study of human rights; examining how these elements can be reoriented to a new area of study; illustrating the possibilities for and difficulties of comparative research; and suggesting frameworks for future research which can both extend American political science and develop a systematic body of knowledge about the causes and consequences of cross-national variations in the enunciation and application of fundamental legal rights. Underlying the present effort is the notion that political scientists cannot contribute to the advancement of knowledge about human rights unless questions of rights policy are linked to other central questions and approaches in the discipline. At the same time, American political scientists must be aware of the biases which their discipline brings to the comparative study of human rights, so that their findings will not simply "Americanize" the perspectives within which human rights are understood.

HUMAN RIGHTS IN POLITICAL SCIENCE

In the United States, human rights have become part of political discourse primarily through the constitutional interpretation and law-making activities of the Supreme Court. The major and most controversial initiatives of the Supreme Court in the past generation have involved freedom of expression, racial equal-

353

ity, political and electoral rights, religious freedom, and the rights of the accused.[3] In turn, those political scientists who have taught about the Supreme Court and attempted to explain the behavior of Supreme Court justices have carried the burden of understanding what these rights are. Because the Supreme Court has annexed to the judicial process the specialized political role of guardian of civil liberties and individual rights, public law and judicial behavior specialists have also become the civil liberties policy specialists within political science.[4] They have read the cases, explicated the legal doctrine in undergraduate courses, and placed their research in the context of individual rights.

Yet the contribution which public law and judicial behavior specialists can make to the comparative study of human rights policy is different from the contribution of lawyers. Legal scholarship focuses upon the explication of general legal concepts, and the articulation of those concepts in the context of specific legal systems. Political science scholarship, on the other hand, is concerned with the development of empirically-based theory for the explanation of political events and processes. To provide a theoretical focus within political science, human rights must be conceived as outputs and outcomes of government policy-making, so that variations in human rights—their definition and redefinition, expansion and contraction—can be measured and analyzed. The development of such theory requires the continuation of a number of trends in the subfield of public law and judicial behavior: (1) judicial specialists must develop variables and measures which can be used in cross-national research; (2) judicial specialists must give increasing attention to organizational behavior rather than individual behavior as the unit of analysis in their research; (3) judicial specialists must include in the policy outputs they study the outputs of government bodies other than courts, on matters other than those arising from litigation; (4) judicial specialists must focus on the outcomes of rights policy-making, including questions of implementation and impact; and (5) judicial specialists must consider not only constitutional law, but also other fields of law through which judicial interpretation generates legal policies affecting human rights.

Judicial behavior research in American political science has focused almost entirely upon political phenomena occurring within the United States. The research has been comparative, because the logic of social science research requires comparison: to test an hypothesis which posits a relationship between two variables, one must compare an instance in which the independent variable has a certain value with other instances in which it has different values. Therefore, analysis of the Supreme Court was transformed into analysis of the behavior of individual Supreme Court justices, because their behavior could be compared and then explained. For example, comparison of voting records allowed the categorization of justices as liberals or conservatives; explanations of why the justices voted as they did could refer to variations in their attitudes, social backgrounds, or political party affiliations.[5] Similar research efforts delved into the voting behavior of judges in other federal courts and in state supreme courts.[6] Other techniques added to the reach of the methodology: content analysis allowed the values of judges to be derived from their written opinions as well as their votes; factor and smallest space analysis allowed a number of variables to be related to one another; survey work by questionnaire and interview extended the range of data, allowing the measurement of additional variables.[7] But cross-national research was late in coming. The subfield of public administration developed a comparative component by the mid-1960s, spurred by the application of its approaches to problems of developing nations, and signalled by Ferrel Heady's introductory text on comparative administration published in 1966.[8] No similar sign appeared in the judicial subfield until the publication in 1969 of *Comparative Judicial Behavior,* a set of interrelated "cross-cultural studies of political decision-making in the East and West" edited by Glendon Schubert and David Danelski.[9] Those studies indicate that cross-national research is possible within the framework of existing judicial behavioral variables: a number of the studies are able to obtain data on backgrounds of the judges and on their ideologies (sometimes inferred from decisions, sometimes measured independently).[10] But Schubert and Danelski's efforts have not encouraged increased attention to cross-national research among judicial specialists.[11] One reason may be that judicial specialists have no interesting theoretical questions to explore in cross-national research. Research on courts and law in foreign lands can produce fascinating information which may be new to American political scientists, but if it is done within the existing paradigm of judicial behavior, it introduces few new variables or new directions. Why?

The answer is that judicial theory continues to focus its attention on the behavior of individual judges rather than on the behavior of judicial organizations. The basic question is "why do judges decide the way they do?" rather than "why do court decisions come out the way they do?" or "why are litigated conflicts resolved the way they are?" As a result, techniques to measure variables which explain differences *within* the United States Supreme Court can also be used to explain differences *within* the supreme courts of other countries.[12] But they provide no insight into the differences *between* one supreme court and another. To discover such organizational differences, a researcher would have to consider the decisions of the court rather than the votes of each individual judge, and then consider the variables which might explain the differences in those decisions from nation to nation: differences in the courts' authority, power, functions, and prestige; differences in the organization and operation of other political institutions (legislatures, bureaucracies, and national and local units of government); differences in the historical development of competing legal and political institutions; and differences in the social, economic, and cultural environments (population size and density; wealth; degree of urbanization and industrialization; and racial, religious, or linguistic homogeneity/heterogeneity). Consideration of these variables requires a different level of analysis than that of conventional judicial behavior studies as they developed in American political science after World War II. Earlier scientific study is not therefore invalid; it is simply less interesting because it does not allow the exploration of new questions such as those posed by the comparative study of human rights.

Schubert and Danelski's book focuses almost exclusively on "units of individual behavior."[13] Only one of the studies, Hahm's attempt to relate the judicial decision-making process in Korea to community perspectives of authority, as measured by a national opinion survey, treats the nature of the judicial system—an organizational variable—as a dependent variable. However, the other major cross-national effort by an American judicial specialist, Theodore L. Becker's *Comparative Judicial Politics,* explores a broader range of questions.[14] He defines the central problem for comparative analysis as the study of variations in the political functions of judicial structures. Drawing from a diverse collection of sources in law and political science, Becker is able to see whether different kinds of courts (for example, those with or without the judicial review power) have different effects on the political systems of which they are a part. However, while Becker explores some important organizational-level hypotheses, he rests his definition of judicial structure on social-psychological attributes of individual officerholders: courts exist when officeholders believe in a judicial role—believe "that they should listen to the presentation of facts and apply such cited normative principles impartially, objectively, or with detachment."[15] Becker must therefore rely on perceptual data to determine whether "judicial structure" exists in a given society.[16] His theory-building starts with judges, but it does move on to ask important questions about courts—the kinds of questions which require and therefore can encourage cross-national research.

The systematic study of human rights policy-making requires the use and measurement of organizational-level variables—characteristics of courts rather than of individual judges. But to do cross-national research on human rights policies, the focus cannot be limited to the outputs of judicial organizations. It must extend to legislative and administrative organizations as well. The fact that the United States Supreme Court has provided the major human rights policy initiatives in that political system does not mean that a similar pattern is followed elsewhere. For example, when Canada sought solutions to its major internal conflict between English-speaking and French-speaking Canadians, its Supreme Court played no role. The rights of French-speaking Canadians were enunciated through legislation, the Official Languages Act (1969), one of the Liberal Government's major legislative initiatives. Thus, linguistic rights were introduced into Canadian law outside the courts and free from any judicial prodding or judicial impediments. The contrast with American handling of racial conflicts could not be clearer: in the nineteenth century, the United States Supreme Court struck down both a congressional compromise (in the *Dred Scott Case*) and the broad Civil Rights Act of 1875 (in the *Civil Rights Cases* of 1883). Congress did not move again on civil rights until after new court decisions in the twentieth century spurred new legislation.[17]

Judicial specialists in American political science have become specialists in human rights policy because the American judicial system has also become a specialist in human rights policy-making. But the field of judicial behavior has been and should be much broader. It began as the field of public law, and political scientists who taught and studied public law were among the most important and prominent persons in the discipline.[18] But the teaching of law in the United States during the first half of the twentieth century has been primarily the study of court decisions rather than statutes and administrative regulations. Lawbooks are termed "casebooks" even though they include "cases and materials"; only in recent years have the materials in certain areas of law come to balance out the cases. And public law in political science was increasingly limited to federal constitutional law, largely the preserve of the federal judiciary. The teaching of other branches of public law, such as administrative law, in political science departments is almost extinct. So when political scientists of all sorts began examining processes rather than institutions, the public law specialists studied the courts, leaving legislatures, administrative agencies, executives, parties and so forth to other specialists. Few judicial specialists within political science define their specialty as "law and politics" and attempt to lay claim to studying the law-making process outside the courts. As a result, their focus is narrower than that of sociologists of law or of social science-oriented law professors, who consider legislative and administrative processes as important objects of study.[19]

When they do focus on courts, political scientists also tend to ignore nonconstitutional decision making. Martin Shapiro is an important exception: his work has ranged into administrative law, tax law, and patent law. He has recently argued that political scientists should consider private as well as public law, because that traditional legal distinction obscured the basic fact that courts were in both cases making law which benefitted some interests in society and adversely affected others.[20] However, these other fields of law must not only be seen as instances of the allocation of public benefits and burdens, but must also be evaluated in relation to a theory of human rights policy-making. Although a given court or agency ruling may not be addressed directly to an issue of human rights, would it still have to be classified as advancing or retarding human rights in order to become a useful datum for testing the propositions which make up a theory of human rights. Classification may be relatively easy. For example, the rights of accused persons in criminal proceedings in Canada are not protected by constitutional document, but through judicial interpretation of federal criminal statutes and common law precedent. If an advance in the rights of the accused is considered an advance in the protection of human rights, decisions favorable to the accused in procedural appeals can be classified as advancing human rights. But the classification problems remain: if a decision in favor of an accused person is based on narrow legal grounds, the resulting doctrine may be used to limit human rights in the future by providing a basis for distinguishing the instant case from future cases. Thus, after the U.S. Supreme Court enunciated the right to counsel in a capital case in 1932, the rule was excluded from noncapital cases in 1942. More recently, the reasoning of the justices in outlawing capital punishment has become the basis for new state laws reinstituting the death penalty.[21]

While the structure of the political science discipline has limited the extension of public law enquiries outside the courts, it has invited a new area of study within the field of public law and judicial behavior: "impact" studies. In the past decade, a wide array of books and articles have examined the impact of Supreme Court decisions.[22] The proliferation of impact studies suggests that American political scientists not only realize the differences between the law-on-the-books and the law-in-action, but also are able to study systematically both what those differences are, and what factors are associated with the degree of difference from one legal issue to another from one community to another. With the exception of Danelski's recent paper on the impact of the Japanese Supreme Court, the many impact studies by political scientists have been confined entirely to the United States.

To be of value to building a theory of comparative rights policy, judicial specialists must not only develop a cross-national data base. They must also continue the present movement away from equating impact with compliance, and toward conceiving impact in terms of the effects of alternative legal policies. By the time Wasby gathered the impact literature into a coherent set of propositions in 1970, he could label the traditional impact study a study of compliance—whether subordinate courts or public agencies (police departments, school boards) obeyed or followed a particular decision. But many other effects could also be examined: how do booksellers or publishers respond to obscenity decisions? Does public opinion or the opinion of specific elite groups change following a decision?[23] And the concept of compliance itself could be clarified by inserting the intermediate stage of communicating decisions to those agencies that are expected to comply with them.[24] And impact studies could be broadened to include study of the effects of statutes and administrative action as well as the effects of judicial decisions (not only individually but as patterns of decision). In this way, impact studies evolve into policy analysis that attempts to separate variations attributable to policy change from variations attributable to other factors.[25]

As judicial behavior specialists evolve into policy analysts, they will be able to draw upon the policy literature in other subfields of American political science. For example, the literature on community power and urban policy-making has sought to understand the nonissue: the policy which is controversial in one community but not in another. Beginning with the notion of "two faces of power"—the power which is displayed by the winning of a conflict and the power which prevents conflicts from arising by keeping questions off the public agenda—political scientists have tried to analyze the circumstances under which the second face of power may be the reason why a given issue is not raised.[26]

The concept of a nonissue might provide fresh insight into the cross-national study of human rights policy. Why, for example, was preventive detention—an accepted legal concept in many jurisdictions—moved from the status of nonissue to the status of issue in the United States in the late 1960s? Are certain issues of religious freedom confined to countries with more heterogeneous religious composition? If not, when is religious freedom an issue and when is it a nonissue?

Specialists in public administration have raised human rights questions in their study of nonjudicial remedies such as the ombudsman. That literature is necessarily comparative, since American political science discovered the ombudsman only 150 years after the office was created in Sweden, and a few years after it was extended to other national and subnational units. Again, studies of foreign institutions are not sufficient in themselves to generate a theory of human rights policy-making. The ombudsman must be treated as a variable: the existence or nonexistence of the office must be related to various national economic and political characteristics as independent variables; and the effects of its existence or nonexistence on the quality of individual rights (dependent variable) must be assessed.

The terminology of "impact" and "effects" begs even broader questions, and ones which could provide increased sophistication and decreased ethnocentrism in building rights policy theory. For example, political scientists and other students of human behavior have written about the symbolic functions of various political institutions, including the legal system. When these writers speak of symbolic functions, they refer to another set of effects or impacts of public policies. Thus Edelman has discussed how certain policies create symbolic reassurances necessary to induce mass quiescence.[27] Edelman's analysis suggests questions about human rights. To what extent do the human rights policies of urban industrial societies constitute such symbolic reassurances? And to what extent does the resulting quiescence reduce the level at which individual liberty is protected and enhanced in such a society?

In summary, political scientists can contribute to the understanding of human rights by developing a crossnational empirical theory of human rights policy. By examining human rights in the context of the public policies of various countries, it will be possible to examine the range of independent variables associated with different degrees of protection and enhancement of human rights, and the dependent variables associated with the effects or outcomes of those policies—the extent to which individual freedom, in fact, exists from country to country.

JUDICIAL ACTIVISM IN CANADA AND THE UNITED STATES

As an initial indication of the possibilities of cross-national research on court behavior, this section will analyze comparative data from the Supreme Courts of Canada and the United States. It will focus on the organizational and behavioral characteristics of courts rather than the attitudes, behavior or other character-istics of individual judges. The variation in court behavior to be examined is the level of judicial activism/restraint shown by the two Supreme Courts in constitu-tional cases. The section will begin by testing the proposition that the U.S. Supreme Court exhibits a higher level of judicial activism than the Canadian Supreme Court. Then two variables related to differences between the level of judicial activism in the two courts will be explored. First, the source of the challenged government action (from the national or state/provincial levels of government): are either or both Supreme Courts more active in cases involving state/provincial action than in cases involving national (federal government) action? Second, the age of the courts: does the level of judicial activism of a court of last resort increase as the court increases in age? The findings will then be used to suggest whether a high degree of judicial activism is, as American writers have implied, a necessary condition for the development and preservation of human rights.

Judicial activism occurs when a court makes a decision invalidating the action of another agency or institution of government. Judicial restraint occurs when a court decision validates previous public action.[28] By this definition, inter-mediate appellate courts, supreme courts in constituent states or provinces, and trial courts may also exhibit judicial activism and restraint. Also, judicial activ-ism can occur in other than constitutional cases (such as application of common law to control the action of government officials). However, as a starting point for analysis, only the decisions of the two national supreme courts in constitu-tional cases is dealt with in this study. Constitutional cases represent a specific category of appellate adjudication which is not necessarily representative of the total universe of appellate court decision making. However, inasmuch as consti-tutional cases have traditionally been the special concern of political scientists both in Canada and the United States, they serve as a workable base for a comparative analysis of judicial activism, and for criticism of the political science preoccupation with constitutional law in explicating the content of human rights policies.[29]

Because the degree of judicial activism/restraint is both an organizational and behavioral attribute, it is different from the concept of judicial review, which refers to the formal authority or power of a court to invalidate the actions of other agencies of government on constitutional grounds. Because both the Canadian and U.S. Supreme Courts have some constitutional power of judicial review, the degree to which the exercise of judicial review is active or restrained can be measured cross-nationally by analyzing court decisions. The analysis is facilitated by many similarities between the legal systems of the United States and Canada. For example, among the factors Becker has cited "that seem to be highly associated with the legal existence of judicial review in various forms" are its occurrence "in erstwhile British possessions" and its "very high correlation with federalism."[30] Both would seem to apply to the two countries in the present research. At the same time, the formal characteristics of judicial review in Canada and the United States are similar in a number of respects. Both systems use review "incidenter" (the introduction of constitutional issues "before ordinary tribunals in connection with regular judicial proceedings") rather than review "principaliter" (for example, the use of special constitutional courts).[31] Both systems use decentralized judicial review, in which "the power of control [is given] to *all the judicial organs* of a given legal system," rather than centralized judicial review, which "confines the power of review to *one single judicial organ.*"[32]

There are also important differences in the form which judicial review takes in the two countries. In the United States, judicial review extends to all questions arising under the constitution, which is a specific document rather than a collection of documents or a combination of written and unwritten traditions. In Canada, judicial review is largely limited to questions of the distribution of legislative power between federal and provincial governments under sections 91 and 92 of the British North America Act. (The bulk of Canadian constitutional cases focus on whether a given federal or provincial action is outside—ultra vires—the federal or provincial jurisdiction as enumerated in the headings of 91 and 92.)[33] At the same time, Canadian constitutional law is potentially broader, because the separation between constitutional and other categories of law is less clear in Canada than in the United States. The BNA Act and its amendments are part of the basic law of Canada, but because they are in fact British statutes, they are not in themselves a constitution. For example, even though the Canadian Bill of Rights is a 1960 federal statute, it may be used in certain cases to invalidate other federal legislation.[34] As a result, it takes on the character of basic law, and cases arising under the Bill of Rights are considered part of the body of constitutional law even though they do not arise under the BNA Act.

The Canadian cases analyzed include all constitutional cases handled by the Supreme Court from 1950 through 1972.[35] The 1950 date was used, following Stephen R. Mitchell, as the year when decisions of the Court were no longer appealable to the Judicial Committee of the Privy Council in England.[36] (Even though the Supreme Court of Canada was created in 1875, it did not function as a court of last resort on constitutional matters until the abolition of appeals to the Judicial Committee in 1949).[37] Included in the sample are, however, certain cases heard after 1950 which had been initiated early enough to be still subject to review by the Judicial Committee. A list of cases from 1950–65 was obtained from Mitchell, verified, and brought up to date. Constitutional cases include all cases in the official *Supreme Court Reports* in which the words "Constitutional Law" appeared in a summary paragraph inserted prior to the written opinions in each case decided by the Court. From 1969 on, cases involving the Bill of Rights were no longer classified under the "Constitutional Law" category but under a new category of "Civil Rights."[38] Since Canadian legal scholars generally place those cases under the rubric of constitutional law, that practice is followed here. The sample includes a total of eighty-three cases.

Included in the sample of United States cases are all constitutional cases decided with written opinions (that is, per curiam decisions were excluded) by the U.S. Supreme Court in the October terms of 1950 through 1968, a period of nineteen years covering roughly the same time period as the Canadian cases (October, 1950 to June, 1969). A constitutional case is defined as a case decided on constitutional grounds; cases which raised constitutional issues are not included if the decision rested on nonconstitutional grounds. This standard for inclusion and exclusion lacks the degree of reliability found in classifying Canadian cases through summaries in the official reports. Neither the official reports nor the two privately printed series of U.S. Supreme Court reports contain summaries which can be used in a manner comparable to that of the Canadian summaries. Nevertheless, the percentage of ambiguous U.S. cases is sufficiently low to justify use of the data for the purposes of this paper. The sample includes a total of 576 cases.

The proposition that the U.S. Supreme Court is more active than the Canadian Supreme Court is demonstrated by the findings in table 1.

In the period since 1950, the U.S. Supreme Court has shown a higher level of judicial activism than the Canadian Supreme Court. Government action is more than twice as likely to have been invalidated in constitutional cases before the U.S. Supreme Court than in constitutional cases before the Supreme Court of Canada. Furthermore, the absolute number of cases in which the U.S. Supreme Court has invalidated government action is over fifteen times higher. Thus, whether the level of judicial activism is defined by rate (percent of total cases in which activism is shown) or by quantity (number of cases in which activism is

Table 1. JUDICIAL ACTIVISM IN THE UNITED STATES AND CANADIAN SUPREME COURTS: INVALIDATING PUBLIC ACTION IN CONSTITUTIONAL CASES SINCE 1950

Ruling on Public Action	U.S.[a]		Canada[a]	
	Number	Percent of Applicable Cases	Number	Percent of Applicable Cases
Valid	249	43.2	55	67.9
Part valid/ part invalid	3	0.5	5	6.2
Invalid	324	56.3	21	25.9
Not applicable	0	–	2	–

[a]U.S. cases extend from October 1950 through June 1969. Canadian cases extend from January 1950 through July 1972.

shown), there are significant differences between the supreme courts of the two countries.

It may be argued that because the U.S. cases are drawn almost entirely from the period of Earl Warren's Chief Justiceship (1953 to 69), they may present a period of unusually high judicial activism, which may be decreased with changes in the Court in the years since 1969. Disaggregation of the data in table 1 lends partial support to this argument. In the 1950–52 terms, the last under Chief Justice Fred Vinson, the Supreme Court ruled in favor of the government in sixty-two constitutional cases and against the government in twenty-nine such cases. Thus in that period, the Supreme Court's rate of judicial activism (31.9 percent) was not significantly higher than its Canadian counterpart. However, the quantity of constitutional cases handled in that period (about thirty per year) was as great as in comparable time periods since 1953. As a result, the U.S. Supreme Court in those three terms alone invalidated more government action than the Supreme Court of Canada has in twenty-two years.[39]

While it is possible to speak of a higher level of judicial activism in the United States than in Canada, the concept may still not be accurately represented by the data in table 1. Judicial activism has been used in a political sense: it refers not to how much creative or imaginative new legal doctrine it generates, but to how much it intervenes in the public policy process of the political system. Critics of a quantitative emphasis would argue that the numbers in table 1 do not distinguish important cases from unimportant cases (*Brown* v. *Board* has no more weight than any other case). Such criticism is a reminder that quantitative data must be supplemented by qualitative analysis; inasmuch as qualitative analysis of the political role of both Supreme Courts is plentiful and quantitative output data are rare,[40] the present section emphasizes the quantitative side for the sake of balance and for the sake of theory-building. A more difficult criticism to deal with is that the level of judicial activism—judicial intervention in public policy-making—is measured not simply by the number of judicial interventions alone, but by relating those interventions to activities outside the courts. For example, it may be that more laws are passed in the United States than in Canada. Inasmuch as there are fifty states and only ten provinces, and private members' bills (that is, not presented by the government) rarely pass in the Canadian parliamentary system (federal or provincial), there may be many times more legislation open to challenge in the United States than in Canada. Thus, the number of judicial interventions may be higher in the United States, but may not constitute a higher proportion of the policy decisions made in that country. An adequate political theory of judicial action therefore requires more (not less) quantification, a consideration of a wider range of operationalizable variables, and a more thorough analysis of the relationship of the judiciary to other policy-makers.

One way of relating the court decisions in table 1 to the political systems in which those decisions were made is to divide the decisions into those involving federal action and those involving state or provincial action. In hypothesis form: the level of judicial activism by Canadian and U.S. Supreme Courts varies with the source of the challenged public action, so that both supreme courts will overturn state or provincial action more frequently than federal action.

The conventional understanding of the role of the U.S. Supreme Court would support this proposition. Lawyers and political scientists in the United States agree that their supreme court is an agent for the centralization of power and authority, because it exercises more restraint on matters of federal law than on matters of state law and practice.[41] Recent history confirms this expectation. The major thrusts of judicial activism by the Warren Court—racial segregation, legislative apportionment, and police practices—all were aimed primarily at the invalidation of state action. The findings from the U.S. Supreme Court data used here add further confirmation. As table 2 shows, action was invalidated by the U.S. Supreme Court almost twice as frequently as federal action. While federal action had almost a two to one chance of being upheld, the odds were almost two to one against state action being upheld in that court's constitutional decisions.

The conventional understanding of the role of the Supreme Court of Canada does not produce similarly clear expectations. The decisions of the Judicial Committee of the Privy Council have traditionally been viewed as favoring provincial power and reducing federal power. Although the transfer of final appellate authority on constitutional matters from the Judicial Committee to the Supreme Court of Canada may alter this direction, most legal analysts would argue that such a new direction has not yet been established. The Supreme Court of Canada is viewed as continuing the Judicial Committee's trend toward "limiting the powers of the general government."[42]

Table 2. JUDICIAL ACTIVISM IN THE UNITED STATES SUPREME COURT: INVALIDATING STATE AND FEDERAL ACTION IN CONSTITUTIONAL CASES SINCE 1950.[a]

| Ruling on Public Action | Type of Public Action | | | | Percent State Action Minus Percent Federal Action |
| | State | | Federal | | |
	Number	Percent	Number	Percent	
Valid	140	34.6	109	63.7	−29.1
Part valid/ part invalid	1	0.2	2	1.2	−
Invalid	264	65.2	60	35.1	+30.1

[a]Cases extend from October 1950 through June 1969.

Table 3. JUDICIAL ACTIVISM IN THE SUPREME COURT OF CANADA: INVALIDAT-
ING PROVINCIAL AND FEDERAL ACTION IN CONSTITUTIONAL CASES SINCE
1950[a]

| | Type of Public Action | | | | |
| | Provincial | | Federal | | |
Ruling on Public Action	Number	Percent	Number	Percent	Percent Provincial Action Minus Percent Federal Action
Valid	29	54.7	29	93.5	−38.8
Part valid/ part invalid	4	7.6	0	0.0	−
Invalid	20	37.7	2	6.5	+31.2

[a]Cases extend from January 1950 through July 1972. Two "not applicable" cases are omitted. Three cases involving both federal and provincial action are double coded: *P.E.I. Potato Marketing Board* v. *Willis*, [1952] 2 S.C.R. 392; *The Queen* v. *Smith*, [1972] S.C.R. 359; *Brownridge* v. *The Queen* [1972] S.C.R. 926. As a result, the totals in this table (federal plus provincial) will exceed by three the totals in table 1.

The data, however, do not bear out this view of the Supreme Court of Canada in over twenty years since abolition of appeals to the Judicial Committee. Table 3 shows provincial action invalidated substantially more frequently than federal action. Thus, both the Canadian and U.S. Supreme Courts invalidated state/provincial action more frequently than federal action; furthermore, the extent to which state/provincial action was invalidated more frequently than federal action is similar in both countries. (Compare the percentage differences in the right-hand columns of tables 2 and 3: 31.2 percent and 30.1 percent.)

An examination of the Canadian cases involving federal action reinforces the finding that the Supreme Court of Canada has exercised judicial restraint on federal matters. The only two cases in which federal action was held invalid were *Canadian Wheat Board* v. *Nolan et al.*,[43] which invalidated an Order-in-Council under the National Emergency Transitional Powers Act, and *The Queen* v. *Drybones*, which invalidated a provision of the federal Indian Act by applying the Bill of Rights. In both cases, the Supreme Court affirmed the decision of the last court below, and neither case involved the interpretation of the British North American Act. In three other cases, the Supreme Court had to reverse the last court below in order to uphold federal action.[44] On the other hand, the Supreme Court has invalidated a substantial number of provincial actions and has upheld federal claims in conflict with provincial claims.[45]

Because the data in tables 2 and 3 refer to the action at issue rather than the position of the governments involved, it may not reveal the full extent of federal influence over constitutional decisions in the two supreme courts. In both countries, it is common for a federal official (the Attorney General in Canada and the Solicitor General in the United States) to present the position of the Department or Ministry of Justice to the supreme court in a case where state or provincial (but no federal) action is being considered. The role of the Solicitor General in the United States expanded considerably during the Kennedy and Johnson Administrations, coinciding with an even greater level of judicial activism on state matters by the Warren Court.[46] Conversely, states or provinces may organize and submit briefs opposing the validity of an exercise of federal power.[47] Thus, to obtain a more complete sense of federal government influence, data should be obtained about whether federal or state/provincial officials intervened in cases involving action at the other level, and what results ensued. It may be that state/provincial action was held invalid at a higher rate when federal officials intervened on behalf of the parties opposing such action.[48]

What emerges from the data is a pattern of court behavior in which national courts in a federal system function to centralize authority and power in the general government. Because the Supreme Court of Canada has been a court of last resort for such a short time, it may not yet have reversed the direction of legal doctrine established by the Judicial Committee of the Privy Council, which, as an external court of last resort, did not perform the centralizing function characteristic of national courts. But its decision-making pattern indicates that the Supreme Court of Canada is moving in the same direction as the Supreme Court of the United States.

Thus the direction of judicial activism (against state/provincial more frequently than federal action) is the same in both countries. It is the extent of judicial activism (how often it occurs) which is different. The usual explanation for this difference is the legal one: judicial review is narrower in scope in Canada than in the United States. But before taking our findings and relating them to human rights policy in the two courts, it is necessary to consider whether any alternative rival hypotheses may explain the cross-national difference in the extent of judicial activism.[49] One variable will be examined here: the age of the Supreme Court. Stated in hypothesis form, the older the Supreme Court, the more active it will be. This hypothesis is based on the notion that a judicial body, without its own means of enforcement, is likely to increase its power over time as it becomes institutionalized—as it becomes valued in itself by the society. Thus, as a judicial body becomes an established political institution, it is more likely to withstand criticism on specific decisions, and its potential for activism increases. The age of the institution may be more important than its constitutional powers.

To test this hypothesis, data were gathered on U.S. Supreme Court activism/restraint in the nineteenth century, that is, when that Court was comparable in age to the present Supreme Court of Canada. Such comparison would be imprecise, because the Canadian data would represent the first two decades in which that Court has been a court of last resort, but seventy-five years after it was first established. Rather than utilize U.S. data beginning in either 1789 or

1864, it was decided to collect data from some period between those two dates. To avoid biasing the results in the hypothesized direction, the period had to represent a hard case: a time that the researcher believed would be least likely to support his initial proposition. Such a hard case had to be drawn from the Chief Justiceship of John Marshall (1801–35) rather than that of Roger B. Taney (1836–64), inasmuch as Marshall was considered to be the leader of a much more activist court. Specifically, the hard case had to be drawn from a period after Marshall's Court was established, particularly after the appointment of Justice Joseph Story in 1811, and during a period when a number of the Court's most famous early decisions were made. Based on these criteria, the twelve years from 1816 to 1827, coinciding with the twelve volumes of Wheaton's Reports, were chosen.

A last operational question was how to define a constitutional case. Because the issues in litigation at that time could have been much different from those in the present U.S. Supreme Court, it was considered inadvisable for the researcher alone to separate constitutional and nonconstitutional cases. Inasmuch as the Lawyers' Edition of the Wheaton's Reports, published in 1882 by the Lawyers' Cooperative Publishing Company of New York, contains headnotes at the top of each case stating the field or fields of law involved in the case in a manner similar to the summaries in the Canadian Supreme Court Reports, it was decided to use these headings to define a constitutional case.[50]

The nineteenth century findings are summarized in table 4. Just over one-half of the cases labelled constitutional in the reports and included in table 4 did not involve an applicable constitutional issue. Eleven cases turned on jurisdictional issues;[51] in the other fourteen nonapplicable cases, the decision also did not turn on a specific constitutional provision mentioned or discussed in the opinion or opinions. Thus the percentages used for comparative purposes are based on only the twenty-four cases which could be coded in terms of the

Table 4. JUDICIAL ACTIVISM IN THE UNITED STATES SUPREME COURT: INVALIDATING PUBLIC ACTION IN CONSTITUTIONAL CASES, 1816–27

Ruling on Public Action	Number of Cases	Percent of Total Cases	Percent of Applicable Cases
Valid	12	24.5	50.0
Part valid/part invalid	3	6.1	12.5
Invalid	9	18.4	37.5
N.A. jurisdictional issue	11	22.4	–
N.A.: Constitutional question not basis of decision	14	28.6	–

validity or invalidity of public action. The rate of judicial activism in the Marshall Court falls roughly halfway between the rates of the contemporary Canadian and U.S. Supreme Courts. Measured by quantity, the judicial activism of the Marshall Court is closer to that of the Supreme Court of Canada. Between 1816 and 1827, the Marshall Court dealt with two constitutional issues per year, invalidating government action about once per year. Since 1950, the Canadian Supreme Court has averaged three and one-half constitutional cases annually, invalidating government action also about once per year.

Furthermore, the Marshall Court, like both contemporary courts, was less active on federal issues than on state/provincial issues. Table 5 is built on the twenty-four applicable cases shown in table 4, with certain alterations.[52] It shows a greater difference between activism on state and federal issues than was shown in either the current U.S. or Canadian Supreme Courts. This lends support to the view that the Marshall Court was decisively important in building a strong central government. The 1816–27 court invalidated state action at a rate almost as high as the post-1950 U.S. Supreme Court. At the same time, however, the Marshall Court was 100 percent restrained on federal action, more closely approximating the Supreme Court of Canada.

In terms of both rate and quantity, the Marshall Court's activism resembles that of contemporary Canada rather than the United States. A period in which the Supreme Court could have been expected to be more active than in any other in the first seventy-five years of U.S. history was still consistently less active than the current period. The Marshall Court had greater impact upon the development of the American political system than the contemporary Canadian Supreme Court is likely to have on the Canadian political system, not because of a lower degree of judicial activism, but because the Canadian court was unable to exercise its influence in the early years of Canadian political development. The data presented here suggest that the Supreme Court of Canada, even with a

Table 5. JUDICIAL ACTIVISM IN THE UNITED STATES SUPREME COURT: INVALIDATION OF STATE AND FEDERAL ACTION IN CONSTITUTIONAL CASES, 1816–27

Ruling on Public Action	Type of Public Action			
	State		Federal	
	Number	Percent	Number	Percent
Valid	6	35.3	7	100.0
Part valid/part invalid	1	5.9	0	0.0
Invalid	10	58.8	0	0.0

narrower scope of formal judicial review than in the United States, is likely to grow in activism and importance—as a sign of its institutionalization over time.

JUDICIAL ACTIVISM, FEDERALISM, AND HUMAN RIGHTS

How is judicial activism in constitutional cases linked to the enunciation and enforcement of human rights policy in Canada and the United States? In the United States today, judicial activism is seen as a central institutional protection of human rights. In Canada, judicial activism is given less emphasis, both because it has not existed to a high degree in the past, and because alternative strategies have been sought. Again, the difference between the two countries has been attributed to constitutional differences, chiefly the limited form of judicial review operating in Canadä. Thus for example, an issue of defendant's rights in a criminal proceeding would be dealt with as a fourteenth amendment (or fourth-eighth amendment) question in the United States. In Canada, however, nonconstitutional principles of common and statute law would be applied.[53] One of the leading civil liberties cases in Canada centered on the discretion of licensing authorities, and resulted in the Supreme Court upholding the assessment of money damages against the Premier of Quebec.[54] In Canada, provincial practices in possible violation of human rights can be reviewed by the national Supreme Court and overturned on the basis of provincial law, providing an alternative to the application of general constitutional principles. In contrast, the U.S. Supreme Court is limited in the extent to which it can interpret state law differently than the highest state court; thus the national Supreme Court must constitutionalize the state issue to deal with it. The fourteenth amendment therefore becomes a device to transform a human rights issue under state law (for instance, the law of evidence) to a human rights issue under the federal constitution (for instance, fourteenth amendment due process). Thus, a full understanding of the role of national supreme courts in the protection of human rights would require consideration of available nonconstitutional strategies for human rights enunciation and enforcement. It may be that fewer such techniques are available in the United States than in Canada.[55]

At the same time, the Canadian deemphasis on constitutional enforcement of human rights may be accounted for in developmental terms, rather than in terms of cross-national differences in the constitutional framework for judicial review. Again, a comparison of the present Canadian Supreme Court and the early nineteenth century U.S. Supreme Court is instructive. In both of those courts, constitutional cases which raised human rights issues were in the minority. At the same time, both courts deemphasized the human rights issues that did exist. The important difference between those two courts and the modern U.S. Supreme Court is not that the issues are different, but that the major preoccupation of the Court with the establishment and consolidation of national power has not shifted to a similar preoccupation with human rights.[56] As a result, the development of human rights policy is episodic and peripheral in those national supreme courts in their first stage of development: that of defining national power in a federal system.

For example, the Marshall Court of 1816–27 heard only a handful of constitutional cases in which human rights issues were raised, but those cases included issues of right to jury trial,[57] limits on methods of seizing property,[58] limits on the contempt power of Congress,[59] and state debtor's relief and militia statutes.[60] The 1827 case of *Martin* v. *Mott* has an especially modern ring. Martin, a deputy United States marshal, seized Mott's goods in payment of fine for the latter's refusal to go into the War of 1812 when the New York state militia was ordered into that war by the President under a 1795 federal statute. Two state courts upheld Mott's action to recover his belongings, only to have the U.S. Supreme Court, in a unanimous opinion by Justice Story, reverse on the grounds that the federal law was clearly constitutional, and the president, not an individual soldier, is the one who judges whether it applies.[61] Thus cases with implications for human rights came before the Marshall Court. They were decided, however, with an eye to their impact on national power in a federal system.

Similarly, the Canadian Supreme Court has dealt with few constitutional cases since 1950 in which human rights issues were raised (less than one in three) and even fewer constitutional cases which turned on a human rights issue. In one case, discussion of the treaty rights of native Indians was replaced by discussion of whether a dead duck had been a wild duck within the terms of federal regulations. (Had the duck been tame, the Indian defendant may not have violated the Migratory Birds Convention Act.)[62] More commonly, cases in which an interpretation of the BNA Act affected human rights (about one in five cases) turned on the distribution of legislative powers. For example, a provision of the Saskatchewan Vehicles Act which allowed suspension or revocation of a driver's license for refusing a breath test was found valid as a provincial regulation of local highway traffic under section 92 (10).[63] But Saskatchewan legislation compelling a person accused of murder to testify at a coroner's inquest was held invalid, not on human rights grounds, but because it was a matter of criminal law and procedure and, thus, the exclusive jurisdiction of the federal government under section 91 (27).[64]

The two post-1950 cases in which the Supreme Court of Canada dealt with limitations on free expression both rested on interpretations of provincial jurisdiction. In *Switzman* v. *Elbling,* the Quebec "Padlock Law" (officially the *Act Respecting Communistic Propaganda*) was found ultra vires the provincial government as criminal law. In *Saumur* v. *Quebec,* a Jehovah's Witness challenged a municipal ordinance requiring permission of the Chief of Police to distribute literature on public streets. The deciding vote in the five to four decision ruled that the bylaw conflicted with a provincial statute.[65] In *Switz-*

man, three justices, led by Ivan C. Rand, attempted to apply a notion of fundamental rights, guaranteed by the preamble of the BNA Act, to invalidate the Padlock Law. Rand brought a fourth judge behind that same argument in *Saumur.* While his opinions in those cases are often cited as important statements of the constitutional basis of civil liberties in Canada, they have not yet become a basis for a constitutional jurisprudence of human rights in Canada. Rand recognized these difficulties at the time. On October 23, 1953, he received a letter to "My dear Brother Rand" from U.S. Supreme Court Justice Felix Frankfurter requesting a copy of the decision:

The New York Times the other day, with teasing brevity, reported a decision in your Court in a *Jehovah Witnesses* case. In due course doubtless the case will be reported in your advance sheets, but my interest is so keen about the case and particularly about what you have written, that I should be grateful for copies both of your opinion and the dissenter's, if you can conveniently furnish them.

Rand replied on October 26:

I have just today received the mimeographed copies of the reasons and I am enclosing one set. There are some features of the judgement about which I am not at all too happy. As you can see, these questions are now being faced in this country for the first time, and I have little doubt that to one who has explored them in so many aspects as you have the broad considerations which underlie them are an old story. There is, of course, a material difference in the constitutional background which necessitates a treatment with which you are not troubled, but it is of some interest how the substance in the one situation resembles that of the other.

Frankfurter echoed Rand's observations on November 20.

Many years ago I delivered some lectures at Princeton on aspects of federalism under the Australian, Canadian and United States Constitutions. As a result of studying the cases . . . dealing with the same kind of social and economic problems I was struck with the fact how Courts reach substantially the same conclusions though they get there by very different routes.[66]

The difference in approach, however, produces a difference in outcome. The *Canadian Witnesses Case* is resolved in favor of free expression, but on grounds sufficiently narrow to retard additional litigation. With rare exceptions, the Canadian Supreme Court is still about the task of expanding national power and checking provincial power.[67] With the heritage of the Judicial Committee of the Privy Council behind it, the Canadian Supreme Court has a substantial task indeed. The U.S. Supreme Court did not turn its attention in earnest to civil liberties until the post-1937 Roosevelt Court established broad national powers over economic affairs. It may be that the Supreme Court of Canada will wait for much the same circumstances before it becomes a primary agent for the protection of human rights in its country.

This argument has placed judicial activism, as a method of developing human rights policy in constitutional cases, in a developmental framework; that is, judicial activism on human rights can be expected when the Supreme Court in a federal system reaches a certain stage in its institutional development. As a result, the argument has permitted the statement of an hypothesis which can be tested in additional political systems, as a step in the development of a cross-national theory of human rights policy-making. However, the argument's focus on the development of the judiciary as an institution for making and enforcing human rights policy obscures the possibility of other institutional approaches to human rights. A reading of Canadian literature in the field suggests the importance of nonjudicial institutions such as parliaments and administrative agencies and challenges the use of judicial supremacy in the field of human rights.[68] Beyond differences over methods of enforcement, that literature reflects contrasting assumptions and concepts: human rights policy is discussed in a *minority rights model* rather than an *individual rights model*.

Minority rights and individual rights are usually not separated; both are supported by advocates of human rights. But they imply different modes of enforcement and different priorities. Thus, the individual rights model stresses protection of the individual against government. It is concerned mainly with those occasions when an individual is separated from others—the criminal defendant, the pamphleteer, the object of invasion of privacy. It stresses the judicial process, where, in theory, the plaintiff's or the defendant's case is not weighed on the basis of political power. It requires judicial review, so that government actions can be invalidated if they deprive the individual of his rights. Finally, it demands judicial activism as a key to survival of human rights.

The minority rights model stresses protection of minority groups. It is concerned with structuring the political process so that minorities are not subject to discrimination or suppression, or both, by majority interests and have political institutions which respond to their demands. The rights of racial, ethnic, and religious minorities are the focus here: the occasions when an individual and his rights are defined by his membership in a subpopulation (or aggregate) within the society. The minority rights model stresses fragmentation of political power through devices such as federalism, semiindependent administrative agencies, and legislative or party caucuses. It requires the decentralization of political power so that minorities can maintain or develop their independence and preserve their rights.

The two models are not defined by the substance of the rights involved, but by the ways in which the rights are enunciated and enforced. Thus, the rights of black people in the United States were treated as individual rights—to be ensured through the judicial process—during the post-World War II period, and only in recent years have they been treated as minority rights and protected through the development of administrative agencies and party caucuses and the attainment of local political power. The rights of criminal defendants in the United States is perhaps the classic case of individual rights, but if defendants were to be protected through their own organizations, a minority rights model might emerge. This is precisely the model that may be developed for protecting rights of prisoners and probationers, although the extent of judicial activism has been so great in recent years that the individual rights approach is increasingly used in the postconviction phase as well.[69]

Advocates of the two models tend to obscure their limitations. Thus D. V. Smiley argues that an entrenched Bill of Rights—one of the demands made by advocates of an individual rights approach—would provide less adequate protection than a parliamentary form of government. Yet he cannot deal with a vast inventory of legal rights available to persons in American courts but not in Canadian courts.[70] On the other hand, Joseph Sax argues in *Defending the Environment* that using the courts to stop polluters is more democratic than mobilizing administrative agencies which are beholden to industrial interests.[71] Yet, without a lawyer, a member of the public could not initiate an environmental lawsuit.

More important are the ways in which the two models conflict and even counteract each other. Thus, the minority rights model depends upon the fragmentation of power in a decentralized federal system, although critics of the federal system have often pointed out that it is precisely the isolated and hostile local majorities that may be responsible for the greatest infringements of human rights. For example, the federal system in Canada has provided an important protection for the French-speaking minority, because of its majority status in the large and politically powerful province of Quebec. At the same time, some of the most flagrant abuses of human rights in Canada occurred during the long regime of Quebec Premier Maurice Duplessis.[72] Minorities too small to be protected by existing political structures may be unable to gain redress through the courts; thus the Hutterites in Alberta, a communally-organized religious sect, were subject to provincial legislation prohibiting the purchase of land without authorization from the provincial government, and the Supreme Court of Canada refused to invalidate the statute.[73]

In the same way, the individual rights model may operate to undermine the minority rights model. The data in tables 2, 3, and 5 show the bias of judicial activism against state/provincial action, and for federal action. Because of this, judicial activism has a centralizing tendency. Rather than balancing federalism and administrative autonomy by checking its occasional excesses, judicial activism undercuts state/provincial power without maintaining similar checks on federal power. Historically, a conservative U.S. Supreme Court undercut the power of states to regulate conditions of work until pressure became so great that federal regulation in the same field was accepted. In the recent past, a liberal U.S. Supreme Court has placed limits on the powers of state and local police officials, leading to an increased federal involvement in law enforcement activities that the Court has thus far been unable to control. Thus the mechanism for preserving individual rights, judicial activism, may undermine the mechanism for preserving minority rights, federal decentralization.

Both models were ineffective as approaches to the preservation of human rights during World War II, when persons of Japanese ancestry were interned on the west coasts of Canada and the United States. In the United States, the federal government action was narrowly supported by a plurality in the Supreme Court.[74] In Canada, internment occurred after intense pressure from British Columbia politicians who converted regional sentiment into national policy.[75] In contrast, the minority rights model operated to delay conscription in Canada in both world wars, when French Canadian pressure made it almost politically impossible to draft citizens for a foreign war.[76] In the United States, the individual rights model proved no match for a federal draft law. In its 1917 Selective Service decision,[77] the Supreme Court unanimously upheld the draft, and dismissed thirteenth amendment arguments in one sentence. A constitutional challenge of the draft system was never again heard by the Supreme Court, even when the draft was extended into peacetime.

The Canadian constitution contains certain centralized features which are designed to check federal decentralization without the development of judicial activism. One is the power of disallowance, whereby the federal cabinet can unilaterally nullify any provincial statute within one year after passage. Another feature is the BNA Act provision making criminal law a federal responsibility, so that provincial governments are unable to create crimes, and are therefore deprived of one commonly used technique for dealing with social or political deviance in a manner which threatens human rights. However, these two features of the Canadian constitutional system have had limited impact. The power of disallowance has not been used since before World War II. And the federal responsibility for criminal law has not prevented the development of local ordinances which limit the exercise of human rights. The existence of two different models of human rights policy—the minority rights model and the individual rights model—suggests that political systems dedicated to the preservation and advancement of human rights must deal not only with the supposed weaknesses of human nature but also with the conflicting tendencies of political institutions.

EXTENDING THE STUDY OF HUMAN RIGHTS

The preceding analysis has used Canadian and United States material to suggest concepts and propositions relevant to a cross-national theory of human rights policy-making. The suggestions are hardly complete; rather than set out all the variables which require consideration, the analysis focused on a few for which data were available and from which interesting problems could be raised. A more complete theory would require:

1) Consideration of rights relating to basic economic security. Economic

rights have been given more emphasis in documents such as the Universal Declaration of Human Rights than in American or Canadian constitutional jurisprudence. In the United States, rights to minimum wages and standards of work, old age and disability benefits, housing, work, labor unions and medical services have been dealt with through legislation.[78] Such rights require positive action by government, either to proscribe private conduct or implement public programs, rather than the enactment of principles proscribing government action. As a result, such rights may be part of a third distinct model, a *positive rights model.*[79]

The individual rights and minority rights models were premised on the need to limit the authority of the general government, either by judicial check or by decentralization of authority. The positive rights model focuses on the need for government action to define and enforce human rights. It stresses legislation and regulation, and is embodied in such institutions as human rights (or human relations) commissions, and agencies which enforce minimum standards of treatment or perform basic economic functions directly. It requires adequate governmental authority and will to perform certain social and economic tasks within a political system.

Even though positive rights are usually associated with economic issues, they are linked to traditional rights of due process and free expression as well. In the United States, for example, the right to counsel in criminal cases has come to include the positive responsibility of the state to provide free counsel to indigents. And free expression is the basis for an evolving right of access to the mass media, enforced by federal government regulation of broadcast media.[80]

The conflict between an individual rights and a minority rights model was noted previously. The positive rights model may conflict with both of them. In Canada, one of the major recent federal-provincial conflicts has been over the scope of provincial power in administration of welfare and social services. In the United States, the development of positive rights legislation and administration may face restrictions by a Supreme Court whose activism moves in a conservative direction. Thus the third phase of Supreme Court development (after a national power and then a civil liberties focus) may involve the restriction of positive government, first illustrated in the early twentieth century by such famous cases as *Muller* v. *Oregon* and *Lochner* v. *New York.* For example, a future activist Supreme Court might invalidate compensatory benefit programs for previously deprived minorities, although such programs could be defended as positive action on behalf of human rights.[81] In future cases, then, judicial activism could directly challenge rather than define and defend human rights policies.

2) Consideration of outcomes as well as outputs of policy making. Rights are usually discussed in doctrinal terms; they are written, not performed or behaved. Human rights theory should consider what difference rights make, asking not only how they are enforced, but also how their presence or absence effects

human behavior. What is the behavior of free people? And how is such behavior linked to human rights? These questions require the use of systematic field observation to collect data and the adaptation of sociological concepts to link these behavioral variations to the process and output variables. A prescriptive bias would have to be consciously avoided in problem selection; thus, it is as important to study societies with a low degree of human rights as those in which human rights exist to a higher degree.[82]

3) Human rights outputs and outcomes should also be treated as independent variables. Thus far they have been important as dependent variables—as things to be explained. They are also important for what they can explain about a society and its political system—what is deemed basic or fundamental to social order, where the weaknesses ("tragic flaws") of a society exist. Thus, the most recent occasion in which the Canadian parliament placed statutory limits on the scope of free expression was when it prohibited so called hate propaganda, which reflected the abiding fear of internal divisiveness which characterizes that diverse society.[83] In contrast, the United States has paid little attention to brands of expression which direct scorn upon subgroups within the society, but prohibits similar expression directed at national symbols such as draft cards and the flag. What happens to human rights can teach us about the nature of societies. Human rights theory can become a piece of social theory—instructive as a whole, and invaluable as a part.

NOTES*

* In references to legal periodical literature, the number of the *initial* page of the work cited immediately follows the volume title. Page references to material specifically referred to in the text, if any, follow the initial page citation. Legal case citations correspond to *A Uniform System of Citation,* 11th ed. (Cambridge: The Harvard Law Review Association, 1974).

1. For example, David J. Danelski, "A Behavioral Conception of Human Rights," 3 *Law in Transition Quarterly* 63 (1966); Stuart S. Nagel, "The Social Consequences of Basic Legal Rights," in Human Rights, ed. Ervin H. Pollack (Buffalo, N.Y.: Fay Steward Pub., 1971) pp. 316–18; Arthur N. Holcombe, *Human Rights in the Modern World* (New York: New York University Press, 1948). Danelski and Nagel use human rights in the philosophical sense of rights present "in the inherent nature of man." Canadian legal scholars, e.g., Chief Justice Bora Laskin, sometimes equate human rights with nondiscrimination (egalitarian civil liberties, as distinct from political, legal, and economic civil liberties). This essay defines human rights as the full range of these civil liberties, leaving problematic whether they inhere in human nature or exist as legal rights in any given political system.

2. Ernst Haas, *Human Rights and International Action* (Palo Alto: Stanford University Press, 1970); Vernon Van Dyke, *Human Rights, the United States, and World Community* (Oxford University Press 1970).

3. For the best known example in each field, see: *New York Times* v. *Sullivan,* 376 U.S. 254 (1964); *Brown* v. *Board of Education,* 347 U.S. 483 (1954); *Reynolds* v. *Sims,* 377 U.S. 533 (1964); *Abington Township School District* v. *Schempp,* 374 U.S. 203 (1963); *Miranda* v. *Arizona,* 384 U.S. 436 (1966).

4. The most prominent exceptions to this generalization are Gary Orfield, *The Recon-*

struction of Southern Education (New York: John Wiley, 1969); Isaac D. Balbus, *The Dialectics of Legal Repression: Black Rebels before the American Criminal Courts* (New York: Russell Sage Foundation, 1973); and James Q. Wilson, *Varieties of Police Behavior* (Cambridge: Harvard University Press, 1968).

5. For a useful collection, see Sheldon Goldman and Thomas P. Jahnige, eds., *The Federal Judicial System: Readings in Process and Behavior* (New York: Holt, Rinehart and Winston, 1968), pps. 122–283.

6. Stuart S. Nagel, *The Legal Process from a Behavioral Perspective* (Homewood, Ill.: Dorsey, 1969), pps. 81–112, 193–98, 219–36; Bradley C. Canon, "The Impact of Formal Selection Processes on the Characteristics of Judges," 6 *Law and Society Review* 579 (1972).

7. See Glendon Schubert's extensive bibliographical essay, "Judicial Process and Behavior, 1963–1971," in *Political Science Annual: An International Review,* ed. James A. Robinson vol. 3 (Indianapolis: Bobbs–Merrill, 1972).

8. Ferrel Heady, *Public Administration: A Comparative Perspective* (New York: Prentice–Hall, 1966); Fred W. Riggs, *Administration in Developing Countries: The Theory of Prismatic Society* (Boston: Houghton Mifflin, 1964).

9. Glendon Schubert and David J. Danelski, eds., *Comparative Judicial Behavior* (New York: Oxford University Press, 1969). See also, Joel B. Grossman and Joseph Tanenhaus, eds., *Frontiers of Judicial Research* (New York: John Wiley, 1969), pp. 45–198.

10. See Edward J. Weissman, "Mathematical Theory and Dynamic Models," in Schubert and Danelski, *Judicial Behavior,* especially the summary table at p. 390.

11. While Danelski and Schubert both contributed papers at the International Political Science Association meetings in 1973, no papers with cross-national data on judicial behavior were presented at the 1973 meetings of the American Political Science Association.

12. See Schubert and Danelski, *Judicial Behavior,* pp. 293–334. In this way Sidney R. Peck was able to apply scalogram analysis to the Supreme Court of Canada. However, when Stephen R. Mitchell applied bloc analysis to the Supreme Court of Canada in a 1967 paper, the technique was ineffective because that nine-person court often meets in panels of five and seven. See Stephen R. Mitchell, "The Supreme Court of Canada Since the Abolition of Appeals to the Judicial Committee of the Privy Council: A Quantitative Analysis," paper presented to the annual meeting of the Canadian Political Science Association, June 7, 1967, Carleton University, Ottawa.

13. Danelski, *Judicial Behavior,* p. 398.

14. Theodore Becker, *Comparative Judicial Politics* (New York: Rand McNally, 1970).

15. Ibid., p. 13.

16. As one consequence of this reliance, Becker's work never considers whether judicial structure can cease to exist. For one approach to the nonpersistence of courts, see Carl Baar, "Will Urban Trial Courts Survive the War on Crime?" in *Sage Criminal Justice Systems Annual,* ed. Herbert Jacob, vol. 3 (Beverly Hills, Cal.: Sage Publications, 1974).

17. *Dred Scott* v. *Sanford,* 19 How. 393 (1857); *Civil Rights Cases,* 109 U.S. 1 (1883). The notion that parliamentary supremacy offers better protection of human rights than judicial review is a major theme in Canadian public law. (See n. 68.)

18. C. Herman Pritchett, "Public Law and Judicial Behavior," in Marian Irish, ed., *Political Science: Advance of the Discipline* (New York: Prentice-Hall, 1968), pp. 190–213.

19. Compare the leading judicial process collection in political science, Walter F. Murphy and C. Herman Pritchett, *Courts, Judges, and Politics: An Introduction to the Judicial Process* (New York: Random House, 1961), with the comparable works by law professors: Carl A. Auerbach et al., *The Legal Process: An Introduction to Decision-making by Judicial, Legislative, Executive, and Administrative Agencies* (San Francisco: Chandler, 1961); and Lawrence M. Friedman and Stewart Macauley, *Law and the Behavioral Sciences* (New York: Bobbs–Merrill, 1969). Even a recent text on the legal process by a political scientist, James Eisenstein, *Politics and the Legal Process* (New York: Harper and Row, 1973), is typically restricted to the judicial arena.

20. Martin Shapiro, "From Public Law to Public Policy, or The 'Public' in 'Public Law,'" 5 *PS* 410 (1972), and Martin Shapiro, *The Supreme Court and Administrative Agencies* (New York: The Free Press, 1968).

21. For the right-to-counsel cases, see Anthony Lewis, *Gideon's Trumpet* (New York:

Random House, 1966), pp. 95–101. Regarding death penalty cases, see *Furman* v. *Georgia*, 408 U.S. 238 (1972).

22. For a collection of studies, see Theodore L. Becker and Malcolm M. Feeley, eds., *The Impact of Supreme Court Decisions*, 2d ed., (New York: Oxford University Press, 1973); for an integrative text with extensive bibliography, see Stephen L. Wasby, *The Impact of the United States Supreme Court* (Homewood, Ill.: Dorsey Press, 1970).

23. See James P. Levine and John H. Kessel and Kenneth Dolbeare in Becker and Feeley *Supreme Court Decisions*. Consider generally, Philip Selznick, *TVA and the Grass Roots* (Berkeley: University of California, 1949) for his discussion of the unanticipated consequences of purposive action.

24. See Stephen L. Wasby, "Getting the Message Across: Communicating Court Decisions to the Police," 1 *Justice System Journal* 29 (1974).

25. See Donald T. Campbell, "Legal Reforms as Experiments," 23 *Journal of Legal Education* 217 (1971) and idem. with H. Laurence Ross, "The Connecticut Crackdown on Speeding: Time-Series Data in Quasi-Experimental Analysis," 3 *Law and Society Review* 33 (1968). Stuart Nagel's research has focused significantly on the effects of alternative legal policies; for example, see his "Minimizing Costs and Maximizing Benefits in Providing Legal Services to the Poor," presented at the 1973 annual meeting of the American Political Science Association, New Orleans.

26. Peter Bachrach and Morton S. Baratz, "Two Faces of Power," *American Political Science Review* 56 (1962):947; Matthew A. Crenson, *The Un-Politics of Air Pollution: A Study of Non-Decisionmaking in the Cities* (Baltimore: Johns Hopkins Press, 1971).

27. Murray Edelman, *The Symbolic Uses of Politics* (University of Illinois Press, 1964), pp. 22–43. Becker argues that the concept of function should be used to discuss the effects of structures; see also, Becker, *Judicial Politics*, pp. 4–12.

28. Glendon Schubert, *Judicial Policy-Making* (Chicago: Scott, Foresman, 1965), p. 157. Judicial activism is not defined as either the overruling of a lower court decision or the reversal of a previous precedent (in contrast to other elements of Schubert's definition). Among the reasons for excluding such court behavior from the definition are: (1) In both the United States and Canadian Supreme Courts, judicial restraint is closely related to sustaining the court below and judicial activism is closely related to reversing the court below. (2) The invalidating of government action is more politically significant than the reversal of a lower court. (3) A court which is willing to reverse the court below or its own previous holdings in order to conform to the legislative or administrative policies of the day does not exhibit a high degree of independence.

29. The structure of the hypotheses also assumes that some public action is always at issue in a constitutional case. If a constitution also proscribes private conduct (e.g., denial of equal protection without introducing a concept of state action), the definition of judicial activism would have to be expanded or the range of constitutional cases contracted.

30. Becker, *Judicial Politics*, p. 222. His third factor, "the strong influence (direct and indirect) on the part of American power interests," operates in Canada, but does not explain the existence of judicial review in Canada.

31. The terms are drawn from Mauro Cappelletti, *Judicial Review in the Contemporary World* (Indianapolis: Bobbs–Merrill, 1971), p. 69.

32. Ibid., p. 46 and ibid., pp. 85–96, for other similarities.

33. The major constitutional law casebooks are: Bora Laskin, *Canadian Constitutional Law*, 3d ed. (Toronto: Carswell, 1969), and J. Noel Lyon and Ronald G. Atkey, *Canadian Constitutional Law in a Modern Perspective* (Toronto: University of Toronto Press, 1975).

34. *The Queen* v. *Drybones*, (1970) S.C.R. 282. Volumes of Canadian Supreme Court Reports are numbered by year, although frequently cases decided late in one year (e.g., *Drybones* in November 1969) are reported in the volume(s) of the following year.

35. That is, through the end of the 1972 volume of Supreme Court Reports.

36. See n. 12. Thus the analysis excludes, for example, the Supreme Court of Canada's invalidation of a federal law prohibiting manufacture, offer, sale, or possession for sale of margarine. See *Reference as to the Validity of Section 5(a) of the Dairy Industry Act*, (1949) S.C.R. 1, affirmed by the Judicial Committee of the Privy Council in *Canadian Federation of Agriculture* v. *Attorney General for Quebec*, (1951) A.C. 179.

37. For the most recent discussion of the Judicial Committee's work by a political scientist, see Alan C. Cairns, "The Judicial Committee and Its Critics," *Canadian Journal of Political Science* 4 (1971):301.

38. Contrast *The Queen* v. *Drybones* with the earlier *Robertson and Rosetanni* v. *The Queen,* (1963) S.C.R. 651.

39. Note however that these statements are limited to constitutional adjudication. See footnotes 53 and 54 and text for discussion of nonconstitutional techniques used to invalidate public actions in Canada.

40. An exception is the quantitative data reported annually by the *Harvard Law Review* in its fall review of the work of the previous term of the Supreme Court.

41. Becker, *Judicial Politics,* p. 235.

42. The quoted language is from K.C. Wheare, *Federal Government,* 3d ed. (New York: Oxford University Press, 1953), p. 229.

43. *Canadian Wheat Board* v. *Nolan et al.,* (1951) S.C.R. 81.

44. *P. E. I. Potato Marketing Board* v. *Willis,* (1952) 2 S.C.R. 392; A.G. for *Canada* v. *C. P. R. and C. N. R.,* (1958) S.C.R. 285; and *Procureur General du Canada* v. *La Compagnie de Publication La Presse Ltee,* (1967) S.C.R. 60.

45. See for example, *Attorney General for British Columbia* v. *Smith,* (1967) S.C.R. 702, and *Re Offshore Mineral Rights of British Columbia,* (1967) S.C.R. 792.

46. It was during the tenure of Archibald Cox as Solicitor General that that office filed arguments against the states' positions on legislative apportionment.

47. For contrasting examples, see Lewis, *Gideon's Trumpet,* pp. 139–60 and Manitoba's "chicken and egg war." Manitoba passed a statute identical to a Quebec statute it wished to challenge, and then sought a Supreme Court decision against its own law as ultra vires for trespassing on federal jurisdiction over trade and commerce. The Supreme Court agreed and invalidated the Manitoba law. *Attorney General for Manitoba* v. *Manitoba Egg and Poultry Assn.,* (1971) S.C.R. 689.

48. Other variables which might affect this relationship are evaluated in Carl Baar, "Social Organizational Variables and Court Behavior," paper presented to the annual meeting of the Canadian Political Science Association, June 4, 1970, University of Calgary, Alberta, pp. 10–13.

49. For a discussion of rival hypotheses, see Eugene J. Webb et al., *Unobtrusive Measures* (Chicago: Rand McNally, 1966), pp. 1–36.

50. Thus the operational definition of a constitutional case in the United States Supreme Court is different for the two centuries. However, in both periods, only decisions with full opinions are included (court orders without opinion and per curiam opinions have been omitted).

51. Ten of the eleven involved federal courts, and rested upon the interpretation of the Judiciary Act of 1789 and subsequent practice rather than on article 3 of the Constitution.

52. Two cases were excluded: *Johnson and Graham's Lessee* v. *William M'Intosh,* U.S. 21 (8 Wheat.) 543 (1823), which invalidated a land title granted by an Indian tribe, and *Cassell* v. *Carroll,* U.S. 24 (11 Wheat.) 134 (1826), which applied as valid an Act of the British Parliament. Two cases, *Gibbons* v. *Ogden,* U.S. 22 (9 Wheat.) 1 (1824), and *Osborn* v. *Bank of the United States,* U.S. 22 (9 Wheat.) 738 (1824), were double-coded; in each case, a federal law was upheld and a state law declared unconstitutional.

53. See, for example, *Gordon* v. *The Queen,* (1965) S.C.R. 312 (habitual criminal statute); *Fraser et al.* v. *The Queen,* (1966) S.C.R. 38 (obscenity); *Wilband* v. *The Queen,* (1966) S.C.R. 14 (procedures in psychiatric examination for preventive detention of dangerous sexual offender).

54. *Roncarelli* v. *Duplessis,* (1959) S.C.R. 121.

55. Whether nonconstitutional techniques are used actively in Canada is problematic, and it would be interesting to have activism-restraint data in this area.

56. The difference that does exist is in the frequency with which given issues arise, which may derive in large part from the reaction of litigants who flood national supreme courts with those issues in which the body has expressed interest. Supreme courts do not merely react to cases flowing to them any more than an academic journal simply responds to input. The composition of the input is shaped by the interests of the organization. This

proposition should hold for the Supreme Court of Canada even though that body had no discretionary jurisdiction such as the certiorari jurisdiction of the United States Supreme Court.

57. *The Bank of Columbia* v. *Okely,* 17 U.S. (4 Wheat.) 235 (1819).

58. *Gelston* v. *Hoyt,* 16 U.S. (3 Wheat.) 246 (1818).

59. *Anderson* v. *Dunn,* 19 U.S. (6 Wheat.) 204 (1821).

60. *Farmers and Mechanics Bank of Pennsylvania* v. *Smith,* 19 U.S. (6 Wheat.) 131 (1821), and *Houston* v. *Moore,* 18 U.S. (5 Wheat.) 1 (1820).

61. *Martin* v. *Mott,* 25 U.S. (12 Wheat.) 19 (1827). The case also raised questions of whether a court-martial was lawfully constituted.

62. *Sikyea* v. *The Queen,* (1964) S.C.R. 642.

63. *Validity of Section 92(4) of The Vehicles Act, 1957* (Sask.), (1958) S.C.R. 608.

64. *Batary* v. *Attorney General for Saskatchewan,* (1965) S.C.R. 465. Religious observance legislation in Quebec was invalidated on the same grounds in *Henry Birks and Sons* v. *City of Montreal and Attorney General for Quebec,* (1955) S.C.R. 799.

65. *Switzman* v. *Elbling,* (1957) S.C.R. 285; *Saumur* v. *City of Quebec,* (1953) 2 S.C.R. 299. Both cases are excerpted and discussed in Peter H. Russell, ed., *Leading Constitutional Decisions,* part 5, (Toronto: McClelland and Stewart; Carleton Library Series, 1965), pp. 193–232.

66. Felix Frankfurter Papers, Manuscript Division, Library of Congress, Washington, D.C. (General Correspondence, Container 92, "Rand, I.C."). Frankfurter's Princeton lectures to which he refers were delivered from notes in April 1935 and were never published. No drafts or notes could be found in his papers in the Library of Congress collection.

67. The possibility raised by the *Drybones* decision in 1969 that the federal Bill of Rights would refocus the Court's attention was at least temporarily dashed by the *Lavelle* holding in the summer of 1973.

68. For criticism of an entrenched Bill of Rights which would limit legislative supremacy, see Donald V. Smiley, "The Case Against the Canadian Charter of Human Rights," *Canadian Journal of Political Science* 2 (1969):277; Peter H. Russell, "A Democratic Approach to Civil Liberties," 19 *University of Toronto Law Journal* 109 (1969); and Douglas A. Schmeiser, "Disadvantages of an Entrenched Canadian Bill of Rights," 33 *Saskatchewan Law Review* 249 (1968). The two leading texts on civil rights and liberties in Canada are Douglas A. Schmeiser, *Civil Liberties in Canada* (Glasgow: Oxford University Press 1964), and Walter Tarnopolsky, *The Canadian Bill of Rights* (Toronto: Carswell, 1966). For the official statement on behalf of entrenchment, see the statement by then Minister of Justice Pierre Elliott Trudeau, *A Canadian Charter of Human Rights* (Ottawa: Queen's Printer, 1968).

69. Consider also the free speech campaigns of the I.W.W. from 1908 to 1916, before any first amendment cases were handled by the United States Supreme Court. See Joyce L. Kornbluh, ed., *Rebel Voices: An I.W.W. Anthology* (Ann Arbor: University of Michigan Press, 1964).

70. Opponents of an entrenched Bill of Rights place more emphasis on legislative supremacy than on federalism for protection of human rights, suggesting that they are following a third model, denoted below as a positive rights model. See n. 79 and text.

71. Joseph L. Sax, *Defending the Environment: A Strategy for Citizen Action* (New York: Knopf, 1971).

72. See notes 54 and 65.

73. *Walter* v. *Attorney General for Alberta,* (1969) S.C.R. 383. Note however that the statute was repealed as of January 1, 1973, following the election of a new Progressive Conservative Party government in the province.

74. *Korematsu* v. *United States,* 323 U.S. 214 (1944).

75. See Forrest LaViolette, *The Canadian Japanese and World War II,* Canadian Institute of International Affairs, (Toronto: University of Toronto Press 1948), and Evelyn Kallen et al., "Issei, Nisei, Sansei, Yonsei," in *The Myth of the Mosaic* (Holt, Rinehart and Winston of Canada, to be published). A similar political history for the United States may be found in Morton Grodzins, *Americans Betrayed: Politics and the Japanese Evacuation* (Chicago: University of Chicago Press, 1949).

76. Donald V. Smiley, *The Canadian Political Nationality* (Toronto: Methuen, 1967), pp. 32–34.

77. *Selective Draft Law Cases,* 245 U.S. 366 (1918).

78. For a collection of legal writings integrating economic rights into traditional civil liberties questions, see Norman Dorsen, ed., *The Rights of Americans* (New York: Pantheon Books, 1971), pp. 3–17. For a useful inventory of basic legal rights in the economic sphere, see Nagel, "Social Consequences of Basic Rights," pp. 316–18.

79. Arthur Selwyn Miller, "Toward a Concept of Constitutional Duty," 1968 *Supreme Court Review* 219. Cf. Wallace Mendelson, "Law and the Development of Nations," *Journal of Politics* 32 (1970):223.

80. See John de J. Pemberton, Jr., "The Right of Access to Mass Media," in Dorsen, *Rights of Americans,* pp. 276–96; and *Columbia Broadcasting System* v. *Democratic National Committee,* 412 U.S. 94 (1973).

81. Paul G. Chevigny, staff counsel for the New York Civil Liberties Union, derives such an argument from a reading of John Rawls, *A Theory of Justice* (Cambridge: Harvard University Press, 1972). See Chevigny's book review in *Civil Liberties,* September 1973, pp. 4–5.

82. Jean Laponce has criticized the tendency of social science research to avoid the negative; see his presidential address before the Canadian Political Science Association, August 1973.

83. See *Report of the Special Committee on Hate Propaganda in Canada* (Ottawa: Queen's Printer, 1966). Pierre Elliott Trudeau, then an Associate Professor of Law, was one of seven committee members.

Chapter 15 COMPARATIVE RIGHTS RESEARCH: SOME INTERSECTIONS BETWEEN LAW AND THE SOCIAL SCIENCES

Richard P. Claude

Students of comparative law and students in comparative subfields of the social sciences have long recognized that their disciplines overlap. But the shared territory has been treated as something of a "no man's land." Scholars in the fields of comparative law and of comparative social science are barely on speaking terms with one another. They resemble neighbors not yet properly introduced, and therefore not yet ready to cooperate, to agree to disagree, or even to argue.[1]

Arthur T. Von Mehren of the Harvard Law School recently observed that comparative law, unlike other areas of legal study, has not established a core of information and theory that is carried forward, developed, and refined by succeeding generations of scholars. With rare exceptions, research in comparative law tends to be scattered and diffuse as to topic, legal system, and purpose. Von Mehren writes: "One has the uneasy feeling that comparative law scholarship is always beginning over again, that comparativists lack a shared foundation on which each can build."[2]

Where human rights are concerned, the legal scholar Edmund Cahn and the political science comparativist Ivo Duchacek[3] have effectively shown that bills of rights are invariably indictments of the excesses or deficiencies of past regimes. Each such formulation to safeguard against continued future abuse is embroiled in historically unique circumstances and is deeply affected by the special culture of the peoples involved. Each device to solve a human rights problem is cast in the mold of quite varied legal systems from country to country.[4] As suggested by table 1, the filiation of legal systems worldwide compounds the difficulties of comparison.[5] Because, as the table suggests, the canvas is so broad and because, as Van Mehren observes, the efforts towards comparison heretofore have been so limited, an attempt to portray diversity in generalized comparative terms must be seen as tentative and suggestive rather than as final and definitive. Nevertheless, some observations on human rights

Table 1. A GENETIC SCHEME OF LEGAL SYSTEMS

- **Legal Systems**
  - *Systems of Occidental Culture*
    - *Systems of Roman Law Filiation*
      - *Laws of Latin Origin*
        - *French and Related Systems*
          - France, French Union Countries
          - Italy
        - *Spanish Law*
          - *Ibero-American Systems* — Spain
        - *Systems of Iberic Filiation*
          - *Portuguese Law* — Portugal, Brazil
          - *Systems Influenced by Common Law* — Puerto Rico, Philippines
      - *Romano-German*
        - Austria, Germany, Switzerland
    - *Scandinavian Systems*
      - Sweden and Finland, Norway and Iceland, Denmark
    - *Systems of Anglo-Saxon Filiation*
      - Great Britain — Commonwealth Countries
      - United States
    - *Mixed Roman-Common Law Systems*
      - Scotland, Louisiana, Quebec, South Africa, Israel
  - *Non-Western Systems*
    - *Mixed Oriental-Western Systems*
      - Japan, South Korea
    - *Non-Western Systems*
      - *Hindu Law* — Sri Lanka, India
      - *Islamic Law* — Arab Countries, Pakistan, Indonesia
    - *Socialist Systems*
      - Soviet Union, People's Republic of China, Cuba
      - *East European Countries*

research from the diverse points of view represented by the essays in this volume is now in order, along with some suggestions for future cooperative research.

The kinds of questions that engage scholarly concern in a research area can be decisive in its development. The reason is that, once the focus of inquiry is clear, research may more economically proceed to the fruitful level of problem-oriented description and analysis, if not explanation.

Comparative human rights research can make three particular contributions to efforts to understand the legal order as one facet of the human experience. The first contribution is to direct attention to the basic questions of *institutional development* by clarifying the relationship between institutional forms—the formulated and developed concepts and structures of law and the legal order's institutional arrangements which structure man's effort to provide a just and workable ordering of human affairs. The second contribution is to forward understanding of specific problems of *public policy* that have a bearing on human rights. Consequently our field of knowledge is expanded, and decision-makers in an age of accelerating social and political developments may benefit by the accurate description of alternative approaches to the practical problems of liberty, equality, and human welfare that are common to many countries. The third contribution is to clarify some of the difficult questions relating to the *behavioral dimensions* of the interaction of law and society. Social science research techniques are now sufficiently sophisticated to make material contributions to the systematic study of human rights. Moreover, since the time of Aristotle, comparative study has supplied the firmest basis upon which to develop guiding theory in the social sciences. Here an effort is made to tie together some of the observations made by the essays in this volume as they bear on the questions of (1) institutional development, (2) public policy, and (3) law and society.

INSTITUTIONAL ANALYSIS

A comparative approach to human rights can aid political and institutional analysis. For example, the discussion in Claude's essay (see chapter 1) focuses on the historical emergence in Great Britain, France, and the United States of various rights and liberties. As natural rights concepts in these countries have given way under the press of socioeconomic conditions to changed legal institutions, such claims have been built, to varying degrees, into a new type of higher law that binds government. They have been converted into statutory and, in some instances, constitutional rights. The analysis in Baldwin's essay (see chapter 3) also deals with the effort to constitutionalize various rights, and particularly to set legal limits on government, contingent upon the goals of nation building inherent in the particular stage of socioeconomic and political development involved. His discussion centers on Mexico, the United States, and Uganda.

Several variations on the process of constitutionalizing rights are suggested by the approaches of the countries surveyed in these case studies.

A salient point of comparison at the institutional level is whether specified rights are fixed in documentary constitutional terms requiring extraordinary amending processes (entrenched rights), and whether such limits are applied to government by virtue of judicial review or some comparable mechanism for enforcement.

Consider the British Constitution, a model of flexibility. It does not rely upon a rigid constitutional declaration of rights—that is, a statement of entrenched rights formally binding upon ordinary legislation. Strictly speaking, such landmarks of British constitutional history as the Petition of Right (1628) and the Bill of Rights (1688) have a status no different from that of any other act of Parliament. Honoring the guarantees stipulated by these documents typically becomes an internalized matter of social tradition, education, and general behavior, as Gallatin's study of political socialization reveals (see chapter 12). The principle of parliamentary supremacy forecloses any opportunity to challenge a statute properly enacted by Parliament on the proposition that it contravenes fundamental rights. The principle ensures maximum adaptability over time, and in Great Britain there is no lack of statutory rights ranging from privacy protection to prohibitions on racial discrimination. Where privacy is concerned, the essay by Hutton, Nehra, and Sastri (see chapter 5) indicates that the glare of parliamentary debate and public discussion, supported by cultural predispositions, supplies important remedies in the absence of judicial review. Nanda's essay (see chapter 8) details the administrative remedies available in the system of race relations boards which, he concludes, hear, but do not always effectively arbitrate, discrimination disputes.

Thus in Great Britain, in the absence of entrenched rights and of judicial review, one may nevertheless speak of basic legal rights supported by specific remedies and enforcement techniques. Another example is supplied by the rights of criminal defendants. Although nowhere declared, they are effectively bound up with procedure. Much of the secret of the fairness of a British criminal trial lies in the independence of the judges and such specific detailed rules as the following: the charge must be precise and detailed so that the accused knows what allegations he must meet; the prosecution must prove guilt beyond a reasonable doubt; a confession may not be used against the accused unless it was given voluntarily. Stephens (see chapter 6) notes a recent tendency in Great Britain, as well as in Canada and Australia, to fault trial judges on the use of traditional judicial remedies for over-zealous police activity. Stephens reports that criticism in these countries of the "Judges' Rules" reflects "a growing scepticism about the value and legitimacy of judicial efforts to upgrade police methods."

The British model of rights, dependent upon tradition and common law, has not been widely followed, although variations are obvious in such erstwhile Commonwealth Dominions as Australia and New Zealand.[6] In Israel, civil liberties, although only in part defined in written law, have found recognition in numerous decisions of the courts. There both codified and case law show considerable British influence. As Baldwin's essay notes (see chapter 3), among those nations which have more recently emerged from the British Empire, such as India, Kenya, Nigeria, Uganda, and Malaysia, the tendency has been to enumerate basic rights and freedoms in general written detail. Where the judiciary has been seen as an instrument for containment and repression during the independence struggle, the more popular political branches often have effectively limited judicial discretion with an extensively detailed written and entrenched set of constitutional rights. Baldwin's comments regarding Uganda and the review by Hutton, Nehra, and Sastri (see chapter 5) of judicial review in India bear out this analysis. A second restraint growing out of developmental circumstances affecting judicial review is identified where Canada and the United States are concerned (see chapter 14). Baar's data on judicial activism in these two countries support the hypothesis that, at least where federal systems are concerned, the need for institutional consolidation takes precedence over human rights activism during the early years of constitutional development.

The French system supplies an interesting contrast to that of the British and those which derive from Great Britain. Wenner's comparative analysis of the problems of linguistic minorities in France suggests that the bargaining framework of political parties has supplied the forum for working out both successful and unsuccessful remedies (see chapter 7). As table 2 indicates, the French system supplies an alternative model with variations found in numerous political systems which have adopted written constitutions. The French Constitution of 1958, while rigid insofar as special amending procedures are required (article 89), nevertheless does not provide for judicial review. The review functions of the *Conseil Constitutionnel* are very limited. Only the Chief of State, the Chief of the Cabinet, and the presidents of the two legislative chambers have standing to challenge the constitutionality of a statute.[7] Such preventive review must be exercised prior to promulgation of the law. Still, the fact that a right is

Table 2. COMPARATIVE PATTERNS OF RIGHTS AND REMEDIES

		Entrenched Rights	
		Yes	No
Judicial Review	Yes	United States	Canada
	No	France	Great Britain

proclaimed by the Constitution gives it a "higher law" dignity with two practical consequences. First, any ambiguous law must be interpreted in conformity with the Constitution, and second, its assertion in the Constitution tends to promote recognition and respect on the part of policy makers. Finally, the *Conseil d'Etat,* which has general jurisdiction over administrative action, would be competent to annul an act of the executive unconstitutionally interfering with *garanties fondamentales.* Although beginning from quite different ideological sources, the European people's democracies all have followed France in adopting written constitutions. These constitutions are comparably rigid in their binding force over ordinary legislation and in requiring special procedures and special majorities for amendment. With the sole exception of Yugoslavia, they also follow the French model of not recognizing judicial review.[8]

The third approach, typical of the United States, has been influential in Latin America, Germany, Japan, and Scandinavia. In the United States, a rigid constitution, which entrenches various specific rights and liberties, is combined with a system of judicial review. Going beyond the preventive control available to the French *Conseil Constitutionnel,* but excluding declaratory judgments, the American system is famous for the capacity of the Supreme Court to nullify legislation and administrative action as void, thereby placing the Court in a policy-making position at both the federal and state levels. With noteworthy modifications, the American model of entrenched and judicially enforceable rights is found in many countries. For example, according to Beer (see chapter 4), modern Japan invests all courts with the power to set aside unconstitutional legislation. As illustrated by Schreiber (see chapter 9) and Breeden (see chapter 10), judicial review is also now at work in Norway, Denmark, and Sweden. The Federal Republic of Germany relies upon a written constitution and a centralized system of judicial review.[9] Since 1951 it has even provided for a special proceeding called constitutional recourse (*Verfassungsbeschwerde*) whereby the individual may directly attack any governmental action in the Federal Constitutional Court after the exhaustion of ordinary remedies. A comparable special recourse procedure is also available in Mexico and other Latin American countries.[10] As described by Baldwin (see chapter 3), the *juicio de amparo* originated in Mexico as a differentiated judicial remedy particularly created to guard against state infringement of fundamental rights of the individual.

As table 2 indicates, the Canadian system stands in something of an anomalous position, which, according to Baar's analysis (see chapter 14) may be undergoing a process of gradual change. While Canada has both a rigid constitution and a system of judicial review, the identification of rights in the Bill of Rights of 1960 is not entrenched or fixed in constitutional law except in ordinary statutory form. Some of the consequences of this situation for the right to counsel for criminal defendants are spelled out by Stephens (see chapter 6). The possibility of considerable variation in the ways in which the provinces handle such basic rights as freedom from racial discrimination is detailed by

Nanda (see chapter 8), whose analysis illustrates Canadian resistance to nationalizing human rights and remedies. The Canadian Bill of Rights was not adopted as an amendment to the Constitution and, thus, it appears to be repealable, or open to change, by a simple majority vote of the Parliament. Nevertheless, the Supreme Court of Canada, in a controversial ruling of 1968, has interpreted the Bill of Rights as controlling ordinary legislation in the absence of an express statement of derogatory parliamentary intent.[11]

Judicial review is thought by many, especially Americans, to be an indispensable support for various human rights. Nevertheless, the French, British, and Canadian models described above suggest that this need not necessarily be the case. Clearly, there are institutional and remedial-pattern alternatives. Because of its hybrid quality, the anomalous case of Canada is especially interesting, as suggested in Baar's essay (see chapter 14). The pressures for decentralization which partly explain Canada's unique position in table 2 draw attention to an independent institutional variable affecting judicial review—that is, the extent of government centralization. The impetus behind judicial review appears, in the first instance, to be associated with a general governmental centralizing tendency. The effort to create uniformity in civil, social, and political rights throughout a country may be more a part of a centralizing strategy than a humanitarian movement. Centralization of the rights-defining and rights-adjudicating agencies has the effect of positioning the mass of citizens as legal equals in a direct unmediated relationship to the central political authority.

This situation was originally analyzed by Alexis de Tocqueville. In the 1830s, he anticipated that the demand for citizenship equality could strengthen the claims of centralized government, which in turn would reinforce such civil rights demands in order to undercut interference of intermediary powers, whether feudal, local, or associational. In a typically epigramatic analysis which draws attention to the paradox that the same power that supports civil rights can also come to overshadow them, he wrote:

Every central power which follows its natural instincts loves equality and favors it. For equality singularly facilitates, extends, and secures its influence. . . . I think that in the dawning centuries of democracy, individual independence and local liberties will always be products of art. Centralized government will be the natural thing.[12]

De Tocqueville's view need not be taken somberly to prefigure the inevitable demise of human rights—"the products of art"—by self-aggrandizing centralized government—"the natural thing." His view may be taken to carry the more sanguine suggestion that the art of devising satisfactory institutional arrangements to preserve human rights must, like all arts, continue to be practiced and refined by the changing lights of human creativity. Issues of institutional conflict over centralization, the nationalized uniformity of legal human rights standards, and techniques for enforcement and remedies arise again and again.

This is true in every legal system, no matter what the institutional arrangements, and whether or not there is a formal bill of rights. It is the continuous task of legislators and judges to work out compromises that resolve such conflicts on as fair as possible terms and to give those compromises expression in legal decisions and rules. The prospect for continuing the art of institutional creativity in the service of human rights is subjected to constant challenges. This is made clear in the discussion in the essays in this volume.

It is appropriate to note in this brief discussion of comparative institutional analysis, albeit at a rather abstract level, some of the common ground that has become evident. Shared among the contributors to the volume are the following assumptions about the institutions that are related to human rights. One, a secure legal system for the dispensing of justice and regularized procedures for settling disputes are necessary for a human rights system to prevail. Two, a modernized legal system relies upon institutionally differentiated legal structures and flexible and rational settling procedures for resolving conflict. Three, the more structurally differentiated and flexible the legal system (through the development of legislation, regularized settling procedures, judge-made law, or both) the more capable is the system of response to incremental social and political change. Four, the idea of rule of law associated with setting legal limits upon government, while subject to varying interpretations from country to country, derives from the principles, institutions, and procedures which the experience and traditions of lawyers and other legal actors have shown to be important to protect the individual from arbitrary government. Five, as the typically modern positive rights policies of welfare enlarge side by side with administrative centralization, the organizational needs for program control and supervision tend to conflict with earlier ideas of rule of law and with earlier negative rights standards, such as protecting property and privacy and forbidding discrimination. Consequently, old equilibrium points sometimes reflected in entrenched constitutional principles, may need to be reviewed and altered, especially as more long-lived negative rights come into conflict with newer positive rights. Since the primary agencies for making these adjustments are the legislatures and, in some political systems, the courts, in the end, the best constitutional guarantees of justice are those which enhance the democratic character of legislative bodies and which safeguard the high quality and independence of the courts.

HUMAN RIGHTS AND PUBLIC POLICY

The study of comparative human rights must not only be sensitive to the rule-making and rule-adjudicating functions at the center of institutional analysis, but must also focus on the decisions or policies actually made by the persons who participate at numerous stages of the institutional processes. As has been suggested, the range of possible institutions concerned with human rights is numerous. Certainly the variety of policies covered by the term human rights is also extensive.

To give focus to the matrix of institutional decision-making and its public policy outputs, it is possible, at a very general level, to speak of a human rights system. A human rights system may be defined as a set of institutional arrangements for securing legally binding guarantees beneficial to (a) the individual in his citizenship and private roles and to (b) groups seeking status-equality, nondiscrimination and inclusion in the social, economic, and political process. As *claims against* government, groups, and private individuals, the resulting entitlements may be characterized as *negative rights.* Guarantees to (c) socio-economic welfare policies are *claims upon* government and other organizations which, as *positive rights,* are typically implemented by systems of administrative support.

One of the most difficult problems involved in fleshing out the above definition in specific policy areas, is the problem of mapping the range of human rights. An appropriate beginning can be made by examining the United Nations Declaration of 1948. In its thirty articles, the Universal Declaration of Human Rights sets forth basic rights and fundamental freedoms to which all men and women everywhere are entitled, without any distinction as to race, color, sex, language, religion, birth, or other status. The rights and freedoms of the Declaration are set forth in two broad categories of rights: civil and political rights, and economic, social, and cultural rights. This list has been used by the United Nations and by member governments as a yardstick to measure the compliance by governments and as a model for achievement. Publications and surveys of the United Nations Commission on Human Rights are a beginning data-base upon which careful comparative research can focus. Since 1955, the United Nations has collected data through an international intelligence gathering program with periodic (triennial) reporting by individual states on human rights development, studies of specific rights and groups of rights, and advisory services in the field of human rights.[13]

To date, the most elaborate academic effort to map the policy fields of human rights is that made by Myres S. McDougal, Harold D. Lasswell and Lung-chu Chen in their article on "Human Rights and World Public Order: A Framework for Policy Oriented Inquiry."[14] Their twelve-page typology separates categories of claims relating to (a) power, (b) respect, (c) enlightenment, (d) well-being, (e) wealth, (f) skill, (g) affection, (h) rectitude, and (i) claims relating to "permissible derogations from established standards." The model is characterized by an explicit concept of human nature, logical symmetry, and breadth of scope.

While the McDougal, Lasswell, and Chen typology relies on logically connected criteria for its elaborate taxonomy, the alternative scheme set out below in table 3 is historical. It uses the criteria of negative and positive rights indicated above. Also, it relies on Claude's stipulation (see chapter 1) of the four classical stages of human rights development ranging over four centuries. From the earliest assertion of rights to the most recent, it illustrates the tendency to progress from the satisfaction of sundry claims to be, to have, to do, and to receive. As such, the typology invites comparison with the priority of needs satisfactions stipulated in social psychology by Abraham Maslow.[15] In his analysis, there is a hierarchy of human needs, but where the most basic need to be—survival—is threatened, all others become subordinate in importance.

The conceptual framework and terminology developed by McDougal, Lasswell, and Chen has brought a policy-oriented approach to bear upon international law. Scholars in that field have found it stimulating, but it has been criticised as producing confusion as well as clarity by its tendency toward "formalism" (overconcern for definitional precision) and discursiveness.[16] The McDougal—Lasswell—Chen enterprise, moreover, has offered rather little explicit guidance to the comparative study of human rights. Nevertheless, its emphasis on policy analysis should be taken seriously as the appropriate core for the comparative study of human rights, both in terms of problem-solving and theory-building.

The estrangement of comparative law from the social sciences already noted creates an impediment to a policy approach to comparative human rights. Because of the isolation of comparative law from comparative social science, two distinct perspectives have emerged: an institutional perspective concerned with the rule-making and rule-adjudicating functions associated with legal institutions, and a public policy perspective preoccupied with rule-application and its social and political consequences more common to social science study. Applied to the problems of human rights, such bifurcation results in emphasizing one dimension of rights policy at the expense of others.

The contributors to part 2 of this volume each give intense attention to a single topical area within the field of human rights. The style of analysis among the authors differs from essay to essay. The diverse levels of description and analysis which they employ supply an opportunity to discern and stipulate the dimensions of human rights policy. If we can identify the various dimensions of human rights with sufficient scope, then perhaps the effort to achieve an integrated policy science of human rights can begin. Policy science is an exercise in strategic analysis insofar as it deals with choices which are subject to long and short-term constraints.

Four dimensions of human rights emerge from the discussions of specific policy problems. Selected illustrations are given here, but the reader will be able to discern various of these dimensions differentially used among all of the essays in part 2. These dimensions may be called the *source, content, protection,* and *extension* of human rights. The first of these dimensions relates to political culture and basic law; the second to definitional propositions of the law; the

Table 3. THE STAGES OF HUMAN RIGHTS DEVELOPMENT

		20th century Socioeconomic Rights	19th century Participation Rights	18th century or earlier Civil Liberties	17th century or earlier Political Freedom
PRIVATE RIGHTS	*Against private persons and groups*	Protection from environmental pollution; Security from economic coercion; Protection of children	Protection from involuntary servitude	Protection from libel	Protection from bodily harm
	Against government	Artistic expression; Life style; Inquiry; Information; Participation in cultural life; Privacy; Marriage; Choice of birth control strategies	Teaching; Travel	Security against unfair criminal procedures; Security against unfair civil procedures; Security against arbitrary administrative action	Life; Physical liberty; Religious belief and practice
POLITICAL RIGHTS	*Against government*	Political asylum; Right to retain citizenship; Right of egress	Voting; Political candidacy; Association; Organization	Political discussion; Assembly; Petition; Publication	Security against arbitrary government action
EQUALITY RIGHTS	*Against government*	Freedom from unfair discrimination based on: sex, age, literacy, wealth	Equal opportunity; Civic equality; Freedom from unfair discrimination based on: race, language, ethnic and national origin	Equality before law; Freedom from unfair discrimination based on: religion, status of nobility	
ECONOMIC RIGHTS	*Against government*	Nondiscrimination in government benefits and services	Labor organization	Possession and use of property; Occupation; Buying and selling; Contracting; Copyright	

HUMAN RIGHTS — NEGATIVE RIGHTS

POSITIVE RIGHTS

Adequate income
Health services
Housing
Employment
Insurance against
    financial risk of:
        work injury
        unemployment
        retirement
        ill health
        old age

Education

"Rights to Receive"   "Rights to Do"   "Rights to Have"   "Rights to Be" third to the full panoply of operative sanction-systems; and the fourth to political and sociological elements. These dimensions of human rights are discussed one at a time:

1. Where human rights are concerned, the most obvious long-term constraints on policy-makers derive from the social and legal *sources* of a right. Human rights policy cannot mean simply the most recent single ruling made by executive officials, courts, parliamentary bodies, or other decision-making elites. It also concerns the continuous public commitments inherent in prevailing culture and ideologies as well as the aggregate of ground rules subsumed under the term "constitution"—whether written or nonwritten and customary.[17] If we ask what is the source of a right, we must locate our answers in political culture as well as basic law. Many questions relating to the source of a right are open to scholarly research and field work. To what extent and with what consequences has legal-rational political culture replaced a traditional ideology emphasizing status and mystery? Are the values underlying documentary constitutional rights-guarantees congruent with the values of the prevailing political culture? Are the sources of documentary or customary constitutionalism imbedded in the national symbols of legitimacy? What is the level of rights consciousness within the population?

In his discussion of free expression rights in Japan with comparative reference to the United States, Beer (see chapter 4) illustrates this level of explanation at work. His basic contention is that free expression is now viable in Japan, not only because of the persistence of political conflict, but also by general popular acceptance of the values in the Constitution. Describing the 1947 Constitution as "the most authoritative scripture and theoretical reference point in Japan," Beer says that "it appears in the rhetoric of most political debates." A detailed description is given of the ways in which Japanese people integrate their current consciousness of their rights with the traditions of their political culture and especially with the values associated with the many cohesive groups characteristic of their social structure. A contrast is offered to American rights consciousness (which is also an influence in Japan), which emphasizes the autonomy of the individual and the propriety of individual self-expression. The comparison prompts Beer to conclude that, if expression rights are to be preserved, decision makers must recognize that de-emphasis on man's interdependence by excessive individualism is as destructive of freedom as extreme group dependency.

2. The skills of legal research are especially necessary to examine another dimension of rights: their *content*. The content of a right in any given system refers to the aggregate of legal propositions which describe the right. The content of any right includes the claims which those invoking the right have (against obstruction by others or for the execution of a duty by others) to make good their demand according to applicable law. In asking what are the legally valid claims attendant upon any given right, interdisciplinary research must go beyond mere legal restatement. There are researchable questions of politico-legal

dynamics that can fruitfully be raised as well. How do the institutions of the legal system contribute to defining the content of a right? How do such basic functions of legal decision-making as the intelligence, recommending, prescribing, invoking, applying, appraising, and terminating functions contribute? How do legal functionaries (governmental officials as well as the bar, legal experts, law journals, private groups interested in legal change, and paralegal workers) contribute? What is the milieu of conflict over a policy area out of which definitive legal propositions emerge? In asking these questions, we are asking not only about textbook law, but also about the agents of change who most immediately influence the formulation of the law's requirements. In this context, Ernst Jones aptly observed that propositions of law, "since they represent verbally-frozen policies based upon assumptions that daily become more obsolete in consequence of social change, are in continual need of policy studies."[18]

The essay on privacy rights by Hutton, Nehra, and Sastri (see chapter 5) illustrates this level of explanation at work. In their review of the American, British, and Indian law of privacy, they found considerable difference in the scope of legal development and the volume of applicable rules. While there are rather few laws specifically concerned with privacy in Great Britain, and far fewer in India, scattered common law developments have a bearing in both of these systems. Most recently, however, intensive debate and discussion in parliament, the scholarly journals, and within the British Justice Commission have actively contributed to the formulation of new statutory law. A worldwide comparative survey of privacy rights in countries other than Great Britain was influential in developing statutory refinements. Where the United States is concerned, the authors show that the incremental development of privacy rights derives from scholarly and legislative efforts, but most particularly from Supreme Court case law tracing back to 1895. The result, in comparative terms, is that the United States possesses the most comprehensive range of legal propositions attaching to a "right of privacy." Nevertheless, they say that the greater elaboration of constitutionalized privacy law is no indication that Americans are better respectors of the privacy of others. On the contrary, they conclude that privacy values are better observed by the British (for whom breaches of privacy are inhibited by internalized norms) and by the Indians (whose technological development does not permit the kind of surveillance and sophisticated government invasions of privacy which are said to threaten Americans). Of the three systems, the authors assess the British as having the most "stable and certain body of law."

3. A third dimension of any given right directs our attention to the *administration of protection* or enforcement of rights. Inasmuch as a claim legally clothed as a right is identical with the opportunity of obtaining judgment against another who is duty-bound to respect the right, the enforcement or procedural protection is merely another side of the content of the right. Yet research focusing on rights protection must go beyond inquiry into the content of the

right in terms of the plain meaning of expressed government decisions. Inquiry into rights protection focuses on the structure of sanctions and remedial dynamics behind rights claims and examines how and under what circumstances coercion may be brought to bear in support of public policy.[19] In this context, numerous researchable questions come to light. What is the role and scope of reliance upon legal and extralegal conciliation for the settlement of rights disputes? How open is access for all to enforcement machinery and procedures? What are the costs (in time, personnel, professional skills, and convenience) of enforcement? Relative to costs, what is the pattern of remedial benefits (symbolic and real) to rights-claimants? What is the compliance record in response to the authoritative determination of rights?

Nanda's essay (see chapter 8) focuses specifically on complaint procedures involving racial discrimination in Britain, Canada, and the United States. He notes that various experiments with conciliation mechanisms show that they play a vital part in educating people, in breaking racial barriers, and in bringing the promise of nondiscrimination policies into the local community. He particularly details British, Canadian, and American experience with conciliation machinery and enforcement techniques, and he assesses the utility of various protection approaches. Since 1968, the British Race Relations Board has gone beyond a policy of open access to complaints, and it now investigates problems on its own initiative. The pattern of remedies is wide-ranging—from written assurances against repetition of unlawful acts to the initiation of civil or criminal court proceedings. Even broader than the British Race Relations Board are the powers of various Canadian boards, particularly the Ontario Human Rights Commission. Nanda notes that administrative streamlining of that body has nevertheless opened it to criticisms of unfairness in that the same Commission members entrusted with investigation may also be given conciliation powers. Until recent years, the laissez-faire approach in the United States, which Nanda says puts unwarranted reliance on good faith, has been responsible for unenforced laws and a lack of ingenuity in developing protective institutional structures. This condition continues to prevail in many of the American states. However, the affirmative action approach newly associated with the federal Equal Employment Opportunities Commission makes a major contribution to the development of civil rights remedies. Nanda concludes that the resulting compliance with EEOC proceedings is superior to conciliation techniques for enforcement. In his judgment, it supplies a worthwhile model for emulation elsewhere.

4. A fourth policy dimension of any given right focuses on the *extension* of the right to ever-larger circles of people. Here we are concerned with the ways in which new groups are assimilated into the system of rights guarantees and the social and political processes involved in the succession to rights. While the administration of protection noted above examines the impact of rights on the politico-legal system, the focus of the extension of rights is instead directed

forward toward elements of the social process.[20] Again, researchable questions available for comparative research are numerous. What social divisions and political cleavages or historical forces impede the application of rights to some groups but extend them to others? Who are the social elites who act as brokers or change-agents in the extension of rights? How is the symbolism and rhetoric of equal rights ideals used to promote various policy interests in the name of broadened rights?

Wenner's essay on linguistic minorities in Europe (see chapter 7) is effective at this level of analysis. He suggests a variety of reasons for the increasing stridency of groups asserting minority rights—the Flemish in Belgium, the Basques in Spain, and the inhabitants of the Jura in Switzerland. In each of these and many other cases, a differentiating characteristic of the involved groups is their language affinity. Many explanations have been suggested for intensified interest on the part of these and other linguistic minorities in asserting special minority rights: diminished minority influence in national affairs due to European integration; the psychology of rising expectations; the focus which the mass media has newly brought to bear upon anticolonialist successes around the world, and the like. To examine these kinds of questions, Wenner particularly concentrates upon linguistic minorities such as the Bretons in France, and the Welsh in Great Britain. He finds that there appear to be no patently evident socioeconomic and political correlates to heightened demands for minority rights. Yet he finds that whereas in France increased levels of activism have produced little improvement in relative minority positions, in Great Britain increased activism has produced an obvious improvement in the rights and language-related privileges which minorities enjoy. The explanation for such differences he locates in the different political cultures involved, in special historical factors such as the traditional continuities in the approach to colonial and minority issues, and in varying activities of political entrepreneurs who assume more or less effective leadership positions. In the absence of serious federalization plans that would ensure the devolution of decision making in response to local participation, Wenner sees the aims of linguistic minorities in terms of a political process aimed at institutionalizing legal standards for group equality.

Human rights may be described and analyzed, with varying utility, at several levels. As the preceding discussion suggests, it would be misleading to propose that only one line of emphasis is correct in the study of any given right. The source, content, protection, and extension of rights are distinguishable components, and no analysis of these four dimensions can be conducted by reliance simply upon one narrowly defined academic discipline. These four categories of analysis are drawn, in part, from the study of rights offered by Alf Ross in his book, *On Justice*.[21] Reflecting Ross's Danish analytical bent and his philosophic distaste for legal idealism, the terms are value-neutral. We employ them here, framed alongside rather traditional-style questions, because in them we have a net tight enough to collect relevant information for purposes of studying public policy but loose enough to angle among very diverse politico-legal systems. By themselves, these categories and the questions we have related to them surely fall short of Professor Ross's long-range objective: to devise categories of analysis that will order data so as to further the scientific task of foreseeing how public opinion will affect fundamental rights and how decisional bodies concerned with rights will act in the future. Only in recent years have behavioral scientists begun to fish in these deeper waters.

BEHAVIORAL DIMENSIONS OF HUMAN RIGHTS IN LAW AND SOCIETY

From the level of institutional analysis and that of public policy studies, it is not possible to deal systematically with the study of human behavior. Those who wish to explore individual decisions by linking personality and the other individual causal factors that may lie behind discrete decisions do not find much usable knowledge at the level of constitutions, legal pleading, or the canons of statutory construction. In their approach to legal phenomena, the behavioral sciences have sought, if not to jettison the study of public law, at least to consider rules and legal formalities as mere statements of belief; yet such beliefs are but one of the elements that individuals receive and process in their efforts to cope with the problems of their immediate environment. The reasons and causes of such legal phenomena as human rights cannot be explained solely by reference to the institutions of the law but must also be explained in terms of the law's creator, man, and the study of man, social science.

The social sciences must be brought to bear upon the study of human rights. In a special issue of *Revue des droits de l'homme* [*Human Rights Journal*] devoted to methodology, in review of various trends in comparative and international research in the 1970s, M. J. B. Marie wrote: "It is the social sciences which, precisely because of the techniques which they have developed recently, now permit research on certain aspects of reality bearing importantly on the subject of human rights" [trans. Richard P. Claude].[22] However data-rich research cognate to the study of human rights may have become in recent years, it is nevertheless correct to acknowledge that the field remains theory-poor. The problem of developing an integrated theory of human rights addressed to questions of explanation derives from basic difficulties not fully resolved by the philosophy of social science. Should the foundation for explanatory theory be elicited from the ways in which men understand and justify their behavior, or should the measurable externalities of behavior form the basis for theorizing? Should the focus be upon personal motives or social effects?

Social science inquiry into human rights, like social science inquiry generally, may be conducted at two levels.[23] At one level, observation of behavior is carried out by considering the actions studied in the perspective in which it has meaning for the actor. The psychological, cultural, and indeed, moral dimensions of the actions are taken into account by reference to the individual participant in the social process. Second, observation is pursued in terms of the empirically verifiable features of human interaction which sustain or nullify hypotheses framed to explain the larger processes of change in society at large. The political, economic, and perhaps anthropological dimensions of the actions studied are taken into account by reference to societal processes. From this analysis, it is clear that when a social scientist understands behavior connected with human rights, two kinds of interpretation may flow from observation of the same actions. One, the social scientist may study certain actions in terms of their having a specific meaning for the actors: going to court instead of accepting an apology for a racially discriminatory affront as a vindication of the principle of equality; marking the ballot as a vote; heckling an official as a gesture of protest. In these instances, the observer has interpreted the meaning of the acts involved, and the interpretation supplies the social scientist with the subject matter for his theory. Two, the social scientist may interpret the litigation behavior as a reflection of the status inconsistencies in social cleavages; the vote as a reflection of resurgent nationalism; the protest as a symptom of social class alienation. These latter interpretations are the meanings attached to action assigned by the observer, not the observed. The point here is that a balanced social science of human rights should attempt to build theory at both of these levels of interpretation. There follow some exploratory ideas along these lines to promote future research; first, under the guidance of an interaction theory of human rights and, second, at the level of human rights development theory.

An interaction theory of human rights. During the past decade, increasing attention has been given to the systematic analysis of psychological, political, and sociological aspects of human rights in terms of political socialization, public opinion, and political action. Of these areas, perhaps the least work has been done on socialization—the process of learning society's norms for relating to proper patterns of participation and for relating to authority. Few comparative efforts have been made to delineate the process of socialization to the norms underlying the various human rights such as tolerance, liberty, and human dignity. The work of Gallatin (see chapter 12) seeks to assess the role that cultural variables play in such cognitive development. By conducting similar survey studies among adolescents in the United States, West Germany, and Great Britain, she has been able to develop some precise comparisons from one system to another. Reassuringly, she finds that in these three western democracies respect for human dignity, as tested by questions on rights and reciprocal duties, is gradually inculcated in the young. But she finds statistically significant the differences among age and nationality groups in the justifications they offer for holding human rights in a position of esteem. Insofar as she identifies the varigated cultural views peculiar to each country, her study supports the comments of Patrice Gélard. In his attempt to sensitize students of comparative law to the behavioral components of their discipline, he observed that, in the framework of our multistate society, "the collective traditions of the peoples will retain differences which may be only minor, but which will subsist in the legal system."[24]

Complementary to the original research done by Gallatin is the literature review by Devall (see chapter 13). He explores the extent to which social scientists have succeeded in developing comparative techniques for the study of public opinion supportive of human rights. Devall reports on numerous such opinion studies, and he also analyzes the attitudes of various elites regarding human rights. Thus, he identifies educational and intellectual elites, in particular, as agents for attitude change, for example, with regard to emerging rights to freedom of lifestyle. Devall's review of cross-national opinion surveying, in combination with Gallatin's field work, helps to give vitality to the appeal by Alf Ross to study the links in the processes of opinion and policy change from the basis of underlying personal interests and attitudes to the end results of cognition and political action.

To the extent that the study of human rights can use rigorous social science research techniques, it must break down behavior relevant to human rights into its component elements. In his analysis of "cognition and action" in law and politics, Ross argues that a dynamic study of legal politics takes more than legal doctrine into account. The researcher should recognize that the activity of those involved in the legal process, like "all conscious activity, must be rooted in an attitude."[25] Thus, the study of legal phenomenon must somehow (and Ross does not say exactly how) be positioned to take attitudes and interests into consideration.

In Ross's view of psychology, attitudes shaped by interests and perceptions of need motivate behavior: "cognition can never motivate an action, but assuming a given motive (perceived interest) it can direct the activity released." As suggested schematically by table 4, the behavioral components in the psychological and social processes of what Ross called "cognition and action" are complex and multifaceted. In behavioral terms, the process requires that the morally motivated behavior of the individual be translated at several levels (ranging from perception, expression, and cognition of needs and interest) into effective political behavior. The components and sequence of this individual and collective process of moving from moral endorsements of various claims to legal recognition of rights may be diagrammed with deceptive simplicity. Social science has only recently begun to itemize (but not yet to explain) the concrete processes of exchange and direction that are involved in this complex of behavioral interaction.

C. Thomas Dienes has elaborated an interaction scheme adaptable to the format of table 4.[26] In terms of Dienes's analysis, the arrows in table 4 which point from moral response to legal response are characterized in terms of various functional types of behavior leading from society to a variety of "legal actors." At the basic level of perceiving needs and interests, an intelligence function must

Table 4. STIMULUS-RESPONSE MODEL OF HUMAN RIGHTS DEVELOPMENT

Stimulus	Response	(Moral Response)	(Legal Response)
	Types of Behavior	Moral-Political Behavior	Politico-Legal Behavior
Socioeconomic and Political Problems	Perception	Perception of needs (interests) in political terms ⟶	Intelligence and problem-related fact-finding
	Expression	Articulation of claims and demands for remedies ⟶	Technical formulation of rights and sanctions
	Cognition	Moral deliberation and endorsement (in terms of ⟶ attitude sets prevalent in the political culture)	Legislative/ constitutional adoption and judicial/ administrative recognition
	Action Response	Political debate and ⟶ promotion of resolution	Sanctioned government enforcement of rights

be performed in making community and political leaders, legislators, and judicial decision makers aware of the problem-related facts. The initial recommending function is essentially a communication problem: needs produced by changing social conditions are communicated to legal actors in the expectation that they will restate these needs in the technical language of public policy, rights, and duties. The policy prescription function is directed at the final prescriptive behavior of the particular legal actor. For example, the legislator or constitution-maker assesses the perceived political consequence of a particular action (such as constituency pressures). Moreover, he is affected by his personal values, and he must operate within a set of institutional role-expectations and "rules of the game." As Baar's review of judicial behavior literature suggests (see chapter 14), similar external forces also affect the judicial actor, although the salience of such considerations may be quite different.

Except for the McDougal-Lasswell-Chen typology referred to earlier, no theory of human rights public policy has been rigorously formulated. Other than their rather diffuse exercise in the mapping of human rights, there is no taxonomy comprehensive enough and sufficiently differentiated to place in a coherent context the kinds of stimuli which produce a rights response, either at the individual-moral level or the collective-legal level. It is possible that this gap in theoretical knowledge cannot be remedied. The reason is to be found in politics, the central and intermediary position of which is suggested in table 4. The task of politics is conditioned by a multiplicity of individual, group, and institutional needs that do not constitute a system, but rather a conglomeration. On analyzing a specific demand for rights, myriad motivational components are found. Their variety reflects not merely the interests and opinions of different social groups, but also (as Devall documents in chapter 13), in many cases, a diversity of needs and opinions within the same group. Thus, the progression from moral response to legal response, shown in the table is inevitably complicated by the insertion of politics at its core. Since the political task is always one of integration, the political response to expressed social needs always has the character of a resolution of conflict, not of a solution (such as the technical solution of how a rights guarantee shall be formulated). With the range of conflicting interests and needs emerging from society ever variable, it is pretentious to suggest that the range of human rights has been captured graphically in a finite chart or taxonomic listing. What can be said, however, is that the behavior of legal actors responding to changing and emerging social needs ultimately serves human rights when that behavior functions to resolve, rather than to create, conflict and to integrate diverse needs and interests.

Human rights development theory. Clearly, these modest generalizations about the framework for the small-scale or microscopic study of interaction between segments of society and various legal actors have not focused on the context of politico-legal and socioeconomic development which inevitably conditions these internal workings from system to system. By contrast to such interaction theory, a behavioral theory of human rights development does not consider rights and liberties from the point of view of the claimants or individuals involved. Rather its perspective is macroscopic, considering human rights from the standpoint of the social system as a whole.[27] In this light, it appears that where human rights have developed, they have come into existence as a part of a political system's response to changing socioeconomic and cultural conditions. Stipulating and correlating the relevant variables assignable to such a societal analysis is a challenge to the field of social science as well as to the field of history.

Increasingly scholars who devote themselves to explaining the complex genesis of real political institutions have turned to systematic comparative history. The attraction of using historical method applied to comparative research, according to the French scholar André Hariou, is that it permits inquiry "by a kind of sequential experimentation which is otherwise practically impossible in the social and especially political sciences."[28] The hope is to identify and analyze a manageable number of underlying social processes so as to explain change in multivariant structures. To this end, complex quantitative analysis, little developed in research on human rights, can aid in the kind of exploration Hariou recommends. In chapter 2 Strouse and Claude press forward the theme of the opening essay on comparative history by focusing on human rights in the context of political and economic development. Their findings regarding the negative result of rapid economic development and the positive effect for human rights of communications development invite replication and may assist in efforts at causal modeling. It is hoped that the suggestive regression analysis set out will stimulate future cumulative work. The analysis illustrates the kind of technical comparative research that remains on the frontier of future exploration.

The comparative study of political development has undergone considerable change in recent years. In the field of legal institutions, comparative research has a venerable tradition which reflects the original preoccupation of political science with public law. The list of innovative public law comparativists concerned with the topic of rights includes Georg Jellinek, Rudolph von Ihering, René Cassin and Edward McWhinney.[29] The problems of rights and liberties which have interested these legalists carry a preoccupation with the negative side of democratic institutions and the freedom from various government restrictions which they entail. The positive side of democracy—popular participation in the selection of political decision-makers—has especially interested contemporary comparativists in the social sciences. Prominent in the field of the comparative development of democracy are Jean Blondel, Seymour Martin Lipset, Stein Rokkan, Dankwart Rustow, and Giovanni Sartori.[30] Comparative history has also captured the interest of a number of contemporary scholars concerned with the process of political modernization. Among them are Cyril Black, Samuel Huntington, Barrington Moore, and the members of the Committee on Comparative Politics of the Social Science Research Council (SSRC) in the United States.[31]

Particularly productive have been the efforts of various of these comparativists to categorize patterns of development by general stages or phases through which different societies have passed on the way toward legal democracy and modernization. Two examples serve to illustrate.

In legal scholarship, Georg Jellinek, writing in 1892, developed a well-known classification of legal rights (subjektiven öffentlichen Rechte).[32] He surveyed four stages of achievements or "statuses:" passive status (which defines the role of the individual in terms of general subjection to the state); negative status (which assures rights or protection from the state); active status (which extends rights of political and electoral participation), and positive status (which guarantees rights to positive actions by the state). Jellinek, however, provided no clear guidelines for social scientists trying to interconnect social processes with the development of the juridical concepts which he described. As a result, his work lacks dynamic capacity to explain change and falls short of what his colleague at Heidelberg, Max Weber, called an "ideal type."

No field of theoretical interest in comparative politics draws the attention of more political scientists than the study of political development. The scope of this topic is very broad since the process of modernization which it studies transcends the regime categories associated with liberal democracy, authoritarianism, and communism. According to Samuel Huntington, the modern polity is characterized by rationalized authority, differential structure, mass participation, and a consequent capacity to accomplish a broad range of goals.[33] The SSRC Committee has focused on political development defined in these terms. Comparative political development is the particular focus of the group in its publication, *Crises and Sequences in Political Development*.[34] The contributors identify a series of crises with which societies must cope in the transition from traditionalism to modernization. These involve critical changes (a) of identity from the parochial to the societal; (b) in legitimacy from transcendental to immanent sources; (c) in distribution from status and privilege to ability and achievement in the control and management of capital; (d) in political participation from elite to mass; and (e) in the degree of administrative and legal penetration into the social structure.

Clearly efforts such as those reviewed above to explain change in legal, political, and administrative institutions should redirect the attention of social scientists in search of theory to the study of history. Success in such a venture will require a new reliance upon quantitative modes of comparative analysis. If stages of politico-legal development may fairly be fixed and linked with independent socioeconomic variables, we may in the future even be able to ask questions, more precisely than heretofore has been possible, about the timing, pace, and direction of human rights development. Today, however, the state of research is such that social scientists, historians, and legal scholars are still without the theoretical framework to enable them to generalize about human rights development under compression, that is, when nearly simultaneous development of various stages of human rights implementation is attempted (as in the case of modern Japan); in fixation, that is, when directional change seems arrested (as in the case of American reluctance to enter the field of positive socioeconomic rights); or undergoing regression, that is, when a collapse or reversal of stages takes place (as with Brazil, Uganda, or the Weimar Republic in Germany). With serial data on economic, social, and political indicators becoming available, social scientists may be expected increasingly to follow the fruitful research approach of exploring problems along the lines of interrelated processes, development variations, and crisis sequences.

In summary, let us emphasize that the process of conducting research in the field of comparative human rights is challenging and difficult. Certainly it is multifaceted. In the manifest absence of any commanding holistic view of the relationship between law and human rights development in society, research must be eclectic in method.[35] This review of institutional description, policy analysis, and behavioral inquiry suggests that in fully integrated research, there should be three principal operations involved to explicate comparative human rights. The first operation, *institutional description,* entails the assessment of divergencies and resemblances in the institutions, concepts, and norms concerned with the resolution of human rights problems. The second operation, *policy analysis,* is concerned with the identification of differences and similarities between systems compared as to the functionally equivalent ways in which discrete policy problems are handled under circumstances of existing constraints upon policy-makers. The third operation, *behavioral explanation,* is directed at accounting for the divergencies and resemblances among different systems in their processing of human rights problems, particularly in terms of two levels of focus. These are, on the one hand, behavioral factors indigenous to those involved in decision making, and on the other, socioeconomic and political influences which have exogenous bearing on societal development at large. In all of these areas the most difficult task, that of constructing explanatory theory, has barely begun.

These operations—institutional description, policy analysis, and behavioral explanation—are analytically distinct. However, if comparative human rights is to flourish as a field of study, all must be included or acknowledged in any effort at systematic research. Thus, the capacity of the field to develop depends upon the recognition by interested scholars that the law and its processes both affect and are deeply affected by the extralegal social factors that surround it. Until such time as this recognition shapes cross-national scholarly work, a costly irony will continue to prevail: while the appeal of human rights is worldwide, the understanding of human rights dynamics is too primitive to ensure effective international development.

NOTES*

* In references to legal periodical literature, the number of the *initial* page of the work cited immediately follows the volume title. Page references to material specifically referred to in the text, if any, follow the initial page citation. Legal case citations correspond to *A Uniform System of Citation,* 11th ed. (Cambridge: The Harvard Law Review Association, 1974).

1. See *Revue des droits de l'homme* (Human Rights Journal) 6 (March 1973):65–70.
2. Arthur T. Von Mehren, "An Academic Tradition for Comparative Law?" *American Journal of Comparative Law* 19 (1970):624–33.
3. Edmund Cahn, *The Sense of Injustice* (New York: New York University Press, 1949); Ivo A. Duchacek, *Rights and Liberties in the World Today* (Santa Barbara: American Bibliographical Center - Clio Press, 1973).
4. See generally, Louis L. Jaffe, *English and American Judges as Lawmakers* (Oxford at the Clarendon Press, 1969).
5. See generally, René David and John E. C. Brierly, *Major Legal Systems in the World Today* (New York: The Free Press, 1968).
6. James Dixon, "The Common Law as an Ultimate Constitutional Foundation," 31 *Australian Law Journal* 24 (1957). See generally Edward McWhinney, *Judicial Review in the English Speaking World* (Toronto: University of Toronto Press, 1960). Cf. Glendon Schubert, "Two Causal Models of Decision-Making by the High Court of Australia," in *Compara-*

tive Judicial Behavior, ed. Glendon Schubert and David Danelski (New York: Oxford University Press, 1969).

7. Maxime Letourneur, "The French Conseil d'Etat," *Journal of the International Commission of Jurists* 8 (Special Issue, 1968):85–112. See also, Jean Rivero, *Les libertés publiques* (Paris: Presses Universitaires de France, 1973).

8. Dimitrije Kulic, "The Constitutional Court of Yugoslavia in the Protection of Human Rights," 22 *Osgoode Hall Law Journal* 275 (1973).

9. Valuable comparison of Germany, Austria, and Switzerland is offered in A. H. Schuler, *Die Verfassungsbeschwerde in der Schweiz, der Bundesrepublik Deutschland und Österreich* (Zurich: Hafner, 1968). See also Fritz Baur, "Les Garanties Fondamentales des parties dans le Proces Civil en Republique Federale d'Allemagne" in *Fundamental Guarantees of the Parties in Civil Litigation,* ed. Mauro Cappelletti and Denis Tallon (Dobbs Ferry, New York: Oceana Publications, 1973), pp. 1–30.

10. Ignacio Burgoa, *Las garantías individuales,* 8th ed. (Mexico City: Editorial Porrua, 1973). More general is the analysis of Héctor Fix-Zamudio "Les Garanties Constitutionelles des parties dans le Proces Civil en Amerique Latine," in Cappelletti and Tallon, *Fundamental Guarantees,* pp. 31–100.

11. *The Queen* v. *Drybones* S.C.R. 282 (1970). See also Walter Tarnopolsky, *Some Civil Liberties Issues of the Seventies* (Toronto: York University, 1975).

12. Alexis de Tocqueville, *Democracy in America,* ed. J. P. Mayer, trans. George Lawrence (Garden City, New York: Doubleday, 1969), pp. 673–74.

13. United Nations, Commission on Human Rights, *Human Rights Yearbook,* 1958 to date.

14. Myres S. McDougal, Harold D. Lasswell, and Lung-chu Chen, "Human Rights and World Public Order: A Framework for Policy-Oriented Inquiry," 63 *The American Journal of International Law* 237 (1969).

15. Abraham Maslow, *Motivation and Personality* (New York: Harper and Row, 1954). Cf. Hadley Cantril, *The Pattern of Human Concerns* (New Brunswick, N.J.: Rutgers University Press), pp. 315–22. See also, Christian Bay, *The Structure of Freedom* (New York: Atheneum, 1966). See also, Karl Fox, *Social Indicators and Social Theory* (New York: John Wiley and Sons, Wiley Inter-Science Publications, 1975), pp. 8–28.

16. See generally, "Symposium on the Lasswell-McDougal Approach," 14 *Virginia Journal of International Law* 387 (1974).

17. Sidney Verba, "Comparative Political Culture," in *Political Culture and Political Development,* ed. Lucien Pye and Sidney Verba (Princeton: Princeton University Press, 1965), pp. 512–60.

18. Ernst Jones, "Law, Political Science, and Policy Studies," *Policy Studies Journal* 2 (1973):56–60.

19. H. M. Hart and A. M. Sacks, *The Legal Process: Basic Problems in the Making and Application of Law* (Cambridge: Harvard University Press, 1958).

20. Robert B. Yegge, "What Has Social Science to Offer Law," *Law and Society Review* 3 (1969):484; idem., "What Has Law to Offer Social Science," *Law and Society Review* 4 (1969):36; and idem., "Caveats to the Interface of Law and Social Science," *Law and Society Review* 4 (1969):163.

21. Alf Ross, *On Law and Justice* (Berkeley: University of California Press, 1959), pp. 170–88.

22. M. J. B. Marie, "Une methodologie pour une science des droits de l'homme," *Revue des droits de l'homme, Human Rights Journal* 6 (March 1973):109.

23. Abraham Kaplan, *The Conduct of Inquiry* (San Francisco: Chandler Publishing Co., 1964), pp. 139–41.

24. Patrice Gélard, "Droit comparé et psychologie des peuples," *Revue de Psychologie des Peuples,* 25 (1970):18–45, at 21.

25. Ross, *Laws and Justice,* pp. 299–300.

26. C. Thomas Dienes, "Judges, Legislators and Social Change," in *Law and Social Change,* ed. Stuart S. Nagel (Beverly Hills: Sage Publications, 1970), pp. 33–44. Cf. A. J. M. Milne, "Philosophy and Political Action: The Case of Civil Rights," *Political Studies* 21 (1973):453–66.

27. See "Modernization and Political Development" in *Comparative Politics, The Quest for Theory,* ed. James A. Bill and Robert L. Hardgrave, Jr., (Columbus, Ohio: Charles E. Merrill, 1973), pp. 43–84. Fred Riggs, "The Comparison of Whole Political Systems" in *The Methodology of Comparative Research,* ed. Robert T. Holt and John E. Turner (New York: The Free Press, 1970), pp. 73–122, "Comparative Research and Social Science Theory" in *The Logic of Comparative Social Inquiry,* ed. Adam Przeworski and Henry Teune (New York: John Wiley and Sons, 1970), pp. 17–30.

28. André Hariou, "Recherches sur une problématique et une méthodologie applicable à l'analyse des institutions politiques," *Revue de droit public et de la science politiques,* March, 1971, pp. 305–47. [Editor's translation.]

29. Georg Jellinek, *Allgemaine Staatslehre* (Berlin: O. Haring, 1908); *(Die Erklärung der Menschen-und Bürgerrechte) [The Declaration of the Rights of Man and of the Citizen]* trans. Max Farrand (New York: Henry Holt, 1901); idem., *The Rights of Minorities,* trans. A. M. Baty and T. Baty (London: P. S. King, 1921); idem., *System der subjektiven öffentlichen Rechte (Freiburg: B. Mohr, 1892).* Rudolph von Ihering, *Geist des römischen Rechts* (Leipzig: Breitkopf und Härtel, 1888). A complete bibliography of the works of the Nobel laureate, René Cassin, is set out in the volume honoring him, René Cassin Amicorum Discipulorumque, *Liber* I, *Problemes de Protection Internationale des droits de l'homme* (Paris: A Pédone, 1971), pp. *ii–x.* Among the comparative works of a Candian scholar, see Edward McWhinney, *Comparative Federalism* (Toronto: University of Toronto Press, 1962); idem., *Federal Constitution-Making for a Multinational World* (Leyden: A. W. Sijthoff, 1966); and idem., *Judicial Review,* 4th ed. (Toronto: University of Toronto Press, 1969).

30. Jean Blondel, *Comparative Legislatures* (Englewood Cliffs, N.J.: Prentice–Hall, 1973); idem., *Comparative Political Systems* (New York: Praeger, 1972); idem., *Democracy in Crisis* (Notre Dame: Notre Dame University Press, 1971); Seymour Martin Lipset, *The First New Nation* (New York: Basic Books, 1963); idem., *Political Man* (Garden City, New York: Doubleday 1960); Stein Rokkan, ed. *Party Systems and Voter Alignments* (New York: The Free Press, 1967); J. Linz, *The Social Bases of Political Diversity* (Stanford: Center for Advanced Study in Behavioral Sciences, 1956); Stein Rokkan, *Citizens Elections Parties* (New York: McKay, 1970); idem., ed., *Comparative Research across Cultures and Nations* (New Haven: Yale University Press, 1966); Dankwart Rustow, *Middle Eastern Political Systems* (Englewood Cliffs, New Jersey: Prentice-Hall, 1971); idem., *Philosophers and Kings* (New York: G. Braziller, 1970); idem., *A World of Nations* (Washington, D.C.: Brookings Institution, 1967); and Giovanni Sartori, *Democratic Theory* (New York: Praeger, 1965).

31. Cyril Black, *The Dynamics of Modernization* (New York: Harper Row, 1966); idem., *The Future of the International Legal Order* (Princeton, N.J.: Princeton University Press, 1969); idem., *Twentieth Century Europe,* 4th ed., (New York: Knopf, 1972); Samuel Huntington, *Political Order in Changing Societies* (New Haven: Yale University Press, 1968); Barrington Moore, *Political Power and Social Theory: Six Studies* (Cambridge: Harvard University Press, 1958); and idem., *Social Origins of Dictatorship and Democracy* (Boston: Beacon Press, 1966).

32. Jellinek, *System.*

33. Huntington, *Political Order,* pp. 32–37.

34. Leonard Binder et al., eds., *Crises and Sequences in Political Development* (Princeton: Committee on Comparative Politics of the Social Science Research Council, Princeton University Press, 1971).

35. See David M. Trubek and Marc Galanter, "Scholars in Self-Estrangement: Some Reflections on the Crisis in Law and Development Studies in the United States," 1974 *Wisconsin Law Review* 1062, 1099–1100.

NOTE ON THE CONTRIBUTORS

Carl Baar, A.B. (1961), U.C.L.A.; M.A. (1963), Ph.D. (1969), University of Chicago. Baar is Associate Professor in the Department of Politics, Brock University, Ontario, Canada. His publications reflect an interest in judicial administration and management. During 1970, he was a Russell Sage Fellow in Law and Social Science at the Yale Law School. He is at present editor-in-chief of the *Justice System Journal.*

Fletcher N. Baldwin, Jr., B.A. (1958), J.D. (1961), University of Georgia; L.L.M. (1962), University of Illinois; L.L.M. (1968), Yale University. Baldwin is Professor of Law at the University of Florida Law School where he has been instrumental in the establishment of the Center for Governmental Responsibility. In 1969, he was a Fulbright Professor at Makerere University, Kampala, Uganda and in 1972, Professor, Escuela Libre de Derecho, Mexico City.

Lawrence W. Beer, A.B. (1956), M.A. (1957), Gonzaga University; Ph.D. (1966), University of Washington (Seattle). Beer is Professor of Political Science at the University of Colorado at Boulder. He has published many articles on Japanese law, society, and politics. He is the Chairman of the Committee on Asian Law, Association for Asian Studies, and is a member of the editorial board of *Law in Japan: An Annual.*

Linda Breeden, A.B. (1966), Stanford University; J.D. (1969), Hastings College of Law. Breeden is a member of the California State Bar and practices law in Palo Alto, California. A specialist in labor and environment law, she was a staff attorney until 1974 for the Congressional Research Service, American Law Division, Library of Congress in Washington, D.C.

Richard P. Claude, B.A. (1956), College of St. Thomas; M.S. (1959), Florida State University; Ph.D. (1964), University of Virginia. Claude is Associate Professor of Government and Politics at the University of Maryland. He has published articles on public law in French, Spanish, and American journals, and he is the author of *The Supreme Court and the Electoral Process.* Currently he is director of the Comparative Human Rights Project, Bethesda, Maryland.

William B. Devall, B.A. (1960), University of Kansas; M.A. (1962), University of Hawaii; Ph.D. (1970), University of Oregon. Devall is Associate Professor of Sociology at Humboldt State University, and he was recently Visiting Professor at Simon Fraser University in British Columbia. His publications reflect an interest in political sociology and the sociology of civil liberties. Recently he edited a special issue of the *Humboldt Journal on Social Relations* devoted to social behavior and natural environments.

Judith Gallatin, B.A. (1962), M.A. (1963), Ph.D. (1967), University of Michigan. Gallatin is Associate Professor of Psychology at Eastern Michigan University. Trained as a clinical psychologist, she has turned in her research to the field of political socialization. Her work with Joseph Adelson on the comparative psychology of urban adolescents is well known. Her most recent publication is *Adolescence and Individuality* (1975).

E. Jeremy Hutton, B.A. (1963), Colgate University; J.D. (1966), Duke University. Hutton is an attorney and Legislative Attorney for the Congressional Research Service, American Law Division, Library of Congress. He is an active member of the District of Columbia Bar, the United States Supreme Court Bar, and the American Bar and Federal Bar Associations.

Ved P. Nanda, B.A.,M.A. (1956), Punjab University; LL.B., L.L.M. (1958), Delhi University; L.L.M. (1962), Northwestern University. Nanda is Professor of Law and Director of the International Legal Studies Program, University of Denver, College of Law, and he has been Visiting Professor of Law, University of Iowa. He has written extensively on the topics of human rights, population policy, and environment. He is coeditor of the two-volume *Treatise on International Criminal Law* (1973) and is a member of the editorial board of the *American Journal of Comparative Law.*

Krishan S. Nehra, B.Sc. (1947), Punjab University; LL.B. (1955), Delhi University. Nehra is a Senior Legal Specialist in the Research Section of the American-British Law Division, Law Library of the Library of Congress, which he joined in 1971. He practiced at the Kenya Bar in Nairobi (1958–64), and at the Indian Bar in the Punjab (1956–57 and 1964–71) where he also served as a State Counsel. He was a lecturer in the Department of Laws of the Punjab University, Chandigarh, India, between 1965 and 71.

Durvasula S. Sastri, L.L.B. (1957), Andhra University; L.L.M. (1971), National Law Center, George Washington University. Sastri has served on the faculty of George Washington University and has practiced law in India. As his publications and present affiliation as Associate General Counsel to the Maryland National Capital Park and Planning Commission attest, he is actively involved with urban and environment law.

Anna P. Schreiber, B.A. (1963), Middlebury College; M.A. (1965), Ph.D. (1969), Columbia University. Schreiber is an International Public Affairs Advisor for the Mobil Oil Corporation. She previously taught political science at Rutgers University and Vassar College. In 1970, she was affiliated with the Royal

Institute of International Affairs, Chatham House, London. She is the author of *The Inter-American Commission on Human Rights* (1970).

Jay Adrian Sigler, B.A. (1954), J.D. (1957), Ph.D. (1962), Rutgers, The State University of New Jersey. Sigler is Professor of Political Science in the Camden College of Arts and Sciences, Rutgers. A member of the King's Bench Law Fraternity, Sigler's interest in comparative rights is evidenced in his articles in Indian, Asian, Mexican, and British journals and in his most recent book, *American Rights Policies* (1975), which contains a useful comparative rights bibliography.

Otis H. Stephens, Jr., A.B. (1957), M.A. (1958), University of Georgia; Ph.D. (1963), Johns Hopkins University. Stephens is Professor of Political Science at the University of Tennessee. His principal fields of research and teaching are constitutional law and the judicial process. He has contributed many articles on criminal justice to various law reviews, and he is the author of *The Supreme Court and Confessions of Guilt* (1973).

James C. Strouse, B.A. (1966), M.A. (1967), University of Maryland; Ph.D. (1970), University of North Carolina. Strouse is Assistant Professor of Government and Politics at the University of Maryland where he teaches political statistics. His research and publications reflect an interest in public opinion analysis. He is the author of *Mass Media, Public Opinion, Public Policy Analysis: Linkage Explorations* (1975).

Manfred W. Wenner, B.A. (1956), Oberlin College; M.A. (1958), Johns Hopkins School of Advanced International Studies; Ph.D. (1965), Johns Hopkins University. Wenner is Associate Professor of Political Science at Northern Illinois University. His several publications range among the fields of international law and comparative ethnic and minority politics. He is the author of *Yemen and the People's Republic of South Yemen* (1971).

Library of Congress Cataloging in Publication Data

Main entry under title:

Comparative human rights.

   1. Civil rights—Addresses, essays, lectures.
2. Comparative government—Addresses, essays,
lectures. I. Claude, Richard, 1934–
JC571.C643   323.4   76–7043
ISBN 0–8018–1784–6